PHILOSOPHIC THOUGHT
IN FRANCE AND THE
UNITED STATES

PHILOSOPHIC THOUGHT IN FRANCE AND THE UNITED STATES

ESSAYS REPRESENTING MAJOR TRENDS IN CONTEMPORARY FRENCH AND AMERICAN PHILOSOPHY

Edited by
MARVIN FARBER

STATE UNIVERSITY OF NEW YORK PRESS
ALBANY

190
F22p
74713
July, 1971

FOREWORD

The publication of a second edition of *Philosophic Thought in France and the United States* provides a suitable occasion for recalling the role played by the first edition, which appeared in 1950. It was evident that the essays making up the volume met a long-felt need, as shown by the warm reception and the continuing interest in them. There had been all too little knowledge of French philosophy in America, and even less knowledge of American philosophy in France. It was to be expected that the philosophical confrontation of scholars from two countries in which there had been such enormous cultural vitality and intellectual change would meet with much interest.

For practical reasons, but also because of personal difficulties and even misfortunes on the part of invited contributors, there were unavoidable omissions. The richness of the content nevertheless amply justified the publication, and its timeliness made up for the elements of incompleteness. The contributors to the volume are truly representative of the major trends in their respective countries, but it is by no means implied that they constitute an exhaustive list of the significant contemporary philosophers, and it is obvious that any selection would entail important omissions. The various contributors are sufficiently representative to illustrate the lack of unity of philosophy in each country. There is no unified "French philosophy"; and similarly, there is no "American philosophy." The issues raised by existentialism in its various forms, in the arguments of its defenders and attackers, play a prominent role in French thought. For America, on the other hand, one may point to the sustained interest in the construction of a philosophy conditioned by logic and the special sciences in opposition to the tradition of spiritualism. The careful reader will not fail to discern elements of resemblance and mutual relevance, and will seek special explanations — socioeconomic, historical, or scientific — for the most striking differences.

Special acknowledgment of indebtedness is due to the Division of Humanities of the Rockefeller Foundation for its generous and thoughtful support of the project. As originally planned, the book was also published in French, in two volumes, by the Presses Universitaires de France (Paris, 1950), under the title *L'activité philosophique contemporaine en France et aux Etats-Unis*.

The major changes and developments which have occurred since 1950 serve to emphasize the relevance of the publication. The upsurge of the new literature devoted to phenomenology and existential philosophy in both countries is especially noteworthy. Formerly regarded as primarily European, it has now been recognized as also grounded in an American tradition including Peirce, James, and Royce. The receptivity of some American philosophers to an "existential" type of phenomenology is historically significant in connection with the tradition of idealism, which had gradually all but disappeared from the philosophic scene. Also noteworthy is the tremendous expansion of interest in analytic and linguistic philosophy, as well as the philosophy of science. The formation of the Society for the Philosophical Study of Dialectical Materialism and the recent increase of the scholarly literature devoted to the subject by such writers as Somerville, Hodges, and Parsons, along with the publication of the periodical *Soviet Studies in Philosophy,* are an indication of the development of an interest that had been relatively more prominent in France in 1950. The rapid growth of institutions of higher learning has made possible a substantial increase in the number of professional philosophers deriving influences from numerous countries. This has resulted in the establishment of several new journals and the encouragement of interest in Eastern philosophy. Thus, although the judgment will still stand that there is no unified French or American philosophy, the philosophers of the two countries tend to display comparable spreads from "conservative" to "radical." As in the case of the French literature, where writers such as Merleau-Ponty and Sartre reacted to Marxist motives, prominently represented by Lefebvre, Garaudy, Cornu, and Wallon, American philosophers may be expected to react from within to a greater extent than heretofore. This also applies to phenomenology and the philosophy of existence, which must eventually be subsumed under a more general pluralistic conception of methods of inquiry, allowing for the relative autonomy of special procedures. The ultimate unity of philosophy in any or all countries, if it is to be achieved, must be a collective type of unity, allowing for a diversity of problems, methods, and selective subject matters. This has been set forth by the present writer in recent publications, including *Phenomenology and Existence* (New York: Harper & Row, 1967) and the third edition of *The Foundation of Phenomenology* (Albany: State University of New York Press, 1967). The striking development of philosophy in France since 1950 is indicated by Professor Gilbert Varet's bibliography, included as a supplement in the present new edition.

Marvin Farber

Buffalo, New York
November 27, 1967

CONTENTS

IX

PART II: CONTEMPORARY AMERICAN PHILOSOPHY

PART I

CONTEMPORARY
FRENCH PHILOSOPHY

FRENCH PHILOSOPHICAL TRADITON BETWEEN THE TWO WARS

Jacques Havet*

TO CLAUDE ROUSSEL

It may appear a hopeless enterprise to attempt to give a true, objective, and complete picture of philosophical developments in a period so close to our own. Whoever undertakes this task is not only faced by a superabundance of material, but finds it almost impossible to set aside his personal predilections. And, in a deeper sense, through his person, today is passing judgment upon yesterday, and this close-up view is likely to falsify perspectives and to be contradicted by history, which will restore values to their right places. The pages that follow, therefore, make no attempt to adopt a universal point of view of French philosophy between the two wars. To go to the roots of the matter meant extracting whatever appears to have preserved significance for philosophy today from what was only a little while ago topical philosophical speculation.

Another difficulty was to decide upon a general plan which should illumine, without distorting, the complexity of philosophic evolution. To render the movement of life would involve following, abandoning, and then retracing a hundred different paths; it would mean going outside of France and analyzing the influence of foreign philosophies on *French tradition;* and, finally, a period such as this does not constitute a whole in itself: the two outside dates, 1919 and 1939, do not indicate breaks in the continuity of philosophical evolution.

Nevertheless, in this particular case, the shocks caused by the First War and the anxious awaiting of another upheaval mark clearly enough a natural period of history, a period of investigation rather than one of

* Born in 1919. Received his higher education in the École Normale Supérieure, Paris, and in the Sorbonne, and became an Agrégé de Philosophie. At present a member of the Unesco Secretariat in Paris, and deals specially with the programme of Unesco in the field of Philosophy and Humanistic Studies. Author of *Kant et le problème du temps* (1947).

constructive stability. It was, in the first place, a crisis of conscience faced with the outbreak of violence, the abandonment of humanitarian optimism; a crisis of science, leading to an astonishing rejuvenation; the scientist abandoned his part of humdrum official in a stable administration and become a pioneer, almost an adventurer; positivism was assailed by the lessons of scientific creation, and no longer from without by the claims of the spiritualists and religious minds. This was shortly followed by a recovery of confidence in the capacity of the mind and of man himself for self-renewal, which, although it illustrated the temporal nature and the historicity of man, also emphasized the dramatic discontinuity of existence. There was a clearer awareness of the external and internal conditions by which action is governed. The postulation of liberty and the need for a justification of values clashed with everything in man which eludes his own immediate grasp. The central problem of the age was embodied in a concept with many meanings—*the condition of man*—the proper field for a philosophy newly conscious of its mission and specific task—a philosophy which, refusing to build all sciences after the pattern of natural sciences, and coming back to the experience of things themselves, endeavors to found the various human and social sciences as autonomous studies, and to offer an understanding of man as such.

This study does not extend beyond the constructs of general philosophy, but we should not forget, for instance, the metaphysical importance of such a radical experiment in poetry as surrealism, with its employment of nonconceptual methods. As for Freudianism and Marxism, they set themselves up, from different points of view, as the guilty conscience of spiritualism and intellectualism, before they inspired and penetrated a part of the philosophic movement shortly before the Second World War. Mention should further be made of the connections between the more and more metaphysical trend of the novel and the drama, and a philosophy which sought an ever closer experience of life; also of the increasing pressure of political, social, and cultural problems—the crisis of civilization, as it has been said—upon abstract thinking. Such are a few of the characteristics which determine the style of the period.

While spiritualism has bent all its energies upon purification and has sought to preserve spiritual life from all contamination by the modalities of internal life and to ensure its full independence, and while the personalists, as well as the representatives of the philosophy of the spirit, have tried to reassure man and to safeguard his destiny as a thinking being, there is a growing feeling today that human existence cannot be altogether assumed or justified by pure reason. As a result, some invoke some kind of transcendence; others define human liberty as abysmal liberty, prior to reasons and motives. Others, again, endeavor to investigate the economic or affective substructure underlying the processes of thought, and from which thought can only escape by integrating them in a dialectic lived, in his own time, by the individual, or, in history, by all mankind.

I. SPIRITUALISTIC REALISM—HENRI BERGSON AND MAURICE BLONDEL

At the same time, 1919 does not mark a clear beginning in the history of philosophical ideas. It is possible to speak of a *French tradition,* not only because many newcomers are following the paths cleared by their elders, and in their turn displaying those constants in what is commonly called the *French genius,* but also because much philosophical meditation which started before the beginning of the century blossomed and bore its fruit in the years that followed. That, however, was not the case with Hamelin, who died accidentally in 1907 after his *Essai sur les éléments principaux de la représentation* had done no more than lay the logical and dialectical foundations of what would have been a general philosophy.

The philosophy of Bergson,[1] already very popular in 1919, exercised a visible liberating influence not only upon abstract thinking and on psychiatry,[2] but on the novel (Proust), art, and the whole sensibility of the age. Bergson had already written most of his important work. But, although the main themes of his thought were well known and it could be foreseen that the concepts of creation, vital impulse, and tension would form the core of any Bergsonian theory of behavior, yet no one could anticipate the future developments of a personal dialectic which had already carried the philosopher from the self-awareness of the "consciousness"—in his *Essai sur les données immédiates de la conscience*—to a study of the link between the three factors of time lived—in *Matière et mémoire*—and thence to the theory of evolution and man's place in life—in *L'évolution créatrice.* What are the moral deductions from Bergsonism? Is it a form of spiritualism, as some Bergsonians such as Le Roy[3] and Segond declare, or, on the contrary, a form of naturalism? Are life and the vital impulse, according to Bergson, the source and guarantee of higher values?

a. Bergsonian Ethics and Religion.

Bergson's own answer to these questions did not follow until the publication of the *Deux sources* in 1932. The passage of twenty-five years since *L'évolution créatrice* shows that the new work had been pondered at length. Though Bergson had not been silent all that time, his *Duex sources* sounded a new note. With its publication, his philosophy appeared in its complete form as spiritual realism; consciousness of the creative life had extended and grown into an aspiration that is of a mystical character.

No philosophy is more monistic than this, yet none accents more strongly the duality of direction, as compared with the unity of source. Tension and relaxation, continuity and discontinuity, aspiration and relapse, impulse and sclerosis, these dynamic opposites endow the doctrine with its live and dramatic character. We shall find in Bergson's conception of morality and religion the reflection of this dual direction which destroys the original unity of the vital impulse: on the one hand, instinct, a process of adaptation without inventive capacity, by which the progress of life, while reaching its farthest point, reunites with the inertia of matter, and by which the individual, himself barely individualized, blindly executes a never-changing gesture for the survival of the species; on the other hand, intelligence, ever imperfect and ever-developing, an infinite capacity for invention, yet ever dogged by another sclerosis, should it become the prisoner of its own mechanisms, and lose contact with the fullness of life. This duality imposes a further opposition in the field of relations between the individual and society.

As opposed to *"closed" morality,* which is nothing but the pressure of society upon the individual to defend itself against chaos, Bergson invokes the secret forces of renewal implanted in the individual by the impulse, and the expanding or *"open" morality* in which this aspiration finds expression. While respecting the legitimacy of "closed" morality at its own level, he refuses to regard it, like Durkheim, as the whole of morality, and he tries to prove that the human individual has in him the means of transcending that morality and reaching a higher plane. Whereas "closed" morality is a negation of the individual for the benefit of the community, something that mirrors the imperatives of the instinct, a war morality expressing the life of a limited group and incapable of expanding to the dimensions of humanity as a whole, "open" morality is, on the contrary, an individual invention, but is valid for others and is coextensive with humanity. It denotes the presence in the individual of a potential infinity, which will find its ultimate expression in mysticism, the supreme form of religion.

Religion, in its commonest forms, is a *closed religion,* an instrument of conservation, but not of progress: *unconscious fable-making,* the spontaneous creation of myths safeguards man against the disintegrating influence of the critical intelligence; an animal has no religion and does not need one. But man, a restless animal, is not only capable of religion, but he has the spark of mysticism in him which enables him to pass beyond the myths that he receives ready-made from society. *Open religion* "sustains man by the very movement it imparts to him, as it renews his place in the vital impulse, and not by the myths and legends to which it directs his activity in his immobile state."

When Bergson defines the great mystic as "an individuality which would transcend the bounds set to the human species by its material substance and which would continue and thus prolong divine action," he is far from reducing moral and religious aspiration to the level of life regarded as a *nature;* on the contrary, he transfigures life by associating with it a spiritual creative power, by revealing in operation at all stages of development an impulse which, although vital in its most elementary manifestations, is none the less of like nature with the spirituality of the divine.

b. Bergson's Philosophic Method.

L'énergie spirituelle was a collection in one volume of essays and lectures which had not been included among Bergson's main works, but in his second volume of essays, *La pensée et le mouvant,* the philosopher at the end of his life delivers his authentic *Discourse on Method,* the fruit of his constant meditation on the essence and justification of his metaphysical approach. Only intuition as opposed to the philosophic concept of the schools, is an experience of the moving, of creative duration, of quality and continuum; it therefore permits of a coincidence with reality in its nascent phase; finally it is the foundation of a deep communion with everything that *is,* i.e., with everything that becomes, a communion that encompasses the whole universe and is comparable with the moral and religious inspiration of the *Deux sources.* If the philosopher penetrates to the heart of reality, it is not after the manner of the scientist by the detachment of a more indifferent onlooker or by regarding it as a field open to technical conquest, but through attuning himself to it, because he is himself a part of that reality, immersed in the world and propelled by the vital impulse. By showing the subject as a fragment of the universe, but endowed with consciousness, Bergson is not initiating a dialectic of the relations between consciousness and its object; on the contrary, he takes his stand firmly on realism.

It is obvious, of course, that, in this statement of his method and in discrediting the discontinuous nature of conceptual knowledge, Bergson was criticizing only the traditional conception of science, and in particular positivism. Moreover, it would be idle to ask what would have been his attitude if he had not been required at the beginning of his career to align himself against a certain narrow positivism by joining the tradition of Ravaisson, Boutroux, and Lachelier, and if at the outset he had made the acquaintance of a science purged of the inertia of the "thing," inspired by a quasi-ontological ambition, constrained to a constant renewal of its concepts in obedience to the claims of its subject matter and respectful of the independence of philosophic thought. We shall see that certain philosophers, reflecting upon the scientific revolution of the day, in their turn encountered themes already developed by Bergsonism and succeeded in making those themes the components of an intellectualism which reintroduces life and motion into the very concept of reason.

c. *Maurice Blondel's Philosophy of Action and Ontology.*

In a passage inspired by Bergsonism, Edouard Le Roy wrote these words, which exactly apply to the philosophy of Maurice Blondel: "In my opinion, the powerful originality and solid truth of the new philosophy are that it recognized the subordination of the idea to the real and of reality to action." The resemblances between Bergsonism and the philosophy of Blondel are unmistakable.[4] Nevertheless, Maurice Blondel must be given a place of his own, for, by condemning the inadequacy of philosophy regarded as pure speculation, and by making it a *life* and not a *view,* a practice and not a theory of practice, he renewed the meaning of philosophic activity itself. For him, the essence of modern conscience, moulded by Christianity, is to be militant and to endure suffering, to feel itself responsible for and one with the entire creation, and to be unable to be satisfied with the notional ideal of Greek speculation.

His first work, *Action,* published in 1893, contained as though in their natural state the themes which were to be developed and substantiated, after forty years of quasi-silence and meditation, in a vast ontological structure. Taking as its subject action itself, and not the concept of action, the thesis of 1893 presented it as irreducible to terms of thought, as the effective snatching away of the individual from himself; intent upon filling the gulf between power and will, action is inevitably unsatisfied, ever haunted by the infinite. "Summoned by infinity, and at the same time its echo, action proceeds thence and departs thither." Hence the philosophy of action, and the resources of human reason, lead us only to the threshold of the true life: the function of philosophy is to create the void which faith will fill; it cannot do more.

In the years between this thesis, at the time a novel one, and the vast
.structure with which Blondel presented the public during the years preceding the Second World War, his thought had grown enormously in
stature and possibly in moderation, though it remained true to its initial
inspiration. For in this ontology, which might be thought pure speculation, action is ever present.

With *La pensée,* we come to the gradual ascent of conscious thought,
from its humblest origins, from that *cosmic thought* where there already
exists *in posse* the full illumination which finds there the basis and the
roots necessary to its ascent: a thought which can find completion and
rest only when it reaches, "beyond all reality experienced or known," the
infinity from which it issues. The destiny of thought is therefore strictly
parallel with that of action. Haunted by the cleavage which divides its
universal aspect from its individual aspect, it cannot of itself bridge this
gulf and attain repose; only a being that transcends us, but which is ever
immanent in our total impulse of free will and our power of choice, only
God can reconcile thought with itself. The destination of thought is its
choice of the infinite, but a choice made "by traversing and sublimating
the universe." Its whole itinerary lies within the being, but throughout
its ascent it is steeped in the plenitude of infinite thought and can only
find its completion by attaching itself to the divine act of charity without
which it would not exist.

The ascent of thought therefore requires a theory of being, a theory,
above all, in Blondel's dynamic view, of the relation between the being
and beings, incommensurable but compatible; at least if we believe in the
inability of any finite being to exist unless penetrated by the absolute
being, and in a hierarchy among beings which makes of them steps in an
ascent. All creation is permeated by an impulse toward God. "Matter is
that which can be vitalized, life is that which can be spiritualized, and
the spirit is that which can be deified." The essence being postulated as
a norm and not as a lifeless definition, ontology ceases to be mere description; it becomes an apprehension, through coincidence with its impulse
of the destination of every being; it is a normative, "a systematic investigation for the purpose of studying the normal process whereby beings
realize the design of which they are a product and the destiny which
awaits them."

Thus buttressed by a clear apperception of the destiny of thought
and by its living ontology, the new *Action,* instead of, like the old,
directly embarking upon the explanation of human acts, can at once take
its stand on the absolute of *pure Acting,* that point of completion at which

action no longer proceeds from itself to be lost in some ulterior effect, but consists of an interior impulse, fully self-sufficient. This pure Acting is what permeates the finite consciousness and makes it capable itself of acting, capable of becoming the enemy of God as well as of rediscovering Him in the course of its ascent. Action is therefore that which integrates us most completely in being. Here we meet once more, based upon the realism of a dynamic ontology, the themes formerly presented dramatically from the point of view of man in the thesis of 1893. And philosophy carries us to the threshold of the supreme experience of total surrender, but only Christian faith can fill the void dug by the exercise of reason and explain what the latter has only been able to postulate as an unknown.

II. THE NEW INTELLECTUALISM AND CONTEMPORARY SCIENCE

a. *The Scientific Revolution.*

In spite of the resemblances between them, Bergson's philosophy and that of Blondel were very different in origin, and it may be said that the ghost of positivism never ceased to haunt Bergson, while Blondel remained more or less indifferent to the problems of science. Admittedly, Bergson's philosophy had developed far beyond the implications of its historical premises; otherwise, as a philosopher he would have been really dead, as soon as his opponent was no longer there; for, as is now a commonplace, our knowledge of the physical world has gradually entirely altered its character since the beginning of the century, and the general conception of the nature of scientific thought, the scientist's work, and the value of science has undergone a profound revision.

The positivism of Comte's followers was bound up with a certain conception of science and, at the same time, with the condemnation of purely philosophic speculation. Science was supposed to have reached its final form, at the end of its historical evolution, and no further revolution was to overthrow the conceptual structure it employed, nor to challenge its results, from the technical application of which it had derived such prestige. As its value consisted partly in its intrinsic clarity and partly in the fact that it endowed man, within the range of his senses, with mastery over the world in which he lives, all science had to do was to fit phenomena into a system of laws, without troubling about the nature or ultimate structure of the underlying reality; even the idea of cause was rejected as being foreign and anthropomorphic. But the paradox of positivism is that this modest conception of scientific truth was coupled with a condemnation of any other effort, by reason or otherwise, to explore deeper into truth.

Even at the end of the nineteenth century, the pretensions of this circumscribed rationalism, known as "scientism," had been challenged by the spiritualists, who championed against science the rights of philosophic reflection or those of religion or moral intuition, which are at issue with the premises and methods of science. This reaction found its most fruitful expression in thinkers such as Boutroux, Lachelier, Lagneau, and Bergson. But, apart from those great philosophies, the defense of the *rights of the soul,* against the cold, surface reasoning of science, was, unfortunately, a flag under which anyone could sail. As Léon Brunschvicg wrote, "an intense inner life is no guarantee of the real value of the life of the spirit." There was a danger that the only result of the pretensions of science might be a recrudescence of an inferior brand of obscurantism, and that positivism might discredit the spirit of free inquiry and so fortify authority, as the guardian of values.

However, and more significantly, shortly afterward scientific theorists found themselves assailed by doubt, as by a presentiment of the impending scientific revolution. For Henri Poincaré, for instance, a so-called "true" proposition is in fact only the most convenient convention to explain phenomena; thus, without appearing to break with positivism, Poincaré was already sketching in the idea of a life of reason, stressing reason's readiness to accept the lessons of experience and criticizing the application of scientific concepts out of their proper sphere; this less rigid attitude in rationalism was, however, attained at the cost of the introductiòn of a sort of semi-skepticism. Meanwhile, the most radical thought on the activity of the mind was proceeding in Germany; Husserl must be given credit for having returned before the crisis of science to the root problem—namely, the transcendental origin of the object—and for having rejoined the great tradition of philosophy by rediscovering the inspiration of a *return to things in themselves,* as we actually experience them. Paradoxically, however, although the phenomenological movement had a tremendous influence on French thought, it was felt in quite different fields, and it would be useless to try to find a connection, which would be quite unsupported by historical fact, between that inspiration and the revival of rationalism in France, in face of the scientific revolution, in the period between the two World Wars.[5]

When Einstein's relativity theory appeared, it destroyed the privilege conferred by Newton to an absolute standard of reference for space and time; by combining all possible standards of reference in a single formula, it restored, in one way, a certain realism; but by including the observer's means of observation (e.g., the speed of light) in that formula, it implanted a sort of idealism in the formulation of scientific truth. Generalized relativity, by exploding the concept of mass, attacked the very root of the belief in a *thing* as an object of scientific study, being the same as the object of ordinary perception, but, at the same time, forbade its replacement by the interaction of convergent univocal laws. The idea was already emerging that it is impossible to separate the framework of experience and its contents, and that, in the dialectic of scientific progress, both are constantly interrelated.

The crisis over scientific truth became still more acute with the appearance of the quantum theory, which gave a new meaning to the concept of discontinuity, shattered classical determinism, made it necessary to combine explanatory systems which had hitherto been considered mutually exclusive in order to comprehend nature, and made experiment, as a means of *intervention,* an essential component of the contents of experience. It appeared that, contrary to Poincaré's assertion, astronomy had been a false counsellor in microscopic physics and its lessons had been tainted with anthropomorphic imagination.

However, the disconcertment of the theorists, faced with this *crisis of foundations,* was soon superseded by a sense of triumph when it was discovered that the new science enabled an unprecedented exploration of the very heart of physical reality. Furthermore, one of the most significant lessons of that crisis was the idea that consideration of the intellectual instrument must be an integral part of scientific activity. In the course of this evolution, science rediscovered its ontological vocation, while reason, in the midst of its triumphs, was subjected to constant examination. The result was the emergence of two contrasting attitudes in philosophy: for some, human truth was to reside in the free movement and development of rational consciousness, at grips with the problems of physical reality in a science freed from narrow positivism; others were to apply independent speculation, set free from *a priori* assumptions on scientific truth, to the consideration of specific problems, which Louis Lavelle[6] lists very correctly as follows: the absolute, the transcendent, the individual, being and value, existence; for science is so highly specialized that it does not enter into the consideration of most men. That was the source of the fresh proliferation of religious philosophies, and theories of value, and finally of existentialism, with its far greater concern with perception, imagination, or certain immediate experiences, than with the evolution of physical science.

b. Philosophies of Identity. Émile Meyerson and André Lalande.

It is remarkable that one of the strongest reactions against positivist epistemology should have resulted from reflections on traditional science, whose conclusions were to be seriously challenged by the scientific revolution itself. Émile Meyerson[7] is not trying to introduce innovations: he merely seeks to rediscover the traditional inspiration of the theory of knowledge from the time of the Greek philosophers onward, by combating positivism, pragmatism, and evolutionism. In the positivist view, the task of science should be confined to the discovery of laws, without considering the problems of object and cause; Meyerson reintroduces the concept of the thing. For pragmatism, the incentive to intellectual activity is the desire to find what is useful; Meyerson says the first vocation of reason is pure knowledge, explanation, for both common sense and the scientific mind. Meyerson thus implies the full restoration of reason as a mode of learning. In his view, reason is no more or less than the power of identification, whose special task is to seek continually, from the variety of concrete experience with which it is faced, the common term by which all may be brought to identity—the only legitimate intellection. As reality constantly supplies new irrationalities to be resolved, reason is involved in the continual exercise of invention, and science moves onward, although reason, as such, cannot change its nature. That is the theory of knowledge which was expounded, as early as 1908, in *Identité et réalité,* and which has been verified and expanded in works published between the two World Wars. The theory is strongly opposed to evolutionism, for science cannot take account of change and time in themselves: it has to reduce differences to identity, the present and the future to the past; no explanation can therefore be founded on evolution. And, although the description of scientific thought given by Meyerson is not unlike Bergson's, Meyerson regards this type of thought as the only valid means of understanding; in particular, Bergson's concept of creative evolution is a myth which, though possibly attractive, has no intellectual coherence.

This clear-cut philosophy, self-styled an optimism in the name of reason, reveals, on the contrary, a sort of agnosticism, since the content of knowledge has no connection with reality, the characteristic of which appears to be its irreducible diversity; unless the content of knowledge is postulated as the only true reality, the phenomenon being only a pretext, unknowable in itself, and, in the fact, illusory; but this revival of the tenets of the Eleatic and Megaric schools, which cannot "save the phenomena," is more or less opposed to the implications of modern experimental science. Moreover, science itself embarrasses the philosophy of identity, since the latter cannot account for the second law of thermo-dynamics, that of the dissipation of energy, which reestablishes the irre-versibility of time and the irreducibility of quality. Classical science thus faced Meyerson with serious problems; modern science raises others and, although *La déduction relativiste* might suggest an interpretation of Einstein's theories, the content of the quantum theories appears perma-nently to impair the validity of the epistemology of identity.

André Lalande,[8] who has greatly influenced French university phi-losophy, may be associated with the same line of development; but, in *Les illusions évolutionistes,* which takes up again a thesis of 1899, his standpoint is as much ontological and ethical as epistemological. Although life seems to introduce an element of differentiation into the material world, which is gradually becoming uniform (in this instance, the law of the dissipation of energy is used constructively), it is always only an uncertain triumph over death. And intellect reaches out, across life, to matter, ever seeking the ideal of identification; similarly morality re-quires that the individual difference should not be considered as a value (except when it consists in an intellectual or moral superiority), and it aims at reestablishing peace which the natural ambition of the living be-ing endlessly aims at disturbing. This philosophy is essentially contrary to Bergson's, as it is to any metaphysics of life; it denies the possibility of salvation for the individual but is, however, very different from the social ethics of a Durkheim, since the latter wants the individualism of men to be repressed for the sake of a superior individual, Society; while Lalande's ethics is not less hostile to the individuality and intrinsic value of collective organisms than to those of mere individuals.

Representing an important element of French philosophy between the two wars, the philosophies of identity, therefore, express essentially a value judgement, and not the affirmation of a metaphysical and static identity of beings; Meyerson has often protested that he pointed only at a character of the work of intelligence in the sciences, which can be con-firmed in history, though its indefinite maintenance is by no means cer-tain; Lalande, who aims at covering not only science, but also art and social ideals in that movement of "involution," has insisted on the fact that it implies the reality of its opposite as a "given" on which it works. The only thing which does not vary is the "constituting reason"; but the "constituted reason" is in constant change, though its change is from the "other" to the "same." This fundamental thesis, recently restated by Lalande in *La raison et les normes,* has found an enthusiastic advocate in Julien Benda.

Meanwhile, time and history are becoming more and more the pivots of all the theories of consciousness and scientific reason. The great problem with which French intellectualists have been grappling is the reconciliation of the belief in absolute truth with the actual history, and indeed the noncontinuous development, of human knowledge. The key figure in the endeavor to breathe new life into intellectualism, and to relax the rigidity of reason, while purifying consciousness, is Léon Brunschvicg.

c. Léon Brunschvicg and the Philosophy of Relation.

Léon Brunschvicg had already described his general theory of scientific truth in *La modalité du jugement* in 1897, and to a large extent, his other works have merely expanded and enriched an intuitive understanding, clear from the very beginning, of the way thought works in the various fields to which it is applied. As an alternative to absolute idealism and naive realism, constantly alternating with one another, he lays the foundations of a relative idealism: the existence of the objects of knowledge is entirely relative to the truth of the judgment attesting them; the judgment precedes the terms which it brings together and the copula "is" has no force of existence, but simply expresses the act of synthesis which is the proper function of the mind. The truth of the judgment or, in other words, the objectivity of knowledge and, equally, the validity of the assertion of an object's existence, can derive only from the mutual correspondence between the series of relationships united in a single synthesis As Albert Lautman has so well expressed it, the truth of a particular judgment is recognized by the mind through *reflection,* which situates it at the center of a world scheme, in which its implications correspond with those of an infinite number of other judgments. It is thus quite as useless to relate a judgment to a purely material reality, postulated as anterior to the judgment, as to relate it to an intelligible universe, which cannot be tested against direct experience: there is no pure fact any more than there is pure logic. However, a finite mind cannot postulate, in a single nontemporal operation, the infinite number of relationships implied in the world scheme: knowledge is always incomplete; consciousness, in its endeavor to assimilate reality, is engaged in an historical progression; reason must continually be renewed at the source of experience; in short, the modality of judgment is never reality or necessity, but possibility. If truth may be compassed by the human mind, it is because the "cogito" contains, so to speak, the infinite "cogitatio," which nevertheless transcends it, but scholars on earth are not fighting a battle already won in heaven; the progress of knowledge is, in very truth, the creation of intelligibility.

The early book *Les étapes de la philosophie mathématique* (1912) caught the mathematical mind in the very creation of living concepts, such as that of number, given new force by the progress of the operations carried out with it. *L'expérience humaine et la causalité physique* shows a constant flux and reflux between reason and experience in the building up of physical science: space is not prior to the objects scattered through it, nor number to numerable objects; it is incorrect to postulate, *a priori,* a system of reference, into which experience is to be fitted, as the Newtonian school of physics tried to do, or to attempt to confine a concept to one of its transient acceptations; for instance, the idea of causality, which was falsely and systematically presented in Mill's empiricism, and which has been fitted successively to certain selected experiences, although it has been impossible to reduce it to any one of them. Brunschvicg finds the most striking confirmation of his views in the new science initiated by Einstein, which replaces the obscurity of physics by the open intelligibility of geometry and shows reason actually evolving the means of progressively assimilating reality to a system of relationships which is transparent and homogeneous to the mind; with Einstein, science rejoins its true line of development and links up, across Newton, with the Cartesian tradition.

Brunschvicg's most important work, *Le progrès de la conscience dans la philosophie occidentale,* greatly widens the scope of analysis, showing the mind at work in all fields and establishing a relation between the authenticity of knowledge and that of the life of the mind going back to the history of ideas. Brunschvicg shows that any clear-cut scientific advance is accompanied by a fortification of the spiritual life: an historical process of reflection, "interiorization," and "totalization," not continuous but interrupted by stages of slackness and dimness, in which the mind sinks back into an abstract and lifeless conceptualism, instead of keeping pace with the clear development of the act of judgment. According to Spinoza's teaching, knowledge makes possible the passage from an individual "cogito" in which consciousness apprehends itself in a state of "inadequatio," to a universal "cogito," in which it is identified with the pure "cogitatio": hence the favored position of the mathematical and physical sciences. Jean Nabert has given a penetrating description (in the *Revue de métaphysique et de morale,* 1928) of how, in the dynamism of Brunschvicg's analysis, history is illuminated by an original conception of the nature of thought, which, at the same time, helps to confirm for Brunschvicg, that the liberating value of a system is intimately dependent on the "mental function" on which it relies; hence the "exclusions," which are merely the result of the original light which the system throws on the development of the mind.

Interchange between reason and experience has its extension in a gradually broadening enlightenment of consciousness, culminating in the creation of an intellectual system of transparent relationships, and simultaneously, of universal love and charity relationships. God is immanent in our judgment, since, in us, judgment proceeds from the presence of the universal "cogitatio"; the gradual attainment of pure and universal judgment of ideas assumes the existence of universal harmony of minds; here God is no longer the God of religious revelation, but an immanent deity, at the heart of the ideal of man.

Thus we see in *Le progrès de la conscience* the first expression of themes which are further developed in *La connaissance de soi* and *La raison et la religion;* progress from an inner life, falsified by the vestiges of animality, to a spiritual life finally stripped of its accretions, when man, rising above his own individuality, embraces all humanity in a network of interrelations, in which love born of intellectual communion preserves the universal character of duty, and adds its own peculiar warmth. *La connaissance de soi* is not a textbook of introspection; nothing is more foreign to Brunschvicg's outlook than a complacent concentration upon the nuances of the inner life; the point is to bet on oneself, to see in oneself the universal essence of man, which provides a guiding thread to lead us through the avatars of man, from the animal state, through the stages of conversion, liberation, and purification, at the end of which life becomes reason in man. The work of men such as Lucien Lévy-Bruhl on primitive mentality,[10] Jean Piaget on child psychology and logic,[11] converge in the spiritualism of *Les âges de l'intelligence,* which is indeed true to Lachelier's reflexive method, but infinitely freer from the temptations of vitalism. That desire for purity shows still more clearly in Brunschvicg's conception of religion, in his refusal to commit religious life to a fixed ritual or to an anthropomorphic creed, even if it were only the belief in a personal God whom man could ask to answer his love with love. The source of religion is the presence within us of reason, which nevertheless transcends us *as* individuals. At the end of the advance of consciousness, in the final illumination, intelligence is thus identified with love; charity is the apprehension of the network of interrelationships in which humanity, as a community of rational beings, is enmeshed; and faith is but the certainty of an indefinite progress of knowledge and morality, a certainty which cannot be conferred by emotional, mystical experience, as the latter fluctuates perpetually "from anguish to ecstasy." [12]

Although based on the exercise of the intellect alone, this philosophy is yet full of warmth and dynamism; fed by reading and meditation on the classics, it gives back to Plato, Descartes, Spinoza, and Kant the life it draws from them; rich and comprehensive, it is nevertheless inflexible in its exclusions; its fundamental obsession is purity, its aim to show that the life of the spirit is the true life.

On the other hand, the main concern of thinkers like Bergson was the effort to maintain contact, in the biological depths, with the fresh spring of life; but one is struck, here and there, in Brunschvicg's writings, by certain themes with which one has become familiar in reading Bergson, particularly the integration of becoming in the picture of consciousness. In Brunschvicg's view, the privilege of Bergsonian intuition should be allowed to a purified intellect, fully possessed of itself; that alone has any criterion of truth and can enable man to rise above the animal state and attain that generosity which perhaps would not be so very far removed from the "élan" of *Les deux sources*.

d. The "New Scientific Attitude."

It is largely due to Brunschvicg that many French scientists have become philosophers in the midst of their scientific work. Louis de Broglie,[13] for instance, reviews coherently the concepts of object, cause, law, the principle of contradiction, the forms of space and time. This has given rise to a new conception of the interrelations of reality and mind. Gaston Bachelard,[14] however, has become the principal theorist of the new scientific attitude. Rejecting both immediate realism and immediate rationalism, Bachelard has endeavored to show how scientific advance revolutionizes the conception one may have of the relations between the mind and nature. "Thus, when we think about scientific activity, we perceive at once that realism and rationalism are constantly advising one another." Science is in fact an activity which, by building up a body of experience, seeks to realize a particular rationale; it is thus never the interaction of an awakened mind and a purely natural object, but of a mind developed and equipped by its earlier scientific inventions and an object constructed by an existing science. "Immediate reality is simply an occasion for scientific thought, and no longer an object of knowledge. . . Scientific reality is in dialectical relation with scientific reason." It would then be useless to claim that one is giving a closed theory of the scientific mind, since the characteristic of such a spirit is to rejuvenate itself by a constant interchange with a reality which, in its turn, can be defined only in terms of that dialectic. Bachelard thus realizes that modern science goes farther than the classical theories; in the *Philosophie du non* he shows that if science rejects the postulates and principles in which the classical scientist tried to confine it, it is not a mere denial, but because those same classical concepts have found their place and a new meaning in a vaster whole. Science is movement, reason is invention, and there is no justification for asserting that those quantum theories which cannot be fitted into Meyerson's analysis, are only a momentary aberration which will one day fit into their place in territory gained by an unchanging reason. Bachelard would like to subordinate to the new scientific attitude a new system of teaching which would give the human mind final mastery over the instruments it has itself created and which still hold surprises for it. For, he says, in an outburst of faith in the future of science, "if we were able to reinforce objective culture with psychological culture, by devoting all the energies of life to scientific research, we should experience the sudden animation which the creative syntheses of mathematical physics give the mind."

With new foundations, after a probably unprecedented crisis, freed from the narrow confines of Comtist positivism and epistemology of identity, science thus offers philosophers great hopes. Of course, no one can foresee what its later developments will be, or whether this period of revolutionary ferment will be followed by a period of codification and axiomatization.

The new positivism of the Vienna Group reacts violently against the philosophies of consciousness and the various dialectics, presenting science as consisting of a body of theories capable of formal statement, the purpose of experiment being to enable us to make a choice between all the logically possible theories; this represents, in itself, the replacement of a theory of truth in the process of constitution by one of truth as already constituted. It remains, however, that the scientific revolution has given rise to a profound revision of the theory of the mind and of reality. This still astonishing structure restores to science its repute, while science's new awareness of the nature of the intellectual instrument it employs, forbids it to condemn other forms of mental activity.

III. TRANSCENDENCE AND EXPERIENCE

Hence philosophic speculation has not been confined to providing a metaphysical background for modern science. On the one hand, a wide variety of routes has been adopted in the quest for an Absolute which shall supply an answer to the eternal query on the meaning of destiny, whence spring speculation on Being and Value, the rationalist metaphysic of the "Philosophy of the Spirit," as well as the new trends in Catholic thought. On the other hand, the greater technicality of scientific thought has caused the crystallization of a movement for a return to the immediacy of the lived experience, in the various types of existentialism; science is becoming increasingly *terra incognita* to the non-specialist, but the bewilderment of Man—actor in a drama whose premises he cannot grasp, and whose meaning seems often to escape him—is becoming constant in current thought. Hence the success of philosophies claiming either to remedy the ill through some form of transcendence or by an appeal to courage, or to be a medium for the comprehension of a condition which is dramatic indeed, but at the very least purged of its worst features by being faced without illusions.

a. *The Philosophy of the Spirit.*

The philosophers who, in 1934, founded the fairly comprehensive school known as the "Philosophy of the Spirit," faithful to the spiritualistic tradition, did not burden the new group with a rigid doctrine; as Louis Lavelle, one of the group's moving spirits (the other is René Le Senne) has said, their object is "the rehabilitation of the spirit conceived as its own perennial source, that is, the source of all motions of the mind and will." The Spirit is activity and light; there is such a thing as a genuine spiritual experience. These doctrines bear a singular resemblence to those of Brunschvicg; however, the Philosophy of the Spirit is suspicious alike of intellectualism, which it deems arid, and of the pretensions of science, which it regards as a danger to the life of the spirit. This school seeks to preserve the independence of ethical reflection and establish its connection with metaphysical speculation. Without losing touch with the concrete and personal aspects of subjective spirituality, emphasis is laid on the importance of values, at once immanent and transcendent, which, though their actualization is conditional upon our effective acceptance of them, yet stand out as absolutes which give its meaning to the act.

René Le Senne[15] was brought up in the solid school of the Hamelin dialectic. In 1925, the same year as Hamelin's *Essay* was reprinted, he published his *Introduction à la philosophie,* which still bore the strong imprint of his master's rationalism . Here he takes up the description of the life of the spirit where Hamelin left off, at the theory of individual existence and liberty (the existentialist dialectic of contradiction as opposed to the logical dialectic of contraries) and shows reason in action for the overcoming of the unending contradictions raised against it by the contact of the spirit with the world.

This is the starting point, and thereafter his philosophy evolves toward an increasingly fruitful integration of subjective experience and a keen awareness of the drama of human existence. *Le devoir* enlarges on the concept of contradiction, by analysis of doubt, of suffering, of the distinction between subject and object, of the conflict of individual selves, of remoteness from God. Contradiction cannot be annihilated, but duty, in knowledge, moral life, love, and religion alike, consist in rising above it by accepting it without reserve as the essence of our condition, recognizing its basic nature and giving it a positive value.

In his most significant work, *Obstacle et valeur*, where his thought had attained the fullness of its form, Le Senne was to cast aside the intellectualism still latent in the concepts of contradiction and duty, in favor of a widened experience of obstacle and value. The life of the spirit then takes on the aspect of a surpassing of oneself, made possible by encounter with the obstacle eternally renewed, which makes us sharers in the universal value thus reduced to particular terms. Le Senne's philosophy is a philosophy of the heroic operation of the consciousness accepting its state of diversion as the starting point for the working out of its own salvation, and is the most dramatic element in the Philosophy of the Spirit; hence the debate within the group between the drama of Le Senne and Lavelle's plenitude; Louis Lavelle's [16] optimistic approach underscores the positive experiences of the consciousness and especially the first and basic experience of participation, on the background of which the only contradiction is a withheld joy, but a joy which always exists *in posse*. "Grace is ever present: it suffices to be willing to receive it."

b. The Church and Philosophy.

By its insistence on the transcendency and universality of value, the Philosophy of the Spirit sought to establish the validity of individual choice in terms of the absolute and to exorcise in advance the absurdity of free acting and existentialist anguish. Official Catholicism goes further in its desire to present to the individual a coherent picture of a world justified by the fact of its divine creation. Admittedly, Thomism, which the Encyclical *Aeterni Patris* established as the Church's official philosophy in 1897, can be given widely different interpretations. The version which has been the most general in France is neo-Thomism, whose first exponents were Fathers Sertillange and Garrigou-Lagrange; its opponents have sometimes complained that it borrowed from Bergsonism the concepts of an understanding of being anterior and superior to the formal sciences, and that of a nature in continuous process of becoming, which never achieves complete fulfillment. However, as early as 1914, Jacques Maritain,[17] one of this school's most brilliant members between the two wars, had set up his own intellectualistic realism in opposition to Bergsonian vitalism. In a series of brilliant works further embellished by the literary taste and artistic sensibility of their author, he has made it his task to demonstrate the richness of the Thomist concept of life and the world, and to defend the solid structure of the *Summa* against the errors of the Cartesian tradition. From a different angle, the personalists, led by Emmanuel Mounier, have taken the antithesis between the individual given over to his own egoism and the person permeated with the presence of God, and built thereon an ethical and political system which makes them in some sort the Left Wing of Catholicism.

c. *The Christian Existentialism of Gabriel Marcel.*

The official philosophy of the Church, then, is mainly concerned with supplying the framework of synthesis of knowledge and the possibility of finding a rational explanation of practical life. Also a Catholic, Gabriel Marcel, the first man in France to assume the name of Existentialist, discusses in his *Journal métaphysique* the philosopher's quest within himself for being. Though the *Journal* is not autobiography, nevertheless the philosopher's choice of this form is not without significance; it is the accurate apprehension of our inner being which admits us to full communion with the universe: thus subjectivity does not turn in upon itself; it has a metaphysical dimension and is in itself transcendence; and the whole of Marcel's speculation is concerned with bringing out its inner meaning.

The *Journal métaphysique* is in two parts. The first, and more dialectical, takes the traditional concepts and shows that they are inadequate to the apprehension of being as such. This part is the essential introduction to the second, which directly utilizes subjective experience as the key to a positive knowledge of being. The writer's distance from the whole idealist school, and from Brunschvicg in particular, can be appreciated from such a sentence as the following, which is in some sort the cornerstone of existentialist realism: "Never, in any circumstances whatever, can affirmation conceive itself to be the begetter of the thing affirmed."

The distinction between reality and appearance is a true one only if it is sought to apprehend reality by the development of concepts. Otherwise reality is, in fact, identical with the appearance which is brought to light by subjective experiences, provided the latter be not distorted. But how do we, within our unsatisfied desires, our troubled hearts, and our instability, apprehend an "Essential Being" who is immutable and eternal fulfillment? If we suffer the pangs of solitude and exile, our suffering is relative to the experience of plenitude, without which any feeling of want would be inconceivable. Alike in the realm of theory and in daily life, we all know the state of abundant fulfillment whose criterion is happiness: the plunge into truth, which is the characteristic of the intelligence, the possession by the free will of the object which itself creates.

Thus, the *Journal métaphysique* passes from the stage of pure description to that of existential analysis, which holds that there can be no field of psychology which is self-contained like an empirical object. Human subjectivity not only in itself reveals being, but it is traversed by the stream of the transcendent: the presence of being, realization of value, winning of salvation are no more than three ways of expressing the same thing. And as salvation consists in submitting to that transcendence which animates us and apart from which we are nothing, then, if salvation is will, it is not keyed-up effort, but consent and relaxation.

Yet, despite its deeply religious spirit and its constant reference to quasi-mystical experience, it would be wrong to assume that this is an ascetic philosophy glorifying the spirit at the expense of the body. Undoubtedly, one of the most novel features of Marcel's philosophy is his attempt to revive awareness of the body in its true perspective and the values which that body "lives." Here sensation is on the same footing as the exercise of the will or the illumination of the intelligence. To regard the body as belonging exclusively to the physical world is to yield to a prejudice which is an unfortunate by-product of the prestige of science. Its description is utterly falsified if we neglect its quality of immediate actuality, whose metaphysical importance must not be overlooked. For that quality is an indisputable revelation of my own existence, admittedly giving me no knowledge properly so called, but ever bringing with it a content of rich and irreplaceable emotions. Those inner feelings are in some sort Gabriel Marcel's equivalent for "cogito," and he makes them the cornerstone in his description of being.

How then are we reconcile these two concepts of sensualism and voluntarism in metaphysics? The fact is that the very transcendency of the will which permeates us forces it to become flesh that it may enter into us and make us what we are. Hence the individual can only apprehend the fact of his own existence through the individual coloration which sensation gives to that will within himself. Therefore sensation and will together will be the foundation of love, whose object can only be the being; the immediate apprehension of being is love, when his presence is the object of a feeling and a will identified in us. And that love is the evidential feeling which shows me the reality of the others, of the "thou," of my neighbor, as an intuitive apprehension as indisputable as that of my own existence, but which still gives me no analytical conceptual knowledge of the other's self. In the final end love in its true fullness is the love of God, whose capture of the self takes the shape of religious ecstasy, the profoundest experience of the inner life.

d. Two "Existentialisms" or One?

That, then, is the first form taken by existentialism, the philosophy which, under other forms, was to achieve such a degree of popular favor, and to become almost the symbol of our age. But what is the common factor which entitles both of two philosophies as fundamentally dissimilar as Marcel's and Sartre's to the name "existentialism"? For the former school no apprehension of the immanent is possible without the enlightenment deriving from the presence of the transcendent; the sense of nonplenitude inherent in finite life becomes perceptible only through contrast with that plenitude whose highest point is religious ecstasy. Whereas to the second school it is of the essence of consciousness that it enclose a void, and it is a contradiction in terms to postulate a consciousness possessing full plenitude, though it were but in moments of special grace separated by long periods of solitude and exile; and that contradiction defines at once the drama and the essence of the consciousness which achieves self-awareness only in its nostalgia for the *in-se,* from which it is sundered by the void making it consciousness, and with which it would fain be united without surrendering its full transparence. To the first school the Being is God, who dwells in us and fills our hearts with joy; to the second the Being *in-se* is a vast profusion of purposeless and irrational existence surrounding us. To the first, our neighbor reveals himself to us in an act of love; to the second, the eyes of others, crystallizing us as what we are, and from whose sight we ever seek to withhold ourselves, are literally hell (Sartre, *Huis-clos,* "Hell is other people . . ."). Marcel is fundamentally optimistic, since, although his starting point is the negative experience of the tragedy of consciousness, he has the sense of security emanating from the certainty of salvation through submission to the transcendent; the new existentialism, on the other hand, presents a pitiless picture of consciousness entangled beyond remedy in the web of its own innate unhappiness, its oneness severed, burdened with an abysmal liberty, which is no more than a lack of being not to be escaped from, responsible for values which itself evolves unaided by the touchstone of the transcendent and whose implications it accepts to the point of heroism, part of a human world, and responsible for the destiny of a human world which it never willed, faced almost inevitably with cowardice and insincerity—in a word, enduring an existence in which there is neither God nor reason to justify. The first school writes with the feeling and spiritual warmth of the great mystics; the second adopts the hard and unfeeling tone of a prosecuting counsel. The first, the Right Wing of existentialism, is of the lineage of Christianity's apostles of consolation; Left-Wing existentialism sets up as the guilty conscience of our age and our contemporaries; it pushes to its ultimate limits the willed denial of all complacency, all accomodations, all excuses, and teaches that man's salvation depends not on submission or reconciliation, but on courage, namely, the clear-eyed acceptance of all the facets of an existence without mitigation.

Nevertheless, it is no misuse of words to bracket these two philosophies under the same label. Admittedly, the definition of existence by Jean Wahl in *Recherches philosophiques* is probably too full to apply to any other philosophy than that writer's own, which follows closely in the steps of Kierkegaard.[20] "To exist," he says, "is to choose; to feel emotion; to become; to be isolated, and to be subjective; to be perpetually concerned with oneself; to know oneself a sinner; to stand in the presence of God." That definition makes too much of the negative side of inner experience to meet the view of Gabriel Marcel; and there is too much talk of God to satisfy Jean-Paul Sartre.

Though Kierkegaard's theses recur more or less in all French existentialists, in Marcel they lack the ring of despair, which is probably part of the Protestant heritage; as far as Sartre is concerned, before reappearing in his work, they have been through the crucible of Heidegger's atheism, and have been conceptualized in the school of phenomenology whose founder is Husserl. But the assertion—vehement in Kierkegaard's case—that the most significant aspects of existence cannot be reduced to a general concept nor universalized according to the rules of reason, is still the basis of all the existentialist schools. There is yet further common ground: the real is held to reveal itself in certain immediate or affective experiences (*Erlebnisse*) which it would be erroneous to regard as no more than "states" of consciousness without any objective value, since they give us completer, truer, and more immediate access to reality than do intellectual concepts; again, all use the "cogito" as giving access to being as such, and not allowing the apprehension of the presence in ourselves of "cogitatio." Time is given a position of primacy; the correlation between the consciousness and the world is emphasized; all existentialists share the concept of the density of the real, of the infinity of the thing, which is ever greater than that part of it we apprehend. All agree, too, on the freedom of the consciousness, a consciousness which, though transparent to itself, cannot assign itself a definable essence; all stress the unique and ineffable character of personal existence; all describe with scrupulous care the actual experience of one's body, basic to the apprehension of any object in perception; all give a privilege to negative experiences, at least as the starting-point for reflection; finally, all show the apprehension of individual existence, of the "being-in-the-world," as amounting to a perpetual choice, which is always anguished because it is always free. That, then, is the existentialist philosophy, and, from its very nature, because a single lived experience reveals Being in all its depth, novels and plays are as much used for expressing it as are formal theoretical treatises.

e. *Psychological Research and the Birth of Atheistic Existentialism.*

In 1939, Jean-Paul Sartre[21] had not yet given himself out to be an existentialist; he was a follower of Husserl and was engaged in applying to psychology the method of radical phenomenological reassessment, which he contended was the only way of making it an authentic science. The concept of a stream of consciousness derived from James and Bergson; the Freudian attempt at exhaustive explanation of the Ego; the endeavor by the Behaviorists to cast out utterly from the subject's methodology the use of the inner sense as a medium for investigation and explanation; the Gestaltists' general application of the notion of form or structure; all are elements, often contradictory, in a revolution in psychology. But all agree in condemning psychological "atomism" and associationism. Thus Sartre's earlier work already follows an existing tradition. Of the many works which make it up, mention should be made of A. Spaier's[22] treatise on *Concrete Thought,* inspired by Bergsonism. Paul Guillaume[23] introduced the theory of form into France and dissected the foundations of the psychological method. Henri Wallon[24] was chiefly concerned with the genetic study of the beginnings of thought in children. A. Dalbiez[25] was to write a thesis, soon to become a classic, drawing the distinction between Freud's method and his doctrine. But the most far-reaching attempt to renew the bases of psychology was Georges Politzer's.[26] In 1928 he published the first, and only completed, volume of his *Critique des fondements de la psychologie,* in which he endeavored to expound coherently the consequences to psychology of the psychoanalytical revolution; "concrete psychology" seeking, with the help of concepts such as drama and narrative, to give a comprehensive interpretation of the effective life of the Ego, is calculated to furnish a true picture of human life and to make possible practical applications of this comparable to those of other sciences.

What emerges in various degrees of diffuseness from the rich collection of contemporary works is psychology's need to come of age as an authentic science. In Husserl's procedure, in the "return to the thing itself," in the abandonment of the natural attitude, in the primacy of the notion of intentionality, Sartre saw the possibility of erecting a new psychology. But rather than analyze the bases themselves, he preferred to test the new method by the study of specific psychological problems, beginning with the imagination. "We must. . .rid ourselves of our almost habitual way of conceiving all modes of existence in terms of physical existence." The image is, in essence, not a thing, but a mode of existence of the object, and no criteria are necessary to distinguish it from the object perceived; "recognition of the image as such is a datum of the inner sense." His book *L'imagination* is a polemical work covering the ground from the refutation of the *a priori* theory which "conceives of the image as *a* thing," and fidelity to the intuitive awareness which "teaches us that the image is not *the* thing," to the point where the site is sufficiently cleared, the remaining problems (e.g., the *"hylè"*) sufficiently delimited for the erection of a positive theory of the image, the imagination, and the "imaginary life" to be possible; the second stage was only to be attained in 1940 with the publication of *L'imaginaire.*

To Jean-Paul Sartre the imagination was not just a problem of psychology; the image being in an ambiguous way the position of an object absent, there is implicit in it the notion of annihilation (*néantisation*), and it is a special case to exhibit the nature of consciousness; and, as the image is a mode of existence for the object, so is "the imaginary" a mode of existence for the subject. That in its earliest stages was the "climate" of the burgeoning philosophy of existentialism. Phenomenological psychology, soon to become existentialist philosophy, attracted the attention of the young as being an original and rigorous method alert to seize upon lived experience, and an unlooked-for chance to rise above the stagnant antitheses of the philosophy of academic people and that of the society people, to clean up the world of things and the world of ideas by placing each problem in its right perspective. Sartre's incisive and irreverent article in the *Nouvelle revue française* maintaining the basic ideas of Husserl's philosophy against the "digestive" philosophies of assimilation honored by the theorists of knowledge, set the tone of that atmosphere of intellectual exaltation which one must have known in order to understand the strange fascination the movement has since had for the public, despite the technical difficulties with which the key works essential for its comprehension bristle.

In 1939 existentialism was not yet a form of humanism; such emotional idealism was left to the "autodidact," a character in *La nausée*. However, certain of its later theses were already appearing, were it only as mental attitudes described in phenomenological terms. Three instances will suffice: in *Le mur* we have the absurdity of history—an ideal Camus was to emphasize more than Sartre—and the significance of commitment (*engagement*), an idea treated from the negative angle in *Erostrate,* a short story in the same book; elsewhere we get the existentialist sentiment of nausea, which "puts across" to us the unwarrantable glut of the being-in-se hemming us in and the "not-being" of the consciousness produced by the formation of the void in a crowded world; it is this nausea which recalls the hero, cut off from the distractions of daily life, to the true destiny of consciousness.

Even in the first part of *L'imagination* the same distinction is made between the *pro-se* and the *in-se,* which was to appear again in *L'être et le néant;* in another work emotion was defined as "moved-consciousness-of-the-world"; the notion of the captive consciousness, victim of its own magical conduct, was already emerging; emotion was "an organic form of human existence," and Sartre was already talking about "man-in-situation." It seemed that for him phenomenology must resolve into an existentialist theory which alone would make it possible to transcend the inherent difficulties of those remnants of idealism from which Husserl had not yet managed to free himself entirely.[27]

From this point of view, the article entitled *Transcendance de l'égo* is of outstanding significance. Sartre sees the Ego not as the essential mode of existence of consciousness, but as a quasi-object, a unifying pole emerging only as the correlative of the reflexive consciousness. Sartre's attack on the theoretical problem of the unification of the content of consciousness, finally solved by Husserl (as it had been by Kant) by recourse to a unifying Ego, lays the foundations of his existential theory of consciousness of self, of the impossibility of perfect coincidence between the consciousness and itself in reflection. So, far from interpreting this impossibility of grasping oneself immediately as an "I" as establishing the superiority of spiritual life over interior life (cf. Brunschvicg), he only rejects the immediacy and special evidence of the interior life, to bind more firmly on the consciousness the burden of its own liberty and make it face the eyes of others. In these technical studies, apparently confined to single specific problems, Sartre, without yet explicitly meeting the nihilism of the age and without offering a remedy for it within the self, was already *in posse* the philosopher whom his ontology in part, but chiefly his articles and literary works were to make famous.

Today the general public has a clearer idea of the significance of the new philosophies which have attained explicit statement, and can perceive what they owe to the French tradition. However, account must be taken of the late war; the death of some and the survival of others are empirical phenomena, and, on this plane where the destiny of a given mind is worked out amid bombs and political police, and not in the arena of intellectual competition, it would be hard to dispute the absurdity of history. Take Cavaillès,[28] or Lautman,[29] whose theses on the nature of mathematical being held out promise, certainly, of new philosophies of knowledge, and probably of new general systems; or Politzer, who was starting the erection of a new general philosophy in the Marxist tradition (a design since continued by Henri Lefebvre[30]); if they and many others had not disappeared just because they were the best, or if such as Raymond Aron [31] had pursued his strictly philosophic work which a meditation on history began, contemporary French philosophy would be infinitely richer.

And yet, so much does the historical situation appear to be the governing factor, transcending the free choice of individuals, that perhaps the general character of our present epoch would not have differed greatly. Perhaps the preeminent power of historical reality explains the renewed favor Hegel enjoys in France[32] (the Hegel of the *Phenomenology of Mind,* pre-existentialist to one party and pre-Marxist to the other). If there be a drama of contemporary philosophy, it is only the most emphatic expression of the drama of the whole epoch, and philosophy has become the most coherent, but not the only, exposition of the need for each man to choose his side in face of the problem of mankind's condition. Philosophy is no longer the unforced movement of an ascetic liberty to separate itself from the hold of intellectual comfort and the security of traditional values. No longer, like Descartes, can the philosopher elect to withdraw himself from the world, even if it be held that philosophy stems from the abandonment of the natural attitude. It is the world itself which questions man and awakens the consciousness, by assailing the security of life and value at all levels.

The search for a concrete understanding of man; the impossibility of treating a specific problem (even purely logical) separately from the general problem of existence; the need for an immanentist philosophy of action; the link between philosophy and politics; the requirement that thought be of the most all-round human significance which forbids withdrawal into a pure life of the mind, as opposed to the life of the whole man—all that may portend more than a revolution in the concepts within philosophy; it may mean a completely new definition of philosophy itself, the practice of philosophy being the effort toward integral self-awareness of a being who apprehends himself as involved or committed ("engagé"), but, simultaneously, as ever retaining the power, not to know himself free, but to free himself effectively in a dialectic of the mind linked inseparably to that dialectic which is lived in action. Perhaps the distress and anxiety of our age will later be seen to be a temporary and superficial symptom of its confusion before the necessary coming of a new Idea of Man.

SELECTED BIBLIOGRAPHY

(1)   Bergson, Henri. *Les deux sources de la morale et de la religion.* Paris, Presses Universitaires de France, 1932.

————. *L'énergie spirituelle.* Paris, Presses Universitaires de France, 1919.

————. *La pensée et le mouvant.* Paris, Presses Universitaires de France, 1927.

(2)   Minkowski, Dr. Eugène. *La schizophrénie.* Paris, Payot, 1927.

(3)   Le Roy, Edouard. See the bibliography for Wahl's essay.

(4)   Blondel, Maurice. See the bibliographies for Berger's and Duméry's essays.

————. *La philosophie et l'esprit chrétien.* Paris, Presses Universitaires de France, 1944.

(5)   As his admirable posthumous work, *Sur la logique et la théorie de la science* (Paris, Presses Universitaires de France) was not published until 1947, we shall not deal here with *Jean Cavaillès's* late philosophic evolution. However, let us mention that the problem of the impact of phenomenology on the theory of scientific truth is one of the main points in this book. (See Cavaillès's other works in note 28.)

(6) Lavelle, Louis. *La philosophie française entre les deux guerres.* Paris, Aubier, 1942.

(7) Meyerson, Émile. See André Lalande's bibliography for philosophy of science.

(8) Lalande, André. See André Lalande's bibliography for philosophy of science.

———. *Vocabulaire technique et critique de la philosophie.* Paris, Presses Universitaires de France, 1926.

(9) Brunschvicg, Léon. *Nature et liberté.* Paris, Flammarion, 1921.

———. *L'expérience humaine et la causalité physique.* Paris, Presses Universitaires de France, 1922.

———. *Le progrès de la conscience dans la philosophie occidentale.* Paris, Presses Universitaires de France, 1927.

———. *La connaissance de soi.* Paris, Presses Universitaires de France, 1931.

———. *Les âges de l'intelligence.* Paris, Presses Universitaires de France, 1934.

———. *La raison et la religion.* Paris, Presses Universitaires de France, 1939.

Articles in philosophical periodicals: unfortunateely, these articles, though important, have not yet been republished in book form:

———. "L'orientation du rationalisme contemporain." *Revue de métaphysique et de morale,* Paris, Armand Colin, 1920.

———. "La relation entre la mathématique et la physique." *Revue de métaphysique et de morale,* Paris, 1923.

———. "Vie intérieure et vie spirituelle." *Revue de métaphysique et de morale,* Paris, 1925.

———. "De la vraie et de la fausse conversion." *Revue de métaphysique et de morale,* Paris, 1930, 1931, 1932.

See also *Discussions of the French Philosophical Society*: "La querelle de l'athéisme," *Bulletin de la Société française de philosophie,* May-June, 1928; "Discussion with Edouard Le Roy," (*ibid.,* 1931).

(10) Lévy-Bruhl, Lucien. *La mentalité primitive.* Paris, Presses Universitaires de France, 1922.

———. *L'âme primitive.* Paris, Presses Universitaries de France, 1927.

———. *Le surnaturel et la nature dans la pensée primitive.* Paris, Presses Universitaires de France, 1931.

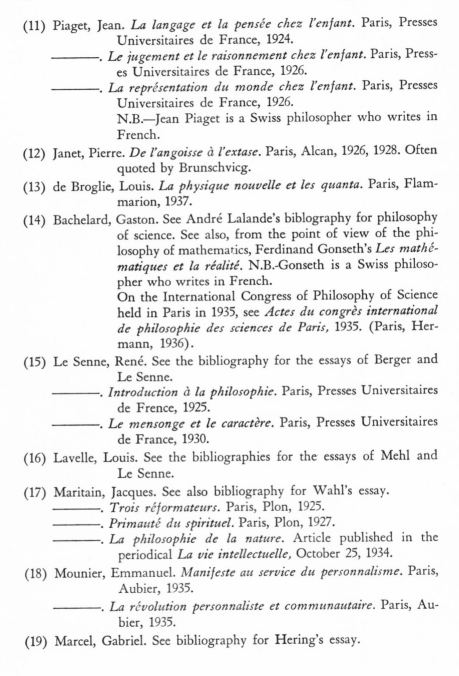

(11) Piaget, Jean. *La langage et la pensée chez l'enfant*. Paris, Presses Universitaires de France, 1924.

———. *Le jugement et le raisonnement chez l'enfant*. Paris, Presses Universitaires de France, 1926.

———. *La représentation du monde chez l'enfant*. Paris, Presses Universitaires de France, 1926.

N.B.—Jean Piaget is a Swiss philosopher who writes in French.

(12) Janet, Pierre. *De l'angoisse à l'extase*. Paris, Alcan, 1926, 1928. Often quoted by Brunschvicg.

(13) de Broglie, Louis. *La physique nouvelle et les quanta*. Paris, Flammarion, 1937.

(14) Bachelard, Gaston. See André Lalande's bibliography for philosophy of science. See also, from the point of view of the philosophy of mathematics, Ferdinand Gonseth's *Les mathématiques et la réalité*. N.B.-Gonseth is a Swiss philosopher who writes in French.

On the International Congress of Philosophy of Science held in Paris in 1935, see *Actes du congrès international de philosophie des sciences de Paris, 1935*. (Paris, Hermann, 1936).

(15) Le Senne, René. See the bibliography for the essays of Berger and Le Senne.

———. *Introduction à la philosophie*. Paris, Presses Universitaires de Frence, 1925.

———. *Le mensonge et le caractère*. Paris, Presses Universitaires de France, 1930.

(16) Lavelle, Louis. See the bibliographies for the essays of Mehl and Le Senne.

(17) Maritain, Jacques. See also bibliography for Wahl's essay.

———. *Trois réformateurs*. Paris, Plon, 1925.

———. *Primauté du spirituel*. Paris, Plon, 1927.

———. *La philosophie de la nature*. Article published in the periodical *La vie intellectuelle*, October 25, 1934.

(18) Mounier, Emmanuel. *Manifeste au service du personnalisme*. Paris, Aubier, 1935.

———. *La révolution personnaliste et communautaire*. Paris, Aubier, 1935.

(19) Marcel, Gabriel. See bibliography for Hering's essay.

(20) Wahl, Jean. *Études kierkegaardiennes.* Paris, Aubier, 1938.

(21) Sartre, Jean-Paul. See also bibliography for Campbell's essay.

————. *Une idée fondamentale de la phénoménologie de Husserl: L'intentionnalité.* Article published in the periodical *Nouvelle revue française,* January, 1939—republished in *Situations I,* Paris, Gallimard, 1947.

To the existentialist research may be linked Jankélévitch's *L'alternative* (Paris, Alcan, 1938).

(22) Spaier, A. *La pensée concrète.* Paris, Presses Universitaires de France, 1927.

See also Pradines's *Philosophie de la sensation.* Strasbourg, Éd. de l'Université de Strasbourg, 1928.

(23) Guillaume, Paul. *La psychologie de la forme.* Paris, Flammarion, 1927.

————. *Introduction à la psychologie.* Paris, Presses Universitaires de France, 1942.

(24) Wallon, Henri. *De l'acte à la pensée.* Paris, Flammarion, 1942.

Gives a good idea of his method and previous works.

(25) Dalbiez, A. *La méthode psychanalytique et la doctrine freudienne.* Paris, Descleé de Brower, 1936.

(26) Politzer, Georges. (victim of Nazism). *Critique des fondements de la psychologie.* Paris, Rieder—Presses Universitaires de France, 1928.

(27) Sartre, Jean-Paul. See bibliography for Campbell's essay.

Note a similar evolution from Maurice Merleau-Ponty's *La structure du comportement* (Paris, Presses Universitaires de France, 1942)— where he avoids the temptation of neo-Kantism, to his *Phénoménologie de la perception* (Paris, Gallimard, 1947), where he brings fully existentialist solutions.

(28) Cavaillès, Jean. (victim of Nazism). *Méthode axiomatique et formalisme.* Paris, Hermann, 1938.

————. *Sur la logique et la théorie de la science.* (A posthumous work written in a German jail). Paris, Presses Universitaires de France, 1947.

(29) Lautman, Albert (victim of Nazism). *Essai sur les notions de structure et d'existence en mathématiques.* Paris, Hermann, 1938.

(30) Lefebvre, Henri. *Logique formelle, logique dialectique.* Paris, Éditions sociales, 1947.

(31) Aron, Raymond. *Introduction à la philosophie de l'histoire*. Paris, Gallimard, 1938.

(32) Hyppolite, Jean. *Genèse et structure de la "Phénoménologie de l'Esprit" de Hegel*. Paris, Aubier, 1947.

Kojève, Alexandre. *Introduction à la lecture de Hegel*. Paris, Gallimard, 1947. The publication of a course given in the twenties which had an important influence on a number of contemporary French minds.

THE PRESENT SITUATION
AND THE PRESENT
FUTURE OF FRENCH
PHILOSOPHY

*Jean Wahl**

L et us see what has become of the most important tendencies of which
Mr. Havet has spoken, and first of what he has called "The Spiritualistic Realism of Bergson." Although this philosophy did so
much for the liberation of the mind, we have to take account of the
fact that on some very important problems it gives quite definite conclusions which one has to adopt if one wishes to be called a Bergsonian. So,
there are not many disciples of Bergson in the quite strict sense of the
word. But first there are important works dedicated to the study of his
philosophy; let us mention two of them. The very beautiful book of
Thibaudet, *Le bergsonisme,* with many rich developments bearing on the
relations between Bergson and the other great philosophers from Parmeni-
des and Heraclitus to Spencer and Hegel; and the one of Jankélévitch with
its deep probings into the most difficult regions of Bergsonian thought.
Secondly, we have the growth of the conceptions of Le Roy. Thirdly,
Dr. Minkowski has continued his endeavor toward the foundation of a
Bergsonian psychiatry, the enlargement of the conception of a qualitative
time with recognition of qualitative space, and the formulation in Bergsonian language of the idea of "Being in the world." So, he arrives at a
combination of psychological and cosmological ideas. Fourthly, we have
to take account of the influence, not always clearly recognized, of Bergson

* Born in 1888. Professor at the Sorbonne. Ousted from the Sorbonne by the
Vichy government, by order of the Germans; imprisoned by the Germans in 1941 as an
active anti-collaborationist. Owed his life to friends who secured for him an appointment
as a professor in the New School for Social Research, New York. Dr. Wahl also taught
at Mt. Holyoke College, Smith College, and the University of Chicago. Upon his return
to Paris, he founded the *Collège Philosophique.* Author of *Pluralistic Philosophies in England
and America* (published in English), *Vers le concret, Études Kierkegaardiennes, The
Philosopher's Way* (published in English), and of numerous other works, including a
book of poems (*Connaître sans connaître,* 1938).

on existentialist philosophy, on the one hand, the religious existentialism of Marcel, on the other hand the nonreligious existentialism of Sartre and Merleau-Ponty, who sometimes criticize very harshly Bergsonian conceptions but whose teachings coincide on some important points with those of Bergson. (Let us mention, for example, the ideas of the last one of these philosophers on the motor character of memory.) Fifthly, some philosophers like Ruyer and Canguilhem, when they stress the irreducibility of vital phenomena to mechanistic phenomena, find themselves in agreement with Bergsonian theories.

We may now turn to what might appear to be the other extreme of philosophy, that is intellectualism. But we will find that intellectualism has tended more toward an enlargement of its conception, be it Nogué, a disciple of Pradines, who combines his teachings with those of Lavelle; of Étienne Souriau, who tries to found an intellectualistic esthetics and a general esthetic theory of the world; or Ruyer, who having first formulated a kind of structural theory of the world, has moved, as we have said already, toward placing an emphasis on the irreducibility of vital phenomena to mechanistic explanations.

Now we come to all those philosophers who are influenced by the intellectualism of Brunschvicg. Brunschvicg, who was very much opposed to Bergson for a long time, finally saw some deep relations between Bergson's philosophy and his own, particularly the fact that they both denied any static being. Let us notice that starting from the thought of Brunschvicg, many philosophers developed theories that take account of elements in reality which are not reducible at all to pure intelligence. This is the case first of all for the important thinker, Bachelard, who in different realms of thought stresses either the subtle relations toward which science tends and which are not amenable to classical concepts; or the complexes of imagination which form the background of poetical consciousness; or finally some universal concepts which dominate, according to him, human thought, like those of the discontinous instant or of negation. He has developed what he calls a superrationalistic theory.

If we take three disciples of Brunschvicg such as Raymond Aron, Cavaillès, and Canguilhem, we observe that the first, influenced by German conceptions of the philosophy of history, has emphasized the necessity of completing the purely intellectualistic scheme with a consideration of a past which is not fixed but which we, up to a certain point, constitute by our personal decisions, although we are immersed in it; he tends toward what may be called an existentialist conception of history.

The second examines the presuppositions of intellectualistic thought in the light of phenomenology and of the last results of the logisticians; and he seems to come to abandon some of these presuppositions. The last, under the influence of biological studies, affirms (like Ruyer) the irreducibility of life and stresses the value of biological phenomena as giving us a richer idea of reality than the one which was given by pure intellectualism.

If we wish to give a representative of Cartesian and Spinozistic intellectualism, we must turn to Alquié who, having left his former surrealistic conceptions, has found a personal defense and a universal guarantee of human knowledge in the affirmation of classical reason. Also we must turn to A. Patri; and, in the esthetic field, to Roger Caillois.

Needless to say the examination and criticism of science has been continued, particularly in the works of Louis de Broglie who shows the complementarity of the different designs which man can use in order to understand the real, and the limits which science, not contingently, but necessarily, encounters.

If we now examine Catholic philosophers, we find first the continuation of the works of Maritain, who in his last volume examines existentialism from a Christian point of view and distinguishes an authentic, nonprofessional, and non-ontological existentialism which in fact is religious, and a professional existentialism which is irreligious and ontological. The last book of Gilson, a very beautiful book on essence and existence, develops and renders more precise some analogous ideas. He seeks the historical background far down into the history of philosophy. Both Maritain and Gilson insist on what has been sometimes called the existentialist aspects of Thomism, since for both of them the whole world depends on one act which is the act of God, the act of existing, superior to every conceptual determination. These are the representatives of Thomism. But for the last ten years or more, a movement has developed within the Church which is nearly anti-Thomistic and which favors a return to the Greek Fathers. This is advocated particularly by Father De Lubac who has written admirable works on the Social Theory of Christianity, on Atheistic Humanism (an examination of Nietzsche and some others), and on Proudhon. Another defender of this movement is Father Daniélou. Father Teilhard de Chardin proposes a rather bold combination of science and religion. He is led by a great faith in both of them and presents to us in these hard times a progressive and optimistic theory. Father Fessard, also a Jesuit, tries to unite Hegel and Christianity, turning to one of the origins of Hegelianism which started from religious thought.

Emmanuel Mounier has studied the different forms of existentialism from what he has called the personalistic point of view.

A personalist also, the Swiss, De Rougemont, is influenced by Karl Barth and Kierkegaard and has written an interpretation of the formation of the idea of love in modern times, and a book on the presence, in modern times also, of the devil. He advocates a concrete mode of thought.

We might say something here about what is called Christian existentialism. By this is meant mostly the existentialism of Gabriel Marcel. But this has been examined in other studies in this volume. A book on Marcel, under this title, has been published and contains some fine articles. Two disciples of Marcel, Dufrenne and Ricoeur, have also written a book on Jaspers in which there are many comparisons between him and Marcel.

Let us mention the developments which a negative theology is taking, particularly in the historical works of Losski and in the philosophic, but still rather tentative, meditations of Morot-Sir.

Face to face with these religious thinkers, most of them Catholic (one of them, De Rougemont, a Protestant), we find dialectical materialism. Unhappily there are not many authoritative formulations of this theory. The most interesting of the materialist authors, Politzer, was killed by the Germans. In his first published work he tried to unite, in a very original manner, Freud and Marx. One of the most prolific and certainly clever exponents of materialist doctrine is Henri Lefebvre. Mougin has given an interesting and amusing history of the growth of existentialism from the Marxian point of view.

We might say that intellectual youth in France seems to be divided into three parties: the Catholic, the communist, and the existentialist. Let us come now to the last of these. In order to understand its development, we must first consider several philosophers born in Germany or in Russia who, having studied under German masters, came to France between the two wars. Groethuysen, a friend of Max Scheler and an admirer of Heidegger, had a great influence in literary circles and launched, we might say, the career of Sartre as well as of many others. Landsberg, a disciple of Scheler, was a friend of Mounier and developed the ideas of personalism. Koyré, a disciple of Husserl, studied Jacob Böhme after having examined the paradoxes of the infinite and turned finally to studies of Plato, Descartes, and of the first developments of modern science in Galileo. Georges Gurvitch, whom we might classify in provisory manner as a disciple of Fichte, on whom he wrote a beautiful book (and also of Simon Franck), gave us the first authoritative book on German philosophy, particularly phenomenology; and then, turning to sociology, he advanced a theory of collective superrational consciousness, somewhat related to that of Durkheim but nevertheless quite different from it. Two Russian philosophers have to be named here—Berdiaeff, an inspirer of the personalism of Mounier and the author of many profound, far-reaching works, and Chestov, the creator of a philosophy of absurdity of which we will find echoes in Fondane, in Camus, and in Rachel Bespalof.

We need not discourse on the ideas of Sartre and Simone de Beauvoir since their ideas have been touched on elsewhere.

Among the books on existentialism, we might mention, in addition to those already named, Campbell's book on Sartre, quite clear and instructive, and also that of Jeanson on the ethical problem in Sartre's philosophy. A disciple of Sartre, Pouillon, has studied the idea and the representation of time in recent novels, with particular reference to Faulkner. Roland Caillois has explained in some articles what he understands as the essence of the thought of Merleau-Ponty.

Merleau-Ponty thinks that we have to start from a fundamental phenomenon which is perception. In this manner, he opposes rationalism and intellectualism with their presupposition of a transcendental ego, which would be an interiority without exteriority. But he equally opposes empiricism, which indeed does not take experience at its primary level but experience as it is understood by means of scientific categories. What he wants to study is the preobjective realm, the living world which comes before the objective one, the antepredicative preconscious world. He is helped in this matter by the work of Gestaltists and of men like Gelb, Kurt Goldstein, F. Fischer, Katz, Werner, and equally by that of Minkowski and Binswanger. For him, as for Husserl in his last works, man is essentially in the world and intentionality is explained by this being in the world which Husserl, in fact, conceived as the real basis of intentionality. The ideas of unreflectedness, of implicitness, of immediacy are all important in this philosophy, since for it the act of reflection is always a reflection upon an unreflected element which it cannot absorb completely.

Indeterminateness and ambiguity are also fundamental facts of consciousness, since we are at the same time body and mind, necessity and freedom, completely the one and completely the other. Not only this, but our perception does not give us these precise distinctions which only a later knowledge based on science will allow us to gain. There are vague fields, maldetermined spaces. All this makes us understand the idea of existence as it is understood by Merleau-Ponty. Existence is the ambiguous milieu of the incarnation of contraries, and dialectics is the very being of existence. He would not completely accept the distinction made by Sartre between *en soi* and *pour soi;* there is no pure *en soi,* and no pure *pour soi.* In the motion of existence the union of mind and body fulfills itself at every moment.

Existence is precisely the name of this equivocal union of the *en soi* and the *pour soi,* of automatism and consciousness. Existential analysis allows us to go beyond the classical opposition of empiricism and intellectualism.

Our body is the expression of our modes of existence. Psychic illnesses are to be explained as expressions of existential attitudes. Body is existence stabilized.

Perception is first anonymous, a kind of invasion of ourselves by the world, a depersonalization. In it we are spellbound by the exterior object. On the other hand, there is a oneness of perception; we mean by this that under the differentiation of the senses, there is a common ground by which each of the senses communicates with the others and which expresses itself in the synesthetic phenomena. By these ideas we are led to the affirmation that perception is linked with meaning. To perceive is not to judge, as the idealists have said, but to catch a signification immanent in and prior to judgment.

From this point of view of pure perception as opposed to all its scientific explanations, our body will be our means of communication with time and space, with the world. Our body is the very fact that we are in the world. In the theory of the *corps propre,* Merleau-Ponty's presentation might be compared with those of Maine de Biran and later of Gabriel Marcel. In place of the Kantian synthesis by means of intellectual categories, he would put a bodily synthesis by means of our organism. For him as for James, body has a particular feeling of space or voluminosity.

We have spoken of existence but there are different fields of existence, each one infinite in this sense at least, that we can push explanation by means of it as far as we wish. So, there will be economic and sexual and intellectual explanations. We can understand by this what Merleau-Ponty conceives as the highest expression of the will of man — that is the act by which we take upon ourselves and affirm and intellectualize either our economic or our sexual or any other situation. We make necessary meanings out of contingent data. This is the very condition and essence of man. We take upon ourselves our own condition and assume our finiteness.

The here and the now take a new meaning in this phenomenology. They are not inferior realities nor vanishing generalities but fundamental starting points. The idea of thing will not vanish either; things are realities from the perceptive point of view which Merleau-Ponty chooses to accept. If there were no things, we could not create illusions of things. A thing is an organism of colors, of sounds, of touch experiences, which symbolize and modify each other. Things are not reducible to laws, as Kant had thought, and instead of the transcendental object standing face to face with the transcendental ego, we have the concrete thing face to face with the *corps propre.*

A new conception of space, or rather of space-time, and a conception of movement, not without similarities to that of Bergson, accompany these ideas. There is a preobjective space without univocal position. The dimension of depth will be explained not by any reasoning, as it was by the rationalists, but by the presence of the object, since any other explanation would be the transformation of the third dimension into one of the two others.

Perception, we have said, is the fundamental phenomenon; but it is not a phenomenon enclosed in itself. First, it is always related to other things; it has an essential intentionality as well as an essential finitude, and always implies a *more,* inside of which it always takes place. Second, perception is naturally creative of worlds, all kinds of worlds, linguistic, artistic, religious, and so on. This is the very phenomenon of transcendence, the power of projection, which is inherent in our essence and which *is* our very essence. And this power of projection itself can only be understood by the fact that we are free and temporal beings; and this again makes us return to the idea of existence as being originally the fact that we go outside of ourselves by what we might call an act of immanent transcendence.

So, we see in this philosophy of Merleau-Ponty anew, and for the moment, a last step in the evolution of existentialism. Already Jaspers, Heidegger, and Sartre had insisted on historicity and communication and in this manner had completed in a non-Kierkegaardian way the philosophy of Kierkegaard. Merleau-Ponty emphasizes some elements which contribute to render this-worldly a thought which was primarily a flight from the world. He binds with perception the thought of existence which first was found to be an element of faith. From this point, new developments of existentialist philosophy seem to become possible; and the *impasse,* which in *L'être et le néant* seemed to hinder the thought of Sartre from going toward more and more positive results, seems no longer to be the necessary final point of an existentialist meditation.

One question which might be put to the author is whether there can be, from the phenomenological point of view, many precise things said about perception itself. In fact, Merleau-Ponty says much about the conditions and the objects of perception. But perception itself has to remain something mysterious, accepted in a kind of silence. This does not mean that these researches are out of the field of philosophy; but one has to widen the customary idea of philosophy, to leave a purely intellectualistic conception in order to make a place for givenness and a kind of intuition.

Moreover one has to ask whether there does not remain in the presentation of Merleau-Ponty some idealistic presupposition; perhaps when one is freed from it, there would be a possibility of going toward still more radical conclusions.

Now let us examine some individual philosophers who cannot be classified anywhere, although they are related, all of them, at least by some of their characters, to existentialist tendencies. First, Jankélévitch, whose work on Bergson we have already quoted and who, by brilliant analyses, tries to express fugitive and eternal essences of the human mind: irony, choice, evil, the struggle in us betwen opposite forces, the maladies of our inner consciousness and our striving toward harmonizing our inner chaos either by art or by virtues. Jean Grenier is most interesting when he tries, opposing himself to the dryness of pure intellectualism, to emphasize our kinship with the world in its deepest and subtlest aspects. In some juvenile and ardent pages, Sinding has also described this kinship with nature. It is in language, identical for him with reason as the Greeks and Hegel understood it, that Brice Parain sees the essence of human thought.

Let us come now to Emmanuel Levinas who, after having written studies on Husserl and also on Heidegger, has in his recent volume[1] presented his own vision of the world. The question from which he starts is the one which for Heidegger is the fundamental question of philosophy: What is being? "The question of being is the very experience of being in its strangeness. This question is a manner of assuming being." From the start Levinas knows that such a question will never

---

1. *De l'existence à l'existant,* Paris, Fontaine, 1947.

have an answer. "Being is without answer because being is essentially foreign to us and hurts and shocks us." We will see little by little that what we have to do is to go beyond being in order to find, not an answer, but something which might lead us toward the vanishing of the question and of the answer. This something Plato has tried to find, and he called it the Good. So, to assume being, then to go beyond it, will be the direction of Levinas' thought.

A disciple of Husserl, he insists on the notion of intention, but he affirms the necessity of taking intention not in any neutralized and disincarnated meaning but as the stimulus of desire (page 56). Intentionality becomes identical with being in the world, even with a kind of possession of the world by an annihilation of distance (page 72). By this we come to the idea of meaning which plays a great role in the thought of Levinas as well as in that of Merleau-Ponty, another follower of Husserl. "Meaning is the fact by which something exterior refers to interiority. It is a kind of transparency, a kind of illumination" (page 74).

This idea of intention and meaning presupposes a duality. In a more general manner, the fact of existing implies a distance between the existing being and existence. Existence is never at one with itself (page 37); and if we have the feeling that we are in the world, this very fact implies that we are a little out of the world in order to feel that we are in it (pages 64, 70, 72). We have already said that there is a distance between us and the world; we can touch exterior things; we can even penetrate into them; nevertheless we cannot break their form and our actions glide over them (pages 73, 77, 78). Light is the manifestation of this distance, of this exteriority which characterizes our interiority (page 79).

Hence we can see how for Levinas, as for Merleau-Ponty, there is a communication of consciousness and unconsciousness. Consciousness is always directed toward this depth which is under it (page 77). And, on the other hand, at its highest point it vanishes and fades; it appears then as a spark which comes from unconsciousness and goes toward unconsciousness.

Consciousness itself is this light, this act of opening our eyes which Heidegger tries to describe as being-in-the-truth (page 27). Thought is always light. The synthesis is not worked at the level of understanding as in Kant, but at the level of synthesis of intuition, and by the very opening of our eyes (page 76), as it is conceived also by Merleau-Ponty.

In order to see what the world really is, we have to go out of the sphere of utility, of what Heidegger called "zuhanden." A house is not a means of staying in one place; food is not simply something which has to satisfy our appetite (page 65).

Finally, we will see that we have to go beyond any determination. Levinas tries to show us that being and nothingness, which Heidegger had correlated, are phases of something more general in which subjective existence, as it is understood by existential philosophers, and objective existence, as it was understood by former realism, are united. This something he calls the *Il y a* (page 20). By this he signifies the anonymous stream of being which at some moments invades and submerges every subject. Night, which is not an object nor the quality of an object, dissolves all forms. In this universal absence, we discover the unavoidable presence of the *It is,* a field of force, a heavy climate, the anonymous rumor of existence. It is not God but rather the absence of God, such as may have been felt by primitive people before any word of God could have been heard. It is the horror of night. It is not at all the anguish as described by Heidegger, says Levinas, because it is a horror in the presence of being and not a horror of being. It remains to be seen whether in Heidegger anguish is not finally something very similar to this anguish in presence of being which Levinas describes (pages 94, 95, 99, 102, 109).

In this context Levinas refers to the works of the writer Blanchot, one of the most remarkable French contemporary essayists and novelists who, particularly in *Thomas l'obscur,* describes this presence of absence, of night, the reality of unreality. [2]

Now being takes place between the night of the *It is* and the ecstasy of existence and the world. Being is the very remaining in itself, the position of itself. Outside the *It is,* which can only be designated as a verb, there is being which is a substantive. So, before we go toward the ecstasy of existence, we have the hypostasis of substance or being (pages 138, 139, 140). To this idea of hypostasis and position are related the two ideas of the here and the now. We find there a polemic against idealism, which we might compare again to the polemics of Merleau-Ponty. "Thought which idealism has accustomed us to place outside space is

---

2. In art, intentionality instead of going toward the object, directs itself to sensation, and it is this wandering in the presence of sensation, which produces the esthetic effect (page 85). In the art of today the ambition is nevertheless a little different. Rather than toward the beginning of things, it goes very often toward the end of things, presenting to us a ruined world where there are cracks and wounds (page 90). Hence the discontinous character of modern painting—its liking of broken lines, its presentation of blocks and cubes and planes and triangles without transition, thrown in a certain manner upon ourselves, naked and absolute elements, affirmation of something which is not ourselves, which is not an object, which is without any name—its striving toward the representation of the sickness, the coarseness, the massivity, the misery, and absurdity of being.

essentially here—the deepest teaching of the *cogito* of Descartes consists in its affirmation of thought as substance, that is, as a thing which posits itself." Thought has a starting point. This is not a question of a consciousness of localization, but of a localization of consciousness (page 117).

In the same manner as there is a here, there is a now which cuts the Gordian knot of time (page 125). Every instant is a beginning, a birth. And the evanescence of the instant constitutes its very presence. We say that the present is absolute; we do not say that it does not vanish and that it lasts (pages 130, 132, 137).

By these affimations of the here and the now, we come to the idea of position. The place, before being a geometrical space, or even the concrete environment of the Heideggerian world, is according to Levinas a basis, the bodily basis of consciousness. Body is not a thing but an event; it is position itself. As a symbol of this, Levinas takes the statues of Rodin which characterize themselves much more by the abrupt relation to their basis than by the presence in them of a soul. Now in our sleep we reestablish our fundamental relation with our place as a basis. Here again in this emphasis put on the now, on our bodily basis, we find affinities with phenomenology as it is understood by Merleau-Ponty.

Equally, they are at one when he emphasizes in sensation all that part of it which seemed sheer confusion for Descartes and which for him is its special depth and taste.

There is a natural decaying of existence by which its freedom falls into a necessity, a captivity (page 134). Nevertheless, we have to be conscious of the fact that this decay which characterizes our everyday life has its own metaphysical status. The everyday world has its equilibrium, its harmony, its own ontological function. It would be a mistake to call it unauthentic. It would be to close our eyes to the value and dignity of ordinary man (page 69). It is the virtue of Marxism to have emphasized the right of this everyday world (pages 69, 80).

But we have to go from the sphere in which we are lost in our environment toward a freer sphere. As we had made of freedom a necessity, we have to make of necessity a freedom. The paradox of freedom is that only the free being is responsible, that is, ceases to be free (page 35). He has to "engage" himself.

We have now to reintroduce in the exposition of this theory the presence of persons other than ourselves. Here a new range of problems presents itself to Levinas. We have to find a relation between ourselves and the others. We leave the realm of light, which according to him is also the realm of solitude (pages 144, 145).

We have to go, also, beyond the economic consideration, beyond the sphere where one thing can be exchanged for another (page 155). We have to go beyond the computation of chances, and also beyond despair. Our hope will not be directed toward the future. "To hope is to hope the repair of what is irreparable. So, to hope is to hope for the present" (pages 156, 158).

There is a relation between the I and the Thou quite different from the dialogue inside myself in the terms of which classical philosophy described thought (page 161), quite different also from a participation that would be explained by a third term which is the common object of the two selves (pages 161, 162). This communion is no more a fusion for Levinas than for Scheler or for D. H. Lawrence. There is a distance between us and the other, and the pathos of love is made of both this proximity and this duality of existing being. "What is presented ordinarily as the failure of communication in love constitutes precisely the positivity of this relation; this absence of the other is precisely its presence as other" (page 163).

Levinas tells us that this philosophy has to be continued by more concrete affirmations of the link between one person and another person, under the form of a union of the masculine and the feminine, as producing a new otherness which is the child. But this is an aspect of his philosophy he has not yet quite developed. At the end of this first part of his presentation is the affirmation that the substantiality of the subject is not closed in itself and nevertheless has a kind of stability (page 168), that there is a starting point which is our position and basis and which is manifested by the obscurity of our feelings; these testify to an event prior to our reason and our reasonings. [3]

We feel that it was rather important to consider Merleau-Ponty on the one hand, and Levinas on the other; they might be both taken as examples of the importance of perception in recent French philosophy.

We might also draw attention to the insistence on negative thought. We find this insistence in Sartre as well as in Merleau-Ponty and Levinas —three philosophers who are influenced by Heidegger—and in Bachelard in his book entitled, *Le philosophie du non,* in the book by Morot-Sir on

---

3. We understand by this the place which the idea of equivocacy or ambiguity has in the philosophy of Levinas as in the philosophy of Merleau-Ponty. There is an ambiguity of time (page 126); there is an ambiguity of the word, inasmuch as it has a multiplicity of meanings which is essential to it (page 87).

La pensée négative, in the one by Polin on *Le laid, le mal, et le faux,* and in the one by Jankélévitch on *Le mal.* All these authors explore, and in the case of Bachelard and Jankélévitch with a particular depth, what might be called the negative region of reality. Is this interest taken in negation a sign of the crisis of our time? The question might be posed.

We might here say some words about the attempt, not completely successful, of Malcolm de Chazal. It may be explained in part by the influence of some occultist and theosophist theories. He tries to make us realize the relation of the senses to one another. "I start from this principle that sight, hearing, smelling, tasting, and touch cannot be understood except if they are put into relation one with the other." There are subterranean passages between them which can only be guessed by our unconscious. On the other hand, there is a relation between man and the universe such that he is a kind of microcosm representing the macrocosm. In his research a kind of preciousness is used as a means for discovering subtle relations, moving relations between the parts of the universe. We might compare this attempt with that of Bachelard when he tries, with the help of the poets, to make us realize what the value of the four elements is for a kind of study of imagination and for an ontological understanding, or rather imagining, of the essences which make up our watery, aerial, fiery, and earthly world. We might compare it also with what Maurice Leenhardt has said about the imagination of primitives when they represent to themselves space and time, persons and things. And we might remember equally what the surrealists have presented to us as being the fundamental relation between man and the most obscure parts of the world. They try to go toward a new understanding of space and matter and mind. (We allude here particularly to sayings of André Breton and Paul Eluard.) We see the importance of this study of perception and imagination in present philosophical thought as well as in present poetical thought.

This is an occasion for us to go backward a little toward two great literary names of the prior generation, Claudel and Valéry. Both of them are, and still more will be, great inspirations for the thought of philosophers, the one showing the reality of a dense opaque feeling of the world, the other the reality of subtle relations whose moving intricacy and infinite complexity are the explanations, if they may be called explantations, of our pluralistic universe. Léon Brunschvicg liked to invoke the testimony of Valéry; and on the other hand, there are great affinities between some aspects of Valéry's thought and some theories of Sartre.

Bachelard often refers to Claudel. They both have to be added to what we have to say about perception in recent French thought.

Let us take another step farther back in the past. We have to take account of the interest in the mystical background of such poets as Rimbaud, Baudelaire, and Nerval. These mystical backgrounds have been studied by Pommier, Roland De Reneville, Gengoux, and some others. The outcome of these studies goes in the same direction as the reflections of the surrealists toward an affirmation of an occult mode of knowledge reserved for poets.

In the same manner as we have drawn the attention toward the relations of philosophy and poetry, we might draw it toward its relations with painting. There was certainly in Cézanne an endeavor toward a rendering of things as they are in themselves, independently of the habits of ordinary human perception. There was in Van Gogh an effort toward catching the atmosphere and landscapes in their movements. Later, cubism may be interpreted either as a tendency toward an intellectualization of perception or as a tendency toward a disintellectualization of it, since it tries to give us all the perspectives of a thing—those which are called illusory as well as those which are named normal and real. So philosophy, although it remains a special activity which has to be considered in its relation to truth, may also be regarded historically as part of a general movement of the mind, visible equally in other activities.

We should at least mention some of the French works bearing on the history of philosophy. Starting from the period which is nearest to ours, we have the volumes of Berger on Husserl; the work of Jankélévitch on Schelling; of Niel, Kojève, and Hyppolite on Hegel; of Susini on Baader; of Gueroult on Fichte; of Lachièze-Rey on Kant. No doubt Kojève ties the thought of Hegel to its starting point too strictly and is not mindful enough of its dialectical ascension. Hyppolite's book also leans too much toward an interpretation of Hegel which would make of his philosophy a kind of naturalistic humanism, but it is wider in its outlook by the very ambiguity, not always quite satisfactory, in which it remains. The work of Gilson, a monument dedicated to the thought of the Middle Ages and its sources and its consequences, is already well-known in America and will remain as the proof of the vitality of deep philosophical studies in contemporary France. Father Daniélou and his co-workers have turned to the study of the Greek Fathers. There is a particularly good book on Aristotle by Father Le Blond, who shows the conflict of diverse schemes of thought in this thinker. On Greek philosophy in general, we have to mention the books of Père Festugière (particularly his book on the life of contemplation in Plato, which might rank with the works of A. E. Taylor and Friedlaender), of Robin, and Rivaud.

Without drawing any formal conclusion, we may say that we have seen the range of French philosophical thought from Plato to Rimbaud, from the study of perception to the study of imagination and science. Many influences mix with one another. Many consequences have yet to be drawn. Some more positive elements seem to emerge just now. If we endeavor to describe them more definitely, if we assert that French philosophical thought directs itself more and more toward the concrete aspects of imagination and perception, and of the world in general, we risk falling into error; but let us take this risk. The history of contemporary philosophy implies a kind of prophecy of at least the immediate future.

SELECTED BIBLIOGRAPHY

Thibaudet, Albert. *Le Bergsonisme.* Paris, Gallimard, 1923.

Le Roy, Edouard. *Une philosophie nouvelle: H. Bergson.* Paris, Alcan, 1912.

——————. *L'exigence idéaliste et le fait de l'évolution.* Paris, Boivin, 1927.

——————. *Les origines humaines et l'évolution de l'intelligence.* Paris, Boivin, 1928.

——————. *La pensée intuitive, I et II.* Paris, Boivin, 1929.

——————. *Le problème de Dieu.* Paris, L'Artisan du Livre, 1930.

——————. *Introduction à l'étude du problème religieux.* Paris, Aubier, 1944.

Minkowski, Eugène. *La schizophrénie.* Paris, Payot, 1927.

——————. *Le temps vécu.* Paris, D'Artrey, 1933.

——————. *Vers une cosmologie.* Paris, Aubier, 1939.

——————. *"L'aspect lunaire, l'aspect solaire, l'aspect humain du monde."* Paris, *Deucalion* No. 2, 1947.

Nogué, Jean. *Esquisse d'un système des qualités sensibles.* Paris, Presses Universitaires, 1943.

Souriau, Étienne. *L'abstraction sentimentale.* Paris, Alcan, 1925.

——————. *Pensée vivante et pensée formelle.* Paris, Alcan, 1925.

——————. *L'avenir de l'esthétique.* Paris, Alcan, 1925.

——————. *Avoir une âme, essai sur les existence virtuelles.* Paris, Belles Lettres, 1938.

——————. *L'instauration philosophique*. Paris, Alcan, 1939.

——————. *Les différents modes d'existence*. Paris, Presses Universitaires, 1943.

——————. *La correspondence des arts*. Paris, Flammarion, 1947.

Ruyer, R. *Esquisse d'une philosophie de la structure*. Paris, Alcan, 1930.

——————. *La conscience et le corps*. Paris, Alcan, 1937.

——————. *Éléments de psychobiologie*. Paris, Presses Universitaires, 1946.

——————. *Le monde des valeurs*. Paris, Aubier, 1948.

——————. *La place des valeurs vitales*. *Deucalion,* No. 1, 1946.

Bachelard, Gaston. *L'intuition de l'instant*. Paris, Stock, 1932.

——————. *La psychanalyse du feu*. Paris, Gallimard, 1938.

——————. *Lautréamont*. Paris, Corti, 1939.

——————. *La philosophie du non*. Paris, Alcan, 1940.

——————. *L'eau et les rêves*. Paris, Corti, 1942.

——————. *L'air et les songes*. Paris, Corti, 1943.

——————. *La terre et les rêveries de la volonté*. Paris, Corti, 1948.

——————. *La terre et les rêveries du repos*. Paris, Corti, 1948.

——————. See also Lalande's bibliography for philosophy of science.

Aron, Raymond. *La sociologie allemande contemporaine*. Paris, Alcan, 1935.

——————. *Essai sur la théorie de l'histoire dans l'Allemagne contemporaine*. Paris, Vrin, 1938.

——————. *Introduction à la philosophie de l'histoire*. Paris, Gallimard, 1938.

Cavaillès, Jean. *Remarques sur la formation de la théorie des ensembles transfinis*. Paris, Hermann, 1938.

——————. *Transfini et continu*. Paris, Hermann, 1947.

——————. See also Lalande's bibliography for philosophy of science.

Canguilhem, Georges. *Essai sur quelques problèmes concernant le normal et le pathologique*. Paris, Clermont-Ferrand, Belles Lettres, 1943.

Alquié, Ferdinand. *Le désir d'éternité*. Paris, Presses Universitaires, 1943.

——————. *Humanisme surréaliste et humanisme existentialiste*. Cahiers du Collège Philosophique, Arthaud, 1948.

——————. *"Solitude de la raison."* Paris, *Deucalion* No. 1, 1946.

Patri, Aimé. *Sur les notions d'essence et d'existence*. Cahiers du Collège Philosophique, Arthaud, 1948.

——————. *"Sur une nouvelle doctrine de la liberté."* Paris, *Deucalion,* No. 1, 1946.

Caillois, Roger. *La mante religieuse*. Paris, Gallimard, 1937.
—————. *Le mythe et l'homme*. Paris, Gallimard, 1938.
—————. *L'homme et le sacré*. Paris, Leroux, 1939.
—————. *Vocabulaire esthétique*. Paris, Fontaine, 1946.
de Broglie, Louis. *Matière et lumière*. Paris, Albin Michel, 1932.
—————. *La physique nouvelle et les quanta*. Paris, Flammarion, 1937.
—————. *Continu et discontinu en physique moderne*. Paris, Albin Michel, 1941.
—————. *Physique et microphysique*. Paris, Albin Michel, 1947.
—————. *Ondes, electrons, corpuscules*. Paris, Albin Michel, 1948.
—————. *"Les révelations de la microphysique."* Paris, *Deucalion* No. 1, 1947.
Maritain, Jacques. *La philosophie bergsonienne*. Paris, Rivière, 1914.
—————. *Art et scholastique*. Paris, Rouart, 1920.
—————. *Théonas* (English translation: *Theonas; Conversations of a Sage*). Paris, Nouvelle librairie, 1921.
—————. *Antimoderne*. Paris, Revue des jeunes, 1922.
—————. *Réponse à Jean Cocteau*. Paris, Stock, 1926.
—————. *Réflexions sur l'intelligence*. Paris, Nouvelle librairie nationale, 1926.
—————. *Frontières de la poésie*. Paris, Plon, 1927.
—————. *Eléments de philosophie I et II*. Paris, Téqui.
—————. *Le songe de Descartes* (English translation: *The Dream of Descartes*). Paris, R. A. Corrêa, 1932.
—————. *Distinguer pour unir ou les degrés du savior. Paris, Desclée, 1932.
—————. *De la philosophie chrétienne*. Paris, Desclée, 1933.
—————. *Sept leçons sur l'être*. Paris, Téqui, 1934.
—————. *La philosophie de la nature*. Paris, Téqui, 1935.
—————. *Science et sagesse* (English translation: *Science and Wisdom*). Paris, Labergerie, 1935.
—————. *Humanisme intégral* (English translation: *True Humanism*). Paris, Aubier, 1936.
—————. *Lettre sur l'indépendance*. Paris, Desclée, 1935.
—————. *Court traité de l'existence et de l'existant*. Paris, Hartmann, 1947.
—————. *Raison et raisons*. Fribourg, L V F, 1947.
Gilson, Etienne. *Le Thomisme*. Paris, Belles Lettres, 1921.
—————. *Études de philosophie médiévale*. Paris, Belles Lettres, 1921.

—————. *La philosophie au moyen-âge.* Second edition, Paris, Payot, 1944.

—————. *La philosophie de saint Bonaventure* (English translation: *The Philosophy of Saint Bonaventure*). Paris, Vrin, 1932.

—————. *Saint Thomas d'Aquin* (English translation: *The Philosophy of St. Thomas Aquinas*). Paris, Vrin, 1925.

—————. *Introduction à l'étude de saint Augustin.* Paris, Vrin, 1929.

—————. *Le réalisme méthodique.* Paris, Vrin, 1948.

—————. *Les idées et les lettres.* Paris, Vrin, 1932.

—————. *L'esprit de la philosophie médiévale* (English translation: *The Spirit of Mediaeval Philosophy*). Paris, Vrin, 1932.

—————. *La théologie mystique de saint Bernard* (English translation: *The Mystical Theology of Saint Bernard*). Paris, Vrin, 1934.

—————. *Christianisme et philosophie.* Paris, Vrin, 1936.

—————. *Héloise et Abélard.* Paris, Vrin, 1938.

—————. *Dante et la philosophie.* Paris, Vrin, 1939.

—————. *Réalisme thomiste et critique de la connaissance.* Paris, Vrin, 1939.

—————. *Théologie et histoire de la spiritualité.* Paris, Vrin, 1943.

—————. *L'essence et l'existence.* Paris, Vrin, 1948.

de Lubac, Henri. *Catholicisme.* Paris, Cerf, 1937.

—————. *Corpus mysticum.* Paris, Aubier, third edition, 1944.

—————. *Le drame de l'humanisme athée.* Paris, Éditions Spes, 1945.

—————. *Proudhon et le christianisme.* Paris, Seuil, 1945.

—————. *Paradoxes.* Paris, Le caillou blanc, 1946.

—————. *Surnaturel.* Paris, Aubier, 1946.

Fessard, G. *Pax nostra.* Paris, Grasset, 1936.

Mounier, Emmanuel. *La Pensée de Charles Péguy.* Paris, Seuil, 1946.

—————. *Révolution personnaliste et communautaire.* Paris, Temps Présent, 1947.

—————. *Introduction aux Existentialismes.* Paris, Denoël, 1947.

—————. *Qu'est ce que le personnalisme?* Paris, Seuil, 1947.

de Rougemont, Denis. *Politique de la personne.* Paris, Je sers, 1934.

—————. *Penser avec les mains.* Paris, Albin Michel, 1936.

—————. *L'Amour et l'Occident.* Paris, Plon, 1939.

—————. *Les personnes du drame.* New York, Schiffin, 1944.

—————. *La part du diable.* New York, Brentanos, 1944.

Marcel, Gabriel. *L'existentialisme chrétien* en collaboration avec Jeanne Delhomme, Roger Troisfontaines, Pierre Collin. Paris, Plon, 1947.

Morot-Sir, Edouard. *La pensée négative.* Paris, Aubier, 1948.

——————. *Philosophie et mystique.* Paris, Aubier, 1948.

Losski, Vladimir. *Essai sur la théorie mystique de l'Eglise d'orient.* Paris, Aubier, 1944.

Politzer, Georges. *Critique des fondements de la psychologie I.* Paris, Rieder, 1928.

——————. *Critique de la psychologie contemporaine.* Paris, Editions sociales, 1947.

Lefebvre, Henri. *Le materialisme dialectique.* Paris, Presses Universitaires de France, 1940.

——————. *Le marxisme.* Paris, Presses Universitaires de France, 1948.

Lefebvre, Henri and Guterman, Norbert. *La conscience mystifiée.* Paris, Gallimard, 1936.

Mougin, Henri. *La sainte famille existentialiste.* Paris, Editions sociales, 1947.

Groethuysen, Bernard. *Introduction à la pensée allemande depuis Nietzsche.* Paris, Stock, 1926.

——————. *Origine de l'esprit bourrgeois en France.* Paris, Gallimard.

——————. *Mythes et portraits.* Paris, Gallimard, 1947.

——————. *"L'enfant et le métaphysicien."* Paris, *Deucalion* No. 2, 1947.

Koyré, Alexandre. *Essai sur l'idée de Dieu et les preuves de son existence chez Descartes.* Paris, Leroux, 1922.

——————. *L'idée de Dieu dans la philosophie de saint Anselme.* Paris, Vrin, 1923.

——————. *La philosophie de Jacob Böhme.* Paris, Vrin, 1929.

——————. *Études galiléennes.* Paris, Hermann, 1939.

——————. *Introduction à la lecture de Platon.* New York, Brentanos, 1945.

——————. *Épiménide le menteur.* Paris, Hermann, 1947.

Gurvitch, Georges. *Fichtes System der konkreten Ethik.* Tübingen, Mohr, 1924.

——————. *Le temps présent et l'idée de droit social.* Paris, Vrin, 1931.

——————. *La déclaration des droits sociaux.* Paris, Vrin, 1936.

——————. *L'idée du droit social.* Paris, Recueil Sirey, 1932.

——————. *Morale théorique et science des moeurs.* Paris, Alcan, 1937.

——————. *Essais de sociologie.* Paris, Recueil Sirey, 1938.

――――――. *Eléments de sociologie juridique.* Paris, Aubier, 1938.

Bespalof, Rachel. *Cheminements et carrefours.* Paris, Vrin, 1930.

――――――. *"Réflexions sur l'esprit de la tragédie."* Paris, *Deucalion,* No. 2, 1947.

Fondane, Benjamin. *Rimbaud le voyou.* Paris, Denoël, 1933.

――――――. *La conscience malheureuse.* Paris, Denoël, 1936.

――――――. *Faux traité d'esthétique.* Paris, Denoël, 1938.

――――――. *Baudelaire et l'expérience du gouffre.* Paris, Seghers, 1947.

Campbell, Robert. *J.-P. Sartre ou une littérature philosophique.* Paris, Pierre Ardent, 1944.

Jeanson, Francis. *Sartre et le problème moral.* Paris, Le Myrte, 1946.

Pouillon, Jean. *Temps et Roman.* Paris, Gallimard, 1946.

Caillois, Roland. *Le monde vécu et l'histoire dans "l'homme, le monde, et l'histoire."* Arthaud, 1948.

――――――. *"De la perception à l'histoire."* Paris, *Deucalion* No. 2, 1947.

――――――. *"Notes sur l'analyse reflexive."* Paris, *Deucalion* No. 1, 1946.

Merleau-Ponty, Maurice. See bibliography for Campbell's essay.

Jankélévitch, Vladimir. *Bergson.* Paris, Alcan, 1931.

――――――. *L'odyssée de la conscience dans la dernière philosophie de Schelling.* Paris, Alcan, 1932.

――――――. *L'ironie.* Paris, Alcan, 1935.

――――――. *L'alternative.* Paris, Alcan, 1938.

――――――. *Du mensonge.* Lyon, Confluences, 1942.

――――――. *Le mal.* Paris, Arthaud, 1947.

――――――. *La mauvaise conscience.* Paris, Alcan, 1933.

Grenier, Jean. *Les îles.* Paris, Gallimard, 1933.

――――――. *Essai sur l'esprit d'orthodoxie.* Paris, Gallimard, 1938.

――――――. *Le choix.* Paris, Presses Universitaires, 1941.

Parain, Brice. *Essai sur le logos platonicien.* Paris, Gallimard, 1942.

――――――. *Recherches sur la nature et les fonctions du langage.* Paris Gallimard, 1943.

――――――. *L'embarras du choix.* Paris, Gallimard, 1946.

Levinas, Emmanuel. *La théorie de l'intuition chez Husserl.* Paris, F. Alcan, 1930.

――――――. *"L'autre dans Proust."* Paris, *Decalion,* No. 2, 1947.

――――――. *De l'existence à l'existant.* Paris, Vrin, 1947.

de Chazal, Malcolm. *Sens plastique.* Port Louis, Ile Maurice, 1947.

Leenhardt, Maurice. *Do Kamo.* Paris, Gallimard, 1947.

Gengoux, Jacques. *La symbolique de Rimbaud.* La Colombe, 1947.

THE SPIRIT OF THE HISTORY
OF PHILOSOPHY AND
OF THE SCIENCES
IN FRANCE

*Émile Bréhier**

In the second half of the nineteenth century, in France as elsewhere, the idea of an *a priori* reconstruction of the past of philosophy was completely discredited, along with that of a general philosophy of history. At the end of this century and the beginning of our own, we see the development of the great works which employ, in the handling and interpretation of text, the rigorous critical method of the historian. In the history of the sciences, in antiquity and the Middle Ages, Paul Tannery and Pierre Duhem have produced admirable works which have become classics, as have Victor Brochard, Hamelin, and Léon Robin in the history of Greek philosophy. It must be added that the spiritualistic generations which preceded them had made a positive contribution, far from negligible, to the history of philosophy. The historical works of Victor Cousin, of Ravaisson, and of Francisque Bouillier opened up many a new path in the history of philosophy both ancient and modern.

It is out of the question to enumerate here, in detail, just what of the novel France has contributed to this field during the last ten or twenty years. There have been studies and articles without number, due chiefly to the great importance our universities continue to attach to the teaching of the history of philosophy and of the sciences, and to the taste of an enlightened public for the history of ideas. It will be more useful, after

* Born in 1876. Member of the Institute of France. Honorary Professor at the Sorbonne. Editor of the *Revue philosophique*. Author of *Histoire de la philosophie*, 7 vols. (1926-1932); *La philosophie et son passé* (1940); *Les idées philosophiques et religieuses de Philon d'Alexandrie* (1907); *Chrysippe* (1910); *La philosophie de Plotin* (1928); *Plotin Eunéades, Notices, Texte et Traduction*, 7 vols. (1924-1938); *Science et humanisme* (1948); *La philosophie du Moyen Age* (1937); and "Y a-t-il une philosophie chrétienne?" in *Revue de métaphysique*, 1930.

having indicated the main directions in which research has been developed, to determine the character of these studies, and especially to put the history of philosophy in its proper place with regard to philosophy, itself, after the great upheaval which left it a separate matter.

I

The first thing to strike us in these contemporary studies is the lowering of the barriers which used to exist between history of philosophy and the other historical disciplines. Let us first state the case:

Thanks to the joint efforts of scholars and philosophers, the study of Greek philosophy thrives in the atmosphere of humanism which is still that of French culture. There is the "Guillaume Budé Collection" which publishes, along with Homer and the Greek Tragedies, the works of Plato, Aristotle, Plotinus, Marcus Aurelius, Seneca, and Epictetus; and there is the "Pleiade" which provides for all who would read them, the translation of Plato's *Dialogues* and will very shortly bring out translations of the Stoic texts. The most recent studies, those of P.M. Schuhl, on the origins of Greek philosophy and on Plato, are the work of a philosopher with a singularly inquiring mind, self-initiated into erudition, including even archeology: those of Victor Goldschmidt on the *Dialogues* of Plato, the work of a scholar who, through a minutely detailed analysis, rediscovered Plato's general method and so came over to philosophy.

A serious barrier, that of the Oriental languages, both ancient and modern, has always made access to the non-Hellenic civilizations of Asia and Africa difficult for philosophers. To be sure, this barrier has not been removed; but the great Belgian philologists, Franz Cumont and Joseph Bidez, by establishing the field of their studies in that Greco-Roman period where the Oriental influence is widespread, give new bases for the history of Hellenistic thought. Egyptologists, such as Sainte Fare Garnot, are taking an interest in Egyptian thought. The philosopher Masson-Oursel turns Orientalist: he plans and is beginning work upon a vast comparative history of philosophy, in which he shows that analogy of the curve of development of thought between the Occident and the Orient. And it is as philosopher that Olivier Lacombe studies an Indian philosopher of the medieval epoch. There is, here, a very wide field of research, hardly explored, notably in that which concerns the reciprocal relations between Hellenic Neoplatonism and the Near or Far East.

Between the Middle Ages and ourselves, our classic century had raised a barrier which long prevented us from seeing the full import of medieval philosophy. Already, however, in the nineteenth century, the spiritualists of the school of Cousin began to take an interest in it: romanticism had brought back into fashion the art and literature of that supposedly barbarous period. But in the twentieth century, France has taken an extremely important part in the studies of medieval philosophy, at first centered around Thomism, but soon extended either in the direction of the origins, or toward the fourteenth century and the Renaissance. Picavet had shown how the Neoplatonic image of the world had maintained itself up to the Middle Ages. The work of Maurice de Wulf and of Étienne Gilson, the publication of numerous texts (which is very far from being completed) beside the German publications, have contributed toward disclosing, not only the mystical thought, but also the real—though somewhat exaggerated—richness of this philosophical thought. Let us add that Gilson has shown the active survival of scholasticism in Descartes.

That which, at the present time, gives new impetus to the history of modern philosophy in France, is assuredly its close connection with the history of the sciences, the history of religion, the history of literature, and even the history of art. It is thus that, thanks to the magnificent Adam-Tannery edition of the works of Descartes, the philosophy of our great thinker could be studied in its relationship to the sciences by Gabriel Milhaud. Father Lenoble has revealed, in his *Mersenne,* the little suspected diversity of the tendencies of the scientific mind at the beginning of the seventeenth century. Jean Laporte's *Le rationalisme de Descartes* owes much to his preliminary studies of the Jansenist movement; and this movement was the subject of the recent works of Oreibal. Books such as those of R. Pintard (*Le libertinage érudit dans la première moitié du XVIIe siècle*), of Paul Hazard (*La crise de la conscience européenne, La pensée européenne au XVIIIe siècle*), and of Auguste Viatte on preromanticism, make clear how much the history of philosophy can be indebted to the historians of literature. Henri Gouhier, on the other hand, devotes very detailed researches to religious philosophy in France in the work of Descartes, of Malebranche, of August Comte, of Maine de Biran. Finally, political philosophy, especially that of Rousseau, is, at the present time, the subject of important studies.

It is partly upon the historian that falls the ever more difficult but very necessary task of not permitting peoples who are kept apart by their languages, their traditions, and their politics, to remain ignorant of each other's thoughts. Such philosophers as Spinoza and Leibniz, Locke,

Berkeley and Hume, and Kant are, of course, considered among us as classics, as is proved by the works, already old, of Léon Delbos and Couturat; by those, more recent, of André Leroy, and, finally by *L'idéalisme kantien* of Lachièze-Rey, based upon the posthumous Opus. But we must mention, also, the studies of J. Chaix-Ruy on the great Vico, on Croce, and on Italian philosophy in general; those of Jean Wahl on the pluralistic philosophies in Anglo-Saxon countries, and finally, following upon the excellent volumes of Xavier Léon and M. Gueroult on Fichte, Charles Andler's books on Nietzsche, and the revival of Hegelian studies in the works of Jean Hyppolite.

II

The profuse wealth of so many studies does not fail to cause us some anxiety through the very diversity of their orientation. That which is most immediately striking is the variety of interests which direct attention toward the history of philosophy. To be sure, that system of knowledge of the past which is called history can hardly be said to be used in a vacuum: the past is never investigated for its own sake, but always with an eye toward the present. Let us admit that history is, in the main, less the history of facts than the history of values (political, national, human, scientific, religious, philosophical, etc. . . , the whole range of titles of histories); and, if these values were not current at the present time (whether they are regarded with sympathy or antipathy is of little importance), it is not likely that we would endeavor to find out just what they meant in the past. Let us add that these values attain to full reality only in a certain thickness of time, and that, in order to understand any one among them—the value, "democracy," for example—history is necessary; for we cannot see what it could mean for us, taken in its abstract formula, apart from its historical manifestations.

It is, then, natural for philosophy to insist upon knowledge of its own proper history, and that the past should be present, explicitly or implicity, in the present thought of the philosopher. But what is remarkable is that the impetus toward historical research in philosophy comes from the crossing of very different interests, many of which are not of the philosophical order.

The most striking example is the extraordinary upswing of the study of medieval philosophy, due, according to all evidence, to the recognition by Leo XIII of Thomism as the official philosophy of Catholicism. After having been disregarded for three centuries (apart from a few exceptions and despite certain survivals), the revived Thomist doctrine is accompanied by an historical study of the writings of St. Thomas, which study goes beyond its bounds in the direction of the antecedents. Aristotle holds high rank in the works of Catholic savants such as Mansion or Father Le Blond; the struggles between ideas in the thirteenth century lead to the study of the different currents of Aristotelianism, Augustinianism, Neoplatonism, and Averroism. Better still, the interest directed upon Thomism goes on to create new and unexpected perspectives in the whole of the history of philosophy. Gilson sees St. Thomas as the initiator of modern philosophy, and it is by relation to him that he judges the whole development of modern thought. Suarez, in the sixteenth century, by making the essences of realities distinct from existences, would have been at the origin of that anti-Thomistic idealism which we see progressing from Descartes to Hegel, until the existentialism of Kierkegaard comes along to renew Thomistic existentialism. Such is, in brief, the thesis of Gilson's latest book.

But it is not the sole example. The critique of the sciences, the increased need, which the sciences themselves feel, of reflecting upon the validity of their principles by going to the particulars of their formation, has brought about a great development of the history of the sciences. We know how Meyerson has made use of this history, and how Abel Rey, Paul Mouy, and G. Bachelard have developed it. It has, also, strongly influenced the history of philosophy, by occasioning a search to determine what contribution each philosopher has made to the sciences and what scientific base underlies each philosophy. Mathematics for Plato, medicine and biology for Aristotle and the Stoics, medieval cosmology and the rapid growth of the positive sciences since the Renaissance, have been, as it were, revealers which have brought to light new features of the philosophical doctrines. But this enrichment has not been without its reverse: there is at times a tendency to absorb the history of philosophy in that of the sciences, or at least to disregard, as without value, whatever in philosophy does not tie up with the effective development of positive knowledge . For Léon Brunschvicg, the facts upon which man's spiritual progress depends are the discoveries of the physico-mathematical sciences, which give us a view of the ensemble of the history of philosophy turning on an axis wholly different from that of Thomism.

Another and quite different interest which at present leads toward the history of philosophy, is assuredly the growth of religious values. Bear in mind, in fact, that it is among the philosophers and bound up with their philosophy, that the highest religious values, those of mysticism, are to be found—especially in antiquity. It is from Plato, from Plutarch, from Philo, from Plotinus, that the historians of religion draw important data for their science. In the history of modern times, it is the same; we seek with curiosity the religious (or irreligious) basis of philosophies; we raise questions concerning the religious sincerity of Gassendi or Descartes, or the religious nuances of the philosophy of Leibniz, Spinoza, or Kant. An actual present interest is involved in these researches; for the dominant philosophy of our epoch, which has taken Kierkegaard as its announcing herald, sets out to be passionately affirmative or negative concerning religious values (whether Christian or atheistic existentialism is in question), and that which is, for it, the center, that sort of affective ontology which consists in the attitude of refusal or of invocation, the historian looks for in the philosophies of the past. Metaphysics no longer appears, as used to be said, as an abstract and dried up religion, but as concrete belief or experience.

These three considerations (it would be possible to add others) will suffice to justify our anxiety. The history of philosophy, however numerous and brilliant the studies to which it gives rise may be, is crumbling from day to day, not for the simple reason that each of its parts now exacts a specialization, formerly unknown, but because of doctrinal divisions, each of which has, so to speak, a history of thought of its very own. Thus, we have three Platos, one to correspond to each of the three interests I have pointed out: the pre-Aristotelian Plato, author of the theory of forms; the Plato who is mathematician and idealist, of Couturat, Brunschvicg, and Joseph Moreau; and the Plato of the myths of destiny, who was evolved by the Alexandrians and the Christian Fathers. In this pulling to pieces, what becomes of the Plato of whom Péguy said: "If Plato had never existed, who, and through what miserable mixtures, supposedly scientific, through what poor combinations, even truly scientific, would have been able to make anything comparable to this wonderful invention?"

We see here a contrast between the perfection of a method which manifests itself by works, both numerous and of the highest value (from the publications of texts up to brilliant interpretations of past doctrines), and the uncertainty in which we stand as to the meaning this past has for us. It seems as though, the more it is investigated in detail, the more this meaning escapes us. There is, here, a direction which is not without danger and which would lead, if it were followed to its conclusion, to the cultivation of knowledge of the past for its own sake: or at least one would be caught between two equally regrettable tendencies, one to use history as a justification of one's own doctrine, which would lead to falsifying it by eliminating everything which might be contrary to this, and the other to reduce history to a mere philological research.

III

We can ask ourselves to just what point the philosophical tendencies of our times are favorable to this sort of integration of the history of philosophy with philosophy, integration which certainly dominated the nineteenth century, in which history had become an organ of philosophical thought. This integration assumed, in a more or less precise fashion, the existence of a universal thought, of which the successive doctrines represented different moments and of which the philosophers were, as one might say, only the carriers and the manifestations. It was then believed possible to divest these doctrines of the individual circumstances in which they were produced, and correlatively, there was admitted to be, from one to the other, a certain progress which was the very progress of the human mind.

This sort of disincarnated philosophy whose ideas have, as it is said today, a subject in the "third person," is, for reason which it would take too long to examine here, much criticized in our times; and it is, under close scrutiny, this criticism which strikes at our history of philosophy and destroys its unity.

Henri Bergson has evidently done much to separate philosophy from that which the historian, with his own proper method, can grasp of it through the study of texts. He has an idea of the past of philosophy which, in certain respects, renders him independent of chronology and the progress of time. He has expressed himself with vigor on this point at the end of *Creative Evolution*. Following a tendency, which is also to be found in Nietzsche, he sees, in the majority of doctrines, philosophies of concept, dissociating the real, and slaves of the practical nature of human intelligence. The philosopher reader must hunt for the effective intuitions or the traces of intuition which are hidden under these formulas, and find them, less through the objective method of the philologists, than through a sort of sympathy which renders them immediate to him. Not that the philological method is useless, it is even, by way of preliminary, indispensable, and all Bergson's pupils know that he made very skillful use of it; but it gives only external indications, brings formulas together, clears up the origins of texts. It lets escape the principal thing, which is, for the great philosopher, the intuition of the real, from which springs the doctrine. Now, intuitions can be confirmed, but they do not govern each other. There is, from one to the other, no progress, dialectic or otherwise. Péguy seems to me to express an authentically Bergsonian notion when he writes: "When it is truly a question of metaphysics and philosophy, when it is a question of theories, there is neither going beyond nor doubling back. Neither linear progress nor the power to return. . . ; one sees only that no man, nor any humanity, in a certain sense, which is not derogatory, could ever boast of having gone beyond Plato. I will go further and add that a truly cultivated man does not understand, cannot even imagine what it would really mean to claim to have gone beyond Plato." (*Cahiers de la Quinzaine,* Feb., 1907.)

We see to what point Bergsonian thought disparages the *historia judicans,* which flattered itself upon discerning a progress which permitted the assignment of each philosophy to its role and place, as though chronology were put in advance, in agreement with dialectic to bring forth, at the chosen moment, the one who must occupy it. *Historia judicans* becomes *historia judicata.* The philosophical past is no longer like a rising tide which carries you along, but like a society of minds, a society of Unique Spirits, let us say, with whom we can communicate across time, thanks to the monuments they have left behind. From this comes the great importance assumed, in France, by the monographs which search texts and investigate influences (which is where the philological method retains all its importance), only in order to arrive at individual traits. It is a question of preparing the way for the philosopher.

Can the history of philosophy, on the other hand, keep the sort of autonomy it possessed as the "history of pure reason," to use Kant's phrase? This autonomy seems to have been struck a hard blow by some directions of thought, issuing from Marxism. In general, Karl Marx replaces the word, philosophy, by the word, ideology; but we have not here, a simple changing of vocabulary. Ideology designates doubtless, materially speaking, the same works as philosophy; but, instead of taking the doctrines in themselves or in their mutual relationship, Marx considers them as inseparable from a given social and economic situation, and evolving with it. Not, as has often been thought mistakenly, that ideology is, for Marx, a mere product or effect of the economic situation which it would follow as a reflection or an epiphenomenon. As has been again pointed out recently by Merleau-Ponty (*Sens et non-sens*) that is only a "skeletonized" Marxism, which makes of the economic regime an independent variable, a cause of which the ideology would be the effect. It must rather be said (and this is the opinion of the best interpreters of Marx) that the ideology is a factor inseparable from the other factors which constitute a culture; but, whether or not one is conscious of it, the ideology is the justification of that culture. One sees the complete transformation of the history of philosophy which would result from this view. Taken in itself, this history would be that of an abstraction. Now, this idea is not without influence in France, as in many other countries. One becomes accustomed, even outside of Marxism, to using this term, "ideology." It appears in current conversations, and one meets with it in all the deliberations of UNESCO, where it designates philosophy, inasmuch as philosophy is the expression of a certain social grouping, of a nation. While philosophy would seem, as making appeal to reason, to be of necessity a connecting link, ideology is, rather, a barrier which separates and whose effect can be nullified only by tolerance. These views on ideology, whether they be Marxist or nationalist, meet, in France, with those of historical relativism, such as Taine, in particular, has presented them; philosophy forms part of a structure of civilization, which attaches itself to the society and the race and cannot be isolated from them.

I could not avoid speaking (with a brevity which I hope will be pardoned) of a powerful movement which explains certain characters of our history of philosophy; notably the taste for what I call "horizontal history," which reintegrates doctrines into the civilization which is contemporary with it, rather than "vertical history," the traditional history, which displays systems according to chronological order, not without trying to find a certain rational connection between them. Here, as elsewhere, one looks for structures rather than developments. And this is also why one sees, in historical researches, that mutual penetration of the components of culture of a different nature—religion, art, economic, or political institutions. In truth, more than philosophy, properly so-called, which is a Greek and European thing, the word, ideology, tends to designate a certain average of opinions which is expressed collectively. The danger is clear: it is the confusion of collective opinions and beliefs with philosophy. While admitting that the true Marxism (Karl Marx, himself, thought that the Greeks of the fifth century had attained eternal values) does not commit such an error, who will be able to see what it is worth only when there shall have been accomplished those detailed researches implied by its thesis, and by the abiding method of all history, the philological and critical method. Now, a history of this sort, with Marxist inspiration, is far from being written in France, although one already sees indications in the studies of L. Goldmann, written under the influence of the Hungarian, Lukács. The Marxist thesis here becomes a leading idea which requires the objective control of criticism; no historian would be ready to consider it as a dogma to be admitted offhand.

Existentialism, in the form it has taken in France with J. P. Sartre, is much more deeply penetrated by erudition and historical knowledge than would be suspected by a lay reader of *L'être et le néant*: the theory of non-being in Plato's *Sophist,* the Cartesian thesis of the dualism of thought and extension, the Kantian theory of intelligible character, all these have inspired the author of this celebrated book. He is not, however, very favorable to the history of philosophy; existentialism is, in effect, an actualism which wishes to consider man only as engaged, morally and physically, in a present and determined situation; as has been said, existence, for it, is not anything but presence; there is not (Nietszche had already said this) any pure thought; so much so, it seems, that we would not be able truly to understand the thought of another, engaged otherwise than ourselves, and still less the doctrines of the past; they float within us like phantoms, like those specters of memory of which Ellenberger speaks. Existentialism does not offer us any interpretation of history as does Marxism; it is simply antihistorical, and the "historicity," characteristic of man, of which it often speaks, is less a going back over the past than a movement toward the transcendence of the future. I cannot, here, discuss these theses nor show, especially, that the present can have a certain density only thanks to the past with which it is swollen, like the surface of a pool of water which cannot be lifted up except by a movement coming from the depths. It is enough for us to have shown that the disfavor in which he holds the history of philosophy does not prevent his having found it necessary to use it, in formulating his own thought.

One sees then (and this will be my twofold conclusion which will lead back to the present situation of the history of philosophy in France) that, on the one hand, it is passing through a crisis, due to the very evolution of philosophy, which, quite naturally, wishes to free itself from the heavy burden of the past and think for itself and not through the interpretation of others; but that, on the other hand, restored to its just import by the employment of the properly historical method, purified of the dross which has too often been mixed with it, by doctrines seeking to make use of it as proofs, it remains an indispensable element of philosophic thought. Add that, in the country of Paul Valéry and of so many critics of history, nowhere more than in France, there is a failure to take fully into account the limits of the history of doctrines: the chance which has presided over the conservation of documents, the fortuitousness in the appearance of geniuses and the elaboration of their doctrine, the difficulty of ancient or foreign languages, the painful passage from one stage of civilization to another. These are all so many difficulties which become more obtrusive the more one enters into detail. And this is why our historians of philosophy, for the very benefit of philosophy, continue to remain historians as far from an *a priori* reconstruction of history as from a skepticism which would violently detach the present from the past.

SELECTED BIBLIOGRAPHY

(1) Detailed bibliographical information in Émile Bréhier, *Histoire de la philosophie* (for the entire period) and in Albert Rivaud, *Histoire de la philosophie* (only volume I covering antiquity has appeared).

(2) Collections:
   Collection Guillaume Budé. Paris, Belles-Lettres (Plato, Plotinus, Marcus Aurelius, Lucretius, Seneca, Cicero).
   Les classiques de la philosophie, published under the editorship of V. Delbos, A. Lalande, and X. Léon, Paris, A. Colin, *Bibliotheque des textes philosophiques* (H. Gouhier, editor), Paris, Vrin.
   Corpus général des philosophes français. (R. Bayer, editor) Paris, Presses Universitaires de France—of this corpus only volume XXXIII on Condillac has appeared.

(3) Masson-Oursel, P. *L'Inde antique et la civilisation indienne.* Paris, A. Michel, 1933.
   ————. *Les philosophies orientales.* Paris, Hermann, 1940.

(4) Robin, L. *La pensée grecque et les origines de l'esprit scientifique.* Paris, A Michel, 1928.

(5) Schuhl, P.-M. *La formation de la pensée grecque.* Paris, Alcan, 1934.

(6) Moreau, J. *Construction de l'idéalisme platonicien.* Paris, Boivin, 1939.

(7) Goldschmidt, V. *Les dialogues de Platon.* Paris, Presses Universitaires de France, 1948.

(8) Gilson, Ét. La philosophie du Moyen-Age. Second edition, Paris, Payot, 1944.

(9) Landry, B. *Duns Scot.* Paris, Firmin-Didot, 1922.
   ————. *L'idee de chrétienté chez les scolastiques du XIIIe Siècle.* Paris, Alcan, 1929.

(10) de Gandillac, M. *La philosophie de Nicolas de Cuès*. Paris, Aubier,
      1941.
(11) Laporte, J. *Le rationalisme de Descartes*. Paris, Presses Universi-
      taires de France, 1945.
(12) Gouhier, H. *La philosophie de Malebranche*. Paris, Vrin, 1926.
(13) Baruzi, Jean. *Leibniz et l'organisation religieuse de la terre*. Paris,
      1907.
(14) Lachiéze-Rey, P. *L'idéalisme Kantien*. Paris, Alcan, 1931.
(15) Mouy, P. *Le développement de la physique cartesienne*. Paris, Vrin,
      1934.
(16) Gouhier, H. *La jeunesse d'Auguste Comte et la formation du posi-
      tivisme*. Paris, Vrin, 1934-1941.
(17) Goldmann, L. *"Matérialisme dialectique et Histoire de la philoso-
      phie."* Revue Philosophique, 1948, p. 160.
(18) Hyppolite, J. *Genèse et structure de la philosophie chez Hegel*. Paris,
      Aubier, 1946.

PHENOMENOLOGY
IN FRANCE

*Jean Hering**

"For myself, Philosophy is a manner of seizing things, a mode of perceiving reality. It does not create Nature, or Man, or God, but finds them and tries to understand them. . . . Philosophy is the ideal reconstruction of consciousness, it is consciousness understanding itself with all that it contains."
Frédéric Amiel, *Journal*, December 26, 1852.

SECTION 1. INTRODUCTION: PRELIMINARY REMARKS.

If we were allowed to give on these pages a historical sketch of the antecedents of phenomenology in France, we evidently would have to speak of the influence of Bergson's intuitionism which has prepared the ground for a philosophy hostile to any abstract construction and to purely rational deductions. But we cannot undertake such a study here. We shall only point out, on one side, that the theme of the *cogito* was developed in an original manner by Mr. Edouard Le Roy in his lectures at the Collège de France in 1919/20 (see his *Problème de Dieu* [Artisan du Livre, 1930], p. 131); on the other hand, we must not forget the fundamental hostility of Bergsonism to the philosophy of essences which separates it radically from phenomenology.[1]

As concerns the philosophy of Edmund Husserl and of Max Scheler, it became known in France only after 1918,[2] not without the agency of the Faculty of Protestant Theology, University of Strasbourg, which once

---

* Born in 1890. Student in philosophy, history, and theology at Strasbourg, Heidelberg, Göttingen, and Paris. Agrégé ès-Lettres, 1914. Graduate of École Pratique des Hautes Études de Paris, 1923. Licencié en Théologie, 1926. Doctor of Theology, 1937. Professor, Protestant Theological School, University of Strasbourg. Author of *Phenomenologie et philosophie religieuse* (1926), *Le royaume de Dieu selon Jésus et l'apôtre Paul* (1937), and *Commentaire de la Ire Épitre de Paul aux Corinthiens* (1949).

1. On this point, we refer the reader to the elaborate study of the Polish philosopher Roman Ingarden: "Intuition und Intellekt bei Henri Bergson" (*Jahrb.f.Phil.u.phän. Forschg*, Vol. VI).

2. The critical study of Victor Delbos on the "Logical Investigations" by Husserl (see *Revue de métaphysique et de morale*, 1911, pp. 685-698), concerns only the first volume of that work in which there is yet no question of phenomenology.

again transmitted to France the knowledge of certain currents in the thought of central Europe.[3] However, it was only since the publication of Husserl's *Méditations cartésiennes,* as well as of the translation of certain books of Max Scheler—*Nature et forme de la sympathie* and *Le sens de la souffrance* (the first published by Messrs. Payot, 1928, the second in *Philosophie de l'Esprit,* 1936)—that the interest in phenomenology became more general. The works of Georges Gurvitch, Emmanuel Levinas, and Z. W. Elbert, the "Journées d'Etudes Thomistes" (Meetings for Thomist studies — see bibliography at the end of this article) and above all, the *Recherches philosophiques,* edited by A. Koyré, Ch. Puech, and A. Spaier (since 1931/32) also largely contributed to promote the knowledge and discussion of the phenomenological movement.

Although there are in France very few philosophers who could be qualified as phenomenologists in the strict sense of the word, such as E. Husserl, M. Scheler, A. Pfaender, and A. Reinach, still the number of those who are more or less strongly influenced by that movement is considerable. Among the works published in the series, *Philosophie de l'Esprit* (Paris, Aubier), there are many who show that influence, such as Berdiaeff, Lavelle, Le Senne, Jean Wahl, and others.

Among the contemporary publications, we still may point out the essay of Gaston Berger on *Le cogito dans la philosophie de Husserl* (Paris, Aubier, 1941), which is the most conscientious study on Husserl's phenomenology in the French language; also the first number of the review *Deucalion* (Paris, Revue Fontaine), which provides very good information on the phenomenological movement to the French reader, and the elaborate critical study on Husserl's transcendental logic by Jean Cavaillès (see bibliography).

As there can be no question of giving here an exhaustive study on the influence of phenomenology in France, we shall content ourselves with giving some examples which appear to us as typical. We need not say that this necessary selection by no means implies any disparaging judgment on such works as cannot be dealt with here.[4]

---

3. Cf. our essay "Phénoménologie et philosophie religieuse," 1925. This work being out of print and no longer up to date, we only mention it for memory's sake.

4. This study being dedicated exclusively to philosophy in France, we cannot deal with philosophy written in French in Belgium, Switzerland, and Canada. However, it is impossible not to mention the fine issue of the *Revue internationale de philosophie* (No. 2, Brussels, Jan., 1939).

PART I: TENDENCIES AND METHODS

SECTION 2. THE SITUATION OF PROTESTANT THEOLOGY: PHENOMENOLOGY OR BARTHISM?

The respective situations of a Barthian and a phenomenological theology are neither complementary nor contradictory; they are rather made out of competition and rivalry. Both of them break with the psychological explication of religious truth, still rather popular in the beginning of this century and even nowadays with certain circles somewhat behind the times. Barthism, however, phenomenologists will say, is not yet radically rid of psychologism. It readily affirms that without faith, we would be obliged to admit as true the psychological, and perhaps even psychiatrical, explication of religious life in general and of religious knowledge in particular. Barthians concede everything to subjectivism, with the purpose of taking refuge in a certain fideism, whereas phenomenologists concede nothing at all to it. For what they are reproaching subjectivism with is an inexact, and often dishonest, description of the religious phenomenon — any conscientious phenomenological description having to recognize the presence in religion of data inexplicable in a psychological way. In consequence, even the nonbelieving philosopher, provided his analyses be honest and well documented, should disapprove of psychologism. Certainly, he will not be able to decipher the enigmas of religious life, but he will admit their existence.

In the last analysis, it would be possible to show that the divergence of views between phenomenology and Barthism is due to the fact that the latter ignores the intentional structure of consciousness, an essential topic of phenomenological reasearches.[5] This is the reason why the theologians belonging to the so-called "Nouvelle École de Strasbourg" (New School of Strasbourg), which is represented chiefly by the Professors Hauter, Mehl, Ménégoz, and Will, were able to surmount psychologism without appealing to the method of Karl Barth.[6]

Another reason which induced phenomenological theology to choose different ways is the fact that Karl Barth, who is a disciple of Hermann Cohen, has remained a neo-Kantian to the backbone, easily introducing the opposition between time and eternity, the finite and the infinite, the

---

5. It stands to reason that this underlying subjectivism also destroys any theoretical philosophy. If the Barthians do not become aware of this, it is because they easily accept in that sphere the Kantian solution, according to which man applies only the laws of his own mind to sensation. But this shift seems to them, for evident reasons, inadmissible in the theological field.

6. Cf. bibliography.

limited and the unlimited with which, according to the above-named theologians (to whom we still must add Mr. Oscar Cullmann, in particular), it has nothing to do.[7]

On the other hand, phenomenological intentionalism will allow justice to be done to a thinker whom Karl Barth and his former companion Emil Brunner could but attack violently because they ignored any other interpretation of his philosophy of religion than that prompted by his rather subjectivist language, namely Schleiermacher. In fact, under his habit of posing all problems in terms of consciousness ("das' fromme Bewusstsein," "das christliche Bewusstsein," "das sittliche Bewusstsein"), a phenomenologist will guess a concern of a phenomenological order: namely, the refusal to build a philosophy of religion on the speculation which pretends to cast a look behind the veil, as well as the desire to stick to the data really revealed to consciousness. This attempt of Schleiermacher and his disciples unluckily failed because of their naive and nonintentionalist conception of consciousness, bringing them always back to a purely subjectivist philosophy of experience. On the contrary, a phenomenologist, whenever he thinks it appropriate to speak of experience, will insist on the objective realities of which the subject makes an experience. He thereby surmounts the sterile opposition between "Theology of Experience" and "Positive Theology" with which the philosophy of religion of the nineteenth century was struggling.

If we do not consider these questions any longer, it is because special articles are dedicated in this volume to questions connected with philosophy of religion. We thought it best, however, to give at least these indications.

Section 3. Phenomenology and History of Philosophy: Alexandre Koyré.

As phenomenology is not a philosophical system but rather a particular attitude toward problems, its influence on the history of philosophy became inevitable. Nothing is more characteristic in this respect than the numerous and solid studies of Mr. Alexandre Koyré,[8] an immediate disciple of Husserl in the epoch before 1914. France, to be sure, always had illustrious historians of philosophy, but none of them, as much as Mr.

---

7. See Jean Hering, *Le royaume de Dieu selon Jésus et l'Apôtre Paul.* chap. x, EHPR No. 35 (Paris, Alcan, 1937); Oscar Cullmann, *Le Christ et le Temps.* (Neuchâtel, Delachaux et Niestlé, 1948); Charles Hauter, RHPR (1925), p. 500 (see bibliography).

8. Among the important number of Mr. Koyré's works, a certain amount are purely systematic. But here we limit ourselves to his most important works dealing with history of philosophy (see bibliography).

Koyré, has so completely broken with certain presuppositions too easily admitted before him — and without abandoning in the least the correct historical method. The prejudices we have in view could in fact be reduced to a single one: namely, that a philosophical system could be understood in the same measure in which it can be explained by the historical influences the thinker had undergone, as well as by his intellectual temperament. On the contrary, a phenomenologist thinks that the desire of explaining everything (in that way) means the danger of understanding nothing at all. For important though the historical and psychological method may be for showing the route traversed by a philosopher (and many times in spite of the influences he underwent!), in order to reach the point where he came in contact with truth, it would be vain thus to attempt to explain truth itself as well as its recognition by the philosopher. In the end, it is only the errors (as well as truths borrowed from others but not really thought) that could be explained (according to phenomenologists) in studying the influences of the surroundings.

It is for that reason that the historical studies of Mr. Koyré, whether they deal with Plato, St. Anselm, Descartes, Jacob Boehme, or Galileo, put us in immediate relation not only with the era of those philosophers but also with a certain field of philosophical problems itself. *Philosophica philosophice interpretanda:* rarely has that motto been taken so seriously as in the phenomenological movement, the more so because the problems again discovered by it often proved identical with those treated by the great thinkers of the past. It is noteworthy, above all, to what extent the study of "essences" by the phenomenologists has prepared them to understand and to appreciate the Platonic ideology, as well as the discussions on universals, and also a great many related questions in medieval scholasticism. Neither is it forbidden to think that it was an important event in the history of French philiosophy when it succeeded in reestablishing, through the pen of a thinker not addicted to any theological party, the prestige of the famous ontological argument for the existence of God.[9]

Besides, the historical method itself, even where it was justified, displayed a curious deviation under the influence of a superficial determinism which always looked for a medium between causes and effects distant in time. Had not one gone sufficiently far in the contemporary world of a philosopher for Platonic or Aristotelian influences, even when

9. See A. Koyré, *La philosophie de St. Anselme*, p. 195-240; *idem.*, *L'idée de Dieu dans la philosophie de Descartes*. We also refer the reader to the capital essay by Mr. Koyré on Jacob Böhme (see bibliography), especially the beautiful chapter on the origin of the notion of God, in order to consider the fine perspectives opened by such a collaboration between phenomenologist and historian united in a single person.

it was evident that the philosopher himself had read the works of those masters of antiquity? It is against that prejudice that Mr. Koyré has also strenuously fought in reminding us that the contemporaries of a philosopher are all those authors he has read. He thereby contributed to re-establishing a sound comprehension of the historical development of thought, and brought about an amendment bearing a certain analogy with that suggested by Max Scheler in the psychological sphere, when the latter states that our distant psychological past may influence the present directly, even when it is separated therefrom by a lapse of time more or less long, and a stream of phenomena more or less rich (cf. the first twenty pages in his analysis of "Repentance" in the volume entitled *The Sense of Suffering*).

For all these reasons we think that the works of Mr. Koyré are extremely characteristic of the happy influence which phenomenology has already exercised, and still will exercise, on the history of philosophy.

SECTION 4. PHENOMENOLOGY AND EXISTENTIALISM: J.-P. SARTRE.

In what measure has the existentialist movement in France, chiefly represented by J.-P. Sartre, been influenced by Husserl or Scheler? We think that French existentialists have learned a good many things from those two thinkers, but not insofar as they are existentialists. This is the reason why: phenomenology, in spite of the transcendental reduction of Husserl, is certainly not hostile to the study of being in its essence. It even affirms that it alone is capable of elucidating in a definite manner the signification of the terms "To be" and "Existence," often utilized in a thoughtless manner by the realists as well as their adversaries, since only the study of certain structures of consciousness can give the key to those terms. Heidegger himself, insofar as he was a philosopher of being, never went beyond the limits of a sound phenomenology.

But what characterizes existentialists as such, Heidegger above all, is—as Jean Wahl has brilliantly demonstrated in an article entitled "Freedom and Existence in Some Recent Philosophies," in *Philosophy and Phenomenological Research* (Vol. VIII, No. 4, pp. 538 ff.)—a kind of obsession with their own real existence, which gives to their philosophy the character of a "clenched" egocentrism, thoroughly unknown by the classical representatives of the "ego cogito." What is more serious is their incapacity to distinguish between the essential and the accidental in the analysis of existence. We are going to make ourselves clear. After having chosen, among all kinds of possible lives, that which is perhaps the most complicated, the most abstruse, one even might say, the least typical, namely, human life in our actual aeon (and no doubt we must add, in our occidental world *hic et nunc*), they see in its particular characteristics (described with great talent), and especially in anguish and nausea,[10] the essential features of life in general; somehow like that famous Englishman who, after landing at Calais, wrote down in his notebook, after one single observation: "French women have red hair." Sartre shares that erroneous "intuition of essences" ("Wesensschau") with Heidegger but not with Kierkegaard, who was still better advised and to whom existentialists wrongly appeal in this respect.

On the contrary, phenomenologists, without rejecting the valid intuition concerning "anguish" and the fact "to be cast into the world," claim a deeper signification to be given those phenomena, capable of leading farther and, particularly, of discovering the real anomalies of our life.[11] For does not anguish imply the intuition of something that is anomalous with respect to the life for which we are destined? Yet the refusal to utilize any of the suggestions implied in those phenomena is quite characteristic of Heidegger's and Sartre's existentialism, which well deserve to be qualified as "obscurantist" (this term being understood in the etymological sense and of course without any injurious character) because of its way of obscuring the windows through which some light could enter. On the contrary, phenomenology represents the "philosophy of enlightenment" in the full sense of the term, for it never eliminates any light, wherever it comes from.

All this, let us repeat, cannot prevent us from stating that a great number of analyses in detail, contained in *L'être et le néant* and *L'imaginaire,* Sartre's chief works, belong to genuine phenomenology, particularly for their refusal to be imprisoned in the absolute dilemma between rationalism and irrationalism, as well as for their purpose of posing the problem of perception, representation, memory, and of numerous analogous problems, *in terms of consciousness.* It is those analyses which, we think,

---

10. Besides, we think that it is not only the configuration of our world which, according to Sartre, is nauseous, but also the insolence with which it dares really exist. Should not a nightmare be fugitive and ephemeral? No doubt Sartre has in view a phenomenon analogous to that which Gustav Meyrink, that great novelist of the fantastic, has expressed in the words: "The world is a petrified nightmare." See his tragi-comical narration in "Der Saturning," in the collection, *Des deutschen Spiessers Wunderhorn,* Vol. I, 1913, p. 92.

11. We cannot enter into further details, but refer the reader to the suggestive observations presented by Mr. Jean Wahl in his report at the Club "Maintenant" as well as to the interesting debate by which it was followed, especially the remarks of Berdiaeff and Gabriel Marcel. The whole is reproduced in *A Short History of Existentialism,* by Jean Wahl (New York, Philosophical Library, 1949).

will continue to be studied with considerable profit by future generations, even at a time when existentialism as such will have been ranked among mere historical curiosities.[12]

SECTION 5. AN INDEPENDENT PHENOMENOLOGIST: GABRIEL MARCEL.

What assigns to Gabriel Marcel an eminent place in the philosophical thinking of France, is the fact that he practiced the phenomenological method long before his acquaintance with the philosophy of Husserl, Scheler, and their disciples. What characterizes him as a genuine phenomenologist is, first of all, his constant concern for research and for exploring the "essence" of things, without separating them from the consciousness that presents them to us. It is furthermore his absolute professional honesty which resists the temptation to advance at an exaggerated speed, like "those philosophers who are impatient to overtake the *cogito* in order to construct their imaginary castles" (Berger *dixit*).[13] Does he not agree, in this, with one of the deepest preoccupations of Edmund Husserl? Does not the philosophy of the twentieth century, the latter asked himself in his lectures,[14] find itself somewhat in the same situation as physics did during the Renaissance? They were numerous then, the builders of "Systems of Nature," both grandiose and ephemeral, which now are only mentioned for curiosity's sake. But what was it that permitted modern physics to be edified little by little? It was the disinterested, laborious work of detail, often ignored or unacknowledged by the great public, of the disciples of Galileo and Newton. It is a similar work of the laboratory, often ungrateful, regarded perhaps as tedious by the unsympathetic (done according to the phenomenological method, of course), and continued during several centuries (so he added), which might permit the building-up of a solid philosophy.

It appears as if Gabriel Marcel had also understood the inanity of that "Weltanschauungs-Philosophie," not less pretentious than fragile, and not less superficial than obscure.[15] The sincerity of his arguments, which he does not hesitate to retract when he believes he has chosen a false way, his refusal to enunciate any truth not yet sufficiently upheld by cor-

12. See my article, "Concerning Image, Idea, and Dream," *Philosophy and Phenomenological Research,* Vol. VIII, No. 2, (December, 1947), pp. 188 ff.
13. Cf. *Revue philosophique* (1948), pp. 92 ff.
14. See also his famous article on "Philosophie als strenge Wissenschaft," *Logos,* Vol. I (1911).
15. Is there a need to emphasize that profundity ("die Tiefe" and not "der Tiefsinn") is never obscure? It is enough to remember, for that purpose, the works of Gaston Bachelard: *L'eau et les rêves* (Paris, José Conti, 1942), *L'air et les songes* (José Conti, 1943), *La terre et les rêveries de la volonté* (José Conti, 1948).

rect analyses—we fain would say: not yet fully lived, if that term were not liable to misunderstanding— is perhaps what is most admirable in the progress of his thinking. But what, on the other hand, distinguishes his *Journal métaphysique* from the journal of a man like Amiel, is his constant concern for describing the objective contents of his experience. It never is the thinker's psychology which stands in the center of interest, as is the case with Amiel, who is nearly always careful to mention the way in which he has profited by the experiences wherein his personality is being made or unmade.

These, however, are still generalities. We think that it would be possible, by examining Marcel's study on the phenomenon of *having* (*Etre et avoir,* pp. 223-255) to show, even in the slightest details, the genuinely phenomenological character of his proceedings and of his concerns. Never does the author make the slightest concession to the sophism of those who juggle away every philosophical question by declaring that "it depends on the definition you give"—as if a definition not prepared by phenomenological analyses, and therefore greatly arbitrary, could ever resolve a philosophical question. Indeed he does not undertake any logical constructions but observations, more and more precise, of a phenomenon, the latter being given mostly by the meaning (*das Meinen*) of a term, or of the different phenomena which the multiplicity of a sense allows us to distinguish, as is the case with all that concerns "having."

In the very study of phenomena it is noteworthy with what care G. Marcel refuses to indulge in the too widespread mania for reducing one fact to another, by which we risk losing sight of what is most original in it. As he explains himself, it is necessary to recognize what a given fact has of the irreducible in it; we must never remove the difficulties nor try to simplify them, which would still be a way of denying them. On the other hand, we must never content ourselves with pointing them out as irrational, but we must show how data logically contradictory, or pseudocontradictory, *coexist in fact.* Even his marked preference for those essences which bear a reputation for being obscure and impossible to define accurately is of truly phenomenological inspiration. When philosophers are frightened by an obscurity, Husserl said, then the phenomenologist has the duty to grapple with it.

For all these reasons, we believe we may affirm that, even if German phenomenology (to suppose the impossible) had remained unknown in France, nevertheless a phenomenology would have been constituted there; and this, to a large extent, would be due to the influence of Gabriel Marcel.

PART II: PROBLEMS AND RESEARCHES

SECTION 6.   A CRITICAL STUDY OF THE "COGITO": MR. MERLEAU-PONTY.

If Mr. Berger has given the most elaborage analysis of Husserl's *cogito,* it is Mr. Merleau-Ponty who, if we are not mistaken, has furnished the most interesting critical study of it in one of the last chapters of his work *Phénoménologie de la perception,* (pp. 423-468). We shall try to examine the points where he respectively agrees, or disagrees, with the master. Like the latter, he rejects, of course, any attempt to explain the subject-object relation as an intra-mundane relation, e.g., of cause-effect. "To the image of knowledge we have obtained in describing the subject situated in its world we should as it seems, substitute another one according to which it constructs or constitutes this very world; and this one is more genuine that the other, since an intercourse of the subjects with the things by which it is surrounded is only possible if first of all it makes them exist for itself, disposes them around itself, and draws them out of its own ground" (p. 424).[16] By this, he rejects, of course, also every other kind of naive realism which tries to explain the consciousness of the world by the mere fact that the latter exists. "If I meet with things around myself, this cannot be because they are actually there, for of this actual existence (by hypothesis) I know nothing" (*ibid.*).

The author thus implicitly admits the justification of the famous transcendental reduction which forbids regarding the world as metaphysically existent. The continuation of his developments shows, besides, that, like Husserl, he considers it impossible to speak of the existence of the world for another reason still: we do not know what an existence of that kind could be before having studied, in a phenomenological way, the meaning of the acts of consciousness which allow us to understand that existence. But, once "existence" is taken in its phenomenologically justified signification, it will become clear that "transcendental idealism is an absolute realism" (p. 430).

There is also admitted the impossibility of studying a *cogitatio* without considering the ego, upon which the philosopher of Göttingen had insisted, if not in the beginning of his phenomenological researches, at least after the publication of his *Ideen.* "Every thought of something is at the same time consciousness of oneself, otherwise it could have no object. At

---

16. If Mr. Merleau-Ponty speaks of the construction or constitution of the perceived by the perceiving consciousness, he does so apparently always in a transcendental sense, which has nothing to do with the cause-effect category nor with any activity whatsoever in the realist sense of this term.

the root of all our experiences and of all our reflections, we therefore find a being which recognizes itself immediately. . . . Self-consciousness is the very being of mind in action" (p. 426).

In turn, the author, without designating Husserl directly but aiming at him implicitly, stands against any absolutist and "eternalizing" interpretation of consciousness. Such a standpoint would lead to the thesis of more than one absolute. "But how could there be more than one absolute?" (p. 427). The plurality of consciousness is impossible if I have an absolute consciousness of myself. On the contrary, "Perception is just that kind of act where there cannot be question of the act itself apart from the term concerned by it. Perception and the perceived necessarily have *the same existential modality*" (p. 492). If the author is right, this simply means the failure of the thesis of Husserl's *Ideen* on the primacy of consciousness, expressed in a classical way on page 92 in these terms: "The immanent being therefore is undoubtedly an absolute being in the sense that it *nulla re indiget ad existendum*" ("Das immanente Sein ist also zweifellos in dem Sinne absolutes Sein, dass es *nulla re indiget ad existendum*"). The reader will remember that immediately after the publication of the *Ideen,* it was about the absolutist interpretation of consciousness (and about transcendental studies in themselves, as a badly informed historiography goes on affirming) that many disciples of Husserl felt scruples and doubts. There is nothing astonishing therefore, if Mr. Merleau-Ponty has attacked it in his turn.

But there is another point where the developments of this philosopher deserve special attention. If he admits, in accordance with the *Ideen,* the essential inadequateness of the so-called external perception, he extends this thesis to the perception called internal. "What is lived does not present itself, " says Husserl in his *Ideen* (p. 81), ". . . a feeling-experience is not adumbrated. . . . What stands before one's view is there absolute with its qualities, its intensity, etc." "Nothing that is lived and substantially given can also not be" (*ibid.,* p. 86). Mr. Merleau-Ponty, in cleverly utilizing certain suggestions of Max Scheler, explains how illusion is possible also in that sphere. I may be mistaken about my own feelings, I may take for a real love what afterwards, when disillusion has come, unveils itself as a false feeling, a feeling where my ego was not really engaged. The difference between reality and appearance, therefore, certainly also has its place here. To these developments Husserl (in his last period) could have answered undoubtedly that there is nothing astonishing, since the human soul with the feelings it undergoes is an object constituted as "mundane" too, which can be but imperfectly perceived and must be bracketed itself (see the article in the review, *Phi-losophia,* Vol. I, 1936, "Die Krisis der europäischen Wissenschaften," etc., especially pp. 18-20). But it is just that reason Mr. Merleau-Ponty does not set forth. If the internal perception is inadequate, it is, on the contrary, because "I am not an object that can be perceived, because I make my reality and reach myself only in the act." It therefore is not the inadequateness in the presentation which allows doubt, but the im-possibility to live the act profoundly enough. Besides, the author ex-tends his thesis expressly to the *dubito,* the basis of the whole doctrine of the *cogito.* According to him, I may, in opposition to Descartes and Husserl, believe that I am doubting without doing so. "There is no other way of annulling any doubt with regard to that proposition ("I doubt") than to doubt in effect, to become engaged in the experience of doubt and thus to give this doubt the certainty of doubting" (pp 438-439). In the end, it is therefore only by deciding ourselves to be, to think, to act truly, that we can overcome the incertitudes of internal perception. In the proposition: "I think, I am," both affirmations are truly equivalent, other-wise there would be no *cogito.* Still, however, it is necessary to understand each other about the sense of this equivalence: "it is not the *I think* that eminently contains the *I am;* it is not my existence that is reduced to the consciousness I have of it: it is inversely the *I think* that is reinstated in the movement of transcendence of the *I am,* and consciousness into ex-istence" (p. 439).

It is for that reason that evidence, though irresistible in fact when lived, is theoretically exceptionable in any syhere. It always is possible to correct evidence by later evidence (see p. 454).[17]

No doubt, a strict disciple of Husserl's transcendentalism could answer that what interests a phenomenologist above all is the *essence* of doubt, apart from its reality, and would call to mind that it is in the realm of fiction where a phenomenologist is really in his element (cf. *Ideen,* p. 132). But Mr. Merleau-Ponty absolutely denies the necessity of a tie between the two famous reductions. According to him, the phenomenological re-duction neither presupposes nor implies the eidectic reduction: "It would be contradictory to affirm at the same time that the world is being consti-tuted by myself and that I can seize but the outlines and the essential structures of that constitutive operation, such as, e.g., Husserl does when he admits that any transcendental reduction is at the same time an

---

17. Mr. Merleau-Ponty certainly will not refuse to confront one day that affirmation with the very much shaded doctrine of evidences as developed by Husserl in his *Formale und Transzendentale Logik.*

eidetic reduction. The necessity of passing through the essence, the definitive opacity of existences cannot be taken as facts needless of explanation . . . . *I think* is not *I am* if I cannot equal by thought the concrete abundance of the world and absorb facticity" (pp. 430 ff. and note).

Certainly, Mr. Merleau-Ponty will not claim to have finished the present debate but is it not meritorious to have it reopened?

SECTION 7. "I" AND "THOU": FROM GABRIEL MARCEL TO MAURICE NÉDONCELLE.

It is well known that the problem of the knowledge of Others had been particularly dealt with by Scheler, who had done away with a certain number of traditional theories contrary to a correct phenomenological description and explaining, in fact, nothing at all. This question was taken up again by several French philosophers, most recently by J. P. Sartre (*L'être et le néant,* third part) and Merleau-Ponty (*Phénoménologie de la perception,* pp. 398 ff.)

But it was Gabriel Marcel who opened new perspectives in this field by examining the problem concerning the intellectual and human relations between subjects. This question has been surprisingly neglected by theoretical philosophy. As for moralists, they evidently were obliged to speak of the moral relations between persons but they had to build on psychological bases which were not solid and had never been examined exhaustively.

The first phenomenon which gained this author's attention was what we may term *the constitution of the second person.* Science knows but of the third person; but then, any relation between persons becomes incomprehensible. "When I speak of somebody in the third person, I treat him as independent, as absent, as separated; more exactly, I implicitly define him as external to a dialogue which may be a dialogue with myself . . . . I have a tendency for treating reality, the universe, like a third person with relation to the dialogue I am pursuing with myself. The 'Thou,' on the contrary, implies a relation with the 'I' " (*Journal métaphysique,* p. 137). Thus, philosophy sometimes agrees to speak in the first person, but opposing it only to the third person ('world,' 'men,' 'my friend,' etc.), and never to the second one. "It seems that we are here in the presence of a world still little explored" (*ibid.,* p. 137).

What characterizes above all the relation between the first and second person is the fact that the *Thou* is considered as capable of answering a question. "I address myself using the second person only to what is considered by me as capable of answering in any way—even if that answer is an 'intelligent silence.' Where no answer is possible, there is only place for a 'He'" (*ibid.*, p. 138). The fecundity of that manner of setting the problem which, besides, has gained adherents, is evident. It leads the author rapidly to formulate certain theses implied in this attitude. The latter above all supposes a minimum of faith in liberty and the value of the *Thou*. It is here that doubt may intervene but not insofar as the problem of the existence of Others is concerned which, as Merleau-Ponty has explained, is always pre-given to the philosopher. The true solipsist is he who has no faith in Others.

It therefore is not by the recognition of the phenomenon of *We* that Marcel attempts to overcome solipsism, nor even by the study of transcendental intersubjectivity such as Husserl put it. The "I" and the "Thou" are supporting each other in a certain way mutually before, and independently of, the constitution of whatever collectivity or, if you prefer, of no other collectivity than the dyad.

Starting from that basis, the author studies other and rather new problems, as, e.g., that of the belonging of the "I" to the "Thou," [18] always following the method of a prudent phenomenological "grubbing," as hostile to logical simplifications as to superficial paradoxes often originating from a refusal to explore the ground of phenomena, but equally far from any metaphysical timidity of Kantian or positivist origin.

Naturally, I may always transform the "Thou" back into a "He." However, there is one exception, namely the case of God. What characterizes divinity, according to Marcel, is its refusal to allow itself to be considered as a "He." "God is reality insofar as it can absolutely not be treated as itself" (p 155). "As soon as God is treated as a metaphysical This to which one makes judgments refer which are supposed to necessarily agree with each other, everything becomes chaotic. . . . If I wrote formerly: 'There is no truth possible about God,' I wanted to say in fact that He cannot be thought as 'This'" (p 254). Thus, the author accepts a certain dialectical conception of the existence of God cherished by Kierkegaard which is, however, far from leading to subjectivism. One also conceives how, from that basis, he arrives at conceding a primary place to prayer in religious life and knowledge, thus joining the theses of Fernand Ménégoz. But we need not say that the God in question never is the "God of Philosophers" (who, according to Marcel, perhaps

---

18. See his paper *Appartenance et disponibilité,* reproduced in RHPR (1939), pp. 55 ff.

does not exist at all) but the "God of Abraham, Isaac, and Jacob" (to speak with Pascal), or the God of mystics (according to Bergson's terminology).

To return, on the other hand, to the problem of human relations, there is nothing astonishing in the fact that the author frequently has chosen the dramatic form in order to express his anthropological and moral ideas. For is not drama the most direct and most striking way of presenting us with the dialectical interaction between persons, the latter alone being capable, according to the author, of elucidating the problems of practical philosophy? Thus one could draw from his tragedies and comedies quite a collection of philosophical thoughts. The crops would be abundant, although we cannot gather them in here.

Moved by analogous concerns, Mr. Maurice Nédoncelle gave us in *La réciprocité des consciences* the results of investigations so rich and at the same time so concise that it is impossible to give a brief summary of them. Suffice it to point out some results considered by the author as fundamental. Just as for Gabriel Marcel, it is the problem of the relations between "Thou" and "I" which is the starting point of his analyses. For him, these relations constitute themselves essentially in Love. Love is, in truth, the access of "I" to "Thou" (inversely, the dyad is the only known form of real reciprocity). Therefore, "personal love has immediately (*d'emblée*) an interpersonal nucleus" (p. 16). The criterion of love, namely true devotedness, is also the touchstone of reciprocity.

But Mr. Nédoncelle goes farther. The "I" itself can fully constitute itself only in love. "It (the loving reciprocity) is not the effect but the cause of personal identity" (p. 22). "To have an 'I,' it is necessary to be 'willed' by other 'I's,' and to 'will' them also ("pour avoir un Moi, il faut être voulu par d'autres Moi et les vouloir à son tour"); it is necessary to have some consciousness, if only obscure, of the Other-than-Oneself ("L'autre que soi") and of the relations connecting between each other the terms of that spiritual network. The communion of consciousness is the primitive fact, the *cogito* has immediately (*d'emblée*) a character of reciprocity" (p. 319).

Of course, we must carefully distinguish Love from Passion, the latter being but the caricature of the former (see the analyses pp. 25 ff.), and also true communion between persons from anything which is but participation and assimilation. In these researches, Mr. Nédoncelle has utilized, in giving them a greater precision, the developments of Max Scheler contained in his work on *Sympathy*.

The solution of problems thus considered allows a light to be cast upon the question of human destiny. For "personal communion entails the feeling of being ahead of oneself and withdraws from the future its possibility of disconcerting" (p. 23). Then, the author examines the growth of personality in relation to nature and to values. In these developments he goes beyond, in correcting them, the researches of Scheler and of Gurvitch, both of whom he reproaches, among other things for not having always exactly distinguished between "value" and "valuation." Finally, his results lead him to examine the way in which personality inserts itself into God.

One may regret that the author has not always given *in extenso* all phenomenological analyses on which he bases his theories. Nevertheless, it is certain that every chapter of his book will furnish matter for fruitful meditation to philosophers.[19]

SELECTED BIBLIOGRAPHY

(a)   Abbreviations.

B I — Bibliothèque des Idées (Paris, Gallimard)

EHPR — Études d'histoire et de philosophie religieuses, éditées par la Faculté de Théologie protestante de Strasbourg (Paris, Presses Universitaires).

Ph.E. — Philosophie de l'Esprit, series published by Messrs. Aubier, Paris.

RHPR — Revue d'Histoire et de Philosophie religieuses, published by the above named Faculty of Strasbourg (Paris, Presses Universitaires).

R.Ph. — Revue Philosophique.

(b)   For Section 1.

Husserl, E. *Méditations Cartésiennes.* Paris, Armond Colin, 1931.

Scheler, Max. *Nature et Formes de la Sympathie.* Paris, Payot, 1928.

——————. *Le sens de la souffrance. Ph.E.,* 1936.—This volume contains, in addition to the essay entitled as before, two other studies, *viz.,* "Repentir et renaissance" and "Amour et connaissance."

Gurvitch, Georges. *Les tendances actuelles de la philosophie allemande.* Paris, Vrin, 1930.

---

19. It was inevitable that Mr. Nédoncelle was led to confront his notion of Love with that of *Agapê,* as presented by Mr. Anders Nygren in his famous book *Eros and Agapê* (French translation published by Messrs. Aubier, Paris, w.d.; a more complete English translation has been published by the "Society for Promoting Christian Knowledge," 1939). See: Nédoncelle, "Vers une philosophie de l'amour," *Ph. E.,* 1946.

Levinas, Emmanuel. *La théorie de l'intuition dans la phénoménologie de Husserl.* Thèse, Faculté des Lettres de Strasbourg. Paris, Presses Universitaires, 1930.

Elbert, Z. W. *Étude sur la phénoménologie.* Thèse, Faculté des Lettres de Nancy, 1931.

Journées d'études de la société thomiste, Vol. I: *Phénoménologie.* Juvisy, Editions du Cerf, 1932.

Recherches philosophiques, yearly publication beginning with 1931 (5 vols. published). Edited by Messrs. A. Koyré, C. Puech, and A. Spaier. Vol. I contains an important article by Hedwig Conrad-Martius: *L'existence, la substantialité et l'âme,* Paris, Boivin, pp. 148-182.

Berger, Gaston. "Le cogito dans la philosophie de Husserl," *Ph.E.,* 1941.

Deucalion. Paris, Revue Fontaine. Periodical edited by Jean Wahl. The first issue contains important studies on phenomenology and existentialism.

Cavaillès, Jean. *La logique et la théorie des sciences.* Paris, Presses Universitaires le France, 1947 (posthumous). This important essay contains among others a criticism of Husserl's logic and utilizes his article *Die Krisis der Europäischen Wissenschaften, etc.* (in the review *Philosophia,* Vol. I, fasc. 1, Belgrade, 1936).

Wahl, Jean. *Tableau de la philosophie française.* Paris, Fontaine, 1946.

(c) For Section 2.

Hauter, Charles. *Religion et réalité.* EHPR, Vol. V, 1922.

——————.*Essai sur l'objet religieux.* EHPR, Vol. XVII, 1928.

——————.Important review of a work by Strauch on the theology of Karl Barth, RHPR, 1925, pp. 500 f.

Hering, Jean. *Phénoménologie et philosophie religieuse.* EHPR, Vol. XV, 1925.

Mehl, Roger. *La condition du philosophe chrétien.* Neuchatel, Delachaux et Niestle, 1947.

Ménégoz, Fernand. *La prière.* Second edition. EHPR, Vol. XIII, 1932.

Will, Robert. *Le culte,* 3 vols. EHPR, Vols. X, XXI, XXIX; 1925, 1929, 1935.

(d) For Section 3.

Koyré, Alexandre. *Essai sur l'idée de dieu et les preuves de son existence chez Descartes.* Bibliothèque de l'École des Hautes Études, Sciences religieuses, Vol XXIII. Paris, Leroux, 1922.

—————. *La philosophie de saint Anselme.* Paris, Leroux, 1923.

—————. *La philosophie de Jacob Böhme.* Paris, Vrin, 1929.

—————. *Trois leçons sur Descartes.* Published by the Faculty of Letters, University of Cairo, 1937.

—————. *Études galiléennes — Actualités scientifiques et industrielles,* No. 852, 853, 854; Hermann and Co., 1939.

—————. *Discovering Plato.* New York, Columbia University Press, 1945.

(e) *For Section 4.*

Sartre, J. P. See bibliography for Campbell's essay.

Waelhens, J. E. "Heidegger et Sartre," *Deucalion I,* Paris, Revue Fontaine.

—————. "De la phénoménologie à l'existentialisme," in: *Le choix, le monde, l'existence.* Paris, Arthaud.

Wahl, Jean. *A Short History of Existentialism.* New York, Philosophical Library, 1949.

—————. "Heidegger et Kierkegaard," in *Recherches philosophiques,* Vol. II, pp. 349-370.

(f) *For Section 5.*

Marcel, Gabriel. *Journal métaphysique.* B I, 1927.

—————. *Etre et avoir.* Ph.E., 1935.

—————. *Du refus à l'invocation.* Paris, Gallimard, 1940.

—————. *Homo viator.* Ph.E., 1945.

—————. "De l'audace en métaphysique" in *Revue de métaphysique et de morale,* 1947, pp. 233 ff.

—————. "Appartenance et disponibilité," RHPR, 1939, pp. 55 ff.

Existentialisme chrétien. Volume dedicated to G. Marcel and presented by E. Gilson.[20] Paris, Plon, 1947.

Wahl, Jean. "Le journal métaphysique de Gabriel Marcel," in: *Vers le concret.* Paris, Vrin, 1932.

Ricoeur, Paul. *Gabriel Marcel et Karl Jaspers.* Paris, Ed. du Temps Présent, 1947.

(g) *For Section 6.*

Merleau-Ponty, Maurice. *Phénoménologie de la Perception.* B I, 1945.

(h) *For Section 7.*

Nédoncelle, Maurice. *La réciprocité des consciences.* Ph.E., 1942.

---

20. The authors of this book take the term of "Existentialism" in a much wider sense than ourselves. It results from our observations in § 4, why we cannot accept this terminology.

———————. *La personne humaine et la nature.* Paris, Presses Universitaires de France, 1943.

———————. *Vers une philosophie de l'amour.* Ph.E., 1946.

Gurvitch, Georges. *Morale théorique et science des moeurs.* Paris, Alcan, 1937.

(i) *Addendum.*

We are informed that the two following works of Edmund Husserl have been translated into French:

(1) The "Krisis" essay in *Philosophia,* translated by Professor Gerrer, under the supervision of Professor Canguilhem, of the University of Strasbourg;

(2) The "Ideen" (Husserl's *Jahrbuch,* Vol. I), translated by Professor Ricoeur, recently appointed professor at Strasbourg.

EXPERIENCE
AND TRANSCENDENCE

*Gaston Berger**

Philosophy is reflection which does not accept limitations from the outside, and the philosopher is a man who puts questions to their last end. That is why all philosophers find themselves confronted with the same problems, and their particular fields cannot be distinguished by their content. The variety comes only from the starting point, the chosen order, and the recommended procedures. But it is always the same matter which is considered. It is just looked at from different viewpoints and with different eyes.

In a book like this, repetitions are, of course, unavoidable. We shall try only to limit them. To speak of Experience and Transcendence is to state the problem of the validity and of the nature of metaphysics. As some of the greatest French metaphysicians of the moment have personally explained their theories in this volume, and as some contributors, like MM. Havet and Duméry have given a general review of French contemporary philosophy in fields closely related with metaphysics, we shall find ourselves excused from giving here a summary of all the doctrines. Therefore we shall restrict our historical account to what is necessary in order to understand the present situation; we shall describe, afterward, this situation; we shall point out finally which statements seem to be valid and which tasks should be fulfilled.

I. IMMANENCE AND TRANSCENDENCE

A complete positivism begins by eliminating metaphysics, and suppresses, by and by, all philosophical research. It tries to demonstrate that philosophical problems are nothing but pseudo-problems, the delusive character of which could be established by a strict logical analysis: science is thus the only useful and valid knowledge. Any pretension to

---

* Born in 1896. Professor of philosophy, University of Aix-Marseille. President of the *Society of Philosophical Research*. Editor of the quarterly review *Les études philosophiques*. Author of *Recherches sur les conditions de la connaissance* (1941), and *Le cogito dans la phénoménologie de Husserl* (1941).

go beyond scientific investigation, to "transcend" science, is only an effect of an emotional temperament, which can bring forth pleasant creations in fine arts or in poetry, but which is absolutely irrelevant for a research concerned only with truth.

Such a "scientism" does not discuss the reasons of metaphysics; it will disregard them, consider them as childish, or at least as out of date. Time has passed, history has been going on, and metaphysicians are nothing but old-fashioned thinkers with a primitive mentality or with an obsolete medieval turn of mind. And you don't discuss with a child; you just wait until he arrives at the age of reason. Sociology has to explain metaphysics—and perhaps psychiatry should. . . .

In this way, "transcendence" gets its first sense: it means the desire to go beyond the limits of scientific research. Let us say at once that this meaning is not the most important now. A complete scientism, severely criticized between 1890 and 1910, has lost all consideration among French philosophers.

We can give only one prominent name, and still with very important reservations: that of Edmond Goblot (1858-1935). He was very positivistic and respected only scientific knowledge. But he paid great attention to philosophical criticisms, did not believe in the almighty power of the "given," and considered as irrelevant all irrational arguments. Thus, unconsciously, "value" was playing the part of "fact" and rationalism was replacing positivism. But rationalism is not a suppression of philosophy; it is just a particular type of philosophy.

The form taken by the conflict between empiricism and the philosophies of transcendence, in the first forty years of the twentieth century, is less that of a fight between science and philosophy than between idealism and realism, and more precisely still, between immanence and transcendence.

It generally happens, in philosophical questions, that the problems change while the discussion is going on. Each time real progress is obtained, the problems of existence, which are stated at the beginning, are transformed into problems of meaning. Instead of asking, "Does the soul exist?" or "Does the exterior world exist?" philosophers put their questions in this way: "What do I mean when I say that I exist?" or, "What kind of existence belongs to material things?" or more generally, "What is the meaning of existence?"

This effort for elucidating meanings showed rapidly that the same word, "Idealism," designated many diverse attitudes and theories. Léon

Brunschvicg (1869-1944) pointed out the differences which exist between an idealism based upon sensory perception, like Berkeley's, and an idealism of intelligence like his own. And that is still too vague. Among the intellectualistic idealisms, he wanted to distinguish and even to oppose the idealism of intelligible objects, which stresses concepts and develops on an Aristotelian basis (the system of Hamelin is in France the best example of this trend), and the idealism of actual intelligence, which is of a Cartesian and mathematical type and which he himself tried to promote. This last form of thought is liberated from the illusions coming from society and from the language, and it shows how the mind does not discover but invents and creates, freely and without limit, structures and methods.

This kind of scientific idealism locates science in the mind and not in things. It attributes to imagination all the realistic beliefs. For Louis Weber's standpoint, idealism, refusing all the uncontrollable hypotheses, is the only authentic positivism, and it develops into a theory of knowledge and of science. With different statements, Brunschvicg goes the same way: idealism considers "relations without substances." Science is the system of these relations, freely created by the mind and which should not be frozen in illusory "things," transcending the mind. The scientist does not always avoid this unconscious and plain metaphysics, but the philosopher ought to destroy it. Beneath what the scientists say, one must find out what they really think, and what corresponds to their experiments and their discoveries. In this way, scientific idealism wants to build up a philosophy of "complete immanence": nothing intelligible exists outside active intelligence, neither ready-made structures nor immutable concepts or fixed rules. Beyond intellectual activity and beyond the relations it establishes, there is only a world deprived of any meaning, giving simply provocative shocks to the mind.

The trend most opposed to this intellectualistic immanentism is that of Thomist philosophy, of which Jacques Maritain is one of the main representatives. The philosophy of being stood in the way of the philosophy of relation, and it seemed that one had to choose between the objective evidence of "Being is" and the intellectual evidence of "I think."

The alternative appeared to be so strict that the thought of Maurice Blondel (1861-1949), as it was formulated in his famous thesis on *Action* (*L'action*, 1893), was at the time absolutely misunderstood. Many believed they would find there a philosophy of immanence only because they were confronted with a personal and spiritual dynamism which it was very difficult to reduce to the objective evidence of being. For that reason the innovations of this philosophy remained long unnoticed, as well as the possibilities it afforded to demonstrate both the insufficiency of immanence and the true rationality of what comes from the transcendence.

Failing to recognize the opportunities given by Blondel's philosophy, the thought of the twentieth century had to reestablish a connection between a realism of transcendence, concerned with metaphysics and even with theology, and an idealism of intellectual activity, interested in science but looking for the origin of science in human subjectivity.

That was realized by the evolution of idealism into spiritualism.

The transformation is already obvious in Octave Hamelin's (1856-1907) Idealism, which is both absolute and personal. In that philosophy the dialetical process binds the notions together, by thesis, antithesis, and synthesis, in the Hegelian way. But the identity of contradictory terms, which was, in Hegel, a logical scandal, is replaced by the integration of simply contrary notions. However the dialectical process does not continue indefinitely; nor does it vanish into the mystery of Absolute Spirit. It leads to personal consciousness which then comes into existence, and which is accompanied by contingency. At that moment, as Hamelin says: "instead of remaining abstract, logic becomes concrete and existential."

On the other hand, beyond the personal and individual consciousness, the consciousness of God is required by the system, and their mutual distinction suppresses any possibility of pantheism and brings transcendence back into idealism. We are no longer in an immanentist system; we have a personalism.

A disciple of Hamelin, Dominique Parodi, inspired by purely rational motives, independent of any religious preoccupations, comes also to personalistic conclusions and tries to show that any true idealism is really a spiritualism.

But it was probably René Le Senne and Louis Lavelle who have made the most effective effort to demonstrate the impossibility of developing a philosophy of absolute immanence or of pure objectivity. The starting point of René Le Senne was Hamelin's idealism, whereas Lavelle started from an uncompromising realism. Both developed their systems in opposite directions without changing their description of the concrete reality of personal mind. Louis Lavelle expands his philosophy into a theory of "participation," while Le Senne, starting from consciousness and subjectivity, shows that any statement, even that which is supposed to be the most objective, involves an evaluation; and to experience a value is to recognize implicitly the transcendence.

For Le Senne, human experience is never that of a fact, passively received and sufficient in itself. It is the experience of "value," which means transcendence invading individual consciousness. This philosophy, presented namely in *Duty* (*Le devoir*, 1930), and in *Obstacle and Value* (*Obstacle et valeur*, 1934), does justice to the reality and importance of the resistance the world puts in our way and which we have to overcome. Human life is not a game of pure ideas, but neither is it the reception of a massive and absurd "given," nor a succession of events deprived of meaning: human life involves an aspect of knowledge and an existentialistic aspect ("elle est idéo-existentielle").

In that way, Le Senne and Lavelle give a description of human consciousness which should not be identified with Blondel's statements, but which is analogous. Blondel, who is now much better understood than he was at the beginning of the century, has recently published a series of important books: *Thought* (*La pensée*, 1934), *Being and Beings* (*L'être et les êtres*, 1935), and a new and much enlarged edition of *Action* (*L'action*, 1936-37). One can find in those books a conception of metaphysics with which many contemporary philosophers would agree, if they mean by metaphysics "the indication of a transcendence, to which we can and we must refer, without being able to reach it otherwise than through its correlative immanence."

We should like to point out also the important works of Jean Laporte, which do not fit into the general scheme we have delineated. He comes back, with very strong arguments and very efficient criticisms, to a position very similar to that of Hume. In his studies on *The Problem of Abstractive Thought* (*Le problème de l'abstraction*, 1940), and on *The Idea of Necessity*, he tries to dispel the metaphors behind which nothing clear and definite can be placed. Repelling all the false constructions of the system-builders, he wants to be faithful to a philosophy of pure experience.

II. THE PROMETHEAN REVOLT

The great syntheses of Maurice Blondel, René Le Senne, and Louis Lavelle do not at this time satisfy all the philosophical minds in France, and we believe that we ought to describe, on the other hand, a broad trend in which many different thinkers are to be found, but the general spirit of which is still relatively simple to catch. It would not be correct to speak of it as "young philosophy," because if some of its partisans are young men, some others are already well-known professors, approaching the age of retirement. Many of its themes, also, are fairly old, even when they appear under new names. We shall not study here, in itself, the existentialist movement, as a special chapter is devoted to it. For the particular subject of our research, we shall not consider the Christian existentialists, who do not share in the revolt against transcendence, which we now want to examine. On the contrary, we can bring closer to the atheistic existentialists the new Marxists who have many points in common with them.

From a methodological point of view, the movement is distinguished by the removal from the Cartesian attitude and by a great suspicion of analytical procedures. "We are convinced," *Jean-Paul Sartre* writes in *Situations* (1948), "that the analytical spirit is now dead and that its only function today is to bring trouble into the revolutionary mind and isolate men from one another, for the benefit of the privileged classes. . . . That is why we appeal, against the analytical spirit, to a synthetic conception of reality, the principle of which is that a whole, whatever it is, is different, in nature, from the sum of its parts." Various influences act together against analysis: the influence of Gestalt psychology, very evident in Sartre and in Merleau-Ponty; that of Bergson's philosophy, manifest in Merleau-Ponty, when he writes, for instance, that "psychological knowledge does not consist any more in decomposing the typical wholes, but rather in feeling them from inside and in understanding them by living them again"; that of Freud's psychoanalysis and of Brunschvicg's Critique, acting together on Gaston Bachelard, to induce in him an epistemology of a non-Cartesian type.

The aversion toward Cartesianism is joined with a return to Hegel and dialectics takes the place of analysis. We ought not develop those considerations in great detail, as they belong to logic and would be somewhat irrelevant to the problem of transcendence. Let us only point out what relation the choice of a method has to do with the attitude toward transcendence: analysis presupposes that all is already existing in the "given" and that the problem is only to find it out; on the other hand, dialectics is a creative method, which is supposed to bring forth entirely new realities. Analysis subordinates man to the object and to something transcendent. Synthesis produces the object and emphasizes our independence. The existentialistic immanentism resumes the theses of Léon Brunschvicg and carries them on beyond the meaning they had in the mind of their inventor.

When Brunschvicg talked about "Spirit," he did not mean a concrete being, outside human individuals, and able to force some rules upon them. He meant the light of intelligence to which we open our minds in theoretical evidence as well as in active generosity. He meant the acting principle, "what is loving in love." Of course, a rational reflection should make the realistic myth of transcendence progressively disappear, but the inward Absolute was still exacting and rigorous: It was a duty to comply with the requirements of truth, by an indefinite improvement of the methods and an indefinite development of the relational system. In the same manner a process of purification should develop on the religious field, turning away from objects and things going beyond formulas and dogmas.

A very serious ambiguity remained in Brunschvicg's philosophy: If I am separated from truth, how can I say that truth is immanent? And if subject and value coincide, how can it be possible to retain the "tension" which is the deepest meaning of human life? Different ideas, which it is very important to separate, are here brought together: (1) the *subject* of the *cogito;* (2) the *act* which creates in the world some kind of reality, a work of art, a judgment, a social organization, etc. . . ; (3) the *value* of the act, of the work, of the judgment. The first is transcendental, the second natural, the third expresses the acknowledgment of a transcendence. The confusion of these three aspects makes it particularly difficult to establish relations between science and history. The light of spirit to which we must accede, and which is exterior and superior to the pure contingency of the events, is still to be looked for in the development of history, that is to say in a purely irrational process. The succession of the facts in history is both an absolute criterion, as it was in positivism, and still it is just a rough draft of the real order, because the historian should distinguish some philosophers who are behind the times, like Hegel or Biran, while others are forerunners, like Descartes.

The reason is that Brunschvicg hesitated between two meanings of immanence, neither of which he consented to abandon: the immanence of the values in man, and the immanence of man in spirit, that is to say in value. This brings back dualism and transcendence.

It is not possible to give here a precise solution which the existentialists would have suggested for this difficulty, because each of them has his particular theory and also because we are speaking of philosophies still in full growth. We do not believe either that a unique and permanent solution could be found in Sartre's books. But the general trend of the answer is very easy to discover: Unity is realized for the benefit of man. One will get rid of the transcendental subject as well as of the absolute and transcendent value. But the notion of man, as being engaged in the world, will be enriched, enlarged, filled with vital meanings. Man will be endowed with prerogatives of the vanishing transcendental and of the disappearing transcendent. From the transcendental ego, he will keep the privilege of being without interior nature, and of enjoying an absolute liberty. And he will replace the transcendent in the function of being the origin of the values.

In Brunschvicg's philosophy, spirit only answered for spirit, that is to say, spirit alone was sufficient, was independent. For existentialism, man only answers for man. The first books of Sartre, such as *Nausea* (1938) and even *Being and Nothingness* (1943), gave a pessimistic impression. But in his more recent writings, which are much more positive, for example, *Existentialism* (1946) and his papers in the monthly review, *Les temps modernes,* the doctrine is really a "Humanism," as its author wants it to be. What it declares is the self-sufficiency of man.

Man, of course, does not pretend to have created himself. He received his existence, without knowing how or why. Neither has he created the world with which he is confronted and of which he is aware. But, without his own action, which unveils it, the world would be only a shapeless chaos, a big viscous heap, a hostile disorder, inhuman and absurd. Human action, suppressing some aspects of the world, annihilating ("néantisant") them, gives a meaning to the world. The exercise of human "projects" reveals the intelligible relations and, with an absolute freedom, creates the values: "in man—and in man alone—existence precedes essence." Man is thrown down into existence; it is up to him to make what he wants out of this existence.

The main interest of existentialism will now bear on the problem of values. To repudiate any transcendence is not to deny the existence of the world, but to deny the existence of a given order and of absolute rules.

For existentialism, man does not discover the values: he creates them. Various philosophers, fairly different from one another, emphasize this very idea, each in his own field. Raymond Polin, strongly influenced by Sartre, tries to show how the values are created, and why they still seem to be transcendent. Their human origin gives to all the values, without exception, a character of relativity. Truth has no more privileges than beauty or duty. Roland Caillois writes: "Most of us have ceased to believe in transcendent God, in the bosom of whom would lie an eternal truth, true before man, true after man, and of which man would be only the provisional guardian. For us, now, man creates his truth and his destiny in a fight to reach himself." And Gaston Bachelard, taking over and developing Brunschvicg's ideas, strives to demonstrate that there are neither stable reason, nor permanent intellectual categories. Moreover, for him, to be a real scientist, "to possess the spirit of invention, is to believe in the evolution of evidence and in the plasticity of reason." There is nothing like a unique type of reason, but different forms of reason, each of which corresponds to a different human attitude; and psychoanalysis can help us to recognize the character and the origin of these attitudes.

It is perhaps in the esthetic field that we can best see that the belief in the human origin of values, which refuses to recognize their transcendence, is a general trend of opinion more than a philosophical theory. The same desire is at work, more or less unconsciously, both in poetry and in plastic arts. The point is to trespass the old rules of significance and likeness and to liberate oneself here from meaning and there from resemblance. The artist no longer wants to look at the things in order to copy them, or to reflect upon the ideas in order to express them. In his *Psychology of Art* (1948) André Malraux deliberately projects into the past the impression he receives from the present, and tries to show that the artists never wanted to copy the living beings nor the objects, except by chance and in the moments when their inspiration was relaxing.

This human origin of the values, this replacing of God by man is quite well suggested by this sally of Malraux: "Every artichoke has in itself an acanthus leaf, and the acanthus is what man would have done with the articoke if God had taken his advice."

It is perhaps Sartre's play *The Flies* (1942) which expresses, both with the greatest strength and in the clearest way, the meaning of the change we are required to accomplish. One of the most important passages is the discussion between Jupiter and the rebelling Orestes—an Orestes whose vengeance is not in the core of the drama, but whose revolt against God is the more characteristic feature—an Orestes who should better be called "Prometheus," because he says the words of the rebellious Titan, as they come from the ancient tradition and as they have been expressed by Goethe in modern times: "Suddenly," Orestes says to Jupiter, "out of the blue, freedom crashed down on me and swept me off my feet. Nature sprang back, my youth, my youth went with the wind, and I knew myself alone, utterly alone, in the middle of this well-meaning little universe of yours. I was like a man who's lost his shadow. And there was nothing left in heaven, no right or wrong, nor anyone to give me orders." And, a little further on Orestes says to Jupiter that he knows perfectly that his human condition is "beyond remedy, except what remedy I find within myself. But I shall not return under your law; I am doomed to have no other law but mine. Nor shall I come back to nature. . . . For I, Jupiter, am a man, and every man must find out his own way. . . ."

The importance of existentialism comes from the fact that it is not contented with shouting its revolt. It tries to discover and to give to man *inside the world* a kind of "metaphysical thickness." As Gusdorf says, we have to elucidate the mystery or reason "in the direction of the immanence of man to his own experience." Metaphysics will no longer rest on transcendence or even on the transcendental, but on man. It will develop out of anthropology. A metaphysics which pretends to go beyond human experience reveals a lack of honesty. It is "the realization of a guilty consciousness, unable to develop its life under the given conditions, and which appeals, for its egoistic comfort, to the pretences of eschatological myths."

It is perhaps too early to ask existentialism for a general theory. But it is easy to see what a momentous part the intersubjective relations will play in the constitution of a "metaphysics immanent to man."[1] M. Merleau-Ponty explains that to believe in the Absolute "is nothing but to experience my harmony with myself and with other people," and he emphasizes the importance of "dialogue" between human beings and of a common human destiny.

We can find among the Marxists the same denial of transcendence as in existentialism. As they are afraid to be surpassed in the field of action and practical problems, the existentialists exaggerate their attacks against bourgeois thought and frequently shift the emphasis from theoretical discussions to historical and social questions. But, on the other hand, the Marxists, who have definite rules for political action, feel more and more the desire to give them a philosophical background, and they try to rethink Hegelian philosophy and to carry on the development of dialectics in the line of Marx's doctrine.

If Jean Wahl had not himself written an essay in this book developing his own theory, it would have been necessary to devote a part of this study to his rich and highly elaborated thought. Closer to Kierkegaard than Sartre or Merleau-Ponty, he gives more importance to transcendence,

---

1. Merleau-Ponty, "La métaphysique dans l'homme," in *Revue de métaphysique et de morale* (July-October, 1947).

in which we are immersed, than to the immanence of values in man. He thinks that "the tension which characterizes subjectivity" is explained by the presence of transcendence, but he tries to liberate the transcendence from any theology and considers poetry "which comes from what is beyond the world and goes beyond the world" as the best human expression of the feeling of transcendence.

III. HUMAN EXPERIENCE

We shall now try to consider the problem in itself. French philosophy—like French literature—has always paid great attention to introspection. That is why it has frequently been tempted to assimilate "interior" life with "spiritual" life, as Brunschvicg pointed out. Psychological activity is then in great danger of being confounded with the value of thought, and the stream of consciousness with the intellectual awareness. We could believe in the delusive reality of an "interior world," which would be the world of our thoughts, distinct from a problematical "exterior world," the existence of which would be asserted by a highly disputable argument. In this conception, philosophy ought to choose between idealism and realism, between immanence *to thought* or transcendence of things.

But the alternative comes from a false expression of what experience really gives: it is supposed that we never know anything but our thoughts, and that this statement is immediately evident. In fact, one inserts between mind and things the "representations," the ideas, the images of the things which would exist in our minds and which would be the only reality we could directly reach.

This is a good example of the way in which philosophical routines have progressively created unnoticed prejudices. We believe, on the contrary that a description of experience which would perform the "philosophical reduction" of the prejudices, would present it as the immediate grasp and awareness not, of course, of distinct and separate objects being their own guarantee, but at least of an *existential continuity*, inside which things are progressively delineated by our intentions and by our remembrances, by our instincts and our habits. Then thoughts are no longer particular types of being, they are just different *ways* of seizing the world. We do not think the thoughts, we think *by* the thoughts, and the phenomenon ceases to be a kind of phantom-like being (a theory which is sometimes attributed to Kant) and takes anew its true meaning of "manifestation of being."

Before a fresh and unprejudiced view, the pseudo-reality called "fact of consciousness" vanishes,[2] and we can perceive the real structure of consciousness: a world of interrelated elements is presented to a mind without any interiority, which is simply the origin of a "view" and perhaps of a particular activity. One of the forms which is frequently taken by the problem of transcendence disappears at the same time, on the ground that there is no psychological immanence and that knowledge is always knowledge of something other than the knower: the body, the social relations, the remembrance are as exterior to the subject, the "ego," the "I," as the table, the dog, or the sky, though they exist, of course, in different ways.[3] To be very precise, we should not say that they are "exterior," nor that they are "outside" the subject, nor "in front" of him. All those expressions are purely analogical, just as all other prepositions would be: prepositions are intended to state particular relations inside the given world; they fail to express relations between the given world and the knower.

Husserl's phenomenology brings a valuable support to these Cartesian-like considerations. It emphasizes the necessity to abandon all the images presenting consciousness as an extended reality, it helps to overcome "psychologism" and to recognize the originality of a transcendental "ego," which is neither a reality inside the world, nor a reality subsisting outside and independently of the world, but always connected with it.

In that way, the transcendental ego derives its meaning from its relation to the given world; and so does transcendence.

The word "metaphysics," which suggests the idea of trespassing, of "going beyond," seems to suit the reflection upon transcendence. We must confess that the burden of proof—as far as the validity of metaphysics is concerned—lies on metaphysics itself. If experience, as it is given to and felt by the subject, were "self-sufficient," there would be no reason whatsoever to look for something else.

But it is evident that the "given" is nothing we can be contented with. Everywhere and in all cases we complete it by "something else," which is beyond the given and affords to it the meaning and validity we are in search of. From the very beginning of reflection we are confronted with this somewhat paradoxical statement that the non-given supports, explains, justifies the given.

---

2. M. Blanché has afforded a very keen critical examination of the so-called "fact" of consciousness.
3. See the study of *Les différents modes de l'existence*, by Étienne Souriau. Paris, Presses Universitaires de France, 1943.

Let us point out that the question is not to go beyond the given because it would not be sufficient *for us*. Our desires do not matter at all, and it is not at all evident that our desires have to be fulfilled by the world. What we have to note is that the given is insufficient *in itself*. It is never independent, it always refers to something else, either to support its existence, or to endow it with meaning.

Of course, some of these requirements can be satisfied by a simple change of the content of experience. This object is a book, because it gives me the possibility to open it, to turn its pages and to see the printed words. And I can, actually, take the book and read. But we must consider two facts: first, new requirements, new "intentions" appear when the first ones are satisfied and this goes on indefinitely; and secondly certain intentions can never be "fulfilled" (as Husserl very clearly pointed out). For instance, we can never grasp, as something given, the consciousness of the other people, nor our own existence as a knower, nor the existence of the past. It belongs *to the essence* of the ego that it can never be an object, *to the essence* of a fellow being to transcend my direct awareness, *to the essence* of the past to refuse the existence in the present. And, of course, we do not forget the existence of the psychological dispositions called reflection, sympathy, and memory. But they do not suppress these essential transcendences because they do not give anything but indirect knowledge. Thus transcendence is really "beyond" actual consciousness, without constituting this illusory "Back-world" criticized by Nietzsche and more recently by the existentialists. On the contrary, transcendence is always in close relation with this world, of which it is the necessary complement.

"Value" is another expression of transcendence of a totally different type. Let us try to describe faithfully what a man really experiences when he has a feeling of value. Or let us reflect upon the essential implications of the idea of value. In both cases we come to the same conclusion, which we can only give here without the concrete examples and the intentional analyses which would explain and support it: value is never something given; it is a relation between a certain given structure, and an ideal requirement to which we compare the given.

There is a criticism which has been renewed very often and which pretends to suppress the reality of the values, while it shows the historical decline and the provisional character of the particular forms taken by that value at different moments of social evolution. It rests on the false belief that the values are just things; they are more or less conceived as material standards, as precise social regulations, as perceptible models with which it would be possible to compare the work to be done. But that has never been assumed by any philosopher of values. The process of indefinite improvement, by which the mind repels the old imperfect formulas, to create new ones, is precisely the expression of the requirements of the transcendent value, as it is evident when we recognize the value is a norm and not a model, an incitation to invent and not a ready-made solution or a lazy conservatism.

What is tragic in human life—or more simply what is serious—is that we feel the importance of the request without knowing exactly *what* has to be done, to be loved, to be believed, in the particular circumstances under which we are placed. We must do our duty. We are sure of that and we know that, in our concrete situation, certain things should be avoided. But we are never sure we have discovered the *true* behavior, the *true* proof, the *true* beauty. Value is neither given, before the action as a model, nor after the action as a given aspect. From this uncertainty comes the feeling of responsibility. That is why any choice is momentous: if we should choose the *wrong* solution! . . . When we believe we are honest, we are perhaps unfaithful . . . . Man experiences his "tension" between the *general* call which comes from the value and the *precise* answer he himself has to invent. And it is, of course, possible that sometimes the feeling of the importance of the decision becomes anxiety. But if there were no call coming from the value, if there were no hidden order to be discovered, and not to be arbitrarily created, anxiety would be absurd.

We are not the origin of the values. Neither do we create the order of the structures in the field of values we are considering. We have not even the power to choose our projects as we please. Man is really in the world, and as such he has a nature, which makes him nearly unconscious of certain impressions and very sensitive to particular influences. Personality and character are not artificial schemes and their actions have to be felt even in the manner in which philosophers select their fundamental experiences, their evident principles, and their favorite procedures. And it is their characters which induce this philosopher to stick to analysis and that one to dislike precise decompositions.

Man who has not created himself but has received his existence, man who is surrounded by nature on all sides and is commanded by a value which is beyond himself, seems not to be qualified as independent and self-sufficient being and absolute reality — because the idea of sufficiency cannot be separated from the idea of the Absolute. And if the lack of sufficiency is the real agent of any philosophical research, how could philosophy dispense with a reflection on the idea of sufficiency, that is to say, on the idea of the Absolute?

We believe that philosophers do not have to be shy and afraid of words. They must dare to be metaphysicians, without trying to minimize the importance of that deed, and with a clear consciousness that metaphysics is a reflection on the Absolute. This does not at all imply the suspension of any critical activity and the vanishing of intellectual precision in darkness and in emotion. The question is to push to the most extreme consequences the search for meanings and to develop an unsparing criticism against all the pseudo-evidences of the things which are "*beyond* discussion": that would be the only type of transcendence metaphysics should not admit, for *a priori* reasons.

Every-day life will profit as philosophy will fulfill its mission, because life never stops, and when action is concerned, some very uncertain assertions are considered as *practically* sufficient. And this is not without danger.

Metaphysics, promoted by the idea of sufficiency and insufficiency, will criticize the illegitimate premises. It will fight the fascination of instinctive impulses which are sometimes presented as validating processes, and the power of the prejudices coming from society.

And also, putting the Absolute in its place, beyond the world which we experience, metaphysics will liberate us from any fanaticism, which always comes from the feeling of self-sufficiency given by certain impressions, certain objects or certain social realities: state, party, race, pleasure, history. The illusory Absolutes are not missing nowadays. That is why we are in great need of an active and daring metaphysics.

SELECTED BIBLIOGRAPHY

Bachelard, Gaston. *Le nouvel esprit scientifique.* Paris, Presses Universitaires de France, 1934.

Blondel, Maurice. *L'action.* Paris, Presses Universitaires de France, first edition, 1893; second edition, 1936-37.

——————. *La pensée.* Paris, Presses Universitaires de France, 1934.

——————. *L'être et les êtres.* Paris, Presses Universitaires de France, 1935.

Brunschvicg, Léon. *L'idéalisme contemporain.* Paris, Presses Universitaires de France, 1921.

——————. *Le progrès de la conscience dans la philosophie occidentale.* Paris, Presses Universitaires de France, 1927.

Berger, Gaston. *Recherches sur les conditions de la connaissance.* Paris, Presses Universitaires de France, 1941.

Goblot, Edmond. *Traité de logique.* Paris, A. Colin, 1917.

Hamelin, Octave. *Essai sur les éléments principaux de la représentation.* Paris, Presses Universitaires de France, 1907.

Laporte, Jean. *Le problème de l'abstraction.* Paris, Presses Universitaires de France, 1940.

Lavelle, Louis. *Introduction à l'ontologie.* Paris, Presses Universitaires de France, 1947.

——————. See also the bibliographies for the essays of Le Senne and Mehl.

Le Senne, René. *Le devoir.* Paris, Presses Universitaires de France, 1930.

——————. *Obstacle et valeur.* Paris, Aubier, 1934.

Merleau-Ponty, Maurice. See bibliography for Campbell's essay.

Paliard, Jacques. *Intuition et réflexion.* Paris, Presses Universitaires de France, 1925.

Polin, Raymond. *La création des valeurs.* Paris, Presses Universitaires de France, 1944.

Sartre, Jean-Paul. *L'être et le néant.* Paris, Gallimard, 1943.

——————. *L'existentialisme est un humanisme.* Paris, Nagel, 1946.

Wahl, Jean. *Existence humaine et transcendance.* Neuchatel, La Baconniere, 1944.

Weber, Louis. *Vers le positivisme absolu par l'idéalisme.* Paris, Presses Universitaires de France, 1903.

LA PHILOSPHIE
DE L'ESPRIT

*René Le Senne**

It would require extensive analysis to study and clarify the relation between a people and its philosophy. France has been so fortunate as to
have found, as early as the seventeenth century, an expression in
which she has never ceased to recognize herself. To follow the development of French philosophy, from Malebranche to Hamelin, or even Bergson, is to realize the fecundity of Cartesianism. It would seem to be the
fixed axis of a tradition which the thinkers of different epochs have been
more anxious to adapt to the needs and conditions of their times than
to replace. Even today, Cartesianism, more than any other doctrine, sets
the pattern for the teaching of philosophy in French schools and colleges;
and it could be argued that, were France to forget Cartesianism, her
whole character would change.

I
THE CARTESIAN TRADITION

What do we mean by this term, Cartesianism, when we have divested
the work of Descartes of the extraneous elements imposed upon it by his
education and the period in which he lived? We mean essentially two
theses.

1. The first is that of the *cogito*. For Descartes, the primary truth is
not a principle from which, as a beginning, the structure of reality must be
built by deduction. It is an experience or, rather, *the* experience, whose
peculiar property is that it is to be found in *every* experience: the experience of thought in thinking. The genetic necessity of all philosophy is
not the logical and propulsive force of an axiom, but the fact, impossible
to deny, of a lived and living experience. I cannot doubt that I am, for, the

---

* Born in 1882. Student of Rauh and Hamelin at the *École Normale Supérieure*. With
Louis Lavelle, directs the "Philosophie de l'Esprit." Professor of ethics, Sorbonne. Member
of the Institute of France. A moralist, he endeavors to connect the concrete study of man
with a metaphysic of values. Author of *Introduction à la Philosophie, Le Devoir,* and
Traités de Morale générale et de Caractériologie.

more strongly I doubt anything whatsoever, the more clearly is impressed upon me the certitude that I am thinking; and, in this very act of thinking, I grasp my existence.

By the *cogito,* human thought (and this must be taken in its most comprehensive meaning, to include feeling and will as well as intellectual activity) is considered, not alone as the initial condition of all philosophy, but as the perpetual act through which truth becomes accessible to us. It will be necessary for this thought to discover the absolute source of its value, for, in the very act of doubting, the hypothesis has been formed that an "evil genius" can lead it astray: but since this "evil genius" can do nothing against the immediacy, the indivisibility of the act through which I grasp my thinking existence, it is indeed the human reality of this act which presents itself as the matrix of knowledge.

How, after this beginning, could the reality and the dignity of man ever be put in question? No unknown, no nature, no tyranny will ever be authorized to substitute itself for personal reflection and the critical spirit. If it should happen that man, betraying the teaching of the *cogito,* were to abdicate his right and his responsibility to be critically reflective, to profess his own worthlessness, this very avowal would give the lie to its content; since it would reveal that neither any affirmation nor any negation is possible which does not contain within itself the act of thinking which manifests the essence of the human being. This act of thinking is, indeed, universal: it is not something special to Descartes, that Poitevin gentleman, born into the French nation and the Catholic religion. It constitutes Descartes, inasmuch as he thinks and what he is thinking, that is to say, Descartes in that he possesses the humanity common to all men.

2. Thus Descartes is existential and it would only be necessary to accentuate, just a little, the vicissitudes of the meditation whose stages he describes to us, to put, for example, emphasis upon doubt and anxiety, upon discovery of the self in rebirth, to reveal the kinship of his philosophy with contemporary descriptions of human existence. But if he can be called or, more simply, if he is existential, he is not an existentialist, and this he cannot be because the universality of the *cogito* already holds him within the universality of truth.

The second essential feature of Cartesianism is the movement through which the human mind, making the inventory of its content, therein discovers an idea whose "objective" reality, that is to say its representation in our mind, reveals its "formal" reality, its reality independent of us, a reality which of necessity sets itself up as transcending us. This is the idea of the infinite and perfect Being, the conception of whom, by a finite and imperfect being, reveals to him the extrinsic nature and the superiority of that which it signifies. Through this discovery which operates within itself, the thinking I makes itself knowledgeable in attaining to the foundation of knowledge and of all that which knowledge supports. The perfection of God brings with it his truth; and the divine truth guarantees the certitude of our knowledge when we are on our guard against precipitancy and prejudice. Evidence of the I thinking of itself will develop into evidence of the truth of "simple natures" and of their ties, in the measure to which thought shall attain clear and distinct ideas, and to which deductions from one to another shall be gathered together into an intellectual intuition.

Two misunderstandings of the *cogito* are thus definitively avoided. There is, on the one hand, what might be called bad subjectivism, that which, under pretext of the primacy of the thinking I, would authorize an arbitrary individualism, the right of each individual to affirm and to do no matter what. Recognition of the freedom immanent in the act of thinking is not approval of caprice, of passion or any form of irrationality whatsoever. "Uncontrolled passions" are no more authorized in the search for truth than they are in political life. The human soul in action and already knowing must be capacity founded upon rational evidence, which objectifies itself in the immanence of the mathematics of nature. The Cartesian ideal, as an ideal of culture, is a surveillance over the self, a critical control of resolving itself into the light of intelligence and generosity of action.

But, on the other hand, there is no reason to fear that the human being if he remains Cartesian should make, of the knowledge he obtains of himself in the *cogito,* a reason for discrediting himself, for cutting himself off from being and from value, for developing a distaste for existence, in short, for despair. Once cleared, by rational evidence, of those fallacies which are the product of our imagination, the world stands clear before us as an order which can be understood: God has set up the system of eternal verities, over which he reigns in his infinity, and the divine truth is our guarantee that he will be faithful to it. Through acquaintance with the laws which are the elements of this order, man will be able to acquire, by degrees, domination over nature, but without "alienating" himself from it, since he goes beyond it by his will and generally by his thinking. The union of soul and body is, for Descartes, an original indivisibility, one mere fact and nothing more than a fact, whose persistence is contingent for us since it depends upon the divine will. Of itself, the soul is entirely incorporeal and, with the body, it makes two; and, at death, it will, as in true knowledge, be liberated from the pressure of the imagination which manifests our present subjection to matter.

Thus, at the heart of this "bicentric" philosophy, the human personality is joined to that universality whose origin is in God and of which the world is the realization. Spinoza falsified Cartesianism by sacrificing the human pole to the divine: man deprived of initiative becomes a mode of substance wherein God naturalizes himself. In our day, J.-P. Sartre sacrifices the divine to the human pole: human initiative becomes arbitrary, irrational, and foolish. Descartes was able to bring together harmoniously the two components of French culture: the humanist component, derived from our Greco-Latin culture and revivified in the thirteenth century and the Renaissance; and the Christian component which, while conferring upon man a depth and a destiny beyond the natural, also, by subordinating metaphysical confidence to disinterestedness, turns him aside from making of himself the egoistic end of his thought and activity.

II

A tradition is not an inertia; it is not transmitted in the same manner as a thing. It exacts from each generation an intelligent and loving effort which not only assures its conservation, but works it over to bring it into accord with the needs and conditions of the epoch and regenerate its fecundity. Should it become scholastic, crystallized into invariable formulas, it would, from that moment, begin to die. Because of this, it must always be threatened to be forced into constant renewal. Outside influences may seek to stifle it: the maladroitness of those disciples who do not understand the solidarity of its elements may compromise it by their partiality for such and such among them. Never can these dangers be more pressing than during those epochs when a foreign power, before or during an invasion, seeks to destroy or to corrupt the spirit of the people it wishes to conquer.

Thus, the *psycho-metaphysical* tradition which France inherits from Descartes has found itself threatened, during the contemporary period, by several dangers, certain of which result from the very development of civilization and others of which manifest the disorder of minds thrown into confusion by the train of events. Three of these must be specifically noted.

1. The first of these menaces comes from *the very progress of science and technique*. Not only has natural science become progressively more

extensive in breadth and depth, but it has, since the beginning of the twentieth century, been multiplying its applications. Now, the special characteristic of science is that it gives prerogative to the object of perception, to the spatial immensity of nature. All this is very well as long as thought bears only upon the world exterior to human consciousness. But when, through attachment to objectivity, through passion for extraversion, one passes up from nature to man and submits him to the ways of thinking characteristic of physics, one is fatally led to reduce him to that which makes of him an object of perception, his body: and, having thus narrowed the I into the organism, one can no longer consider it as anything but a bit of nature; and, as a counterpart to this, everything will be depreciated which can be grasped only in the innerness of personal consciousness. Whether this positivism, in the Comtist sense of the term, takes the from of a logical positivism, after the manner of the Vienna Circle; or of a biological positivism, as usually happens in medical thought; or of a psychological positivism, as in the case of Watsonian behaviorism; or, again, of a sociological positivism, it ends by sacrificing the subject in man to the object; and this partiality inevitably entails the gravest consequences.

There are, first, certain *theoretical* consequences. In assimilating man to a natural object, it is implied that a well-conducted analysis could break him up into a complex of laws, through whose functioning it would be possible to understand his behavior as the doctor understands the reaction of a body through the conditions of its being; and the *cogito* will be forgotten, that inner and infinite power of thought which enfolds liberty. Through this liberty, it may be that man can establish new relations among the events he apprehends, or, on the contrary, sever relations previously established. Because of this he escapes determinism and, eventually, tyranny. In all science, on the contrary, there is an implied idolatry of the concept, its adequation to the real: it is hoped, by the addition of concept to concept, to reconstruct reality. But in the very midst of man's being, the spirit harbors a virtually infinite power of passing beyond all conceptualizations.

This is verified when we arrive at the *practical* consequences of positivism. If it were true that man was nothing more than an objective complex of laws, then one would be able to achieve a technique which would make it possible to make him out completely and then use him with surety. Thus, positivism must favor the setting up of techniques of all sorts, psychological or sociological, whose end would be to bring man under the domination of the man of science. Thus did professional psychologists put themselves at the service of Nazi propaganda. But since this postulate is verified only to the extent to which individuals, themselves, reduce themselves to the automatism of the laws by means of which it is sought to manoeuver them, the desire to determine the nature of man by his conditions usually works itself out by the more or less explicit attempt to simplify him psychologically, in order to render him subject to the jurisdiction of a science simpler than himself.

From this has resulted that most serious of *spiritual* consequences: the tendency to enucleate man of his mental innerness. At the heart of all behaviors, in increasing degree as they become higher and more complex, are secret dialectics, elaborated by the solitary activity of the spirit; and it is in the maturing, the expanding, the control of these inner processes that, before manifesting itself, the human being engenders and cultivates itself. But objective science remains a stranger to these inner movements, is forever suspicious of introspection and looks for human reality in its spatial outlines. This is to misunderstand the transcendence of the spirit in relation to all its spoken or actual manifestations; to deprive it of its initiative and its responsibility; in short, to diffuse all those ways of thinking which lead to suppressing man's personality, in order to consider only nature from which it springs.

2. This positivism tends naturally toward totalitarianism. In effect, by condemning metaphysics, it has suppressed recourse to any unity superior to the objective or subjective offerings of experience. One no longer speaks of the Absolute, God, the One, the concrete Universal, except to cast them back beyond the bounds of useful and practical thought and quickly forget them. But this elimination cannot be complete; for one cannot, merely by refusing to reflect on these supreme and classic modes of unification, do away with the intellectual and moral need of systematization. This exigency, as Comte's positivism made clear for the first time, then finds nothing with which to satisfy itself except the State, in fact the highest of systematizations; and this State takes the place and assumes the characters which man formerly attributed to the divine Absolute. This results, as is clearly evidenced by the contemporary examples of totalitarianism, in a monstrous alliance between science and the State: the former furnishes the technical knowledge and the latter makes of it the instrument of its despotic caprice. Undoubtedly in the occidental civilizations, Anglo-Saxon, French, and Latin, where the personalistic influence of Christianity has remained quite strong and where critical reflection arms the citizens, this convergence of the science of man and the State is still only a tendency. The invincible feeling of freedom and of the dignity of man keeps this

tendency from arriving at its goal. But, quite otherwise, in those countries in which the critical spirit either grows weak or remains rudimentary, the mechanization of individuals works itself out in their enslavement. When theoretical thought has reduced man to the condition of a thing, how should practical thought not end by treating him as a thing?

3. One cannot maltreat a subject without the subject crying out. It is easy to see how, through a dialectic of opposition, absolute determinism, which tends to destroy the intrinsically spiritual subject by reducing him to the intersection of a larger or smaller number of natural laws, provokes the upsurge of an *absolute subjectivism,* which, forgetting the role of heredity and of nature, generally, in our very existence, replaces idolatry of determinism by idolatry of the arbitrary. When, as a result of this replacement, the I is separated from the not-I, world or value, there is engendered the illusion of a freedom which, claiming to be independent of everything in its decisions as it is in its initative, and having no longer any goal except its own exercise, proclaims itself absolute. As though each I, born in a certain body, at a certain epoch, and having received a certain education, were not tied to a situation which he can improve and dominate only by beginning with recognizing it and admitting its reality. As a matter of fact, every I is a mixture of being and ought-to-be; and, such being his situation, it is only through the illumination or inspiration of a value revealing to him, at the end of the research through which he renders himself really worthy of that revelation—truth or beauty, the good or love—that his value comes to give a meaning to his action and to transfigure his freedom of initiative into rational and spiritual freedom. One does not escape bias by replacing the positivist bias for the object by anarchistic bias for the subject; for this latter will be condemned no less for the vanity of its separate existence than for its alienation in nature.

Historically, every philosophy, however biased and therefore incomplete, has at least the usefulness of a symptom. This individualism without counterbalance, this individualism of the self above all, which goes from Stirner to Gide and Sartre, only makes manifest that hyperesthesia and that hypertrophy of the self which is to be found at the root of the social ambition of the despot and the pleasure, gross or refined, of the hedonist. In classic thought, such principles as the Good, duty, and the like formed so many norms to which the individual was persuaded to submit after having recognized their rationality and their divinity. He lived intent upon *something more than human;* and, for him, social power as well as the activity of the citizen had legitimacy only on condition of being authorized by ideas whose authority came from above man, but which constrained him only after having required his judgment. The slow continuous, ever more serious enfeebling of religion and the metaphysics which enfolds it, followed by the lessening of the mutual support they gave each other with the purpose of disciplining human activities through education, gave the individual over, increasingly, to his impulses. This could only result in that instability of social conditions, that competition between ambitious men, conquering or revolutionary, that deification of individual caprice, which, little by little, have worn away the universal forms destined to put the individual at the service of the public good, to provide a foundation for arbitration between individual or collective greeds for the sake of establishing peace, to lead the different elements of humanity to seek their own prosperity only in the common prosperity; all of which forms the most intelligent and most Christian way of life. On the contrary, following Nietzschean teaching, people have ended by professing that values were only human creations, as though man could decree what should be the true, the just, the beautiful, what should be worthy of love, according to his own good pleasure.

Such, in brief review, are the most accentuated features of an intellectual and moral situation by which France, in the years which followed her sacrifices during the first World War, years already darkened by the approach of the second, has felt herself menaced. Against this menace, which put in question the whole French psycho-metaphysical tradition, of Cartesian and even pre-Cartesian origin, the "Philosophie de l'Esprit," launched in March, 1934, by Louis Lavelle and myself, has been an act of reaction. The new war soon intervened and, for a long time, cut us off from the rest of the philosophic world. In spite of this isolation our collection, though we doubted that it would go beyond the tenth issue, as happens to so many collections, has just published the fifty-second. In the second part of this article, I shall give a resumé of the doctrine, or rather the tendency, at once as resolute and as open as possible, which has determined its orientation.

III
LA PHILOSOPHIE DE L'ESPRIT

In naming it *Philosophie de l'Esprit,* our dominant desire was to put spirit in its place, which seemed to us to be first place, whether from the point of view of knowledge or the point of view of value, whether this "first place" were regarded as the origin or as the end term of the efforts of reflection. The notion of spirit is that which embraces all that can be felt, thought or surmised, since all the contrasts by which philosophic thought lives are sustained and animated by spirit. In French, the word, "esprit" means both "mind" and "spirit," the distinction between which is the same as that to be found between the two French adjectives, "mental," whose significance is the more empirical, more psychological, more cognitive; and "spiritual," which is accepted as loftier, more metaphysical, even somewhat religious. Thus, the use of the word, *esprit,* permits one who writes in the French language to write in one word that which relates to mind in its human form and that which, in this same mind, manifests a value superior to man's mental activity.

The first result of this ambivalence has been to condemn all those abstractions which have been made into a reason for discrediting mind: such as matter in materialism, industrial economy in Marxism; the body in physiologism; nature in positivism; the thing-in-itself in agnosticism; and, as a culmination, the Power of the State in totalitarianism. Not, indeed, that any philosophy could misunderstand their importance and whatever, in the mind, may be additional or opposed to them; it is quite another matter to seek out and define what role they play in the spirit itself. In recognizing these notions within itself, along with the group of experiences with which each is linked, the mind accepts them as mental: it absorbs them as the elements, positive or negative, of its life. This way of taking the questions at once related us to that absolute idealism, personalist in opposition to Hegel, of which Hamelin gave a systematized expression in France at the beginning of this century. But, following the example of Descartes, whose great care was never to disregard any mode of knowing nor any aspect of reality, we could, in opposing the innerness of the mind to its abstract and ideological expressions, combine with this idealism, after the manner taught us by the Cartesian Malebranche, a phase of intuitionism.

There remained the bivalence of the term, *esprit.* Just as every determination is—where our mind grasps it—such a definite identity and not any other; but that this determination, in reference to the universal Spirit which must make the reality of truth in thinking it, is true or false, so the word, *esprit,* may signify the mind of a man, even the mind of some particular man, in which the true is contaminated by the illusory; or, on the contrary, it may signify the absolute, universal Spirit, in which truth and beauty, the good and love find the principle of their value. This, then, is their relation, the man-with-God-relation, made alternatively of separations and unions between subordinate, limited, human minds and the universal Spirit in which these human minds may eventually participate, with which they must cooperate through all forms of morality, which is presented as the axis of *Philosophie de l'Esprit.* Upon this relation can be developed a philosophy bent upon never giving up the consideration of human existence, without excluding from that existence either the unfortunate proofs of its shortcomings or evidence of the union of the self whether with the ideas which constitute the warp and weft of the universe, or with the life of the absolute Spirit. Positivism tends to dissolve, in the indifference of objectivity, that affectivity, that sensibility which is the perception, deep within ourselves, of powerful differences. Existentialism has aggravated to the limit the "bad conscience" and the feeling of distress. Neither of them fulfills the purpose of philosophy, which is to further the search for truth, the service of duty, and the joy and confidence for the lack of which humanity is abandoned to war and men to frustration.

IV
THE PHILOSOPHY OF MIND IN ITS HUMAN ASPECT

Insofar as *la Philosophie de l'Esprit* concerns the mind such as it is actualized in a consciousness more or less similar to our own, it approaches psychology. But it must correct its faults; for psychology has only too often made the mistake of reducing man to that which, of his total experiences, most directly manifests the influence of his body or forms his motor activity. In reality, human existence is made up of all the relationships which unite a man to the world, to other men and, also, to the ideal. In him, the mechanism is orientated and, as it were, upheld, by purposes, aims, and aspirations which are not less worthy of consideration than the conditions which make up the situations in which he acts. Science draws man toward nature; but man lives in nature only to rise above it. It is therefore necessary that anyone wishing to understand him should seek beyond biology and anthropology, in order to grasp those activities which are motivated by the highest human ambitions. This effort made, he will not fail to recognize that these ambitions always contain implicitly a conception of the relation of man to the absolute reality, that is to say, a metaphysics. Before revealing itself as the relation of the Absolute to ourself, metaphysics, *a parte hominis,* presents itself as an attitude of man, himself, as an activity advancing from the lower toward the higher extremity of that relation. Before becoming a transcendent manifestation, of more than human origin, it is a belief, a feature of human life; and of this aspect even a positivist, indifferent to values but faithful of facts, must take account in his descriptions.

While psychology is most often suspected of pulling man toward his body and, consequently, of treating mind as an epiphenomenon, it also applies to human experience the concepts worked out by physics and biology, forgetting that, in passing from a lower to a higher phase of reality, one is bound to encounter something new, which requires that the seeker after knowledge adopt new attitudes and new methods. The psychological formula for man only too often makes of him a construction of functions, which substitutes, for the complication and subtlety of mental life, an abstract schema altogether inferior to its rich variety. Without doubt, biology, physiological analysis, endocrinology, and characterology—which is somewhat nearer to individual originality—do find, in the substratum of human life, objects for their study. But, to the degree in which the importance of cerebral conditioning—which we cannot even seize directly in its proper working—is increased by the organic development and the activity of the subject, the human consciousness expands to a dialectic richness which philosophic knowledge *must* explore with the utmost precision if it would avoid substituting a caricature for the true picture of man, considered in his higher modes of being; of man, not merely normal, but inventive, generous, spiritual.

This effort toward concrete man leads to qualitative consciousness; and it is evidently this ascent which has, in our times, as existentialism proves, brought together philosophy and literature. Both seek knowledge of the living consciousness, recognized through that which quality gives it of variety; while the inequalities of level, the modifications of tension, the conflicts through which man reenters the universal dynamism, add their power and their vicissitudes. The writer, whether poet, novelist, or dramatist, seeks to suggest this qualitative diversity, to build up sympathy for these vicissitudes. Usually, he is more of a pessimist than necessary, because men are more easily moved by accentuating the pathos of their life and highlighting the tragic side of the picture.

But a profounder reason inclines him toward this pessimisim; which is that, at the end of the count, he remains a slave, like the man he depicts, like the reader for whom he writes. He surrenders to that which happens to him, for he is more intent on reflecting life than on reflecting upon it: on experiencing it than on thinking about it or bettering it.

On the contrary, the philosopher, resembling in this the man of science, seeks to understand, because he knows that by understanding he will begin to make himself master of that which he understands. Thus, the man of science advances in knowledge of nature by discovering its laws; and, by this analytical discovery, he puts himself into position for

using these laws to foresee and to produce events which nature would
not have produced without his intervention. By means of that intellectual
analysis to which the writer refuses to have recourse, because it would remove from the experiences of every day the very quality of which art
makes the object of enjoyment, the philosopher puts himself into condition
to discern the abstract dialectics which form the moving framework, the
trajectories of the concrete movements of consciousness. This is still to be
an idealist; but an idealist who, instead of holding idealism to the level
of categories of the mind, raises it to the stage of the mind's livelist activity. Through this discernment, it becomes possible for the mind, which
draws from it the most determinate knowledge of itself, to judge its dialectics and, with the aid of morality, to make the choice between those which
increase his ability to live and act well and those which, on the contrary,
begin his demoralization. Thus, insensibly, *Philosophie de l'Esprit,* from
being speculative, becomes normative and could become pedagogic.

One immediately perceives the kinship of *Philosophie de l'Esprit,*
thus understood, with phenomenology. But as a matter of fact, this concrete idealism can hardly be said to have proceeded, in France, from the
influence of German phenomenology. Just as Kierkegaard has had less
influence upon French thought than upon that of central Europe, because
we already had Pascal, so we were already prepared for phenomonological
analysis, first as being pupils of Descartes—whose examples Husserl later
invoked—and following Descartes, of Maine de Biran, whose influence
has not ceased to increase in France, for more than a century. It is only
upon the more recent existentialists that the German influence of Jaspers
and Heidegger has made itself felt. Therefore, it would not do to assimilate *Philosophie de l'Esprit* to phenomenology without examination. There
is between them, from the beginning, the capital difference that phenomenology aims at extending science, while *Philosophie de l'Esprit* is orientated toward metaphysics conceived as the supreme mission of philosophy.

In fact, Husserl came to phenomenological analysis from reflection
upon arithmetic and moved, himself, by a logical intentionality had as his
avowed purpose the aim of properly scientific objectivity. He has expressly
stated that his object was to make of phenomenology a rigorous science, of
which one had, doubtless, to expect that it would do away with the disputes between philosophers. This claim was made many times before
Husserl and always shown to be false, as it is, here, once again. Phenomenology has, by itself and by its existential prolongation, sufficiently manifested, in the works it has produced, the individual subjectivity of phenomenological analysis. How, indeed, could any phenomenological analysis,

seeing that here it is concrete consciousness which is concerned, be independent of the proper personality of the one who conducted the analysis? But, likewise, can a concrete movement of the personality show itself without involving the main preferences of the human being? And, by degrees, these preferences always imply an attitude toward the Absolute. Now, the Absolute is "put in parentheses" by Husserl. But is this not a paradox? If the Absolute has a meaning, it is not only that it must enter into the heart of all relations, but also that it confers reality upon them. By essence, it forbids the philosopher, whose task is precisely to take into account all abstractions, to abstract himself from it. Therefore, the philosopher must interrogate himself concerning the Absolute; and metaphysics mixes itself with phenomenology, not to do away with it, but to perfect it. Complete analysis of mental experience must comprise the study of metaphysical dialectics; and transcendental subjectivity cannot, in short, be other than the geometric meeting place for psychological subjects and the Absolute, trans-objective and trans-subjective, but everywhere sought and everywhere present.

Therefore, much better to acknowledge it. Every description is inseparable from an appreciation. To begin with, the practice of natural science manifests certain evaluations; that knowledge is good, for example, that orderly thought is better than incoherence, and the like. This is why Descartes maintained that a mathematician cannot be an atheist. With greater reason, knowledge of men, who pursue many other values besides truth, should put to the fore the consideration of those values through which they seek to participate in the Absolute. If, then, one wishes to create unity of minds, one will not seek it in an identification which would exclude their heterogeneity, which is precious and should, in consequence, be respected and esteemed. One will expect it, rather, from the convergence of efforts and values into a sovereign unity—Being, Action, absolute Value, God—from which radiates inexhaustible diversity, individual minds and norms, by following which each of these minds pursues the determined value which its character, its historical situation, and its election assign it. Thus, still following the Cartesian schema, personality and universality are reconciled, without universality denying the freedom indispensable to the personality's empirical and spiritual realization and without having freedom become, in the world, the source of greed, of oppression, and war.

V

THE *Philosophie de l'Esprit* AS UNIVERSAL

We have just been considering the relation between man and the Absolute, beginning with man. Metaphysics appears in man as a belief, an aspiration, as the need to attain the supreme Good, which would be his guarantee of conformity between the Real and his value requirements, in order that these should not, lacking this guarantee, be condemned to absurdity and defeat. But what would be the value of what was only a subjective belief? It is essential to any sincere belief, to any belief upon which one would be ready to risk one's life, that it should, to some extent, contain affirmation of the value of that which it professes. I do not continue to walk forward upon ground when I no longer think it will bear my weight. A belief which professed itself illusory would be an unbelief. Thus, when a person declares that one should live to seek truth, discover beauty, bestow charity, do good, he implies by this declaration, that truth, beauty, the good, and love are not appearances, but that they must gradually reveal themselves as manifesting the Absolute. But if the Absolute is such that our minds draw from it that which makes their value, it is because the Absolute is, of itself, spirituality in its supreme form. It is the universal, first, and sovereign Spirit; and our minds, in that which is best in them, appear as images, expressions, reductions of its infinite Unity. Thus, after having considered mind in man, a *Philosophie de l'Esprit* must consider it in its superhuman, universal, and absolute aspect.

To make meditation upon the Absolute the supreme goal of thought, in an epoch when the pursuit of utility, production, and efficiency is the principal and almost the sole preoccupation of mankind, is to risk turning aside, from any philosophy which presumes to return to this thesis, those who are most legitimately attached to empirical and social reality. But it is precisely to these realists that the *Philosophie de l'Esprit* is addressed, in the effort to convince them that the pursuit of utility, production, and efficiency must necessarily turn to man's destruction and abasement, if metaphysics be not added to science and technique to give them a moral and spiritual soul. It would be necessary to analyze a thousand cases to convince everyone of this; and we have space, here, for its verification, to describe only one, and that summarily.

Let us consider divorce. In the United States and elsewhere, psychologists, sociologists, and moralists are alarmed by the multiplication of divorces. A divorce is a failure and has the seriousness of all failures. A man and woman hoped to find happiness in their union; they admit that they have not attained it. It is also a social evil. A family is broken up and, if children have been born, they suffer from it; while society loses a source of procreation and education. How can we serve family happiness and the social interest by making divorce rarer? Psychological and sociological analysis seeks to determine the conditions of divorce: a characterology will attempt to recognize the affinities of likeness or complementariness which inter-characterology supposes between the partners of a durable, happy, and fruitful marriage. But can this scientific analysis be sufficient? It would suffice if it were a question of things, for things are integrally determined by the conditions which bring them into being. In contrast to the thing, man is conscious; he *knows* himself to be eventually determined or determinable; and by his initiative, in whatever fashion it exerts itself, he cooperates with the conditions under which he lives, to modify their effects, for example, by adding the action of other conditions. Thus, along with this initiative, aims intervene, which add to it morality, dream, feelings, the whole of metaphysics.

Thus, in the case with which we are concerned, every family meets with favorable or unfavorable conditions for persistence and evolution. The essential thing is that the members of the family, like the passengers on a boat which is in danger, should unite their thoughts and endeavors, even against certain traits of their own proper characters, to assure the predominance of the favorable over the unfavorable conditions. The family will fall apart if each of its members sees in it only an association of egoistic interests, to be maintained just as long as it is useful to this association. On the contrary, the family will endure, consolidate itself, and expand, if it is for all, parents and children alike, beyond utility, a value which they must serve: if they love its devotion to a tradition, as the bridge between the past and future of their country, the cradle of a nobler humanity, the very creation of the continuity of time in the human community; in short, a metaphysical participation in the blossoming of the living eternity, which in history displays the divine fecundity. To diffuse these feelings among all men through education would be to build a metaphysics of the family, one of the thousand chapters in general metaphysics.

The generalization from this summary example: Metaphysics has two main purposes. It must direct man's efforts toward value, and it must assist the convergence of our efforts toward any particular value by turning them toward the unity of all values. Through these two purposes, it is the highest mediation of courage and peace. Let us begin by considering the first purposes. In setting up this supreme unity above all empirical or subjective factors, it precludes the idolatry of any special feature of nature, state, or individual. It renews the invitation to aim beyond that which may already be attained or conceived. Freedom can not give way on any point and remain freedom. Insofar as it elevates the Absolute, considered in its indetermination and mystery, above all the determinations to which one might wish to reduce it, metaphysics, in such case negative, opens before the human being an infinite quest. So Gabriel Marcel was right in underlining the "metaproblematic mystery" of the Absolute. But negative metaphysics makes appeal to positive metaphysics, for the infinite has its danger: Greek thought feared it as the source of destruction and disorder. Also, in his turn, Louis Lavelle is right in emphasizing the other mission of metaphysics, which is to waken man to the feeling of the ontological reality of the One, whose worth is to recall us to the duty of coherence and cooperation. Every man is destined to seek his value; but no value remains such except by reason of the transparency through which it permits us to perceive the absolute Value from which it draws its right to impose obligations upon us and its power to inspire us.

In conclusion, let us now bring together *Philosophie de l'Esprit,* as complete description of the human mind, and *Philosophie de l'Esprit* as meditation upon nature and aspects of the metaphysical principle of things and selves; as we must do, since it is their relation which constitutes the axis of human life. The *Philosophie de l'Esprit* appears, definitively, as the doctrine of salvation.

This is what philosophy has always been when it has not abused its name. Above all particular disciplines of knowledge, such as logic or acoustics, and of activity, such as medicine or politics, philosophy has presented itself as the synthetic reflection whose task it is to equilibrate all these branches of knowledge and all these activities into an impartial body of thought as well as into joyous and harmonious conduct. Knowledge turns back toward that which is past, that which has been accomplished, that which is: action leans forward toward the desirable, the future it projects before itself: the present, from which we can never escape, balances, one against the other, that which is with that which should be, in such a way as to forward development of the spirit. When this balancing is successful, the human being makes his escape from all that menaced him, in stimulating his research, from obstacles which checked him, from contradictions which rent him, from the nothingness which made him giddy. It is its capacity to crown this *rescue* by *salvation* which measures the value of every philosophy.

If it be asked what is the social ideal toward which the French *Philosophie de l'Esprit* claims to be working, it is toward an oecumenical spiritualism which, defending the spirit against whatever denies it, recognizes that every man, every nation, has the right to come to spirituality by those ways which are best suited to them; but imperatively exacts of each that he coordinate his research with that of others, because this spiritualism shows that, in becoming reconciled among themselves, men become reconciled with the metaphysical Source of all that makes the value of existence.

SELECTED BIBLIOGRAPHY

Lavelle, Louis. *La présence totale*. Paris, Aubier, 1934, in collection "Philosophie de l'Esprit."

——————. *La dialectique de l'éternel present*:
    I. *De l'être*. Paris, Presses Universitaires, 1928.
    II. *De l'acte*. Paris, Aubier, 1937.
    III. *Du temps et de l'éternité*. Paris, Aubier, 1945.

Le Senne, René. *Obstacle et Valeur*. Paris, Aubier, 1934.

Marcel, Gabriel. See bibliography for Hering's essay.

Forest, Aimé. *Du consentement à l'être*. Paris, Aubier, 1936.

——————. *Consentement et création*. Paris, Aubier, 1943.

Minkowski, Eugène. *Vers une cosmologie*. Paris, Aubier, 1939.

Nédoncelle, Maurice. *La reciprocité des consciences*. Paris, Aubier, 1942.

Morot-Sir, Edouard. *La pensée négative*. Paris, Aubier, 1948.

——————. *Philosophie et mysticisme*. Paris, Aubier, 1948.

Paliard, Jacques. *Théorème de la connaissance*. Paris, Aubier, 1942.

Valensin, Auguste. *Balthasar*. Paris, Aubier, 1934.

Berger, Gaston. *Le cogito dans la phénoménologie de Husserl*. Paris, Aubier, 1941.

de Gandillac, Maurice. *La philosophie de Nicolas de Cues*. Paris, Aubier, 1941.

Gerard, Jacques. *La métaphysique de Paul Decoster*. Paris, Aubier, 1945.

Marcel, Gabriel. *La métaphysique de Royce*. Paris, Aubier, 1945.

Royce, Josiah. *La philosophie du loyalisme* (French translation).

Wahl, Jean. *Études Kierkegaardiennes*. Paris, Aubier, 1938.

Lavelle, Louis. *La conscience de soi*. Paris, Grasset, 1938.

——————. *L'erreur de Narcisse*. Paris, Grasset, 1939.

——————. *Les puissances du moi*. Paris, Flammarion.

Le Senne, René. *Introduction à la philosophie*. (Coll. Logos) Paris, Presses Universitaires, 1925.

——————. *Traité de morale générale*. Paris, Presses Universitaires, 1942.

——————. *Traité de caractérologie*. Paris, Presses Universitaires, 1945.

Berger, Gaston. *Recherches sur les conditions de la connaissance.* Paris,
    Presses Universitaires, 1941.

Revue internationale de philosophie. Brussels, October, 1939. Devoted to
    "Philosophie de l'Esprit."

THE THREE STAGES
OF
METAPHYSICS

*Louis Lavelle**

I t is useless to try to define metaphysics and to inquire into its possibility before undertaking to *make* it. These preliminary investigations merely delay and confuse reflection: by questioning the legitimacy of an object to which we have not yet given existence, we necessarily conclude in the negative. Here as always, there is no other method than to push thought as far as it can go. It will soon appear what results it obtains, and whether the term "metaphysics" is suitable to cover them. Here as always it is by moving that we prove movement; we show its possibility by making it actual.

Now in the affirmation of being there seem to be three different stages for (1) being reveals itself to me at the outset by the *very power I have to say I,* which bears within it, from the moment that it begins to operate, the very act which causes me to be. But, (2) in this very experience which I have of it, my being is infinitely overwhelmed by a being which contains it and exceeds it, from which I derive my own power to be and hence to say I, in which I continually participate, which can never be considered as an object, which on the contrary should be defined as *pure inwardness,* that is, as an act free from all passivity and from which all particular acts derive the very possibility of being accomplished. (3) Between the act of participation which enables me to say I and the omnipresent and absolute subject which is its basis and continually supports it, there is *an infinite interval which nothing other than the world comes to fill up*: it can only present itself to me in the form of an outwardness which I always seek to penetrate and to reduce.

I. The Power I Have To Say I

From Descartes to Husserl it can be said that the indivisibly onto-

* Born in 1883. Professor at the Collège de France; Member of the Institute of France. Director, with René Le Senne, of the collection "Philosophie de l'Esprit." Author of *La parole et l'écriture* (1942), and of other works listed in the bibliographies.

logical and gnosiological primacy of the self-affirmation of the subject has always been recognized. It has been taken for granted and forgotten rather than disputed. And the objections directed against it bear against its sterility when the attempt is made to isolate it from an object to which it applies and yet with respect to which it can define itself only by opposition, or against the possibility of objectivizing itself, which, despite the prejudice which links existence to objectivity, strengthens its originality rather than weakens it. For *the first stage of metaphysical thought lies precisely in the discovery of oneself as consciousness and as act, and in uniting the two terms as genesis of oneself.* Whereas we almost always consider consciousness as being merely the condition of our access to being, which it acquaints us with, we should say with respect to access to being that it is not only *by consciousness* but primarily *in consciousness* that it is realized. We can make no assertions regarding being as such, where it differs from us who think it, and where consequently, insofar as being, it has an existence independent of us which we can only know as external to us: we can only reach it, then, as image or as concept, that is, by a representation which aims at it, but without containing it. On the contrary, in the act of consciousness I give myself being: I cannot say I, except *by* and *in* that every act. And the basic error into which common sense and philosophy continually relapse is to believe that that act of consciousness is nothing more than a power to think things different from myself and, among other things, the thing which is yet myself. But if being consists in outwardness, we need not be suprised that, of all the objects in the world, the ego is the only one which always eludes us. The essence of philosophical invention is continually to re-climb this slope: to recognize, as happens in the most lucid and secret moments of my personal existence, that for me there can be actual presence of being only in that being which is mine, that this being consists in a presence to itself which gives me an incomparable emotion, which does not conceal an unknown being whose reactions can surprise me; (for such a being is a part of nature; I only undergo it; it is so far from being identical with me that it is in relation to it, with it, for it or against it, that I define what I am); whereas the ego consists in a being always being born, with the very consciousness it has of itself, and which, at every instant, assumes the responsibility of what it is going to be.

In such a discovery the ego grasps itself as pure activity, that is, as an activity which before giving rise to any effect first gives rise to itself. Now, if such an activity is constitutive of the ego, if we do not have the right to pronounce the word I except at the point where this activity comes into play, then we can say that the ego is really heterogeneous to every object and that we should never hope, therefore, to obtain any sort of representation of it; but if there is no representation except in relation to it, the reason is that it posited itself at the outset as a real being which is not the representation of anything. And despite appearances, the paradox here is on the part of common sense, which considers as the model of being that being which I have in my purview, of which I know only that it is not my being, and of which I can have only an image, instead of seeing that the being which I myself am constitutes the only domain in which being is really present to me in its own genesis. On the contrary, I posit an *object* of knowledge only where I discover that I am not myself coextensive with the totality of being. It appears then that it should be an undisputed result of metaphysics that it is by the ego that we have access to being, but to a being such that it is never a being-object because it can never be distinguished from the act which causes it to be and that, far from being alien to knowledge, it should be considered as being the very source of knowledge.

This analysis succeeds in eliminating the classic notion of substance considered by a sort of contradiction as a *transcendent object,* that is, a term which by definition is the point of application of our experience and which yet is intrinsically outside of every possible experience. But the object is always before us and never behind; and this objectivizing procedure of consciousness must be very essential to it if it prefers to expel itself from being rather than accept its inability to convert itself into an object. This is seen not only in the materialists but in all those who wish to reduce the subject to a purely formal existence.

Nevertheless, if on the contrary self-consciouness is the only road which enables us to enter into being, that means not, as is thought, that it gives us merely the means of knowing being, but that it is already the very presence of being, or again that my awareness of the totality of being is not different from my own being. I cannot, where I am concerned, make the distinction between the ego who gives the awareness and the ego to whom it gives it, as when my awareness of a thing is involved; but this impossibility is instructive. It shows that the awareness consists in an act of attention which always revives, which gives rise to myself in giving rise to the show of things, which cannot give way without my existence giving way, in which I continually accept the responsibility of making myself in the double and invisible power of thinking whatever is and of willing what I am.

It will be said: this is the extremity of being, but it requires an immense substructure. At the least it must be recognized that the being we are seeking, the only one which merits the name of being, the one to which metaphysics gives the name of absolute, since it is necessarily internal to itself, can only be grasped in the form of inwardness. *Absolute and interior to itself have the same meaning.* Kant made a mistake in introducing the name of "thing in itself" into philosophy, for metaphysical being is almost always represented to oneself under the form of the thing in itself; but the expression is a contradiction in terms. A thing is what is never in itself, which has no self, which is never itself. It is what never is, except for a subject or an "in itself" which, positing it outside of itself, although in relation with itself, defines it precisely as a thing. In other words, entering into being is entering into a world which, since it is self-interiority, is the basis of my interiority to myself; and if this is the world which precisely we call the spiritual world, we must say that there is an *identity between the discovery of being and the discovery of spirituality.*

One thus realizes that the direction of metaphysical thought is just the opposite of that in which it is almost always used, but which is seen at once to be a blind alley. For, in meditating on the nature of the object which is held to furnish us with the very type of being, one sees very soon that it is subject to certain conditions which the subject places on it: we try to separate it from those conditions and thus one comes to imagine a being which should be a pure object, liberated from all the subjective conditions which enable one to think of it as object. But this is a chimera. It is not enough to say with regard to such an object that it is unknowable: it is impossible; it is still I the subject who posits it as beyond all knowledge, as self-sufficient without me. This is what was formerly called an imaginary entity (*être de raison*), but one which is equally alien to all intelligibility and to any experience. The only way which is open to metaphysics is the opposite one: since in subjectivity itself, even though it is often impure, being is always present as "self," absolute being can be reached only where subjectivity is most complete and most unadorned. *Being in itself consists, therefore, in utmost subjectivity and not in utmost objectivity.* The more thought objectifies itself, the more it turns away from being toward the spectacle, the image, or the concept; the more it concentrates on its own subjectivity, the nearer it comes to the source where being is constantly being born to itself and to the multiplicity of its modes. The objection should not be made that we are as unable to find pure subjectivity as pure objectivity, for these two contraries cannot be compared. For if the object can only be posited in its relation to us, an absolute object deprived of all relation with us is nothing. Whereas if the subject is our self, the absolute subject is an awareness which goes beyond us, but into which we penetrate and which becomes ours as we increasingly participate in it.

However, the word "subjectivity" acquires a more insidious connotation, and one more in accordance with the common prejudice, when it is reduced to the states which we experience, which we feel as ours and which each of us knows by himself alone. The observation could already be made that this does not diminish their reality, as is believed, but on the contrary means "living" them, experiencing their being at the precise point where it is one and the same thing to say that they are and that we feel them. But this is not possible unless I feel them as mine. At any rate, true subjectivity consists only in the very act which enables me to say I, that is to experience my states and to say of this representation that it is mine, while the object it represents is not mine. Now this power consists in a pure initiative which is inseparable from its exercise, which can always be more or less blocked but which for this reason continually contrasts itself to objects which appear to it, to states which affect it; but it is the only experience we have of true being where it becomes our own being, i.e., its own beginning, without there being anything whose modality or phenomenon it can be, even though there is nothing which goes beyond it and in relation to it does not become modality or phenomenon. All objects, all states express the limitation of the being which is I, which consists exclusively in the act which causes it to be, without one's being able, however, to ignore the fact that whatever limits it also brings it the experience of what it lacks: all the objects I find in front of me form a world which precisely in going beyond me discloses to me the richness of being, all the states which I experience within myself from the content of my life, continually developing and growing with its contact with the world.

II. Pure Inwardness

It is not for exclusively logical reasons that I am compelled to grant that there is no contact with being except in the being which I am, where being asserts itself as ego. There is no emotion comparable to that given, not exactly by the discovery of the states which I feel are mine, through which I pass in succession, but by the power I have to call them mine, which is inseparable from an initiative in which I enlist all my responsibility and which is the being which I call "I." Of the ego I shall say that it is the only place where I can deal with the "in itself" or the "self" of being, at least if the universe which surrounds me only exists in relation to it, that is to say, is for it only a phenomenon, whereas the ego who thinks this universe makes me enter, by the fact of its existence, into absolute existence, which is the existence of pure inwardness. We like to speak of the limits of subjectivity as if the real world of the object and subjectivity were nothing but a perspective we have of it, from which we do not succeed in escaping and yet which we should have to surmount in order to meet being as it really is. Thus subjectivity would shut us up in a solitude which would forever separate us from being. Yet it is our very being. *It is an absolute of our own which introduces us into the absolute of being.* And it is for that reason that, once the field of subjectivity is opened to us, we see it immediately as susceptible of being indefinitely extended. We should not say that it turns us in upon ourselves, but on the contrary that it enables us to penetrate everywhere. For the being which it discloses to us is the univalent being which puts us on the same plane with all of being, where we unendingly move and expand.

Here however the difficulties begin. If there is a universality of the *self* into which the ego constantly gives us entry, the comparison inevitably arises of the ego with the body which occupies a determinate place in the immense universe. But the comparison does not hold, for, in enlarging subjectivity beyond our own limits, I am not dealing with a spiritual immensity of which I represent a small corner, but with an infinite power which I put in operation at the very point where I can say I. It is in this sense alone that one has the right to say of the ego that it can only assert itself in the interior and by means of a subjectivity which infinitely exceeds it, whence it unendingly draws its nourishment, as Fichte says of this *Ichheit,* from which it continually draws the power of saying I. But for this reason, as I penetrate further into the intimacy of the pure Ego, I unceasingly go into the depths of my own intimacy. I enlist my body in the universe, but it always remains a body exterior to me; on the contrary, as I go further down into that primeval subjectivity from which I draw the subjectivity which is my own, I increasingly divest myself of all that in any way was exterior to me, of all that was only appearance or state in respect to me, I coincide more and more rigorously with what I am, and in the act which causes me to be, I recognize the presence of the same act which gives being to whatever is.

But then the difficulties redouble, instead of disappearing. What right could I still have to say I beyond the very act that I perform? And beyond that act how could everything not be exterior for me, that is, object? Nevertheless exteriority, objectivity is precisely that in which I do not participate, which I continually put away from me, even though I cannot define them except in their relationship to me. But subjectivity, intimacy, on the contrary, constitute the essence of what I am, even though, in the experiences I have of them, they are never pure and are always subject to some limitation, that is to say, some contamination with the external. But there the word "participation" will find its adequate connotation. For this word seems to express the only means by which particular being can act, that is to say, enter into communication with what exceeds it, but in order to make it its own. Thus, every act is in a way an act of participation. Inversely, participation is always effected by an act; and this is so true that, in order to say of being that it does not act or remains inert, we say merely that it no longer participates in anything. But the nature of participation is to presuppose an activity rightfully common to all and offered to everyone, which can be engaged in without us, but also with us and by us and which is always available to all, although everyone may take it up in his own way. If all our acts are imperfect and unfinished, or, what comes to the same thing, if they always enclose within themselves an object to which they apply, that is no obstacle to their having a common origin from which they draw that which makes them acts, which is the very power of acting. And it will readily be granted even that, in activity as such, it is impossible to conceive any particular determination, so that it may equally be said of it that it does not apply to anything and that it can be applied to everything: which explains why we cannot define ourselves as act without setting ourselves equal to the all, not actually no doubt, but potentially and in that infinite ambition which forms man's ambiguous essence and the source at once of his greatness and his wretchedness.

One could justify this analysis in another way, and show that the experience we have of ourselves is the experience of an activity which unendingly supplies us and which we never use more than partially, that is the experience of an infinite possibility which we can make use of up to a certain point. And just as our body, the only one we experience as real, is inserted into a universe which is present to us in its entirety, but only in the form of representation, the act which we perform is itself inserted into a universe which is the universe of possibility that each one makes actual according to his powers. But, as there is a being of representation, there is also a being of possibility, far from possibility's being a pure chimera or an unintelligible middle term between being and nothing. No doubt the possible can be reduced to a pure object of thought, but its secret is only grasped in the act which causes it to be in us: *it is this act which, in being performed, reveals to us the very intimacy of being.* For, first of all, what does our being itself, which is never a thing, consist in except in the being of something possible, which is in process and which it is up to us to realize? I have no right, it is true, to consider this possible thing as something determined in advance, entrusted exclusively to me and to which I would have the sterile task of giving a form in the visible world. The word "possible" has meaning only in the plural. The infinitude of the possible is an infinite multiplicity of possibles among which I always have to choose that possible which shall be mine. It must be said too that this world of possibles is the totality of being insofar as that totality is the basis of the existence of an ego whose destiny it is to realize itself by an act of participation, just as the world of represented things is the totality of being insofar as it is the basis of the existence of my own body, that is of a body by which the ego is unceasingly affected. But that does not mean that possibilities, any more than things, ever have a separate existence. For if there is always, as Bergson believed, an artifice, based on the nature of my physical needs, in the division of the world into an infinity of different objects, there is the same artifice based on the internal requirements of participation, in the division of pure activity into an infinite diversity of possibles.

Thus, I could maintain in a sense that all possibles derive from my invention. It is still necessary that this invention should not be arbitrary, that the very constitution of the all should have certain characters which justify my invention and correspond to it. It is still necessary that there should be in us a power to produce it which we feel belongs to us, since it is we who exercise it, and that it comes nevertheless from higher up, since we have received it. Actually, we cannot say that we originate possibility; it imposes itself on us with the same rigor as does objectivity. Like the object, but better than the object, which it always surpasses, it bears witness to that sort of omnipresent infinity which is the very mark of the absolute, whose exterior and given manifestation only is disclosed to us by the object, and the internal and creative power by the possible. It is the possible, not as pure object of thought, but as a proposal for our activity which discloses to us, in its relations with us, the very intimacy of the being in which we participate. The word "possibility," like the word "representation," seems to express a diminished existence which is only in its relation to us, but it is in order that by their mediation we may form, in the totality of being, precisely that double corporal and spiritual existence which is ours.

It will be said again that if the possible is before us without being us, if it is unceasingly offered us and set before us, even though there is nothing, even as possible, outside of our thinking, we must at least consider the act which realizes it as our own act, so that if the intimacy of being, precisely insofar as it goes beyond us internally, is enclosed to us only as the infinite of possibility, the operation by which we make a choice among possibles in order to adopt that possible of which we will make our very being belongs to us alone. Participation would then play a part in the evocation of possibilities, but not in their actualization. However matters are much less simple. For one thing, possibility is not, as one might suppose, a pure object of contemplation: it is itself an active possibility, or at least one which has meaning only with relation to the act which realizes it: it already invites me, and if I have the power to repress it, it is always a virtualness in waiting, never a spectacle given to me. Finally, at the very moment I act, that act by which I actualize it puts into motion a power which is not mine, or at least one which notably exceeds mine, whose efficacy fills me with astonishment and admiration when I think back to it, but which becomes mine as soon as I grant it my consent. This consent can never be forced: it alone constitutes my own being and bases my personal subjectivity in the total subjectivity.

At the point we have reached we have not only discovered in the intimacy of the ego our first encounter with being, but we have shown that if that intimacy is always imperfect it participates in a pure intimacy which itself consists in an act which creates itself rather than anything exterior to itself, which is consequently the eternal beginning of oneself, from which too I draw that power of being the first beginning of myself, that is of discerning that possibility out of which I, by consenting to actualize it, will make an existence which is mine.

III. The Externality of the World, or the Interval Between the Ego and Pure Inwardness

This metaphysical analysis has thus far remained acosmic: it is a dialectic of intimacy, that is, of correlation within the intimacy between the individual and the universal. However, the world continues to be present to us. In following our analysis we have continually used comparisons drawn from the relations of our body with the world. And it would be rash to think that it is the characteristic of metaphysical thought to abolish the world in behalf of a spirituality which it would never succeed in isolating, whatever its efforts toward purification or *askesis*.

We must now prove finally that the real world comes as an immense datum between the infinite act and the finite ego, filling the interval which separates them, that the ego always tries to fill up this interval without ever succeeding, but that the efforts it makes toward that goal explain at once both the evolution of the world and the progress of humanity, for the world is continually being humanized and spiritualized; I penetrate it gradually by knowledge. I constantly reform it to make it conform to my purposes, that is, not only the most pressing needs of my body but also the most delicate requirements of my thought. It is understandable then how *from within being should appear to me as a system of possibilities and from without as a system of things.* But not all possibility is actualized. Yet it must be capable of actualization; and it never finishes the process; thus the world will never have finished its course. It can be said of all these possibilities that they can never be considered as given; otherwise their actualization would not add anything. In this sense they are perpetually invented, that is, isolated from each other within the sovereign act which contains them all, and that is the proper object of our intelligence; but we continually choose among them, and that is the object of our will. That explains also why the world of possibilities not only appears legitimately as infinitely more ample than the world of things but also how there is in it a dynamic power which uplifts the world of things and continually moves it onward. Finally, we realize that, if the secret of existence comes down for us to the relation between the pure act and the act which participates, the former supplying the latter with all the possibilities it actualizes, we still do not succeed in explaining the shape of the world unless we also realize, first, that all these free actions fit into each other, that is, have to limit each other in order to come together, which is an adequate explanation of the degree of necessity which reigns in the world; and secondly, that the very exercise of liberty requires, as its precondition, the actualization of certain possibilities which it continually makes use of and goes beyond, which is an adequate explanation of why there is an evolution of the world, whose liberty at each point can never be regarded as anything but the utmost point. Thus we can say of liberty that it governs the world because it is liberty which draws out of infinite possibility, as the condition of its own elevation, those first sketches of existence on which it has to rely in order to go beyond them by means of denying them.

We shall now show that the world possesses three properties which suffice to define it: for it is at once an appearance and a trial for each consciousness, and an instrument of mediation among different consciousnesses.

(1) *The world is an appearance.* The act which lies at the basis of my interiority to myself does not coincide with the infinite act, that is, with the inwardness of whatever is, although it participates in it; but yet it cannot be separated from it. And the very indivisibility of the all requires it to be present to me, even though it always exceeds me. I can neither confuse it with myself, nor *know* it as it is in itself. This amounts to saying that it can only be present to me in its relation to me, which may be expressed by saying that it is for me an object, a phenomenon or an appearance. All of being must therefore become for me a spectacle or an immense datum which as such is linked to inwardness only by my own thought, without which no spectacle would ever be presented to me. I should add that I have to make myself a part of this world of objects, that is, I must be able to become an object for others, but also for myself to the extent that the act which creates me, although always unfinished, should still at every instant be present to itself. I express this by saying that I have a body. From this analysis can be deduced the nature of attachment, which superadds itself to the representation which I have of my body, and by continually setting a limit to the very act by which I make myself as I, will enable me to say that it is mine. Thus the ego is legitimately reduced to the body by all those who think that there is no other existence than that of the object.

From the fact that each being has its own characteristic representation of the world, it cannot be inferred that the world in which it lives has existence only for it: for that representation is of a non-ego which is common to all consciousness, precisely because it expresses them all in going beyond them, that is, in changing itself into a datum for them, the act from which each of them borrows precisely the power to say I. We cannot yield to a certain realism which seems to be inseparable from scientific research, and according to which it is the characteristic of the spirit to go behind the layer of appearance as it takes form under the action of our senses, to reach the objects that in themselves they are. There can be no object with which knowledge will coincide one day: for knowledge is knowledge only if it is distinguished from its object. But we can easily understand that the part played by an ever deeper and more delicate experience, the use of tools, the very artifices which thought continually uses to obtain more and more precision and coherence, continually change the representation we form of things, but still do not take from them the character of being a representation. The conception which science forms of the world does not do away with the image which the senses give us. The image remains when we consider the immediate relation which things have to our body: it is on these things that the acts of our most accustomed life are based. The image seems to vanish, but what we should say is only that it opens when we bring new means of investigation into play; then our action requires more power and finesse. But all these successive representations are equally true: we pass from one to the other as method and point of view change: they admirably express the infinite multiplicity of possibilities which the all continually offers for participation.

However, it will be observed that as our knowledge becomes more complex the role of the spirit's operations continually increases. Whereas if we thought we could reach the thing as it is, it would seem that we should on the contrary break off all those operations and break them down in a sort of receptivity toward the thing itself with which consciousness would mysteriously come to coincide. On the contrary, when we come to the highest degree of knowledge, the thing itself seems to have evaporated, to have resolved itself into a pure object of thought: which would favor a return to Platonism, that is, to the conception which identifies the real with the idea. We should moreover try to show that the idea is never a thing which the spirit just runs up against; there is in it, it is true, a certain opacity which always remains and which is like an irreducible residue of sensible experience; but as it becomes more transparent, it is no longer distinct from the operation of the spirit which thinks it, that is, from a pure relation between the finite and the infinite in the very act which causes us to be.

(2) *The world is a trial.* It is sometimes thought that by saying of the world that it is an appearance, we attenuate its existence: and it is held that every appearance is an illusion. But that is impossible. The appearances are in fact things. Or in other words, things only subsist in the very appearance they give us. One would like then to know what it is they are appearances of; but the word "appearance" indicates only that they have no existence except for a subject capable of saying I as the inwardness of his being enlists itself in the inwardness of all of being which, beyond the limits in which the ego continually confines itself, takes on the character of externality and turns into a world which seems to come to it from without. Hence the density and depth which such a world has for us. At each instant it is only a vanishing appearance. Yet it is always reborn and has an immense reserve. It never fails to provide for me; it brings me a revelation which continually astonishes

and enriches me. I always begin to discover it anew. I shall never succeed in exhausting it. It has eternal novelty for me. It comes about then that my existence may seem poor and pale by comparison, being only a pure possibility. Once my existence turns in upon itself, once it suspends its relations with the world, it is as nothing. My existence always needs to be actualized, and that can only take place through and by means of the world. And not only is it thanks to the world that my being ceases to be a secret being and becomes a manifest being, but it must also be said that this becoming manifest is essential to my secret being, which without it would be rather as aspiration to being than a veritable being.

Here we grasp in the profoundest manner the relation between the being which is and the being which appears; here we can give the world which appears its true meaning. We should in no way impair the principle that being is internal to itself, but this inwardness consists in the very power it has to make itself. Now if we admit that such a proposition can be conceded by all, it seems possible to draw from it two opposite consequences, against each of which we must defend ourselves: the first is that externality is an illusion we must learn to free ourselves from; the second that it alone enables inwardness to realize itself. But in both cases the meaning of the world escapes us. We cannot say that the ego should give its attention principally to never going outside of itself, nor that it is only in the world that it finds its existence. *The world is a tool for it, not a place to stay.* For (a) we have no right to despise the world as a phantasmagory which takes the ego away from itself: to the extent that it is a given, not a created presence, it is all the being which I feel infinitely exceeds me and continually instructs me. I find in myself only a virtual infinity; but it can only actualize itself by the stimulus which the world brings it and to which I constantly respond. (b) Inversely, it would be a contradiction to desire, as often happens, that the destiny of the ego should be achieved outside of the ego, namely in the world where all its actions come to receive a material form. For, on the contrary, it is well known that all the efforts of knowledge, will, and love aim, by means of the world, at giving us a spiritual satisfaction without which the world would have no sense for us. This is a conclusion which the most hardened materialist, who asks only one thing, to change the world, cannot avoid. This is the reason why the shape of the world constantly passes away, as we so often complain; but the world must pass in order to be at once passed through and surpassed. The material world is the place where the conversion of my spiritual possibility into my spiritual existence continually takes place; it is the place where the spirit realizes itself.

(3) *The world is an instrument of mediation among consciousnesses.* Up to now we have considered each consciousness as if it were alone over against the world. And it is from this relation with the absolute that we have derived the existence of the world. It will be readily understood that we do not have the immediate experience of any other finite existence than our own. But perhaps we can show that the existence of only one finite being implies the existence of an infinity of finite beings, as if the infinity of the multiple were nothing more than a manner of putting the infinity of the one to work.

However, it is through the world that we learn of the existence of other consciousnesses, that is, of other existences internal to themselves from which we remain separated, but yet with which we can communicate. It will be said that this experience is indirect and hypothetical, for it takes place by means of the manifestation, that is of the body behind which we imagine a secret life comparable to ours. But that is not enough. For one thing, if the ego is always a possibility of realizing itself, we cannot ignore the fact that there are still of right within each ego all the possibilities at once, so that what you are I am too, or at least could be in some way; which confirms the view that all being is present in every point, and that still it is by liberty, that is by the actualization of different possibilities, that particular beings come to establish their separate existence. And again, it is illegitimate, as the objectivist prejudice so often leads us to do, to consider the ego as capable of entering into relation only with things and not with beings. For, as has been shown, outside the ego there is nothing but things whose relations with me constitute what we call representations. But the relations of the ego with another ego are of a different nature. The being that I am and the being that you are, in the degree that each of them on its own initiative assumes the existence proper to it, are infinitely farther apart than the subject and the object of knowledge can be. And yet between these two beings there is a much greater affinity than between the ego and a thing. The difference there is between you and me, the debate I have with you, are also a difference that exists between me and myself and a debate I have with myself. And as there is in me a part of myself which only has meaning by its relations with an object which is at once external and represented, there is also a part of myself of which I can say that instead of confining me within myself, it gets me out of myself, not, it is true, in order to set before me a thing which I contemplate as a spectacle, but in order to set before me another being I set myself up against, but with which I communicate.

We now see that there is the closest unity between the affirmation of the existence of the world and the affirmation of an infinite plurality of beings who, like me, can say I. But it is on condition of not limiting oneself to saying that these other beings are a part of this world that I see, because in that case they would be nothing more than things among other things. Like me they think the world and they contribute to modifying it, but it is thanks to it that they constitute what they are. They are therefore not simply a fragment of it. It is as ego in this world that they have to express themselves, that is to manifest themselves; and that expression or that manifestation is indispensable for their entering into relationship with each other and with me. This no doubt is the reason why Hegel considered as the motive force of the development of consciousness and perhaps even of the evolution of the world *the desire to be recognized*. But that is not enough. The relation which two beings have with each other and with the world is much deeper. The world brings them the presence of the all, which is a unique presence, but only a given presence, in the face of which each one remains unequal, but which applies each one with the career in which his destiny is involved. They find there a source of material which continually enriches them, provided that they themselves continually spiritualize it. Each one of them has a perspective of its own on the world. Nevertheless all these perspectives must be in agreement. They are only perspectives. We say that they open out on the same world: it would be truer to say that they open out on the same being, which, to the extent that it goes beyond all particular beings, presents itself to them in the form of a world. Therefore it is because there is a world that consciousnesses are separated from each other instead of fusing in the unity of the pure spirit, and it is also because there is a world that they can enter into communication with each other; but it is because it is an instrument of mediation among them that it has become the foundation of human society.

EXISTENTIALISM IN FRANCE
SINCE THE LIBERATION

*Robert Campbell**

I n philosophy, especially since the end of the war, we have witnessed a
general reaction against the systematizing mind, and perhaps even
against science itself. It is probably because the passion for final and
totalitarian truths has become so pervasive that the individual, threatened by the generality and abstraction which are shutting him in, is
fighting a fight of the last hour against his imminent drowning in universal laws.

Therefore, existence (and particularly human existence) in philosophy has been suddenly provided with a new priority; it is no longer
included in nature as a particular organ that would be accounted for by
all that precedes it, as we may see in the traditional systems of Hegel and
Spinoza. For present philosophies, *existence* is ever *here,* first of all
(Heidegger says ever already-here).[1] It appears before everything; it
precedes every "essence." We cannot reduce it to some other principle
which would account for it; quite the contrary, it is existence itself which
is absolute, and cannot be rationally deduced. It is irrational, or again,
gratuitous and unjustified, full and opaque, chaotic and obscene: It *IS:*
my cat, my child are here; these are existing beings; they are here, but
we might conceive they might not be; that character of existence is called
"contingency" and seems to be the utmost limit of every philosophical
explanation.[2]

Every question concerning what could exist "beyond," that is, what
could clear up the origin or the cause of existence is to be regarded as

---

* Born in 1913. Agrégé de mathématiques, docteur ès-sciences, engaged in research
at the *Centre national de la recherche scientifique.* In addition to mathematical publications,
author of *Jean-Paul Sartre ou une littérature philosophique* (1945), *L'existentialisme* (1947),
and of critical literary essays in the review *Paru* (1947, 1948).
1. Here we may recall the use of the word "Dasein" in Jaspers's and Heidegger's
philosophy.
2. Absolute or absurd! Absurd, irreducible! Nothing, not even a deep and secret
madness of nature could explain it! (Sartre, *La nausée,* p. 156).

devoid of any human meaning.[3] This already makes us infer that this philosophy could not provide a large place for God. And, indeed, in it both absence of God and irrationalism come in the first place. It takes up again mystical and religious themes, but emptied of any divine trace; it comes from St. Augustine, Pascal, Kierkegaard, but it was born after the death of God. The "Widower of God!" exclaims G. Bataille,[4] speaking of himself, who, in spite of his recent denials, is one of the most representative figures of "existentialism," since, having been a pious Christian, he has come, in his books today, to sing his own love of irreligion.

Jean-Paul Sartre:

J.-P. Sartre's literary and philosophical success has made him the most quoted representative of existentialism in France. In his magisterial work *L'être et le néant* there rings a really Pascalian undertone; but we have chiefly to notice with it the rigorous, strong, and even "rational" character of his argument and analysis.

It is essentially with the Cartesian qualities of mind that Sartre takes on this fundamentally anti-Cartesian (and anti-Kantian) doctrine. In Sartre, a great, almost morbid, emotional sensitiveness is combined with a very sharp and keen understanding and with an acute critical faculty, trained in the traditions of Alain and Husserl, so that when he appeals to the readers' feeling in order to *persuade* them, he cannot help appealing at the same time to their "esprit de géométrie" in order to *convince* them.

The basic truth of which he wishes to convince (or to persuade) us is that "man is free." We know that such is the theme of his first play, *The Flies,* and of his last essay, "What is Literature?" But such is also the message in all his novels and the very foundation of all his philosophy.

In this way, and in spite of his irrationalism, Sartre has recently declared himself a disciple of Descartes, whose famous aphorism he recalls: "Our freedom is known without any proof and by our mere experience of it." We know that, according to Descartes, the essence of human reason is divine; that means, for instance, that mathematics is true because God has established that it must be and that there cannot be any other criterion of truth but divine freedom. It is precisely on this point that today Sartre sees a kind of aberration. For him, man himself

---

3. Cf. Heidegger. Existence or *Dasein* as selfness and freedom is taken away from this very freedom and lies without a ground. It is abandonment (dereliction), powerlessness, abyss (*Vom Wesen des Grundes,* p. 110).
4. In his book on Nietzsche, p. 114.

can *alone* decide on truth. And God's freedom, such as Descartes alludes to, man cannot know, except by the idea or the experience he can have of his own.

Therefore, it is in man's freedom (and not in God's) that we must look for the foundations of principles of reason. Sartre concludes his essay on Descartes by noticing that the great philosopher has really given God what is man's own attribute; [it is not a question of reproaching him with it, but rather of admiring him for his having thus driven the concept of 'autonomy' to its utmost consequences, and having understood, two centuries before Heidegger (cf. *Vom Wesen des Grundes*) that the unique foundation of being was freedom.[5]]

We may easily conceive here that there could not be a more systematic atheism (or, if one prefers, a more coherent humanism). When Sartre says, "man is free," it is exactly the same as when he says, "God is not." Besides, that human step which he denounces, and which consists in endowing God with specifically human attributes, is, according to him, a very general tendency of the human condition. For man suffers from feeling himself free and tries to prove to himself that he is not really free. He aspires to be merely a simple creature, homogeneous with the whole of nature that he may perceive around him. And so, for instance, he builds philosophical systems in which he integrates himself as an object. Man has a longing for things, for these things by which he is surrounded, because they have *being,* he has but *existence.* Things are already what they are; and man is never anything but what he has chosen to make himself and even then he is never completed, except at his death, at which moment he is precisely no more. So the modus of the being of man is not being, but becoming (and he is even the free maker of that kind of becoming). Being fails him, he misses being, or, he is a void of being, a *hole* in being, like a cleft in a hard rock. It is man who falsifies the homogeneity of the rest of the world. If we had to represent being in general as a fruit, man would be the inner worm gnawing at it. And it would be a worm which could not help being a worm, which would know it is a worm, and assume itself to be a worm.

That nothing that apprehends itself as a nothing (as Pascal's reed thought of itself as a reed), Sartre calls a *For-Itself.* All that is not man in the world, and therefore is not conscious of itself, is called by contrast

---

5. We use the word "freedom" in its usual sense in philosophy. Nevertheless we have to remember Eduard Nicol's recent paper in *Philosophy and Phenomenological Research,* Vol. VIII (June, 1948), p. 552: "Liberty as a Fact, Freedom as a Right." With this distinction, the freedom of which Sartre speaks would be rather a liberty.

an *In-Itself*. With that terminology, a principal feature of Sartre's philosophy can be summed up in this formula: "Man is a For-Itself that wants
to be an In-Itself." That means exactly that man denies his own freedom
and envies that impassive irresponsibility, that whole and clean being of
nature, with its set, lasting, and reassuring laws.

That vacuous, ever-present and always-starting-again freedom stays
within us like the obsession of an abyss, of a desert, of a vertiginous
void. It is no longer the silence of the endless spaces which is frighten-
ing us, it is that of our nothingness, our non-being. To be more precise,
it is not so much a question of fright, but of "anguish" (fright being
caused by an object of the world, and anguish by ourselves). So it is
our own anguish we flee from, by evading our freedom in making ourselves exist after the manner of things, according to an "essence" which
would be given and immutable. This tendency of man in setting himself free from his own freedom is what Sartre calls "bad faith" (*mauvaise
foi*). And here we may say that for Freud's psychoanalysis he has substituted a new kind of psychoanalysis (which he himself calls "existential"). In this one, man does not covet the lost bliss of prenatal life
(Freud's golden age), but the quiet state of things: "The Being of In-
Itself." And that passive condition, man seeks by all means—whether
he is obeying instituted laws or other men whom he acknowledges as his
masters, or identifies himself with his own body and so makes himself
a thing in the glance of another, or still when with the imagination, he
creates obligations which would be supposed to come from nature or from
God. The notion of "bad faith" here plays a part somewhat similar to
Freud's censor (and Sartre has no difficulty in showing the great logical
superiority the former has acquired over the latter) and appears as a general invention and testifies to the power of his exceptional insight and
psychological observation. It is the fundamental (and fundamentally
new) point of his philosophy.

Sartre himself applies his method to an explanation of Baudelaire's
life and works; and Mrs. Simone de Beauvoir, loyal (and close) disciple
of Sartre, derives inspiration with great subtlety to interpret some ancestral myths which tradition brings us, about woman[6] and her part in the
world (as mother, wife, or mistress), sexual customs, "taboos," and complexes. Moreover, the range of that new psychological method has already even drawn the attention of psychiatrists since a real therapeutic
value has been imputed to them.

---

6. "La femme et les mythes," *Les Temps Modernes* (May, June, July, 1948).

From the point of view of ethics, one easily conceives that the first moral step of man is to get rid of his bad faith. Few are those who succeed in doing it; most of us live as nameless organs of a great system, according to that modus of existence that Sartre, after Heidegger, calls "inauthentic." These authentically free acts (Sartre gives some examples of them in his literary works: the murder of Orestes in *Les mouches,* Ines's wickedness in *Huis-clos,* the final resolution of Canoris in *Morts sans sépulture,* and some of Mathieu's "choices" in *Les chemins de la liberté,* are those in which freedom, which has acknowledged itself, asserts itself and assumes itself as such. In such an act, the individual finds in himself, and in himself alone, the motives of his resolution and remains alone to create what he acknowledges as his own values.

However, that man, who decides alone, was born in a determinate place and time, in the midst of a given family, with a given heredity. Such a complex of circumstances makes up his "situation," and it is that situation as such to which freedom must cling. For it is the freedom which acknowledges the situation and, in a certain manner, makes it exist. But, on the other hand, without the situation, freedom could not exist, for freedom implies obstacles against which it can stumble. And the more difficult the obstacles, the more authentic the liberty. So Sartre wrote in 1944: "Never have we been more free than under the German occupation." And, in fact, in that time, the least act of a man 'committed' his whole life. The freedom of man implies his being 'committed'; at any moment of his life he must choose; deceitfulness itself is a choice; abstention is a choice. A simple choice is forbidden to man (as, in the earthly Paradise, there was one single forbidden fruit): the choice which would *allow him not to choose,* to resign his freedom. The fallen man in the Christian religion has been replaced by the deceitful man, but with this distinction: the fallen man of the Genesis is forever so, whereas the deceitful man is so only until he will agree to change. It rests with him to put an end to his sin. Here is the fundamentally optimistic point of that philosophy (always called "hopeless philosophy"): in it *the stakes are never laid down.* Sartre himself has said: "Existence begins beyond despair"; but here he has only meant that, if man will exist authentically, he must have understood that he cannot place hope in anything that would be situated outside of himself (for instance, in God) but that he is able, and will ever be able, to rely on nothing but himself.

Merleau-Ponty:

The philosophical position of Merleau-Ponty is very close to that which we have just presented. According to him, every human undertaking is built on the ground of existing, existing situated outside of man, and empty of sense: in a senseless background. But on that meaningless foundation "man," he says, "is condemned to meaning" (Sartre says, "condemned to be free"). Thus the tone of Merleau-Ponty is more intellectualistic. He has remained closer than Sartre to Husserlian phenomenology, as his forceful work, *Phénoménologie de la perception,* testifies. But his own ethical concerns are directed more toward the social and political part of existentialism. He wishes to see it draw nearer to Marxism, and even to collaborate with it. His deep knowledge of Marx allows him to assert that in Marx's thought, as in Sartre's, it is man who has to make history, and man *alone,* in the middle of a situation given by his time, with economic, scientific, industrial, and sociological data. Therefore, it is man alone who is able to lead history toward social revolution and must do so, but with this restriction, that he must not believe too candidly that the success of this revolution is already secure now. This certainty of success would imply that history admits some logic, that reason or science are capable of showing the issue of an enterprise; but history is still in the making and the stakes are never laid down and probably never will be, for if they were ever laid down, there could be no more liberty and it would be the death of man. And there we see Merleau-Ponty part from the Marxists who do not want (and cannot want) to reveal to workers such a doctrine of revolution which is so little strengthened by the assurance of success. The working masses are very fond of all that is scientific and that can be shown. And this "contingency" of history would depress them. According to Merleau-Ponty, there is precisely too much reason in the world, one can ever show that reason is almost everywhere in mankind, that men are entangled in it. What he wishes to be realized is a widening of the realm of possibilities and that is what Marxism is to preconize. Marxism is not an optimistic philosophy; it is only the idea that "another history" is possible, that there is no fate, that the existence of man is open. It is the resolute attempt of this future, which nobody, either in the world or outside it, is able to know *whether* it will be, or *what* it will be.

Rather than a philosophy of anguish, one may say that it is a philosophy of *risk,* or of *anxiety,* or, as Ferdinand Alquié[7] has tried to show, of *ambiguity* or contradiction. However irrationalistic he is, Merleau-Ponty is still tormented every time he meets with a contradiction,

7. *Fontaine,* No. 59.

either that of morals and history (which constitutes the foundation of his essay "Humanism and Terror"), or that of transcendence and immanence (beyond which he tries to reach in his *Phénoménologie de la perception*), or that of situation and freedom (in Sartre) which leads him to identify (or nearly so) existence with the fundamental ambiguity in time. (We have still to notice the analogy of this conclusion with that of Heidegger, though the thought of the latter seems to be far from it.)   Merleau-Ponty has devoted a long paper to Cézanne, who seems to him to be the very type of artist who has evolved and has made himself in the risk, in the idea that nobody can be sure of reaching his end.   Thus Cézanne appears as the expressive symbol of man (the man of good will), the man who hurls himself against chance.   Like Sartre's thought, which is not rosy-colored but not hopeless, this one incites man to risk himself, and without any assurance of success but without any certainty of failure.   As Koestler has said in his novel, *Darkness at Noon:* "Nobody can know who will be right in the end.   But meanwhile one must act on credit and sell one's soul to the devil."

Cézanne has triumphed against chance.   Existence is not a mathematically assured success, but it is also other than a long misfortune.

Georges Bataille:

Want to chance!   Such is the subtitle M. Bataille has chosen for his last work, *On Nietzsche.*   For him also, man at any moment is facing his possibilities, and the possible is only a chance "which cannot be taken without danger, frail chance that is always to be played, always fascinating and exhausting me, . . . for the better and the worse, and that wants to be played till its end."[8]

M. Bataille is the man who teaches us how to go to the end of the possible, to make, as he says, an *experiment* — to go to the end of the possible freedom from delusion and fear, and here he condemns, as "being of bad faith," *the project of life* which gives a respite to life.   The project, he says, consists in the putting of existence to a later date, the burking of existence.   To project is to go into this extinct and quiet world where we usually drag along.   Here all is in suspense; the "inner experience" is the denunciation of the truce; it is the being-without-reprieve.[9]

And here we see how Bataille identifies the project with that modus of being which Sartre, following Heidegger, calls "inauthentic."   But

---

8. *Sur Nietzsche*, p. 152.
9. *Ibid.*, p. 76.

among all possible projects, the one which seems to him to be the most blamable is the *Salvation*.

"To work out one's Salvation," that seems to him the crowning of deceitfulness. "Of all the shortcuts, this is the most hateful." Sartre has answered that concept of project in a long and strong paper (with that trenchant style he uses when he has to show he is right) and where in the last analysis it is Bataille who is convicted of his own deceitfulness; first because "he teaches one to turn anxiety into delight" (which is not an honest way of facing it), then because he preaches the "non-knowing," and places himself in the night, to begin to speak of the day; the "non-knowing," that is the excuse for the *escape* of Bataille, who is called, in the conclusion, "a black pantheist."

If the manners of thinking of Sartre and Bataille are similar (atheism, antirationalism, and that endless taste for an endless freedom), their persons are different, we would wish to say, "by their essence" if we were not speaking of men who do not believe in "essence." The more Apollonian is Nietzsche's influence on Sartre; the Bacchic, Dionysiac, passional is the loan which Bataille makes from the philosopher of *Fröhliche Wissenschaft*. Whereas the former rather belongs to Descartes, Husserl, and Heidegger, the latter would rather stand like Kierkegaard's "subjective thinker" or a kind of inversed St. Augustine who would have put God away to devote himself to a laughing and tortured erotism. One would imagine Bataille, in the midst of one of those antic or wild feasts, where gladness of living exasperates itself to the point of the taste for mutilation, finally to die "for nothing" in the paroxysm of a sexual excess, in a terrific burst of laughter. There is no page in all his books in which M. Bataille does not laugh, with a total, mystical, distorted laugh, with the laugh of a man on the rack. For, *torture or laughter,* it is the same thing for this man who "crucifies himself at his pleasure."

In this ineluctable pain of remaining "the widower of God," M. Bataille never ceases to be a merry widower; but he never ceases to loathe both being a widower and being merry. However, if as Kierkegaard says, "he who has lost his passion, has lost more than he who has lost himself in his passion," Bataille moreover remains the least impoverished of all widowers, and the least lessened; for, if he has indeed passionately loved this God who is dead, he is nevertheless consumed with love for that absurd life of the man who knows nothing, of the man forsaken under a sky henceforth silent, indifferent, and emptied.

Albert Camus:

If a passion for the absurd can indeed exist, M. Bataille has a serious rival (and that he knows) in M. Albert Camus.

One seldom speaks of the former without alluding to the latter. Yet, contrary to his emulator, M. Camus never laughs (neither does he cry), he hates the violent manifestation of feelings; and on that account, he is a classical writer. Moreover, if we are accustomed to compare his novels with those of Sartre (because they also express a philosophy), we have to notice that the style of *L'étranger* and chiefly of *La peste* does not recall that of *Le mur* or of *Les chemins de la libertée* (which derives from Faulkner or Dos Passos), but seems to us to be pretty anachronistic today, for it would rather remind us of Voltaire or Mme. de la Lafayette. And although he is akin to Bataille, Camus is visibly not a disciple of Nietzsche (M. Wahl says he is a disciple of Chestov), he would rather be a kind of Kierkegaardian, whose *despair has become secular.*

Rather than resign oneself to lie, the absurd mind, he says, prefers to adopt without trembling Kierkegaard's answer: despair. But Camus also is a descendant of Hegel, inasmuch as he behaves as a "contrite consciousness." He appears as a lucid reason which feels alien in the world of history, but which, however, does not identify reason with the historic while, in order to give up the contradiction. And it is this denial before taking the Hegelian step which ranks him within the existentialist tradition (in spite of his recent denials). Nevertheless he parts from Heidegger in this point at least, that for him the human creature is dreadfully enclosed in itself, whereas for the author of *Sein und Zeit,* quite the contrary is the case. The human creature is always "outside itself." In this respect Camus is a disciple of Leibniz, whom Heidegger expressly wishes to oppose.

Two attitudes are possible for man, in his complete abandonment: "suicide," or the opposite behavior, which consists in assuming the absurd as such, and accepting its consequences to the limit, that is, till *revolt.* And it is the latter attitude Camus has described in *L'étranger* or in *Caligula;* it is characterized by the destroying of every aspiration and by the acceptance of an overwhelming fate, without any trace of resignation. A man who would reach such a condition without failing (that is to say, who would not kill himself, and that is the case in *L'étranger*), would be surely condemned to death.

This revolt is the first principle of Camus's philosophy. For him, it has the same significance as the "cogito" (he himself says, "the cogito itself is revolt"[10]). The admirable play, *Caligula*, seems, in the evolution of Camus's thought — between his first works and his last novel, *La peste* — to play an intermediate part (we might almost say a moral part) insofar as Caligula appears to have given his author a lesson while driving the absurdity to the point of dying mad. For, in *La peste* Camus seems to have given up this monadism we have spoken of, so that he draws nearer, if not to Heidegger, at least to a position which is not without connection with that of Merleau-Ponty. In *La peste* one can first find the idea that a man never is alone in struggling against the absurd, that he always has neighbors who are striving also against a similar oppression, and second, this idea, that the life of a man is not a revolt *by itself,* but a revolt *among others.* "The evil hitherto experienced by a single man becomes a collective Pest. Man alone is worthy of having man sacrificed to him."[11]

In the world of *La peste,* nothing can have a meaning, but man himself who precisely gives it one, and who gives it freely and within a freedom full of risks and facing up against chance (the end of the struggle being not necessarily failure). We here again meet the "symbole Cézanne." However, counter to Merleau-Ponty, Camus declines all totalitarian, scientific, or rationalistic explanations, like those of Marx's disciples, and declares that his own intention is toward "Kierkegaardian subjectivity." The final revolution cannot be but pessimistic, and pessimistic so far as it concerns human condition, but *decidedly optimistic* when concerning his own action. In the last analysis, Camus's thought, like Sartre's, seems optimistic indeed, since it denies that men can ever be accused or guilty.

Gabriel Marcel: [12]

Although he points up the differences between Bataille and Camus, it is nevertheless in the same paper that, in 1943, Gabriel Marcel has challenged the doctrines of both.

Violently against Bataille, he makes an obvious allowance for Camus whom he has very much admired since his last novel *La peste.* We have also to recall that Gabriel Marcel is the oldest of the French existentialist thinkers, since his *Journal Métaphysique* was published over twenty years ago; and he is the only one among them for whom God has already

---

10. *Remarques sur la révolte,* p. 13.
11. *Ibid.,* p. 12.
12. Marcel's thought has been considered elsewhere in this volume, so that it is sufficient merely to indicate it in the present context.

been resuscitated. (Gabriel Marcel was converted when about forty.)   He denounces the attractive and inexpugnable character of those philosophies the essence of which is "to deny." For, according to him, if you could find a man caught in such an asphyxiating thought and if you could demonstrate to him that he will never be able to live and will have to break open the windows, this man would answer you that this human condition is precisely inhuman as soon as one tries to think it to the end, and that this is just what he wishes to show.   Thus, a dialectic able to triumph over such a blinded thought can never exist.   And the fact which makes the apparent strength of it is that it presents itself as facing truth and confronting man with his situation, such as it actually is.   But to come back to the fundamental presuppositions of phenomenology, here M. Gabriel Marcel recalls Sartre, Bataille, and Camus, for here there cannot be any question of seizing a truth (in terms of scientific meanings). The situation of man cannot be divided from the very standpoint man himself has already chosen to consider; pure objectivity is not concerned here.   According to Marcel, it is not the "self" which is the center of the ontology, but the Being; and we may acknowledge here the philosophers for whom the "cogito" chiefly reveals the existence of *Other*.   We see that the former reproach with which he somewhat wrongly loads Sartre is chiefly to be applied to the monadist, Camus, to whom we have alluded, and much less to the Camus of *La peste*.   But this in no way lessens the accuracy of the objection of Gabriel Marcel, who here seems to be a faithful disciple of Husserl. For him, the point of view that man takes upon his situation is *intentional;* and so, Camus's absurdity is not an absurdity included within the world, but an absurdity chosen by himself in his own relationship with the world.   This remark, which drives human freedom on to its utmost limits, would be worthy of Sartre; and we are astonished when the same Gabriel Marcel comes to reproach Sartre with exaggerating human liberty, to put it everywhere and so to devaluate it. It seems we are witnessing a struggle between him, Sartre, and Camus, the aim of which would be to discover who is the most authentic phenomenologist of the three.   But here the very arbitrator who points out the victor would have already been acknowledged as a greater phenomenologist that the three others; and so may we ask ourselves whether, in the last analysis, Camus would not be both victor and arbitrator, when he decrees that no man here below can ever *judge* or *be judged.*

All these philosophers of existence, we see, set man too high to let him sink into a process of scientific, economic, or social rules.   All speak to us of man in terms which are extremely old and extremely new, as if every instant, because it is lived, would resume in its unique tone the whole eternity of mind. Sartre, in his exacting demand of authenticity, Merleau-Ponty in his portrait of the hero, Camus in his ethic of holiness out of God, all draw for man a figure which is undoubtedly proud (since God is dead) but without any allowance, overwhelming but strengthening. Perhaps all (other than Bataille, who rather looks for ecstasy), inheriting from Descartes and Husserl rather than from Kierkegaard and Nietzsche, only celebrate with different tunes in that human existence, which surpasses all, this extraordinary, sparkling lucidity.

SELECTED BIBLIOGRAPHY *

WORKS OF SARTRE:

Since 1937, Sartre has alternately published books on philosophy and literary works.

> *L'imagination* (philosophical essay). Paris, Alcan 1937.
> *La nausée* (*Nausea*). Paris, Gallimard, 1938.
> *Esquisse d'une théorie des émotions* (*The Emotions: Outline of Theory*). Paris, Hermann, 1939.
> *Le mur* (*The Wall and Other Tales*). Paris, Gallimard, 1939.
> *L'imaginaire*: *essai sur une phénoménologie de l'imagination* (*The Psychology of Imagination*). Paris, Gallimard, 1940.

UNDER GERMAN OCCUPATION:

> *Les mouches* (*The Flies*), played at the Charles Dullin theatre. Paris, Gallimard, 1942.
> *L'être et le néant*: *essai d'ontologie phénoménologique*. Paris, Gallimard, 1943.
> *Huis-clos* (*No Exit*), played at the Vieux-Colombier theatre. Paris, Gallimard, 1944.

SINCE THE LIBERATION: The philosophical production of Sartre is not yet published. He is working on a large book on ethics; but he has published novels and plays:

> *Les chemins de la liberté* (*The Roads to Freedom; Age of Reason; The Reprieve*). Paris, Gallimard, 1945.
> *Morts sans sepulture; La putain respectueuse* (*The Respectful Prostitute*), played at the Antoine theatre. Paris, Gallaimard, 1946.

---

* The titles of works translated into English are given in parentheses.

Les jeux sont faits (The Chips are Down), film. 1947.

Les mains sales (Red Gloves), played at the Antoine theatre.

Besides, Sartre has edited a review, *Les temps modernes,* where he has himself published philosophical and critical essays which he has recently assembled in two books, *Situations I* (Paris, Gallimard, 1947), and *II* (1948). The first contains articles published before and during the war in many reviews (*Nouvelle revue francaise, Cahiers du Sud*) on Mauriac, Bataille, Blanchot, Kafka, Faulkner). The second contains essays published after the war: "Engagement de la littérature," "Materialisme et revolution," and a large essay: *Qu'est-ce que la littérature? (What is Literature?)*. Sartre has also published a work on *Baudelaire* (1947) in the collection *Les essais* (Paris, Gallimard) and an *Introduction to Descartes* (Les classiques de la liberté, Geneva), which one may read in *Situations II.*

WORKS OF SIMONE DE BEAUVOIR:

Mrs. Simone de Beauvior also uses literature to express her philosophy. In addition to her existentialist essays:

> *Pyrrhus et Cinéas,* Paris, Gallimard, Collection les essais, 1945,
> *L'existentialisme et la sagesse des nations,* Paris, Nagel, 1947,
> *Pour une morale de l'ambiguité (For an Ethic of Ambiguity),*
> Paris, Gallimard, 1946,

and a report published in *Les temps modernes,* "L'Amerique au jour le jour," she is the author of a play, *Les bouches inutiles,* played at the Bouffes du Nord theatre in 1945, and of several novels, unequally interesting, but all intended to corroborate Sartre's philosophical arguments:

> *L'invitée.* Paris, Gallimard, 1943.
> *Le sang des autres (The Blood of the Others).* Lausanne, Marguerat, 1946.
> *Tous les hommes sont mortels.* Paris, Gallimard, 1946.

In *Les temps modernes* last year she published a long paper, "La femme et les mythes," of which we have already spoken.

WORKS OF MERLEAU-PONTY:

Counter to Sartre and Simone de Beauvoir, Merleau-Ponty does not publish literary works; he keeps himself to philosophy. In addition to his principal work:

> *La phénoménologie de la perception,* Paris, NRF, 1946, he has
> published
> *La structure du comportement.* Paris, Alcan, 1943.
> *Humanisme et terreur.* Paris, NRF, Collection les essais, 1947.

A political essay previously appeared in *Les temps modernes* with the title "Le yogi et le prolétaire."

> *Sens et non-sens*. Paris, Nagel, 1948, Collection Pensées, assembles thirteen articles which previously appeared in several reviews.

WORKS OF BATAILLE:

The philosophical essays of G. Bataille which appeared in the NRF are:

> *L'expérience intérieure*. 1943.
> *Le coupable*. Collection les essais.
> *Sur Nietzsche*. 1945.

Other works:

> *L'anus solaire*. Galeries Simon.
> *L'archangélique*. Message.

Besides, since the war, M. Bataille has edited a review, *Critique*.

WORKS OF ALBERT CAMUS:

Novels:

> *L'étranger* (*The Stranger*). Paris, Gallimard, 1942.
> *La peste* (*The Plague*). Paris, Gallimard, 1947.

Plays:

> *Le malentendu* (*Cross Purpose*). Paris, Gallimard, 1944.
> *Caligula* (*Caligula*). Paris, Gallimard, 1944.
> *L'état de siege*. 1948. (Adaptation of *La peste*.)

Philosophical essays:

> *Le mythe de Sisyphe*. Paris, Gallimard, Collection les essais, 1943.
> "Remarques sur la révolte," published in *Existence, 1946*.

Other essays:

> *L'envers et l'endroit*. Paris, Charlot.
> *Noces*. Paris, Charlot, 1945.
> *Le minotaure ou la halte d'Oran*.
> *Lettre à un ami allemand*. Paris, Gallimard, 1945.

BERSGONIANISM AND EXISTENTIALISM

Auguste Cornu[*]

INTRODUCTION

This study of the evolution of French bourgeois thought from the eighteenth to the twentieth centuries, from rationalism to Bergsonianism and existentialism has the last two doctrines as its principal theme. It is written from the point of view of Marxist criticism, which does not deal with an undifferentiated humanity but with a society which is differentiated by the conflicts of classes. Marxist criticism holds that movements of thought can in the last analysis only be explained by the development of economic and social life and hence by the struggles of classes, which constitute the driving force of that development.

Obviously, any attempt to relate an ideological movement to a social and economic movement must avoid the danger of trying mechanically to establish a rigorous parallelism between the two movements; such an effort could not but be arbitrary and false. We should simply strive to show the close but broad connections which tie the development of spiritual life to the development of social life as seen in its class differentiations.

Contemporary French idealist philosophy, whose essential representatives are, first Bergsonianism, and then existentialism, is the ideology of the bourgeoisie, which was revolutionary during the rise of the class and conservative during its dominance, becomes reactionary during the phase of decadence, a phase marked by the disintegration of the capitalist system, more and more deeply undermined by economic and social contradictions. Bourgeois ideology no longer tends to change or to justify the real, but to escape from it.

---

[*] Born in 1888. Until recently, professor of German at the Lycée Buffon in Paris. At present, professor of literature and comparative civilization at the University of Leipzig. Author of two theses for the doctor's degree, *La jeunesse de K. Marx,* and *M. Hess et la gauche hégélienne,* and also of *Utopisme et marxisme* (1937), *K. Marx et la revolution de 1848 en France, La Pensée,* (1948), and *K. Marx et la pensée moderne* (1948).

I. RATIONALISM

Ideology of the Rising Bourgeoisie

The ideology of the rising bourgeoisie was rationalism, which by rejecting the notion of a preestablished, immovable, eternal order enabled the bourgeoisie to combat the feudal regime in the name of reason, and to set up against it a new regime embodying its class aims.

Rationalism found its highest expression in the French Encyclopedic movement, which was formed at a moment when the bourgeoisie's action assumed a revolutionary character, as is shown in its emphasis on the idea of progress, in the philosophical and scientific realm as well as in the economic, political, and social fields.

Since it was a justification of the economic and social regime of the bourgeoisie, rationalism could not rise above the contradiction inherent in the capitalist system, between a mode of production which is increasingly collective, which brings men together in their work and integrates them by means of their work into their natural and social environment, and on the other hand an individualistic mode of appropriation which isolates them and sets them against each other.

This rationalism was therefore unable to arrive at the conception of an effective and total integration into the world, and remained essentially dualist, subordinating either nature to mind or mind to nature.

Meanwhile, the development of production, in virtue of man's increasing integration in the world and the increasingly powerful action it enables him to exert on the world, implied the surmounting of the dualistic rationalism which contraposes man to nature, mind to matter, and its replacement by an organic conception of the world.

This step forward was made by the German idealist philosophy, in particular Hegel's, which rejects the mechanist conception of the world and considers it instead from the point of view of its organic change and its historical development. But Hegel, like the rationalists, remained within the framework of the capitalist system, and thus was unable to get around its inherent contradiction. His organic conception of the world is only imaginary, reducing the totality of the real to the mind, and thus integrating man in an illusory world.

Subsequently, Karl Marx, giving voice to the aims of the proletariat and no longer to those of the bourgeoisie, surmounts this contradiction by showing how effective integration of man into the world and into the historical process is achieved by concrete practical activity.

II. POSITIVISM

Ideology of the Bourgeoisie when Dominant

Upon taking power, the bourgeoisie ceases to be revolutionary and becomes conservative. This tendency is accentuated as the development of the new system of production entailed the formation of a stronger and more numerous proletariat, which becomes an increasing menace to the bourgeoisie.

Rationalism, because of its revolutionary character, now becomes a danger to the bourgeoisie, and not a tool. The bourgeoisie abandons it; condemns progress on the social plane; and tries to restore it to the technical and scientific field where it is indispensable to the development of production.

An ideology which suits the bourgeoisie's new class interests now replaces rationalism. The essential expression of this ideology is Comte's positivism at first, and then the scientism inspired by positivism. The characteristic property of positivism and scientism is their attitude toward the sciences; they want to help science to advance, while trying to prevent conclusions being drawn from it which might be prejudicial to the class interests of the bourgeoisie.

In contrast to rationalism, positivism studies reality in its historical development; but since its bourgeois inspiration keeps it from seeing contradictions as the essential sources of changes in reality, it gives historical development a continuous and regular cast, an evolutionary character, which is explained by a mechanist determinism.

Positivism influenced a whole series of thinkers and scientists during the course of the nineteenth century: Renan, Taine, Claude Bernard, Durkheim, who strove to give a scientific form to the whole of human knowledge, but were, like Comte, conservatives on the political and social plane. This conservatism, which inclines them toward finalism, tends to bring their ideas closer to the ideas of objective idealism which, as the ideological expression of the initial stage of the bourgeoisie's decadence, succeeds positivism.

III. IDEALISM

Ideology of the Bourgeoisie in Decadence

a. *Objective Idealism.*

The scare of 1848 was followed by a period of relative stability which lasted up to the last third of the nineteenth century. Thereafter the capitalist system was more and more deeply undermined by the aggravated crises, class struggles, and national rivalries which mark the era of imperialism. Menaced in its position as dominant class by the rise of the proletariat, and losing its faith in progress because of the exacerbation of crises, the bourgeoisie turns from being conservative to being reactionary.

This evolution is expressed on the philosophical level by an agnosticism which takes the form of a sweeping critique of the value and significance of science. After Renouvier and Cournot, who show the impossibility of obtaining a strictly scientific conception of the universe because of the large part of liberty and chance it contains, Ribot and Janet stress the outstanding role that the subconscious plays in the mental life. While Poincaré brings out the conventional nature of the great theories enunciated by the mathematicians and physicists of the nineteenth century, Hannequin and Meyerson show that the phenomena of nature cannot be reduced to science, because of the inability of the mind to reduce the totality of the real to the quantitative and measurable.

Skepticism as to science is accompanied by an evolution from positivism to objective idealism, which is considered a surer means of defense against the revolutionary steps forward taken by science and history. This transition from positivism to an idealism which asserts the priority of consciousness over existence marks a complete turnabout in the bourgeoisie's attitude toward reality; for when it was in the ascendant along with empiricism and materialism, it asserted the priority of existence over consciousness. The transition made by Lachelier and Boutroux records on the ideological level the movement of the bourgeoisie away from concrete reality.

Lachelier considers spirit as the essential reality and makes it the creative element of the world, which thus appears as ruled and directed in its evolution not by a mechanical causality, by determination, but by a reason which is conscious of aims to be reached, by finalism. Inasmuch as there is no impersonal consciousness, independent of the human mind, Lachelier, like all objective idealists, and in particular Hegel, is forced to resort to a myth to explain the existence and formation of the world. But in Hegel, who gave a revolutionary interpretation of the development of mind and the world, the myth was charged with all historical concrete reality; whereas in Lachelier, who divorces the idea from the concretely real, the myth degenerates into an abstract and empty notion.

The same idea of liberty, conceived of metaphysically in the framework of an absolute opposition between free will and determinism, and implying a finalist conception of evolution, dominates Boutroux's doctrine. He too considers the spiritual reality as the essential factor and thereby reduces the development of the world, in what is fundamental in it, to the development of ideas. Boutroux rises up against mechanism, which undertakes to reduce all reality to quantitative and measurable elements, and against determinism, which undertakes to explain all change by a strict causality, by a chain of necessity which it only establishes by an arbitrary restriction of the data of experience. In point of fact, determinism applies only to inorganic matter; the nearer one gets to life and thought, the more necessity and causality yield to a finality which makes the world evolve toward liberty.

This disjunction between concrete reality and the idea is more strongly accentuated in the idealist philosophers who come after Lachelier and Boutroux, and whose doctrines mark the step from objective idealism to subjective spiritualism, a step which is determined both by the need for freeing the mind from its impersonal character, which makes it impossible to explain the individuality of human consciousness, and also by the intensification of the contradictions of capitalism, leading the decadent bourgeoisie to detach itself more and more from reality, an isolation expressed on the ideological level by the opposition set up between the mind and concrete reality.

This last rupture is effected by neo-Kantianism, which gives phenomenology a new meaning. For, whereas Kant held that knowledge, although relative, corresponds to the universal laws of the world, neo-Kantian idealist philosophy makes use of phenomenology to reduce essential reality to the thinking subject. Going further than Kant, these philosophers (Blondel, Hamelin, Brunschvicg) take their inspiration from Hegel in solving the problem of time, the fundamental problem set for modern thought by the passage from the static to the dynamic conception of the world.

But Hegel had solved the problem by using his conception of the historical and dialectical development of the world to attain a new type of rational thought adapted to the notion of time, while these philosophers dissociate the essential themes of the Hegelian philosophy: action, dialectics, and history, and give them a metaphysical and absolute character; and are therefore unable to arrive at a rational solution of the basic problem that each one sets himself.

Blondel, by separating action from concrete practical activity, reduces the problem of action to that of the will, considered by itself: to be is to act, not in accordance with the data of concrete reality and science, but according to the postulates of a higher will, implying as final cause the existence of God who alone gives life a meaning.

Brunschvicg treats the problem of history outside of dialectics and thus reduces history to the progress of consciousness considered by itself, apart from practical activity and economic and social development. He thus proceeds from Hegelian objective idealism to a subjective idealism.

Hamelin on the other hand treats the problem of dialectics outside of history and so deforms it. He replaces the dialectics of contradictories, which implies the surmounting of each successive stage, by a dialectics of correlative contraries which are complementary; therewith he suppresses the active element in contradiction. Again, by reducing dialectics to a conceptual development which issues in an existential reality, i. e., a personal consciousness which is self-sufficient and beyond which there is nothing, he, like Brunschvicg, passes from objective idealism to a subjective idealism which is not very far from Bergson's subjective spiritualism. [1]

b. Bergsonianism.

The transition from objective idealism to subjective spiritualism was made by Bergson, who thus broke the trail for existentialism. Even more than objective idealism this spiritualism is the ideological expression of the decadent bourgeoisie, which feels that it is less and less master of the forces of production and so turns more and more from concrete practical activity, escaping from reality by turning in on itself.

To the man engaged in action which integrates him into the world, Bergson contrasts the individual considered only as such, reduced to an Ego whose activity is confined to the spiritual domain and outside of concrete reality.

Like the idealist philosophers who preceded him, Bergson is inspired by Kant's phenomenology to reduce essential reality to the knowing subject. He divorces this subject from its object, concrete reality, and out of all reality retains only the states of consciousness and the activity of the Ego, which he makes the manifestation of a creative force, an *élan vital*.

Bergson separates human life from reality and concrete activity, which seem to him secondary and superficial; he replaces rational knowledge of the world by direct perception of the continuous unfolding of life, by the immediate intuition of what is lived through. The anti-intellectual and

---

1. For these philosophers, cf. H. Mougin's penetrating study in *La sainte famille existentialiste*, pp. 44, 56 (see bibliography for all works cited.).

anti-scientific offensive is reinforced by a severer criticism of intelligence and science, which he regards as incapable of grasping life, which cannot be reduced to the abstractions of thought and physical mechanism. He rejects deterministic rationalism, which considers the word from a mechanical and spatial point of view.

The intelligence applies to a practical activity. It is a superficial form of the spirit, with a utilitarian character; its function is to transform the representations of objects with determinate and stable forms, located in space, into concepts which serve as tools for practical activity. It gives thought a spatial form, fixing it in things; and conceives of space and movement only as functions of space, by giving them a linear configuration which decomposes them and immobilizes them in juxtaposition. Rendered incapable thereby of seizing the living and moving reality in its fluidity and continuity, the intelligence reduces that reality to inert matter, takes up a materialistic and deterministic point of view in order to study matter and arrives, along with the science founded on it, at a universal mechanism, mutilating and deforming whatever has life.

Since intelligence and science leave nothing of reality but the quantitative, material, inert elements, Bergson opposes to them a vitalist conception of the world, which he borrows from reactionary German romanticism and which reduces the essence of reality to the life of the spirit.[2] This life is held to be a pure effusion of the *élan vital*, of the deeper Ego; it is located, not in space and the objective time which serve as framework for material reality and as basis for rational thought, but in subjective time, in the time which is lived through and is identical with the duration of states of consciousness.

To seize a spiritual life unfolding in its indivisible continuity, we must depart from abstract intelligence, which separates the states of consciousness, deforms them by the reduction of the qualitative to the quantitative and freezes them in stability and uniformity; we must penetrate, by a sort of inversion of consciousness, into the inmost recesses of the Ego and arrive at the immediate intuition of duration, of the unending unfolding of states of consciousness.

Retaining nothing of reality by what is experienced, Bergson seeks first of all to recover the states of consciousness in their original purity, qualitative heterogeneity and continuity, which distinguish them from

---

2. On the different aspects of the irrationalist trend in contemporary philosophy, in particular Bergson's, cf. A. Cuvillier, *Les courants irrationalistes de la philosophie contemporaine*, pp. 56, 58-62, 63-70, 71-76, 78 f.; and G. Lukács, *Existentialisme ou marxisme*, pp. 58, 64.

homogeneous and discontinuous concrete reality. He locates these states not in space and objective time, which are composed of juxtapositions, but in duration, which is indistinguishable from the flow of spiritual life.

Duration is the living unity of the totality of states of consciousness which interpenetrate and fuse, unceasingly changing. Beneath the superficial ego, strained for action, it shows us an inner ego which constitutes the essence of the individual and gives him his personality.

Duration is preserved indefinitely in memory, whose constant connection between present and past insures the continuity of human life. Memory is not localized in the brain which, being oriented toward action, uses only recollections which are useful in active life; memory forms the infinity of the subconscious, the seat of the inner ego, which reveals itself in those moments when consciousness, losing interest in action, possesses itself and relaxes.

Memory, while inserted in the present by means of recollections, reaches out toward the future by means of duration, which is an infinite development of our ego. This development appears in the form of the ebullition of the *élan vital* which, instead of ending up in immobility, as in the plant, or in stagnation, as in the animal, has a creative character in man, by reason of the freedom of choice peculiar to consciousness, by means of which man triumphs over the inertia of matter and frees himself from determinism, to become master of his destiny.

To be free, we must turn from the world of things, clear ourselves of the concepts created in their image which bind us to them, and merge in the *élan vital* which indefinitely renews our ego in an act of spontaneous creation. This implies going beyond the intelligence which is adapted to an inorganic matter made up of immobility of repetition, and hence cannot comprehend the moving, the living; it implies too a recourse to intuition which enters into the very life of the spirit and makes it possible to seize it immediately and to follow its infinite development.

This intimate contact with the experienced, with the pure welling-up of our life, enables us to attain the absolute by way of the identity established both between the knowing subject and the object known and between the Ego and the universal life. For intuition, in making us penetrate into the innermost regions of our being, does not lock us up within the narrow limits of our ego; it gives us access to the source of universal life and thus expands our ego to all creation.

It is to this totality that the *élan vital* tends; at the same time that it disperses into a multiplicity of individuals, it passes beyond them to merge with the creative evolution which gives rise to the world by the union of individual energies.

This passage and this union are realized at once by art, which liberates us from action and reveals to us the full life of the spirit; by morality, whose imperative becomes more and more universal in character; and by religion, whose highest form is found in the great mystics who live the experience of the divine.

By this philosophy of the experienced, which derives from the vitalist world conception of the German romantic philosophy, especially that of Schelling, Bergson completes his criticism of deterministic rationalism, which considers the world in its mechanical and spatial aspect; by this criticism he passes from objective idealism to a subjective spiritualism.

Hegelianism and Marxism had based their criticism of mechanistic rationalism on the connection between the notions of space and of time. This made it possible to consider concrete reality in its dialectical development and to adapt a new mode of thought to this conception of the world. Bergson, however, bases his criticism on the opposition which he sets up between objective time, which serves as the framework for the development of the concrete reality, and subjective time, lived-through time, duration; this opposition leads him to limit human life to the succession of states of consciousness. Preferring instinct and the immediately experienced, he belittles intelligence and reason, and denies science true knowledge of the world. This latter capacity he transfers to the intuition, an extra-rational faculty which enables us immediately to grasp the living flux. Whereas knowledge is the result of an effort of the intelligence which passes beyond the data of sense and the contradictions inherent in the real to give a rational interpretation of the world and life by raising the sensible to the intelligible, Bergson expects intuition to resolve the contradictions by making them live, and thereby he transforms knowledge into a sentimental revery.

At the same time that he criticizes intelligence and science, Bergson condemns the practical activity which turns man from his true destiny and prevents him from grasping, within himself, in the intuition of his states of consciousness, the *élan vital* which makes him commune with universal life.

Separating human life in this way from concrete reality and practical activity, and reducing it to the experiencing of duration, to the continual flux of states of consciousness, Bergson at the last resorts, like every idealist philosopher, to the myth which assigns mental constructs the role of reality in explaining the world.

Despite his efforts to go beyond traditional philosophy, which he censures for its abstractness, and reach a philosophy of the concrete, he does not work free from abstractions and, like classical psychology, he merely generalizes such abstractions as the qualitative, duration, the *élan vital,* seeking to put life into them by plunging them into the immediately experienced, and applying them uniformly to all individuals.

Coming down from these abstract generalities to particular lives, Bergson professes to explain psychic reality by means of them; but since he leaves unspecified that which is actually experienced by the individual, and considers only the way in which the psychic states are experienced, he comes finally, not to the concretely real, the individual grasped in his particular determinateness, but to abstraction, the Ego conceived in its generality. [3]

To this philosophy of the immediately experienced and the *élan vital,* which makes the climb to life the great law of the world, there corresponds a conception of liberty which considers it not dialectically, in its connections with determinism, represented by man's necessary relations with his natural and social environment, but metaphysically, in isolation.[4] Liberty, identified with the welling-up of the inner Ego to Life, takes on an absolute character; it is realized totally in each individual thanks to the possibility each has of determining himself autonomously; it becomes a property of every consciousness, which to be free has only to turn from the world of things and grasp the creative drive within itself. Because Bergson considers life and liberty in this abstract way, he is unable to lay the foundations of a genuine morality, since the purpose of morality is to regulate men's behavior and thereby to modify their way of life. His morality is established not for man but about man. It lies outside concrete action, and its object is the pure activity of the Ego, something which has nothing in common with practical activity guided by a rational will. This morality is based on an abstract and absurd liberty, set up in contrast to a rigid determinism; like life, in which the unconscious holds sway, it has an irrational character. Since its aim is no man's effective liberation but a total and unreal autonomy of the Ego, taken absolutely, it actually comes to terms with the worst slavery to the extent that consciousness accepts it;

---

3. On the abstract and mythical character of the Bergsonian psychology, see G. Politzer, *Le bergsonisme:une mystification philosophique,* in particular pp. 28, 32.

4. G. Lukács, *op. cit.,* p. 69.

this morality thus constitutes an indirect justification of the established order.[5]

All in all, this philosophy, which culminates in a speculative phenomenology, contemplative of reality, and in a counterfeit of life and progress, by transforming abstractions into realities which determine the course of human existence, this philosophy testifies on the ideological plane to the intensification of the bourgeoisie's decadence. The bourgeoisie, confronted by the aggravation of the economic and social contradictions which had led to the first World War and ended by seriously weakening its own position, tends to escape from a reality it is less and less able to cope with, and to which it can only oppose the abstract imperative of its will.

By its passage from objective idealism to subjective spiritualism and by the basic irrationalism to which it leads both on the conceptual and the moral levels, Bergsonianism serves as a prelude to existentialism, whose coming it prepares by the substitution of the individual subject for the transcendental subject of idealism as expression of essential reality.

c. *Existentialism.*

Existentialism succeeded Bergsonianism at a time when the breaking-down of the capitalist system had been accelerated by the two World Wars. Existentialism is the expression on the ideological plane of the failure of the bourgeoisie, no longer able rationally to manage the forces of production because of the increasing aggravation of the internal contradictions which dislocate the capitalist system and prevent it from working within the framework of liberty of production and exchange which are of its essence.

The contradictions are accompanied by a concentration of capital. As a result, capitalism develops toward monopoly, which has the effect of assuring the supremacy of the United States, the country with the greatest concentration of capital. This supremacy is expressed on the ideological plane by pragmatism, the apologetics of utilitarian action, while in other countries, in particular those conquered and war-impoverished, the decomposition of the capitalist system increasingly takes the form in the bourgeoisie, especially in the lower bourgeoisie, hopelessly ruined by competition and inflation, of resignation to defeat.

The loss of the solid economic base which had previously assured its class dominion arouses in this bourgeoisie, along with a more serious

---

5. G. Politzer, *op. cit.,* pp. 70, 80.

doubt in the value of reality and a distrust of it, the desire to get away from it.

Bergsonianism had already contrasted the concrete man, engaged in practical activity, with abstract individuality, the Ego, whose action is essentially restricted to the spiritual domain; now this doubt, this distrust, this escape from reality find their final expression in existentialism.

Existentialism first developed in Germany, and especially after the first World War, which ruined the German petty bourgeoisie; after the second World War, it became the favorite philosophy of the French bourgeoisie, and in general of the bourgeoisie of all the countries in which this class had been ruined.

The scope of this article does not allow an analysis of all the forms which existentialism has taken in France. We shall confine ourselves to a brief study of the doctrine of J.-P. Sartre, which has the most influence there.

Sartre does not show how man integrates himself in the external world which he adapts to his needs, transforming himself in the process; nor does he use the fact of this adaptation to connect the development of knowledge with the development of experience, the development of liberty with the progressive liberation from instinct and the external world. Instead, Sartre separates man from his natural and social environment and opposes him to it, making of him an isolated individual, an absolute subject with his *raison d'être* in himself.

This philosophy of the subject is based, as was Bergsonianism, on a phenomenalism which starts from the proposition that nothing is given to man outside of his subjective impressions; it reduces life and the world to states of consciousness experienced by the self-existent Ego enclosed in its subjectivity.

Sartre pushed phenomenalism to its extreme, thereby giving ideological expression to the aggravation of the capitalist system's decomposition. It is not enough for him to deny all substantive reality to the external world; he finds the Ego itself has an essentially phenomenal character, and deprives it of all substance, reducing it thus not to the inner Ego, as Bergson did, but to Nothingness.

The point of departure of this philosophy of Nothingness is the opposition which J. P. Sartre sets up between essence, *viz.,* an ensemble of properties common to beings of the same species, and existence, which is a particular and original mode of being. In a reaction against the conceptualism which reduces man to an essence of the type, he subordinates the essence in man to existence, which constitutes his true reality.

In contrast to other beings, whose existence is preceded and determined by the essence which they reproduce indefinitely, man is not determined by his essence, which is only virtual in him and only becomes real through existence. Sartre, thus dissociating existence and essence, postulates existence without essence, man, being-for-himself, on one hand; and on the other, essence without existence, being-in-itself, which is absolute being, immobile, without relations.

This opposition of the for-himself and the in-itself, conceived metaphysically in the absolute, leads Sartre, in order to justify the existence of each of the terms of the opposition, to adopt a double idealism: an objective idealism of the in-itself which enables him, surmounting subjective spiritualism, to attribute at least a relative value to external reality and the transcendental Ego; and a subjective idealism of the for-itself, which enables him to transform the transcendental and impersonal subject of objective idealism into an existential subject. But Sartre's philosophy really tends to Nothingness; and in adopting this double idealism he actually does away with both by a total relativism which denies the absolute value both of inwardness and externality.

For, since he attributes an objective reality to the external world which exists outside us, but which we know only in its phenomenal aspect, he replaces the reality of things by the objectivity of phenomena, which do not reveal to the subject the essential being as identified with the transcendental subject. Rejecting objective idealism by stressing the phenomenal character of the external world, he rejects subjective idealism as well by showing that the phenomenon is relative not only to the subject of knowledge but also to the transcendental subject. [6]

In virtue of this total relativism, the world and man lose all substantiality. The world is but an absurd chaos before the intervention of consciousness. It only takes on significance and attains existence by way of the Ego, which transforms it into a phenomenal world, which for us is the true world; and the world accordingly depends on us, for each of us chooses it in what it signifies for him, not in what it is in itself, which explains why the world varies according to the particular ends each one sets himself.

The essential reality is thus the single ego, being-for-itself, consciousness conceived as consciousness of self, freely determining itself by a con-

---

6. H. Mougin, *op. cit.*, pp. 118-122, 166 f.

stant choice which prevents it from freezing in a final attitude and enables it to realize its essence by the continual creation of its existence.

No more than the world does the Ego, being-for-itself, constitute a substantive reality; like the world, it has a phenomenal nature and is identified with the spurting into life by which it posits itself as existent. Consciousness, in effect, exists only to the extent that it reveals itself to itself, and affirms itself by a choice; as its choice always envisages an object which is foreign to it, it appears empty and without content, and so can define itself only from the point of view of nothingness, as consciousness of not being that which it knows.

To the existential subject, the for-itself, reduced to phenomenal consciousness, Sartre contraposes being-in-itself, the transcendental subject which remains identical to itself, with no reason for being, without either cause or goal. The existential subject, for-itself, devoid of all substantive reality and a prey to the anxiety which the feeling of nothingness arouses in it, continually seeks to escape this anxiety and nothingness, to merge with the transcendental subject and attain the reality of the in-itself by becoming a for-itself in-itself. But this attempt necessarily is doomed to failure, for the for-itself, which presupposes a break or fissure with the in-itself, cannot merge with it without abolishing itself. [7]

Sartre's absolute subjectivism condemns man to an absurd existence, and reduces the subject to a tortured consciousness, in despair because of its pursuit of a goal which remains inaccessible to it, and making the wretchedness of consciousness the very essence of existence; existence thereby has the character of a pointless drama.

This wretchedness of consciousness, this pathos of despair, this tragedy of an uncaused and purposeless existence, which constitutes the basis of the existential subject, is a translation of the drama of the isolated man of decadent bourgeois society, who, up against a world which abandons him and which he no longer recognizes, rejects that world, declaring it absurd, and, in order to escape the anxiety which is crushing him, seeks refuge in isolation and inwardness. [8]

In Bergson, this turning-in of man upon himself enables him to reach his inner Ego; in Sartre, it only leads him face to face with Nothingness, which thus becomes the basic category, determining man's attitude toward the external world and toward himself.

Sartre exhibits even more clearly than Bergsonianism the decomposi-

7. H. Mougin, *op. cit.*, pp. 147 f.
8. J. Kanapa, *L'existentialisme n'est pas un humanisme*, pp. 65 f.

tion of bourgeois society after the course of history has deprived it of any reason for existence and any future prospects. Sartre makes this concept of Nothingness universal, taking all concrete content out of human life and the world, and making Nothingness the general law of existence.[9] Existence reduces to a purely formal activity, the exercise of a liberty of choice which is not motivated by anything, is located in the absolute, outside of concrete activity, and answers on the plane of action to a conception of the world expressed by nothingness and absurdity. As choice has no object and no aim except for the individual who chooses, and as it is unpredictable anyway, the result is that human activity has a subjective and arbitrary nature, and action loses all its social import.

The only distinction one can draw among actions derives not from their object and efficacy, but from the subjective interest which determined them, the intention which attended their being chosen. They thus become equivalent practically, and this equivalence leads to an indifferentism and thence to a fatalism which, far from setting man free, rather bends him to every servitude.[10]

This morality of intention thus eventuates in a nihilism based on the fundamental irrationality of existence, which like every irrationalism finds its natural and necessary conclusions in fideism. In Sartre this is seen in the aspiration of the for-itself to rise to the in-itself, an aspiration which is but a philosophical variant of the religious theme of man's return to God.

In modern society this hope is an expression of man's desire to recover his alienated essence. Sartre, by assuming that the project cannot be carried out, makes the alienation of the individual, which is a social phenomenon peculiar to the capitalist system, into a metaphysical and eternal phenomenon.[11] He thus condemns man to a futile effort to realize his essence, to an illusory and absurd activity which deprives life of all meaning and so of necessity inclines man to renunciation, solitude, and despair.

This radical failure in which individual life culminates, and which Sartre sums up in the aphorism, "Every existent is born, lives and dies without cause and without reason," is accompanied by a parallel failure in social life. Reducing social relations to relations among individuals as such, he shows that every Ego by its projects reduces other men to the role of means or tools, and in turn is reduced to that role by others;

9. G. Lukács, *op. cit.*, pp. 88, 103.
10. J. Kanapa, *op. cit.*, pp. 70, 74.
11. J. Kanapa, *op. cit.*, pp. 87-90.

therewith a permanent conflict among individuals is engendered which constitutes the very center of social life.[12]

By this conception, which is a restatement of the struggle among individuals which competition gives rise to in capitalist society, Sartre arrives at an individualist anarchism which he seeks to rise above by trying to coordinate the existence of the for-itself with that of the in-itself and harmonizing the individual act with collective activity.

In his work *L'existentialism est un humanisme,* he makes the attempt to give his existentialism the character of humanism, proclaiming rules for action inspired by the Kantian ethics, which declares that every man be treated not as a means but as an end.[13] This existentialism, now no longer oriented toward an evasion of reality but toward action, still remains profoundly anti-humanist, in view of the fact that it continues to be based on a conception of isolated man and a world which sums up to Nothingness and absurdity, so that it can ascribe only a useless and futile character to action.

True humanism integrates man in his natural and social milieu and conceives action as the concrete practical activity which enables man to transform this milieu by adapting it to his needs. Existentialism makes man an isolated individual, and human activity the expression of an arbitrary and absolute will; this activity consequently is subordinated to a subjective intentional morality, whereas what is important for humanism is not the intention but the efficacy of the act, the goal to attain and the degree to which it has been attained.

Sartre's existentialism thus appears, in sum, as the ideological expression of the decadent bourgeoisie at the period when capitalism is breaking up. He translates this decadence into the escape from the real, the isolation of the individual, and the affirmation of the Ego's absolute autonomy and superiority to the world, which it can mould at its pleasure. Thus he combines (and this is what constitutes the originality of the system) all the characteristic traits of the ideology of decadent classes, an ideology marked by an egocentrism expressed either in an escape from reality by way of dream, renunciation, or death, or in a utopian voluntarism which tends arbitrarily to impose its rules on the world.

By a phenomenalism recalling that of Schopenhauer, he reduces the external world to a simple appearance masking an absurd reality; over against this world he erects the Ego as the only true reality, as Stirner

---

12. J. Kanapa, *op. cit.,* p. 79.
13. Sartre, *op. cit.,* "Nothing can be good for me without being so for others" (p. 25); "I am obliged to wish the liberty of others in the act of wishing liberty" (p. 83).

before him had done in *The Ego and His Own;* and finally, following Nietzsche, he affirms the possibility for the Ego of dominating and transforming the world by the assertion of a will to power posited in the absolute.

But since he speaks for a class which has lost its reason for existence, he deprives both the world and the Ego of all substantive reality; thus he makes Nothingness the basic relation of man with himself and with the world, and reduces the will to power to a freedom of choice without reason and without goal, to a useless activity in an absurd world.

In Sartre the tendency of idealism to impoverish reality reaches its highest point. He reduces concrete reality to abstractions even more than Bergson does; like Bergson, he resorts to the myth in his explanation of the world, and makes of these abstractions—the in-itself, the for-itself, choice, anxiety, and Nothingness—realities which determine the course of human life.

But while in Bergson this myth leads to the assertion of an inner Ego constituting the essence of man, in Sartre it ends in the total negation of all substantive reality, in the Nothingness of an absurd world and of a human existence devoted to the vain search for a goal which cannot be reached.

*   *   *

This brief account of the evolution of bourgeois thought from rationalism to existentialism shows that it follows exactly the economic and social development of the bourgeoisie.

A rising and therefore revolutionary class in the eighteenth century, it finds its ideological expression in rationalism, which has a revolutionary character, as well on the economic and scientific levels as on the political and social level.

A dominant and therefore conservative class after the Revolution of 1789, it finds its ideological expression in positivism, which remains revolutionary on the economic and scientific plane, but is politically and socially conservative.

The accentuation of the economic and social contradictions in the last third of the nineteenth century evokes a growing doubt in the idea of progress, the reality of the sensible world, and the value of science, a doubt which batters down the foundations of positivism and furthers the evolution of bourgeois thought toward idealism.

Idealism, which corresponds to the decadent phase of the bourgeoisie, first takes the form of objective idealism, which undertakes to bring under the spirit a reality which the bourgeois feels is escaping from its domination and guidance.

The transformation, in Bergson, of objective idealism into a subjective spiritualism which impoverishes reality even more, reducing it essentially to the Ego, reflects, on the ideological plane, both the increased powerlessness of the bourgeoisie to control a system being crushed by the pre-World War I contradictions, and its tendency to escape from a world which has become hostile to it.

Finally, the breakdown of the capitalist system, accelerated by World War II, finds its ideological expression in the existentialism of J.-P. Sartre, who deprives both external world and Ego of all substantive reality and thus reduces both to absurdity and Nothingness.

SELECTED BIBLIOGRAPHY

Parodi, D. *La philosophie contemporaine en France*. Paris, Alcan, 1919.

Cuvillier, A. *Les courants irrationalistes dans la philosophie contemporaine*. Les cahiers rationalistes.

Politzer, G. *Le bergsonisme: une mystification philosophique*. Paris, Editions sociales, 1947.

Mougin, H. *La sainte famille existentialiste*. Paris, Editions sociales, 1947.

Lefebvre, Henri. *L'existentialisme*. Paris, Editions du Sagittaire, 1946.

Kanapa, J. *L'existentialisme n'est pas un humanisme*. Paris, Editions sociales, 1947.

Lukács, G. *Existentialisme ou marxisme?* Paris, Nagel, 1948.

PRINCIPAL PUBLICATIONS ON THE PHILOSOPHY OF THE SCIENCES BROUGHT OUT IN FRANCE SINCE 1900*

*André Lalande***

We include, here, under the title, Philosophy of the Sciences, (1) studies concerning the nature, structure, and method of the sciences, to which strict French usage gives the name, "epistemology" (in the etymological meaning of this word and contrary to English usage which employs it to designate theory of knowledge); (2) philosophical studies concerning mathematics and the physical sciences, which, through a rather regrettable usage, are intended when the word is unmodified, as in Academy of the Sciences, Faculty of the Sciences, and the like. It would be impossible to include everything which touches upon the "moral sciences," for this bibliography would then have to cover almost all philosophy.

In the second division, yet another distinction must be made, between questions relative to the constitution or method of these sciences, taken separately, this being a specification of epistemology as defined above; and attempts at philosophical synthesis of the "results" of any particular class of scientific research. But we have not felt it possible to mention

---

* Professor Gaston Bachelard, who was to have written an article on Philosophy of Science in France, was prevented from doing so by accidental circumstances, to our great regret. The time not having permitted asking another writer to take his place, we are presenting herewith a bibliography of works which would have provided the materials. It has been contributed by Professor André Lalande.

** Born in 1867. Agrégé de Philosophie, 1888; Docteur ès-Lettres, Sorbonne, 1899. Formerly Director of Philosophical Studies at the Sorbonne. Member of the Institute of France. Besides the works mentioned in the bibliographies, he is the author of: *Précis raisonné de morale pratique*, 1907; *La psychologie des jugements de valeur*, 1929; and many papers in the *Revue philosophique, Revue de métaphysique et de morale, The Philosophical Review*, etc.

these separately, for reasons which will be easy to understand, as the same works often include these two classes of considerations.

This bibliography is far from being exhaustive: we have confined it to those works or articles which seemed to us most characteristic, or those which we thought were of particular interest on some special point. It does not include works of pure logic, such as, for example, *Le problème logique de l'induction,* by J. Nicod; or philosophical researches upon any particular point in the history of the sciences such as *Études galiléennes* by M. A. Koyré. Finally, it comprises only the publications of French authors, or of foreign authors but written in French and published in France. In the latter case they are indicated by the letter, (E).

The works of each author are put together in the same paragraph, and these are arranged chronologically, beginning with the date of the first work cited.

Abbreviations:

> Act.—*Actualités scientifiques,* published by Hermann.
> Bull.—*Bulletin de la Société française de philosophie,* published by Armand Colin.
> R.M.M.—*Revue de métaphysique et de morale,* Armand Colin.
> R. Ph.—*Revue philosophique,* published first by Alcan, later by Presses.
> Presses—*"Les Presses Universitaires de France."*

GENERAL QUESTIONS

Poincaré, Henri, *La science et l'hypothèse* (Science and Hypothesis), Paris, Flammarion, 1902; *La valeur de la science* (*The Value of Science*), *ibid.,* 1906; *Science et méthode* (*Science and Method*), *ibid.,* 1908; *Dernières pensées* (*Last Thoughts*), *ibid.,* 1913. Collections of articles brought out in the last years of the nineteenth century and the first years of the twentieth. They exerted an influence of the first importance, (1) by bringing out the role of "conventions" and convenience in the mathematical and physical sciences; (2) by creating a lively interest in the critique of the sciences and by attenuating the character of absolutely true knowledge which had been attributed to them by "scientism" in the preceding period; (3) by encouraging professional scholars, even without special philosophical training, to publish their reflections on their own science.

Le Roy, Edouard, *Un positivisme nouveau* (*A New Positivism*),

R.M.M., 1901; *Sur la logique de l'invention* (*The Logic of Invention*), R.M.M., 1905. Reprinted, revised and completed, in *La pensée intuitive,* tome II (*Intuitive Thought,* Vol. II.); *Invention et vérification* (*Invention and Verification*), Paris, Boivin, 1930. Belongs to the same movement of critique of the sciences, and is, moreover, related to Bergsonism. Discussion of belief in the rationality and absolute objectivity of the sciences. Cf. below, *Physics,* 1901.

Milhaud, Gaston, *Études sur la pensée scientifique* (*Studies on Scientific Thought*), *Société française de librairie,* 1906. Mainly historical, but the first chapter, "De la science" ("Concerning Science"), which was a communication to the Congress of Geneva in 1904, has wide import. The author had previously published an *Essai sur les conditions et les limites de la certitude logique* (*Essay on the Conditions and Limits of Logical Certainty*), and a collection of articles, *Le Rationnel* (*The Rational*), Alcan, 1894 and 1898. All these works are inspired, on the whole, with the same relativistic spirit as those of the two preceding authors.

Picard, Émile, *La science moderne* (*Modern Science*), Paris, Flammarion, 1905.

Lalande, André, *Lectures sur la philosophie des sciences* (*Readings on the Philosophy of the Sciences*), Paris, Hachette, 1907. (A first edition had appeared in 1893). Personal studies, serving as framework for numerous texts from scholars. Republished in fourteen revised editions, with a fifteenth in press. *Les théories de l'induction et de l'expérimentation* (*The Theories of Induction and Experimentation*), Paris, Boivin, 1929. Historical, with theoretical and critical conclusions, chapters XI and XII. *Les illusions évolutionnistes* (*Evolutionistic Illusions*), Alcan, 1930. This is a new edition, revised and abridged, of *La dissolution opposée à l'évolution dans les sciences physiques et morales* (*Dissolution Opposed to Evolution in the Physical and Moral Sciences*), Alcan, 1899.

Meyerson, Émile, *Identité et réalité* (*Identity and Reality*), Alcan, 1908; *De l'explication dans les sciences* (*Interpretation in the Sciences*), Payot, 1921. This work is especially characteristic of the ideas of the author. *Le cheminement de la pensée,* 3 vols. (*The Progress of Thought,* 3 vols.), Alcan, 1931. These works are a vigorous and well-documented exposition of the thesis according to which search for the identical and the permanent is the essential motive power of the sciences. Cf. André Metz, *Meyerson, une nouvelle philosophie de la connaissance* (*Meyerson, A New Philosophy of Knowledge*), Alcan, 1934; André Lalande, *L'épistémologie de M. Meyerson et sa portée philosophique* (*Meyerson's Epist-*

emology and Its Philosophical Import), R. Ph., 1922; *Une philosophie de l'intellect* (*A Philosophy of the Intellect*), R. Ph., 1937.

Maugé, F., *L'hypothèse rationaliste et la méthode expérimentale* (*The Rationalistic Hypothesis and Experimental Method*),Alcan, 1909; *La systématisation dans les sciences* (*Systematization in the Sciences*), id., same year. *L'esprit et le réel perçu* (*Mind and Perceived Reality*), Alcan, 1937. Cf. below, *Mathematics, 1937.*

Boutroux, Émile, *Du rapport de la philosophie aux sciences* (*The Relation of Philosophy to the Sciences*), R.M.M., 1911.

Darbon, André, *L'explication mécanique et le nominalisme* (*Mechanical Interpretation and Nominalism*), Alcan, 1910. Now outdistanced, but very interesting for the controversy, which seems not yet to be ended, between the partisans of hypotheses of structure, and the partisans of exclusive research for merely functional laws connecting actually perceived phenomena.

Tannery, Jules, *Science et philosophie* (*Science and Philosophy*), Armand Colin, 1912.

Goblot, E., *Traité de logique* (*Treatise on Logic*), Armand Colin, 1918. Especially chaps. XI-XVIII, on the method of the mathematical and experimental sciences. *Le système des sciences* (*The System of the Sciences*), Armand Colin, 1930. Partial reprint of the subject treated in his *Essai sur la classification des sciences* (*Essay on the Classification of the Sciences*), Alcan, 1898, whose first part contains a remarkable exposition of the relation between the deductive and the experimental method. It abounds with ideas, based upon precise facts, which have become classic in France.

Brunschvicg, Léon, *L'expérience humaine et la causalité physique* (*Human Experience and Physical Causality*), Alcan, 1922. Historical, in the first three parts; but the second half bears upon central questions of the philosophy of the sciences. A work which has exerted a great influence. Cf. by the same author, the Introduction to the collection, *L'orientation actuelle des sciences* (*Present-Day Orientation of the Sciences*), Alcan, 1930. He has, also, done much, in this matter, through his teaching at the Sorbonne, where he was professor of the History of Philosophy from 1909 to 1939.

(E). Dupréel, Eugène, *Convention et raison* (*Convention and Reason*), R.M.M., 1925.

Metzger, H., *Les concepts scientifiques* (*Scientific Concepts*), Alcan, 1926.

Dorolle, M., *Les problèmes de l'induction* (*The Problems of Induction*), Alcan, 1926; *La valeur de l'observation* (*The Value of Observation*), R. Ph., 2 articles, 1945.

Bachelard, G., *Essai sur la connaissance approchée* (*Essay on Approximative Knowledge*), Vrin, 1928; *Le nouvel esprit scientifique* (*The New Scientific Spirit*), Alcan, 1934; *La formation de l'esprit scientifique* (*The Formation of the Scientific Mind*), Vrin, 1938; *Philosophie du non* (*The Philosophy of No*), Presses, 1940. Cf. the last chapter of *Nouvel esprit scientifique* (*The New Scientific Spirit*), which is entitled, "L'épistémologie non-cartésienne" (*Non-Cartesian Epistemology"*). *Le rationalisme appliqué* (*Applied Rationalism*), Presses, 1949. See also below, *Physics,* 1932. These are works which are very much read at the present time, and which exert a great influence. M. Bachelard's philosophy of the sciences is the one which goes the farthest, in the direction of relativity, of dynamism, of continual movement of reconstruction of the sciences. It ties in with the ideas of Boutroux — *De la contingence des lois de la nature,* 1874 (*The Contingency of the Laws of Nature*)—of Poincaré, Milhaud (mentioned above), and Brunschvicg; particularly in that which concerns the mobility of reason. It has, also, a certain kinship with Bergson. Cf. *La pensée et le mouvant* (*Thought and Movement*), Alcan, 1934. The idea of supplying, of "dialectizing" scientific notions plays a large role in it, as well as "psychoanalytic" exploration of scholars' ways of thinking. But this radical mobilism of the reason is compensated, with Bachelard as with Brunschvicg, (1) by the thesis that mathematics is the sole true language of science; (2) by confidence in reason as the supreme authority in scientific and philosophical matters.

Poirier, René, *La philosophie de la science,* Extraits de savants et de philosophes français du XXe siècle (*The Philosophy of Science,* Selections from French Philosophers and Scholars of the Twentieth Century), Alcan, 1926. *Essai sur quelques caractères des notions d'espace et de temps* (*Essay on Some Characters of the Notions of Space and Time*), Vrin, 1931. This work is extremely rich in technical knowledge and in ideas. *Remarques sur la probabilité des inductions* (*Remarks on the Probability of Inductions*), *id.,* same year.. See below, *Mathematics, 1938.*

Picard, Jacques, *Essai sur l'invention dans les sciences,* 2 vols. I. *Les conditions positives de l'invention;* II. *La logique de l'invention* (*Essay on Invention in the Sciences,* 2 vols.: I. *Positive Conditions of Invention;* II. *The Logic of Invention*), Berthod, 1928.

Maritain, J., *La philosophie de la nature* (*The Philosophy of Nature*), Téqui, 1935.

Matisse, G., *La philosophie de la nature, identité du monde et de la connaissance* (*The Philosophy of Nature, Identity of the World and Knowledge*), Alcan, 1938. See below *Biology,* 1947.

Mouy, P., *Logique et philosophie des sciences* (*Logic and Philosophy of the Sciences*), Hachette, 1944. This is a synthetic work, designed for teaching, written by a philosopher and historian of the sciences, very well informed concerning the contemporary scientific movement.

(E). Reymond, Arnold, *Philosophie spiritualiste,* Tome II, 2e partie: *La vérité et l'activité rationnelle de juger;* 4e partie: *Philosophie et sciences.* (*Spiritualistic Philosophy,* Vol. II, 2nd part: *Truth and the Rational Activity of Judging;* 4th part: *Philosophy and Science*), Vrin, 1942. See below, *Mathematics,* 1932.

Vouillemin, Général, *Science et philosophie* (*Science and Philosophy*), Albin Michel, 1945. The author is the principal translator and interpreter, in France, of the works of the *Wiener Kreis* (*Qu'est-ce que le science? La logique de la science et l'école de Vienne,* [*What is Science? The Logic of Science and the Vienna School*]). See, also, below, *Congrès de philosophie scientifique de 1935* (*Congress of Scientific Philosophy of 1935*).

Gérard, R., *Les chemins divers de la connaissance* (*The Diverse Paths of Knowledge*), Alcan, 1945.

Vendryés, Pierre, *L'acquisition de la science* (*The Acquisition of Science*), Albin Michel, 1946.

COLLECTIVE PUBLICATIONS

With two exceptions, easily recognizable, these publications in no way present the doctrines of a philosophical group, as was done, in America, in "The New Realism," or the "Essays in Critical Realism." They are the studies of scholars or philosophers, often of very different tendencies, on subjects concerning their specialty.

De la méthode dans les sciences (*Methods in the Sciences*). A collection of articles, of which thirteen concern the mathematical or experimental sciences, the majority being the work of eminent specialists (notably Émile Picard, Jules Tannery, Le Dantec, and Jean Perrin), 2 vols., Alcan, 1909 and 1911.

L'orientation actuelle des sciences (*Present-day Orientation of the*

Sciences), lectures with a view to the examination for a degree in philosophy, by J. Perrin, P. Langevin, G. Urbain, L. Lapicque, Ch. Pérez, and L. Plantefol, with an introduction by Léon Brunschvicg, Alcan, 1930.

A la lumière du marxisme (*In the Light of Marxism*), by Messrs. Baby, Cohen, Friedmann, Labérenne, Langevin, Maublanc, Mineur, Parain, Prenant, Lauvageot, and Wallon, Éditions sociales internationales (International Social Editions), 1935.

Le centre de synthèse (The Center of Synthesis), under the direction of Henri Berr, has organized, since 1929, *Semaines de synthèse* (*Weekly Symposiums*) with lectures and discussions on a predetermined scientific subject; and the proceedings of these meetings have been edited by him.

Congrès internationaux de philosophie (International Congresses of Philosophy), founded in 1900 by Xavier Léon. The first of these Congresses (Proceedings published by Armand Colin, 4 vols., 1900-1903) and the ninth (Congrès Descartes [Congress on Descartes], 1937; proceedings published by Hermann, Act., fascicles 530 to 541, 1937) were held at Paris. All have included a section for the philosophy of the sciences.

Congrès de philosophie scientifique, (Congress of Scientific Philosophy) organized at Paris, in 1935, by M. Louis Rougier, in the spirit and with the cooperation of several members of the *Wiener Kreis*. Proceedings published by Hermann, Act., fascicules 388 to 395, 1936. See also, below, *Biology, 1927.*

PHILOSOPHY OF THE MATHEMATICAL SCIENCES

Couturat, L., *Les principes des mathématiques* (*The Principles of Mathematics*), Armand Colin, 1905.

Winter, M., *La méthode dans la philosophie des mathématiques* (*Method in the Philosophy of Mathematics*), Alcan, 1911.

Brunschvicg, L., *Les étapes de la philosophie des mathématiques* (*Stages in the Philosophy of Mathematics*), Alcan, 1912. This work more especially concerns the stages in the development of mathematics, considered philosophically. This important work was republished in 1949.

Boutroux, P., *Les principes de l'analyse mathématique,* 2 vols. (*Principles of Mathematical Analysis,* 2 vols.), Hermann, 1914 and 1919. *L'idéal scientifiques des mathématiciens* (*The Scientific Ideal of the Mathematicians*), *Alcan,* 1920. The author—professor of mathematics at the Collège de France, son of the philosopher, Émile Boutroux and nephew of Henri Poincaré—handles the different forms with quite remarkable mastery.

Nicod, Jean, *La géométrie dans le monde sensible* (*Geometry in the Sensible World*), Alcan, 1924.

Rougier, Louis, *La structure des théories déductives* (*The Structure of Deductive Theories*), Alcan, 1929.

(E). Reymond, Arnold, *Les principes de la logique et la critique contemporaine* (*The Principles of Logic and the Contemporary Critique*), Boivin, 1932.

Weber, L., *Pensée symbolique et pensée opératrice,* (*Symbolic and Operational Thought*), Bull., 1935.

(E). Gonseth, F., *Les mathématiques et la réalité, essai sur la méthode axiomatique* (*Mathematics and Reality, an Essay on the Axiomatic Method*), Alcan, 1936. *Philosophie mathématique,* (*Mathematical Philosophy*), Act., 1939.

Maugé, F., *L'esprit et le réel dans les limites du nombre et de la grandeur* (*The Mind and Reality in the Limits of Number and Size*), Alcan, 1937.

Poirier, René, *Le Nombre* (*Number*), Presses, 1938. Very instructive.

Cavaillès, J., *Méthode axiomatique et formalisme* (*Axiomatic Method and Formalism*), Hermann, 1937. *La théorie des ensembles, étude historique et critique* (*The Theory of Ensembles, Historical and Critical Study*), ibid., same year. *La pensée mathématique* (*Mathematical Thought*), Bull., 1939. *Du collectif au pari* (*théories des probabilités*), (*From the Collective to the Wager* [*Theories of Probabilities*]), R.M.M., 1940. *Sur la logique et la théorie de la science,* (*Logic and the Theory of Science*), Presses, 1947.

Lautman, A., *Sur les notions de structure et d'existence en mathématiques* (*Notions of Structure and Existence in Mathematics*), Hermann, 1937. *Essai sur l'unité des sciences mathématiques dans leur état actuel* (*Essay of the Unity of the Mathematical Sciences at the Present Time*), ibid., same year. *Nouvelles recherches sur la structure dialectique des mathématiques* (*New Inquiries into the Dialectical Structure of Mathematics*), ibid., 1939. *Symétrie et dissymétrie en mathématiques et en physique* (*Symmetry and Dissymmetry in Mathematics and Physics*), Act., 1946.

Bouligand, G., *Les aspects intuitifs de la mathématique* (*The Intuitive Aspects of Mathematics*), Gallimard, 1944.

Daval, R., and Guilbaud, G. T., *Le raisonnement mathématique* (*Mathematical Reasoning*), Presses, 1945.

Gendre, J. L., *Contribution à l'étude du jugement probable* (*A Contribution to the Study of Probable Judgment*), Presses, 1947.

Darbon, A., *La philosophie des sciences mathématiques* (*The Philosophy of the Mathematical Sciences*), Presses, 1949. (Posthumous).

PHILOSOPHY OF THE EXPERIMENTAL SCIENCES: PHYSICS AND CHEMISTRY

Duhem, P., *La théorie physique, son objet et sa structure* (*Physical Theory, Its Object and Structure*), Chevalier et Rivière, 1906. This is a collection of articles which had appeared in the preceding fifteen years. This work, very critical in spirit, has much shaken belief in the absolute value of physico-mathematical science. After having been vigorously discussed and considered as a polemical contribution to the religious campaign denouncing "the bankruptcy of science" (Brunetière, 1895), it has exerted a great influence over subsequent scientific philosophy.

Le Roy, Ed., *Sur la valeur objective des lois physiques* (*The Objective Value of Physical Laws*), Bull., 1901.

Rey, Abel, *La théorie de la physique chez les physiciens contemporains* (*The Theory of Physics Among Contemporary Physicists*), Alcan, 1907. Second edition, revised and much augmented, 1908. *Le retour éternel et la philosophie de la physique* (*The Eternal Recurrence and the Philosophy of Physics*), Flammarion, 1927.

Perrin, Jean, *Les Atomes* (*Atoms*), Alcan, 1912. This is a celebrated work, mainly technical, but set forth in a very philosophical spirit. Important for the discussion already mentioned (see above, Darbon) upon the legitimacy and utility of hypotheses of structure. It is to be remembered that Hannequin in *L'hypothèse des atomes* (*The Hypothesis of Atoms*), 1895, had maintained, with considerable success, that they should not be considered as physical realities.

Rougier, L., *En marge de Curie, de Carnot et d'Einstein* (*Notes on Curie, Carnot, and Einstein*), Chiron, 1920.

Urbain, G., *Les disciplines d'une science: la chimie* (*The Disciplines of a Science: Chemistry*), Doin, 1921. *Remarques sur l'orientation des doctrines chimiques* (*Observations on the Orientation of Chemical Doctrines*), R.M.M., 1929.

Bergson, H., *Durée et simultanéité, à propos de la théorie d'Einstein* (*Duration and Simultaneity, with Regard to the Einstein Theory*), Alcan, 1922.

Borel, Émile, *L'espace et le temps* (*Space and Time*), Alcan, 1922.

Langevin, P., *La physique depuis vingt ans* (*Physics in the Last Twenty Years*), Doin, 1923.

Meyerson, Émile, *La déduction relativiste* (*Relativist Deduction*), Payot, 1925. *Réel et déterminisme dans la physique quantique* (*Reality and Determinism in Quantic Physics*), Hermann, 1933.

de Broglie, Louis, *Déterminisme et causalité dans la physique contemporaine* (*Determinism and Causality in Contemporary Physics*), Bull., 1929 and 1930. A long and important discussion. *La physique nouvelle et les quanta* (*The New Physics and Quanta*), Flammarion, 1937. This collection of articles is valuable from the philosophical point of view, both for the great competence of the author and the character of the exposition. *Matière et lumière* (*Matter and Light*), Albin Michel, 1932. *Les conceptions de la physique contemporaine et les idées de Bergson* (*The Conceptions of Contemporary Physics and the Ideas of Bergson*), R.M.M., 1941. *Physique et microphysique* (*Physics and Microphysics*), ibid., 1947.

Bachelard, G., *Le pluralisme cohérent de la chimie moderne* (*The Coherent Pluralism of Modern Chemistry*), Vrin, 1932. *Les intuitions atomistiques* (*Atomistic Intuitions*), Boivin, 1933. *La continuité et la multiplicité temporelles* (*Temporal Continuity and Multiplicity*), Bull., 1937. *L'expérience de l'espace dans la physique contemporaine* (*The Experience of Space in Contemporary Physics*), Presses, 1937.

Brunschvicg, L., *La physique du XXe siècle et la philosophie* (*Twentieth Century Physics and Philosophy*), Act., 1936.

Boutaric, A., *Les conceptions actuelles de la physique* (*Present-Day Conceptions of Physics*), Flammarion, 1936.

Destouches, J. L., *Essai sur la forme générale des théories physiques* (*Essay on the General Form of Physical Theories*), Hermann, 1938. *Principes fondamentaux de la physique théorique; 3 vols.: Orientation préalable; Physique du solitaire; Physique collective* (*Fundamental Principles of Theoretical Physics, 3 vols.: Preliminary Orientation; Physics of the Individual; Statistical Physics*), Hermann, 1942.

Boll, Marcel, *Les quatre faces de la physique* (*The Four Aspects of Physics*), Rieder, 1939.

Mouy, P., *Les diverses formes de déterminisme dans la science moderne* (*The Divers Forms of Determinism in Modern Science*), R.M.M., 1944.

Daujat, J., *L'oeuvre de l'intelligence en physique* (*The Work of the*

Intelligence in Physics), Presses, 1946. With an extensive bibliography, going back beyond 1900.

Blanché, R., *La science physique et la réalité* (*Physical Science and Reality*), Presses, 1948. This work is founded upon solid scholarship and is of a high philosophical level.

NATURAL SCIENCE: BIOLOGY

Delarge, Yves, *L'hérédité et les grands problèmes de la biologie générale* (*Heredity and the Major Problems of General Biology*), Schleicher, 1903. This is a considerably enlarged reedition of an important work published first in 1895.

Goblot, E., *La finalité en biologie* (*Finality in Biology*), R. Ph., 2 articles, 1903 and 1904.

Le Dantec, F., *Les lois naturelles, réflexions d'un biologiste sur la science* (*Natural Laws, a Biologist's Reflections upon Science*), Alcan, 1904. *Éléments de philosophie biologique* (*Elements of Biological Philosophy*), Alcan, 1907. This is a leading work. *La stabilité de la vie* (*The Stability of Life*), Alcan, 1910.

Bergson, H., *L'évolution créatrice* (English translation, *Creative Evolution*), Alcan, 1907.

Rabaud, E., *Le transformisme et l'expérience* (*Transformism and Experience*), Alcan, 1911. *Éléments de biologie générale* (*Elements of General Biology*), Alcan, 1928.

de Launay, L., *La science géologique* (*Geological Science*), Armand Colin, 1913.

Caullery, M., *La nature des lois biologique* (*The Nature of Biological Laws*), R.M.M., 1914. *Le problème de l'évolution* (*The Problem of Evolution*), Payot, 1931. *Les conceptions modernes de l'hérédite* (*Modern Conceptions of Heredity*), Flammarion, 1935. *L'embryologie expérimentale* (*Experimental Embryology*), Flammarion, 1939. *Les étapes de la biologie* (*The Stages of Biology*), Presses, 1943.

Blaringhem, L., *Les problèmes de l'hérédité expérimentale* (*The Problems of Experimental Heredity*), Flammarion, 1919. *Évolution par mosaïque* (*Evolution by Way of Mosaic*), a discussion with René Berthelot, Bull., 1926.

Cooperative volume, *Le transformisme* (*Transformism*) by Messrs. Cuénot, Dalbiez, Gagnebin, Rabaud, Thompson, Vialleton; Vrin, 1927.

Le Roy, Ed., *L'exigence idéaliste et le fait de l'évolution* (*Idealist Exigency and the Fact of Evolution*), Paris, Boivin, 1927.

La vie et l'évolution, études sur la philosophie biologique (publication collective) (Life and Evolution, Studies on Biological Philosophy [Collective publication]), *Archives de Philosophie,* Bauchesne, 1928.

Vialleton, L., *L'origine des êtres vivants (The Origin of Living Creatures),* Plon, 1929.

Rostand, Jean, *L'homme, Introduction à l'étude de la biologie humaine (Man, an Introduction to the Study of Human Biology),* Gallimard, 1930.

Cuénot, L., *Invention et finalité en biologie (Invention and Finality in Biology),* Flammarion, 1931.

Lecomte du Noüy, P., *Le temps et la vie (Time and Life),*Gallimard, 1935. *L'homme devant la science (Man before Science),* Flammarion, 1939.

Guyénot, E., *L'hérédité (Heredity),* Doin, 1942. New edition, revised and augmented, of a work brought out in 1931.

(E). Guye, Ch. E., *L'évolution physico-chimique (Physico-Chemical Evolution),* Hermann, 1942.

Ruyer, R., *Éléments de psychobiologie (Elements of Psychobiology),* Presses, 1946. Researches of the greatest interest; novel and well-documented views on the nature of biological phenomena, and their relation to thought. Cf., Bull., 1939.

Matisse, G., *Le rameau vivant du monde:* I. *Le déchiffrement des faits,* Presses, 1947; II. *Philosophie biologique, ibid.,* 1949, *(The Living Branch of the World:* I. *The Deciphering of the Facts,* Presses, 1947; II. *Biological Philosophy, ibid.,* 1949).

LOGIC IN FRANCE IN THE TWENTIETH CENTURY

Marcel Boll* and Jacques Reinhart**

French-speaking philosophers are fortunate in the possession of an exceptionally rich and reliable reference book: The *Vocabulaire technique et critique de la philosophie*[1] published by André Lalande and constantly kept up to date since it was started (July, 1902). In it the article on Logic testifies to the fact that there is a constant tendency in France to take this word in a wider meaning than anywhere else. Thus, under this same heading, comes formal logic as well as general logic. This is probably characteristic of the French way of thinking: never to have lost sight—even while studying (in formal logic) the abstract processes of reasoning, and however reminiscent of algebra the way of formulating them might be—of the fact that this reasoning must, in the end, contribute to the further development of science; it being admitted that the analysis (by general logic) of the methods peculiar to each science opens the way for new emendations of and a more searching inquiry into the formal structure of reasoning. It must be understood that it is out of the question to limit the scope of general logic to this kind of analysis, as it has at the same time the purpose of forming a general estimate of the value and aims of science, an estimate which in its turn will not fail to influence all views on the further development of formal logic.

Consequently, in France, formal logic has hardly ever escaped the effects of a critical point of view which has probably hampered the conception of great systematizations comparable to those of Russell and Hilbert— the weaknesses or shortcomings of which did not escape the notice

---

* Born in 1886. Early in life, devoted himself to teaching and research. Author of numerous works on natural science, mathematics, psychology, epistemology, and logic (*Manuel de logique scientifique*, second edition, 1948). Editor of the French translations of the manifestos and declarations of the Viennese school of thinkers (Hermann).

** Born in 1918. Found his attention especially attracted toward the axiomatization of mathematics and has published in collaboration: *La conquête de la vérité* (1947), *Les étapes de la logique* (second edition, 1948), the chapter dealing with logic in *Les grands courants de la pensée mathématique* (1948), and is now preparing a comprehensive treatise on logic.

1. Presses Universitaires, fifth edition, Paris, 1947.

of exacting contemporary philosophers. Does this imply that no valuable contribution has been made in this country to the contemporary progress of logic, and that while observing a wholly negative attitude toward the purely formal problems which were being studied elsewhere, philosophers here were content with paraphrasing the latest findings of science or with drawing out more or less hazy generalizations while we realize that both forms of activity could in no way lead to an improvement of our knowledge of ways of reasoning? Certainly not, and though the French have often had the reputation of being inclined to denigrate their own countrymen, our definite purpose will, on the contrary, be to try to show that the contribution of our compatriots was by no means negligible or trifling but much rather underestimated or ignored.

Our intention here is not exactly to give an exhaustive list of all publications in French on logic, or to examine down to the most minute details the contributions of its chief representatives. We shall be content with giving a clear outline of the main currents of thought, going over the original conceptions of major thinkers. And though, in order to have an overall picture of logical studies in France in its true perspective, it would seem necessary to make a careful drawing of that framework with which general logic provides it, we shall have to limit ourselves[2] to mentioning a few names:[3] Milhaud, Louis Weber,[4] Poincaré, Brunschvicg,[5] Lalande,[6] André Darbon,[7] Abel Rey,[8] Meyerson,[9] Rougier, Koyré, Bachelard,[10] Serrus, Poirier, Blanché. To characterize, within a few words, such original tendencies is of course out of the question, though their common denominator would seem to be (as it has often been pointed out) the more or less important part played by idealism, and namely, critical idealism. This is quite what might be expected. Was not Brunschvicg's definition of it, the thesis maintaining that "all metaphysics can be re-

---

2. For this subject is not, properly speaking, our own.
3. We shall be content for the moment with mentioning a few books by those authors, books that will not be mentioned again below.
4. *Vers le positivisme absolu par l'idéalisme*, Paris, Alcan, 1903.
5. *L'idéalisme contemporain*, Paris, Alcan, 1905; *Le progrès de la conscience dans la philosophie occidentale*, Paris, Alcan, 1927; *Héritages de mots, héritages d'idées*, Paris, Presses Universitaires, 1945.
6. *La dissolution opposée à l'évolution dans les sciences physiques et morales*, Paris, Alcan, 1899.
7. *L'explication mécanique et le nominalisme*, Paris, Alcan, 1910; *Une philosophie de l'expérience*, Paris, Presses Universitaires, 1946.
8. *La philosophie moderne*, Paris, Flammarion, 1908; *La théorie de la physique chez les physiciens contemporains*, Paris, Alcan, 1924.
9. *Identité et réalité*, Paris, Alcan, 1912; *De l'explication dans les sciences*, Paris, Payot, 1921; *Du cheminement de la pensée*, 3 vols., Paris, Alcan, 1931.
10. *Le nouvel esprit scientifique*, Paris, Alcan, 1934.

duced to a theory of knowledge"? Such a theory finds, on the other hand, its deeper motives in a wealth of studies devoted by Blanché to *La science physique et la réalité*.[11]

It is likewise to the influence of idealism that we may attribute the magnificent part played by a group of historians of ideas of which Rey[12] was such a typical member. Side by side with the effort tending to reproduce the evolution of conceptions as each successive discovery was bringing them to the test and making it necessary to revise them completely, it is quite as interesting to describe accurately what, in those very conceptions, pertains to the very structure of our mental mechanisms. Besides Brunschvicg who precisely expatiated on *Les âges de l'intelligence* (being very careful to specify that however high the qualities of the soul, they should not go without the corresponding qualities in the mind), we have to put in the very first rank the very original study which serves as an opening piece to the *Introduction à la psychologie*[13] by Paul Guillaume.

Centered as they were on the activity of the mind, on the balance between "la raison constituante" and "la raison constituée," our logicians' studies were to follow very closely the general drift of the revolution then taking place in formal logic, and were reconsidering, with all due attention, the problems raised by logical induction, problems which in the past had hardly been given anything but superficial solutions, superficial even if consecrated as canons.

To one wanting in our time to characterize the state of formal logic at the beginning of the present century, it would appear necessary to lay stress on the preeminence, still practically undisputed, of Aristotelian thought. Not that there were not any attempts to deviate from it when possible, taking into consideration certain of John Stuart Mill's theses for instance. Elie Rabier's *Logique*,[14] while distinctly incorporating the various contemporary tendencies to renovate the subject, is nevertheless an attempt to make them fit into the only slightly widened framework of an Aristotelian body of doctrine. The significant influence in that period was chiefly that of Jules Lachelier, who in particular gave the syllogism an interpretation which has remained the standard view on the subject. Even in these early times, he was already trying to break away from the rigid framework to which Aristotelian analysis had been confined and,

---

11. Paris, Presses Universitaires, 1948.
12. *La science dans l'antiquité*, 5 vols., Paris, Albin Michel; the first of a series which was to continue up to our time and which the author was not able to finish.
13. Paris, Vrin, 1942.
14. Paris, Hachette, 1886.

when examining relational propositions, observed that they could not be classified in the same pigeonhole with predicative propositions (of the form subject-copula-predicate). But the latter observation, the consequences of which were soon to be minimized by neo-Thomist logicians[15] with narrower Aristotelian allegiances, was doomed never to bring about any positive improvement.

Aristotelianism was to run its course for some time yet, owing to its momentum, and furthermore at a time when many of the best scholars still held and took for granted that all mathematical demonstrations were reducible to a syllogistic form. True, not all were absolutely faithful to this prolonged Aristotelianism. A particularly interesting effort to rejuvenate it was made by Edmond Goblot in his lectures at the University of Lyon the substance of which appeared in his *Traité de logique.*[16] This treatise, however, did not consist of logic so much as of thoughts about logic. The latter part of this work ingeniously throws light on a number of points and for that reason remains a book which the beginner should consult. Many aspects of it have, however, rapidly become obsolete —such for instance is the case of the sociological standpoint which it was then fashionable to adopt when inquiring into any subject. Equally outdated is his analysis of mathematical reasoning, in which he opposes Henri Poincaré's views, and reveals himself as never having commanded an intimate knowledge of higher mathematics. Asserting the predominance of judgment over concept, Goblot reached conclusions comparable to Russell's theses, but he did so by joining forces with the psychologists and not, as Russell had done, by carefully analyzing formal mechanisms. Working in this roundabout way, he was finally led to defend the particular original point of view of the anteriority of propositional logic as compared with predicative logic, thus moving the center of gravity away from Aristotle toward the Stoics. On closer examination, this was no great novelty; and Goblot, in fact, remained a prisoner inside the formal framework within which thought had been running in a circle ever since ancient times. Some of his conclusions, as we said, seemed to reach out toward logistic; but though he was not unacquainted with the latter, and alluded to it, he seemed to see in it only an array of symbols. The shortcomings which we have just pointed out in his conception of mathematics are possibly the signs in this otherwise distinguished mind of

---

15. Who remark, on more or less justified grounds, that the study of the handling of relations had already been taken up and partly dealt with in the theory of "oblique syllogisms."

16. Paris, Armand Collin, 1918.

an incapacity, which he perhaps never quite surmounted, to overcome the elementary difficulty of training oneself to thinking by symbols. It is probably to the same reason that one might ascribe his rather unexpected blindness to the new realities formulated by logistic.

With Goblot we come to something very much akin to the logistic movement. Before entering upon the discussion of the latter, we should mention, by the way, a stiffening, apparently unexpected, of the stricter Aristotelian tradition—to wit, the neo-Thomist interlude. In fact this tradition had never been extinct and had always been kept alive in Catholic educational institutions in which Aristotelianism and Thomism constituted the principal items of what was there termed a sound "philosophical" and theological training. But this tradition, kept up mainly for teaching purposes, had not for a long time produced any original representative, and was rather looked upon as a long-lived anachronism. One of the many reactions against positivism, introduced by quite an extraneous combination of circumstances due to the inner life of the Church, was to take the form of a pseudo-revival of Thomism. This is how—as Aristotelian logic had remained (only there and probably nowhere else) the essential foundation of intellectual training—there came about a relatively strong opposition to the vagaries of logic such as it was at the time. The general outlines of this Aristotelo-Thomist logic are probably best described in the *Logique*[17] by the Belgian Cardinal Désiré Mercier, but the more controversial exposition adopted by Jacques Maritain[18] is better suited to give a clear idea of the tendencies of this movement in its attacks against other French logicians. Still, it would not be appropriate to start a discussion of it here since this doctrine identifies itself with an ontology and, what is more, with a well specified ontology.[19] No doubt, a system of logic may quite well imply a system of metaphysics, and furthermore, according to certain opinions, any system of logic might be regarded as constituting, in a way, a system of metaphysics. But what is more questionable is the tendency to associate an ontology with it as closely as neo-Thomism does. All the more so, one might say, as the ontology in question has been considered by many who, in that, followed Léon Brunschvicg—as an "instinctive realism" incapable of distinguish-

---

17. Paris, Alcan, 1912.
18. *Petite logique,* Paris, Trequi, 1923.
19. It would be adequate to make the same remark about Marxist neo-Hegelianism represented by George Politzer, René Maublanc, Henri Lefebvre, ... But can one's attention be arrested by a neoplastic proliferation (born of fortuitous circumstances) of aberrant dialectics, bold enough to appear in the nineteenth century when Aristotle alone would have been able to reduce all its sophisms to nothingness?

ing between the process of speech and the process of thought, and impervious to the understanding of anything outside the preestablished framework of language.[20]

Let us specify that the attitude toward logistic, from the condescending attitude it had been with Goblot, had become with Maritain resolutely hostile. "Logic is an art devised to serve intelligence not to replace it." We agree; but he adds, rather recklessly, that its task is not to supply us with self-sufficient formulae, to furnish us with an algorithmic mechanism which works all by itself, intelligence remaining idle and a mere agency to control its workings. One might then wonder why some mathematicians have become famous for their work in algebra if discovery in that line were automatic. But this mental attitude reflects at the same time a deep misapprehension of the part played by symbolism in logic as well as in mathematics, a misapprehension which is rather widespread and which we shall discuss later. This is also the source of some people's strange opinion that while formal logic must not be disloyal to intelligence, yet logistic could never avoid doing so unless it were at the cost of "fantastic complication." Whoever has had the opportunity of comparing the heavy and confused plodding of thought in a classical treatise of formal logic with the terse single chapter sufficient in logistic to set forth, amend, and refer to the whole subject (which occupies only an insignificant position in its whole), needs no answer to such an objection.

In spite of these differences and antipathies, the development of logic has been carried on now for sixty years—and here as elsewhere the center of interest has been logistic.

We cannot, of course, hold Boole solely responsible for the rise of the latter, though he carried on most of his work without knowing the scattered or even unpublished fragments of his predecessors. There nevertheless remains the fact that all that was to become for a long time the essential building materials of logistic is to be found in his book. These materials remained for a time mere objects of curiosity and were at the beginning but slowly elaborated, thanks to efforts in which, we regret to say, France took no part. These effervescent ideas did not become acclaimed in our country till the publication of some work by Peano,[21] for instance, followed or even accompanied by a swarm of studies of the same kind in foreign periodicals. An enthusiastic initiator in this branch was

---

20. *Les âges l'intelligence,* Paris, Alcan, 1934, in which one can also read "Aristotle had demonstrated the merely verbal character of his own ontology and, probably, of any ontology."

21. Whose *Formulaire de mathématiques* was in the same year published in Turin and Paris.

Louis Couturat, a philosopher endowed with a mathematical culture far above the average.[22]   He led to the discovery—nearly simultaneously with Russell but independently of him—of the basic and essential influence on Leibniz of a special preoccupation with various points of logic, bringing to light a mass of hitherto unpublished papers, and showing Leibniz to be the great precursor of algorithmic logic.[23]   At the same time, in widely noticed articles for *La Revue de Métaphysique et de Morale,* Couturat made a critical survey of the findings of foreign research workers; he also published *L'algèbre de la logique,*[24] unfinished because of accidental death (1914), and part of which was to appear in that very same *Revue de Métaphysique.*   Rarely has a brilliant cause found a more ardent exponent and apostle.   In perfect harmony with the Leibnizian tradition, he saw logic as the matchless, irreplaceable instrument [25] for the unification of "thought and the harmony of words."   "Logic first teaches us to distinguish judgments which are right from those which are wrong; one acquires habits of rigorous and accurate thinking; one cultivates within oneself the sense of truth; one acquires a keener power for discrimination, a more acute critical insight. Each separate cog in the system of logic is relatively simple, but their various combinations lead to results of an incredible richness and variety.   Nothing is more different from that pseudo-reason, elusive, overflexible, and easily bent in every direction, invented for the needs of an impressionistic philosophy." [26] Therefore, if French logisticians of our times were in want of a patron, it would be very legitimate that they should resort to Louis Couturat.

Many have been pleased to call him dogmatic, which might have implied something harsh and jerky in his thought and expression. But as a matter of fact, his was much rather the case of one struggling toward clearness in the exposition of matters which had all too often been treated in a confused way, and the later evolution of his theses reveals in him a constant preoccupation with perfection and an intellectual honesty very

----

22. The subject of his doctorate dissertation, *De l'infini mathématique,* Paris, Alcan, 1896, has been the occasion for highly interesting discussions among specialists.   The theses which he set forth in this piece of work were to change largely, moving toward a point of view very close to that of Russell.

23. *La logique de Leibniz,* Paris, Alcan, 1902; *Opuscules et fragments inédits de Leibniz, ibid.,* 1903.

24. Paris, Gauthier-Villars, 1905 and 1914.

25. He made vigorous efforts to supplement logic with an international language which should have profited by its improvements and the vocabulary of which would have been intensely rationalized without being a mere reflection of the various particular idioms. With a similar intention, he wrote most of the first articles on logic in Lalande's *Vocabulaire philosophique,* which in its editor's intention was an answer to the same preoccupations.

26. The opening lesson of a course of lectures delivered (1905-06) at the Collège de France, while acting professor in Bergson's chair.

much akin to Russell's. It is all the more to be regretted that his premature death should have prevented Couturat from achieving really creative work in the treatment of technical problems concerning formalism, in which field he gave every mark of being destined to do great work.

After Couturat's death, the study of logical forms was to remain for a long time under a shadow. Henri Dufumier, who wrote a number of very promising articles, was not (he died in World War I) to carry out the work he had planned. Jean Nicod, who attracted attention by demonstrating that propositional logic (Russell's logic) can be condensed into a single axiom, disappeared from the scene when still quite young, a victim of tuberculosis. Louis Rougier, about whom more will be said later on, gave, in *La structure des théories déductives,*[27] a mere summary of the fundamental notions of Russell's logic. *La logique formelle*[28] by Georges-Henri Luquet bears a more individual stamp, though still remaining very elementary (propositional logic plus the rudiments of the logic of classes).

To what cause may we attribute this stagnation? Mainly, it is probable, to the influence exerted by Henri Poincaré, even if there were crtain apparent misunderstandings about the latter's ideas. Couturat's insistent efforts had in fact been looked upon with some reserve, partly due, as we must say, to the novelty of his ideas. And if certain scholars, however eminent in other branches of knowledge, admitted them but reluctantly, the grounds for this attitude might be called in question. The minds of a good many of them were ill-prepared for this sort of problem —whether they had been too intensely nurtured on previous doctrines into which logistic could not fit, or were insufficiently informed in those major sciences susceptible to become the test-benches, so to speak, for this new technique of reasoning; or lastly were too acutely specialized and unable to dissect processes of thought which they nevertheless made use of. We have, earlier in this work, pointed out a few characteristic oppositions, coming from minor authorities. Quite on another scale, Émile Meyerson's opinion would seem to have more weight. However highly one may esteem the other aspects of his lifework, it cannot be denied that this former chemist labored under a perfectly Hegelian "intellectual deafness" where mathematics was concerned and was thus grossly misled in his considerations on the latter science or, as a natural consequence, on logic. One may think it astonishing to find, in the ranks of the enemy, Pierre Boutroux whose remarks on mathematics and deep historico-critical

27. Paris, Alcan, 1921.
28. Paris, Alcan, 1925.

analysis of their principles might have given him an inkling that logistic was very different from a mere stenography (that is to say an indispensable technical process), however useful he has conceded it to be.[29]

But, side by side with those oppositions, rather due to mode or temperament, a few better-grounded critiques did not fail to lay stress on defects to which French minds might be particularly sensitive. The sources of a good many of them may be found in philosophical articles [30] by Poincaré, who, taking advantage of his half-way position as a professional mathematician and a philosopher by inclination, was then the most authorized person to judge this new science in the making. These articles are not always devoid of polemical intentions. Besides, we are not to forget "that we are in the presence of a mathematician, not a philosopher; that, deep under sentences apparently so clear and comprehensive runs, as an undercurrent, a complex experience of mathematical thinking; that he did not explicitly say everything but was often content with suggesting; that he seems quite often to have written just what occurred to him as his pen ran, without always demanding of his philosophical style that it should have the same rigorous accuracy as that of his mathematical demonstrations; that he has retained above all, as a specialist would, a habit of completely trusting his reader for being perpetually and deeply attentive. To make more explicit the involutions of his thought, far more complex than it appears at first, is indispensable for those who want to seize the spirit of it, not the letter. One has often been mistaken for the other and certain people have been led into simplifying to an excess a theory which is richer, fuller of fine shades of meaning than is commonly thought." [31] Poincaré has watched with a keen interest the developments of Peano's, Whitehead's,

---

29 The authors who have resorted to the protection of Pierre Boutroux's authority have in general made an unlucky choice—in fact they never fail to reproduce one of the rare mistakes committed by this mathematician, who had a sound knowledge of Schröder's, Peano's, and Russell's work. (He gave a summary account of the latter's doctrine.) "Given any relation, there exists another relation which is the converse of the former." But, Boutroux objects, a function is a special instance of a relation, and this would-be general law does not apply in this case. A function has not necessarily another function as its converse. Any logician will, of course, have remarked that, in the making of a function a particular instance of the general law, the formal rules of logic allow one to replace the word *relation* by the word function only the first time when it is used in the sentence between quotation marks. Let the noninitiated for whom these indications are not sufficient to reveal the underlying sophism try the parallel proposition: "Given any man, there exists another man who is the father of the former," with reference to the fact that, for instance, a general is a man.

30. Later collected in volume form (Paris, Flammarion): *Science et hypothése* (1902); *La valeur de la science* (1905); *Science et méthode* (1908); *Dernières pensées* (posthumous, 1913). (English translations of the first three have appeared, under the titles: *Science and Hypothesis; The Value of Science; Science and Method.*)

31. Roger Daval and Georges Guilbaud. *Le raisonnement mathématique*. Paris, Presses Universitaires, 1945.

Russell's, and Hilbert's thought, and has discussed their doctrines, in the course of famous controversies with Couturat; he has been quite willing to acknowledge the extension given by these authors to the syllogism which Kant had still found satisfactory, and himself stressed the interest of this extension. Not that he did not inveigh against the excessive optimism professed by the first protagonists of logistic. It has often been recalled that "he declared that he could not understand the Peanian," [32] while, as a matter of fact, he has ever protested against the habit of certain authors who, replacing a sentence in ordinary language by a symbol, thought that in so doing every obstacle had been overcome: he called that *christening* difficulties, not solving them.

The creator of ideas for Poincaré, could not help objecting to the opinion initially maintained by Russell and more emphatically expressed by Couturat, according to which logistic lends wings to invention. "Well," he exclaimed, pointing out that Peano had published his *Formulaire* ten years before, "now you have been equipped with wings for ten years and you have not yet begun flying!" Let us grant that the early logisticians, inheritors as they were of the old Cartesian and Leibnizian myth, believed a little naively in discoveries contrived in a purely mechanical way, thanks to the play of substitutions and inferences authorized by the usual rules. Poincaré has made a timely remark in stating that, behind the scenes, there was the logician or mathematician, who *directed* the applications, and *chose the results*. He has also made felicitous disquisitions on the *creation* of new concepts, out of those which were taken as starting points, showing that the true source of fruitful logical and mathematical reasoning lies in the more or less felicitous character of those creations.

On the subject of this fecundity, Poincaré was the first to insist so forcibly on the part played by recurrence in reasoning; and he found it amusing to bring to light the vicious circles contrived, at the beginning, by Russell and Hilbert, with a view to relating this very special type of reasoning to more general logical laws. Here there seems to have been a most remarkable anticipation, as it is well known that ulterior research work on metalogical matters carried on by Hilbert's school or cognate thinkers, has regularly failed to justify the axiom of recurrence. One may, by the way, think that the problem which was then raised has not yet ceased giving scope to the perspicacity of research workers: one may, in fact, doubt whether reasoning by recurrence shall be reduced

---

32. More exactly he wrote: "My understanding of *Peanian* is too bad for me to be bold enough to raise an objection . . .," a sally which, set in its context, is very typical of his slightly ironical turn of mind.

to the utilization of the axiom bearing the same name and, according to all likelihood, it probably hides another form of reasoning, analogous but of a superior nature, and no longer resting on axioms but rules.

Poincaré has also, for a long time, been preoccupied with antinomies, though he never took them seriously: "Logistic is no longer barren, it has given birth to antinomies." The Russellian theory of types he has always looked upon with a certain amount of skepticism, and he could not help seeing it as a base imitation of the solutions adopted by mathematicians when certain difficulties got in their way. In his opinion, for instance, negative or complex numbers were not "creations" *ad hoc* or arbitrary: they were discoveries (the theory of types never seemed to him worthy of the latter name). From the technical point of view his main effort was circumscribing the intervention of the infinite in famous controversies with the Cantorians as he termed them; he could never bring himself to accept the conception of the infinite, and he never ceased to consider the infinite as a distinctive character of a certain type of reasoning, while nevertheless maintaining that all reasoning can bear on a finite number of objects only. Finally, he had to call in question the notion of "ensemble" (i.e., collection) introduced by the Cantorians. Making drastic restrictions on this notion, he has exclusively used in his critical study of Zermelo's axioms the German word "Menge," for which he refused to accept the French translation "ensemble" in the usual sense of the word.

One must not forget the important part played by Poincaré's conventionalism in the current of contemporary thought. True conventionalism does not belong to him alone, and on various points it found a better or more accurate exponent in the works of Gaston Milhaud,[33] Léon Brunschvicg,[34] and René Berthelot.[35] Still, Poincaré had the merit of expressing this thesis under the most general form, carefully avoiding the excess of which Pierre Duhem and Edouard Le Roy have been guilty.

With Peano, logistic appeared preeminently as a technique; with Russell and Couturat, it included metaphysical considerations, which undoubtedly were not all necessarily related to it and caused considerable prejudice against it. Destructive criticism (from a philosophical standpoint) emanating from Poincaré and Brunschvicg involuntarily brought discredit upon this science in the eyes of people of superficial or hasty

---

33. *Essai sur les conditions et les limites de la certitude logique,* Paris, Alcan, 1891; *Le rationnel,* Paris, F. Alcan, 1898; *Le positivisme et le progrès de l'esprit,* Paris, F. Alcan, 1902.

34. *Les étapes de la philosophie mathématique.* Paris, Alcan, 1912.

35. *Un romantisme utilitaire.* Tome I, Paris, Alcan, 1911.

judgment. Hence the withdrawal of French research workers from this branch of learning even while the logistic movement was being brilliantly launched in German- and English-speaking countries, as well as in Poland and Holland. The only tribute to this international current at that time was to be the work [36] of Jacques Herbrand (1908-1931), which was left unfinished. Though related to Hilbert's school of thought, Herbrand was to bring a contribution typical of French lucidity: the outcome of research in mathematics, his work allowed one to presage a widening of general views which has been denied to us. Jean Cavaillès too was to call back the public's attention to the results which had been recently attained abroad: his were books of information,[37] and the documentation they brought was precious if one considers the difficulty of consulting the sources themselves. However, the part reserved to criticism was often of a lesser interest[38] in spite of the high mathematical culture this philosopher had acquired. Notwithstanding the deep and justified sympathy of all those who knew him, we may doubt whether this man who died a victim of the Nazis would ever have been able to play as significant a part as Couturat had played in his own time.

Men like Herbrand or Cavaillès constitute, as it were, accidents in our logical thought, owing to their more definite allegiance to foreign schools of thought. And if we have indicated a momentary slackening of interest in the study of logic, that does not mean that studies were not carried on, preserving their original character which differentiates them rather sharply from all similar studies abroad. In particular, one of the definite purposes of these studies — during the interregnum which took place after World War I — was to define with greater accuracy the nature of principles and the foundation of logic. And this is the right occasion for mentioning the importance of the critical studies published by André Lalande,[39] Arnold Reymond,[40] Ferdinand Gonseth,[41] Jean Laporte.[42] But

---

36. *Recherches sur la théorie de la démonstration.* Thèse, Paris, 1930. "Les bases de la logique hilbertienne," *Revue de métaphysique et de morale* (1930).

37. *Remarques sur la formation de la théorie abstraite des ensembles,* Paris, Hermann, 1938; *Axiomatique et formalisme* (1938); *Transfini et continu* (Posthumous, 1940).

38. His article (*Revue philosophique,* 1937), "Logique mathématique et syllogisme," betrays some difficulty in keeping a strict control over symbolism applying his theories to specific cases.

39. "Logique normative et vérité de fait," *Revue Philosophique,* (March, 1929); *La raison et les normes,* Paris, Hachette, 1948.

40. *Les principes de la logique et la critique contemporaine,* Paris, Boivin, 1932; *Une philosophie spiritualiste,* Tome I, Paris, Vrin, 1942.

41. *Les fondements des mathématiques,* Paris, Blanchard, 1926; *Les mathématiques et la réalité,* Paris Alcan, 1936; *Qu'est-ce que la logique?* Paris, Hermann, 1937; *Philosophie mathématique,* Paris, Hermann, 1939.

42. *Le problème de l'abstraction,* Paris, Presses Universitaires, 1940; *L'idée de nécessité,* (1942).

while Gonseth, a mathematician, considers logic more specifically as a "physical theory of the indeterminate object," the two first-mentioned philosophers caution us against forgetting that logic plays the part of a legislator, creating norms. This twofold aspect, a physical theory on one hand, a normative science on the other, can be reconciled with the value— more or less absolute according to the author you consider — which is ascribed to logical principles. On the contrary, Louis Rougier, a stricter follower of the idealist tradition which has left, as has been said before, such a deep mark on the evolution of philosophy in France, and manifestly influenced by Poincaré's conceptions,[43] rather considers those principles as conventions (in Poincaré's rigorous and accurate conception of the term): taking this as his starting point, and proceeding by the light of the last findings in logic, Rougier launches on a thorough examination of major past errors of realism,[44] or even of Thomism.[45] However devoted to idealism all these authors might be, they have all allowed for the necessities of experimentation freely enough not to be led as far as nominalism. That is why, even if some of the theses they present seem parallel to those set forth by the school of Viennese thinkers, the latter's final evolution made it impossible for it to find any definite response in France.

One might even think that the original intention (with its intellectualistic and experimentalistic characters) of the Viennese movement had been more faithfully adhered to and preserved by French logic, which, moreover, had adopted it independently, not to say anteriorly.

On the other hand Rougier had had an opportunity (see note 27) to refute Goblot's views on mathematical reasoning, while Roger Daval and Georges Guilbaud, focussing their attention on the same subject and conducting a contrasting study of Poincaré's views on it, gave a very brilliant analysis of them (see note 31): these views are the object of almost a rediscovery, the depth of insight they reveal not having, so it seems, been estimated at its real value for almost two generations. This is a definite sign of the present-day value of the monumental work elaborated by this intellectual giant: Henri Poincaré.

If not drawing inspiration directly from it, at least by keeping close to the same line of inspiration, the technical study of the various problems offered by formal logic was resumed only shortly before the second World War. We have mentioned above one of the reasons for this delay; we

43. *La philosophe geométrique d'Henri Poincaré.* Paris, Alcan, 1920.
44. *Les paralogismes du rationalisme.* Paris, Alcan, 1920.
45. *La scolastique et le thomisme.* Paris, Gauthier-Villars, 1925.

must add that the progress of formalism, on which attention had been closely focussed in other countries, was rather minimized by French logicians. As regards formal logic, almost all the essential material was to be found in works by various authors from Boole and DeMorgan to Schröder, Peano, and Frege. The original contribution of Whitehead and Russell,[46] as well as that of Hilbert and his disciples, appears after all as rather limited. Let us, for the moment, be content with only mentioning many-valued logical systems, about which we shall have more to say; what had the relish of novelty was the research work done on metalogic (or we might say metamathematics), metalanguage, or even semantics, with which logical formalism is only indirectly concerned, and which have not yet reached a sufficiently advanced stage for one to make an estimate of their definite value. The aim in general was not, properly speaking, to improve the instrument which formal logic is, but much rather to set up a theory of its possibilities and its limitations. Here we may say that outside of the remarkable contribution, already alluded to, of Jacques Herbrand, French specialists evinced a kind of skepticism, discrete but inflexible, concerning researches of such an order. Must one consider them completely wrong? It scarcely happens that a theory can be built up before the limits of its object have been defined or its substance carefully explored. Not that we must discard all theory as long as this task has not been carried out, since the former and the latter, after a certain stage has been attained, progress together. Yet logistic, such as it appears in the essential treatises of Whitehead, Russell, or Hilbert, may be regarded as having reached a state sufficiently advanced to account for the swarm of theoretical studies which were carried on in the last twenty-five years. Let us notice however that most of them deliberately limited themselves to propositional logic — a particularly barren patch of the whole field — so that one may well wonder with Lalande what is the use of the creation of a special set of symbols, if one must go no further. The way in which, in this country, the various systems of many-valued logic have come to grief is significant of this state of affairs. Thus it is that, from the very beginning, Brouwer's intuitionism was successfully attacked by practitioners of mathematics such as Émile Borel, Paul Levy, Marcel Barzin, and Alfred Errera in a controversy[47] with Rolin Wavre, who was endeavoring to launch this movement in France. Besides the

46. Of course, it is far from our intention to minimize the interest presented by their analyses of mathematical notions in purely logical terms.

47. Several articles and notes (1926-27), the essential matter of which can be found in: Émile Borel, *Leçons sur la théorie des fonctions* (note 7), 3rd edition, Paris, Gauthier-Villars, 1928.

mitigated restrictions made by Gonseth (1939) on the intellectual processes then in use among Dutch and Polish logicians to try and bolster up systems of many-valued logic, René Poirier[48] took the timely decision to devote himself to the preliminary criticism of the notion of *truth*, which has constantly been used in an ambiguous sense[49] in the aforesaid innovations.[50] How far-reaching the work later on achieved by Poirier may be, it is unfortunately difficult to ascertain, for his *Traité de logique*, though it has been due for quite a while, has not yet come out.[51] The authors of the present study have, for their own part, insisted on the fact that the slightest transcription in logical terms of a scientific reasoning process demands, almost in every instance, the use of words with quantitative implications such as "all" and "some." It is owing to the imperfectly defined importance[52] of the latter that they attribute the over-simple character which has raised strong objections against the analyses or models proposed for scientific demonstrations, as well as the difficulties met with in expressing the basic notions which systems of many-valued logic have to handle. Besides, without resorting to any new indefinable element, they in their turn, offer a logical system of *modalities*, which can be adequately resorted to in solving the decision problem and to which is appended a logic of probability.[53] Under those conditions, systems of many-valued logic seem no longer to clash with two-valued logic (the *problem of experimental verification*) since they are the direct outcome of the latter and, as can be seen, have quite a different field.

Another instance quite typical of the French standpoint is that of antinomies. Just as for Poincaré, our logicians were very reluctant to have any faith in it. Charles Perelmann had drawn (1936-37) our attention to the fact that they were all built on the same model, and the sophisms which they contain were going to be pointed out in books written sep-

---

48. *Essais sur quelques caractères des notions d'espace et de temps*, Paris, Vrin, 1932; *Le nombre*, Paris, Alcan, 1938.

49. It is a similar case for the "three-valued" logic (1937) of Paulette Février, who elaborated it with the special purpose of applying it to microphysics, and similar productions by Jean-Louis Destouches.

50. Charles Serrus, whose death was deeply regretted and whose early work in places was quite remarkable, published just before he died, a *Traité de logique* (Paris, Aubier, 1945). Unfortunately it was written hastily owing to circumstances, so that he failed to preserve the cautious attitude demanded by such delicate subjects.

51. His teaching allows one to suppose that he has attempted a systematization in terms of symbols of which we possess no detailed account.

52. It is quite certain that Russell was right and Lewis wrong (when the former maintained the simplicity of material implication), and that one must take this "material implication" as a starting point for defining "strict implication." There nevertheless remains the fact that, practically speaking, it is always the latter that presents itself and sets forth the relation of reason to consequence.

53. In the case in which a "statistical" decision is the only possible issue.

arately.[54] Thus Poirier observed (1938) that Epimenides's paradox rests on the error which consists in considering a contrary as contradictory,[55] an objection repeated, under different forms, by the present authors (1946) and Alexandre Koyré.[56] They agree in finding it, just as Lalande had done (1945), a mere witticism for the use of the scholastic students. Koyré has also applied his energies to showing the vacuity of other "classical" antinomies, in most of which appears the violation of rules known even among ancient philosophers; he remarks that in this definite instance, the use of symbols has rather hampered the investigators, who have forfeited all critical acumen after they had clumsily transposed their subject matter into formulae, thus sharing in the illusion denounced by Poincaré, as we have already seen. The authors of the present article reaching the same result, have insistently drawn attention to the fact that, if (as is ascertained by Koyré) "I lie" has no meaning whatever in ordinary language, that is a thing impossible to formulate in logistic, which assertion would tend to establish the superiority of symbolism as well as the astounding lack of skill of many who use it. In 1931, Poirier had already asserted that "the percentage of errors committed by students, when asked to judge the validity of ways of reasoning, the reliability of which has been questioned, however simple, is astounding. To tell the truth, in the case of grown-ups, even well-educated grown-ups, this percentage is not much lower, and the study of mathematics does not diminish it." Therefore it is probably legitimate to attribute the origin of those phantasms,[57] which have so much hampered the progress and diffusion of logistic, to a deficiency in the present-day methods of intellectual training.

One should consequently be cautioned against seeing these examples

---

54. Which sets off the fictitious difficulty of his question.

55. If one holds "Cretans always tell the truth" as the negation of "Cretans always lie," while this negation is effectively "There are Cretans who sometimes tell the truth."

56. *Épimenide, le menteur.* Paris, Hermann, 1947.

57. The present authors have shown that we should identify with a sophism — in every respect comparable to that of Epimenides — the apparent cornerstone of all objections raised by mathematicians such as Birkhoff and Von Neumann (*Ann. of Math.,* 1936) against the application of bivalent logic to microphysics. Do not the latter go to the extreme of stating that the negation of "the experimental observation of a train of waves Ψ on one side of a plane in ordinary space" is: "the observation of Ψ on the other side"? They contradict themselves shortly afterwards when mentioning as possible "The observation of Ψ in a state symmetrical about the said plane" (a possibility which when contrasted with the foregoing "premises" manifestly leads us — through a plain Aristotelian dilemma — to an apparent antinomy) — while a negation must include *all possible* cases excluded by the corresponding affirmation. The correct negation is: "The observation of at least part of Ψ on the other side."

It is nonetheless rather strange that this blunder should have been repeated or quoted approvingly on various occasions (Albert Lautman, Jean-Louis Destouches, to mention none but French writers).

as a condemnation of the use of symbolism itself in matters of logic: only a limited group of logicians have brought upon themselves the mentioned reproaches. Their case is similar to that of a certain eminent scientist who used to declare: "Tensor calculus has a more accurate knowledge of physics than the physicist himself"; that may be sarcasm, but if we were to give credit to it, we should feel compelled to add "alas!" On the contrary, it seems likely, as has already been pointed out, that what would be chiefly criticized in contemporary logic is to have explored too narrow a field, devoid of any interest of its own, and not to have sufficiently profited by the possibilities of the language of symbols to analyze the basic notions of ulterior sciences. Russell and Whitehead — in a more significant way than the followers of Peano — had broken ground which has too long remained uncultivated by French logicians since then. Yet France may be proud of the mass of work achieved (under the collective pen name of Nicolas Bourbaki) by a team of brilliant young mathematicians (Henri Cartan, Jean Dieudonné, Charles Ehresmann, André Weil, ...). Their *Éléments de mathématiques*[58] constitutes an admirable instrument for all research workers in that field. It tends toward a complete survey of all fundamental parts of mathematics at present, and rests entirely on the theory of "ensembles." This survey is only semiformal in the more minute details of the reasoning process adopted. One might remark that some of the demonstrations might as a consequence of this have been made less weighty — while this semiformal process has perhaps prevented the team from clearly delineating certain of the characteristics of mathematics. In spite of that, the above mentioned attempt clearly shows that what is essential to the science of mathematics consists to a great extent in elaborating its *contents* under new forms.

Does that mean that this remarkable reconstruction gives every satisfaction to our French critical minds? The very foundation of it seems to have caused some embarassment to the team, which—in what regards the theory of "ensembles"—did not venture further than drawing up a plain *fascicle of results,* which we must add, is on the whole quite classical. This very classicality and conformity to accepted theories may cause some uneasiness; we have mentioned above Poincaré's restrictions, and Brunschvicg too has pointed out the radical difference which separates "a logical class" from "a mathematical class." Looking from another angle, Koyré maintains that some of the classes used by mathematics are

58. Nine pamphlets up to this day, published without interruption since 1939 in spite of the hardships of German occupation and the enormous difficulties due to it (Paris, Hermann).

not "totalizable." The question here examined is rather delicate to analyze; let us just mention that the authors of the present article have set forth a logic of "ensembles," taking the word in its usual sense of *"collections,"* and showing that it is possible to start from this notion to define the "ensembles-Mengen" of the classical theory of "ensembles." Still they limit both notions to the *finite,* not having yet published any final account of the theory in the special case, when the notion of the so-called "infinite" is brought into play. They have just produced, on the subject, a sketch of the theory of powers, laying stress on the fact that this theory covers the entire range of the usual arithmetic of the integer without ever resorting to the "infinite series of powers."

Besides the reservations which concern the foundations themselves, it is important to notice the uneasiness felt by several mathematicians concerning some of the reconstructions which have been drawn up, for they are not sure of recognizing in them the objects of their usual studies. Such is the case of the notion of *number*: the unity of this notion, which appears as certain to most scientists, finds itself in Bourbaki's work (as happens in the studies of many investigators, though starting from different definitions) somewhat scattered and clouded. Many are the scientists who believe that the notion of number is far richer than that purely formal "counterfeit" as they even term it. The vivacity of such objections shows, moreover, that the axiomatization of mathematics remains a fruitful field full of life and promise, which confirms the presumption already expressed, that it might be quite premature to discuss its methods dogmatically.

So we have seen that demonstrative logic has enjoyed rather an original life [59] in our country. Classically, demonstration is opposed to induction (the two together covering the whole field of deduction on condition that one should consider hypothetico-demonstration as an element common to both) and many logicians have dreamed, following John Stuart Mill, of giving an account of induction similar to that which is given of demonstration. Still the problem is somewhat different, and André Lalande [60] has dealt with various widespread illusions on the subject. His semihistorical exposition is the quarry from which are extracted materials for most new studies of any account in this field. He had made the French public discover Whewell's views, so startling in their present-

59. Let us incidentally mention the beginnings of new developments in connection with psychology in recent work by Jean Piaget — especially in *Classes, relations et nombres,* (Paris, Vrin, 1942), a book that a logician, however, may find questionable in places.
60. *Les théories de l'induction et de l'expérimentation,* Paris, Boivin, 1929 [rewritten from notes for lectures which had been delivered in 1921-1922].

day value, and first described the growing awareness, all through the evolution of logic, of the major part played by hypothesis in the inductive process. Taking up again the ideas still in a relatively entangled state which had been propounded by Lachelier, he also most felicitously endeavored to draw a distinction between the problem of *foundation* and that of *principle*.

Let us also mention the fine opuscule of criticism published by Maurice Dorolle[61] together with the *Essai sur la connaissance approché*[62] by Gaston Bachelard—the latter being definitely more attracted toward questions of methodology in experimental science, a subject which, in other publications, is liable to become an excuse for more or less laborious compilations done by persons rather devoid of real scientific culture, at least of the kind required for the working out of these general surveys. Hence it is fitting that some diffidence should be shown with respect to anything published which borrows too many examples from the minor sciences, among which one must count, for the time being, descriptive chemistry and biology. It is probably useful for a physician to know Claude Bernard's writings, but a logician, by adhering too closely to them, would thereby betray a rather rudimentary knowledge of the general form and of the motives of present-day scientific knowledge. Meyerson himself, owing to his early technical training, has often remained in his historico-critical work, *Le cheminement de la pensée,* all unconsciously, at a stage of thinking which contemporary physics has long since outgrown; in this branch of science he has too often been obliged to resort to the confidences of some research worker playing the truant out of his laboratory and ill-prepared for philosophical considerations. If, on the other hand, his partial realism, his perfectly Aristotelian substantialism—giving him a justified and sufficient outlook when dealing with chemistry such as it was in 1880—were subsequently fortified by his long and painstaking inquiries, one may suspect that he was but ill-trained for seeing anything beyond that. Yet, the perusal of Meyerson's work remains profitable, but for other reasons and from a different standpoint.

Likewise, on the subject of induction in general, it is profitable to refer frequently to the work of the philosophers mentioned quite at the beginning: *L'expérience humaine et la causalité physique*[63] by Léon Brunschvicg will, for instance, be specially worth reading in this respect. We also have at our disposal books more definitely centered on the meth-

61. *Les problèmes de l'induction.* Paris, Alcan, 1925.
62. Paris, Vrin, 1928.
63. Paris, Alcan, 1922.

odology of one special branch of science or other; they are often collections of studies by various authors [64] or the records of discussions between specialists which unfortunately rarely bring anything beyond passably heterogeneous documentations destined to be used in future syntheses.[65]

The principles of induction have also attracted the attention of Jean Nicod,[66] who, deeply influenced by Keynes's conceptions, made an attempt to widen their scope. The gist of this essay, which consists in making induction rest on what René Berthelot terms "numerical probabilities," has been contested even beforehand by the latter, who had already had the opportunity to admonish Poincaré for having been slightly inaccurate in the expression of his thought on the subject: referring to a distinction made by Augustin Cournot, he opposed to the above-mentioned probabilities "ordinal probabilities" and showed that they alone come into play in the process of induction. This point of view was confirmed (quite independently) by a critical inquiry by Poirier,[67] in which he ruins, resorting to definite examples, the probabilistic interpretation that is sometimes quite imprudently given of them. Robert Blanché, the author of a fragmentary translation of Whewell's *Novum organum renovatum,* had previously given to the public an important study on *Le rationalisme de Whewell*[68] in which the sections devoted to the views on induction of the English philosopher and the new depth of meaning given by him to the term *colligation* often bear an individual stamp without deviating from the original. The authors of the present study have, on their part, tried to delineate the structure of inductive inferences.[69] The outline they have given shows among other things that this very way of having recourse to colligation springs from an allegiance to formal rules, and abundantly insists on its preeminent importance: would not Aristotle have been, in this case too, a precursor in spite of the sarcasm that was showered on him for asking that the horse should be seen in Bucephalus and the man in Socrates?

Through this rapid survey of contemporary French logic we hope to have shown clearly that this department of knowledge has preserved an

64. Typical of this kind of work (though in parts obsolescent) are the two volumes published under the title *De la méthode dans les sciences,* Paris, Alcan, 1908 and 1911.

65. As for the considerations concerning microphysics — a science the matter of which has not at present been quite clearly worked out — the less said about them, probably the better.

66. *Le problème de l'induction.* Paris, Alcan, 1926.

67. *Remarques sur la probabilité des inductions.* Paris, Vrin, 1931.

68. Paris, Alcan, 1935.

69. Problems which had already been tackled by Luquet, *Revue philosophique* (1935), and in which work, according to his own confession, he had but half succeeded (that might partly be imputed to the fact that he restricted himself to the use of material implication).

intense life of its own, though the voices of its representatives are rarely heard in international circles. We have given a few circumstantial reasons for it. There are others which are deeper, and pertain to the characteristics of our intellectual background. A time-honored tradition, the long habit of hearing clearness and coherence praised, make French workers abstain from making an indiscriminate use of any material that may be at hand or building in a confused way without any general plan, or progressing by blind leaps in the dark. University training in France has a tendency to encyclopedism, a defect with which it has often been reproached. It is certain that when one wants to train highly specialized engineers and technicians, this tendency may present serious inconveniences and occasion an excessive proportion of failures. Yet it becomes obvious that as a person's field of action grows wider, this kind of intellectual formation seems to create the best preliminary conditions that could be wished. If we consider the outstanding names mentioned in the course of this article,[70] is it not patent, in fact, that active research workers in logic come, almost exclusively, either from the ranks of mathematicians well trained in the critical discussion of philosophical questions, or from those philosophers endowed with a personal experience in mathematics?[71] In particular, the existence of well-attended courses in philosophy in secondary schools [72] helps many a scientist in avoiding excessive naiveté where general ideas are concerned, or in the rediscovery (on their own account) of an empiricism comparable to Hume's—a narrow empiricism which seems to be the spontaneous ontology of the adult once he has set foot in a laboratory, just as Aristotelism is the ontology of a child once he has learned how to speak (an Aryan language).

We therefore feel fully assured that, as soon as all the preliminary work which is now in progress has reached its ends, the French influence shall felicitously bring its contribution to the activity of the other nations.

---

70. Theirs are very probably the only works in which posterity shall look for what will have been valid and effective in the contemporary French philosophical movement.

71. The first as well as the others must of course be sufficiently conversant with the problems of ulterior sciences, especially with those of physics.

72. In spite of its several shortcomings and its scholasticism. But might not one utter the same opinion on the way in which mathematics is taught?

THE PHILOSOPHY OF
VALUES IN FRANCE

*Raymond Polin**

hereas, outside France, axiological research had been in full swing from the beginning of the century, French philosophers only began to devote themselves to the study of values, considered as such, at a very recent date. C. Bouglé looked like a forerunner, even in 1922, when he gave one of his books the title of *Leçons de sociologie sur l'évolution des valeurs.* So that, in a country where philosophic traditions have always had peculiar prestige and influence, the contemporary philosophy of values in France finds itself without any direct tradition and always seems to apply, more or less, for its source to doctrines imported from abroad.

No doubt, it might be said that literature has been, for a long time, open to widely axiological preoccupations. The immoralism of a writer like Gide, or the manifestations of surrealism are questioning values viewed as a whole, either by creating between them a vast osmosis, and stressing their specific originality, or by treating them all, whatsoever they may be, with the same destructive rage and the same nihilism.

It seems, on the other hand, that one has met, on the part of the philosophy experts, with a systematic refusal to think in terms of values for a much longer period than in any other country. The influence of Nietzsche's *Umwertung aller Werte* has proved to be negligible with all of them, to such an extent that his claim to be a philosopher is still sometimes questioned, and that he is acknowledged and praised merely as a poet.[1] Even in 1938, E. Bréhier, in a well-known article strongly criticized the notion of value which, he thought, would lead to outdated, verbal, or indefinite solutions.[2] Two essential reasons, though seemingly contradictory, concur to render traditional French spiritualism hostile to

* Born in 1910. Student at the École Normale Supérieure. Agrégé de philosophie; docteur ès-lettres. Formerly professor of philosophy at the lycées Rollin and Condorcet, Paris. Professor of ethics, University of Lille. Author of works listed in the bibliography.
    1. A. Lalande, *La raison et les normes* (Paris, Librairie Hachette, 1948), p. 25.
    2. E. Bréhier, "Doutes sur la philosophie des valeurs," in *Revue de métaphysique et de morale,* (1939).

the use of the notion of value as an instrument of philosophical reflection, and to the specificity and concrete signification of this concept.

On one hand, the French tradition gives such a considerable place to moral phenomena, that it seems inadmissible not to study them for themselves, since they are at once important and concretely apprehensible: the goods, the rights, the ideals, the duties, the virtues, the moral facts are "pre-given" in a concrete and sufficient manner. Why should we complicate reflection and make it indirect by using an additional, more abstract concept? Could it be to realize a more systematic conceptualization?

But, on the other hand, the unity of the different types of values is often proclaimed so categorically that it becomes useless to create a concept of value, with the intention of making it, and it alone, on principle, capable of subsuming the different species of values, whether moral, esthetic, logical, sacred, etc. . . . If the true or the beautiful may be reduced to the good, or, eventually, two of these values to the third, we need not consider values as a species: the only authentic species is thus that of the goods, or truths, or beauties.

Now, it is the species of the goods that has prevailed generally, and the ethical systems which have been elaborated, being self-sufficient, precluded all attempts at a systematic axiology. The more so as those systems, by denying any specificity to the goods themselves as well as to all the other values, endeavor to reduce the moral question to two key problems and generally attempt to solve the first by the second: how is the validity of the goods to be founded? How can they be known? Such are the typical themes of all the contemplative ethical systems in the French tradition.

It is on these themes that a typical conflict has been taking place, for some years. And if we group in two directions the present trends of the French philosophy of values, we may put together, on one side, those attempting to maintain the traditional positions, using a new language if necessary, and, on the other side, those attempting to overthrow them and adopting attitudes if not new, at least revolutionary as far as France is concerned. We shall use this simplification, though with caution, for it corresponds to a doctrinal and methodological conflict, and, at the same time, to a discussion between two generations: that which preceded the two World Wars, and that which followed.

I. THE TRADITION OF OBJECTIVE AXIOLOGIES

One might say, in other terms, that the scission appears, if one traces it back to its origin, between those who believe in an objective foundation for values, and those who uphold their more or less radical subjectivity. Let us first consider those who, according to the traditions handed down to them, endeavor to found the legitimacy of values and their existence on their participation in a given transcendent, absolute in one way or another, as if the presence of an absolute entirely *other* were for man, and for each man, the sole guarantee and foundation of his values.

The seekers of the absolute had received support, not very long ago, from illustrious names, and encouragement from the extreme poles of French philosophy.

At the positivist pole, Durkheim himself had gradually come to seek the foundation of moral facts in the reality, incommensurable with individual consciousness, of a collective consciousness, the object of a mystic desire and a source of obligation, which, though it was a "fact" in Durkheim's opinion, nevertheless, played the part, in his system, of a given transcendent. When in his last works, he longed to transpose into social terms the unaccounted-for *a priori's* of Kantism, he would show their validity only by constructing a real metaphysics and by founding the objectivity of values on the absolute exteriority of the social, and finding again in the collective conscience the perfection of the sovereign good and the creative power, which are the ordinary attributes of the deity.

At the opposite pole, the belated message of Bergson also summons moralists to the quest for the absolute, the transcendent object presented as the source of all moral and religious virtues. No doubt, the absolute constitutes the keystone of his system; and in the divine absolute, Bergson will find the principle of all life and all creation—life itself, this vital impetus the origin of which he now sees in the divine creative impetus, which is a love impetus because it is creative and a creative impetus because it is love.

Yet his main effort at elucidation does not bear on this transcendent object which makes men sure of themselves because it is better than they, but on the quest for and the experience of this transcendent. The main point is less to find God and the guarantee implied in Him, than to seek Him and feel Him. The stress is placed, not on the divine object, but on the subjective experience of the mystic who, in the creative emotion, participates in its objectivity. That is the reason why Bergson can assert that values spring from a mystic creation, this creation being understood as coinciding in part with the creative vital effort. ("This effort

is of God, if not God himself." [3] Values *have* value because they manifest the creative love of great mystics, but this love would have no sense
if it had no object.) So the Bergsonian description of mysticism is chiefly
concerned with showing that it does not achieve its end in ecstasy, in the
passive contemplation of the object, but in action which unites creative
energy and love, on one hand, and on the other, the divine objective will.
Thus mysticism would cease to lose itself in the sands of mystery or to
become frozen in the motionless ice of the object, but would irrigate,
with its lifegiving waters, practical values and a system of ethics.

One thus realizes that what divides the objectivist philosophers is far
less the nature of the objective transcendent reality or the kind of guarantee it brings to values—indeed, Bergson reveals this proximity when he
links together "the two sources of morality"—than the way in which man
and values participate in it. Since the objectivist presentation of the problem reduces the research for the foundation of values to a problem of
knowledge, it is about the method and scope of this knowledge that the
present divergences may be observed among philosophers; and they are
so great that even among the seekers of the absolute, it is diversity carried
to the point of disorder that is the clearest characteristic of contemporary
French thought. Thus, we see the philosophers of mystery walking side
by side with the philosophers of lucid reason, and monists opposed to
dialecticians, whereas sociology is persistently maintaining its position.

Meanwhile, Georges Gurvitch, aided by a scholarly, international
culture had, even before the war, attempted a vast synthesis. In his
opinion, values are the magnetic poles of individual aspirations, and also
of collective aspirations; they are subjective and projected by the "closed
consciousness," but objective too and given by the "open consciousness."
After all, the objectivity of values only means that they cannot be resisted
or substituted within a system of equivalent values. Consequently, they
are neither absolute nor immutable, but relative, at least because they are
"lived" in acts which experiment and test them. And what is important
for Gurvitch is precisely the nature of the immediate experience in which
one lives them, now an affective intuition, now a "volitive intuition," the
decision to act also constituting an intuition of value. At the extreme, by
participating in the creation of fresh values, the subject supremely experiences the "trans-personal flux of creative liberty," as foreseen by
Fichte.

———

3. *The Two Sources of Morality and Religion*, translated by R. A. Audra (New York,
Henry Holt and Co., 1935).

Between the revolutionary experience of moral values and the conservative experience of judicial values there is room to found a sociological description.

That was the main purpose of Gurvitch. But as a doctrine of values, such an eclecticism has encountered all the difficulties common to all kinds of eclecticism, within which the most ingenious notions are counterbalanced and annihilated by their neighbors, and where the answers are less striking than the questions they raise. Contemporary French philosophers have generally been less preoccupied with synthesis and continuity, than with carrying their ideas to a logical conclusion, as if to put them to the test. And, following them, we shall rather try to point out extreme positions and to study borderline cases.

Insofar as we may reduce to an outline the thought of Gabriel Marcel, we might describe it as a forward-and-backward movement composed of "calls" and invocations from the ontological mystery to the mystery of incarnation and from the mystery of incarnation to the ontological mystery. In this direction, he does not meet with an actual moral doctrine, but, every minute his footsteps rouse moral echoes and axiological vibrations; he tries concretely to approach the ontological mystery by meditating on faithfulness, hope, and love. The axiological situations constitute the favorite themes of his analyses for they allow him to suggest the fundamental mystery of a call which is a call only because it is called, of a creation which is a creation only because it is created and an acknowledgment of creation, of a liberty which is belonging to God, and which belongs to itself only if it belongs to Him.

Values have no sense except in relation to man, but they are valid only through God; they express less a "synthesis" than a "contact," a communication with the absolute "Thou." It is the presence of this unfathomable reality that endows one's experience with its values and their dense and mysterious concreteness. The characteristic of human values is to be beyond the human, to be *"between"*: hope is hope only if it is more than hope, if it is not truly a hope but the irradiation, creative of hope, of an absolute presence.

One realizes that, from this standpoint, acts are not considered in their objective, creative efficiency, but in their ability to realize values, since the latter exist in God sufficiently, before any human act: action is the means whereby, by engaging itself, the personality constitutes, assumes, and incarnates itself. Instead of ending with an ethical system, Gabriel Marcel overflows with an affective effusion that constitutes both the favorite "milieu" for the analyses in which he excels, and eventually their strictly traditional theme, which is no other than the dialectics of desire and its object. Values are illumined but they become diffused and are dissolved until they lose themselves in their affective halo.

In a completely different climate—such as might make possible a Cartesian who has frequented surrealism—Ferdinand Alquié tries to solve the same problem and finds the same difficulties. It is the same problem, since values are in his view specifications of the Spirit, that is to say of the eternal and infinite transcendent, of which man is so willing to make a God; they are eternal and universal like Him. Action is nothing but the moral process moving from the universal to the individual and from the eternal to the temporal, which imposes values on concrete reality. In the human sphere, there is no act but through the intervention, within an individual self, of the Spirit that inserts this individual self into the general course of the world. Thus, according to Descartes, God is pure action and man is His own image only insofar as he wills.

But if the Cartesian monism of reason proposed a solution of the problems by considering knowledge as the pure form of action and its vehicle, according to Alquié, the concept of action remains ambiguous, and so do values. For he professes, at the same time, that only the act is the free action of the eternal Spirit, and that, however, there is no act but through the agency of man. As for values, they are both eternal and realizable in time; they are at the origin of the act, but though they be values, they cannot serve as its ends. And what can be said of this human subject through whom the action of the Spirit exerts itself in the world, but which is suppressed and obliterated all the more completely as it acts more effectively? With a fine and accurate sensibility, Alquié evokes the irreconcilable themes of the doctrines of objective values, but he succeeds in evoking with them the mere ghost of a reconciliation.

Thus the neo-Cartesian call for the absolute is answered by the same silence as the mystic call. Could the use of dialectics enable us to reconcile these irreconcilable themes? Such is the hope of René Le Senne when he asserts that every value appears as a relation between a transcendent, "the Absolute, unknowable in its superabundant plenitude," and an immanence, the testing and the experience of an individual value by a given subject in a definite historical situation: in a double dialectic process, the Absolute emits the value and creates the self, the self tests and experiences the value through participating in its creation. From the self originates the quest, from the Absolute, the grace that rewards it.

So that value is neither a mere knowledge, though it may grasp the absolute in an intuition of a mystic character, nor a mere existence. Every substance seems to be axiological, and every existence may be found between infinite value and nothingness ("néant"); reality, for instance, results from a cross-section of value made by theoretical knowledge.

In every value, therefore, is manifested absolute value, for value is absolute or else it is not value. And as soon as the Absolute presents itself as the source of values, it appears as Perfection and should be named God. For value is personal and connects personal existences. By creating the human Self, value gives itself to him and unites him existentially with God. R. Le Senne sometimes defines it as the existential union of God and Self, that is to say, of two persons. God who is the totality of experience, insofar as he is value, is thus the *I* of value. *My Self* confronted with an obstacle tests and experiences value, which ceases to be an ideal, and becomes a creative experience in the love and action it inspires.

Thus, the two key notions of Le Senne's system seems to be this personal axiological Absolute and the existential dialectics which unites it to the creature in the form of value. Now, this Absolute is threatened with sterility by the following dilemma: either it is radically transcendent and different, and it can create and found values, but we cannot reach it and it is totally exterior and incommunicable, like its creations. Or, the existential dialectics enables us to reach it, but it ceases to be transcendent; it comes within the scope of man and becomes neither more nor less capable than he is of founding values. If dialectics succeeded in establishing a relation of interiority between the Absolute and individual consciousness, it would deteriorate into a mere knowledge—does not R. Le Senne himself define value as the knowledge of the Absolute?—and would degrade the Absolute until it became something immanent, imperfect, useless, and inefficient. If it does not succeed, it runs the risk of not really leaving the convenient paradise of the Absolute, and of never touching the earth where men live, uncertain and imperfect but concrete, with their hazardous actions.

Is there not an irreducible solution of continuity between Le Senne's axiology and his fine and profound characterology, so full of human meaning, and so unconcerned with the Absolute? Or could it be that he has sought, in a systematic attempt at understanding human individuals, a satisfaction that he has been unable to find in his meditations, however brilliant they may be, on value, the ever absolute value? In spite of dialectics, the irreconcilable notions are in danger of remaining completely apart. The pluralistic objectivism of values finds its unity only at the risk of sacrificing its concrete signification and its practical efficiency.

Louis Lavelle would perhaps explain that the question has been put in a wrong way, and that it should have been formulated, from the outset, in monistic terms. For him, indeed, everything is action, original indivisible activity, which creates itself, and founds itself and wills itself, creating itself, which is wholly its own sufficient reason, its intelligibility and its end. The Absolute, perfection, God, such are a few of its names.

The being is action considered in its source, in its universal interiority; it coincides with the good, since it is a sufficient reason and an end. The good is absolute will in action, in other words, the whole world willed by all the individual wills. For individual existences are nothing but the acts through which participation in action takes place. They realize actions engaged in the participation, and the good presents itself to them in the form of values. The latter realize in their turn the good engaged in the participation and the sufficient reason of existences in the situation where the act becomes individualized in them.

We feel in this series of definitions the development of an identity action=action=action, which makes its theoretical strength, but also its practical weakness. In this monolithic block, individual existences, their values, and their ideals are absorbed and fused. What is the good of knowing that values are founded by their participation in the Absolute, if they become devoid of significance in their singularity and their historical situation? No doubt the ideal invites us to go beyond reality, the act always being beyond what is accomplished. But even if the call to participate in action is necessarily indeterminate, it is paradoxically answered before being heard, since we exist and have a value only by virtue of this participation. By enclosing oneself within a metaphysical system of unity—even if it is the unity of action—one suppresses the opportunity for the act, as well as its terms, and ethics becomes useless.

It seems that these various philosophers, by adopting the Platonic view of an objective axiological transcendent, have inevitably encountered a series of problems. Either they maintain a plurality between the Absolute, values, and men, and encounter the insoluble difficulties of participation; or they lose themselves in the contemplation of an ineffable sovereign good, and they never emerge from it. In both cases, the more they resort to the Absolute, the better they suppress the problems of axiology and ethics. But they do not solve them, nevertheless.

II. THE SUBJECTIVIST AXIOLOGIES

This has been deeply felt by some philosophers, brought up in the meditation over the disorders which have prepared or accompanied the last World War. They have generally thought that a great distance separated the objectivist philosophers from the actual history of our time and its moral problems, as if the gigantic wings of these metaphysicians, meant to frequent the transcendent and consort with the Absolute, prevented them from walking on the earth and through history. They have been tempted to inaugurate their philosophical life by systematically doubting the transcendent objectivity of values, and by a refusal, temporary at least, to resort to the Absolute. Thus have been gradually built axiologies which are subjectivist in a great variety of ways.

Some have succumbed to the extreme temptation of nihilism, and have concentrated their thought on the non-being of values. Such is Jean Grenier, who, attentive to Indian philosophy, takes pleasure in demonstrating the vanity of all values. Indeed, they annul one another, so diverse are they and so many irreducible disagreements exist between men on that subject. Each existence goes beyond its reason for existing. To conceive these means reducing them to being. Now, the being is the indifferent. Would not wisdom, if one may hazard this too sublime word, consist in acknowledging the vanity of all values, going beyond the illusory exigencies of a purely apparent choice, and living in indifference? The advantage would be to free oneself from the pathetic and, perhaps, by abandoning oneself to the given situation, we could play more fully our human part, without according more value to it on that account.

One feels indeed that Jean Grenier is often tempted to seek peace and serenity in this abandonment to his *Karman,* but also in the renunciation of action and of the self. But this nihilism represents for him a passively experienced temptation rather than an active attempt.

On the contrary, Albert Camus's nihilism attests a kind of harsh, cold rage; it resembles a denunciation directed against the meaning of values rather than against their metaphysical essence—a denunciation of the absurdity of all the values scattered in an absurd universe, in a chaotic world where chance is king—a denunciation of a world where out of the anarchy of values is born their equivalence and their nonbeing is confirmed; where everything is given, where there is, consequently, no room for values and ideals, where thoughts as well as lives are deprived of a future. The only kind of liberty accessible to man is the state of "readiness" (*"disponibilité"*) which, arising from a total lack of attachment and interest toward everything, deprives the values of their meaning and of their illusory hierarchies. For man who lives without an Absolute and, consequently, without the necessary obedience, there is no ethics, no justification, no commandment. The only creative action which "the absurd man" is allowed to practice is re-creation, i.e., the mimicry and repetition of its own reality. "Absurd man" is neither responsible, nor guilty, since action has no meaning: he lives in innocence and may find in his lucidity the source of a bitter joy.

But, by a process very typical of contemporary French ethical doctrines, if Camus adopts nihilism for a while, he does not persist in it, in his philosophic reflection or his personal life. For there is no question of abandoning oneself to nothingness and to that death which he hates so intensely. The problem is to live—which is possible only through revolt that becomes, because of this choice, the foremost truth and fundamental value of clear-headed man, superior to his destiny—a revolt against the given order, reputed sacred and divine, in the name of a human order. As if, with Camus, under the influence of love (and perhaps of pity), the value of man were assuming form and dignity. We must therefore understand revolt, out of absurdity, but against absurdity, as a value through which man goes beyond himself. In particular, revolt gives back to action its very meaning even if it does not take away its vanity, for it permits us to justify ourselves through a protest against the world. We must know how to revolt with only the hope of going beyond "the anguish of feeling limited" (*angoisse*) and beyond eternity, understanding and assuming our human condition, in the quest for inner peace.

No doubt the work of Albert Camus is more remarkable for its wealth of philosophic intentions and acts—political acts, artistic creations —than for the systematic elaboration of a doctrine. Going beyond the nihilism of the absurd implies an apparent incoherence, if not in its intention at least in its form. But we can find in the system of Jean-Paul Sartre the same reversal of position and the same attempt to change over from a nihilism of values to a morality of action. Sartre does not approach the axiological problem directly; he solves it rather by way of consequence. He starts from an ontology and one feels he is entirely preoccupied with static, motionless being. Now, value is precisely what is not, what is beyond being and what has to be; rather, since Sartre can admit nothing but the being, value has this double character, this fundamental ambiguity of being unconditionally and of not being. It can thus be revealed only by "human-reality" by the being-for-itself whose nature consists in being cognizant of itself as a lack of being, as a "want." What the being-for-itself wants, what it at once a "want" and a failure, (*le manqué de tous les manques*) is indeed value understood as the impossible totality of the being-in-itself and of the being-for-itself, as their impossible synthesis, that which is sometimes called God. Value at its origin, the supreme value, is the *beyond* and the *toward* of transcendence, the beyond that calls for and goes beyond all transcendencies.

As such, value which is given with the self (from the original stage of the non-thetic self-consciousness) constitutes the absolute being of the self, its cause and foundation. It is the being that the being-for-itslf has to be and which he makes itself be by going beyond itself and "annihilating" itself (*néantir*). Value haunts the being-for-itself insofar as it founds itself only because it is liberty. Value exists only through liberty, liberty exists only for the sake of value.

But we must not lose sight of the fact that value is, at the same time, rejected from the being, expelled even from any possible realization. There is no value except in what is different from reality, in "imaginary creations" (*l'imaginaire*). Is not imagination total consciousness as it transcends itself and realizes its liberty? Now, once reduced to imaginary creations, all values are equivalent; and consequently, no longer exist in relation to one another. Imaginary creation is always an effect and never a cause. One cannot proceed from imaginary creation to reality. No axiological motive has any meaning, no imaginary creation prepares for a future action. The values which "haunt" the being-for-itself are only phantoms. Value is given with the self, but together with its non-being. We understand Sartre's condemnation of the "seriousness" (*esprit de sérieux*) which, on the contrary, considers imaginary values as transcendent realities and desirable objectives in conformity with the nature of things. And seriousness is never without unconscious double-dealing (*mauvaise foi*) for every now and then it undertakes to defend objects and ignores the essential subjectivity of values.

Now, far from refusing every form of ethics, Jean-Paul Sartre, assisted by Simone de Beauvoir, starts precisely from the subjectivity of imaginary values, and from each man's "situation" in the world, to announce ethical researches. The choice of an ethical system—for there shall no longer be any universal moral law—will depend on the ambiguity of the ontological situation proper to "human reality." Since the self *is* only because it makes itself and exists only by reaching beyond itself toward the impossible value, since all its projects are illusions and find no objective support anywhere, its existence is manifested in a situation by which it finds itself effectively "engaged." In his vain attempt to realize value as the totality of the being-in-itself and the being-for-itself, and in order to be God, each human individual makes himself exist as a man. The individual only is capable of founding his own existence. It is for him to assume his ambiguity, to accept the inevitable limitation of his human achievement, to exercise his liberty not in order to "capture" the being, but to "unveil" it.

It is liberty which constitutes, after all, the central theme of a Sartrian ethics—not the central value since man *is* free and even condemned to *being* free—the liberty which one assumes, which one reconquers from the "facticity" (*facticité*) of existence, and for which one accepts the absolute and final responsibility; which means, no doubt, that this liberty is the stuff of my being as a man, since it coincides essentially with the nothingness that is in my inmost self. This liberty which is given me, I have to be, instead of ignoring it "with unconscious double-dealing" or running away from it. An endless task, a permanent and ambiguous conquest, since it consists in being endlessly other than I am. To assume its liberty is for "human reality" to understand itself and choose itself such as it is—by renouncing supreme value, as well as all values, to accept to be its own being for itself and to be *it* totally.

It seems as though, having begun with a description of being, Sartre could not join values, action, the flux of history. He runs the risk of immobilizing man under color of apprehending him better. Driven to reject values out of the being, he finds room for them only in "imaginary creation." But the more he confuses them with this creation, the more he is menaced with losing all sense of effective action, which transforms reality, and loses all grip on it. To assume one's humanity, to accept the responsibility of one's individual situation, is not to act; we can even ask ourselves what is the use of prizing so highly a liberty since it is given to us. If we identify liberty with the being-for-itself, choice with consciousness, are we not led to confuse action with existence totally for itself, and, in the end, to reduce this existentialist ethics to an ethics of lucid self-knowledge?

That is why some have thought that, in order to understand values and to arrive at an ethics of action, one should start neither from transcendent Absolute, nor from a static ontology, but from the values themselves, or rather from evaluation understood as the dialectic unity of value, action, and achievement. Values are nothing, if they are not potential actions, their mimicry, and in fact their preparation. At least that is what is revealed by their phenomenological analysis, as we have ourselves endeavored to show. One notices, in effect, that a value, for the consciousness which thinks about it, coincides with its signification. It exists as an actual consciousness. Man is originally an axiological consciousness, which is the same as saying that he cannot but think in terms of values. They constitute for each consciousness its history as existence, and its history as thought; they are human and subjective like it. But the only concrete phenomenon, i.e., the only phenomenon, forming an independent whole, that can be thought of separately, is the creative process by which consciousness raises itself beyond the given reality, invents a value, then, according to this evaluation, attempts to act on the given and to impose upon it an order that should be its own work. This process arises from the dialectic succession of transcendencies owing to which creative consciousness goes beyond itself, and, at the same time, beyond all the given reality, to invent the *other,* intentionally to create between the imagined *other* and reality a hierarchical relationship, and to transform in an effort of effective and efficient transcendence the given reality in accordance with the chosen imaginary project. Value is therefore the very opposite of a knowledge through immanence aiming at a transcendent in one way or another; it is itself, a transcendence in action, creative of a hierarchy, it must be thought of as a kind of action.

But it goes without saying that, if the existence and the signification of a value depend on its original creation, the transcending impetus which animates it cannot exert itself without undergoing exterior pressures, and becoming heavier with extraneous attractions. Thus, the dialectics of transcendence and desire, essential to consciousness, is embodied in the existential dialectics of values and tendencies, which tends to transform the original and changing axiological creations into stable and communicable *goods* linked with affective attractions or repulsions. Or else, by reflecting or redoubling itself, the hierarchy-making activity of transcendence tends to present itself to itself as a kind of given transcendent in the shape of a *norm.* It is indeed in the form of goods and, even more often, of implicit or explicit norms, that the presence of others manifests itself axiologically, and that a crude communication takes place between one consciousness and another, each one tending to impose on the other its own transcendence and values. In the shape of goods and norms, values gradually lose all their axiological virtue and originality, and only maintain a more and more mechanical power of compulsion.

The historical situation of each results from the attractions and pressures he suffers, and from the more or less keen effort made to transcend them by creating personal values. The irreducible pluralism of values, which is a consequence of that, brings about an irreducible individualism of human consciousnesses. That is why a doctrine of the creation of values must be doubled by an explanation of their comprehension. The subtle comprehension of values and of another's consciousness demands the gradual reconstitution of the world of his axiological intentions and of the order he creates. The comprehension of a value will not attempt the impossible knowledge of it, but will strive to reconstitute the creative attitude of the original inventor and to recreate, not a value identical with the former value, but a value intentionally in harmony and axiological coherence with it. To understand a value is not to realize its authentic resurrection; it is to re-invent the axiological attitude and the law of transcendence peculiar to its creation.

Thus are defined some central themes of a radical subjectivistic un-realism of values, for which, obviously, every value is of necessity uncertain and devoid of any foundation. It may be added that, since any knowledge of values is impossible, the notion of the truth of values is meaningless. But such are precisely the only conditions permitting the elaboration of an ethics of practical liberty, which envisages action neither in the absolute, nor in the eternal, but in the relative and the temporal peculiar to a man who tries to be a man and not God or beast. One cannot act in a human way, one cannot transform the given world except by starting from subjective values, deliberately false and inadequate in comparison with this given: how can one transform reality according to a truth which could only be its revelation? Action, in accomplishing value, makes it real, but in realizing it, it exhausts in it the axiological potential which animated action. One could not act in the evidence of objective values that would cause a serene contemplation and immobility. The uncertainty of subjective values alone expresses the unsatisfied climate of action, which is a climate of adventure and of risk, where everyone is called upon, at any moment, to assume his responsibility in obscure and hypothetical conditions. For the man who, in order to act, has given up looking for a light, a fallacious guarantee and protection in the obedience to something transcendent, has also resolved, once and for all, not to seek for the foundation of the values he attempts to realize, beyond his decision to act.

An ethics of practical liberty will not choose, as its supreme object, a liberty that, as such, would be either given, or gratuitous; liberty will be only the necessary means and the method of action. To choose an ethics is first to appreciate its human character, to choose a human value and a manlike way of acting. This choice is both an ethical as well as a metaphysical choice, and one through the other. It is to elaborate one's ethics just like one's human existence and to create oneself as a man, choosing for one's principles, in relation to oneself, a principle of coherence, with others, a principle of comprehension: only intentionally-sought coherence permits one to live with oneself and to build the sole order compatible with the radical subjectivity of one's own values. Only the will for mutual comprehension, sought ever more deeply, permits one to live with others.

A conclusion should be expected here. Yet it is an obvious and typical fact that, if it is desirable to take sides boldly—and we have just done so —one must beware of any conclusion or final solution. In the present French philosophy of values, no dogma prevails, no school holds ascendency, the notion of a science of values as the source of a new orthodoxy is rejected or considered as outdated.

The diversity of subjective axiologies, in spite of their dynamism, is just as great, we realize, as that of objective axiologies, which are more in conformity with tradition. No doubt there is a rather unfavorable presumption in the fact of not agreeing with one another when people appeal, all together, to an objective and absolute transcendent, while diversity is no longer a sign of disorder for philosophers who support the idea of a radical subjectivity of value; it appears to them, on the contrary, as the necessary condition of reflection and action. But in both groups, philosophies are practiced that look toward the future, toward hope and effective action, and their diversity is at least a proof of a common eagerness in their research, and of a common demand for liberty.

SELECTED BIBLIOGRAPHY

Alquié, Ferdinand. *Le désir d'éternité*. Paris, Presses Universitaires de France, 1943.
Beauvoir, Simone de. See bibliography for Campbell's essay.
Bréhier, Émile. "Doutes sur la philosophie des valeurs." *Revue de métaphysique et de morale*. Juillet, 1939.
Camus, Albert. See bibliography for Campbell's essay.
Grenier, Jean. *Le choix*. Paris, Gallimard, 1941.
——————. *L'indifférence*. Paris, Gallimard, 1946.
Gurvitch, Georges. *Morale théorique et science des moeurs*. Paris, Presses Universitaires, 1937.

Lalande, André. *La raison et les normes*. Paris, Hachette, 1948.

Lavelle, Louis. See bibliography for Le Senne's essay.

Le Senne, René. *Qu'est-ce que la valeur?* Bulletin de la Société française de philosophie, 1946.

——————. See also bibliography for Le Senne's essay.

Marcel, Gabriel. *Homo viator*. Paris, Aubier, 1944.

Nabert, Jean. *Eléments pour une éthique*. Paris, Presses Universitaires, 1943.

Parodi, Dominique. *La conduite humaine et les valeurs idéales*. Paris, Presses Universitaires, 1937.

Polin, Raymond. *La création des valeurs*. Recherches sur le fondement de l'objectivité axiologique. Paris, Presses Universitaires, 1944.

——————. *La compréhension des valeurs*. Paris, Presses Universitaires, 1945.

——————. *Du laid, du mal, du faux*. Paris, Presses Universitaires, 1948.

Ruyer, Raymond. *Le monde des valeurs*. Paris, Aubier, 1949.

Sartre, Jean-Paul. *L'existentialisme est un humanisme*. Paris, Nagel, 1946.

——————. See also bibliography for Campbell's essay.

CATHOLIC PHILOSOPHY
IN FRANCE

Henry Duméry *

Those who look upon Christian philosophies from the standpoint of an outsider are apt to confuse them one with another: for have they not the common will to reserve a place, beyond that accorded reason, for the legitimate functioning of a superior order? However, as soon as these philosophies are scrutinized from within, it is at once recognized that, while alike as *Christian,* they are, nevertheless, different as *philosophies.* The explanation of this is simple: a philosophy is to be judged by its methods and its inner logic, not by its results, however important these may be. It is not, then, surprising that one finds, in France, many thinkers who are brothers in belief and antagonists in philosophy. By this very fact, they make manifest that Catholic doctrine does not lend itself to a sole and invariable projection on the plane of reason. Not only does the diversity of their philosophical perspectives fail to injure their community of faith, but it clearly establishes its transcendence. It is, therefore, possible to present the Catholic thinkers of present-day France, in all their individual originality, without fearing—indeed, quite to the contrary—to cast reflection upon the purity of their Christian inspiration.

In order to avoid the easy fashion of a catalogue, we shall, in this chapter, limit ourselves to the mention of very few names. It is preferable to be very incomplete than to be superficial. Moreover, the merit of those workers who are not mentioned here cannot, by this fact, be diminished: what is said cannot prejudice that which is left unsaid of necessity. Limit-

* Born in 1920. Doctor of the University of Paris; Professor, Stanislas College; Director of Studies (philosophy section) of E.A.F.; Secretary of the Catholic School of Family Sciences. Author of *La philosophie de l'action, Les trois tentations de l'apostolate moderne, L'itinéraire de l'esprit vers Dieu d'après St. Bonaventure* (forthcoming).

ed to a few of its bridgeheads[1] Christian philosophy, in present-day France, can be reduced to four principal tendencies which, again, can be grouped under a handful of names: Maritain and Gilson for Thomism; Marcel for existentialism; Nédoncelle for personalism; and Blondel for the philosophy of action and religion.[2]

I. THE THOMIST CURRENTS: JACQUES MARITAIN AND ÉTIENNE GILSON

French neo-Thomism is a particularly lively philosophical current. The works of Rousselot and Sertillanges are universally known: and thinkers of their persuasion are legion.[3] If, upon this watchtower, I set only two masters from among so many, it is, doubtless, partly because they have become so well known, but it is, more especially, because they complement each other admirably and, in a suggestive diptych, symbolize, in and of themselves, the twofold effort made, in France, to restore, on both the doctrinal and the historical level, the ensemble of the Thomist synthesis.

Maritain[4] is as distinguished in America as in France. Philosopher,

---

1. Without wishing to annex the very high inspiration of Louis Lavelle and René Le Senne, one must seize the present occasion to render homage to these two masters, who, on their own avowal, think in the Christian clime. One must equally mention the name of Edouard Le Roy, of the French Academy, to whom all the world renders homage for his penetration of mind and his fine loyalty; but whose effort in religious philosophy has long been compromised by his harsh anti-intellectualism. Recently, his critique of the intelligence was decanted and the Reverend Father Rideau, S. J., debated it deservedly in the *Études*. Finally, I note, only *in memoriam,* and by exception (for I am to speak here only of the living) the name of Father Laberthonnière, dead in 1932, who was for several years the companion in arms of Maurice Blondel, but who separated from him because of the profound divergencies which revealed themselves between the two thinkers. More moralist than metaphysician, burning apostle of love but redoubtable polemist, Father Laberthonnière became hardened in voluntaristic positions which were never those of the true "philosophy of action."

2. I warn the reader that my sole concern in these pages is to sketch, in broad outlines, the physiognomy of each doctrine, but not to speak its language. While sticking as closely as possible to the thought, I have kept as far as possible from literal expression. Fidelity need not be servile.

3. It might be useful to indicate that French neo-Thomism employs two methods of working, which are quite different and sometimes in conflict: the one of historical inspiration, which is the achievement of specialized medievalists and which tends to recover the message of St. Thomas in its context and its historical relativity; the other of scholastic inspiration, which presents Thomism as a doctrinal block, formed not only by St. Thomas but by the whole School. Separate mention should be made of Aimé Forest, professor at the University of Montpellier, who often recuts Thomist perspectives by those of Malebranche or even Hamelin.

4. Born at Paris, November 18th, 1882. Former professor at the *Institut Catholique* at Paris; former Ambassador of France to the Holy See; teaching, at the present time, in the United States. Principal works (in chronological order): *La philosophie bergsonienne; Antimoderne; Introduction générale à la philosophie*; Petite logique*; Art et scolastique*; Réflexions sur l'intelligence et sur sa vie propre; Trois réformateurs: Luther, Descartes, Rousseau*; Primauté du spirituel*; Le Docteur Angelique*; Religion et culture*; Distinguer pour unir ou les degrés du savoir*; Le songe de Descartes*; Sept leçons sur l'être et les premiers principes de la raison speculative; L'humanisme intégral; Science et sagesse; Raison et Raisons.* (Works translated into English are marked by asterisks.)

artist, and mystic, he began with Bergsonism; but he advanced far beyond this and has ended by taking a position opposed to it. Indeed, in his particular case, conversion to Catholicism involved conversion to Thomism. Certain people have pretended to see, in this last affiliation, the swaddling of the neophyte and a certain prepossession for those positions which facilitated the rupture with his former views. But this explanation has been proved to be a bit of wishful thinking, for it very soon appeared that there was something very like a preestablished harmony between Thomism and the aspirations of Maritain. In short, it would be hard to imagine Maritain as other than a Thomist, that is to say, a defender of intellectualism and a methodical classifier of the degrees of knowledge.

This is because Maritain—and I say it to his honor—seems to us, first and foremost, a logician.[5] If he has set himself against Bergsonian intuitionism and, in general, against the modern spirit, it was to refuse, for good cause, to give primacy to feeling. And if he has enrolled himself under the banner of St. Thomas, it is precisely because this philosopher puts the act of intellection above everything else. But acknowledgment of the primacy of intelligence may be made in various ways. Idealism is also, and, perhaps, above all, *intellectualist.* Why then, does Maritain pursue it with the same sarcasm as the vitalism of Bergson or, again, of Luther and Rousseau? Simply in the name of a logic of which he recognizes the universal value. The idealism of Descartes dissolves being in the *Cogito,* that which amounts, on the logical plane, to reabsorbing the classification of the sciences into the unity of a mind which creates them all with the same claim. On the contrary, for Maritain, logic has not the right to confine the reality of things in a series of purely intellectual relations: it has for its mission to attest that every judgment refers its terms

---

5. It is especially in unedited fashion that I address myself, under the bias of logic, to the justly renowned work of Maritain. But I insist that, to appreciate this doctrine at its true value, it is necessary to go a great way beyond the restricted point of view from which I give it here, under title of review. The vision of the world, offered by the Thomism of Maritain, is nourishment for the soul as well as food for the mind. One could not recommend too highly the reading of the recent work by Madame Raïssa Maritain, *Les grandes amitiés* (first brought out in New York, then in Paris, by Desclée), whose vibrant but restrained fervor gives back the veritable physiognomy of the intrepid lieutenant of St. Thomas Aquinas. Maritain's doctrinal effort appears, then, as an attempt to carry out Thomism in its entirety and to establish it in a perfect philosophical autonomy. "He (Maritain) has become more and more persuaded that the philosophy of St. Thomas, with its incomparably powerful structure, has remained, through the centuries, enveloped in the forms of theology, without making the most of itself, according to its essence; and that the time has come for it to reveal its proper form, its inner organization, and its autonomous development as philosophy. It is upon this task that he has entered, and he believes that it will be the great task of the philosophers of the future, if the future does not betray itself, and if workers are not wanting." (*Les grandes amitiés,* French edition, p. 466.)

—subject and predicate—to a being which is imposed upon the mind as a given and which it suffices to lay bare by abstraction. The classification of the sciences finds again, through this, a diversity articulated according to the very diversity of experience, and not prematurely unified in the bosom of a constituting spiritual activity. It is, thus, solely for a logical and ontological reason that Maritain rejects idealism and subscribes to Thomism.

Moreover, Thomism is the chosen ground of a logicism of distinction, always for this same reason, that, contrary to the identifying mind of the idealist type, the logic derived from Aristotle and regardful of the pluralism of the experimental relations, is led to establish hierarchies, to set up scales, to allow everywhere for planes of cleavage. In a word, like Aristotelianism, Thomism is essentially a classifier. Now, this is precisely where Maritain's logical mind enjoys its greatest triumph. In short, he never does other than classify, that is to say, measure, the degree of being or of intelligibility and place it in a subtly gradated system. Thus, from physics to metaphysics and even to mysticism, the question is to show what, by order, are all the steps to be progressively climbed. So, one obtains a complete topography of the activities of the mind, an exact map of knowledge. The logician is satisfied and also the esthetician.

It will, perhaps, occasion surprise to find us insisting upon this logical aspect of Maritain's thought; for it is customary to emphasize, rather, the metaphysical aptitude of Thomist philosophers. I would reply that the one does not exclude the other, and even that they make a distinct appeal, each to the other, especially when it is a question of Thomism, whose very ontology is a separating and arranging of structures. In any case, faced with the magisterial work of Maritain, it would be grave disloyalty to pass over in silence the unremitting care he has always had to seek first the specifying principle of each reality or of each activity. In fact, has he ever attempted anything other than to open to the light and to order the formal constituents of the various intelligible realities? Think of the importance which, with good cause, questions of frontiers take on for him: it is a matter of delimiting, with precision, the contours of art and mortality, of spiritual and temporal, of faith and reason, and so on. Everywhere is made the implacable effort to distinguish, to purify, to put everything where it belongs; being very well aware, moreover, that proper arrangement is the first step in integration: to distinguish and to unite are one.

However, there is at least one case where zeal for good order runs the risk of giving spatial juxtaposition the preference over organic union.

It is recognized that it is a matter of distinguishing between theology and philosophy, or, better, faith and reason, without producing a play of duplication in the consciousness. Nevertheless, Maritain is willing to take this risk, so imperious is his logical exigency. In his eyes, the philosopher who is a believer is assuredly in a privileged position; for his faith "comforts" him by suggesting what direction can finally assure the entire rectitude of his reason, though this comforting does not go beyond the scope of a subjective aid. The *Christian philosopher* is a philosopher who, because of being Christian in his conscience, will philosophize in security: he is not a Christian who, as philosopher, will fundamentally alter the groundwork of his whole philosophy in the light of the Christian economy. On this point, Maritain refuses, in effect, to ask himself whether reason, *without ceasing to be itself* (which is, indeed, the condition of philosophy) cannot or ought not justify, in its own eyes, its necessary opening up to the supernatural; and whether this ultimate justification is not further inscribed in the record of the most autonomous philosopher. But this refusal on Maritain's part is nothing other than the proper suspicion of a very classic logician, who fears a disarrangement of cadres at the very moment when it is most expedient to anticipate borderline incidents.

Thus, we may say that the great merit of Maritain's philosophical work—leaving aside his social and political works which have become authorities on two continents—is to have restored, in our generation, a certain logical and methodological sense of which we have had and still have too little. In this, Maritain could pass as being more of a Cartesian that he would like to be. But it is certain that liking for the clear and the distinct has, with him, a different savor than with Descartes. With the latter, whom he accuses of "angelism," logic is a triumphal distribution: with Maritain, it is an onerous restitution, an order to retrieve from confusion, not to create imperially. There is, finally, a lesson in modesty which emanates from this patient and impassioned work. We may find charm in the technical aridity of the logician and salute the courage of the thinker as well as the generosity of the Christian.

With Gilson,[6] we pass from the plane of personal reflection to the

---

6. Born at Paris, June 13th, 1884. Professor at the Collège de France. Director of the Institute for Medieval Studies of Toronto. Councilor of the Republic. Member of the French Academy.
    Principal works: *La philosophie au moyen âge; La philosophie de saint Bonaventure*; Introduction à l'étude de saint Augustin; La théologie mystique de saint Bernard*; L'esprit de la philosophie médiévale*; La liberté chez Descartes; Index scolastico-cartesien; Études sur le rôle de la pensée médiévale dans la formation du système cartesien; Les idées et les lettres; Heloise et Abélard; Christianisme et philosophie*; Le realisme méthodique; L'être et l'essence.* (Works translated into English are marked by asterisks.)

plane of historical reconstruction. Now, Gilson set out from Descartes
and parted from him only to turn back, immediately, to retrace the same
stream. For Cartesianism, in which certain thinkers would like to see
an absolute beginning, appeared to him as though filled, at least in its
terminology, with notions borrowed from the scholastics of the middle
ages; wherefore, it became a matter of interest to go back to the source.
There is a certain piquancy in the fact that, after having discovered it,
Gilson remained with it. As he, himself, explains it, in figurative language, what is the use of turning taps when one has a spring within reach
of one's hand?

For Gilson, the spring in question is no other than the doctrine of
St. Thomas Aquinas, replaced in its context and its historic meaning. The
Thomism of history is that marvellous feat which consisted in constituting,
with one same stroke, thanks to the Aristotelian instrument, in distinct
and solidary *sciences,* theology and philosophy. Up to the time of St.
Thomas, according to Gilson, Platonism had been quite successful in constructing a distinctly Christian spirituality and mode of thought. It had
even arrived, under the dominance of St. Augustine, at the elaboration
of several harmonious syntheses, of which the richest and most precise,
from the double viewpoint of philosophy and theology, is that of St. Bonaventura. But only the clear distinction of formal objects, formulated by
Albert the Great and Thomas Aquinas, permits the fixing of properly
scientific statutes, suited to theology and philosophy. From that time, by
a stroke of genius which anticipated modern rationalism, these two sciences found themselves made specific in their matter and form and exacted,
for their valid practice, that their method should first be penetrated. This
was at once to guarantee their fecundity and preserve their integrity.

There is no question of recapitulating, here, or even of giving in brief
summary, Gilson's minutely detailed exposition of Thomism. But two
observations, from the point of view of method, and two others, from
the point of view of doctrine, must be made. Then one will realize the
immense service the historian can render the philosopher.

The first observation concerns Gilson's sagacity and his refusal of all
eclecticism. The positions of the great thinkers are positions pure and
unalloyed: it serves no purpose to confuse them with collusions of viewpoints; it is important, on the contrary, to keep them scraped as bare as
possible. When St. Thomas is in question, that "admirable strategist,"
as Gilson calls him, who was able to tell, at any moment, the full bearing
of the least of his affirmations and to delimit exactly the contour of the

enemy, one must be doubly exacting of precision. Gilson is thus, constantly employed in drawing, from all points, a line of demarcation between the Christian thinkers who are apt to be confused with one another: St. Augustine, St. Bonaventura, and St. Thomas. He follows back, in their entirety, the threads of their respective logics, in order to establish the fact that that which they call by the same name changes meaning according to the light, and that, finally, the methods face each other, foot to foot, drawing from very different propensities the deductive effort of each system. No other historian of Christian philosophy has given such proof as Gilson that thinkers, as we suggested at the beginning of this study, may be in perfect accord as believers while they are opposed to each other as philosophers.

Naturally, Gilson is everywhere occupied with hunting down eclecticism and always with the same vigor. He denounces all the contaminations: those affected by too easy-going historians; those, also, attempted by false disciples of the great masters. He ruins the hybridization of Platonic, Cartesian, and Kantian Thomism, he shoves aside the *cogito* critics who cloak themselves in the name of St. Thomas; he vigorously condemns what he calls inverted realisms. After which, one is sure of seeing more clearly into the matter and prefers to an accord in confusion, a "good disagreement," which is, in short, after the Socratic manner, a harmony created on discord.

But it must not be believed that this praiseworthy passion for ordering data could harden, with Gilson, into exclusivism. Quite the contrary is true, and this second observation is needed to complete the first. The most lucid mind is also the most receptive; for true open-mindedness is discernment. Gilson, then, can be at once the perfect geometer, who immediately grasps the historical coordinates of each system and the perfect honest man, who, without preconceived opinion, penetrates, to the bottom, the various points of view, to delight himself with all perspectives. Thomist with St. Thomas, he makes himself Augustinian with St. Augustine; and his studies of St. Bonaventura and St. Bernard have the same fervor as his presentation of the humanism of Abelard or the Franciscanism of Rabelais. If the gift of sympathy, joined to the faculty of discrimination, defines the true historian of ideas, then it must be said that Gilson was born to carry his specialty to perfection. His example should be eminently profitable to the philosopher always tempted to shut himself up in his starting point and to shut up with him the totality of the tradition. On the contrary, to know, on the one hand, that one cannot win on all the boards, and that one must choose between Plato and

Aristotle, St. Augustine and St. Thomas; and, on the other hand, that the option taken does not abolish the variety of options which could be and are taken up by neighbors, is the sole means of progressing in a straight line and respecting the trajectory of other minds. We shall repeat, in consequence, that Gilson's great merit has been to give us understanding of the selected position as completely differentiated, as impossible to tear apart as to fuse. At the heart of Christian faith, itself, beyond any particular point of view, are a couple of complementary tendencies which, from one end of history to the other, exercise their beneficent antagonism. Let us seek neither to separate nor to blend their components, for, indeed, they can, as Gilson very well expressed it, "neither exclude each other nor coincide."

To these two observations, which give an account of Gilson's method-ological attitude, it will suffice to add, as promised, two others concern-ing the doctrine. In the first place, Gilson, in his character of historian, has given an original interpretation of the relations between reason and faith. He affirms that there is, historically, a *Christian philosophy,* be-cause, historically, there has been a renewal of philosophy, thanks to the contribution of Christianity. Revelation conveying, along with trans-cendent and irreducible truths, certain rational elements, these latter were immediately claimed and assimilated by philosophy, as, for example, the idea of creation. Is there, in addition, an influence exerted by dogma, as such, upon reflection, as might be suggested by the expression, "faith generator of reason"? For this, there is undoubtedly a good claim, even from Gilson's point of view, since it is, in fact, manifest, in some degree, notably in ontology and in theodicy, where the conception of the Christ-ian God brought about an authentic metaphysical revolution. But Gilson is careful to entrench himself in historical perspective and does not attack the question for the sake of dealing with it. It would, indeed, be nec-essary to elaborate a new problematics which would lead to determining the conditions under which reason is able to enrich itself by the contact with faith. This would leave the plane of historic facts, which, upon this point, Gilson has not permitted himself to do, or has permitted him-self only incidentally.

He is certainly less timid on another point. Estimating that the last word of Thomist metaphysics is the discovery of the act of existing, he has launched the idea that Thomism is a philosophy of existence, op-posed to doctrines of essence of the Platonic type. At a stroke, we be-hold intellectualism and existentialism paradoxically reconciled. If the intelligence seeks essences, it is always in the concrete apprehension of a certain existential reality, which forces it to a standstill and constrains it to abstract. The shock of contingence would play, in Thomism, a role analagous to that which it holds in contemporary existentialism. But of course the orientation is different, and one does not stumble upon the existent except in a wholesome rough-and-tumble, which breaks forth providentially in representation and expands in dialectics. For, in fact, existence is never given us in the pure state, but caged in a determination, whence the grasping, at once disjunctive and simultaneous of an essence and an existent; whence, also, the necessary reference of every existent whose essence does not equal existence to the pure act of existing, in which essence and existence are but one. Thus, there would be, in Thomism, a "radical primacy of existence over essence," existing originating everything which is, and the being being this or that only because it, in the first place, is or exists.

Proceeding from history, and remaining faithful to it, Gilson thus succeeds, with rare good fortune, in catching up with preoccupations which are very much of the present day. He has been reproached with having inspired too many pure historians and not enough disciples willing to think problems through again. But it must be declared, on the contrary, that his work follows quite another bent. Gilson has never considered the history of ideas as being mere erudition, and he has definitely given proof that the history of philosophy would cease to be authentic history if it ceased to be philosophy.

II. CHRISTIAN EXISTENTIALISM: GABRIEL MARCEL[7]

We have observed Gilson finding existential resonances in Thomism. They are to be found, at present, in all contemporary works. But, in the days when Marcel launched, in France, the existentialist label, which Sartre has since revamped, the matter seemed new and daring. What, then, did it signify in the beginning, and what is the precise meaning which the Marcelian venture has for us today?

The multiform work of Marcel, who is at once philosopher, dramatist, literary critic, and musician, is not other than a long spiritual itiner-

---

7. Born at Paris, December 7th, 1889, *agrégé de philosophie,* former lycée professor, on indefinite leave of absence since 1923; adherent of Catholicism since 1929.
     Principal philosophical works: *Journal métaphysique* (1927); *Etre et avoir* (1935); *Du refus à l'invocation* (1940); *Homo Viator* (1944); *La métaphysique de Royce* (1947).
     Principal works for the theatre: *Le seuil invisible; Le quatuor en fa diège; Trois pièces; L'iconoclaste; Le coeur des autres; Un homme de Dieu; Le monde cassé* (followed by *Position et approches concrètes du mystère ontologique; Le dard; Le fanal; La soif; Théatre comique.*

ary. To seek to systematize a body of thought which deliberately sets out to be a-systematic would be a prime inaccuracy. One can only separate out certain lines of emphasis whose convergence expresses the only possible unity, that which is not reduction, but center of attraction.

A first fact is worthy of note: Marcel, while yet an unbeliever (he was not converted until 1929), began with a reflection upon the essence of religious faith. Now, this research resulted very soon, at least confusedly, in revealing the incommensurability of faith with the order of objective and impersonal verifications. The relation of the believer with the Absolute, indeed, in no way presents itself, even looked at from outside, as adhesion to a verity spread out upon the plane of facts, supported by an empirical criterion and coinable from individual to individual. It is enough to suspect an order of subjectivity which frustrates all controls, refuses analysis and inventory, in a word, ruins the imperialism of objective knowledge. One can, without doubt, affirm that Marcel's point of departure is there: in the restoration of a zone of obscurity, which is, nevertheless, the source of ulterior light, which envelops and overflows the borderland of empirical clarity, where the science of things unfolds freely. The experience of the believer reveals a spiritual dimension unknown to the world of attestations, of factual registry and of the manipulation of solids.

From this moment, mystery becomes a central pivot, around which the conscience, henceforth, will be gravitating. If it is true that man is not reduced to the man of science, what, then, is he besides? What signifies his attitude of interrogation or, as Marcel says, of invocation, in the midst of a mysterious reciprocation? It is the expectation of a communion, the presentiment that he will be able to realize himself only in a spiritual communication. Man is, then, only an active appeal, for which the awaited response is already creation of self: he is the term of a dialogue whose ceaseless alternation, which resounds not at all in the thickness of things, elevates him to spiritual dignity; in short, he is a *person*.

But how does it happen that man is so tardy in discovering his veritable essence? It comes from the very ambiguity of his condition. My body is at the juncture of the subjective and the objective: I can say of it, by turns, *I* or *it;* it is, alternatively, function of the soul and a solid among solids, means of action upon them. I have, thus, the double and redoubtable possibility of degrading myself into body or of spiritualizing my incarnation; but, of itself, the body proper leaves me tranquil in the face of bifurcation.

Likewise, the hostile encounter with the other does not, of itself, dictate any decisive conduct. Language, which is made up of utilitarian countersigns (this is why Marcel is perpetually employed with polishing up words) inclines constantly to the degraduation of *thou* into *it* and of *we* into the impersonal *they*. With greater reason, material socialization is a spontaneous factor of depersonalization. Thus, everything in myself and outside myself, if I penetrate the sense of mystery, which that is of spiritual relief, bends me back toward objective platitude. Placed in a world of things, I set about becoming a thing, myself: I "reify" myself.

However, I can escape from the menace, on the trying condition of turning my back on objective illuminations. To do this, I must work out a complete valuation of my most familiar categories: I must substitute, for the *problem,* which is given, enumerable, localizable, entirely calculable, the *mystery,* which is never given, because it is giving; never encircled, because it is enveloping and conditioning; never exhausted, because it is the very source of existence. Likewise, I must prefer *being* to *having,* or roughly speaking, the act to the object; the movement of creation, which is unlimited production, to its products, which are derived, always limited, and which fall lower than myself as soon as I possess them.

This turning about of categories alone can lead me, at last, to see existence and all existents on the right side. The other person no longer "poses" before me, which would mean that I objectify him: he is a *thou* as I am an *I,* and we exist truly, one and the other, only on condition of being such, that is to say, of existing, one for the other, one by the other. Passage from the third to the second person is, thus, entry into subjectivity for each, through the intersubjectivity of all.

However, it would be a mistake, from Marcel's point of view, to believe that the promotion of subjects is done through a horizontal intersubjective causality. Once more that would be to spread out in display that which can operate only in depth. Always it is tension toward mystery, toward the beyond, which must account for admission to being. This is why the "thou" and the "I" must confess their illusion to valorize themselves, mutually, from equal to equal: in reality, they can maintain themselves at the level of subjectivity only through reference to a more profound *we,* which renders possible their proper discovery and unceasingly revictuals their fervor, too ready to return to solitude. The intersubjective bond must not appear as a bridge, flung across the interval, for no spiritual separation, as opposed to spatial exteriority, could be surmounted: unity must precede union and community, communion.

Moreover, if it could be otherwise, the bond between subjects would very soon no longer have the privilege of freedom. If consciousnesses had to engraft themselves upon each other from the outside, the rapprochement would be utilitarian need and conjugated passivity. On the contrary, it is disinterested alertness, in the measure to which it is a matter of participating in a same plenitude, to which each yields himself completely, to discover that to find oneself, therein, is to find, at the same stroke, all others, in an autonomy, inexhaustible and shared. This plenitude is, moreover, nothing other than God, source and home of the mystery of existence.

Naturally, this access to ontological plenitude, to this realm of communion, involves an onerous austerity. Existence, like liberty, is never a possession: except for the absolute, everything is always being brought back into question. And, in relation to this, it may be emphasized that Marcel has had, as much and more than Sartre, the feeling of the precariousness of the spiritual adventure. That which is always lying in wait for consciousness is the retrogression of being toward the multiple degradations of thinghood, of spatialization and having.

There are, at least, certain appreciable stages on the road to conversion. It may be said that they are of two sorts and, doubtless, of unequal value. There are, first of all, the privileged experiences, love, musical creation, the presence of another beyond death, perhaps, even, according to Marcel, the study of metapsychical facts: there are, especially, the spiritual contacts with the Absolute; faith, "absolute refusal to put in question," that is to say, to debate ontological reality on a level with that which has not its foundation in it; the creative fidelity which, positing that which is not yet, holds already that what should be will be; the witness which is not a passive reading of facts, but engagement of the whole self; the sacrifice and the prayer, in fine, which are renunciation and awaiting; which amounts to saying recognition of the unique efficacy of ontological mystery, which does not tolerate the stamp of the immediate (this is why prayer is neither magic nor working technique) but cherishes, all the more, the realization of those values which are worth preservation.

I have said that these different means seemed to be of unequal value, and this leads to the admission that, with Marcel, the "metaphysics of hope" retains, as ally, a certain empiricism. In the one case, in effect, one preserves the taste for the experimental to assure oneself of metempirics, itself; in the other, one draws the ladder up after oneself, in order to keep the conviction that the mystery is accessible only beyond all support. Is there a contradiction here? Perhaps not, if it is taken into account that the Marcelian method has, in sum, two aspects: it discovers the mystery of uniqueness in the savor of experiences situated, and most pertinently, in *my* precise condition, which privileges my situation and all that pertains to it; but it cannot plumb uniqueness to the bottom, as the relation of the "I" and the "thou" has demonstrated, except by bringing into light the patent universal, which makes crop out in me, as in all, the presence of the Absolute. Hence, the unique and the universal march, paradoxically, in the same direction: experience and existence rise to the encounter with each other. It could, then, be sustained that there is a double approach to ontological mystery which ends, however, at the same vista. Nevertheless, when the source of being is reached, only the descending way is imposed and prescribed: in the blazing forth of all nature and the surpassing of all experience, it is the hearthfire of existence which illumines the entire field of that which is. "Sanctity as introduction to ontology," such is the supreme formula, for access to the pure freedom of God is a direct responsibility laid upon all that which participates, to whatever degree, in his existence.

Marcelian existentialism ends with this; not with critical justification of the destiny of the person in the universe but with the effective engagement of the human being in the long course which must lead him even to the ultimate summit where "the opposition between willing and knowing" shall be transcended. Borne up by hope, carried by faith, and purified by trial, man, according to Marcel, advances in a close-drawn network from which he cannot escape, but in which the decision to advance, in spite of temptations to draw back is strengthened at each step by the certitude that salvation lies in communion, of which we receive, from the moment of engagement, the pledge and the first fruits.

Thus the salutary work of Marcel presents itself. He has been reproached with marking out for us an itinerary of life, there, where the technicians of philosophy advertise a dialectic path. But one should recall that Marcel's attempt was born of a refusal to separate theory and practice, and from the intuition that, in the long run, lived practice reveals itself as the living soul of all theory. It is true that it still remains to justify, rationally, this noetic value of practice; but it is, surely, already a great deal to have discerned its function and affirmed its importance.

France is honored, in any case, to possess one of the most courageous pioneers of the philosophy of existence, who, before Jaspers, has spoken of situation and engagement, and who has dispensed Christians, for good and all, from having to submit to Heidegger or his disciples.

III. SPIRITUAL PERSONALISM: MAURICE NÉDONCELLE[8]

Though Marcel, as I have shown, has worked with success upon the emergence of personalism, he has nevertheless refused to write its systematics. He had excellent reasons for this. However, this enormous task has been attempted, these last years, by Nédoncelle. It is worth the effort to find out if he has been successful.[9]

Catholic priest and famous expositor of Newman, Nédoncelle found himself prepared, by virtue of his theological and philosophical make-up, to get a good grasp on certain of the fundamental demands of personalism. The notion of person is, in effect, of Christian importation. The doctrines of antiquity did not anticipate it, and even Christian philosophers have been, only too often, content to express personal values in ancient language, especially the Aristotelian. Nédoncelle comprehended that this was a case of ready-made clothing, wherefore, he set himself to elaborate, for the person, a standard better adapted and, as it were, made to measure.

Marcel had presented the illuminating distinction between *being* and *having*. And it is certain that it is useful to take, in the lump, a first trick in personal values and natural qualities. But, according to Nédoncelle, the *being* and *having* correlation must be criticized in its turn; for, if *having* designates, without equivocation, the ensemble of natural qualities possessed by the subject — which is what Aristotle's logic expresses by a judgment of inclusion or inherence — the notion of being, for its part, remains ambiguous, with an ambiguity which benefits the logic of the schools, complaisant to the *quid pro quos* of grammar but which risks altering gravely the definition of the person. In effect, what do we understand by *being?* If it is equivalent to the assignment of the predi-

---

8. Born at Roubaix, October 30, 1905: Professor at the *Faculté Catholique* of the University of Strasbourg.
   Principal works: *La réciprocité des consciences (thesis), La personne humaine et la nature; La philosophie religieuse en Grande Bretagne de 1850 à nos jours; La pensée religieuse de F. von Hügel; Newman, Apologia, commentaire; Oeuvres choisies de Newman, Introduction; Vers une philosophie de l'amour.*
9. The work of Nédoncelle, for all that it is so originally expressive, did not form itself in a closed vessel. Personalist researches abounded around him: we have just noted the example of Marcel. But we must mention other thinkers equally Catholic: Gabriel Medinier in *Conscience et amour;* Jean Lacroix, in *Personne et amour;* and, also, Emmanuel Mounier, pioneer of the *Esprit* movement, who was the first to engage upon the trail, with *Révolution personnaliste et communautaire.* Moreover, one can point out certain consonances between the thought of Nédoncelle and the doctrine of Blondel, and certain less overt correspondences with the reflexive Biranism of Jacques Paliard, perhaps, even, with the Augustinianism of Jean Guitton.

cate to the subject, one falls back, unfortunately, into the category of *having;* and the person, confused with the qualities of which he has been shown to be the proprietor, is nothing more than a natural being. If, now, through a sort of artificial dehiscence, being is made to split into *essence* and *existence,* one does not know to which term one should reattach reality; for essence, which should play a determining role, is extenuated in the abstract; and existence, of which one enjoys the experimental savor, no longer expresses more than a brute fact which does not account for anything. In short, for having bid double on an idea, which is pulled in opposite directions, one loses on both tables. It is too easy to play upon words and pass clandestinely from being-idea to being-fact: this leaves untouched the opposition of the real and the ideal.

What, then, is to be done? Convince oneself, once and for all, that if logic continues blissfully digesting grammar, being will remain another name for having, and reality a decalcomania of observable experience, by means of which one will manipulate the person as a thing, in the manner of the physician or the mathematician. There is only one way of getting out of this impasse, that is by recreating logic on a personalistic pattern, that is to say, by inventing original categories and perceiving, in the first place, that at the level of a person, being is a spiritual *act*—an act conditioned at the bottom, since the I is incarnated, and yet unconditional cause at the top, since, in the last analysis, itself posits the conditions for positing itself. In this way, the distinction between essence and existence (elsewhere convenient at times in reserving the transcendence of God) is passed by or, at the very least, invalidated in its ambiguity; for we know that the *act* exalts essence to the height of a working perfection, and, also, redeems empirical existence by incorporating, through the assumption of qualities, nature with the person.[10] Under these conditions,

---

10. Seen from this angle, Nédoncelle's personalism, in spite of the author's apparent preference for inner experience, is opposed to the existentialism of "being-there." Factual existence is subordinated, in his eyes, to the ideal essence, which is the true principle of realization: "We regard the ideal I as the superior form and, as it were, the source of psychological reality. Now, in this case, essence is, in no way, opposed to existence: it is opposed to the empirical situation or to the exteriority of existence. It is not existence diminished, but existence perfect, in its eternal principle, which illumines its temporal manifestations and permits them to be perceived" (*La personne humaine et la nature,* p. 57). I quote this with pleasure for it forcefully establishes the metaphysical, and not psycho-empirical, character of spiritual personalism. Nédoncelle avoids, by this return to Platonism, the disadvantages of vitalistic personalisms, which, better to sensibilize apperception of the individual *I,* end by making it only an efflorescence of nature, which becomes contradictory to the very idea of person. Moreover, the Nédoncellian conception of essence is so free from all empirical contamination that the affirmation of essence, which is expressed in the demand for the ideal I constitutive of the person, at once returns to positing, as source of actualization, the existence of perfection, in such wise that every person, if scrutinized to the depth, is an *ontological proof* by act of God.

the initial step of spiritual personalism consists in a complete overturning of the logic and the ontology of the schools. For the *logic of identity* which takes, as a concrete norm and a real cause, the constructed legalism which we project into things in order to maneuver them at our ease, must be substituted the *logic of faith,* which can say pertinently that there is no cause but the personal; no effectiveness except through internal coherence; no judgment except an onerous equation with self; no subsistence in all orders and of definitive permanence except within spiritual immanence, wherein duration is taken up, the diverse become unified, nature, entire, flows back for its salvation.

But when one has succeeded in purifying the person from the dross of interior logic, there remains the task of scrutinizing it in itself. It is then perceived that the *I* is not completely explained by opposition to the *not-I,* but again, and more intimately, by opposition to the *thou.* This means that it is not enough to divide the *cogito* into subject and object; it must be redoubled by other subjects, whose presence is necessary to every finite spirit to multiply and renew its perspective to infinity, and thus bring it about that it, solidary with all others, cannot will itself without willing them and being willed by them. If the subject remained alone, it would become absorbed in an impersonal perspective, a sort of optical reflection whose specular passivity has no connection with spiritual movement. If, on the contrary, the fundamental subjectivity is a *we,* from which are derived the *I* and the *thou,* each consciousness is awakened by a play of relations which is its very breath. Thus, there is no *I* without preliminary oppositional consciousness of self and of others. It is the dyad not the monad which brings the person into being. The human *cogito* is not solitary, but from the first, reciprocal; not an islet but a network. "The communion of consciousnesses is the primitive fact."

But this primitive communion reveals itself only progressively. "Inwardness is acquired," is Nédoncelle's very expressive way of putting it. Personality must, then, acquire itself by its own efforts. It may remain veiled and misunderstood; it may even be deranged. Plato and Hegel speak of a fall: Christianity speaks of original sin and personal faults. In any event, there is the hostility of nature to be overcome, and especially the divisions interior to the mind itself; in short, evil in all its forms. The sole means, not of denying these obstacles, but of conquering by making use of them, is *love,* since only love, by making persons coincide in a perfect union, which at once respects and resolves their distinction, can assure their mutual advancement. In any event, love cannot act upon the horizontal plane of persons whom it seeks to federate, two by two, in multiple directions, unless, most essentially, it acts upon the vertical plane, in bringing back each consciousness to God, himself; for only this reference to the Absolute, who is subsistent love, gives a foundation for reciprocity and renders it efficacious. Without God, who is the *Thou* par excellence, there would be no *I,* nor any human dyads; for each *I* must be posited as a spiritual center of personification before being promoted through interpersonal reciprocal communications.[11] It is, then, the presence of God and the tender regardfulness of his love, which permit us to love others and to be loved by them, and so to give them being as they make us exist. This reciprocity circulates from us to them and from them to us, because it proceeds from God for each one of us all. The miracle would go still further if, as Christian revelation teaches, God himself were a reciprocity with three pinnacles like a college with a personnel of three and if, through a grace of his pure goodness, a divine Person incarnated himself to stir humanity to a privileged type of reciprocity between God and man, which would permit us, in participating, through love, directly in the divine life, to contribute toward making God, himself, exist. The circle of reciprocity would then be closed, or, rather, it would have no other dimensions than those of perfect love.

We must strain toward this ideal without presuming to lay claim to it. Love springs up in us; it cannot come to completion unless we recognize that it had its beginning in God and descends from him. In the return of the spirit toward its source, we can at least distinguish several stages in the ascent: *science,* which marks a practical prowess over nature, without revealing its essence; *art,* which associates consciousnesses in a common emotion but would not be able to procure for them a stable and definitive unity; and *ethics,* which produces generosity, that is to say, realization of the good, but without succeeding of itself, alone (as stoicism proves), in instituting true reciprocity, which implies recognition of an Absolute of love. One must, then, pass on, finally, to a "metaphysics of love," which Nédoncelle presents, in a very original

---

11. It is a question of knowing whether, from the point of view of a truly spiritual personalism, that is to say, of a personalism anxious to define person through an absolute act, the initiative, anticipated, originated, and maintained by God, which constitutes the personality, must be comprehended as a *given,* even ideal, or, on the contrary, as an active and actual cooperation, analogous to an eternal generation of intelligibility by the spirit united to God. Nédoncelle supplies texts for both interpretations. It would seem that his theory of the *ideal I* tends rather toward the realistic meaning. But, given the incommensurability of person and nature, there would follow, perhaps more rigorously, the notion of a radical spiritual autonomy, for which one would not be able to speak of *given,* but only of giving: the continuous creation of the spirit by the Transcendent would, then, be comprehended as the supreme innerness of the creation of the self by the self and would preserve the personalism from all naturalistic relapse.

fashion, as a sort of esthetics of grace (in the double meaning, profane and theological, of the term). Alone, in effect, God-love can resolve the dualism of nature and the person, and above all (that which is the most acute form of evil and, at bottom, the only one worthy of interest) the internal laceration of the Spirit. The Absolute can redeem all, within us and without: it manages matter, reconciles the mind with itself, or if, unhappily, the consciousness persists in rebellion (which, in Christian parlance, is called hell), it never ceases to keep up its loving advances, which, even when repulsed, solicit as much as they sanction. "To have oneself carried by the love of God and of others without continuing them, such is hell" *(La reciprocité des consciences*, p. 308).

Thus the philosophical work of Nédoncelle, of which we have, as yet, only the beginnings, poses, in all its acuteness, the problem of the person. The first error from which it preserves us is the proud solitariness of the *cogito,* as it is understood since Descartes and Leibniz. No consciousness is made of itself, alone, against the others and against God, nor even alongside of others and at the margin of God. Personalism is intrinsically devoted to community; individualism is the radical negation. The second error from which it frees us is that of the abusive prestige of science: the person cannot be fulfilled by assimilating nature, alone; the *I* is not achieved in the domination of the material not-I, but only in the promotion of the spiritual *thou* and, above all, by intimacy with the divine *Thou.* Finally, the third error which it eliminates is that of the adequacy of time to reabsorb evil (as all the evolutionisms believe) and to make humanity accede to the perfection of life: for it is not enough to compensate for the past by a better future; it is, also, necessary that the past, itself be recovered and transmuted. In other words, only eternity, put into our lives and unceasingly present all along the course of time, can purify, recapitulate, and finally save all. Spiritual personalism is a philosophy of salvation.

IV. THE PHILOSOPHY OF ACTION AND RELIGION: MAURICE BLONDEL[12]

Blondel, celebrated for his thesis on *Action* in 1893, has remained,

---

12. Born at Dijon, November 2, 1861; Professor emeritus of the University of *Aix-Marseilles,* until his death in 1949.
   Principal works: *L'action,* 1893; *Lettre sur l'apologetique,* 1896; *Histoire et dogme,* 1904; *Le procès de l'intelligence,* 1921; *Qu'est-ce que la mystique?,* 1925; *L'itinéraire philosophique,* 1928; *Le Vinculum Substantiale d'après Leibniz,* 1930; *Le problème de la philosophic catholique,* 1932; *La pensée* (2 vols.), *L'être, L'action* (2 vols.) 1934-1937; *La philosophie et l'esprit chrétien* (two volumes published), 1944-1946.
   Some Commentaries: Paul Archambault, *L'oeuvre philosophique de Maurice Blondel;* Paul Archambault, *Initiation à la philosophie blondélienne;* Blaise Romeyer, S. J., *La Philosophie religieuse de Maurice Blondel; Ouvrage Collectif: Hommage à Maurice Blondel* (Blond et Gay).
   One would find a quasi-exhaustive bibliography in my work on *La philosophie de l'action.*

for many, the man of his first book. However, good judges, such as Lachièze-Rey and Paliard, estimate the recent trilogy on *Thought, Being,* and *Action* to be, from the ontological and gnosiological point of view, the real summit of the Blondelian contribution. In reality, the two opinions do not conflict, for Blondel has not had two successive philosophies, but a single position which has been consolidated and deepened in the course of sixty years of research. It is even this example of exceptional precocity and exceptional longevity which has led us to present, last of all, the dean of contemporary French philosophers, as at once the oldest and the most up-to-date.

If one wished to sum up the Blondelian work most briefly, one could say that it is a *philosophy of action* and, also (which is often forgotten), a *philosophy of religion.* But the meaning of these two expressions should be rigorously defined.

It would seem that Blondel's peculiar merit was to understand, from the beginning, that philosophy, as it was practiced in the French university, in the nineteenth century, kept to this side of its legitimate frontiers, in an intermediate zone of abstract clarity, which permits the escape of all the riches of implicit thought. He had, on the contrary, the intuition, that recourse to the double mystery of psycho-organic and religious action would immediately give back to metaphysics its real depth and its true height. Blondelianism, then, presents itself, in its origins, as a deliberate attempt to restore to philosophy the whole of its domain, by introducing reflexive light into the very substrata beneath, and the upper regions above clear thought. If there was ever, in the history of ideas, an authentically intellectualistic reform, was it not this almost rash undertaking to conquer, for intelligence, everything, even that which seems to befog or dazzle it? To accuse Blondel of anti-intellectualism would be to contradict that which was his own purpose and to take his whole effort the wrong way.

But how can such an ambitious project be realized? Is it possible to enlarge philosophy at the bottom and at the top—at the bottom, by fathoming the effectivity of human acts, which always escape analysis— at the top, by submitting the religious dogma to a critical reflection, charged with respecting said dogma's transcendence and yet with increasing, paradoxically, its own proper rationality, by contact with it? To put it another way, are a philosophy of action and a philosophy of religion conceivable, realizable, and viable?

Reflection upon concrete acting has been so well preached by Blondel that it has become common to the ensemble of contemporary philosophers. Since the attempt of 1893, he is no longer a thinker who would refuse to philosophy the right and the duty of entering into the incoherent appearance of acts and conducts, to penetrate into this very subsoil of the consciousness which moves and lifts the weight of the parts. It is true that there are many ways of inscribing acting in one's program, and that, through having chosen one way of doing it, Blondel has preceded rather than prepared certain other procedures, called existentialistic. For, from Blondel's point of view, it is a matter of rendering existing and acting as transparent as possible to thought, by incorporating in them a secret logical framework; while, in the other case, there is no compunction (I am speaking of negative existentialism) about giving them over, bound hand and foot, to the irrational powers of sensation and feeling. Now, with regard to the end pursued, which is to extend rationality to that which seems the most alien to it, one sees immediately which of these two attitudes is the right one. Here, again, it is his intellectualism of principle which saves Blondel from the mistakes of empiricism, whether vitalistic or pragmatic. If the philosophy of action has been able to go so deeply and levelheadedly into the most convoluted folds of incarnated consciousness, it is because it has never lost sight of the essential objective: to enlarge reason, to expand its categories and not derange or dismember them according to the "living force" or the pressures of instinct. Thus, the philosophy of action has never ceased to be a philosophy of spirit. Its single aim has always been to bring light into the subsoil of reflective life and, notably, into that intermediate zone of the psycho-organic, wherein aspirations from above come to grips with resistances from below, before the entire mechanism, through the effect of a rigorous logic, is swept away, in flight or in downfall.

With such a context, one divines that action, for Blondel, signifies something quite other than an irrational compulsion, and that it designates, rather, the spiritual complexity of a dynamism, which, starting with consciousness, must traverse the whole of nature and God, himself, in order, at last, to equate its exigency and its expansion. Action is, in effect, truly a complex spiritual reality, since it can attain to the equation of mind with itself, only at the end of a process, one and diverse, which continually goes beyond the plane of clear thought and even scores an original encroachment upon that of the abstract idea. But how, then, is one to reconcile, anew, the intellectualist perspective with this theory of plus-value, which seems to be of advantage to effective acting but not to disinterested thought? Once again, the Blondelian paradox of an intellectualized or intellectualizable acting seems to be in danger; for it seems to be very near to giving up holding the act and its concept in the same hand.

It is just here, on the contrary, that the true originality of the philosophy of action is confirmed. Blondel is, without doubt, the metaphysician who has most clearly revealed to us that which could be called the pluri-dimensional character of thought. This latter does not display itself in entirety on the plane of discourse: underlying scientific thought, there is an implicit thought, foster mother of the word and spirit of judgment. These thoughts are, as it were, the solidary aspects of integral thinking: they must work together as one, under penalty of juxtaposing an empty clarity and a blind mass. True intellectualism is that very one which does not flatten out thinking according to a single dimension, that is to say, make of it that which never disconnects reflection from its source.

This congenital duality of thought in us once discerned, it remains to show it working functionally; which is what Blondel sets out to do, not only in the two recent volumes of *Pensée,* but also in the *Action* of 1893. One ends, then, with marking two complementary functions, of which one is to put a chain composed of a series of intelligible links from sensation to God, himself; and the other is to follow, not just an analytical and conditioning thread, but a veritable process of realization which descends from Being, absolute and beyond series, down to reality in its lowest depth. But it is impossible to effect this going and return and grasp its terms, without perceiving that this double proceeding of ascent and descent is but a single movement, centered directly upon God: for the Absolute is at the end of the ascension only because he is at the beginning of the procession; and reflection posits him from situation to situation only because he posits himself, unconditionally, in positing all beings. Thence, the only danger for thought would be to seek to remain proudly self-sufficient on the ascending plane, whose reflective power must remain pregnant with the ontological current which proceeds from God. If conceptual dialectics seeks to reject the fruit it carries within itself or, better still, if analysis organizes itself apart from synthesis, it is all over with its real value: it is only an empty shell. On the contrary, reimmersed in the ontological process, to which it is united with full justification, even the most notional dialectics is fully efficacious. In short, not to cut off *thought* from *being* is simply to respect the *being of thought*— that being for which two thoughts are not too much, that is to say, two functions within thinking, to encompass it, one to prove that it is, the other to participate in it and, finally, to force us to recognize that, if the first rejoins it, it is because the second parts from it.

But, in all this, it will be said, where is acting? Is there a place for it in that complex architecture which Blondel must have inherited from Platonism, through the expositions of Boutroux at *l'École normale supérieure?* That which preoccupied us was acting in its specificity, irreducible to abstract thought. Has it not been lost sight of in going back to the double dialectic, ascending and descending? Indeed no, and we have, even, engaged upon the distinction of the two thoughts, only in order to permit the insertion of acting into the dialectic partition. For action is essentially mediatory between the two other terms: analytical thought and implicit thought, pregnant with being; or, put otherwise, between just thought and being. We act only with a view to a coincidence, always closer and more perfect in us, between reflection and life; or, again, between reason constituted and reason constituting. Action is only an effort to equate the word and its Act, that is to say, the movement of expression and the movement of realization.

Thus summed up, in its broad metaphysical lines, the philosophy of action calls for the following remarks: (1) It has nothing to do with activism and even maintains, with regard to the supreme bond of the two gnosio-ontological dialectics, that contemplation is the highest and most efficacious form of acting. (2) It affirms the correlative double primacy of thought and being and, in consequence, holds as undissociable the two complementary points of view, of essence and of existence.[13] (3) It accords an equal supremacy to Action; for, carried to the absolute, the equation of being and thought is effected in the synthesis of acting. (4) It is an *integral intellectualism,* for which thought is called upon to realize itself in plenitude, through a double effort, reflective and moral—moral practice having, itself, the value of a noetic purification, destined to illuminate the obscurities of thought in us.

---

13. Lachièze-Rey sees, in Blondelian ontology, an authentic existentialism, through the fact that the ontological function is, therein, the inalienable prerogative of God and is to be found at work in the mind before the reflexive reaction which it excites in return: the human word would, thus, be only a second consideration of consciousness. Paliard, on the contrary, speaks of the antiexistentialism of Blondel, in noting that the Blondelian ethic (that is to say the function assigned to the practical) has no other aim than to recover a noetic purity, essential to the mind, but contaminated, in fact, by the necessity of coming to terms with experience. These two contrary opinions cannot exclude each other, for, with Blondel, it is true, both that the word has value only through being, and that realization is, nevertheless, given in proportion to reflexive fidelity; this latter, moreover, not necessarily making itself in the scientific fashion, but also in the language of simple souls. It is even a capital point for Blondel, and not one of detail, that spiritual light is homogeneous with the simple as with the learned, which removes the criterion of illumination and sincerity far beyond the scholarly distinction of the schools.

In a word, we assert that philosophy of action is a refusal to give preference to any of the terms which constitute spiritual exigency: it teaches, finally, only one pre-excellence, that of mind. It seems a very vague affirmation, but one which Blondel has labored to render more precise, in renewing, on the philosophic plane, our very notion of spirituality. We have seen how he has been able to extend this latter from below. It remains for us to look briefly upon his effort to extend it, also, from above.

It has not, in effect, been enough for Blondel to carry the torch of reason among the lower irrationals: he has wished to bear it, equally, into the midst of the higher irrationals or, it would be more exact to say, of the transrationals of religious data. Philosophy of action is perfected in philosophy of religion.

But, then, the difficulty redoubles. For the supernatural resists reason in another fashion than does the emotional: it is not of a different degree, but of another order. Faith is, essentially, a distinct order of evidence, endowed with criteria proper to itself and incommensurable with the evidence of pure reason. The easiest thing would be to juxtapose the two planes to avoid shocks and confusions; but this solution is untenable, because the mind permits no compartmenting and can have but one sole end: we know well that there are not two verities nor two Gods, one of nature, the other of grace. There is, indeed, the squaring of the circle! How shall we go about it to have two orders of evidence subsist, in the unity of one same mind, without mixing together and without excluding each other? Blondel responds to this question by two progressive points.

The first point to establish is that the autonomy of the philosopher is in no wise menaced by the apparent heteronomy of the supernatural, quite to the contrary. Indeed, when the mind has taken back unto itself the immense field of the phenomenon, when it has traversed all nature by means of science, art, ethics, metaphysics, all human activities, it remains unsatisfied. The first and the last word of mind is to put everything in question, including its products and its immanence. A single recourse remains to it: to surpass that which it can do by that which it can become; to offer itself to the Absolute to be set free from all nature. Now, this is no mere whim on the part of someone who no longer knows to what saint to vow himself. This solution of disclosure from on high, which is the hypothesis of the supernatural, is inscribed in the very woof of the mind in continuity; not certainly with its exigency (that would have no meaning—the finite does not demand to exhaust the infinite) but with its aspiration which it nowhere succeeds in enclosing: one might even define mind as a power to contest all nature. In the face of this limitless aspiration, the Absolute, rightfully demonstrated as originating Being, presents itself as creative generosity, limitless and pregnant with an inner life, which, beyond our own proper disjunction, is necessarily the harmonious synthesis of thought, being, and acting, and therefore, perfect spirituality, total autonomy. How can we, therefore, refuse to put the supreme question? Why should the mind, which cannot perfect itself in nature, not seek to perfect itself by the grace of God? Why, after having proved that the furthest reach of its effort leaves it still alienated and dispossessed, while the Origin of all autonomy solicits and urges it, should the mind put off solving the problem of its liberation? A reason which does not go as far as to pose this question—which alone is decisive —which stops and takes its stand this side of it, literally commits suicide as reason, for it chooses definitive abdication and alienation instead of throwing overboard the ballast of all empiricism, in declaring for this *supernatural,* which signifies, in effect, passing beyond all natural limits and therefore redemption of all the restrictions imposed upon the incarnate *I.*

But this first point does not, for Blondel, exhaust all the resources of reflection. All has not been said when the metaphysics of insufficiency wrings from reason the confession that reason does not suffice and brings up, from a rational point of view, the problem of gratuitous consummation. In this direction, one marches ahead of the act of faith and also of the theology, which may ensue. But a parallel course is still open to the philosopher, on the margin of the very path he can enter to become a believer; this course is that of philosophy of religion, or autonomous reflection on the data of positive religion; it, and it alone, must permit reason to go to the very end of itself.

Assuredly, the difficulty seems very great in the way of conceiving a philosophy of religion which would not be theology and which would, nevertheless, respect the transcendence of revealed data; or which would be philosophy and yet draw a superaddition of rational illumination from an object which goes beyond reason. It is, however, this very thing which it is important to execute. It must be shown that religious doctrine, without letting itself be either corrupted or reabsorbed, can profit from the very rationality of reason and extend it for the greatest good of philosophy. The paradox becomes progressively more animated. Not long ago, the hypothesis of the supernatural heard favorably the prayer for the autonomy of reason; at the present, dogmatic data seek to strengthen this same autonomy. How is this? Is it even possible to make faith and reason collaborate without contaminating them mutually, or absorbing them one in the other?

Blondel replies in the affirmative: it is possible to have between them heterogeneity and connection, union without confusion. To deprive reason of its autonomy would be to throw the mind of the believer as well as the philosopher into the chaos of the irrational. To deprive faith of its transcendence and naturalize it, after the fashion of Hegel, would be to prejudge that reason closes the circle, though the metaphysics of insufficiency has proved the contrary, and by way of consequence, to disown the legitimacy of the superior order of evidence, after having established it. Reason exacts, then, that faith remain faith, as this latter exacts that reason remain reason, for we have here an *a priori* condition of philosophy of religion, which must no more dissolve the specificity of its data than betray the rationality of its method. There is, then, no danger to fear. There will be neither distortion of reason nor violation of faith.

Will there be, nevertheless, useful and fruitful relations between the two terms? Yes, and here is the authorization. The mysteries of faith are not thick darkness, but inexhaustible intelligibility. Thus, when the reason is finally blocked in an impasse, it comes about that faith presents, in an otherwise irreducible perspective, the key of the enigma. The philosopher, then, is going to be able to conduct his free inquiry in the domain of the theologian with the certitude of drawing therefrom a rational gain. But it is here that it is necessary to understand clearly the nature of this gain, which is not a larceny. It is not a matter of treating reason with faith as though one could transfuse all or part of the superior order into the inferior order. It is a matter of provoking, through contact with faith, a sort of internal maturation of reason. And there is nothing strange in this; we can find both an indirect analogy and a historical verification for it. We assist, in effect, every day, in the intervention of a similar proceeding in the constitution of the new philosophy of the sciences, which, upon information taken from the scientist, invents logical categories, entirely original and sometimes subversive to the established rational order. We note, especially, in the course of history, a progressive expansion of reason in contact with faith. Our theodicy easily admits on its plane, a God-Love and even, according to Blondel (as afterward to Nédoncelle) an Absolute, endowed with internal spiritual relations, while ancient thought contented itself with objectifying a first Intelligibility or entangled itself in a transcendental triplicity. With greater reason, the perspectives of the Incarnation or of the Christian sacramentary have suggested to us considerable alterations in our conceptions of matter, time, history, etc. In this way there has been, without doubt, not rationalization of faith, but growth of the reason through faith. The philosophy of religion has precisely for its goal only to take back upon itself this historical function, and to separate out, explicitly, the method, with a view to systematic applications. Blondel has attempted this in the last pages of the *Action* of 1893, and in the most recent volumes of *Philosophie et l'esprit chrétien*. One will go back to them for details. We must content ourselves with stressing one more word on method.

It is important, in effect, not to make a mistake concerning the mode of influence of faith in such a domain. The philosophy of religion is deliberately a reflection upon positive dogma in its definite literalness, and not a simple philosophical integration of the elements of reason which revelation requires explicitly at the periphery of the mysteries, properly so called, such as the notion of creation or the existence of God. We have there, in fact, verities of full rational right, which the philosopher at once claims as his own, although, in fact, they may at times be whispered to him from without. This segregation terminated—and St. Thomas Aquinas seems to have put an end to it once and for all—the philosopher of religion is ready to begin his task. It is upon mystery itself, that he meditates, being very well aware, however, that it belongs to another order of evidence; and it is through contact with this inviolate source that he endeavors to discover new dimensions in his own reason. Just as, in a game of cards, a swift glance at one's partner's play suffices to render one's own play clearer, so—and without trickery—the detour through dogmatic data leads back to a clearer vision of the rational imperative. The paradox of a real collaboration between faith and reason, distinct and solidary, is no longer monstrous. It expresses merely the ultimate hope reason can have of one day raising itself to its full height, not to keep faith in check, but, on the contrary, to bestow upon it the kiss of the friend and the one under obligations.

If there subsisted a last fear of seeing the philosopher of religion entering into competition with the theologian, it would be easy to dissipate it. Theology belongs to the order of evidence of faith; the philosophy of religion, on the contrary, relies upon the evidence of reason. Assuredly, the metaphysician of dogma receives his object from on high; but he takes it as research hypothesis, after the fashion of the geometer, that is to say that he takes it as a constituted *datum* and that he undertakes to respect it, under penalty, should he falsify the data of the problem, of losing the benefit of the solution. He has not, then, to deal with the act of faith as such, and keeps, as his exclusive goal, the extension of the rational field.

So, with all difficulties set aside, philosophy of religion finally takes its place—the highest place—in philosophy.

Philosopher of action and religion, such is Blondel. Like Einstein in physics, Blondel will live in philosophy as the explorer of a sort of hyperspace of the reason. He has, in fact, extended the frontiers of metaphysics, on all sides, from the narrow rationalism of the nineteenth century. If we wished to sum up his endeavor, at one stroke, we would say that Blondel, who was carelessly accused of Kantianism, has passed his life—perhaps without being fully conscious of this—in refuting and going beyond Kant: (1) by suppressing the dualism of pure Reason and practical Reason, in order to carry reflection into the very heart of acting; (2) by substituting, for the formalism of the Kantian *cogito*, the spiritual plenitude of action; (3) by restoring the ontology compromised by Kant, for whom the transcendental conditions of knowing eclipse those of being;[14] (4) by refusing, above all, to confine religion within the limits of reason, seeing that rationality of the latter has nothing to lose and everything to gain from the transcendence of the former.

But it is useless, after all, to ask oneself whether Blondel is the antithesis of Kant, when we are assured, on the word of his friend, Victor Delbos, the historian, that the philosopher of action did not take, as his point of departure, any preconceived system, but only his Christianity, taking as spiritual guides, St. Paul, St. Bernard, and Pascal.

This bare summary of only five representatives of Christian philosophy in France, during these latter years, will doubtless suffice to convince the reader of the variety of forms and methods which Catholic thought can assume among us. It is probable that the future will be as fruitful; no one of the authors here studied, moreover, has said the last word. But if we seek outside the currents in which they make room for themselves, and which oscillate practically from St. Thomas to Augustine, one never sees appear, among the Christian thinkers of our country,

---

14. Lachièze-Rey, specialist on Kant, has even written that the ontological normative of Blondel was the sole means of filling in the immense lacuna left on this point by Kantianism.

any truly original undertaking.[15] Should we believe that a confrontation of Christianity and Marxism will permit a new systematization? Efforts have been made in this direction. It cannot be said that they have as yet come to anything, except perhaps—invading Marxism—the Hegelian revival of R. P. Fessard, S. J.

France is experiencing, moreover, at the present time, an important theological renewal,[16] which makes one ask oneself whether it will entail a philosophical rebound, or if it is not, rather, a consequence of the extra-ordinary vitality of Christian philosophy in France in the last fifty years. One significant fact should, in any case, be put to the credit of present-day theologians: their works are awakening an active sympathy among the French academic public; it is to be hoped that they will get echoes from this. Now, here is the indication of a progress which has been too little noted: for the first time since the middle ages, at the very least since Malebranche, the theological and philosophical disciplines, though so jealous of their proper prerogatives, seek to join together again. We shall see fewer and fewer theologians avoiding criticism of their philosophical postulates, and fewer believing philosophers putting their faith in parentheses to reconstruct the world in the margin of its true history. The time of concordances is ended; so, also is the time of separatisms.

SELECTED BIBLIOGRAPHY

Archambault, Paul. *Plaidoyer pour l'inquiétude*. Paris, Spes, 1931.
Berger, Gaston. *Le cogito de Husserl*. Paris, Aubier, 1941.
Blondel, Maurice. *Trilogie: La pensée, l'être, et l'action*. Paris, Alcan, 1934-1937.

---

15. I mean from the constructive doctrinal point of view, for works of history superabound, some of excellent quality. I note, however, that the properly doctrinal work of Jacques Paliard, professor at the University of Aix-en-Provence, deserves a wider audience. Ethics, esthetics, and mysticism find themselves conjoined, therein, to support a "psycho-noematics" of perception, which makes the structures which are highest, everywhere present but veiled, react upon inferior structures. I observe, finally, that the ever more influential work of Jean Guitton displays an Augustinian thematics, supple and varied; time, eternity, and love are the author's favorite themes; through and through, researches into Christian origins enrich the reflection of the philosopher of the analyses of the exegete and of the intuitions of mysticism.

16. It is not my task to speak explicitly of theologians and their works, but I feel it necessary to put forward the name of Reverend Father Teilhard de Chardin, S. J., by reason of his renown as a scholar and also because of the paradoxical and at times confusing forms of expression affected by his research. His name is, in any case, synonomous with a reconciliation between science and religion, even more profound that that of Lecomte du Noüy. One can regret, however, the vitalist atmosphere, doubtless in extension of Bergson, which envelopes this effort at synthesis, still more, perhaps, than the methodological autodidacticism, which is, as it were, ransom for the author's genius.

Boyer, Charles. *L'idée de verité dans la philosophie de saint Augustin.* Second edition, Paris, Beauchesne, 1941.

Brunner, R. P. *La personne incarnée.* Paris, Beauchesne, 1941.

Chevalier, Jacques. *Bergson.* Paris, Plon, 1926.

Dies, Mgr., A. *Autour de Platon.* Paris, Beauchesne, 1926.

Etcheverry, Auguste. *L'idéalisme français contemporain.* Paris, Alcan, 1934.

Fessard, Gaston. *La méthode de reflexion chez Maine de Biran.* Paris, Blond et Gay, 1938.

Festugière, A. J. *Liberte et civilisation chez les grecs.* Paris, Édition de la Revue des Jeunes, 1947.

Forest, Aimé. *Du consentement à l'être.* Paris, Aubier, 1936.

de Gandillac, Maurice. *La philosophie de Nicolas de Cuès.* Paris, Aubier, 1941.

Garrigou-Lagrange, R. P. *La sythèse thomiste.* Paris, Desclée, 1947.

Gilson, Étienne. See bibliography for Wahl's essay.

Gouhier, Henri. *La philosophie de Malebranche.* Paris, Vrin, 1926.

Guitton, Jean. *Essai sur l'amour humain.* Paris, Aubier, 1948.

Jolivet, R. *Les doctrines existentialistes.* Paris, Fontenelle, 1948.

Laberthannière, L. *Esquisse d'une philosophie personnaliste.* Paris, Vrin, 1942.

Lachièze-Rey, Pierre. *Le moi, le monde et Dieu.* Paris, Boivin, 1938.

Lacroix, Jean. *Force et faiblesse de la famille.* Paris, Le Seuil, 1949.

Laporte, Jean. *La conscience de la liberté.* Paris, Flammarion, 1947.

Le Blond, J. M. *Logique et méthode chez Aristote.* Paris, Vrin, 1939.

Lenoble, Robert. *Essai sur la notion d'expérience.* Paris, Vrin, 1943.

Le Roy, Edouard. *Introduction à l'étude du problème religieux.* Paris, Aubier, 1944.

de Lubac, Henri. *Le drame de l'humanisme athée.* Paris, Spes, 1945.

Madinier, Gabriel. *Conscience et amour.* Paris, Presses Universitaires de France, 1947.

Marc, André. *Psychologie réflexive.* 2 vols. Paris, Desclée, 1949.

Marcel, Gabriel. *Position et approches concrètes du mystère ontologique.* Paris, Vrin, 1949.

—————. See also bibliography for Hering's essay.

Maritain, Jacques. See bibliography for Wahl's essay.

Marrou, H. I. *Histoire de l'éducation antique.* Paris, Le Seuil, 1948.

Moreau, Joseph. *La construction de l'idéalisme platonicien.* Paris, Boivin, 1939.

Mounier, Emmanuel. *Traité du caractère.* Paris, Le Seuil, 1947.

Nédoncelle, Maurice. *La réciprocité des consciences*. Paris, Aubier, 1942.

——————. See also bibliography for Hering's essay.

Niel, Henri. *De la méditation dans la philosophie de Hegel*. Paris, Aubier, 1941.

Paliard, Jacques. *Théorème de la connaissance*. Paris, Aubier, 1938.

Romeyer, Blaise. *La philosophie chrétienne*. Paris, Blond et Gay. 1937.

Serrus, Ch. *Le parallélisme logico-grammatical*. Paris, Alcan, 1933.

Sertillanges, R. P. *Le christianisme et les philosophies*. Paris, Aubier, 1941.

de Solages, Mgr. *L'analogie*. Paris, Aubier, 1947.

Teilhard de Chardin, Pierre. *Le milieu divin* (not available).

Valensin, Auguste. *Autour de ma foi*. Paris, Aubier, 1948.

Vancourt, Raymond. *Marxisme et pensée chrétienne*. Paris, Blond et Gay, 1948.

Verneaux, Roger. *Les sources cartésiennes et kantiennes de l'idéalisme français*. Paris, Beauchesne, 1936.

Vignaux, Paul. *La pensée au moyen-âge*. Paris, Colin, 1938.

Wahl, Jean. *Études kierkegaardiennes*. Paris, Aubier, 1938.

THE SITUATION OF
RELIGIOUS PHILOSOPHY
IN FRANCE

Roger Mehl *

The title, religious philosophy or philosophy of religion, is, apparently, not one of the most frequent in French philosophy. One might look for it in vain in the majority of our great philosophical reviews.[1] This does not mean that French philosophy is lacking in religious signification. On the contrary, most of the great philosophies of the present day, that of Brunschvicg, of Bergson, of Lavelle, of Le Senne, and that of the existentialists, have a religious problem. But philosophy is averse to calling itself religious. It seems to think it would lose some of its own proper quality and some of its methodical rationality if it took to itself this qualification. It is quite common, in France, for philosophy to pursue a religious aim, while making out that religion has nothing to bestow upon it. It often takes science or art as its object—much less often, religion. With Bergson, religious meditation supports itself much more upon the bases of the system, itself, upon the notion of creative evolution, than upon religion, objectively given and grasped in its specific essence. At the most, this latter happens to bring to the work some apt illustrations (Jewish prophetism, Catholic sainthood).

This paradoxical attitude, which does not show lack of concern on the part of the religious, but disregard of positive religion, is to be explained, perhaps, by a long philosophical tradition which goes back to Descartes, if not to medieval scholasticism. The attitude of Descartes, in fact, is resolutely dualistic: two ways are offered man to attain to God—that of supernatural revelation, for which a more than human assistance is need-

---

* Born in 1912. Agrégé in philosophy; licencié in theology; master of conferences, Faculty of Protestant Theology, University of Strasbourg. Editor of the *Revue d'histoire et de philosophie religieuse*. Author of *La condition du philosophe chrétien* (1947), and *Éthique et théologie* (in a collective volume in the press).
    1. Exception being made of the several yearly volumes of *Recherches philosophiques* and, naturally, of the *Revue d'histoire et de philosophie religieuses*.

ed, and that of natural light, that is to say, of reason, alone. This does
not mean that the second does not, from time to time and on certain
points (proof of the existence of God and the immortality of the soul)
lend the first a certain support, at least on the plane of apologetics, as is
proved by the intention which animates Descartes, offering his *Méditations métaphysiques* to the Paris Faculty of Theology. But each of these
wishes to guard its autonomy and keep its own proper quality unmixed.
Theology and metaphysics certainly apply themselves to the same objective—the Pascalian dissociation between the God of the philosophers and
the God of Biblical revelation has hardly been retained in the philosophic
tradition—but theological thought, as such, does not hold the attention
of the philosopher. Thus, there has been constituted, in France, a religious philosophy which is not a philosophy of religion.

Let us add to this rationalistic influence, that of positivism, which
leads minds curiously to restrict the notion of positive fact. It is evident
that there is, for positivism, no properly religious fact; but that the religious fact dissolves, under analysis, into facts which psychology or,
eventually, sociology, can take over as subject matter, that is to say, dissipate as specific facts. The religious fact is nothing other than a psychological state. It has no objective content properly its own. Here, analyzed by M. Pradines, is the final conclusion reached by such a psychologist
as H. Delacroix, who devoted himself to the study of the great mystics:
"Illumination and ecstasy, and other analogous divided states would seem
simply to express, in certain extraordinary natures—which, from another
point of view, might well be called privileged—the superabundance of an
inner life which divides and lets its proper richness burst forth; and
Delacroix was inclined to think that it is the emotion bound up with
such states which, here, engenders belief and leads the subject, in order
to explain to himself his characteristic disturbance, to believe himself the
object, if not the plaything of a supernatural action of which the luminous
agitation of his consciousness would be the product." [2] Though positivism does not inevitably lead to a denial that these religious facts have
any value, it does tend to despoil them of their nature, to reduce them
to something other than themselves. Some will even go so far as to admit the supernatural, but on condition of its being a psychological category. Such seems to be the postulate which animates Lévy-Bruhl's
analyses of primitive mentality.

Hence, if it is true that the religious life is not orientated toward a

2. M. Pradines, *L'esprit de la religion,* p. 7.

specific reality, then religion can consist only of beliefs, with all the irreducible subjectivity which this term implies: its objectivity, if one wishes to keep this term at any price, would consist solely in its practices and its institutions. The philosopher, as metaphysician, will not, on the side of religion, meet with any of the finalities to which he aspires. The most evident sign of this deficiency on the part of religion is the absence of any Christian philosophy. Christianity has, perhaps, brought us a new type of sensibility, but it has not been able to give birth to any new philosophy: it has succeeded only in giving emotional coloring to certain traditional philosophic positions, precisely because it does not contain any original idea, because it is not the discovery of any objective value. Such is, without doubt, the postulate which cropped out in the memorable discussion which arose between Bréhier and Gilson, at the French Philosophical Society, apropos of Christian philosophy. To deny, as Bréhier did, the existence of a Christian philosophy, is this not definitely to push religion back toward pure emotion, and, at the same time, whether one wills it or not, give the advantage to a positivism which denies all religious reality, all objective religious data? Religion would pertain, then, only to the order of feeling and could be defined only as a psychological function of consciousness. From this, to seeing in it nothing but a sort of projection of ourself is only a step. By a strange detour—the bias of psychologism—positivism rejoins idealism.

However, it was necessary that there should be a turning back. It has not been sufficiently stressed to what degree sociological researches of the Durkheim school have prepared this evolution. For this latter, religion ceases to be pure expansion of the sensibility, purely a private affair: it takes its place in the social universe, which, in many respects, has more reality, in the eyes of the unsound empiricist which Durkheim was, than the empirical universe. The objective is the common: it is that which can be the occasion for communication between consciousnesses; it is, then, the social. And the social comes very near to being confused with the rational, itself, for, like the rational, it is its own justification. Society is, at each moment, at least, in the large, all that it can be. Now, in this social and objective world, religion occupies a position of distinction: it is the matrix of the whole social order, as of the whole rational order. Far from being a creation of individual feeling, it is, for the individual, an objective datum, which informs his consciousness and directs his practice. Here is truly a specificity of the religious phenomenon. We have here, assuredly, quite a new view of things and one which might well have given rise to a religious philosophy, or, at the very least, to an investigation of the type carried on, in Germany, by Rudolf Otto in *Das Heilige*. If this has not happened, it is because, after having authorized the category of the religious, Durkheim has striven to ignore the present importance of positive religions. After having presented religion as sole source of all human activities, he, in a way, beats a retreat: "But, of course, the importance which we thus attribute to religious sociology does not, in the least, imply religion should play, in the societies of the present time, the same role which it played of old. In a sense the opposite conclusion is better founded. Precisely because religion is a primitive fact it must give way, more and more, to the new social forms it has engendered. In order to understand these new forms, it is necessary to connect them with their religious origins, but without confusing them with religious facts, properly so called." [3] Thus, sociology, because of being in the service of an evolutionistic philosophy of history, had to make a quick turn in its effort to perceive the specificity of the religious domain.

Parallel to this performance, which need not immediately yield up all its fruits, one could cite an attempt which would merit being called the exegesis of myths. It is a fact that the most rational philosophy has never been able to rid itself completely of myth. Myth is at the heart of Platonic philosophy, and this very fact does not pass without making an impression upon the philosopher. Must not religion be considered with a quite special earnestness, if we see it as an ordering of myths whose meaning remains valuable; and if we see, in myth, more than idea, even the expression of a fundamental human structure, to which all ideas are linked? It follows that a religious philosophy remains possible, precisely as exegesis of myths. Such seemed to us to be the chief point of interest in the numerous publications which Alain, an atheistic and, by supererogation, anticlerical philosopher, has devoted to religion.

It is Alain's intention to free himself from the philosophical tradition which confuses the true and rational with the probable. He would not have the religious myth, the legendary narrative, set aside, *a priori*, as false: ". . . we are very badly placed for doubting a report. For the object which is in question is that which is lacking to us. . . . And the criticism of the stories is a scholasticism, entirely founded upon the ruinous notions of the probable and the impossible. Going about research in this fashion, one will not avoid the ridiculous idea of a Renan, who gives it as impossible that an amputated leg can grow out again, whereas every-

---

3. E. Durkheim, *Préface de l'année sociologique*, 1897-98, p.v., note.

one knows that the leg of a crayfish does grow out again. . . . A reported miracle can no longer be verified: which is to say that neither can it really be denied. . . . For to deny a report is to lose one's time, and it is even something more: it is to lose one's judgment through negligence; and it is, certainly, to lose an occasion for learning something. . . . When one wishes to gain knowledge about human nature, that which is said, absurd or not, should, in the first place, be left in its naive state, which is worth a hundred times more than a probable arrangement, from which you will draw only commonplaces. . . . These marks left by man, these monuments which are the gods, never tell anything but the truth of history." [4]

It is not very important for our purpose to know what use Alain makes of his special principles. His exegesis of religious myths is, without doubt, too univocal and even monotonous. It would be the fundamental experiences of our childhood which express themselves in religious myths. Grace would be only the echo of and the nostalgia for an age, in which it was possible to gain, by means of certain gestures which cost little, the complaisance of nature and of society. What seems to us more decisive is this insistence upon taking myths seriously, this desire to understand human history and destiny through myths. For it cannot be denied that this attitude has had fortunate extensions. The volume of literature devoted to myth is, today, considerable. The confusion between myth and irrationality, even puerility, is being dissipated. The existential character of myth and of religion, which is its vehicle, is made evident. Myth, which supposes a profound alliance between act and thought, expresses, before any intellectual dissociation, certain profound relations between the human being and the cosmos. Every myth is, in the last analysis, a myth of participation: every myth evokes, then, a religious situation for man. To refuse the myth, or to refuse the myth a meaning, is to preclude understanding of man's existential kernel; it is to deprive man of his deep participations, to shut off access to the mystery of the person. For man is a person only when supported by his myths, integrated in the network of his participations, with a cosmos which is not merely the physical universe. This is explained, with decisive clarity, by Maurice Leenhardt, in connection with Melanesian myths.[5] The exegesis of myths seems to us to be, at the present time, the surest way through which a serious philosophy of religion can be constituted. In order that this way may be opened up, philosophy must renounce all the pretentious ra-

---

4. Alain, *Les dieux,* pp. 17-20, *passim.*
5. Maurice Leenhardt, *Do Kamo.* Paris, Gallimard, 1947.

tionalism, all the naive evolutionism which have kept myths in the twi-
light regions of the prelogical age.   (We learn, through the recent publication of Lévy-Bruhl's philosophical testament, that the eminent sociologist has, himself, categorically condemned the idea of the prelogical
character of primitive mentality.[6])   That there is a mythical dimension
of the human mind and that this dimension is the negation neither of
reason nor of history, is a discovery which forces us to locate religion in
the heart of man and not in the periphery.

To set philosophy a task in the name of exegesis, does not that involve
a definition of philosophy, quite new and unexpected in the French tradition?   It does, indeed.   For, certainly, philosophy in France has presented itself as essentially an effort of dogmatic construction.   Even when
critical, in the Kantian meaning of the term, it has remained dogmatic.
There is, perhaps, only a single great exception to this rule: Maine de
Biran, who, moreover, is found to be, along with Jean-Jacques Rousseau,
one of the few French philosophers who had a philosophy of religion.
Now, at the present time, it is undoubtedly the tradition of Maine de
Biran which, through the meditation of Bergson, carries the day.   In place
of being constructive and dogmatic, philosophy has become descriptive.
Or rather, to recapture a distinction made by Henri Gouhier, there are,
today, side by side with philosophies of truth, philosophies of reality.
For the former, the point, starting with the datum, is to arrive at the
conditions of the datum through reasoning, it is a matter of reconstruct-
ing.   For the second, the point is to explore reality, in order to unveil an
existent still remaining hidden.[7]   Le Senne has not hesitated to define
philosophy as a description of consciousness.   As soon as existence is
taken seriously, the philosopher knows that his whole effort must be directed toward exploring existence in all its dimensions, and elucidating
the meaning of all human situations.   And this is a condition eminently
favorable to the constitution of a philosophy of religion: one will no
longer seek either to demonstrate religious truths or to destroy them, and
philosophy will no longer be an apologetic.   But it will consider religion
as a concrete historical datum; and it will be a matter of perceiving its
meaning with regard to human existence.   We shall be far, then, from
the construction of a Malebranche, from the awkward syntheses between
Greek Logos and Christian Logos.   It is at the meeting point of phenomenology and existential philosophy that the chances for a philosophy
of religion are situated.

---

6. *Revue, Présence africaine*, No. 1.
7. *La philosophie et son histoire*, pp. 26-7.

However, before indicating the general lines of the effort which has been made in this direction, we must take into careful consideration the fact that the secularization of occidental thought forces philosophy to assume an important obligation, which consists in definition of spirituality. And in performing this task, it will come to pass, either that philosophy will set itself against religion and especially against Christianity, or that it will endeavor to accept it, demanding, to be sure, that it make certain sacrifices. There is, thus, in the French philosophical tradition, a quite impressive current which, escaped from positivism but perhaps not quite cured of it, strives to obtain a conjunction with Christianity. The clearest example of this orientation is, without doubt, the religious philosophy of Maurice Pradines.

This thinker is concerned with assuring to morality, which he would have rational, not only a foundation but a veritable effectiveness. Through this, he clearly shows his anxiety to build up a philosophical spirituality. Now, he has been led to note the existence of a deep hiatus between morality and religion, between virtue and saintliness, between penitence and temperance, between mortification and courage, between mystic communion and the community of cooperation. The essential hostility between morality and the religious life can be thus defined: "Morality, which cannot exist without autonomy, does not cease to push back, into the bosom of the religious life, that dependency in which we are submissive to the immediate presence of God and the other forms of mystical participation. It must have a God who is less close to us, and even less sure, who does not weigh down our liberty by his mercies, and who cannot corrupt the spontaneity of our designs by his threats and his promises."[8]

The opposition between the innerness and the autonomy of reason, on the one hand, and the externality and gratuitousness of grace, on the other hand, is profoundly brought to life by Pradines. But elsewhere, he recognizes that a purely rational morality is very inefficacious. Morality needs an external support. "It has, then, searched into mysticism, and, not being able to act sufficiently upon man, has undertaken, first of all, simply to convert God. This first God was only strong; morality had no rest until it had made him holy; and it compelled religion to become moral, in order to assure to itself a supernatural power. The signification of this compulsion should not be disregarded: it expresses the weakness of an activity which will always sense, in the extraneous assistance

---

8. M. Pradines, *L'esprit de la religion*, p. 525.

of God, a condition upon which depends the satisfaction of its ambitions, precisely the most elementary." [9]

From the beginning to end of his vast and imposing inquiry, Pradines does not cease pointing out that "inner enmity" which characterizes the relations between religion and morality. Seeking allies, morality had no choice: paradoxically, it could not have found a more certain one than in that religion, which is, nevertheless, originally opposed to it. For sincere faith easily assumes the negative of all the virtues whose triumph the moral will labors hard to ensure. It is possible that the mystic communion, which always runs the risk of smothering the social order, may, nevertheless, be its cradle. In any case, religion has the merit of inspiring "great abnegations, even in quite little souls." [10]

In short, it is clearly in religion that the author seems to find the essential spiritual force, that which, beyond the very structure of human nature, seeks to restore for man the impossible unity without which he no longer has any spiritual life at all. The moral and religious work of Pradines ends, thus, on a note of which one would not be able to say whether it is more skeptical or more religious: "The evolution of mysticism gives us evidence of an exigency which is stronger than all logical reason; it is the aspiration of human nature toward a unity which the discordance of the principles which constitute it seems to preclude it from attaining; and this aspiration cannot be assuaged except through faith in a power, capable, whether of transforming the heart, or of triumphing over reason, itself." [11] A Christian reader will have difficulty in reading these lines without recognizing the perspective in which we are placed by the question of Nicodemus: "How can a man be born when he is old? Can he enter a second time into his mother's womb and be born?"[12] It is interesting to note that whenever the problem of an authentic spiritual life, that is to say, a spiritual life which is deeply unified, is broached, the problem of the new is found to be posed by the same stroke.

The idea that Christianity would contribute toward receiving true spirituality underlies, also, the religious work of Léon Brunschvicg. For he has the conviction that Christianity could, on condition of purifying itself, or rather of persevering in the continuous movement of purification which is immanent in it, rejoin the great current of occidental spirituality, a current which originates with Plato and culminates with Spinoza. But for this, it would be necessary that the God of Christianity

---

9. *Ibid.*, p. 522.
10. *Ibid.*, p. 511.
11. *Ibid.*, pp. 525-26.

should cease to be the God of the Bible, the God who grants grace, the God who condescends to our weakness, marking thus that His transcendence was only a fallacious exteriority, the God who is a person with whom other persons can enter into relation. For this God is never, in the eyes of Brunschvicg, the God who is truly inner and intimate, whom one can adore only in spirit and in truth. "He is not the superior power toward which turns the being who lives and who prays to be saved from the laws of his living. He is the eternal verity, in which a thinking soul acquires the feeling and the intimate experience of the eternity of thought." [13]

Defining spiritual activity by that activity which is at work in science and which is characterized by a permanent renunciation with regard to anthropomorphic imagination and egoistic sensibility, Brunschvicg essays to discover the truth immanent in that activity and in the progress of the mind which it manifests. And he arrives at the following conclusion: ". . . man, considered in his present-day reality, does not account for himself, . . . the progress of his inner activity would be inexplicable if he had not within him, living spirit, a law which surpasses him and which he obeys in order to surpass himself. The spiritual existence of man implies then, as its condition, the existence of the supreme unity: the truth of spiritualism is that same truth which is at the basis of religion." [14] It is to this supreme unity, which is already immanent in man's spiritual activity, and, is, in addition, the promise and the hope of that activity, that Brunschvicg gave the name of God. And he hoped that the religion of Jesus Christ, which was, for him, the religion of antilegalism, of anti-Pharisaism, of appeal to the inner life, of mistrust with regard to the external works and the anthropomorphic representations of God, would, some day, affirm without reticence the religion of the spirit.

It is, above all, because of this desire and this hope for a convergence, that the work of Brunschvicg is of interest to us here. For they imply an effort or inner comprehension of religion as a positive datum. The admirable penetration which Brunschvicg displayed with regard to the "Thoughts" of Pascal should have served him here. However, his personal philosophical position led him to oppose preliminary denials to this religion which he claimed to understand. And thus, the dialogue between

---

12. *John*, 3-4.
13. Léon Brunschvicg, *La raison et la religion*, p. 74. For a more complete statement of this position of idealism we refer the reader to our study of "Christianisme et spiritualisme" in the *Revue d'histoire et de philosophie religieuses* (1943), pp. 149-156.
14. Léon Brunschvicg, *Introduction à la vie de l'esprit*, third edition, p. 157.

philosophy and Christianity, dialogue which constitutes the most actual aspect of all religious philosophy, had to fall short.

Brunschvicg, in effect, fails to recognize the truly specific aspects of Christianity. He can accord it religious signification only if he first denies that which is its very essence. And from the first, Brunschvicg intends to put Christianity back into an evolutionistic perspective; he demands that it realize and perfect itself, that it be conceived as a moment of the spiritual progress of humanity. We must admit that modern Catholicism, as well as Protestant liberalism, encouraged and authorized such a demand. But it was, nevertheless, to forget that Christianity has always looked upon itself as a revelation and a history of salvation, which are completed. Without doubt, this history really implies an eschatological perspective, but this eschatology is, in no way, an indefinite progress. It is expectation, rather than construction. And it is expectation, not of an indeterminate future, but of a salvation which is already realized and which needs only to become manifest.

If Brunschvicg demands that Christianity think of itself as a historical moment about to be left behind, he, on the other hand, disputes its claim to look for salvation in any historical event whatsoever. Truth, for him, is of the order of eternity, and the first characteristic of eternity is precisely the absence of temporality. That it had been possible for the fullness of eternity to be given in a moment of time, that is to say, that eternity should have been able to assume time and history, this is what he denies categorically. At the origin of the misunderstanding between Brunschvicg and Christianity, there is a judgment of value, bearing upon time and upon history, which for Brunschvicg, as for all Greek philosophy, partakes of unreality.[15]

It results from this that every being which has time as a fabric (the human person) seems to Brunschvicg an insufferable I. The feeling of our inner eternity ought not to be affected by any personal character. At the limit, it is permissible to ask oneself whether Brunschvicg's philosophy gives any place at all to the subject. Subjectivity does not pertain even to God, and that which he most desires to extirpate from positive religion is precisely the idea that there could be person to person relations

---

15. One appreciates apropos of this refusal to signify time and history, the profound truth, despite certain schematizations, of O. Cullmann's excellent book, *Christ et le temps*. It is quite true that Christianity has modified not only our conception of time but our manner of placing ourselves in time.

between God and us. With Spinoza he aims to realize "the reciprocal and perfect renunciation of God and Man." [16]

But, if the religious life is no longer a relation of person to person; if God is not a real and objective presence for man; if God is not he who proposes, imposes, and opposes himself to man; if God is not he who gives himself to man, it is hard to see how, in such a perspective, pure idealism and, in consequence, pure psychologism could be avoided. For Brunschvicg, the religious life is only, in the long run, a certain quality of inner life, without reference to any objectivity whatsoever. Furthermore, to make such reference would be to vitiate the religious life at its root, by reintroducing transcendence, alterity, exteriority. The triple denial of the history, of the person, and of the objective presence of God, precludes Léon Brunschvicg from carrying out his attempt to elucidate the meaning of religion as a datum, and to understand religious objectivities as such. In his last and brilliant leaps, traditional idealism recreates the myth of a spiritual religion, which is only a face of natural religion; but the essences, in the phenomenological meaning of this term, effectively offered by religion, escape him.

The blind alley in which idealism has confined religious philosophy, in France, is certainly upon the point of being by-passed. In this removal of obstacles which has been accomplished, an important place must be given to the work of Bergson. We shall not analyze here the themes, now become classic, of the *Two Sources of Morality and of Religion*. As has been stressed, this book does not contain, perhaps, Bergson's essential statements about religion. His religious philosophy must be sought through his whole work. Without doubt, his inquiry manifests a certain reticence concerning "the revelation which has a date, the institutions which have transmitted and the faith which accepts it." [17]

But despite this affirmation of principle, the Bergsonian philosophy is in a good position for grasping religious reality, for it is a philosophy which seeks, not to construct, but to see and to show. Moreover, it is a meditation which begins with experience, and which does not wish to neglect any of the dimensions of experience. Philosophical enterprise consists in "the resolution once taken to look naively within oneself and around oneself." [18] It is precisely this fresh vision of the universe and of our experience which permits Bergson to rediscover the concrete duration which appeared to him the essence of existence. Now, it is this discovery

16. *La raison et la religion,* p. 73.
17. *Deux sources,* p. 268.
18. Statement by Bergson, quoted by the brothers Tharaud in *Notre cher Péguy.*

which is valuable for religious philosophy. Conformably with the fundamental intuition of Greek thought, philosophy had always considered
that the religious life, confused with the various forms of mystical discipline, consists in an effort to get away from time and find the immobile
eternity; in short, that the purpose of religion was to deify man, by letting him escape from his condition of creature. On the contrary, for
Bergson, all spiritual life consists in rediscovering one's proper duration,
and through this the duration of the universe. At once, duration recovers
its dignity, it ceases to be the screen which separates man from invisible
realities, to become the very ground upon which his spiritual destiny is
fulfilled. If there is an eternity, it is in duration that we must become
acquainted with it. It could not be revealed to us anywhere else.

From this discovery, Bergson drew conclusions which inevitably orientated him toward pantheism. His whole effort, in effect, is going to consist in rediscovering duration, under the superficial crust of the world of
objects, phenomena, and states of consciousness. This duration is going
to become identical with the universe as totality, with the universe such
as it exists, previous to the cutting up which our intelligence has made it
undergo.

And when, this reduction made, Bergson shall have affirmed: "The
universe endures," [19] it will be easy for him to attribute to this duration
as to the consciousness which has rediscovered its inner duration, a creative character, and easy to define the universe as a "continuity of creation." [20] The notions of creative duration and of "élan vital" lead, of
necessity, to a sort of pantheistic immanentism, wherein the universe is
substituted for God. [21] The idea of a creation, which would be the veritable act of a God distinct from his work, seems to us, in spite of the
exegesis attempted by J. Chevalier, foreign to the thought of Bergson,
which rejoined much rather, and very curiously, the Schleiermacher of the
Discourses.

But this singular course, taken by the religious philosophy of Bergson, should not conceal from us his central contribution: the union established between duration and spirituality, which means that, thanks to
Bergson, an end has been put to that strange contempt in which traditional philosophy held time and history. Thus there was found to be
prepared an altogether new understanding of religion in general, and of

19. *Évolution créatrice*, p. 11.
20. *Durée et simultaneité*, p. 83.
21. This is really the impression one gets from Lydie Adolphe's book, *La philosophie religieuse de Bergson*.

Christianity in particular. From this time, the idea that the content of a religion might be neither a system of ideas, nor an ensemble of practices, but really a history, has become acclimatized in our mental economy. A new understanding of theological thought was found to be prepared likewise. Jean Guitton's book, *Le temps et l'éternité chez Plotin et chez St. Augustin,* is one of those best fitted to permit the measuring of the progress realized, following the Bergsonian revolution, in the field of philosophical comprehension of theology.

But French thought was encumbered with another deficiency which prohibits it from constituting a veritable religious philosophy. Its idealism led it to a generalized psychologism so that religion signified for it, essentially, religious life, religious experience, but not religious reality or religious object. Under the influence of this current theologians themselves, such as Sabatier and Henri Bois, had come to the point of considering that religion, in the last analysis, has no other foundation than the religious experience itself, that this latter, alone, can be the norm of truth. Psychologism is, in France, without any doubt, a Cartesian heritage. Which is to say that it is hard to uproot. But phenomenology must, by its doctrine of the intentionality of consciousness, completely modify this philosophical situation. Since 1925, Jean Hering has been recognized as showing all the importance of phenomenology for the constitution of a religious philosophy. If it is true that there is no consciousness except when there is consciousness of something, that there is no consciousness except directed toward an object, one understands that the desire of religion not to let itself be reduced to a mere state of soul, but to assert a transcendence with relation to consciousness, in short, to explain the religious experience by the veritable presence of a specific object, should not be discarded, *a priori,* by the philosopher. On the contrary, to postulate that religion is reducible to a certain quality of subjective or social experience is, at once, to deny it intelligence.

It is even possible to go further and give, on the part of phenomenological method, a description of the religious object. This is what Charles Hauter does. It is not possible for us to set forth, here, the details of his analysis. Let us retain, to underline the fruitfulness of the method, just the affirmation that if one does not distinguish clearly between religion, which is a social and psychological phenomenon, and its object, which is not, one lets escape the historical dialectic which is established between religion and its object, dialectic which is the mainspring of the evolution of religions: "Religion is different from the religious object. The object engenders religion: it could not identify itself with it. Religions are historical phenomena. Once inserted into the evolution of facts, they follow the laws of that evolution and often stray very far from their origin. Modified and transformed, during the course of centuries, they even come to turning their action against the objects which have created them, which they modify and transform, in their turn. Then, the object, if it retains its first force, will react violently, to the point of engendering a new religious current, which according to circumstances, will manifest itself in the old movement or outside it." [22] Thus the religious object has a structure of its own: it distinguishes itself both from religious experience and from the historical and sociological structure of religion. By its nature, it pertains to the "great objectivities" which dominate our lives, while distinguishing itself radically from concrete and historical data. One could even establish its pretension to being a transhistorical reality. It claims to be always displaying itself in history, without being a part of history. Phenomenological analysis must, first of all, put in parentheses the question of the validity of this pretension. But Charles Hauter thinks that this putting in parentheses is not definitive and that new analyses could lead us beyond that inquiry.

But one could not combat psychologism and idealism, solely through a restoration of the transcendence of the object. Religious transcendence is not any transcendence whatsoever: it is not simple exteriority with relation to a subject which would be only an ensemble of bio-psychological and socio-psychological determinations, and, in relation to which, any fact at all can be qualified as transcendent. That is to say that there is imposed the rediscovery of an authentic subject, of a subject of faith which could be put in ontological relation with religious reality. A religious philosophy would not be able to eliminate the problem: how is the religious object *for* my existence? Note that this problem is nowhere brought to light in Bergsonism. Idealism, for its part, is well aware of a reflexive self which knows the empirical self and which judges it, which can even divide itself in order to know the self which judges the empirical self. But precisely because there is, there, the question of a purely cognitive and judicatory activity, a sort of supreme instance, one does not see how it could exist for a transcendence, how it could be situated with regard to a transcendence, which is to say, in the last analysis, put in question by a transcendence. Now, such is the very pretension of religious transcendence: it is put in question by that which is most inner

---

22. C. Hauter, *Essai sur l'objet religieux*, p. 280.

in my existence (this is what is expressed by the relationship of dependence, in which the faithful find themselves with respect to God, this is what all faith signifies). Transcendence for self would no longer be religious, that is to say, transcendence-for-self, if the subject, in himself, and not only in his behavior, did not admit this transcendence to be, also, an interrogation concerning the final meaning of his existence. Now, the subject of idealism refuses to consider this interrogation.

It is essential, then, that a philosophy, which does not wish to postulate or to construct anything, should attempt to grasp the subject in an existential situation, other than the activity of judging, or more exactly, in a situation where the activity of judging, always present, ceases to be the whole of the human situation. Our philosophical generation seems to have found this decisive situation in a certain "fissure" of the self, [23] in a certain experience of contradiction, in which breaks forth the radical insufficiency of the self and the inner unhappiness of consciousness. R. Le Senne has shown how the obstacle arises, which limits all the operations of the intelligence, which prevents its activity from wasting itself, which is always presenting it with new, inexhaustible aspects of the real. He has taught also, that, in our relations with others, and even in love, the union, if it is to remain vital, must remain unachieved. There is, in the community of love, a secret which remains inviolable and, without which, love would lose all that it holds of anxiety and, perhaps, anguish. The meditation of existentialism has only accentuated this analysis, by rejecting even the least hint of a removal of the obstacle, by eliminating the possibility of signifying the obstacle, and, through that very means, of making a rift in the anguish. [24]

But is is to be feared that, in the long run, this anguish may become a sort of essence of the being, and no longer merely a concrete and historical situation, a lived adventure, in such wise that the being, immured in the absurd, can no longer be the subject of any relation whatever, either with others or with God. Philosophy, thenceforward, would no longer be able to comprehend that there could be a God-and-man relation. Doubtless, the work of a religious philosophy is not to render intelligible or to explain the act of grace produced by this relation. But its role is, perhaps, not to give us a view of the subject, such that the act of grace is deprived of signification, because deprived of object.

---

23. Cf., R. Le Senne, *Obstacle et valeur,* pp. 146ff.
24. Certain philosophers remain much preoccupied with making of the obstacle only a provisional reality, on the whole, favorable to a joyous expansion of the I. Cf. on this point, L. Lavelle, *Le moi et son destin,* especially pp. 124-31.

Now, the whole philosophical endeavor of a Gabriel Marcel consists, to the reverse of Sartre, in preserving a hospitable philosophy, a philosophy where there is room for both existence and trancendence, to which it is possible, as in *fidelity*, to have "absolute recourse; humility polarized by the very transcendence of that which it invokes. We are here at the joining of the severest engagement and of the most desperate expectation." [25] From betrayal to fidelity, from despair to hope, from having to love, or, if it be preferred, from reclusion to love, everywhere the subject can recognize those concrete approaches of the transcendence which Marcel endeavors to preserve against the temptation of despair. There are, then, existential situations, whose meaning one would not be able to elucidate without, at the same time, reestablishing a living dialectic or, rather, a communication between the subject, a concrete person, involved in history, assuming his own determinations, but not confused with them, and, on the other hand, a transcendence which is a challenge, a presence, much more than an object or a substance.

This does not mean that such a philosophy leads us to religion, and especially to the Christian Revelation. Between the method of philosophy and the religious method, between the two mysteries, there is only consonance. Reviewing the great themes of Marcellian philosophy (ontological mystery, incarnation, discovery of the relation with the "thou"), a recent interpreter of Gabriel Marcel could write: "The Christian mystery displays itself in the ontological mystery, the incarnation of Christ in the world in which I am incarnate, Redemption in a condition of man in which a thou can be evoked." [26]

* * *

The existentialistic attitude seems to us, in short, extremely favorable to the constitution of a religious philosophy, capable, not of assuming the condition of the religious man, and especially of the Christian man, but of elucidating it, drawing its signification from it. Through doing this, religious philosophy will have attained its goal. And it will no longer be temped, as was so often the case in the French philosophical tradition, to construct a philosophical religion, a natural theology, over against concrete religion and ecclesiastical theology.

SELECTED BIBLIOGRAPHY

Adolphe, Lydie. *La philosophie religieuse de Bergson*. Paris, Presses Universitaires de France, 1946.

---

25. G. Marcel, *Du refus à l'invocation*, p. 21.
26. Paul Ricoeur, *Gabriel Marcel et Karl Jaspers*, p. 274.

Alain (pseud. Émile Chartier). *Les dieux.* Fifth edition. Paris, Gallimard, 1947.

Bergson, Henri. *Durée et simultanéité.* Paris, Alcan, 1923.

——————. *L'évolution créatrice.* First ed., Paris, Alcan, 1907.

——————. *Les deux sources de la morale et de la religion.* First ed., Paris, Alcan, 1932.

Bréhier, Emile. "Y-a-t-il une philosophie chrétienne?" *Revue de métaphysique et de morale,* April-June, 1931, pp. 133-162.

Brunschvicg, Léon. *Introduction à la vie de l'esprit.* Third edition, Paris, Alcan, 1920.

——————. *La raison et la religion.* Paris, Alcan, 1939.

Cullman, Oscar. *Christ et le temps.* Neuchâtel and Paris, Delachaux and Niestlé, 1947.

Delacroix, Henri. *Psychologie et mysticisme.* First edition, Paris, Alcan, 1908.

Descartes, René. *Méditations métaphysiques.* Adam Tannery Edition, Vol VIII.

Durkheim, Émile. *Formes élémentaires de la vie religieuse.* First edition, Paris, Alcan, 1912.

Gilson, Étienne. *Christianisme et philosophie.* Paris, Vrin, 1936.

Gouhier, Henri. *La philosophie et son histoire.* Paris, Vrin, 1944.

Guitton, Jean. *Le temps et l'éternité chez Plotin et St. Augustin.* Paris, Boivin, 1933.

Hauter, Charles. *Essai sur l'objet religieux.* Paris, Alcan, 1928.

Hering, Jean. *Phénoménologie et philosophie religieuse.* Paris, Alcan, 1925.

Lavelle, Louis. *Le moi et son destin.* Paris, Aubier, 1936.

Le Senne, René. *Le devoir.* Paris, Alcan, 1933.

——————. *Obstacle et valeur.* Paris, Aubier, 1934.

Lévy-Bruhl, Lucien. *L'âme primitive.* Paris, Alcan, 1927.

Marcel, Gabriel. See bibliography for Hering's essay.

Mehl, Roger. *La condition du philosophe chrétien.* Neuchâtel and Paris, Delachaux and Niestlé, 1947.

Otto, Rudolf. *Das Heilige.* Breslau, Trewendt and Gramer, 1922.

Pradines, Maurice. *L'esprit de la religion.* Paris, Aubier, 1941.

Ricoeur, Paul. *Gabriel Marcel et Karl Jaspers: philosophie du mystère et philosophie du paradoxe.* Paris, Éditions du Temps Présent, 1947.

RECENT ESTHETIC
THOUGHT IN FRANCE

Raymond Bayer[*]

A backward glance over the esthetics of the period between the two wars will perhaps help toward casting light on the paths into which the last war steered our French esthetics. The years from 1920 to 1940 witnessed a general advent and consecration of the kingdom of the spirit. This was the import, in literature, of the enterprise of a Gide and a Giraudoux; in philosophy, of the development and completion of the critical doctrine of a Léon Brunschvicg; in art history, of the application of the spirit to the world of forms by a Henri Focillon; in esthetics, of the all but dominant new perspective of a Valéry. This, and no other, was the import of the Paris conferences toward a *Policy of the Spirit,* organized by the Institute of Intellectual Cooperation of the League of Nations, and ominous of the cataclysms which were to follow. The straight line, the rigorous *askesis* of a spiritual training, the rectitude of a method and a lucidity, doubtless brought French culture a period of equilibrium which other generations rarely knew. For esthetics, it will remain the equilibrium period of a piece of furniture of the 1925 style, or the *Discours aux esthéticiens* of a Paul Valéry, at the 1937 Congress.

After liberation in 1944, the return to new world conditions endowed the esthetics of recent years with quite opposite characteristics. A traumatism seems to have touched to spirit itself. Without making any value-judgments on more immediate efforts and the new studies on the beautiful and the meaning of art, it is quite obvious that the previous generation's pledge of purism and lucidity has undergone some sort of eclipse. In all directions, and in art too, philosophy loses its most certain autonomy. Confusion of genres and the emotional vibrato of doctrines supplant the speci-

* Born in 1898. Student of Victor Basch and Henri Focillon. Professor of philosophy, Sorbonne. Co-Director of the *Revue d' Esthétique.* General Secretary of the *Société Francaise de Philosophie, of the Fédération Internationale des Sociétés de Philosophie, and of the Société Française d'Esthétique.* Administrator of the *Institut International de Philosophie.* Director of the *Corpus Général des Philosophes Français.* Author of *L'esthétique de la grâce* (1933), and *Léonard de Vinci* (1933).

ficity of doctrines and the lucidity of mastery. Everywhere philosophy ceases to be quite free of literature, and every literature dedicates itself to a
philosophy. This is what our young colleague, Mikel Dufrenne, studying
this new problem, expressed recently in an article in the *Revue d'esthétique.*

Such a traumatism is not without fertility, provided at least that the
spirit do not thereby lose its rights nor rigor its firmness, and that the
shock-emotion be a new self-examination. It is equally evident that for
the younger generation Sartre has taken the place of Léon Brunschvicg
and André Malraux's *Psychologie de l'art* that of Paul Valéry's *Eupalinos.*
Esthetics itself, subjected to all sorts of loyalties, reflects this eclipse of autonomy, and that is the most essential aspect of its history in the decade
we have just passed through.

The evolution of esthetics in France would have to be taken up in
two periods: the war and the post-war. The reprinting of Focillon's *Vie
des formes* in a new edition for the use of philosophers, as well as the publication of the last fragmentary works of Paul Valéry, retouching his conception of art for the last time, marked the first period and kept for those
years, which did not break with the past, a unity of style and intention.
Thus there appeared in *Variété V* (1944) several especially illuminating
and timely fragments of the "Cours de Poétique" given at the Collège de
France; thus too *Tel quel II* (1943) and *Regards sur le monde actuel*
(1945) close the cycle of Valéry's meditations on the fate of the literary
cause by means of considerations which the history surrounding him made
pertinent and influential in the world of letters.

Yet it was the university masters of esthetics who upheld French
esthetics in those disastrous occupation years. Charles Lalo, in particular,
as professor of esthetics and the science of art at the Sorbonne, gave a long
series of psychological studies commencing in 1933 and completed only in
1947. A new era in his scientific work on art is marked by his basic thesis
on the typology of artists, which he develops for the first time in his work,
L'expression de la vie dans l'art (1933). He lists all its resources in four
further works which follow with remarkable regularity: *L'art loin de la
vie* (1939), *L'art près de la vie* (1942), *Les grandes évasions esthétiques*
(1947), *L'économie des passions* (1947). All of Charles Lalo's first line
worked toward elucidating the sociological problems posed by art, in a
way that might sometimes have been envied by the German theoreticians
of *Kunstwissenschaft.* His second course, which we trace out here, is that
of a typological psychology of art: the originality of the entire series of

books is their being based on a typology and studying a psychology of
cases. As for the question, "Does art express life?" for Charles Lalo, the
vitalists' answer, the esthetes' answer, even the expressionists' answer are
equally false for anyone who takes them absolutely, equally correct for
anyone who distinguishes and recognizes the specificity of types. The sociological relativism of M. Lalo's esthetics is well known; here, in his latest
works, is its exact and rigorous counterpart: a pure psychological relativism. In this general relativity, art and life divide: and, far from becoming
confounded with each other, they keep an ever-changing relation. For the
vitalists, the only true art is life itself. To live one's job as aviator intensely
is to be an artist. For the esthetes, at the other end of the horizon, the
artificial play of art, nobly free, suffices unto itself: "One gives all the
aviation in the world for a single good poem about aviation." Between
these opposites, the thesis upheld, more concrete and more subtly shaded,
is that art is neither all of life nor nothing at all of life, but that it expresses something of life. The relativist truth is that the real must be analyzed, not considered as a whole nor held to be homogeneous. From this point
of view, five great complex entities share the organization of art based on
life: there are five types of artists. In each of these great psycho-esthetic
complexes described by Charles Lalo, life and art have different relations
and different reciprocal conditions. The expression of art comes into play,
according to the artists, in connivance with life, or in rejection of life. (1)
The complexes of technique place art, for the first time, outside of life:
art for art's sake, or art for the craft's sake, procures the artist another kind
of life; (2) it is also placed far from life by flight-complexes, in which the
artist aims, by a sort of general esthetics of ennui, at keeping his distance,
thus giving himself, through art, either a game and a diversion, an escape,
or a foretaste of the Beyond; (3) the economy-complexes proceed, by
means of art, by extinction: here action, there passions, often achievement;
imaginative satisfaction takes the place of high-tension activity: one makes
up for one's lack of aptitude by velleity; (4) the complexes of mental
homeopathy should be examined too, attempts at healing life by its likeness in art: "Life confessed is life half-pardoned"; (5) finally, the complexes of egotism, or the culture of the ego "doubling life by an egocentrism,"
wish to be or believe they are rebels against any divorce of art and life.
These last two psycho-esthetic types are those in which art stays *near* life.
In every case, whichever of the complexes is in view, genuine mental
therapy, whether preventive or curative, is going on: immunization, catharsis, stimulation by an exercise which is unreal, or reduced, or homologous, which constitutes, in relation to life, all the exercising of art. The

originality of the method is then to consider the work of artists, the art of nations, and of epochs, parallel with the life of epochs, nations, and artists: and the position adopted makes it possible immediately in concrete cases to support a rich inquiry, to diversify their aspects, to bring out their prodigious variety. The warning must be given however that this bio-typology refers to general esthetics and leads straight to the theories of the metaphysicians. The examination of these complexes is nothing other than relativist history, the posing and psychological transposition of doctrines of art which claimed to be absolute: Platonic idealism, the formalist or evolutionist play-theory, the vitalist theory of naturalism, Aristotelian catharsis, the purgation of the psychoanalysts. "Truth within a complex, error outside of it": there is a basic relativity of all values and all types. And art has many shapes. Art is not life, but being the countersubject of that subject, it remains an answer to life; and praise must be given M. Lalo for having replaced the esthetics of the inspired by a genuinely criti-cal esthetics which purports to know phenomena by their causes.

Lucien Rudrauf, *chargé de recherches* at the University of Strasbourg, defended his two splendid theses during the same period. One was a psychography of *Eugène Delacroix,* admirable in style and breadth of in-formation. M. Rudrauf, resetting his hero in his surrounding romanticism, studies a single type of artist where Charles Lalo sketched the whole pan-orama of artistic typology. He follows very precisely, as a faithful disciple of Baron Ernest Seillière would, a very representative nuance and exam-ple of anti-Rousseauist romanticism: imperialism of art here, and there altogether resistance to the passionate cult of nature. It is perhaps Lucien Rudrauf's complementary thesis on the theme of the Annunciation that deserves close attention. There the author studies carefully and rigorously the entire morphology of a two-character theme, throughout its iconogra-phic history. It is an excellent contribution to the esthetics of plastic dyna-misms and structures. Lucien Rudrauf examines by a systematic method the polarity of the work and its variants, the dynamic charges and the dra-matic tension of the ensemble along with the four rhythmic types for which the iconographic datum of the Annunciation furnishes the occasion. From the outset, and all along, he raises the geometric and plastic problem of space and its properties in relation with the polarized themes. Finally he arrives at the description of the morphological types: gravitating, conver-gent, hybrid, of the very highest comparative interest. This is one of those monographs which we desire and should like to see become general, in France and all over the world, for the sake of the positiveness of future esthetic research. Lucien Rudrauf is thus directly in the lineage of the formalists, like Wölfflin and Henri Focillon for example, who set up their technical esthetics in the course of an iconography and a history. Such an esthetics would, it is true, have to take up a position at the very point where the historicity of the problems and the technique of art come together, if we are to see the essential problems arise which are in the heart of the esthetician and which would at last make the new esthetics: the problem of effects and the problem of styles.

We too, during the war, at the time of the death of the great philosopher, published, in the "Études Bergsoniennes" of the *Revue philosophique,* a long study on *L'esthétique de Henri Bergson.* We sought to show the deep roots of the Bergsonian intuition in accord with the *De Emendatione Perceptionis* which constitutes, by and large, his entire work, but essentially divergent from the goal art sets itself. That qualitative heterogeneity, which would certainly have inspired the master if he had given free rein to the expression of his esthetics, had to encounter the interposition of all the screens which every art proposes. Art is, in a sense, the son of intelligence and industry; the work of art does not arise upon immediate contact with the real, as Bergson would have had it; and the Bergsonian esthetics of perception could not furnish us with a systematic treatment of art. Nor does it give us a theory of genius and a poetics of inspiration. The myth belongs to the world of action, and sets up "that systematically falsified experience" against the immediately real. Everything in art is value and postulation of values, not intuition of essences. Art is not that Veronica's veil; there is no art of pure perception; a perceptionism would only grasp facts; but the beautiful is an apperception of values. Such an esthetics, finally, would be unable to give us the exact physiognomy of the object, as it should appear in the consciousness and for the experience of the auditor. Bergson tells us that there are only two sources, or more accurately two materials, of experience: the sense datum and the internal datum. Now each of these undergoes a refraction of its own in art. The esthetic vision is not the metaphysical organ Bergson believed it was; it does not correspond to the conditions he would require of an ontological instrument. The esthetic vision can be (as we shall show) either pure heterogeneity or pure duration or perception of the quality of objects or direct perception of change in the subject: it cannot even be that regulation of duration which the Bergsonian empathy presupposes; an instantaneous-ism of rhythm, or to put it in a word, an impressionism. The Bergsonian alienation, that manner of being things *sub specie durationis* could not constitute the esthetic perception: at the moment of coincidence, consciousness dissolves itself instead of expanding. The guiding marks disappear, the perspectives fade out; the esthetics of pure perception is impossible, just as a *being* of *change* is contradictory. The Bergsonian substantialism and realism become the stake of an intuitive unrealizable experience; and, more generally, if it is possible that a negative theology, which effaces every attribute of God, is possible, one could not remove every screen from the perception of the work of art, and a negative esthetics, based on contemplative passivity, is impossible. If the artist is an ascetic, he could only be an ascetic *en route;* an ascetic who had got there could only be silent, and art would vanish at once.

The post-war period, on the contrary, between 1946 and 1948, witnessed the invasion of esthetics by literary matters. Philosophy and literature became more and more confused and intertwined with each other, their methods and their disorders passing by osmosis from one to the other, along with the objectivity and their existentialism, as they did in metaphysics too for the matter of that. Thus the names of Sartre, Merleau-Ponty, and André Malraux were mingled with those of the most reputed masters of esthetics at the Sorbonne. Still, the methodical resistance of a positive and formed esthetics to the suggestive and sporadic esthetics of literary estheticism has been successfully, and even strikingly, asserted during the last three years. And the works of the masters were accompanied, filled out, supported by a very brilliant flowering of precise, intelligent, solid technical studies, in which the originality of the methods often rivaled the quality of the results.

In poetry, in particular, J. G. Krafft published, in November, 1944, his curious study on the polyphony of "voices" in poetic counterpoint and entitled the thesis which he sustained at that time *La forme et l'idée dans la poésie*. Studies of poetry have followed uninterruptedly in the last few years, and have had profound repercussions among the cultivated public. Thus the works of a Pius Servien are summed up in a Wisdom, prose and verse mixed, and culminate in striking résumés on rhythm, notably on the rhythm of French verse in *Science et poésie*. But studies of poets too are numerous: the *Baudelaire et l'expérience du gouffre* of Benjamin Fondane calls as if from beyond the tomb, to the *Baudelaire* of Jean-Paul Sartre; speculations in general esthetics continue the remarks of a Maritain and a Raïssa Maritain in the preceding period: for example, the penetrating studies on *Les arts de littérature* by Jean Hytier and on poetic pleasure and poetic creating in *La recherche de la poésie* by Yvon Belaval.

In music too, both in the major philosophical journals and in books, a serious effort at technical analysis has been made: there have been few periods in which, at only a few months' interval such important works have appeared as *Esthétique et création musicale* by Gisèle Brelet, *Schönberg et son école* by Leibowitz, and *Introduction à J. S. Bach* by Boris de Schloezer. On the theatre, André Villiers' two works on *La psychologie du comédien* and the *Prostitution de l'acteur* followed Henri Gouhier's book and preceded Paul Arnold's *L'avenir du théâtre.* Finally, in choreography *L'histoire de la danse* by Léandre Vaillat is closely followed by the *Traité de la danse académique* by Serge Lifar, now in press. As a result of all this activity, the *Revue d'esthétique,* which the Presses Universitaires de France has just brought out under the editorship of Charles Lalo, Étienne Souriau, and Raymond Bayer, professors at the Sorbonne, has published a group of scattered or coherent researches, all however very firmly directed toward a Science of Art, whose inauguration was the transformation of the old *Association pour l'étude des arts* into the *Société française d'esthétique* and the formation of a broad committee for the technical Vocabulary of Esthetics, to be published serially by the Society.

This period was particularly fertile in technical and esthetic researches, even in the provinces, for example at Strasbourg, where the *Cahiers techniques de l'art* were published. To the same period belongs M. Charles Lalo's latest book, *Esthétique du rire,* which is accompanied by two theses for the doctorate defended by E. Aubouin, on *Les genres du risible* and *Technique et psychologie du comique.* Charles Lalo reviews, with the aid of numerous and topical examples, the various classical theories of laughter; there is, to be sure, in laughter a transition from the large to the small, but there is also a transition from seriousness to derision. Thus, all laughter, psychic or social, comes from a devaluation; and it is by a process of devaluation that we should explain the reduction to nothing, so dear to Kant, the fall of the infinite to the finite so dear to the German Romantics, the social fagging of mechanization of the living so dear to Bergson.

Joseph Segond, the old master of Aix-en-Provence, published his *Traité d'esthétique* during the same period. Such a work crowns a career of diligent reflections on the Beautiful, abundantly thrown out in his previous works on *L'esthétique du sentiment, L'imagination, Le problème du génie, La situation de la tragédie.* In his *Traité d'esthétique,* whose two hundred pages do not of course pretend to completeness, Joseph Segond examines with great sagacity, together with some partiality, art as pure play of appearance, the feeling for nature in its relations with art, correspondences "from the bottom of the soul," the classification of the arts, style and its work; but he is a metaphysician before anything else, and his study of the virtual arts as well as his views on art as a "supreme game" in which the world of appearances is "opened by the dream and fashioned by intentional mirages" attest the metaphysical thought which runs through the entire *Traité*.

Étienne Souriau too is a metaphysician, and that without having waited for the collusion of literature and philosophy, but rather in congenial fashion, ever since the time long ago when he wrote *L'abstraction sentimentale* and the more recent era of his concern with *Avoir une âme*. Last year he published his most recent book, on the *Correspondance des arts*. But it should not be forgotten that M. Souriau had also already published his book on *L'instauration philosophique* and that he was already engaged on a general morphology of structures. Thus seeking relations among the arts, he poses several of the principles of a comparative esthetics. The book is rich in suggestions on the activity of establishing. A regrettable feature no doubt is a certain obsession with ontology, which organizes the full existence of the work into four ontic presences: physical and material existence, phenomenal existence by *qualia*, real existence as a thing, finally transcendental existence and messages of super-existence. Such a presential ontology shows us the work of art too vaguely and tells us too much about it: in this way we shall know nothing precise about the object, and nothing specific, through these four canons. No doubt too the play of correspondences is too vague, in turn, and once the game has fixed its analogies as genuine similitudes (which could only happen exceptionally), it must reduce to the resemblance of primary thetic gestures and the primary structure of a veritable metatechnic. But in the course of these difficult searches for a basic architectonics and these metaphysical speculations, the author ingeniously indicates the subtle relations which he sometimes feels he perceives among heterogeneous arts, and sets up classifications more valid than those customarily made, in the heterogeneity of the arts themselves. The evidence for analogy cannot usually be anything more than metaphors; but it must be conceded that Étienne Souriau works diligently in that field, and sometimes with much precious subtlety.

Confronted with the mounting flood of literature and metaphysics, we too have felt that the time has come to recall to mind the foundations of a specific method for esthetics. With respect to the technical vocabulary of notions, we had, even before the war, sent the *Revue internationale de philosophie* of Brussels a long study which was prevented from appearing. It has finally appeared under the title *Esthétique et objectivité*. Its starting point is the double stop to every positive esthetics: the subjective and the qualitative. It seeks to define, taking into account the vocabulary phenomenon of our value judgments and structure judgments in art, the qualita-

tive homogeneity in which notions are born; it thus rises from the subjective comprehension of objects to their decisive comprehension. Finally,
starting with that vocabulary, it determines the principles of an experimental method which permits at once tests and purity. From this to a reestablished objectivity it is only a step, but a step in a new perspective in
which our judicative thought is itself judged: "far from my judgment's
judging the work, my judgment judges me." But the methodological principles of such a science of quality were above all established in our article
in the *Revue philosophique* in 1946 on *"La méthode en esthétique,"* which
took up again the themes of our inaugural lecture at the Sorbonne. After
retracing the stages of the heteronomous method in esthetics from the
origins of speculations on the Beautiful (metaphysical methods, psycho-
physical method, psychological method, sociological method), we showed
the possibility of an autonomous method, based on the esthetic object
alone viewed as such, in the light of an operational realism, a method
which should consider its *aspects,* the principle of its *effects,* the result of
its working. We showed the misdeeds of an esthetics which had for
too long remained mental, and not observational; we indicated that everything is written in the work as an artistic trace, that what is not written
does not count for art, and that therefore we should not go beyond the
strict analysis of operations and of traces. Starting with this sensorial and
patent thing, it is allowable to pose three methodological principles: (1)
To reject any mental esthetics; (2) Not to pose in esthetics any problems
but those which pose themselves; (3) Not to comment on anything but
what one sees. Thus there appears the true countenance of a positive esthetics, and of a motivated and causal interpretation in art: Esthetics is a
science of *effects,* starting with their sure causes.

It is a strange circumstance in literary men who have in recent years
tried their hand in esthetics, that the advantage they have over many
others in knowing the practice of an art and its management has often
taken the place of a genuine philosophy of art. But it is an esthetics which
is "committed" to the spiritual needs of an epoch, and even its tics. The
latest book of Jean-Paul Sartre, *Situations II,* is precisely a manifesto of
"committed" art, or more exactly a "committed" literature. "What is literature? What is writing? Why write? For whom is one writing?" such
is the quadruple question which the writer-philosopher raises, "in the 1947
situation." The frequent flirtation, a sort of misery of love, which he carries on with communism, leads him to considerations of keen and penetrating literary sociology on the state of the French writer in the seventeenth century, then in the eighteenth, finally in the nineteenth. Pro-

found as some of his remarks and analyses may be, their aim is so evident, the commitment so one-sided and near-sighted that one can and should hardly consider them as esthetic studies properly so-called; more as sparkling literary analyses than as attempts at science. From this point of view, I prefer the essays on the directed creation which constitutes the prose work as J.-P. Sartre conceives it. This collaboration of object and subject in the creator, this dialectic of writer and reader in the work are among the best pages that have been written on the art of the prose-writer. In perception, for example, the object is given as essential and the subject as unessential; the latter seeks essentiality in the object and obtains it, but then it is the object which becomes unessential. "I cannot unveil and produce at once." The writer does not foresee nor conjecture: he projects; for the reader of the book, it is quite the contrary. The work of the mind only reaches its end-point as object in this complementary collaboration of author and reader: reading seems the synthesis of perception and creation. Finally, the first part of the work, devoted to the essence of the art of writing, seems to me still more revealing of a genuine esthetician's temperament. The distinction which the author makes between poetry and prose is of the first order. As an authentic writer, he takes note that the poet stops at words as the painter does at colors and the musician at sounds. Fused in the word, absorbed by its sonority or its visual aspect, thickened, degraded, the meaning too is a thing which is uncreated, eternal. For the poet, language is a structure of the external world: for want of knowing how to use it as the sign of one aspect of the world, he sees in the word the image of one of those aspects. He considers it as a trap to catch a fleeting reality. In short, language as a whole is the mirror of the world, in his eyes. The word-things group themselves by magic associations of belonging and not-belonging together, like colors and sounds, they attract, repel and burn one another. Emotion itself becomes a thing, it now has the opacity of things. The prose-writer, on the contrary, illuminates his feelings in the degree that he sets them forth. He expresses himself: the art of prose operates on discourse, its subject matter is essentially significant, that is to say, the words are not primarily objects but designations of objects. And that is why the prose-writer cannot but be committed, and prose is never anything but the privileged instrument of a certain undertaking; whereas it is the task of the poet alone to contemplate words disinterestedly, and it would be rather stupid to demand poetical commitment.

Equally caught between the spiritual needs of a tormented age and the lucid observation of a science, but without that depth of vision perhaps which makes Sartre's book most engaging among its peers, other estheticians of merit have worked. Thus Madame Krestovsky, who had already come to the fore with various articles on esthetics, especially in the *Revue philosophique,* has given us, in the Slavic mode of a confession, two very praiseworthy books on the ugly and the monstrous, which must be read: *La laideur dans l'art à travers les âges* and *Le problème spirituel de la beauté et de la laideur.* Jean-Paul Sartre's brother in existentialism, Maurice Merleau-Ponty, has just given us in *Sens et non-sens* a certain number of essays of an esthetic nature: "Le doute de Cézanne," "Un amateur scandaleux," "Le roman et la métaphysique," "Le cinéma et la nouvelle psychologie." The guiding thread of this new esthetics which Merleau-Ponty, together with those of his generation, sees ahead, is that the hero of our contemporaries "is not Lucifer, is not even Prometheus, it is Man." And in this *tête-à-tête* of man with his singular will there is expressed the revolt of immediate life against reason. More and more, therefore, expression is never completed; the highest reason is close to unreason. "As Cézanne wonders whether what his hands have made has meaning and will be understood. . . the citizen of today is not sure that the human world is possible." In any case, the example of Cézanne shows under what risks expression and communication take place. "It would be necessary that the experience of unreason be not simply forgotten; it would be necessary to form a new idea of reason."

But it is perhaps André Malraux who has seen this esthetic problem most broadly, publishing during this period his two large works on the *Psychologie de l'art (I. Le musée imaginaire, II. La création artistique).* The whole spirit of the age is concentrated there; it is, in every respect, a veritable *humanism* of art. In reaction against every sort of materialism, Malraux lays the foundations of an idealism of art which indicates the relations of each art to its time by showing, in each creator of art, not the work of what they see and what surrounds them, but a veritable vision of the "superhuman." Whether it be the Sumerian or the Byzantine, the Pre-Columbian, or the Gothic, the sovereignty of man is everywhere, the sovereignty of a spirit, of a dream caught sight of, an ideal aimed at; of a man liberated and triumphant, at peace with the world he lives in, even in the coherent deformations of art, each loaded with meanings. Even there, beyond the great previous adventures, is the meaning of the Renaissance and its continuation in the subsequent centuries of "the great individualist adventure"; the universe of the individual succeeds the universes of the religious. Everywhere there appears "the dull presence of a world of which, one feels, this image is but the means of expression." It was the achievement of André Malraux to conceive of great art as an ordered succession of *adventures*. Civilizations and cultures seek each other through the high effort of the spirit. Man, by his intelligence, there takes on a dignity which he imposes on the universe of forms: he seeks his destiny there and imposes the effigies thereof on us. All art is a lesson for the Gods. "May the gods, on Judgment Day, raise up opposite forms which were living, the people of statues!" The great artist is not the transcriber of the universe, he is its rival. For the artist is the "survival of the world's quality by means of a man."

SELECTED BIBLIOGRAPHY

Valéry, Paul. *Tel quel II*. Paris, Gallimard, 1943.

─────────. *Variété V*. Paris, Gallimard, 1944.

─────────. *Regards sur le monde actuel*. Paris, Gallimard, 1945.

Lalo, Charles. *L'art loin de la vie*. Paris, Vrin, 1939.

─────────. *L'art et la vie*. Paris, Vrin.

    a. *L'art près de la vie*. 1942.

    b. *Les grandes évasions esthétiques*. 1947.

    c. *L'économie des passions*. 1947.

Rudrauf, Lucien. *Eugène Delacroix et le problème du romantisme artistique*. Paris, Laurens, 1942.

─────────. *L'Annonciation—étude d'un thème plastique*. Paris, Grou-Radenez, 1943.

Bayer, Raymond. "L'esthétique d'Henri Bergson." Paris, *Revue Philosophique,* May-August, 1941.

Krafft, J. G. *La forme et l'idée en poésie*. Paris, Vrin, 1944.

Servien, Pius. *Sagesse et poésie*. Paris, A. Fayard, 1947.

─────────. *Science et poésie*. Paris, Flammarion, 1947.

Fondane, Benjamin. *Baudelaire et l'expérience du gouffre*. Paris, P. Seghers, 1947.

Sartre, J. P. *Baudelaire*. Paris, Gallimard, 1947.

Hytier, Jean. *Les arts de littérature*. Paris, Charlot, 1945.

Belaval, Yvon. *La recherche de la poésie*. Paris, Gallimard, 1947.

Brelet, Gisèle. *Esthétique et création musicale*. Paris, Presses Universitaires de France, 1946.

Leibowitz, René. *Schönberg et son école*. Paris, J. B. Janin, 1946.

de Schloezer, B. *Introduction à J. S. Bach*. Paris, Gallimard, 1947.

Villiers, André. *Prostitution de l'acteur*. Paris, Le Pavois, 1946.

Arnold, Paul. *L'avenir du théâtre*. Paris, Savel, 1947.

Vaillat, Léandre. *Histoire de la danse*. Paris, Plon, 1942.

Bersier, Jean. *La gravure*. Paris, La Table Ronde, 1947.

Prudhommeau, M. *Le dessin de l'enfant.* Paris, Presses Universitaires de France, 1947.

Lalo, Charles; Souriau, Étienne; Bayer, Raymond. *Revue d'esthétique.* Paris, Presses Universitaires de France, beginning with 1948.

Rumpler, Marg. *Les cahiers techniques de l'art.* Strasbourg, F. X. Le Roux, beginning with 1947.

Lalo, Charles. *Esthétique du rire.* Paris, Flammarion, 1949.

Aubouin, Elie. *Les genres du risible.* Marseille, 1948.

——————. *Technique et psychologie du comique.* Marseille, 1948.

Segond, Joseph. *Traité d'esthétique.* Paris, Aubier, 1947.

Souriau, Étienne. *La correspondance des arts.* Paris, Flammarion, 1947.

Bayer, Raymond. "Esthétique et objectivité." Bruxelles, *Revue Internationale de Philosophie,* January, 1949.

——————. "De le méthode en esthétique." Paris, *Revue Philosophique,* January, 1947.

Sartre, J. P. *Situations II.* Paris, Gallimard, 1948.

Krestovsky, Lydia. *La laideur dans l'art.* Paris, Le Seuil, 1947.

——————. *Le problème spirituel de la beauté et de la laideur.* Paris, Presses Universitaires de France, 1948.

Merleau-Ponty, M. *Sens et non-sens.* Paris, Nagel, 1948.

Malraux, André. *Psychologie de l'art:* I. *Le musée imaginaire,* 1947; II *La création artistique,* 1948. Geneva, Skira.

KNOWLEDGE AND SOCIAL CRITICISM

Henri Lefebvre[*]

I

In simplifying somewhat the philosophical situation, one may say that French philosophy is divided, at the present time, into two tendencies.

One of these tendencies endeavors to find another place for the problem of knowledge; more exactly, it refuses to look for knowledge where it is to be found: in the sciences. It dissociates philosophy and science. It gravitates towards a sentimental description of individual consciousness, or of the relations between individual consciousnesses, or of life in general.

The connection between the "subject" and the "object" ceases in this view to be a knowledge relation or determinable in terms of knowledge. It is considered a relation immediately established in existence: a "dramatic situation," on an individual scale—susceptible of an exhaustive description. The formulation of knowledge, the study of actual connections between human beings, objective description of time and historical situations, are then replaced by an endless account of the anxieties, the hesitations, or the "free" decisions of individuals.

Starting from this postulate, it is easy to mix the abstract impeachment of the "human condition" in general, with the social criticism of present conditions, and to replace the indictment of historically and objectively determined concepts ("bourgeois" concepts) by a questioning of men in general.

Existentialism, for that is what we are considering, is oriented toward a bewildering confusion. It continues a conception of the world which, at least in France, seems to be out-of-date: individualism. For it

[*] Born in 1901. Formerly professor of philosophy in Toulouse. At present, in charge of studies at the *Centre National de la Recherche Scientifique*, sociological section, in Paris. Author of *Nietzsche* (1939), *Le matérialisme dialectique* (1939), *Critique de la vie quotidienne* (1947), *Logique formelle, logique dialectique* (1947), and *Pour connaître la pensée de Marx* (1948).

forever concerns itself with the solitary individual, that is to say, isolated, even when he is considered to be torn from himself by "the other," or by "being," or by "nothingness." To escape the contribution of the sciences of man, existentialism tends to confuse literature with philosophy, and the immediacy with broader questions involving more extensive perspectives.

To all those who have examined texts, documents, facts, data (physical, biological, historical, sociological . . .), the ideas of the existentialists often seem rather childish. In spite of the ingenuity, over even the subtlety of certain works of this school, its tendency is characterized by facility. Is it not much easier to solve questions by consulting one's immediate and, on the whole, subjective impressions, than to patiently decipher the apparent chaos of facts? The existentialist philosopher gives himself complete and full "freedom," but it is an abusive freedom. He misuses freedom of thought; he mystifies it. The process being easy, its success is assured. All those who prefer speeches to intellectual work, and emotions to thought, who like to describe themselves endlessly, and who answer the objective problems with "impressionistic" considerations (concerning their anxieties, their hopes, their freedom, etc.), adopt this tendency. It borrows nothing and returns nothing to knowledge. Really, one might ask if it still concerns itself with philosophy!

Social criticism, that is to say, critical thought which does not place itself on the level of pure thought and abstract reason, but leans on the analysis of the social connections and historical situations, by examining the basis of the social significance of ideas—social criticism characterizes such a tendency as existentialism as a phenomenon of decomposition and crisis. It sees in those who accept existentialism, first of all, a sort of gluttonousness for immediate truths; then, a research often sincere but easily satisfied; and finally, an emptiness easily filled. Sometimes it is simply a question of reassuring oneself, in a rather troubled period, by maintaining some inoffensive anxieties.

The other tendency seeks knowledge where it is to be found, although dispersed in scattered results and mixed with ideological interpretations, namely, *in the sciences,* and secondarily in an activity distinct but not separable from scientific knowledge, the *esthetic creative activity.* This second tendency seeks to associate more and more closely philosophy considered as a general theory of knowledge, with acquired or about to be acquired knowledge.

The vital problem of philosophy and the philosopher presents itself in these terms: abandon the abstractness and the emptiness of immediate description, as well as the emptiness and the abstractness of speculative metaphysics. The philosopher endeavors to link his thought to concrete studies. A difficult task, because these studies are always special and almost always reserved for specialists!

He thus endeavors to approach, by a general methodology, concrete problems which range from mathematical philosophy to the study of art. He wants to build his concept of man and the world upon a thesis in which all the elements from all fields and all boundaries of knowledge will come into their place. An overwhelming task, which is too much for the forces of an isolated individual, and which requires new conditions: a collective effort, socially organized, namely, team work.

Between these two great tendencies, mixed attitudes are interspersed, compromises whose validity does not seem certain. Such and such a philosopher studies theoretical physics, not so much to find elements of knowledge, as to discover some gaps through which to introduce extra-scientific methods, "existential" descriptions of the world. The future will judge of these attempts.

II

France, everyone knows, is an old country (which does not mean at all, an aged one!). This historical situation is not without its disadvantages; it also comprises some advantages. Particularly, the cultural history of France—the succession of eras, of "styles," of "centuries"—offers numerous themes of reflection for the thought which compares and confronts the different aspects of man.

A notion of philosophical origin[1] has gradually descended to the rank of banal truth. Every high school student knows that there is something in common between the architecture of Versailles, the etiquette at the Court of Louis XIV, a tragedy of Racine, a fable of La Fontaine, and even a work of Descartes or Pascal. This common element is the "style" of the "Golden Age," which every author of a textbook professes to define. More generally, all the manifestations of an "era" present a certain unity.

We were saying, that in this form philosophical and historical truth falls to the level of banal affirmation. Still, one must observe that perhaps this notion has not been exhausted; and that the analysis of the "style" of

---

1. Formulated with the greatest clearness by Hegel. Taken up in the realm of literature after the romantics, by Baudelaire (*Correspondances...*). Already popularized by Taine in the realm of literary criticism.

a certain great era, provided that one is not contented with vague analogies and remote correspondences, can still hold uncertainty and surprises. This analysis, even in what concerns the seventeenth century, has been carried into effect, in general, only on a purely literary or esthetic plane, therefore abstract, and by authors fairly ignorant of sociological history. As far as the eighteenth century is concerned, the discovery of nature represents, so it seems, its ideological unity, whether it is a question of philosophy, of science, of art, or of literature. Now, historians and critics have barely begun to rediscover this discovery, to seriously reconstitute the notion of nature in the eighteenth century (for example, the works of Mr. Daniel Mornet, Mr. Paul Hazard, etc.).

Generally speaking, some perspective would seem necessary in order to become aware of what makes the unity of an era. Distance, in a period of history, attenuates differences, tones down details, as in a landscape. This conviction, that historical distance is absolutely required for the global comprehension of an era, prevents us therefore from raising the question in the present. Contemporaries, it seems, lose themselves, and cannot but lose themselves, in the differences of works and men. At the most they might suspect quite subjectively, "affinities," relationships more or less "secret" and "profound," between those men they see living actively and those works which they saw born. Having no certainty whatsoever where the "value" of the works is concerned, how could the contemporaries reveal their essential and common traits? The perspective is lacking. Absorbed by the notation of small individual differences or by vague "spiritual relationships," our contemporaries, even the more clear-minded ones, do not even think of asking the question of essential and common traits.

So that if anyone asked: "Is there a common characteristic between this picture of Picasso and this treatise on undulatory mechanics?" he would perhaps at first cause a certain astonishment; to many the question would appear absurd. And yet, in what way is that question more paradoxical than this one: "Is there a common trait between a work of art of the seventeenth century and a philosophical and scientific treatise of this same period?" Now, we have seen that this question belongs on the level of academic banality and that the answer is considered easy!

The problem cannot be put in the present unless we possess a method which allows us to have the necessary perspectives on the present; and which, by the motivated *criticism* of our times and our *society,* brings intellectually (through an intellectual operation) the perspective and distance which time brings naturally.

Let us, moreover, remark that today the "time" of history is accelerated. The perspective brought by time comes faster, and the settling into place of the elements or aspects of a completed era is carried out with a much greater rapidity than before. It took almost two hundred years to get a general perspective on the seventeenth century. Now, today, we are already beginning to take notice of the characteristic traits of a very near era, which was the "other pre-war" (the period before 1914). The question: "Is there something in common between the philosophy of Bergson, impressionistic painting, and the music of Debussy?" has not only a sense which can be grasped fairly easily; the question answers itself, since it is evident.

Yes, in spite of the profound differences which distinguish these works—if it were only because they belong to distinctive fields—there are common traits: first, a sort of cult of fluidity, of continuous change, therefore without metamorphoses or profound modifications. Then an absence of outline, an absence of forms (we know today that form cannot be completely lacking; it is therefore a question of established forms, confusedly accepted). The absence of definite forms, of structures, accompanies the cult of fluidity. Nothing comes to annihilate, in this thought, or these works of art, outlines which have not been grasped and emphasized. To Bergsonian duration, duration without anything dramatic (Georges Politzer demonstrated it more than twenty years ago), corresponds impressionistic fluidity, notation of colors without contours and instants without structure in the life of the individual. Movement thus set within unseen and unfelt limits gave the impression of the unlimited, of infinite mobilism. It gave the illusion of absolute dynamism, illusion which for us conceals the tranquil security of "intimism," of inwardness established once and for all!

This pure continuity contains a great deal more logic and corresponds to a notion much more definite than Bergson had imagined it! Is it not very remarkable that, during the same period, the investigations of the mathematicians, coming after Dedekind and Cantor, were essentially directed toward the *continuous?* Naturally, the analysis can and should also look for differences. In Debussy one can find more "architectural" indications and especially more sensuality than in Bergson (though, according to Mr. Julien Benda, Bergsonism comprises equally a sensual delectation, a suspicious satisfaction in the inwardness of the "I"). The masterly tenacity of the mathematicians in the profound study of the notion of the transfinite and the continuous does not seem to have anything in common with the apparent spontaneity of pictural impressionism. Nevertheless, the analysis which marks the differences puts, simultaneously, the emphasis on the common element: the presence, the praise, the idolatry of the *continuous*. This period elaborated and carried to the limit a character of reality. Believing that it was grasping concretness and finality, it therefore performed, in its own way, within the limits of unilateralness and abstraction, and within those of the temporary and the relative.

How is one to explain this attitude common to men who are so different? This period thought it was the dawn of a progress, unlimited and unbroken. Was it not, on the contrary, an end of an era, a *fin de siècle?* Instead of the sensational innovations which it thought it was bringing, did it not reach the conclusions of a long effort, and did it not drive them to the critical point where they soon exploded, to leave room for preoccupations truly new? The period which we are concerned with believed in the *continuous* progress within the then existing framework of social and industrial life. This idea, already old, of progress, Bergson in particular worked out by borrowing his guiding schema from a biological evolutionism which was still ignorant of abrupt mutations and genetics. We have, today, the feeling that the thinkers of this period settled themselves calmly without adventure, within established forms of thought and sensibility which they confusedly accepted. They then attempted to insert in these forms, the infinite becoming, the evolution, in which they believed. Since then, these notions have "exploded"; these confused forms have disappeared from our esthetic, scientific, and philosophical horizon.

To understand, to judge this era, we thus establish ourselves in the realm of *social criticism*.

This is not accomplished without certain paradoxes. More than one disciple not only believed in the "Bergsonian revolution" in philosophy, but in painting; for example, the impressionists presented themselves as subversive or at least were considered as such. They were repudiated by the bourgeoisie which obstinately preferred the art of the Academy. Now, social criticism characterizes impressionism as a form of bourgeois art, and even as a typical expression of individual bourgeois sensibility: moments of fervor before the fleeting spectacle of the world, formless and merely "picturesque."

The paradox ceases as soon as one learns how our bourgeoisie does not even recognize those who express its universe. Reciprocally, to express it the latter must go outside of it, or pretend to go outside of it. It is the well-known case of Diderot, or of the romantics, of Flaubert. Our bourgeoisie has always spurned Diderot, has only very slowly accepted romanticism, and has but very slowly found itself in the "romanticism of nonromanticism" of Flaubert.

Can one explain by the mere ennui in the face of a monotonous attitude the fact that for forty years, and especially after the war of 1914-1918, all the "spiritual" preoccupations were not only upset but *reversed?* That everywhere in all fields, the *discontinuous substituted itself for the continuous?* That the quest for form, for structure, for contours, replaced the taste for the fluid and the formless? Could this be a simple "reaction," a general vogue, simply opposed to the preceding one? It seems difficult to limit oneself to such a superficial explanation.

Be that as it may, the change was as rapid as it was profound (though prepared by transitions for which a thorough study would find the succession and the connection).

To "achieve" the change of intellectual and artistic atmosphere, all one needs to do is to place side by side an impressionistic picture and a picture by Picasso! Everyone might have made the experiment and observed the contrast. Yet, we must still analyze it with precision and show that the same contrast — the same change of "atmosphere"— is to be found in music, in romantic literature, in poetry and even in the sciences (taking into account, once more, the specific differences; particularly, the amazing development of the natural sciences and the advance taken by them in most countries, over the sciences of man).

It was around 1910 that Picasso invented what commentators now call "analytical cubism."

He began systematically to accentuate the contours of objects, even to bringing them nearer to the fundamental figures of spacial geometry. By this procedure he intended to "render" on the two dimensions of the picture, the objective three-dimensional spatiality, as well as the forms with which he was concerned. Then he decided to bring to the canvas simultaneously, therefore juxtaposing them, the various aspects of the same object (projecting, thereby, on the plane surface of the picture not what he saw, but what he knew and felt about the object, somewhat in the manner of children and primitives, but with a very clear consciousness of the effect which he wanted to obtain).

Thirty years later, when the critics tried to understand what had happened in modern painting, they significantly compared the studies of Picasso with the "Gestalt theory" and the "Psychology of Form" of Mr.

Paul Guillaume. They insisted on the passing to the foreground of the *formal* properties of the picture and of the problems presented by the canvas, considered as a two-dimensional spatial structure. (Cf. in the important special number of *Confluences* devoted to the problems of painting ["Problèmes de la Peinture"] the clear statements of Mr. Diehl, who proposes to "simultaneously comprehend the totality of the relations which link the parts of the picture," p. 21; of Mr. Dorival, pp. 30f.; of Mr. André Lhote, who insists on the rigorous and necessary organization of lines and forms; of Mr. Michel Florissonne, who writes: "This plane is the site of the world animated with its own life, having its laws, its necessities, its conditions independent of the outside world. The oblong and flat canvas on which the artist paints, demands of each thing that it submit its sketch to a given general organization . . ." [*Ibid.*, p. 133].) The modern artist draws discontinuous contours and creates forms. At the same time he breaks, he tortures, he annihilates the objective forms which he discloses through analysis, to submit them to the privileged structure — equally objective and endowed with formal properties — where is situated his pictural world: the canvas.

The parallel between Picasso and Stravinsky has become a sort of commonplace with our art critics. Let us go on with the analysis a bit further. One may consider as a curious testimony of our times the small book of Igor Stravinsky: *Musical Poetics* (*Poétique musicale*, five conferences given at Harvard University; published in French in 1945, Janin publisher). Stravinsky violently attacks the musical fetish of the preceding period, the "infinite melody," the "perpetual evolution of music which had no excuse for beginning as it had no reason for ending" (p. 96). In his own way, and referring especially to the Wagnerian influence, the famous composer criticizes the fluidity, the absence of contours and structure in the music of the preceding period. He demands (p. 18) a revision of the "musical values," and one sees in what sense: the concepts of structure, of forms, appear immediately with an accurate vocabulary. The creative process in music is manifested by the invention of a form: it is a "formal process" (p. 11), in relation to which the psychic, the affective, the individual process—the inspiration—is only an accident. Music has its structural law, comparable to the laws of the perception of forms in a drawing (p. 54). This musical form possesses its own specific objectivity, though in its own way abstract (p. 17, p. 43).

Musical form, endowed with a sort of objectivity "sui generis," thus creates, in Stravinsky's opinion, a specific musical world; and just as the theorists of painting assert the "irrealism" and abstract idealism of modern painting, likewise Stravinsky asserts a musical idealism (p. 37, p. 43) and goes so far as to attribute an ontological value to pure music (p. 165, etc.).

It matters not whether the work of the famous composer corresponds to this program, and whether one can attribute an "ontological" meaning and value to *Petrouchka*. The important thing is to understand his intentions, so clearly expressed, and their connections with those of the painters and the theorists of modern painting.

The discontinuous — syncopated — and constructive character of "pure" forms of modern music, does not need to be demonstrated. (The discussion by Stravinsky, page 58 and following, of the notion of *atonality* is particularly interesting. He forbids the modern composer, under the pretext of going beyond the tonal system, to deal with the formless; he enjoins him, on the contrary, to accentuate the articulations, the structured combinations, the polarizations, while continually reserving the liberty to knowingly break them.)

More generally, for us time has ceased to define itself, if one might say so, by the interpenetration alone of instants, by succession alone, by the continuity of an infinite melody. Bergsonian duration seems to us a disagreeable mockery: a hazy confusion, an impression of schizophrenia, a terrible mixture of psychologism and vague mysticism. Time, like space, seems to us to be structure. It is a series of moments, not of instants; it is an interaction of forms which are juxtaposed, or are sustained, or, on the contrary, jar and break, and this whether it be a question of biological time, or psychological time, or of historico-social time. It is a time both definite and dramatic. From elementary gestures and behaviors to the most subtly elaborated images, it seems to us made up of "montages," of "cutouts," of "sequences" well defined and very distinct, each one full of an intellectual meaning or an affective efficacity for and by itself. Penetrating into time, the idea of structure has equally penetrated the analysis of emotions and tendencies, of actions, of behaviors, of sensations, of images, of neuroses, or of logical ideas.

About twenty-five years ago, Max Jacob taught young people the meaning, the taste of the discontinuous. He saw in it the sign of "modernism." He said that uneasiness and surprise create the poetic sentiment. He insisted in approximately these words: "Suppress reassuring transitions, reasoned (of the classical type), or sentimental (of the romantic type). Split, break the rhythms. Never let the verse or the phrase resemble a vine, or the poem or page a ball of thread which unwinds. Do not prepare the image and do not continue the metaphor. The poetic image creates a dazzling shock. It should surprise, then disappear, leaving the reader like the poet, surprised, unsatisfied. Poetry is first of all poetical situation. The poem should be situated, should present itself as a whole, as an object, with its form and its contours. . . . ." He said, not without reason, he owed this poetic experience to Guillaume Apollinaire (the first of those who tried to represent graphically, on paper, the poem-object and the poetical form). Surrealism and before it dadaism (Tristan Tzara) gave to the image and even to the isolated word this meaning of poetical shock. One could show the influence of this advice and of these works in all modern French literature and even in the novel and the theatre. Conversely, these works, this influence, corresponded to exigencies which were at first obscure, of the new era.

Let us now consider the province of science and the scientist. It is hardly necessary to recall the introduction of the discontinuous in physics as in biology, and to underline its importance. The fact is so well known that only specific instances can have any interest. Let us then rapidly consider the research on the structure of the atom undertaken since Bohr. Physicists seem to have been guided by an analogy between the movements of the atom and those of a vibrating cord. The latter occupies only a whole and finite number of real positions among the indefiniteness and the continuity of geometrically possible positions. Its movement confers upon it a form, a contour well defined: a structure! Besides, at the same time, it produces a continuous phenomenon (sound undulation). Thus studying a physical fact occupying a spatial form relatively stable and definite, the physicists had to abandon, in part, the procedures of calculation which connect the observable elements of the phenomenon to the successive values of continuous variables. They were particularly led to juxtapose distinct elements, observed or observable, simultaneously on the form or structure of the phenomenon and thus to form *tables*. In this manner there was developed, in modern physics, the calculation of matrices of which undulatory mechanics has made a large use since Heisenberg.

Is it not curious to see the effort of physicists follow—"mutatis mutandis"—the same orientation as that of painters or writers, and tend to present in a simultaneity, aspects of reality, at the same time discontinuous, coexistent, and defined by their form, configuration, and structure. Is this remarkable coincidence simply a result of chance?

We can, it seems, assert that our "modern" era has discovered in all fields, and in obscure or conscious opposition with the preceding era, a new aspect of things and man.

But this affirmation in not sufficient and does not suffice unto itself. Questions throng to our minds. How and why this discovery, at a determined moment, and simultaneously in such different fields? Is this innovation final? Is it a question of essential and lasting discoveries, or merely of temporary results? Was a revolution accomplished in painting, in poetry, in literature, in philosophy—or is it but a passing phase?

In order to answer these questions satisfactorily, one must place oneself little by little on the terrain of social criticism. Knowledge of our times alone will define the contributions of these times to knowledge. We will soon see this, better and better.

III

And firstly, it is not possible to completely eliminate the explanation mentioned above. Our so-called "modern" age opposed itself to the preceding one (which also thought of itself as "modern"). It became conscious of itself like children in connection with their parents: from "a spirit of contradiction." It brought into opposition new attitudes with old, new notions with out-of-date notions. The war of 1914-1918 left its mark upon the generation which lived through it and those which followed. It was the moment and the point of the break.

Is it only a question of a conflict of generations and of the discovery of new attitudes, more restless, more adventurous—looser also—than those of the generation of people settled down in their comfortable inwardness, and their so-called indefinite progress? It seems not. This break, which a detailed ideological history will minutely study, had a profound significance. The ideas— and attitudes—of the preceding period had been exhausted; they seemed irrelevant, without application and without significance and, in short, old-fashioned, and somewhat ridiculous in the new conditions. Thus, after World War I, after the convulsions, the crises, the revolutions, after those historical and social events, Bergsonian interiorism and "continuism" appealed only to a very limited category of young men. The more clear-headed ones revolted. The small book of Georges Politzer, written in 1928, (*Fin d'une parade philosophique, le Bergsonisme*), remains the living testimony of this rebellion.

The progress beyond exhausted ideas (and above all, of the fetish-notion of this period, the continuous and the continuity), therefore necessarily highlighted the antagonistic ideas.   There, on the cultural level, is a remarkable example of historical *dialectics*.

This new aspect of reality—of the world and of man—has it much chance of being final?   Was a cultural revolution accomplished, as so many believed and perhaps still believe?

To take up the analysis again, let us consider once more the case of modern painting.

(The reader has already been able to notice that this account sets aside the "professional" examples, that is to say, the purely philosophical ones, and for several reasons; first of all, so as not to open or reopen polemics.   Secondly, because only a minute, ideological history would establish the real efficacy of philosophy and the real influence of the philosophers.   It is not at all proved that the philosophers caused the upheaval.   The comparison between modern painting and the psychology of forms does not at all prove that the latter influenced the former.   The earlier "modern" pictural research [Cézanne] antedated the first philosophical and psychological studies on structures and forms.   It may also be that the tremendous success, in France, of certain philosophers [Husserl] is a symptom—another symptom—not the cause, of a labor, much vaster and greater than that of the professional philosophers.   Let us notice, finally, that the ideas and words [forms, structures] had belonged for a long time to the research and the vocabulary of the Marxists [social structure and infra-structure—logical, sociological, political forms, etc.] which expressedly discarded the idolatry of the continuous.)

Let us then go back to the example of modern painting (and especially of Picasso). Let us again consider this remarkable fact and experience.

The formal studies (in the sense of pure form) have reached an impasse: abstract painting. The pursuit of form has led to an idolatry of "pure" and "purely" plastic form, therefore emptied, dried up, without any significance, except a cerebral one, without affective "charge," incomprehensible to those who confusedly retain the idea of a "total" work of art. The cult of form leads to a new formalism, not so much in the work of Picasso as in that of his competitors and continuators.   It is significant that this great creator has gone beyond the "analytical" cubism to enter afterwards a phase of synthesis; he reintegrates (or tries to reintegrate) the continuous, emotion, the "subject," that is to say the real object! The astonishing series of drawings and sketches exhibited at the Grimaldi Museum (in Antibes) permits us to study, in Picasso, the process of creative research in full maturity. One sees him emphasizing and underlining the contour of objects, carrying this contour to the point of approximating it to a pure form, for example, an oval, and then, re-covering, so to speak, the expressive and emotive contents (momentarily abandoned) : the oval again becomes a face, or an owl. One sees him thus elaborating, at the same time plastically (formally in the frame of the picture) and expressively, a given theme (at Antibes, the theme of the goat, the theme of the centaur, etc.). From sketch to sketch, he arrives thus at compositions in which is expressed an uneven and sly jubilation— a carnal joy, luminous, pagan. He thus attempted to find again, with his style and his technical means, something of the ancient Greek beauty, and to express his vision of the Mediterranean world. Did he completely succeed? Apropos of Picasso as of Stravinsky, let us put the point aside. It still remains that this painting has ceased to be a game, an abstract writing, a language of pure forms, to become or become again transmis-sion and communication, passing through forms, of contents antedating the work, of a meaning, of an emotion. He remains "figurative"; the pic-ture contains an "anecdote," although stripped, general, significant. And the eye passes behind the canvas to find an object. However, other painters enter into the path of pure abstraction, that is to say of formalism. Now, this "pictural world" only situates itself "purely," only makes itself a "world" at the price of a mutilation. The pictural idealism is founded on the "pure" construction of forms, and on the absolute discontinuity of forms and structures. It implies an absence of content, of emotivity. Under the pretext of avoiding an anecdotal character, the content is eliminated. Under pretext of constructing, of creating, of rejecting the old "imitation of nature," of not making of the picture a simple "hole in the wall," the object is eliminated, and it is the picture which becomes an absolute object, all but mystical (a "world"). The vacuum between the forms, the absence of objects in back of the canvas, cause a sort of emptiness to reign which perhaps thus reveals the emptiness of this completely abstract "pseudo" world. This idealism or "irrealism" is reduced to abstract—mechanical—combinations of lifeness elements (cf. "Problems of Painting" ["Problèmes de la peinture"], *op. cit.,* p. 33, article by Mr. Dorival). It also seems to be used up. New ideas have been pushed to the very extreme point where they burst forth, where they have already burst forth. Was not this idea of "painting-painting," of a pure pictural "essence," of a world purely pictural, impregnated, in spite of itself, with the old *logic?*

Let us go from this exemplary case to other fields of culture.

In each field, the pursuit of structures appropriate to this field, and of specific forms, leads to their isolated determination, cut off from its relations. This field first of all claims to have its autonomy, and there sets itself up as an absolute. Thus in each sector is determined, aside from the relations and the content, a sort of *objectivity* "sui generis" for each field, therefore abstract and only situable to regard to a subjective activity, conceived equally as "sui generis." Culture and the world (reality, human and natural) dissociate themselves then into a juxtaposition of "worlds," each of which presents itself with its independence, its constructive activity, its objectivity, and its own ontology: the pictural world, the musical world, the mathematical world, the physical world, the poetical world, etc. Each one of these "worlds" appears, therefore, with an idealistic interpretation of its own structure.

Pictural idealism was analyzed under the name of *irrealism* by the historians and the theorists of modern art, particularly by Mr. Dorival.

Musical idealism finds its perfect formulation in the work mentioned by Stravinsky (regardless of the fact that the composer gives the impression of wanting to connect himself with the "ontological realism" of scholasticism. But perhaps we should not forget that Stravinsky, like Picasso, has a sense of humor, as well as of the dramatic and of adventure).

Under the auspices of Plato, of Husserl, and of Brunschvicg, Albert Lautman has presented a mathematical idealism founded on the study of structures in mathematical thought. The idealism of Lautman and of Cavaillès differed from that of their master Brunschvicg, in the sense that they did not see in mathematical concepts the product of an intellectual activity immanent to the thinking subject, but mathematical essences, participations in the mathematical "Ideas," thus endowed with structures, form, and with a specific objectivity.

More than in the already remote works of Jeans and Eddington, physical idealism is perhaps the most clearly formulated in the work of Mr. Destouches. This physicist and philosopher of physics has attempted to construct the latter, with a specific objectivity, not starting from the concept of a given objective reality (material), but from the situation of the observer in the world (physical).

We could make the list longer, show how surrealism attempted to define a poetical world with a mixture of ideal objectivity and subjectivity; how Mr. Rolland de Rénéville has attempted to describe a poetical experience "sui generis" and to set up an idealistic metaphysics of poetry; how attempts have been made in France to define a sort of sociological objectivity likewise "sui generis," having nothing in common with the individualistic interpsychology, the "substantialism" of Durkheim, and especially with historical materialism, etc.

Do not these idealisms destroy themselves reciprocally? Or rather, does not this general idealism carry inside itself the virus of its destruction by the fact alone that it dissociates itself into a multiplicity of unconnected "worlds," and it thus dissociates culture?

In fact, in a society where *specialization* (inevitable, necessary, fertile, but which is not without its weak points) and the absence of *universal* ideas were carried to extremes, each speciality was formulated independently. The discovery of the discontinuous was transformed into a discontinuity of the methods of discovery. And in each sector, an interpretation perhaps abusive has metamorphosed the forms newly conquered by analysis—the instruments of research, the specialized techniques—into isolable forms and structures. This, once more, on the basis of a science deprived of a unitary conception and of a universal methodological logic —on the practical basis of a divided work of specialists—even drives the specialists to the point of isolation. Then, the forms and the structures thus defined, isolated, separated from the relations and the content, therefore *abstract,* become static and give, as a matter of fact, the illusion of a specific "ontology."

Pushed to its last consequences, this idealism is led to a sort of crisis which jeopardizes idealism in its entirety, for it represents its failure. Forms and "structures" defined once and for all, and appearing for that reason "ontological," become in actual fact, rigid determinations, which detach themselves at the same time from living man and from living nature. The meaning of the real social man and the meaning of real nature become indistinct simultaneously. A great many specialists, technicians, and even contemporary philosophers, confusedly tend to encompass creative activity—knowledge, production, action—in the limits of perspectives, abstractly limited, of "worlds" or closed universes, foreign to each other, impenetrable to the uninitiated and the nonspecialists. In social conditions which conceal from them the dialectical unity of reality, and through ignorance of social criticism of these conditions, our technicians become the victims of the progress of their techniques and of their instruments of analysis. To abstract painting corresponds a formal poetry, and an abstract music, and a "pure" mathematical abstraction, and a physical abstraction. In each sector, the connections of elaborated forms are transformed into a dry and abstract mechanism, that is to say, into hazardous combinations of fixed elements. Discovery, invention, action would thus be reduced to the application of these "ontological" structures and forms. From there, to assert the extratemporality and the extrahumanity of these forms, there is but a step, quickly taken. An antihumanism, latent even in the abstract and mystified forms of humanism, menaces therefore the existing relationship of man with nature, with his works, with himself. (As a testimony of this antihumanism, one can take the recently published works of Mr. André Malraux on the psychology of art.)

Has not the moment come to return mobility and life to its so-called forms and structures? And while still keeping the technical results of the studies, the instruments of analysis, to return to them their relations and content? This project cannot, moreover, be accomplished except in going beyond the social framework of a static thought: the existing limits of the detailed division of intellectual work, the social conditions of abstraction.

We have already given above the example of Picasso. Other examples are as significant. Even in the extreme formalist idealism of the French contemporary thinkers, there appear—in conflict with their predominant tendency—efforts, incomplete and useless, to restore a content and determine the *dialectical* connections of form and content. The effort and the word appear here and there; among the painters (declarations of Pignon, *Confluences, ibid.,* p. 264); among the musicians (cf. Stravinsky, *op. cit.,* especially p. 80); among the scientists (cf. the very disputable but significant effort of the review *Dialectica*). Even among the existentialists one might mention the studies, likewise questionable but equally significant, of Mr. Merleau-Ponty.

It is not necessary to believe that this transcendence of abstraction, of formalism, of idealistic mechanism, only poses academic questions or indeed remains particular to French culture, or again operates only on a speculative plane, itself abstract, in such a manner that it would only have a limited range, and not a historical and world wide scope.

The famous works of Lysenko have recently showed what all the dialecticians have suspected for a long time. The genetic theory of the discontinuous and of the granular structure of the hereditary living substance leads to mechanism. The organic forms transmitted by heredity would remain, if such were the case, stable, indifferent to the outside world. They would escape from all influence, thus from all action. Lysenko has, on the contrary, shown that the interaction of the external and the internal modify the forms and the structures, that modifications produced by action of the environment on the living being (changes of temperature, etc.) are transmitted by heredity. He has thus restored the content and the mobility to the set forms where formalism had wanted to invalidate the science of life and the living substance itself. These studies and other similiar ones have shown that the question has a world wide scope.

Perhaps here one might put forward a formula and say: it is now necessary to search for *the unity of the discontinuous and the continuous* —and therefore, go over and examine thoroughly the two ideas, including that of continuity. Such was the great idea of Langevin. Such was the program that, in his field, an eminent psychologist, Doctor Wallon, already set for himself several years ago. Examining more closely the concepts of continuity and evolution in psychological development—and those of structures, of specificity, of "type of behavior"—he perceived their unity in a large conception, transcending unilaterality. (Cf. H. Wallon, *Evolution psych. de l'enfant,* Armand Colin, Paris, 1941, pp. 32-33. Cf. also, pages 55 and following, criticism from a formal and static point of view of the Gestalt theory of Koffka, etc.)

The point of view indicated here evidently leads to the abandonment of the research aiming at an absolute transcendence. Who says absolute and transcendence says "alienation" of the human. The unity of man and of the world is opposed to the plurality of "worlds" as well as to the oneness of an absolute transcendence. Man, tied to the world, transcends himself, and transcends the momentary forms of his activities, without denying himself in going out of himself. The "moment of the transcendence," a decisive moment, which poses as primordial, nature (the being), or consciousness (the thought, the mind) must settle the dilemma to the advantage of the first reality, but does not get away from the dialectical unity "nature, man."

IV

In short, this restless and tormented era has discovered, in all things, the uneasy aspects: the discontinuity, the abrupt turnings of the *devenir,* the aspects of crisis.

"Modern" man has thus, by an indirect path, and so to speak, projecting it first of all on the world and on things, little by little become conscious of his own crisis, of the discontinuous in himself. Or, if you wish, in the course of a historical crisis and discontinuousness, "modern" man in France has little by little become uneasily conscious of the discontinuous aspect of all things. And it is thus that culture itself engaged in its own crisis, inseparable from a more general crisis, but characterized on its level by the exhaustion and the rapid bursting forth of new notions (themselves expressive of the historical situation).

In a sense, France of today can justly pass for the center of an exciting experience. Ideas face each other with an acuteness never equaled. The clearest formulas confront each other, and also the varied compromises.

French philosophy was not the first to earn the merit of formulating the new ideas (new yesterday) of form, of structure. French philosophy had neither this honor nor this misfortune. Kantian academic idealism and Bergsonism have for a long time satisfied our philosophers, and sufficed for the tasks which they assigned to themselves (or which were assigned to them without their realizing it, as Lukács showed so well at the beginning of his book, *Existentialisme ou marxisme?*). French philosophy has thus received these ideas from the outside. It then gave them a perfectly clear formulation. Existentialism itself received in France the expression which finally formulates it, clarifies it, exhausts it, and definitely compromises it.

For this reason probably the attempts of criticism and of the transcending of formalism and of abstract "structuralism" have already produced in France concrete results.

But it is probably in the field of the plastic arts (of painting) that for more than three fourths of a century, the contribution of France to culture has been the most important, the most varied, the most criticizable from certain points of view, the most fertile from others. This is why modern French painting—and the work of Picasso—have been taken here as a "model case," worthy of a philosophical analysis.

The "modern" era appeared to itself "purely creative"; as though there could be pure creation! Yielding to an old illusion, it brought to the absolute results, temporary and unilateral, at which it had arrived. What was it? What is it still? A period of transition.

In this period mingle, almost indiscernibly, the elements of decadence —the products of decomposition or of dissolution—and the seeds, the gestating elements, the possibilities, the promises of renewal. It is not a question of an overall condemnation, nor of approving globally, but of judging with the maximum of impartiality the values and the results.

To take up again the same example, a Picasso presents contradictory aspects. On the other hand, he is a man representative of a decadence.

He created abstract art, dried up, inhuman. That he answered the call of snobbism, both by a love of paradox and scandal, and in humor, making fun of snobbism—that he furnished his clients, not without irony, what they expected from him, namely, the new, the unexpected, the bizarre— there is no doubt about it. He has worked at the making of painting a closed language, a repertory of formal signs. "Painting-painting" after Picasso has become painting for painters or the closed circle of privileged amateurs (likewise, pure poetry has become poetry for the poets, etc.).

All that can be said against Picasso is true, but also all that can be said for him!

He was a man of discovery. He attempted an "adventure" esthetically necessary and gave to our instruments of analysis, perceptible reality— the eye, the form—an unequalled sharpness. He had the sense of the tragic as well as a sense of humor. Impossible to get along without him! He haunts young painters who would like to surpass him and he makes them desperate. Perhaps he surpasses himself, in restoring here and there, more or less successfully, content, movement, life. Decadence and abstraction intermingle closely with valuable discoveries.

V

A paradoxical situation which should be again underlined: in this period of crisis, of decline and renewal, many highly cultured men, too occupied by their duties and their works, were not able to clarify themselves, to become conscious of their situation and draw conclusions from it. This consciousness can only be acquired at the price of a very stiff struggle against the forms and the exterior causes of decadence, and also —and often—for each individual against himself. For the social causes and conditions never remain completely exterior to the individuals. In each one it is a struggle for the concrete, for the human and the victory of man who must "engage himself."

Social criticism carries the clue in order to find itself in the labyrinth of our time. In discovering the concrete foundation of activities, it shows that only a historical and objective comprehension makes it possible to go beyond the limited points of view which become immobilized and congealed in falling back on themselves.

Thus, in a way which might seem paradoxical, social criticism becomes, in a certain sense, the keystone of the entire field.

SELECTED BIBLIOGRAPHY

Merleau-Ponty, M. *Sens et non-sens.* Paris, Nagel, 1948. Esp. pp. 143 ff.
Lukács, G. *Existentialisme ou marxisme?* Paris, Nagel, 1948. Last chapter.
Baudelaire, C. *Le peintre de la vie moderne.* Paris, Ed. Pleiade. Vol. II, p. 324 f.
Taine, H. *Essai sur les fables de La Fontaine.* Paris, L. Hachette et Cie., 1861.
Mornet, D. *Origines intellectuelles de la révolution française,* Paris, A. Colin, 1933.
Arouet, F., Politzer, G. *Fin d'une parade philosophique: le bergsonisme.* Paris, "Les Revues," 1929; reissued, 1947.
Benda, J. *Belphegor.* Paris, 1923.
Cavaillès, J. *Formation de la théorie des ensembles; Axiomatique et formalisme; Transfini et continu.* Paris, Hermann, 1938-1947.
Guillaume, Paul. *Psychologie de la forme.* Paris, Flammarion, 1927.
Confluences. Paris, 1943. Special number *Problèmes de la peinture.*
Stravinsky, I. *Poétique musicale.* French edition, Paris, 1945.
de Broglie, Louis. Papers published in *Actualités Scientifiques,* especially "Principe de correspondance et interaction entre matière et rayonnement," pp. 53ff.
Langevin, Paul. *Notions de corpuscule et d'ondes en physique.* Lecture published by *Actualités Scientifiques.* Paris, Hermann, 1934.
Lautman, A. *Schémas de structure, schémas de genèse en mathématiques.* Paris, Hermann, 1938.
Rolland de Rénéville, A. *L'expérience poétique.* Paris, Gallimard, 1938.
Wallon, H. *L'évolution psychique de l'enfant.* Paris, A. Colin, 1941.
Special number of *Europe* devoted to the problems of biology. Paris, 1948.
Malraux, André. *Psychologie de l'art.* Geneva, Skira, 1947.

THE PHILOSOPHY OF HISTORY

*Raymond Aron**

The philosophy of history customarily includes multiple problems which are as difficult to separate completely as to treat simultaneously. One might, for example, distinguish the theory or methodology of historical knowledge, from the concrete interpretation of global history, as has been the practice of St. Augustine or Hegel, Spengler or Toynbee. One might add, eventually, between formal and material philosophy, an intermediate domain, that of the formalism of concrete interpretation: we are thinking of the questions traditionally discussed, such as the role of the individual and the masses, of rationality or contingency, etc.

There is no question of denying the scholarly or pragmatic legitimacy of such a classification. But it would be vain to, expect it to be the object of a unanimous agreement, as if it did not involve the very basis of the dispute. The conception of historical intuition is bound up, for Spengler, with the conception of becoming, of destiny, of symbolism, of analogy. A single metaphysics of time and history commands the theory of historical *knowledge* and that of historical *reality*. Likewise, for Marx, the theory of dialectic arises from the formal philosophy of history, but is inseparable from the philosophy dealing with the concrete. Dialectical materialism sends us back, on the one hand, to a logic of knowledge, on the other, to a certain idea of the proletariat and its mission. The unity of philosophies defies academic distinctions: one makes an uninterrupted transition from formal to material, from analysis of knowing to determination of the meaning of the human adventure through the centuries.

The explanation of this unity of problems seems to me to be the following: the primacy of the material over the formal, of the *ontological* (in the meaning of the phenomenologists) over the logical. Doubtless, it

* Born in 1905. Agrégé de Philosophie, 1928. Formerly professor at the Lycée of Havre and Master of Conferences in social philosophy, Toulouse. At present, contributor to the daily press in France, notably *Combat* and *Figaro*. Author of works on sociology and the philosophy of history, including *Le grand schisme* (1948).

can be said that this primacy is not special to history. In a strict sense, all the sciences spring from a certain manner of interrogating the real and this manner of interrogation is inspired or justified by a certain conception of the structure of reality. It is thus in the case of the physico-mathematical sciences, which were originally bound up with a certain philosophy of nature, even though the success of these sciences has led, gradually, to the forgetting of this philosophy.

The difference between physics and history is not less striking and is of considerable importance. The success of the physicomathematical method of interrogation and explanation is such that the logician or the epistemologist finds himself faced with a structure of uncontested truths (or approximately this). It is, then, permissible for him to make abstraction of the implicit philosophy and elaborate the principles and methods of the effective science, according to the results obtained, as though no philosophy were implicated. A pragmatic methodology, rules of methods such as they are suggested by scientific practice, are possible if not satisfactory.

There is nothing of the sort in the case of history. There is no historical science, whose truth, to a certain degree of approximation, imposes itself upon all. To be sure, facts without number have been established. The despoiling of the past, the deciphering of documents or monuments, have made progress and are continuing to do so. But as soon as one arrives at the interpretations, whether it is a question of the projects of Caesar, the causes of the ruin of the Roman Empire or the origins of the war of 1914, it seems impossible to eliminate uncertainty. Understanding of the workings of minds, reconstitution of social structures and of their evolution, seem to be, by their very nature, imperfect. One would not, then, be able to start out with knowledge, as though it constituted an undisputed ensemble and as though the sole task were to separate out its principles and methods which have been demonstrated by success. It is important, on the contrary, to recover, in the very nature of reality and (or) of historical knowledge, the origin of this essential ambiguity. One is, then, sent back to a theory or phenomenology of history (reality) and of the historian. At the same time, from formal to material, the unity of the problems is reestablished. From hermeneutics to prophesy, the philosophy of history encompasses everything which man stirs up in the way of questions in reflecting, in the course of history, upon himself and upon that which will come to pass, of which he is, in turn, actor and victim; which is at once external to him as a constraining necessity, and present within him, as a part of his deepest self.

In this brief study, which does not aim at resolving any problem but only at analyzing current discussions, we will make use of a classification which will suggest the personal philosophy of the author, but which will have especially as its goal to organize the matter clearly, while showing the bond between the different controversies. The basis of a theory of history would be, in phenomenological terms, an *ontology of historicity*. Ontology—in Heidegger's doctrine, for example—recovers the historicity of *Dasein*, but one encounters this either apropos of temporality or of decision, or following upon the discovery of fellow men (*Mitmensch*) and intersubjectivity. Beginning with the historicity of human existence, one would come up against two themes, linked together, however, of which one would be the phenomenology of the structure of history, the other the theory of historical knowledge. One would arrive, finally, at a double result: one, the philosophy of history, in the classic meaning of the term, that is to say, the global interpretations of the meaning of history; and the other that which I propose to call the ethics of historical man.

I. THE HISTORICITY OF HUMAN EXISTENCE

One would be at a loss to mention French works which, in the course of these last few years, have had as their object precisely the analysis of historicity with a view to establishing history on a philosophical basis. But the existentialists return frequently to the themes of human historicity. Individual historicity, so to speak: each existence is an adventure in which each is, for himself, the responsible actor. The individual makes himself by his decisions, and he remains free to make himself over, to disentangle the threads of complexes or fixations in which he has enmeshed himself. The knowledge he gains of himself, which is a solidary relation between what he is at each instant and the decision which he renews, is an aspect of that existence in becoming which finally blends itself with the person. Intersubjective historicity, in the next place: each one is alone with himself, in the sense that no one decides for him, but each is engaged with others in multiple relations, through which he transforms himself while transforming the others. Not that, strictly speaking, others can ever be integrally cause of that which I am or of that which I do. But others create, in large measure, the situation in which I make my decisions and which restricts or enlarges the margin of my liberty, calls me toward autonomy or inclines me toward alienation. On these two themes, contrary and solidary, of man always alone, and of man always guilty, because the waves of his actions prolong themselves to infinity and influence the destiny of others, the existentialists have multiplied the literary variations.

Les mouches (*The Flies*) of Jean-Paul Sartre is the epic of liberation, *Huis-clos* (*No Exit*), the tragedy of hell through others. *L'invitée* (*The Invited*), of Simone de Beauvoir, bears in exergue the quotation from Hegel: "Each consciousness pursues the death of the other." *Le sang des autres* (*The Blood of Others*) illustrates the responsibility which each one has, whether he wishes or not, with regard to those whom he encounters: whether one acts or abstains from acting, one weighs upon the destiny and is accountable for the life and death of others. This antinomy of solitude and responsibility lends itself marvelously to literary purposes; it would not seem to lead to the foundations of historical reality. The proof of this is the novel of Simone de Beauvoir, *Tous les hommes sont mortels* (*All Men Are Mortal*), which one might call the romance of the essential vanity of history. Each generation gives a meaning to its life in devoting itself to objectives to which it attributes an absolute value, but whose precariousness it would recognize if it lived long enough to assist at the death of its gods, at the swallowing up of cities, the defeat of conquerors, the victory of the vanquished. The succession of empires and of ideas has no global signification: it leads neither to the reconciliation nor to the realization of humanity; it does not arrive at a social order which could pass as the goal of human effort. Men will forever fling themselves toward the future, linking their lot with projects whose futility, imperceptible to the actors engaged, will inevitably be apparent to detached or retrospective observers.

There is, then, neither unity nor end to history, nor even historical progression, nor signification common to separate epochs. The existentialists frequently play with Marxist concepts, without always taking into account the fact that there is no possible agreement between their own philosophy and that of the Marxists.

Doubtless, the ontological potentialities of existentialism are richer than their literary offspring. The themes which we have outlined lend themselves to pathetic developments: the novel of failure is easier to create than the novel of success. On the other hand, even in denying all human nature, even in leaving man the choice of his fundamental projects, he would not be debarred from reintroducing a certain historical continuity, by insisting on the permanence of the problems posed to human existence. History could be conceived as men's struggle for liberty. And though one may have difficulty in conceiving an end for history, in the sense of a total liberation of humanity, one could not exclude, in the cadre of existentialism, a transformation of social structures, designed to assure, to an increasing number of men, situations which permit them to exercise effectively the liberty constitutive of the "for-self."

The limit of this existentialist theory of history remains none the less determined by the Sartrian conception of intersubjectivity. In the relations between men, Sartre seems hardly to be aware of more than a single fundamental relation, that of subjects who take themselves, reciprocally, as objects, and thus destroy each other insofar as they are consciousnesses (or insofar as they are for themselves). The glance which I cast at another transforms him into object. From then on, there subsists, in depth, only a single relationship between consciousnesses: that of conflict. Communication between consciousnesses in freedom and their reciprocal enrichment seem to be excluded. Without doubt, Sartre has borrowed from Hegel the idea that each consciousness pursues the death of the other, just as he found, in the work of the phenomenologists and of Max Weber (or of their disciples), that objectification of the consciousness in the knowledge which others obtain of it. But he has modified the bearing of these ideas in isolating them, in raising them to the level of ontology. The struggle of consciousnesses, in Hegel's philosophy, becomes historical only in the measure in which it is struggle for recognition. The struggle between master and slave is not congealed, once and for all, in a sterile permanence: it is the very mainspring of historical movement. The slave ends by triumphing over his master, in subjugating nature by labor. The triumph of the slave is not a meaningless stage in a dialectic without end. One conceives a reciprocal recognition of consciousnesses which gives a meaning (in the double sense of direction and signification) to historical becoming.

One does not see, in *L'être et le néant,* that recognition is in question or even that it could be in question. Thence, the mere conflict of consciousnesses, through time, would no more constitute a history than would the dialogue of the individual with God (or with the absence of God). History is lavishly divided into projects, into conflicts, of which nothing enables one to envisage the end or the signification.

On the other hand, the reciprocal objectification of consciousnesses is only one aspect of the fundamental relation between consciousnesses. When one makes it almost the sole principle of intersubjectivity, not only does one falsify reality, but one condemns oneself to fail to recognize the collective realities created by interchanges between consciousnesses.

To establish a basis for history, it is, above all, necessary to recognize, at the level which Husserl would have called ontic, the phenomena which constitute the historical dimension of existence. These phenomena have a primary psychological material, but they are not essentially similar to those dealt with by psychology or psychoanalysis. They are constituted by what I shall call the *intelligible structure of human behavior.* That which historical knowledge takes as its first aim, that which constitutes the reality of human becoming, are not the impulses which carry individuals toward crime or heroism, but the systems of ideas or values which are immanent in their consciousness.

Alfred Schuetz, in *Der sinnhafte Aufbau der sozialen Welt,* has provided the most important contribution to a fundamental theory of historical knowledge and also historical reality. Doubtless, this contribution is intentionally limited. It does not broach the ontological problem of the discovery of the other as it is posed by Husserl in *Méditations cartésiennes* or Sartre in *L'être et le néant.* On the other hand, it does not follow intelligible construction of the social world up to the historical ensembles (institutions, economic regimes, etc.). It does not insert knowledge of consciousnesses by each other into the global dialectic of intersubjectivity. None the less, Schuetz has laid hold of the theories of *meaning* and of *comprehension* which seems to me an essential part of every ontology of history.

In effect, these theories not only account for historical knowledge, they show the simultaneous beginning of historical knowledge and historical reality, in the relations of consciousnesses with each other. If there is a historical reality, it is because men understand each other, orientate their behavior toward each other, establish their thoughts in collective works, their conduct in institutions, and benefit, at each instant, from the collective acquisitions. It is, then, one of the constitutive features of historical reality to be the object of knowledge for those who live it. Assuredly, there is an immense distance between this spontaneous and partial knowledge and the science of the human past. But it is certain that the signification of historical science emerges from this spontaneous knowledge. Man is a historical being, not only because his existence is a becoming, because he must choose his destiny, because he is plunged into a social milieu, because he reaps, through the objective mind, the conquests of his ancestors; but because he defines himself by comparison with others, that is to say, by comparison with the past. Historical knowledge is reconstitution of the life of the dead by the living.

These rapid analyses suffice to indicate the three levels upon which the ontological, or ontic, phenomenology of history could be carried on.

(1) The discovery of the other, such as Husserl analyzes it in *Méditations cartésiennes,* is of more importance to constitutive phenomenology than to the phenomenology of history. But analysis of ontological categories, of historicity, of the fellowman, of decision, has a direct relation to the foundation of history. (2) One would have to study the different modes of the reciprocal knowledge of consciousnesses as well as the fundamental types of their relations. It would be possible to recognize, both for solitude and for reciprocations, their right place. (3) Finally, one would extend the intelligible construction of the social world. Beginning with knowledge of the self and of others, one would find, between psychology and metaphysics, the dimension proper to history.

II. THEORY OF KNOWLEDGE

Philosophers and scientists come together when they approach the theory of the sciences, but they seldom understand each other. Even when it is a question of history where technique raises no barriers, historians do not always recognize their own proper preoccupations in the problems discussed by philosophers.

The theory of historical knowledge has been largely tributary, in all countries, to the endeavor of German philosophers and sociologists to elaborate what Dilthey called *a critique of historical reason.* Rickert, Simmel, and Weber, after Dilthey, contributed to its elaboration. Mandelbaum's book, as well as the one I published some ten years ago, *Introduction à la philosophie de l'histoire,* belongs in the extension of these attempts.

Reflecting upon historical knowledge, the philosopher tries to separate out the types of relations which can be established between historical facts. For example, one distinguishes *comprehension*, an intelligible bond, immanent in reality itself, from *causality,* which is regular succession between facts previously isolated and constructed. This schema evidently does not exhaust the complexity of the measures through which one builds up the historical world: it serves merely as an example of logical distinctions. More generally, the philosopher seeks to replace historical science among the activities of man and the functions of societies: he shows the tie between historian and history; the incessant renewal of the past through the changing interests of those who interrogate it; the multiplicity of perspective compatible with the facts established according to systems of concepts and values. Always, every collectivity is remaking for itself a past, in order to seek within it for a model or a justification, in order to discover within it the sacred origin of its being or its ideal.

It goes without saying that the effort toward pure truth, toward the reconstitution of that which has been, *wie es geschehen ist,* is an indispensable element of historical science, as it develops in occidental civilization. It goes without saying that the deformation of facts or interpretations through political prejudices or ideologies is only a sorry caricature of that inevitable relativity of the past to the present, of the dead to the living. If history begins with the myth or the legend, if criticism substitutes precision for fantasy, the third term of the dialectic, recognition of the inevitable role the historian plays in selection and interpretation, does not mark a return to the first term, the sacrifice of criticism to legend. On the contrary, all the requirements of criticism, the will toward impartiality, must be safeguarded. The theory of the limits of historical objectivity merely points out the impossibility and vanity of a pretended integral detachment, of a seizure of a crude pseudofact. Much more, it affirms the positive signification of that solidarity between knowledge and life, between the reconstitution of the past and lived experience. As each individiual defines, at the same time and by the same proceeding, that which he has been and that which he wishes to be, so humanity would not be able to launch itself toward the future, without taking, at each instant, a view of its past, without confronting its intention with the defeats and successes of yesterday.

If many traditional historians have rejected these considerations, in which they have seen a subtle threat against the scientific character of their discipline, this rejection has been very far from being general. One of the most gifted among the younger historians, H. I. Marrou, has taken to himself the principal theses of my book, which he hailed as an introduction to a larger, more fruitful conception of historical knowledge. He has, moreover, interpreted them in a certain sense: the discovery of the *other* is, in his eyes, the essential characteristic, the profound value of historical knowledge. The historian does not set out to discover a humanity of a monotonous sameness, crystallized in its nature; he is in search of other men and other societies, whose otherness will help him to discover himself, and understanding of whom will enrich his understanding of himself and of humanity.

Another historian (specialized in the philosophy of history), the Reverend Father Lenoble, reflecting upon his work after having completed it, has recovered, he also, for his own account, the theses of the philosophers and outlined a theory of historical knowledge, inspired by Roupnel's book, *Histoire et destin,* and by *Introduction à la philosophie de l'histoire.*

In spite of all, these two examples remain exceptions. The book of an excellent historian, Alphen, upon history, confines itself to the classic discussions: the part played by science and by art; severity of criticism and feeling of the historian; uncertainty of causal explanations; role of psychological interpretations, etc.

The most alive and most interesting of the French historical schools, that which had gathered, before the war, around the *Annales d'histoire économique et sociale,* of Marc Bloch and Lucien Febvre, and which, after the tragic death of the former, is again to be found around the *Annales,* edited by the latter, is more careful than the majority of historians to define the object and methods of its work. It remains, however, hostile to theories of historical knowledge, which seem to it equivocal and dangerous. Quite legitimately, it is fond of the problems which arise at the level of research, itself.

It refers frequently to the conceptions of the historical synthesis of Henri Berr. But the essential thing is not the distinction made by this latter, of contingency, necessity, and logic. The essential thing is that, in fact, history should arrive at seizing the historical ensemble in its totality. Whence come the polemics of the school of Lucien Febvre against the traditional ways of writing history (for example, against those which hold to the old framework of diplomatic history). Whence comes insistence upon the economic infrastructure of societies, upon development of techniques, upon the evolution of forms of property. There are some Marxists close to the *Annales,* but neither Lucien Febvre nor his disciples are Marxists, in the orthodox meaning of the term. They have nothing to do with the dogmatism of the dialectic nor with the primacy of the economic. They do not recognize any factor as exclusive nor even as of first importance. They borrow, from Marx, that which every historian must borrow from him: a sharpened consciousness of the importance, through the centuries, of the organization of work in common, according to the available tools and the relations of exchange. But, very far from being materialists in the strict sense, the historians of the *Annales* incline toward recovering, even in the infrastructure, the presence of spirit. In all likelihood they would willingly revive Michelet's formula, integral resurrection of the past, on condition of interpreting it anew. It is not a question of an intuitive reconstitution of the soul of the past; but of a patient reconstruction of the institutions, the customs, the political and economic relations, the ways of thinking, feeling, and dreaming. The end is always to understand men, in their unique existence; but this end is to be attained only through a slow and methodical approach, through the unlimited despoiling of documents and works, through the study of implements and texts, through the ordering of the multitudinous facts which, together, have constituted civilizations which have perished and centuries which have passed away.

Between the philosophical theory of historical knowledge and the methodological painstaking of historical synthesis, there is no opposition. For one thing, these two sorts of consideration are situated on different levels. Experimental physicists have the right to be indifferent to studies of causality, but not to reject them as useless or dangerous. Likewise, working historians often have only contempt for theories of historical causality. When they condemn them, they forget that the purpose of philosophical theory is not, necessarily, to serve the practitioner, but merely to bring to light certain truths. The philosopher proposes, in the first place, to make out what historical comprehension or causality is, and, in the second place, to render the historian more clear about himself. Even supposing that this second objective is not attained, the philosopher is not, thereby, disqualified (for the rest, a scientist such as Max Weber has demonstrated what methodological or logical clear-sightedness can add to research).

Perhaps, moreover, these misunderstandings are more easily dissipated when the theory of historical knowledge comes upon problems which cannot help being posed by the historians themselves. It seems to me, today, that the analysis of historical knowledge could be centered around two inseparable ideas — of historical *ensemble* and of *signification*. Let us reconsider the example, traditional in all books on historical knowledge, of a battle, considered as an elementary fact. This elementary fact is not an atom; it is not the smallest conceivable unity, since it is effectively constituted of a multiplicity of acts, gestures, thoughts, of the individual combatants and their leaders. This fact, although christened elementary is, then, constructed; and this construction is inconceivable without unity of the signification we give to a multitude of material data. Material complexity and significative unity would, then, be the two characteristics of the historical fact, from top to bottom of the scale, from the battle of Marathon to Greek civilization.

On this same example, one could equally well separate out the different modes of comprehension. For, in order to understand a battle, it is necessary to know the instruments of combat, the rules of tactics which result from them, the organization of the combatants in the engagement, the conceptions of the leaders (incomprehensible without anterior information); in short, the unrolling of the battle, just as it proceeds from material, institutional, and psychological data, without counting the accidents, whether extrahuman (atmospheric condition) or human (frenzy or panic among the combatants), capable of influencing the course of events.

On this same example, one could clear up certain of the most difficult problems of the philosophy of history. The battle, reconstituted by the historian, has never been lived by anybody, neither by the soldier nor by the Commander in Chief (although it is nearer to the vision of the latter than of the former). The history of wars is capable of being renewed when the historian has at his disposal original categories which were lacking to his predecessors (the role played by numbers, the relation between the number of combatants and the social organization, tactical or strategic concepts, forgotten by certain epochs and rediscovered by others). Historical comprehension combines comprehension of intelligible structures of behavior (the general's plan) with comprehension of institutions, as they are spontaneously lived by individuals (the organization of armies), and comprehension of natural or human accidents (the arrival of unforseen reenforcements or changes of weather). It is easy to see that, by applying the same method, one could clear up the different aspects of comprehension of an economic or a political regime.

It does not seem to me that anyone has attempted from this slant, a systematic study of historical construction. And yet, this way of approach seems to me promising, capable of interesting philosophers and historians alike. Philosophers would find in it the fundamental propositions of the theory of historical knowledge. The elaboration of history is not comparable to the shaping of a crude datum. Historical facts are complex and significant. There is no battle but only "insensate tumult" for him who stops at sense perception.

At the same time, in the very degree to which one advances in the scale of complexity, one would find again the difficulties known to the historians, themselves. How determine periods? How isolate civilizations? At what moment do we leave the Middle Ages behind? At what moment do we emerge from capitalism? To just what point are these historical unities arbitrary, cut according to the historian's discretion, or inscribed in reality itself?

Thus, the theory of historical knowledge debouches into the phenomenology of the historical structure.

III. PHENOMENOLOGY OF THE HISTORICAL STRUCTURE

Men make their history, but they do not know the history they make. Each generation is born into a situation which it has not chosen and which appears to it as fatality, though it is, after all, only the crystalliza- tion of the past behavior, the objectification of that which men have thought and willed. Often, these men would not recognize themselves in their works. Would Lenin and his early associates recognize themselves in the Stalinist regime?—or the members of the Constituent Assembly in the Republic of '92, the Empire of Napoleon, or even the Monarchy of Louis XVIII?

These two themes—man perpetually attributing a sort of fatality to the crystallization of the past which he observes around him, and man perpetually disappointed by the result of his actions—are at the origin of Marxist thought. This defines itself by the will to put an end to this sterile dialectic. Humanity must organize, rationally, its conditions of existence, without admitting that any may be imposed upon it from out- side. Man must take his destiny in hand, must orientate the course of history, thanks to the knowledge acquired of historical laws.

There is no need for us to take a stand, here, either for or against this rationalistic optimism (hyperrationalism which aspires to complete mas- tery over nature, catastrophic optimism which waits upon this triumph of reason with a series of conflicts and calamities).

We have recalled this Marxist point of departure because it can serve, also, as the point of departure for that which I call phenomenology of historical structure. This latter would have precisely for its object the respective parts of liberty and destiny, of blind forces and conscious free- dom, of individuals and masses, in the unfolding of history. (These three antitheses, whatever may be thought of them at times, are not to be con- fused).

This phenomenology is linked with the theory of historical knowl- edge, of which, to begin with, it constitutes a sort of counterpart. In effect, analysis of historical ensembles brings to light both the reality of these ensembles and the cutting which is the work of the historians. The phenomenology of structure applies itself to determining the proper char- acter of historical ensembles: institutions, political systems, economic regimes, civilizations. It would be absurd to say that only the element is real. (What is the historical element?—the gesture, the thought of the individual? But these are not to be comprehended, such as they are, in their isolation.)

It is no more satisfactory to consider American capitalism as real in the same sense as a tree or a feeling. "Intersubjective realities" lend themselves to a phenomenological consideration, capable of disengaging the originality of each of them.

Beyond the analysis of these intersubjective ensembles, one would have to study the modes of historical continuity or breaking up. Time does not pass at the same pace for the different sectors of history. Between the slow transformation of the social humus (popular manners and customs) and the vertiginous transformation of technical means, one would bring to light the diversity of what will be called historical rhythms. There is no doubt that one of the causes of the troubled state of the world today is the acceleration of the historical rhythm. Each generation lives in several societies, if not in several civilizations. Those statesmen who are more than sixty years old, which is to say the majority of statesmen, received their intellectual formation before 1914, which means before the motorization of economy and of armies, before the onset of the period of monetary instability and of widespread unemployment, before the proliferation of political, religious, and totalitarian tyrannies. Humanity, it has been said, is rarely contemporary with its problems. Formerly, this retardation of thought with regard to the event led to the persistence of the ideas received from the previous generation; today, it can be sufficiently accounted for by the fidelity of each generation to its own youth.

The phenomenology of historical ensembles would be relatively formal, essentially indifferent to the diversity of historically realized structures (although, in the measure to which one drew nearer to the concrete, one would recover this diversity). The phenomenology of historical continuity would, in return, with certain elements valuable for all epochs, be immediately marked by the diversity of times and of societies. Beginning with these fundamental studies, one would rediscover through a positive means, the classical aporias. Instead of endlessly exchanging arguments to demonstrate whether the great man is the creator or the expression of his times, whether economy is the decisive factor, whether politics or ideology rules everything, one will strive to indicate, in what and to just what point, the great man is capable of innovating or of diverting historical destiny, under what circumstances and in what sense economy or politics is the destiny.

In the framework of a given system, economic or political, the effectualness of an individual is strictly limited. It is not in the power of a captain of industry to modify the manner in which French capitalism functions, nor of a party leader to put an end to the decomposition of the Third Republic. As a matter of fact, no one would be able to determine, in advance, the consequences of a change of system, inaugurated by leaders of men when they possess themselves of power. To be sure, this seizing power, in its turn, presupposes favorable circumstances; but the success of political adventures depends, in a measure which it would be difficult to appreciate in general, upon the leader, himself, just as the work accomplished bears his imprint. In the last analysis, one would not be able to draw, in advance, a strict circle around the effectualness of the man who, situated at a strategic point in events, orientates history in one direction or in another.

Neither a politician nor a thinker creates from nothing. But that which accrues to him as his own prolongs his effects indefinitely, without one's being able, unless by an act of faith, to acknowledge a sort of compensation of accidents, capable of releasing the broad features of history, determined by massive forces alone.

Thus, a sort of concrete theory of man's liberty in history could be accounted for. Could one go further and formulate, in general terms, the action of each category of forces? Would it be necessary, after the manner of Scheler, to assign a primacy of efficaciousness to race, to politics, or to economics, according to the centuries?—or to assign this primacy to the same factor throughout all history? Is it possible to develop a general theory, valuable for the whole of history, of the relation between ideas and reality, the former being present at all epochs but expanding in collective existence only in the case where the valves of reality offer them passage?

These interrogations have no other purpose than to indicate the result of this phenomenology of structure. It is not certain that it brings demonstrable and indisputable answers. The further one goes beyond description, the more one risks propositions of universal value, the greater grows the uncertainty. But, in large part, the classical controversies admit of positive analyses. It is not precluded to establish a theory of historical destiny or freedom. If its conclusion is equivocal, it is because it ends by rejoining that which makes the traditional object of the philosophies of history: the interpretation of the totality of human becoming.

IV. GLOBAL INTERPRETATION OF HISTORY

For at least a half century, the philosophy of history (in the traditional sense) has, in France, fallen into disrepute. Academic historians almost unanimously reject it. They have not taken Spengler seriously: they do not read Toynbee. In a short article in the *Revue de métaphysique et de morale,* Lucien Febvre dismissed Spengler and Toynbee, simultaneously, with the classical arguments: these attempts have no scientific character; they rest upon information at second- or third-hand; they make use of vague or ambiguous concepts; they do not advance the progress of science but merely foster myths and ideologies.

Apart from this scientific distrust with regard to philosophy of history, the French have long appeared rebellious toward speculations concerning the course and the signification of history for another reason. Since 1871, they have never ceased to be pessimistic, in their hearts, concerning the future of France. The ascendancy of Germany the relative decline, the demographic stagnation, the slowness of the industrial development of France, have all contributed to convince them that the future of our country would be inferior to its past. Even the victory of 1918, won with the assistance of a coalition not fitted to live and grow, did not modify these deep presentiments. They rejected the philosophy of history because they feared the future.

This state of mind is in process of changing. *L'histoire de l' Europe,* by Emmanuel Berl; the *Bilan de l'histoire,* by René Grousset; the *Grands courants de l'histoire universelle,* by Jacques Pirenne, have been successful publications. All written by nonacademic historians (of unequal ability), they bear witness that the public has begun to welcome that which the scientific historians are loath to give them and continue to proscribe: the global interpretation of becoming.

The reason for this change seems to me to be the following: the crisis is manifest—not that of France, but that of Europe, even that of occidental civilization. Hence, the complex of pessimism is no longer active and ceases to paralyze curiosity. Everyone is conscious of living in a period of troubles, comparable to the sixteenth century or to the decay of the Roman Empire. Everyone is anxious to recover from the past, precedents which would permit the placing and interpreting of our own experience. The fate of France seems, henceforth, to be only one element, among others, of a destiny which goes beyond it.

More or less confusedly, three philosophies of history oppose each other and exercise an influence on French thought: that of Marx, that of Spengler or Toynbee, and that of Burnham. The first passes for optimistic; the last, as commonly interpreted, for pessimistic; the second admits of a pessimistic and a neutral version.

The Marxist philosophy of history has become, today, the quasi-exclusive property of the Communist party and of those who connect themselves with it. The interpretation preserves the same simplicity: the present crisis is that of decadent capitalism; the bourgeoisie as the ruling class has served its time; the Russia of Stalin has taken the lead in universal liberation; stabilization of the new world implies the universal diffusion of communism. In France, as elsewhere, a certain number of intellectuals have rallied to this doctrine, but one could hardly say that they have utilized it to rethink the world. One would hardly be able to name important works of Marxist philosophy of history. There is not even a comprehensive book on the problems of Marxism. Never has the economics of *Capital* and its signification for the present day been studied by an economist of the first rank. The most interesting of the recent Marxist books are still those of Henri Lefebvre.

Burnham's book, *The Managerial Revolution,* has had a real success. One has seen in it, especially, the means of recognizing the indisputable evolution of the liberal and capitalistic societies of the nineteenth century toward another type of society, without, at the same time, subscribing to the mythology of a classless society, or to the tyranny of a single party. Many readers have attributed to Burnham the opinion that the society of managers would inevitably present the characters of the Stalinist regime. At once, they built up a Burnham whose pessimism would be symmetrical with Marxist optimism: the same evolution judged by both to be inevitable would lead, not as Marx said, to a definite end and to the reconciliation of humanity, but to a social structure as unequalitarian as the capitalistic structure and more oppressive.

The philosophy of Spengler and of Toynbee places our epoch in a vaster perspective. Both admit the possibility of a comparative history of cultures; both try to separate out the likenesses presented by the formation and growth of cultures. The former ends up with a radical pessimism, founded not oñly upon the conviction that our occidental culture is entering upon its ultimate phase, but also upon the conception of man as a beast of prey. The latter, who does not subscribe to a biological fatalism and who leaves a wider margin for man's freedom, defines our times through the contact, real for the first time, of all the great cultures which are alive today. Humanity has, or will soon have, at its disposition the means of blasting itself out of existence. Will it answer the challenge thrown at it, or will it succumb?

Though none of these three philosophies belongs properly to France, all three of them have penetrated deeply into French opinion. It is through reference to them that one is able to formulate the problems raised by the global interpretations of human becoming. One will distinguish among them two sets of categories: those which interpret becoming by a relation between man and his vocation, in such wise that unity is imposed upon becoming through the universal value of the idea; and those which find, in becoming, itself, the unity, or rather the unities, which they seek. The comparison of culture does not give us, perhaps, the ultimate signification of the human adventure, but the laws or rules according to which cultures live and die. A philosophy of the Hegelian type pertains to the first set of categories. The philosophy of Spengler is characteristic of the second. The philosophy of Marx pertains to both. In the texts of the young Marx, it depends on the first; but Marx dedicated his life to proving, through sociology and economics, the intuitions of his youth. The rational dialectic which, passing through revolution, led to the reconciliation of humanity with itself, had to be, at the same time, the real dialectic through which capitalism destroyed itself; and the struggles between classes led to a classless society. The vacillation between *rational dialectic* and *causal necessity* is at the origin of the larger part of the philosophical uncertainties of Marxism.

It does not seem to me that the task before the present time is to invent a whole new interpretation of history, which would imply an original idea of man and his destiny, but to work out more rigorously the problems of these interpretations and strike the balance between our knowledge and our ignorance. Never have historians had at their disposal such a wealth of instruments: theory of political systems, theory of economic regimes, theory of classes and of elites, individualistic structure and collective structure, bureaucratic societies and personalistic societies, peace of equilibrium and peace of empires, universal religions and national ideologies, permanence of customs and transformation of techniques. Our concepts of human and social relations are more numerous, more finished than at any other epoch. The most visible aspects of the present crisis admit of all the precedents, suggest comparisons, lend themselves to explanations. The ordering of these partial interpretations, the final judgment, remain ambiguous and controversial. But are not ambiguities and controversies well founded if the truth of a time can be perceived only by those who embrace it in its entirety, if the truth of history finally depends, not upon reality, but upon the vocation which man attributes to himself? For lack of knowing the outcome of the crisis through which we are living, for lack of unanimous adherence to a settled philosophy of man, the diversity of the partial interpretations, favored by the enrichment of our historical and sociological requirements, gives no answer to the final question. The final question is, at bottom, that of men who would put themselves in the place of God and be delivered from the obligations of action.

v. HISTORICAL ETHICS

We shall say a few words, in closing, about problems which usually pass unperceived, to which the events of the war period have given a political and philosophical actuality.

The purge has been practiced in all European countries, following upon the German occupation. It is a permanent practice of the Soviet regime. Doubtless, it is not a new phenomenon. In all epochs, a victorious regime or gang have hunted and driven their vanquished adversaries. From 1789 to 1815, the French did not lack occasion to observe the purge, whether it was a matter of quarrels between revolutionaries, or the revenge of counterrevolutionaries upon revolutionaries (or inversely). The contemporary purges have, none the less, given rise to more philosophical reflections, for two main reasons: in France, the purge has, more than once, struck at collaborators or "Vichyites," whose patriotism was unquestionable, whose disinterestedness was indisputable, who were reproached either with having blindly obeyed the orders of Marshal Pétain, or with having played Germany's game through ideological passion, with the hope of protecting France in case of German victory. In Russia, the accused of the famous Moscow trials pleaded guilty, confessed to acts which they had certainly not committed. Whatever the part played by the staging of the affair, whatever the refinements of physical or mental torture through which the former Bolshevik leaders were brought to these confessions, one is clearly obliged to consider an explanation, which contains at least a part of the truth: these men, who were in opposition to Stalin, but not spies or traitors, in some fashion, judged themselves guilty. It did not seem to them inconceivable that, in certain circumstances, the fact of opposition should be held by governments to be a crime.

These two examples have begun to give rise to unlimited reflections upon the condition of man in history. Historical responsibility is not to be confused with moral responsibility. Without having committed any moral fault, one is susceptible of being accused for acts (or their consequences) accomplished in all good faith and with the intention of serving one's party or one's country. In tranquil epochs, this responsibility does not become penal. It is the historians who reproach you for your errors. In periods of crisis, societies tend to apply the principle: one does not have the right to make mistakes.

Up to what point is it legitimate to apply this principle? The discussions about the Moscow trials and around Koestler's book, have taken up this question from multiple viewpoints. The freedom of the opposition is the dogma of democratic liberals. The obligation to stick to the line, the dogma of the oriental pseudodemocracies. But if one carries to the extreme the dogma of obligatory unanimity, if the power is free to regard all opposition as a crime, under the pretext that it was serviceable to the enemies of the revolution, what guarantee subsists for the citizens? Does not terror become a permement feature of the socialist state?

At the same time, the old questions are revived: of the relation between intentions and acts, between acts and their consequences, the morality of conduct and its efficaciousness, the right of individuals and the exigencies of collectivities (parties and states). Such discussions are not new, but they assume, in the light of events, a tragic acuteness. For everyone, in Europe, knows that, henceforth, he stakes his life in politics.

Much more, historical thought, itself, is put back in question. Marxism knows nothing this side of history or beyond it. Revolution is the goal, the absolute value. The party which deciphers history and shows the way to revolution has a providential mission. Who betrays it, betrays truth. Who serves it, by whatever means, is sanctified by success. These conclusions are logical if one admits the principles. But do not the very consequences (the permanent terror, the war without end up to the universal triumph of the proletariat) react upon the principles?

Can man, should man accept being only a soldier of history? Is history the sole dimension of human existence? That a former communist should come to the point of opposing the Yogi to the Commissar has, perhaps, a more than accidental signification. An integrally historical philosophy has come to the point of disowning itself. The moment has come for the philosophy of history to free itself from the historical absolutism instilled into it by the Marxist tradition.

SELECTED BIBLIOGRAPHY

Aron, Raymond. *Introduction à la philosophie de l'histoire. Essai sur les limites de l'objectivité historique.* Paris, Gallimard, 1938.

————. *Essai sur la théorie de l'histoire dans l'Allemagne contemporaine. La philosophie critique de l'histoire.* Paris, Vrin, 1938.

Berl, Emmanuel. *Histoire de l'Europe.* 2 vols. Paris, Gallimard, 1945-47.

Dardel, E. *L'histoire, science du concert.* Paris, Alcan, 1946.

Febvre, Lucien, *Collection des annales d'histoire économique et social,* and since 1945, *de civilisations.* Paris, Armand Colin.

————. "De Spengler à Toynbee. De quelques philosophies opportunistes de l'histoire." *Revue de métaphysique et de morale,* 1936.

Focillon, Henri. *La vie des formes.* Paris, Alcan, 1939.

Friedmann, Georges. "Jeunesse de l'histoire." *Revue Europe,* 1946.

Grousset, René. *Bilan de l'histoire.* Paris, Plon, 1946.

Halevy, Daniel. *Essai sur l'accélération de l'histoire.* Paris, 1948.

Halphen, Louis. *Introduction à l'histoire.* Paris, Presses Universitaires de France, 1945.

Lenoble, Rev. Father. "Les nouvelles conceptions de l'histoire." *Revue philosophique,* 1945, No. 7-9 et 10-12.

Malaraux, André. *Psychologie de l'art.* 2 vols. I. *Le musée imaginaire,* II. *La création artistique.* Zurich, Skira, 1948-49.

Marrou, H. I. "Tristesse de l'historien." *Revue Espirt,* 1938. (Published under the pseudonym of Davenson.)

Merleau-Ponty, Maurice. *Humanisme et terreur.* Paris, Gallimard, 1947.

Pirenne, J. *Les grands courants de l'histoire universelle.* 3 vols. Neuchatel, Éditions de la Baconnière, 1944.

Sartre, J. P. *L'être et de néant.* Paris, Gallimard, 1943.

THE PHILOSOPHY
OF
EDUCATION IN FRANCE

*Henri Wallon**

T wo definitions of education are possible, and both have their
supporters in France. Durkheim for instance holds that its
aim is to prepare the child for incorporation into the social or
national group he is a part of, with its own "collective representations," beliefs in common, traditions, and tendencies, with an image of
itself and an ideal. It is in the light of this heritage that each of its
members should be formed. A contrary definition starts from the individual and sees him as a being endowed with aptitudes, needs, and aspirations to which education should give all the guidance desirable and
all possible means of development. The collective life should be a result of the competition and emulation among individual activities or in-
itiatives.

Evidently this second conception too, no matter how opposed to the
first it may appear, corresponds to the image which a certain sort of
society forms of itself. It seems less archaic than the other. For it is
in primitive societies that tradition is held to be the supreme law, a vital
necessity. There education properly so-called is replaced by initiation.
More or less esoteric rites serve to attach the individual to his group by
making him share in his ancestors' wisdom. In the caste system, there
is the same overshadowing of the individual by his membership in this
or that social category, whose functions and privileges it is his principal
destiny to maintain.

This state of mind still survives today within nations and among
nations. There are social classes who consider themselves superior, and

* Born in 1879. Agrégé de l'Université; Docteur en Médicine; Docteur ès Lettres.
Professor, Collège de France; Director, École Pratique des Hautes Études; Co-director,
Institut National d'Orientation Professionelle; President de la Commission de la Réforme de
l'Enseignement; President, Société Francaise de Pédagogie; President, Groupe Francais
d'Education Nouvelle. Author of *Psychologie pathologique, Principes de psychologie appli-
quée l'évolution psychologique de l'enfant, De l'acte à la pensée, Les origines du caractère
chez l'enfant, Les origines de la pensée chez l'enfant, L'enfant turbulent*.

desire a different education or at least distinct educational establishments for their children; in many countries there still exists an aristocratic education and a popular education depending on the pupils' family origin. The differences are even sharper among nations, according to whether they are sovereign or dependent, colonial powers or colonies. Here pretexts of race, color, allegedly superior civilization are brought into play: prejudices which spread terribly once their principle is admitted. Even among nations of old civilization they can try to set up discriminations. Sometimes pretended superiority of racial type and sometimes greater technical or economic resources serve as the theme of these pretension to supremacy, which are inevitably reflected in the education children receive.

Individualist education is founded on the denial, at least in theory, of these biological or social predestinations. Every one should have the chance to show what he can do and what he is worth; society should assure each child the education that can best develop his abilities. Society will gain thereby as well as the individual. This principle of justice and utility is not usually disputed in France. However, individualism is not conceived of here as a simple competition among differently endowed persons. It is bound up with a universalism which is just as profound a tendency in the French mind. This has often been remarked: the French, it has been said, tend to consider their case as the case of the human race. If they proclaim their rights, it is because they hold them to be inherent in the nature of man and consequently as valid for everyone. Their individualism is based on humanism. All men have something in common which is the essential thing, which it should always be possible to find in the individual, and which precludes the use of differences to call into contempt his dignity as man.

But in practice what becomes of this principle? Every nation has derived from its history traditions, institutions, an intellectual and moral orientation which gave it its character, and each of which is capable of setting up special obstacles to the changes which have become necessary, or of more or less delaying their adoption. It is evident moreover that for each type of society, and for each stage of social evolution, there should be a system of education which in the main satisfies the needs of the moment. In every nation, each epoch must be the resultant of its history and its actual social structure. Accordingly, French humanism has clothed many very different realities in the course of time. But what have been its origins in the French tradition?

We might speak of the amalgam which has made up the French population over the centuries, by the assimilation of very diverse ethnic fragments, each province drawing within its frontiers disparate elements which melted in the unity of France while preserving the memory of and interest in their original diversity. Undoubtedly, France has a great deal of interest, spontaneous sympathy, and even fraternal feeling for foreign customs and ways of life. Attachment to local traditions and to national spirit does not entail intolerance or an exclusive feeling of superiority. Xenophobia was a theme of political agitation; it could never seriously affect even those sections of the population where it succeeded in getting a foothold.

However, French humanism has more specific historical sources, particularly with respect to culture and education. It derived its forms and its content from the Renaissance. In the sixteenth century two great movements took place in Europe, the Reformation and the Renaissance. Their causes have been variously interpreted according to the point of view; but each of them was in response to a great social change: the entry of the bourgeoisie into the lists as an important factor of political and social life.

In France the bourgeoisie's fight against the feudal power had already begun with the agitation of the communes and the gradual emancipation of the city artisans. But as its power increased, it aimed at mastery of the intellectual weapon as well, and so had to assail the authority of the Church, which had the monopoly of culture in medieval society.

In the countries where the Reformation triumphed this opposition took form within Christianity. It aimed at replacing the teachings of the Church by every man's personal study and interpretation of the sacred texts. Important psychological results followed: an increase in the feeling of personal responsibility in the moral domain, greater assurance in the field of action, the interpretation of success as divine approbation, and the pride which arises from assiduous familiarity with the Bible, the book of the prophets inspired by God, of the people chosen by God. From all this, individuals and people can draw ideas of superiority over other individuals or other peoples, ideas more or less protective but uncompromising, and naturally not incompatible with one's own interests— quite the contrary, since it is success which seems to justify pretensions to supremacy.

In France, it was not the Reformation which triumphed. In the end, the Protestants came to constitute only a small minority, which certainly had an influence, but after the fashion of a minority, that is, in the direction of liberalism and resistance to the principles of dogma and authority. Not being able to hold their own within Christianity, the opposition became external. It was the Renaissance that was the weapon of the bourgeoisie in their thirst for intellectual power and spiritual influence. The Renaissance sought to replace the Christian man of the middle ages by man pure and simple, the complete man; and it looked for examples of him outside of Christion society. This is the reason for the exceptional value the Renaissance placed on antiquity. It did not look for academic themes in antiquity, but for the very nature of man, freed from ecclesiastical restraints. It turned to antiquity as a source of new or renewed life. There it found a morality which was not necessarily ascetic, heroes who were not saints, an enterprising spirit which was not submission to catechising, and in a word, beings for whom the meaning of their activities lay on earth.

The enormous success of Plutarch's *Lives,* which J. J. Rousseau tells us lasted down into the eighteenth century, is not due solely to the charming translation of Amyot, a writer who contributed to the elegance of the French language. The *Lives* furnished the imagination with models of greatness and strength of mind, of generosity and self-denial, of skill and practical subtlety, who had no resemblance whatever to the canonical virtues of the old society.

But the most significant work was that of Rabelais. This has often been the subject of schematic or oversimplifying commentators, each critic seeing in it only the reflection of his own opinions. It is a river into which the tendencies of his times flowed, and if we sometimes seem to find contradictions within it, at least the motion it imparted to them has a very well-defined orientation. Some of its parts have been accused of coarseness and regarded as a precaution taken by the author, giving a tone of farcical pleasantry which unmercifully satirized powers still dangerous, particularly the ecclesiastical authorities of the time. The maneuver may actually have been diversionary, but the diversion was in the true spirit of the work. For all their triviality, which does not seem to have annoyed Rabelais, physical appetites and physiological needs are a part of man just as much as his aspirations to knowledge, wisdom, and concord among men. To Christian man, who regards his body as a perpetual occasion for damnation and his spirit as continually liable to temptation, Rabelais contrasted the man of flesh and reason whose nature is all the justification needed for what he is.

Rabelais's humanism is coupled with naturalism. His program of education proceeds from the same conceptions. He set it forth twice: for the first time, in a rather negative way, in Gargantua's letter to Pantagruel, in which the father congratulates the son on being born in an age when education is no longer, as it was in his time, a sort of physical punishment and intellectual penitence, where the spirit succumbed under formulas empty of all reality, under subtleties foreign to the world of things, under arbitrary precepts unjustifiable in practice. On the contrary, the education which Pantagruel receives from Epistemon and Gymnaste should not neglect any of his physical or mental aptitudes. With the latter he will plunge into all the exercises and all the games which can make his body supple, strong, and untiring. With the former he will devote himself to direct knowledge of nature, all of nature. And finally he will spend a part of his time in visiting craftsmen and learning their techniques.

Certainly this encyclopedic quality is not on the scale of the individual. The giant Pantagruel is a collective symbol, which however represents everyone's requirements. If we must concede the existence of differences and distinctions among men, every man must be able to take part in all the activities which will develop his being over the entire range of his bodily and spiritual nature. Under an obviously chemical and almost mythical form, this is the ideal expressed by the program for the life to be led at the Abbey of Thélème. In every individual there is something universal to respect.

Humanism and naturalism, universalism and encyclopedism—in this way a conception of culture and education takes form which may at times be frustrated or fragmented, but whose memory will persist, even during the most inauspicious phases of social history.

In Descartes the same tendencies appear, but in a clearer and more systematic form. He showed by his own example as well as by his declarations the price he attached to personal action and indeed to physical action: he was in the army, he went to war, he traveled, and he always claimed to be anything but an armchair scientist. Action on things is the aim of his philosophy, and he therefore gives technology an essential place. But the techniques of his time seem ludicrous compared to the changes that a profound study of its laws could impose on nature. Man's power over it, it semed to him, should be unlimited. He cited as an example the prolongation of human life, which seemed to him a legitimate ambition of science.

This study of the physical world was made possible, according to him, by man's capacity for reasoning and constructing mathematics, the key to the other sciences. Reason is characteristic of man; it is common to all men; it can be brought to light and cultivated in everyone provided that the prejudices originating in sense and opinion, which obstruct it, be destroyed. It is to this end that education should apply itself; and evidently it can be extended to all, since reason is universal.

Descartes puts universalism foremost. His humanism is based on reason. He takes a detached view of antiquity; what it says is open to criticism, as it itself served to criticize Christian life. There is no other authority than reason, no other criterion of truth than the principles which make it up. Thus humanism and science seemed about to become one; and this tendency was to persist in the French tradition, although most often submerged by another humanism, the increasingly stultified classical humanism. Descartes himself saw the clash take place. He had been a student of the Jesuits and had converted some of his former teachers to his ideas. They were exiled to Canada, at that time a place for deportation. He thought it more prudent on his part to go to live at the Hague, a Protestant city where he would not have to fear ecclesiastical persecution.

In addition and in contrast to the encyclopedic humanism which Descartes may be said to have originated in France, Renaissance humanism also gave rise to watered-down humanism on the antique model— classical humanism. This was mainly the work of the Jesuits. In line with its customary policy, the Church exerted itself to capture its opposition. After the two great shakings given the world by the Reformation and the Renaissance, the Council of Trent had adopted inevitable condemnations and practicable accommodations. It was of the utmost importance to get education back into its hands, but concessions had to be made to the spirit of the times. The enthusiasm for antiquity was not extinguished, but had to be toned down and filtered, by choosing authors and texts whose precepts were general enough to fit in readily with those of the Church, and above all, by a more formal orientation of classical studies. They had been a means of exploration into a literature rich in human content: what had to be done was to transform them into exercises in expression, and indeed exercises whose interest became more and more expressly grammatical. This development has continued down to the present. Still, indispensable as it was, the undertaking had its dangers; and the Catholic Montalembert reproached the teaching of the

Jesuits with having raised up against the Church adversaries like Voltaire.

As a matter of fact, during the eighteenth century there was no disjunction between encyclopedism and classicism. Education remained classical but the scientific cult ran all through intellectual life. Newton was discussed even in the "salons," which were like little worldly academies where learned men and cultured amateurs came together. The deist Voltaire and the materialist Diderot still marched side by side. However, in the Revolution it was encyclopedism which triumphed. The "Écoles Centrales" were founded, suppressed a few years later by Napoleon, who here as in every other field put a check to the revolutionary drive, in behalf of a bourgeoisie which now had advantages which it tended to maintain as monopolies.

The programs of the *Écoles Centrales* were remarkably novel. They oriented minds toward the study of science and technology, and were inspired by a boldly progressive philosophy, the philosophy of Descartes, Diderot, and Condorcet, in whose eyes reason proves itself by an ever wider knowledge of the world, and knowledge proves itself by the ever greater power of man over things. This confidence in the unbounded development of human civilization was as dangerous for the new powers as it had been for the old. Encyclopedism was thus opposed by classicism, which became the great pedagogical argument of the bourgeoisie, and an argument it still continues to invoke.

From having been, at the beginning of the bourgeoisie's conquering period, an offensive weapon against the spiritual authorities of the times, the return to antiquity became a means of defense. It was now reduced to the study of Greek and Latin, especially of Latin, and in practice, of a very limited number of Latin works. The aim is no longer replacement of an outworn asceticism by the free unfolding of natural needs, of the most diversely earthly interests and activities, but rather the erection of a cultural conformitarianism, outside of which the intelligence was alleged to find no salvation. The aim was no longer initiative but rather a badge of honor, the stamp of good society, the stamp of a select ruling class. Education was valued less for its effects than for its recognized prestige. It no longer consisted in the development of wisdom but in a mere gymnastic of the wits. Instead of knowledge to be obtained, there were exercises to be gone through. Montaigne's formula, *une tête bien faite plutôt qu'une tête bien pleine* (a good head rather than a well-filled head), was interpreted more and more narrowly. Rabelais and Descar-

tes too had condemned the rubbish of scholastic education and its purposeless burdening of the memory; but they did so in order to leave the
intelligence free to study nature in the light of the principle of reason.
Montaigne himself stressed the vast inquiry that man must institute concerning man. A "good head" does not mean an empty head, but good
judgment. Judgment presupposes objects of knowledge and experience
of the real world.

In the *lycées* which Napoleon put in place of the *Écoles Centrales,*
he restored classical education as it had been gradually thinned down by
the Jesuits prior to their expulsion from France in 1762. His conception
of the state was that the Sovereign should have at his disposal agents unable to set their own ideas up against his, but adroit at translating his
wishes into all the forms capable of furthering their execution. Hence
the usefulness of an education based primarily on exercises of linguistic
interpretation. As for the now dominant bourgeoisie, it too had no interest in raising up innovating minds. On the contrary, it esteemed the
qualities of intellectual elegance and ease which classical education can
develop. It thus tended, by ascribing these qualities to itself, to build up
an aristocracy whose superiority the people would have to concede.

This predominantly formal education brought with it, on the philosophical level, consequences which perfectly matched the direction being
taken by social change. An education which professed to cultivate the
mind by detaching it from concrete objects actually pushed it toward
a purely idealistic representation of itself and the world. It professed
to deal with the mind's somehow native or essential aptitudes in order
then to study nature; as if the mind were the lawgiver of nature or had
no function except giving a sensory content to principles derived from
itself. In contradiction to a Descartes, for whom matter has its own
reality and its own laws, which the laws of thought reproduce on the
level of ideas, a Léon Brunschvicg, well-known academic philosopher,
engulfs the entire science of things in a mathematical and axiomatic conception of mind and the world. Likewise, on the economic plane all
the concrete activities of production are absorbed by the speculations of
finance, also an abstract power and also one which believes itself capable
of organizing the life of nations and of persons in accordance with its
own private principles.

But by eliminating all concrete content from specifically intellectual
activity, idealism undermined itself. It fell from rationalism into irrationalism. This evolution appears sensationally in Bergson's philosophy, which is an indictment of reason and consciousness on grounds of

being a mockery of the real and of life, which is said to animate beings and things internally after the fashion of tendencies and instincts, intrinsically indefinable. This theoretical renunciation is matched on the social level by the recognition of forces which the existing economic system is unable to master, despite its ingenious and subtle stratagems: *viz.,* irrepressible urges of production, leading to social conflicts and imperialist wars.

The years around 1900 mark an important date in the history of French education, as in the history of the country as a whole. At the same time that the old certainties are shaken, as the rise of irrationalist doctrines shows, the worth of the classical education is called into question. At least it is no longer considered as adequate to meet all needs. Alongside it in the *lycées* there arises a modern education which gives more attention to the needs of the present time, that is to say, to teaching the sciences and modern languages. This is of course a shamefaced irresolute reform, one limited in its principles and effects by the persistent prestige of classical education, the only one deemed worthy of the most gifted children, and therefore unfortunately demanded for the less gifted, as if it were able to regenerate them. By reason of the idea that classical education alone possesses cultural value, modern education was conceived of in purely utilitarian forms.

However, their coexistence marks a sort of competition or rivalry within the bourgeoisie. By its want of immediate usefulness, classical education was calculated to repel that part of the bourgeoisie whose resources are too limited to allow it to guide its children toward studies whose result after all is uncertain if they are not followed up to the very end. The creation of modern education was a victory for the petty bourgeoisie, echoing, on the academic level, a political victory. For, around 1900 France went through a crisis which had tremendous repercussions, the Dreyfus case. Appealing to reasons of state and the respect due to the institutions which had soiled themselves in the affair, the ruling classes tried to keep in prison an officer unjustly accused of treason. The battle for justice was fought against the oligarchy by the masses of the petty bourgeoisie and the people, who strove to shake the oligarchical authority. The juridical conflict was at once political and social. The triumph of justice was at the same time the triumph of the middle classes. And they gained a foothold in the *lycées* as well, but still in a humble way, as the prestige maintained by classical education shows.

By a sort of paradox, secondary education in France has been far in advance of primary or elementary education, which would seem to be the starting point of all education. Really, the difference is not merely one of level; it is essentially based on the class distinction between the bourgeoisie and the people. Secondary education had and still keeps its elementary classes, but they are only the prelude to an instruction which aims at humanism. If it preceded primary education, the reason was that the bourgeoisie had made it the instrument of its emancipation. It is only very late and by degrees that the bourgeoisie granted education to the people.

The principle of compulsory universal education had indeed been proclaimed at the time of the Revolution. A bill by Le Peletier de St. Fargeau had been put before the Convention by Robespierre. All children from 7 to 14 were to be admitted to the nation's schools to be educated in complete equality. But once the Thermidor had come, all the Revolution's achievements for the people were abandoned or wiped out. Under Napoleon one had to fight, not learn; under the Restoration one had to be a loyal and pious subject. After 1830, under the monarchy of Louis Philippe, who replaced the landowners' rule by the rule of the bankers, the business world felt the need of a less ignorant body of workers and began to express wishes for popular instruction. It was still an optional and purely utilitarian education. The better to restrict its cultural possibilities, Guizot's school laws (1833) and the Falloux law (1849) put the schools under the close supervision of the Church; often the teacher was the curate's beadle.

It was the Paris Commune which for the first time in France undertook to put the "free, secular, and compulsory" school into operation. The Commune went down at the end of several weeks, but the precedent remained, and when at last the republicans came to power, after defeating MacMahon's "moral order," they could not avoid organizing that kind of school. This was affected by the school laws of Jules Ferry (1882-1886).

These laws organized the primary schools completely outside the framework of secondary education. The pupils of the *école primaire* did not enter into secondary schools, with the exception of a few scholarship students. The teachers were trained in normal schools which had no connection with the universities in which the future secondary school teachers studied. The normal school students were recruited from the *Écoles primaires superieures,* where some children from the primary schools continued their studies up to the age of 15 or 16, but with no contact with children of the same age in secondary schools. The difference in examinations prevented any assimilation of the two, for only the examinations of the secondary schools gave admission to the universities.

Education in France has always reflected the political and social situation in a very direct way, and cannot be explained out of connection with the history of the country. So sharp a distinction between primary and secondary education indicates a clear consciousness of the nation's class division into the bourgeoisie and the people. A result is that the primary school, recruiting its pupils and its teachers exclusively among the people, has been very close to them and has developed in the people of France a certain sense of independence, responsibility, dignity, and also a form of humanism whose sources may be near enough to those from which the bourgeoisie's humanism, classical humanism, has come, but which has remained militant. This humanism is what we call the secular spirit.

The public schools in France are secular. This term, which has all too often been given a political sense, denotes one of the great moral achievements which our country is proud of having brought into the world. We are clearly aware of it when we visit other countries where religious sects still dominate public life, morals, or opinion. Laicism or secularism must not be taken to mean either the neutrality to which some would confine it or the anti-religion by which others would like to embarrass it. There have been and there are Christians who are profoundly secularist.

The secular ideal was unquestionably born during the bloody convulsions into which the wars of religion plunged France, menacing its very existence, since behind the Huguenots stood the king of England and behind the Papists the king of Spain. In the writers of the period, in a Montaigne, for instance, the idea can be seen taking form that religious differences should not at any rate disturb public order nor expose the nation to foreign interference. The latter has always had the effect, in our nation, of arousing a violent defense reaction, whatever means and whatever pretext it may have employed.

It was on such occasions that the French learned to reconcile national feeling and a feeling for humanity. On such occasions it became clear that if the cohesion of minds and wills was not broken by differences of dogma and cult, the reason was that there is in man something more essential than the way in which each man happens to translate his preferences or his beliefs. Every personal belief should be the result of a choice. It is this freedom of choice which earns belief the right to be respected.

For the secularist, tolerance is not mere sufferance, nor a more or less sincere indulgence to thoughts and feelings which he does not even try to comprehend. Understanding among individuals cannot be based on the simple prudential precaution of not hurting other people in order not to be hurt. Men are not compartmented off, simply juxtaposed, each caring nothing for the other beyond not getting in the other's way. Tolerance presupposes that everyone be able to make use of his reason; and that implies that reason has not been paralyzed by a dogma imposed on it before it was capable of judgment either to reject or to accept.

Secularism is the basic liberty of conscience, in that it aims at creating free consciences, capable of determining themselves. It aims at arousing in everyone that effort of the reason on which Descartes wished to base his certainties. In the sixteenth, seventeenth, and eighteenth centuries, a whole series of thinkers forged the lay ideal in France, and it is the lay ideal which inspires the schoolteacher today when he tries to make the child think instead of appealing to his docility or his credulity. The lay spirit is the spirit of free inquiry.

In this way there developed in our schools a militant humanism alongside the classic humanism which daily became more conformist and more a stranger to the interest and curiosities aroused in the child by the civilization of our days. But in both cases there is still an aspiration toward the full realization of the humanity in each individual, without limits or exclusions based on the pretext of intrinsic differences or inequalities. The complete man is seen only in his universal form, because man, in his quality as man, should attribute to himself the power of understanding, of reasoning, and of choosing.

Of course this equality exists in principle, not in fact. In France as elsewhere the inequality of material or moral condition is the historical consequence of the relations which obtain among the classes of society; but cultural inequality is seen as shocking as soon as attention is called to it. The provision of two types of schooling, one for the bourgeoisie, the other for the people, has become the symbol of a privilege to be abolished. But the systematic organization of both makes the problem of their fusion a difficult one.

The problem has arisen nevertheless, with increasing force, and especially so after each of the two World Wars, which shook the nation to its foundations and quickened its latent needs. But between the two wars the solution changed. At first it was only a question of equalizing the chances of all pupils, of whatever origin, bourgeois or plain people. All without distinction should attend the *école primaire,* and therefore the elementary classes should be taken out of the secondary schools. Only the best-qualified pupils would then go on to secondary education, meaning that bourgeois children might be rejected and children of the people be chosen. The two schools were simply placed end to end, each one recovering from the other the classes which overlapped its own. Professional training and vocational apprenticeship remained marginal, the latter following directly on elementary school for those who were not admitted to secondary school.

By and large the two levels of culture persisted. The change dealt solely with the question of which children should benefit, of basing the selection on merit and no longer on wealth. Of course the resistance of the formerly privileged group was desperate. They laid special stress on the uncertainty of a definitive judgment on the aptitudes of a child made when he is eleven, which decides his whole future. In any case the reform could only satisfy a certain principle of justice toward individuals and of utility for society, which would in this way recruit the best men for the higher posts. It did not bring with it generalization, nor extension, nor enrichment of culture. Its enactment had hardly begun when the second World War broke out. It was still at the stage of looking for the best way to select the children.

A very different conception arose during the period of resistance to the occupation. Then those who did not accept the enslavement of their country asked themselves what its future should be, what each man's duty was toward the nation, and what the nation's duty was toward each man. At the same time, men who were prevented from meeting for large-scale discussions by the necessities of their mutual security experienced a sort of unanimous inner drive toward that humanism which has been, as it were, the mould of French thought down through its history. The monstrous consequences that racism was exhibiting at this time had something to do with it; but the main factor was the resurrection and renovation of traditional aspirations.

This movement was so strong that after liberation the provisional government named a commission to study educational problems. Its work inevitably concentrated on the conditions required for a larger humanism. It must no longer be the privilege of a few, but should extend to all; everyone, that is, should be given the means of cultivating all the human values, all the intellectual, esthetic, and moral possibilities within him. Culture must be made to be no longer the accompaniment of a certain level of education, or a certain more or less traditional and conventional kind of education. All education can and should have cultural outcomes, every cultural aptitude should and can have instruction designed for it.

All of man's activities have possible prolongations toward culture. It is from all of them, and in particular from the most utilitarian, that men's civilizations have arisen. Techniques and sciences have a large part of their history in common; neither could have developed without the other; the sciences began as rationalizations of techniques. Likewise, the esthetic activities from which art has arisen have their sources in spontaneous needs of expression: rhythms, reproductions, images, which can satisfy impulses which are more or less developed in the individual according to his aptitudes. A genuinely humanist education should not neglect any of these various dispositions which go to make up the complete man, even though they are unequally distributed among individuals.

The task then is to introduce into the school everything that can help the child to develop his natural gifts and tastes. The task is to have the school fulfill all the needs of the child's nature and at the same time all the needs of society, in which the variety of jobs and functions should have scope for continuous expansion.

The conclusions of the commission, which was presided over at first by Langevin and then by me after his death, were that every child should receive all the instruction that his aptitudes make him capable of receiving; that his education should not end with the acquisition of a few minimum essentials, but should continue until the age of eighteen; that the school should give him not only the common instruction that everyone can take, but also and along with it special instruction which he can choose in accordance with his tastes and abilities. The school should therefore include subjects which too often have been strange to it, in particular all those concrete activities which have either been considered as futile because they are different from knowledge narrowly so-called, or abandoned to the confined routines of industrial apprenticeship. Everyone has to arrive at culture by means suited to himself. The school should not neglect any means, nor lack interest in any student. The project is no longer to preserve culture for a more or less select group of individuals, nor to limit culture to a certain luxurious conformity.

Culture should be accessible to all, and realize in everyone the kind of humanism and all the humanism he can attain.

The plan of such an education has been discussed among specialists; it has been sketched in its main lines. It would be the time now to proceed to carry it out. But the political wind has shifted since the liberation; for how long a time? The hope of a second liberation is not dead in our country.

To define the philosophy of education in France it has seemed necessary to show its historical development. It was not a question of giving an ideal definition which might have seemed arbitrary or chimerical, but rather of showing under the pressure of what interests or what dangers it took form as the offensive weapon of a social class eager to free itself and as the defensive weapon of the nation anxious to escape from foreign interference. It had to be shown how, under these two influences, the philosophy of education tended to affirm a basic identity among all men, and also how it could split up and, in its classic form, serve caste spirit, while in its secular form it sought by means of the education given to children to go beyond the dogmas and doctrines which might divide them. Going back over its historical development was needed in order to show that it is not a mystical Decalogue, but the expression of an effort which has fluctuated with the social and political fluctuations of our people, an effort which will continue to the extent that our people do not lose confidence in their civilizing mission.

AN AMERICAN REACTION
TO THE PRESENT SITUATION
IN FRENCH PHILOSOPHY

Richard McKeon*

I. THE STATEMENT OF A PROBLEM

THE effort to organize or unify all aspects of knowledge and experience, which is one of the marks of the philosophic enterprise in even its derivative and casual forms, has always been joined, apparently inseparably, to the examination of the principles of other philosophers and to the demonstration of their insufficiencies and errors. The ideological conflict conspicuous in all fields of discussion and action today may be viewed as an extension of philosophic differences to political, social, scientific, artistic, and religious questions, in which the polemic oppositions of parties are the familiar consequences of efforts to advance the unique and universal use of particular sets of principles in the solution of problems. In the misuse and the controversial denunciation, no less than in the use, of philosophic principles and methods applied to practical action, to art, and to science, philosophy has found new possibilities for the exercise of functions frequently claimed for it. Philosophy in some form will contribute to the constitution of the new world which must emerge, by agreement or by force, from the disputes of the present, for the positions in dispute have been formulated in general and doctrinal terms, and the parties to the discussion are all mankind, grouped according to statements adapted to their aspirations and just claims, their traditions and needs. Philosophic principles and distinc-

* Born in 1900. Ph.D., Columbia University, 1928. Studied from 1922 to 1925 in Paris, where he received the *diplome d'études supérieures* in philosophy at the Sorbonne and the *diplome d'élève titulaire* at the Ecole des Hautes Etudes. Formerly dean, Division of Humanities, and at present Distinguished Service Professor of Greek and Philosophy, University of Chicago. Served as member of the American Delegation to the General Conference of UNESCO. Author of *The Philosophy of Spinoza*, 1928, and of numerous articles in learned journals. Edited and translated *Selections from Medieval Philosophers*, 1929-1930; edited *The Basic Works of Aristotle*, 1941, and *Introduction to Aristotle*, 1947. His "Introduction to the Philosophy of Cicero" will appear in a new translation of Cicero's philosophic works in the autumn of 1949.

tions enter into statements of propaganda; they appear, slightly transformed, in authoritative pronouncements distantly reminiscent of the
philosopher-king and the golden lie and in the preambles of international
organizations dedicated to principles of justice and right; they make the
meetings of diplomats and of international delegations sound like echoes
of Platonic dialogues concerning rights and duties, democracy, freedom,
law, property, justice, and piety; they condition the official actions of
states and non-governmental organizations. Under these circumstances,
when all men have come into contact with philosophy as part of the day's
news, the discussions of philosophers reflect new responsibilities and new
opportunities. Philosophers face new problems as well as new forms of
old problems, and in the process of mutual criticism, which serves to
extend philosophic scope and to test philosophic principles, they are
brought face to face with widely heterogeneous traditions instead of the
limited dialectic developed in a single culture. The problems and the
methods of philosophy have changed, and new cultural and intellectual
instruments exist to bring philosophic distinctions to practical applications.

The function which may be served by this publication on French
and American philosophy during the past thirty years is defined by these
circumstances. The analogies between the spirit of French and American
thought and between the history of the institutions of the two countries
are numerous, yet the differences of philosophic idiom and approach
are so great that they are separated as two distinct philosophic traditions.
In each of these traditions, moreover, particularly as each is viewed from
the vantage point of the other, the changes of the last thirty years are
revolutionary in character, though gradual in accomplishment; yet in
the process of change they have often used opposite elements of the
broader tradition of Western European thought to travel in contrary
directions. The American and the French revolutions, for all the differences of their circumstances and immediate consequences, were the
common source of liberal ideas which were to influence profoundly the
lives and institutions of modern man. During the eighteenth and early
nineteenth centuries, Montesquieu, Rousseau, the *philosophes* and the
idéologues had a profound influence on American statesmen and scholars;
but, after that, the influence of French thought on the development of
American philosophy ceased almost abruptly, for about a hundred years
until, in the last forty years, James recognized fellow spirits in Renouvier
and Bergson; the philosophies of Gilson and Maritain acquired wide
influence in the United States; and, finally, the flood of existentialism

in fiction, drama, and philosophy began to flow in translation. France was almost untouched by Hegelianism and Scottish Common Sense philosophy during the nineteenth and early twentieth centuries when they were important influences in the United States, while today, when the Hegelian marks are not easily discernible in American philosophy, an active Hegelianism has been called into existence in France by the success of the philosophies initiated by Kierkegaard and Marx in reaction to Hegel in order to supply the thesis for their antitheses and has, almost ironically, vindicated the Hegelian dialectic. The positivism of Comte was not a dominant influence in the United States, while the neo-positivism of the Vienna Circle, which took root in the United States, has not been regrafted on the parent trunk. The discussion of "engagement" by existentialists is reminiscent of the discussion of the criterion of "use" by pragmatists thirty years ago, and the history of ideas practised by Marxists in France is not without its analogies to the methods earlier popular with American pragmatists and sociologists. Conversely, contemporary American concern to relate philosophic analysis to the historical developments of doctrines and concepts and to the procedures of the sciences has closer affinities to the methods and materials of Brunschvicg than to the dialectic of contemporary existentialists, Marxists, or philosophers of Spirit.

An American observer of the changes of method and doctrine in French philosophy can easily recognize many of the problems which engage American philosophic inquiry, and he finds stimulation and insight both in the novel methods used in their treatment and the new implications, new relevances, and new problems that are brought to his attention by these differences. The temptation, therefore, is to enter into the discussion of problems and of movements presented so abundantly and so vividly in the foregoing papers, to translate problems of the American tradition into French forms and French statements of problems into American forms, and to estimate their relative values as well as the importance of problems omitted or inadequately treated in one or the other approach. The eighteen essays on recent French philosophy, however, afford an opportunity also to consider, not the problems of philosophy, but the problems of philosophic discussion and communication, for they trace the recent histories of related problems, or schools, or disciplines of philosophy, yet the same philosophies and the same arguments are differently described and evaluated in the various accounts. Bergson, for example, is referred to by many of the authors, sometimes as a basic source of what is sound in contemporary philosophy, sometimes as an historical influence which prepared for a sounder formulation of what was fundamentally the same as his doctrine or method or of what was antithetically opposed to it, sometimes as a sleight-of-hand artist who inspired only confusion and sophistry. Ranges of problems and schools of thought which are important in one statement disappear in others; connections apparent in one version are implausible in others; frequently the history of the period is presented as the epiphenomenal accompaniment of the refutation of a school or a philosopher. The French philosophy which appears from this juxtaposition of eighteen essays can be conceived best on the analogy to a soft polygon—and less subject to radical alterations of state than Descartes' wax—which changes its shape as it is set on various faces: some of the apices and faces can be distinguished, though distorted, in all positions of the polygon; some which are prominent when the polygon is in one position disappear entirely when it comes to rest on another face; sizes change, forms that were similar become incongruent, and lines that were parallel intersect.

The following expression of an American reaction to these essays is an attempt to treat these statements of what has happened in French philosophy as part of the problem of discussion and communication among philosophers and traditions of philosophy. Most philosophers have experienced the difficulties of understanding the statement of problems, the intentions of technical terms, and the structure of systems as well as the difficulties of formulating what is familiar in terms that will be intelligible and yet escape misconceptions based on unaccustomed emphases and interests. They are merely larger and sharper forms of differences which are encountered even in local meetings of philosophers. The accelerating effect of wars and crises on the processes of intellectual history, however, has been, on the one hand, to underline the intellectual and practical pertinence of such differences and difficulties in fields far removed from the analyses of technical philosophy and, on the other hand, to direct attention to the differences of intellectual traditions in the various parts of the world which seem almost to result from shuffling comparable or common elements of interrelated traditions to arrive at arbitrary and ingeniously heterogeneous combinations.

The signs of change in a tradition of thought are more apparent to a foreign observer, since he does not have the impression of continuity which comes with participation in changes, and he tends, therefore, to emphasize the contrasts between extreme points marked for him by his experience of the tradition. Thus, the basic impression which I formed of French philosophy goes back to the three years which I spent as a student in Paris from 1922 to 1925, working on medieval philosophy with Gilson, on Spinoza with Brunschvicg, and on Plato with Robin, and attending courses of Levy-Bruhl and Lalande. It was characteristic of the philosophy of the period that I studied a portion of the history of philosophy with each of these masters and that I also learned from each a method of philosophy and an attitude toward philosophy. The history of philosophy was closely integrated in philosophic inquiry. In my later visits to France and in my later reading in French philosophy I watched what seemed to me to be developments of tendencies with which I had been familiar, until, late in the 1930s, it was apparent that many French philosophers including some of those with whom I was familiar had begun to use a different technical language and to organize their inquiries differently in the treatment of familiar as well as new themes. When I returned to France after the liberation, the contrasts were acute and the differences sharp. Descartes was no longer guilty of having set up an unreal distinction between body and mind; he had laid the foundations of the unity of experience and of metaphysics in the *cogito*. Bergson was no longer the source of insight into what is living and immediate in all fields of human activity; he was guilty of having set up an unreal distinction between reason and intuition. Two of the five philosophers under whom I had studied, Levy-Bruhl and Brunschvicg, were dead. Gilson, while continuing his penetrating philosophic analyses had, like many other philosophers, seen the need to apply philosophic principles to the practical problems of the day: I had encountered him on his way to the Conference of the United Nations at San Francisco in 1945, and I had seen him again across the tables as a member of the French Delegation at the first General Conference of UNESCO in Paris 1946; he was shortly to be elected to the Council of France. In 1947 I was present with other former students and friends of Robin at the celebration of his eightieth birthday (Robin corrected his friends in his reply to Bréhier's eloquent discourse: it was his eighty-first birthday) and his elevation in the Legion of Honor; as Robin talked of his former students—those who had died in the first war, those of the period between the wars, those who were assembled to do him honor—and of the sorrows of his last years, one could not avoid the sense that an era in philosophic and philological studies had closed; Robin has since died, having produced in the last ten years of his life an amazing series of comprehensive and mature works on ancient philosophers. Lalande has continued to adapt his studies of "involution," reason, and terminology to the developments of philosophic thought; he has entered actively in the preparation of this collaboration of retrospect and diagnosis and has contributed to it a revealing commentary on the directions of thought in the philosophy of science.

Such observations tend to direct attention to the value of much that has been abandoned in the reactions of French philosophers against their immediate past as well as to the value of much that has been accomplished recently with a strange method and in an obscure preposition-dotted vocabulary. The experiences determine the point of references from which the following reactions are constructed: a philosophic formation received from Woodbridge (who is not as well known abroad as his influence on American thought merits) and Dewey supplemented by study with some of the masters of French philosophy of the 1920s profoundly altered by the influence of twenty-five years of American philosophic developments brought to bear on contemporary movements of French philosophy which, in so far as they reflect any influence of American thought, are cognizant primarily of the work of American philosophers of the 1920s.

These are comments, then, not on French philosophy as an American views it, but on French philosophy as it is presented in the eighteen papers which are included in this volume. The schematism of the comments, moreover, is suggested by the organization of the papers. Some of the papers, in the first place, expound the doctrines of a single school of philosophy, or differences within a school or between related schools, or oppositions of schools. These papers tend to treat the very nature and purpose of philosophy, and the differences that emerge in them are differences of principles. Some of the papers, in the second place, are organized to treat different approaches to one of the traditional fields of philosophy: logic, esthetics, theory of value, or metaphysics. These papers expound the different structures and contents given to the disciplines of philosophy, and the polemical oppositions concerning principles are translated in them into differences or ambiguities of terms and differences of scope and method. Some of the papers, finally, center attention on some field of knowledge closely related to philosophy: history, science, psychology, social circumstances, art, religion. These papers tend to argue that some subject-matter has a peculiar pertinence to the problems of philosophy or that philosophy has a peculiar contribution to make to some range of problems otherwise determined than by the formal structure of a philosophy or the whim of a philosopher; and the differences of principles and structure are related in these papers to important problems of experience, or life, or the world. These differences are differences of primary emphasis, since all the papers treat, in some fashion, all three problems, and the utility of the distinction comes from the possibility it affords to trace the shifts that occur as problems move from one emphasis to another. The universalism of philosophy and the polemics of philosophers may be stated in terms of principles which organize knowledge and experience, in terms of systems in which a method is applied to the organization of knowledge and experience, and in terms of problems which are solved in the process. The discussion of philosophy is basically a discussion of principles; the task of philosophers is basically the construction of systems or the development of methods congruent with principles; but communication among philosophers who credit different principles and use different methods is basically the discussion of the nature of problems and of the means adapted to their solution. The decision to treat the problems of philosophic discussion rather than the problems of philosophy, therefore, does not mean omitting any of these problems but rather treating them in reverse order. The problems of the treatment of subject-matters and problems, I shall group under the heading, *The Epistemic Grounds of Philosophy*. The problems of the structure and dialectic of philosophic disciplines will be treated under the heading, *The Constitutive Structure of Philosophy*. Finally, such comments concerning principles and fundamental beliefs as emerge from this treatment of the accounts of French philosophy will be made under the heading, *The Pistic Foundations of Philosophy*. Ancient philosophers sometimes made a similar distinction when they differentiated elements, principles, and causes.

II. THE EPISTEMIC GROUNDS OF PHILOSOPHY

The basic differences concerning the epistemic grounds of philosophy which emerge in the eighteen papers are of two sorts. One difference takes the form of denying that a given field or subject-matter is a branch of knowledge, or an important ingredient in experience or, at least, a proper subject-matter for philosophic inquiry and speculation; and this argument is countered by the contention of those who hold the opposed theory that a conception of philosophy which omits that field does not cover the whole of knowledge or experience, or, even, its most important part. The second difference consists in divergences in interpretation of the nature of the fields of knowledge and in conception of their proper methods. History, thus, is treated or used in some fashion in almost all the papers, and the differences concerning history are of the second kind, that is, differences of uses to which philosophers put a branch of knowledge and of principles with which they supply it. Moreover, the enterprise on which the collaborators in these volumes are engaged is itself an enterprise in historical inquiry. The account of French philosophical tradition between the two wars prepared by Jacques Havet provides an excellent starting place for the discussion of history and the recent history of French philosophy. The major figures of the period are arranged suggestively there under three heads: spiritualistic realism, the new intellectualism and contemporary science, transcendency and experience. Even readers who have followed French philosophy closely will find much to learn in this thoughtful and well documented study.

With admirable clarity Émile Bréhier sets forth, not merely the sequence of writings on the history of philosophy and of science, but the spirit which animated the inquiries. His view of the task of the historian might provide the text of this collaborative study of French and American philosophy, for he conceives part of the task of the historian to be to prevent peoples who are kept apart by language, tradition, and politics from remaining ignorant of each other's thoughts. [1] He states, moreover, a profound insight into the nature of history, that it consists less of the narrative of facts than of development of values, since the values of the present determine the effort of the historian to endeavor to find out what they meant in the past. [2] One could not do better than to borrow Bréhier's distinction between "horizontal history," which reintegrates doctrines into the civilization which is contemporary with them, and "vertical history," which traces the chronological sequence of doctrines and methods and the rational connections between them. [3]

Bréhier gives as an example of horizontal history a balanced statement of history as it is practised by Marxist philosophers, but other devices are used in constructing horizontal history, some influenced by Marx, some in radical opposition to Marxist doctrines and presuppositions. Raymond Aron indicates some of the varieties of this horizontal mode of history when he points out that the three philosophies of history, all of them horizontal, that exercise an influence on French thought are those of Marx, of Spengler or Toynbee, or of Burnham, [4] and when he finds a common point of departure for the Marxist conception of history and for his own conception of a phenomenology of historical structure. [5] His discussion of that phenomenological structure is preceded by a considera-

1. Émile Bréhier, "The Spirit of the History of Philosophy in France," p. 57.
2. *Ibid.*, p. 58.
3. *Ibid.*, p. 63.
4. R. Aron, "The Philosophy of History," p. 315.
5. *Ibid.*, p. 312.

tion first, of the ontology of historicity in which he treats approaches to the historicity of human existence, and second, of the nature of historical knowledge, in which he treats the variety of methods that have been used to relate theories of historical knowledge to processes of historical research. The elaboration of the phenomenology of historical structure is a highly significant examination of the ways in which men resolve their dilemma between the apparent fatality of the historical situation in which they find themselves and the indisputable effects of human action making history.[6] Aron presents an illuminating discussion of the applications and of the consequences of history in the few pages in which he considers the ethics of history,[7] and he remains faithful to his subject-matter throughout by arguing that the task of the present is not to invent a new interpretation of history based on a new idea of man and his destiny, but to use the instruments of history abundantly available to resolve the problems presented by the materials of history and their partial interpretations.[8]

Henri Lefebvre makes a brilliant but uncritical use of the devices of horizontal history in his treatment of knowledge and social criticism. Within the framework of a contrast between existentialism (which refuses to look for knowledge in the sciences where it is to be found, but instead dissociates philosophy and science) and Marxist social criticism (which seeks knowledge where it is to be found, that is, in the sciences and in esthetic creative activity, which is inseparable from scientific knowledge), he finds analogies among contemporary intellectual and esthetic theories and products in aspects of discontinuity that replace continuity in the structure and concepts of the arts and sciences. The result is an illuminating discussion of specific features of contemporary culture, in the manner of a Platonic myth or of Henry Adams's broader applications of the same contrasting terms to the thirteenth and twentieth centuries. For Lefebvre, however, it is no philosophic myth but a literal, if not a scientific, explanation in which the etiological factors are the taste of the bourgeoisie, on the one hand, and the dialectical unity of reality, on the other. The temptation to explain an age by a word is recurrent, but when any such word is placed in the context of other technical terms in process of like modification (continuity in the context of infinity, motion, time, space, matter, etc.) and of other schools engaged in speculation concerning them (realists, naturalists, formalists, positivists as well

6. *Ibid.,* p. 312.
7. *Ibid.,* pp. 318 f.
8. *Ibid.,* pp. 317 f.

as the various kinds of Marxists and existentialists), the simple contrarieties lose their explanatory force. A. Cornu uses the same dialectic in a simplified form: where Lefebvre undertakes to study the interrelated ideological factors which constitute a culture, Cornu finds the causes of ideologies in the economic and social conditions of classes without much need for empirical evidence or conceptual analysis. "Rationalism" is "a justification of the economic and social regime of the bourgeoisie" incapable of resolving the dilemma of large scale collective production and individual returns and use.[9] If the origin of a doctrine can be made suspect, there is no need to define or refute it, and any failures can be ascribed to it. The supremacy of capitalism in the United States "is expressed on the ideological plane by pragmatism, the apologetics of utilitarian action."[10] The statement is not invalidated by the fact that many, if not most, American philosophers would agree that pragmatism ceased to be one of the active schools of American philosophy some fifteen or twenty years ago, except for a few attempts to combine the doctrines of Dewey and Marx; sufficient removal from the facts and strong enough faith in a dialectic are grounds to make American philosophers pragmatists whatever doctrines they enunciate. It would seem more profitable to observe that pragmatism and Marxism, in common, have denied this separation of theory and practice and to investigate the different consequences of that denial in the two philosophies and in the cultures of which they were parts. Cornu's paper is a criticism of Bergsonianism and existentialism drawn almost exclusively from the works of men who have attacked those philosophies.

Henri Wallon[11] makes use of a similar history to furnish background for the educational reforms recently sponsored by him and his commission. His statement of the need for a larger humanism, for educational opportunities equally available to all, and for the establishment of relations between culture and all man's activities, has a validity and a moving force which are fortunately independent of the historical background which he supplies for it. If the Renaissance was merely "the weapon of the bourgeoisie in their thirst for intellectual power,"[12] by which they "sought to replace the Christian man of the middle ages by man pure and simple, the complete man" found outside of Christian society, historians will have to eradicate the names of Petrarch, Erasmus, Lefèvre d'Etaples, Colet, and More from the list of Renaissance thinkers. The

9. A. Cornu, "Bergsonianism and Existentialism," p. 152.
10. Ibid., p. 161.
11. H. Wallon, "The Philosophy of Education in France," pp. 321 ff.
12. Ibid., p. 324.

programs of the *lycées* cannot be explained simply by Napoleon's desire for docile agents equipped for the adroit linguistic translation of his ideas, nor are the arguments for the study of Greek and Latin answered simply by branding such education a badge of honor and an instrument of cultural conformitarianism.[13] Most liberal minds will share Wallon's regret that no measure has been taken to improve the structure and contents of French education, but there would not be the same unanimity in attributing the cause of the defeat of Wallon's proposals, as he does, to a shift since the liberation in the "political wind" or in finding the solution for the problems of educational reform in "the hope for a second liberation."[14] A foreigner would hesitate to advance an opinion concerning the intricacies of the winds of French politics, but an educator who has examined the proposed changes may suggest the importance of questions connected with them which Wallon does not mention: (a) some of the defects of the curriculum instituted in the plan which were pointed out in the course of its discussion are not disposed of by allegation of partisan bias, and (b) the centralized state control of education in France, which precludes experimentation in local or partial changes, made the immediate costs of the reform enormous. Politics are often a bar to progress, but they may also be used as an instrument for social change, and the parties united for liberation discover differences in their methods and purposes which are not easily resolved without political instrumentalities and political institutions to permit men of vision, like Wallon, freedom to plan reforms and to express their bitter disappointment at obstacles and failures.

References to the uses of "vertical history" in philosophic inquiry are no less frequent in the eighteen accounts of French philosophy, though they are somewhat less polemically formulated, than the dialectical manipulations of "horizontal history." Henry Duméry analyzes very acutely the part which historical reconstruction plays in the philosophic doctrines of Gilson and the use which Gilson makes of the oppositions of systems to test the validity and credibility of his own formulation of philosophic problems.[15] Jean Hering throws light on the applications to which Koyré puts the phenomenological method to break down the prejudice that a philosophic system or doctrine can be understood only insofar as it can be explained by the historical influences undergone by the thinker.[16] Koyré's studies are directed to making the doctrines of Plato, Anselm, Descartes, Boehme, and Galileo more intelligible in themselves and in

---

13. *Ibid.*, pp. 327 f.
14. *Ibid.*, p. 335.
15. Henry Duméry, "Catholic Philosophy in France," pp 225 ff.
16. Jean Hering, "Phenomenology in France," pp. 70 ff.

their influences on later thinkers, not to explain them by social and political circumstances or by doctrinal analogies while neglecting their relevance to problems of later periods, including the present. René Le Senne traces, in vertical fashion, the modifications undergone by a tradition in the course of its transmission from Descartes, and he recognizes the uses of philosophies historically as symptoms of social situations.

The extremes of horizontal and vertical history are in radical opposition. Vertical history seems to the exponent of horizontal history to trace a thin insubstantial line and to neglect the roots and causes and circumstances of doctrinal changes; horizontal history seems to the exponent of vertical history to provide explanations for doctrines, which men did not hold, frequently by events which did not occur and by institutions which did not exist in a fashion which could be related, except by vague analogy, to the doctrines. The two extremes rarely exist, however, except in the descriptions of polemical critics, and each mode of history could profit from the other, the horizontal tradition to acquire more facts of doctrine and event, the vertical tradition to learn the relations and applications of doctrines.

Science is not as prominent as history in the uses and interpretations found for it in the eighteen essays. The basic ground for the interpretation of the influence of science on French philosophy is provided by André Lalande's admirable annotated bibliography of French publications on the philosophy of science. From it one may recognize the richness of the materials found in this field, the variety of philosophic interpretations of which science is susceptible, and the number of strands of theory and method which have been submitted to philosophic elaboration. One fundamental distinction among the approaches to science appears in the differentiation between schools which separate logic and method from ontology and schools which join or even identify methods of inquiry and proof with processes or stages of reality. Boll and Reinhart contrast their treatment of logistic and logical method on these grounds with the ontological Thomist logic of Mercier and Maritain as well as from the Marxist neo-Hegelianism of Politzer, Maublanc, Lefebvre (which they think unworthy of serious attention by logicians).[17] They differentiate their own position from that of the positivists by their manner of separating the development of method and the investigation of being. Lefebvre, on the other hand, thinks Marxism peculiarly adapted to the facts and developments of science, since dialectical materialism is the method of

---

17. M. Boll and J. Reinhart, "Logic in France in the Twentieth Century," p. 185 and especially footnote 19, p. 185.

science. The difference between the two approaches appears strikingly in Lefebvre's praise of Lysenko's achievements in biology, which show "that the interaction of the external and the internal modify the forms and the structures, that modifications produced by action of the environment on the living being (changes of temperature, etc.) are transmitted by heredity."[18] Many scientists are convinced that these contentions have not been proved—or have been, in part or totally, disproved—by scientific inquiry, and that the merging of political and scientific methods is detrimental to the objectivity of scientific inquiry. The logical positivists have had little influence in France, in spite of their separation of logic from ontology, because their nominalism prevents them from treating adequately the twofold aspect of logic stressed by Boll and Reinhart, as a physical theory and as a normative science.[19] Maritain relates logic and ontology, in opposition to the idealists, by showing that the problems of proof reflect a pluralism of experimental relations, a multiplicity of sciences, and a hierarchy of being.[20] Le Senne recalls the avowed purposes of Husserl's phenomenology to achieve scientific objectivity,[21] and Berger traces the evolution of the philosophy of science in terms of the oppositions of scientific idealism and scientific realism, of immanence and objectivity.[22] Underlying the discussion, and emerging from time to time, are the questions whether philosophy is or should be scientific, and whether any of the proper subject matter of philosophy is inaccessible to the methods of science: in the course of the discussion of these questions neither the methods of science nor the purposes of philosophy have fixed interpretations.

Art is intimately and variously related to philosophy in contemporary French literary and philosophic movements. Raymond Bayer quotes Lalo to trace the interrelations of philosophy, literature, and esthetics by which art is treated as an expression of life—between the two extremes of sociological relativism in which the only true art is life itself and estheticism in which art is removed from life.[23] Jean Wahl, who is a poet as well as a philosopher, views philosophy not only as a special activity directed toward the discovery of truth, but in its relations to poetry and painting.[24] Gabriel Marcel has used philosophy and the drama as media

---

18. H. Lefebvre, "Knowledge and Social Criticism," pp. 296 f.
19. M. Boll and J. Reinhart, *op. cit.,* pp. 192 f.
20. H. Duméry, *op cit.,* pp. 222 f.
21. R. Le Senne, "The Philosophy of Spirit," p. 114.
22. G. Berger, "Experience and Transcendence," pp. 87 ff.
23. R. Bayer, "Recent Esthetic Thought in France," p. 269.
24. J. Wahl, "The Present Situation and the Present Future of French Philosophy," pp. 47 f.

for expression of his ideas, [25] and the doctrines of existentialism are expounded by R. Campbell from materials derived from dramas, novels, and literary criticism as well as from formal philosophic works. [26] This use of the arts to express philosophic truths or to engage in activities closely related to philosophic inquiry is easily distinguished both from Maritain's sensitive esthetic analyses to delimit the contours of art, morality, and science, and from Lefebvre's shrewd use of the arts in close relation to the sciences as subjects to which the methods of dialectical materialism may be applied both for purposes of analysis and development.

Unlike history, science, and art, in which differences are found primarily in the interpretation of their nature and of their relation to philosophy, religion gives rise to differences concerning whether or not it is a proper subject for philosophy. The proponents of Marxism in the foregoing essays do not find occasion to treat the question directly, but the antipathy of existentialism and religion is expounded fully and Sartre's atheism is mentioned, [27] while proponents of the philosophy of the Spirit examine the operations of spirit to show the insufficiencies of positivisms, materialisms, and existentialisms. [28] The two papers on religious philosophy afford interesting insights into the nature of the problem presented by religion. Henry Duméry stresses the point that religion does not commit one to a single philosophy, but that Catholic philosophy in France follows four principal tendencies: Thomism represented by Maritain and Gilson; existentialism by Marcel; personalism by Nédoncelle; and the philosophy of action and religion by Blondel. Roger Mehl, on the other hand, finds an absence of any Christian philosophy, and beginning from the sociology of religion and the analysis of myths, which forces us to locate religion at the very heart of man rather than in the periphery of his interests, he finds the chances for a philosophy of religion "at the meeting point of phenomenology and existential philosophy," [29] where the distortions of Pradines, Brunschvicg, and Bergson may be avoided and where the labors of Hering, Hauter, Le Senne, Lavelle, and Marcel may come together.

III. THE CONSTITUTIVE STRUCTURE OF PHILOSOPHY

The effort to apply philosophy to the problems and subject-matters of

---

25. H. Duméry, *op. cit.,* footnote 7.
26. R. Campbell, "Existentialism in France since the Liberation," *passim;* cf. R. Le Senne, *op. cit.,* p 113.
27. R. Campbell, *op. cit.,* p. 139.
28. R. Le Senne, *op. cit.,* p. 111, and L. Lavelle, "The Three Stages of Metaphysics," p. 135.
29. R. Mehl, "The Situation of Religious Philosophy in France," p. 254.

the arts and sciences, to use scientific methods or literary forms in philosophy, and to establish a close relation or an identity between philosophy
and other disciplines is one of the marks of contemporary philosophic discussion.   Philosophic problems are formulated in ways peculiarly amenable to literary treatment, and the doctrines and methods of science have
approached close to philosophic problems.   A hundred years ago a study
of philosophic movements in France would doubtless have been organized
according to the disciplines or parts of philosophy, probably under three
heads: logic, morals, and psychology (which had taken the place of "physics" in the older "Platonic" classification).   Three of the essays in the
present collection are devoted to surveys of fields of philosophy: logic,
theory of value, and esthetics, while metaphysics comes in for separate
treatment in several papers.   These examinations of the disciplines of
philosophy reflect the applications of philosophy that were discussed in
the consideration of the epistemic grounds of philosophy as well as differences consequent on the dialectical oppositions of the schools of philosophy.

Marcel Boll and Jacques Reinhart set forth the recent history of logic
in France as a development of logistic in opposition to the earlier Aristotelian tradition which persisted in Thomism.   The exposition is of particular interest to an American student of logic and scientific method, for
the authors, while admitting that French logicians did not participate
actively in the creation of logistic techniques, [30] argue that French logicians
have adhered to and preserved the original intention of the logical positivists more faithfully than the Vienna Circle and its descendants.   They
stress the importance of the distinction between formal logic and general
logic, and recall Poincaré's criticism of Russell's theory of types and his
metaphysical commitments.   Their discussion of Poincaré's doctrines is
a useful reminder of the direct pertinence of the views of that incisive
thinker to the recurrent problems of logic, and their brief survey of French
positions on multi-valued logics, antinomies, and induction brings together in a single view some of the controversial contributions of French
logicians to problems discussed internationally.   These logistic contributions are presented in a dialectical frame in which the tradition of logistic
inquiry is first separated from traditions of ontological logic (which include Thomists and Marxists) and is then divided into two parts to distinguish the French tradition from logicians who fall into arbitrary nominalism to effect the separation of logic from ontology.

---

30.   M. Boll and J. Reinhart, *op. cit.*, pp. 191 f.

The presentation of the philosophy of values in France by Raymond Polin falls into a pattern similar to the exposition of developments in logic, both in the respect that it opens with an acknowledgment that French philosophers turned their attention to this field late, and in the respect that schools are opposed in dialectical opposition. The basic distinction is between philosophies in which an objective foundation for values is sought and those based on a more or less radical subjectivity. The objective axiologies, in turn, are divided into positivist efforts, such as Durkheim's, to find a foundation for moral facts in collective consciousness, and idealist efforts, such as Bergson's, to discover the source of moral and religious values in a transcendent object; the distinction between the two consists not so much in the nature of the objective transcendent reality or the guarantee it affords to values but rather in the way in which men and values participate in it. Gurvitch, Marcel, Alquié, Le Senne, and Lavelle complete the oddly assorted group of axiological objectivists, and their doctrines are expounded either by the pairs of opposites which they employ (the two sources of morality, the closed consciousness and the open consciousness, a personal axiological absolute and an existential dialectic) or by a monism of reason or action which unites eternal to temporal, universal to individual. The subjectivist axiologies, in turn, are divided into those committed to nihilism (Grenier, Camus, Sartre, de Beauvoir) and those who, like Polin, start from the values themselves and consider valuation as a dialectical unity of value, action, and achievement. [31] Philosophies (like Thomism) which argue against the reduction of the kinds of value and which therefore separate considerations of ethics, esthetics, politics, and logic are excluded from this schematism; philosophies (like positivism and pragmatism) which seek to apply scientific method to problems of value are not examined because in France the notion of a science of values as the source of a new orthodoxy is rejected or considered outdated;[32] dialectical materialists, who could be fitted in the scheme and who claim a new and universal theory of value, are not mentioned. There are numerous indications in the other papers of problems associated with the discussion of values, but few are more striking than the shifting relations of religion and values, in which Pradines discovers a fundamental inner enmity between religion and morality. [33]

As the discussion of values turns on the place to be given to object, activity, and mode of perception, so too in esthetics, differences of ap-

---

31. R. Polin, "The Philosophy of Values," pp. 215 ff.
32. *Ibid.*, pp. 217 f.
33. R. Mehl, *op. cit.*, p. 255.

proach are determined by the emphasis or central position given to the artificial object, the creative activity, and the esthetic perception.   The interchangeability of art and philosophy, however, is a peculiarity of esthetics: the literary or artistic creation may have philosophic content and the philosophic expression may have artistic form and force.   The relations of art and philosophy which were considered above in the treatment of the epistemic grounds of philosophy, are rich and diversified.   This is a phenomenon which Raymond Bayer, in his clear and comprehensive presentation of the complex movements of esthetic thought in France, refers to in vivid phrases as an "osmosis" or again as a "collusion of philosophy and literature."[34]   He separates the works published during the second World War from those produced since its termination by the increased intrusion of literary matters into esthetics.   Bayer's own critique of Bergson's esthetics and his interest in objectivity and method in esthetics focuses attention on the esthetic object itself by means of an operational realism which uses as polar terms the subjective and the qualitative.   Bayer approves collaboration of object and subject in the creator and the dialectic of writer and reader in the work similarly employed by Sartre, and his survey takes on a final unity from the fact that it begins with the analysis of Lalo's sociological inquiry into the relation of works of artists to the lives of men in different epochs and it closes with the analysis of André Malraux's idealistic psychology of art in which civilizations and cultures are conceived in terms of the creations of spirit.

The constitutive construction of argument and doctrine in any field of philosophy, which is the continuing task of philosophers, is influenced, on the one hand, by the view which the philosopher takes of existential problems, facts, and subject-matters (that is, by the epistemic grounds of his philosophy) and, on the other hand, by the principles which he employs and credits (that is, by the pistic foundations of his philosophy). Philosophers who adhere to the same school or to related schools engaged on problems constitutively similar in formulation may discuss a single problem in comparable terms.   Philosophies based on radically different principles, however, employ different structures of analysis and construction on materials differently organized and related, and their oppositions take the form, not of different solutions to the same problem, but of different formulations of problems, so opposed to each other that each formulation is unreal or trivial by the standards of the opposed principles. One of the characteristics of the philosophy of the recent past is the increased tendency for philosophic discussion to take the second rather than

---

34. R. Bayer, *op. cit.*, pp. 272 and p. 274.

the first form: for discussions of logical problems to turn into discussions of the nature of logic or else to narrow the terms of the problem to the distinctions and the interests of one school; for discussions of moral problems to turn into a hunt for the bases of all values in consciousnesses and objects, or in cultures and ideologies, or into defenses of new or old orthodoxies; and for discussions of metaphysical problems to turn into metaphysical demonstrations of the impossibilty of metaphysics or dialectical demonstrations that all men, short of perversity and error, share the same metaphysics. The result is that principles are applied directly to subject-matters and to specific problems; and, insofar as metaphysics is a science of first principles, all problems become metaphysical problems. In the process, the lines of distinction between the various sciences and the various arts become vague and disappear, and metaphysical inquiry ceases to be an investigation and grounding of the principles of the special disciplines and sciences and becomes a dialectic of opposition of contrary, contradictory, and relative terms. The pattern of oppositions employed to state recent developments in French philosophy in the foregoing papers assumes particular importance, not merely as a sign of metaphysical elements in the discussion of various parts of philosophy, but also an indication of the reason why the pistic oppositions of philosophers appear in all questions and renders a common formulation of problems difficult.

IV. THE PISTIC FOUNDATIONS OF PHILOSOPHY

If the dialectical treatment of fundamental principles is extended — both in the application of principles and in the overthrow of opposed principles—to all subjects and to all problems, the chief single function of philosophy is to relate its arguments to concrete, existential reality. The chief errors to be found in opponents are either some form of separation of inseparable aspects of reality or exclusive concern with one part of an indissoluble whole. Idealists, materialists, and nominalists are guilty of the latter error, and they may be disposed of by pointing out the distortion or irrelevances of philosophies based on purely abstract ideas and rational deductions, or on purely material conditions and dialectical oppositions, or on purely verbal constructions and operations. Errors of the first sort are found in philosophers engaged in the task of encompassing existence as an organic whole and of accounting for all the relations of any part to its conditioning circumstances, for in order to talk about the existential unity it is necessary to differentiate phases or stages—mind and object (or immanence and transcendence), mind and mind, action and action, essence and existence, word and thing—and any such distinction may be an illicit abstraction in a slightly altered dialectic. These dialectical conditions of philosophic discussion serve to explain, at least to a foreign observer, two of the pecularities of contemporary French philosophy: the central position and promethean character of existentialism in contemporary French philosophy and the sharpness and diversity of reactions against recent French idealism. An examination of the shifting terms employed in the investigation of existence and shuffling positions assigned to philosophers in the perspective of changing dialectics may throw light on oppositions of principles in French philosophy.

According to Jean Hering, Bergson's intuitionism prepared the ground for phenomenology in France.[35] Hering differentiates sharply between existentialism, which is possessed by a kind of egocentric obsession with the existence of individual thinkers, and phenomenology, which affords means for the study of being in its essence. He argues that Marcel is a phenomenologist not an existentialist;[36] he accords Merleau-Ponty's discussion of the *cogito* an important place in the phenomenological tradition; and he relates Nédoncelle closely to Marcel in their discussions of the problem of the knowledge of others and the relation of "I" and "Thou." According to Robert Campbell, existentialism is part of the general postwar reaction against the systematizing mind and possibly even against science. Existentialists take existence as an absolute; and, therefore, they regard any questions concerning the origin or cause of existence as devoid of human meaning, whether the answers be sought in nature, God, or reason. According to Campbell, the position of Merleau-Ponty is close to that of Sartre, and Marcel is an existentialist who seeks to recall Sartre, Bataille, and Camus back to the fundamental presuppositions of Husserl and phenomenology. According to Cornu, the transition from objective idealism to subjective spiritualism made by Bergson broke the trail for existentialism. This spiritualism, even more than the objective idealism replaced by it, is the ideological expression of the decadent bourgeoisie, which turns more and more from concrete practical productivity as it becomes less and less master of the forces of production and which, therefore, escapes from reality by turning in on itself. Existentialism is the expression on the ideological plane of the failure of the bourgeoisie to manage the forces of production rationally. The error of Sartre is to separate man from his natural environment and to oppose him to it as an isolated individual, an absolute subject with his *raison d'être* in himself.[37]

---

35. J. Hering, *op. cit.*, p. 67.
36. *Ibid.*, pp. 74, and 84, footnote 20.
37. A. Cornu, *op. cit.*, p. 162.

As a result, he reduces concrete reality to abstractions, [38] and he fails in the task of philosophy to show how man integrates himself in the external world which he adapts to his needs, transforming himself in the process, and to connect, by means of this adaption, the development of knowledge with the development of experience and the development of liberty with the progressive liberation from instinct and the external world.

René Le Senne differentiates existentialism from phenomenology, recognizing a basic kinship between the philosophy of Spirit and phenomenology, but only an opposition between it and existentialism. [39] He makes use of familiar antitheses to trace the evolution of that philosophy from the existential implications of Descartes's *cogito* through the modifications worked on it by cultural changes and scientific advances. These lead to positivism—which by condemning metaphysics suppresses recourse to any unity superior to the objective or subjective offerings of experience —and absolute subjectivism—which forgets the role of heredity and nature in our existence and replaces idolatry of determinism by idolatry of the arbitrary. The philosophy of Spirit is an attempt to remedy this unreal separation by appeal to *esprit,* in its double meaning as "mind" and as "spirit," since by this means abstractions which discredit mind (matter in materialism, industrial economy in Marxism, body in physiologism, nature in positivism, thing-in-itself in agnosticism, power of the state in totalitarianism) may be avoided, while spirit remains, nonetheless, linked to experience as mind. Positivism and existentialism fail to perform the tasks of philosophy, because positivism in its quest for objectivity is unable to treat the sensibilities of the perception of differences, while existentialism has aggravated the sense of bad conscience and the feeling of distress. Philosophy of Spirit, despite its kinship to phenomenology, differs from it in that phenomenology is oriented to extending science, philosophy of Spirit to cultivating metaphysics. [40] Louis Lavelle does not treat of the differences of schools, but expounds such a metaphysics by three steps of a subtle dialectic which analyzes the *cogito* into parts which permit the individual thinker to be related to the absolute and omnipresent subject: (1) the power I have to say I, (2) pure inwardness, and (3) the interval between the Ego and pure inwardness. The world then appears in a triple guise: as appearance, as a trial, and as an instrument of mediation among consciousnesses. As in the case of phenomenology and existentialism, the arguments of Descartes have a profound effect on the development of the philosophy of Spirit: it is a truly French tradition as it is

---

38. *Ibid.,* p. 167.
39. R. Le Senne, *op. cit.,* pp. 111 f. and p. 114.
40. *Ibid.,* p. 114.

formulated by Le Senne and Lavelle (since the American student, for example, would learn that Bacon had performed the tasks of initiating modern philosophic and scientific thought assigned to Descartes in France, while Descartes was a man of doubts who proved thereby that he existed and was led thence to the error of bifurcating body and mind), but it is a tradition in which St. Bernard plays an unacknowledged role almost as important as that of Descartes.

Jean Wahl traces the dialectic of the present situation and the path run by existentialism in another and broader sweep. The intuitionism of Bergson and the intellectualism of Brunschvicg are the polar opposites (with fundamental agreements in their denial of any static being) from which contemporary discussions stem by adapting some aspects of the Bergsonian intuitionism and enlarging the conception of intellectualism. The intellectual youth of France are divided into three parties: the Catholic, the Communist, and the Existentialist. Wahl expounds the Catholic philosophers in terms of existentialism: Maritain's differentiation of a religious and non-ontological existentialism from its irreligious and ontological counterpart; Gilson's study of Thomistic existentialism; Mounier's examination of different forms of existentialism from a personalist point of view; the Christian existentialism of Marcel and of his disciples Dufrenne and Ricoeur. He finds few authoritative formulations of dialectical materialism, and expounds the doctrines of existentialism in an illuminating and subtle analysis of some of the ideas of Merleau-Ponty and Levinas. Gaston Berger uses the three steps of another dialectic to bring together the parts of existence torn asunder by the analyses of philosophers and to reassemble the same cast of philosophers in different groupings. The first step is the opposition of immanence and transcendence, of idealism and realism; the idealism of Brunschvicg was opposed by the Thomist realism, until idealism was transformed into spiritualism, and various efforts were made to unite immanence and objectivity in personalism, in the philosophy of Spirit of Le Senne and Lavelle, and the philosophy of action of Blondel. The second step is the promethean revolt against the great synthesis of Blondel, Le Senne, and Lavelle: it is exemplified in the substitution of synthesis and dialectic for the Cartesian analysis in the existentialism of Sartre and Merleau-Ponty, the substitution of the creation of values by men for their discovery in the doctrines of Polin and Roland Caillois, the substitution of a conception of the evolution of evidence for permanent intellectual categories, in the philosophy of science of Bachélard, and like attempts of André Malraux, Gusdorf, and Jean Wahl to make the transition from the immanence of values in man to some form of transcendence. The final step is accomplished by avoiding the false alternative between idealism and realism by a conception of experience as an existential continuum within which things are progressively delineated by our intentions and our memories, by our instincts and our habits after the manner of Husserl's phenomenology.

Existentialism, approached from another angle by Roger Mehl, is an attitude extremely favorable to the constitution of a religious philosophy, as is evidenced by Le Senne's analysis of obstacles and of our relations to others and by Marcel's treatment of fidelity, hope, and love in terms which place existence and transcendence in concrete relation. Catholic philosophy, in the variety of schools presented by Duméry, has likewise oriented its approach to the problems of concrete existences: Gilson in his original and incisive analysis of the history of the discussion of essence and existence discovered the treatment of the concrete apprehension of existential reality in the heart of the philosophy of St. Thomas Aquinas and joined intellectualism and existentialism; [41] Marcel created an independent Christian existentialism; Nédoncelle concentrated on the intersubjective problems of personalism; Blondel found in action the concrete unity which binds together the inseparable parts of reality separated in other philosophies. Finally, with all these crossings of the domain of the existential and with the consequent rearrangements of the participants in the discussion according to new frames of reference, it is possible to find any of the contrasted terms conjoined: Gilson joins realism to existentialism; Merleau-Ponty combines existentialism and Marxism; Father Fessard, S. J., uses Hegelian dialectic to combine Marxism and Christianity.

V. THE CONDITIONS OF PHILOSOPHIC DISCUSSION

The shifting terms and methods of philosophy and the altering interpretations of the doctrines and purposes of philosophy do not indicate a verbalistic and obsessive weakness of philosophic discussion (as is sometimes intimated by critics of philosophy), but rather its importance and omnipresence. Discussions of the most concrete problems of historical or physical fact, psychological observation or social condition, practical action, verbal statement, or moral intention, become philosophic if they encounter difficulties or are pushed to the extreme; and all men become philosophers, even in the peculiarity of redefining their terms, reinterpreting what other men say, and discovering new principles or new arrangements of old principles. The differences of interpretation given to Des-

41. H. Duméry, *op. cit.,* pp. 226 f.

cartes and Bergson in the eighteen essays do not mean, necessarily, that some of the interpretations are erroneous or that, even when they are historically false on some point, they are without philosophic interest and utility; nor do the differences concerning the principles of philosophy, its nature and methods, and its applications to problems of life, art, and science, mean that its grounds, constructions, and applications are untestable and unusable. Analysis shows, on the contrary, a pattern in these philosophic treatments of the development and interrelations of philosophies, which bear much the same relation to those philosophies as the second intentions of medieval philosophers bear to first intentions. The sketchy reactions set down in the previous pages trace some of the lines of that pattern, but at the risk of making selections and emphases that will seem to the authors of the papers distortions of their meanings similar to the distortions some of them found in philosophic interpretations of philosophers and the doctrines of philosophers. It is impossible to put an end to philosophic inquiry, discussion, and contradiction; but it is sometimes profitable to center it on the nature of the philosophic discussion itself.

Within the broad agreement that a common tradition affords, the philosophies developed recently in France are directed to different purposes—practical, esthetic, and scientific—as evidenced in the differences of their principles and methods. What unites them in the discussion of problems is not agreement on principles, tradition, or purposes, but rather agreement of a very general sort on the criterion by which fundamental principles will be chosen and defended. That criterion specifies that philosophy shall treat of the existential, and therefore of the organic unity in which the inseparable will not be separated, the whole will not be sought in the juxtaposition of parts, and the individual will not be isolated from his circumstances. That criterion, so conceived, accounts for the importance and omnipresence of existentialism in contemporary French thought. It is of interest in considering the nature of philosophic discussion to conceive the criterion in this fashion, since, although existentialism scarcely exists as a philosophy in the United States, the criterion which governs philosophic discussion there may be stated, without excessive distortion, in the same terms; and the relations between French and American philosophy, which are few in direct influence, may be seen to be numerous in analogous standards and devices. American philosophers tend to seek the existential in "relations" rather than in "consciousness"; "experience" is analyzed in terms of "problems" and their solution rather than in terms of "immanence" and "transcendence," and is focused in "events" rather than in "mental acts" and "intentions;" the search for the organic whole moves from the situation to the universe or to the solution rather than from the Ego to the Absolute or to Nothingness. Once these rough equations are made, the American may become aware, in the face of the discussion of existentialism in France, that the similar search for the organic, the existential, and the circumstantial has given to the varieties of realisms and naturalisms in contemporary American philosophy the same central position that is occupied by the varieties of existentialisms in France.

If one were to construct a scheme for American philosophic discussion comparable to the one which has emerged for French philosophy in the foregoing pages, both the diametrical differences and the continuing communications between the two traditions might be made more apparent. In France, if the evidence has been interpreted correctly, there is a great variety of existentialisms and of philosophies of action, person, or spirit, whose approach is similar to existentialism, flanked on the one side by the realism and intellectualism of the Thomists and on the other side by the dialectical materialism of the Marxists. In the United States there is a great variety of realisms and naturalisms, flanked on the one side by the nominalism of the positivists and on the other side by the dialectic of the idealists. There are, apparently, no longer idealists or nominalists in French philosophy, and the problems and language of naturalists are unfamiliar. Thomists and Marxists, on the contrary, have not contributed conspicuously to American philosophy, and existentialism is still a novel and exotic doctrine in all its forms. There is little immediate prospect of communication between French and American philosophers on the problems of existentialism or naturalism, if these may be viewed as centers of their respective interest, yet the criteria which led to the comparison of existentialism and naturalism suggest the subjects on which communication is possible, for existentialists and naturalists are both engaged in investigating problems concerning the nature of "experience," of the "existential," of "engagement." Moreover, the methods employed in the discussion are not dissimilar. Two methods are of particular importance in the existentialist construction: the reflexive argument of the *cogito* in which thought is warrant for existence and the dialectical argument in which opposites like immanence and transcendence are conjoined. American philosophers have expended great ingenuity on two devices: the reflexive argument in which propositions may be true because of the form in which they are cast or false because they are applied to themselves and the dialectical argument in which opposites like knower and known, theoretic and practical, eternal object and actual occasion, are conjoined. The material differences may be more important than the formal similarities, yet it is along such threads of argument and analogy that philosophic traditions grow, and philosophic arguments are frequently transplanted, but seldom cultivated with strict fidelity. Moreover, the negative similarities between the French and American traditions are even more striking when viewed in relation to the tendencies in philosophy which are omitted or stressed lightly in both traditions: the philosophies of independent substances, univocal categories, fixed first principles, causal relations, and independent sciences.

The problems of philosophy are found in the activities of man in the pursuit of his purposes in the situation in which he finds himself: these have been referred to above as the epistemic grounds of philosophy. The proper tasks of philosophy consist in the analyses and constructions by which those problems are rendered more intelligible and by which their solutions are furthered: these have been called the constitutive structures of philosophy. The success of philosophic inquiry depends on the soundness and clarity of the principles which it employs: these have been called the pistic foundations of philosophy. Discussion and cooperation among philosophers may center on any of these three levels. When there is great polemic opposition concerning the principles of philosophy, philosophic discussion turns largely on the basic presuppositions, purposes, and applications of philosophy; there is comparatively little development of the constitutive structure of philosophies when the philosopher must return at each point of the discussion to defend fundamental principles, and the practical utility of philosophy is properly questioned (usually from the point of view of an unacknowledged philosophy) when the whole character and interpretation of the original problems from which the philosophic inquiry took its departure is altered with the shift of philosophic principles. In the periods in which philosophy has contributed significantly to the order of men's lives and thought, there has been at least a minimum common understanding of the opposed principles of philosophers, of the developments dependent on those principles, and of the significances and consequences derived from these developments. What is desirable in philosophic discussion and communication is not necessarily that philosophers use greater objectivity and precision in stating and refuting the principles of other philosophers (even the greatest philosophers have not thought these virtues essential), or that they agree on unambiguous meanings for terms or on common methods of analysis and construction (the ideal of unambiguous terms and constant methods could

be achieved only by avoiding the adjustments of living and the developments of thinking), or that they find the center of their problems and
meanings in the same aspects of man's lives and careers. What is desirable is sufficient pause in the shuttling insistence on new beginnings and
in the presentation of the advantages of peculiar principles to permit examination of the common structure of problems and the particular structure of proposed solutions. The juxtaposition of two related yet radically
different traditions in contemporary philosophy, like the French and the
American, may contribute to such a clarification and may serve as a step
toward the examination of the interrelations of philosophic traditions on
a universal scope.

The discussion of philosophic traditions and systems has further consequences today, however, than clarification of philosophic principles and
critical insight into methods of philosophic analysis and construction. The
chief purposes of philosophers in the discussion of philosophy must continue to be the elucidation of principles and the development of consequences in their effort to convince others of the validity of their principles
or at least of the cogency of their methods and the value of their conclusions. The study of the philosophies of other peoples has two further
consequences in the world today: it may be a means by which to understand the basic convictions and aspirations of peoples and it may provide
the means of cooperating with them in a world which should be one in
understanding as well as in material proximities. There is a tendency to
state the problems of world cooperation and world community in material,
economic, and social terms, and to neglect the place which systems of
values and intellectual constructions have, even in the determination of
material conditions. There is a consequent tendency to think of cooperation exclusively in terms of agreement on the same basic principles and to
neglect the possibilities of cooperation in common action and common life
for different reasons drawn from different social, economic, and philosophic principles. It is possible that there are philosophies which lead to
totally incompatible modes of life—although it is more probable that only
pseudo-philosophies, detectable by philosophic analysis, bear that relationship to other philosophies—but that question of radically and immovably
opposed principles is in itself an inquiry worthy of philosophic analysis
in the broadened frame of a world discussion. In that frame philosophy
may contribute at once to the clarification of basic principles, the construction of systematic explanations, the understanding of peoples, and the
promotion of common action and equitable cooperation.

PART II

CONTEMPORARY
AMERICAN PHILOSOPHY

PHILOSOPHY IN AMERICA
BETWEEN TWO WARS

*A. Cornelius Benjamin**

When one attempts, for the purpose of analysis and description, to extract a segment from the on-going historical process, he is certain to be faced with two important difficulties. In the first place, neither time nor history proceeds by waves or pulsations; there are no fences or signals indicating the beginning or the end of an era. All demarcation of periods, therefore, is more or less arbitrary. In the second place, the closer the historian is to the period which he is examining the more arbitrary his selection will be. Perspective is gained neither from within nor from a close vantage point.

Both these difficulties are apparent in the attempt to carry out the task of this essay. The great wars did not in any obvious way constitute turning points in American philosophy; nothing happened in either case which could be said to have produced the death or the birth of a movement, or to have given philosophical ideas a significant change in direction. The effect was rather on the philosophers than on the philosophies. Students disappeared from classrooms, and money disappeared from budgets; and, as a consequence, many teachers of philosophy, either voluntarily or by the pressure of circumstances, changed their activity to government service in one form or another. This produced in their philosophical outlooks nothing more striking than an increased sense of insecurity, enforced, perhaps, by a clearer recognition of the importance of the problem of evil in an adequate philosophy of life. But rarely was there a fundamental change in metaphysical outlook or in the conception of the task of philosophy. Even pragmatism, which may properly be said to have its roots in the social situation, was little affected by the war since it was already a strong and growing movement by 1917. Such an attitude of aloofness is possible, I presume, only in a country like the Unit-

* Born in 1897. Ph.D., University of Michigan, 1924. Formerly at the Universities of Illinois and Chicago. Professor of Philosophy and chairman of the department, University of Missouri. Guggenheim Fellow, 1930-31; president, Western Division, American Philosophical Association, 1947-48. Author of *Logical Structure of Science* (1936) and *Introduction to the Philosophy of Science* (1937).

ed States where there has never been an "official" philosophy nor even a great concern for a "cultural" philosophy.

Furthermore, it will be impossible until several years have elapsed to evaluate properly what has happened in American philosophy in the last few decades. Tendencies exhibit themselves in great numbers, but their promise is obscure. Some will certainly die without issue; others, already undergoing change, will be further modified in unpredictable directions before presenting their offspring to American thought; still others, apparently barren, may suddenly reproduce in great numbers.

I propose, therefore, in the following pages to interpret my topic somewhat liberally. The period with which I shall be concerned is roughly the second quarter of the present century. This is a somewhat more arbitrary selection than that indicated by the title, but it will permit me occasionally to refer to some of the more recent post-war tendencies. I shall make no attempt to "survey" the field, or to mention all the movements and trends which are evident. The essays which follow will supply the deficiences which are caused by the limitations in my vision or the errors in my evaluation. I can only argue that this is American philosophy in the last quarter-century as I see it now. Others will certainly disagree and tomorrow I, myself, shall probably view it differently.

I

Measured in terms of externals, and judged by purely quantitative criteria, American philosophy passed during these years through a period of rapid growth. Philosophy was continually being done in a bigger, if not a better, way. Except for a few years during the depression in the late twenties and early thirties philosophy prospered. Student enrollments increased; teaching positions were readily procured by graduating Ph.D's; publishers were not too reluctant to accept manuscripts; and, on the whole, the output of the philosophical press was extensive, varied, and of high quality. One important periodical[1] ceased publication, but several[2] were born. Though the American Philosophical Association was already an established organization at the beginning of this period, it proliferated during the ensuing years into three more or less independent divisional groups—Eastern, Western, and Pacific—which together now claim over a thousand members. Local, state, and district philosophical

---

1. *The Monist.*
2. *Philosophy and Phenomenological Research, Philosophy of Science, Journal of Symbolic Logic, Review of Metaphysics, Journal of Aesthetics and Art Criticism, New Scholasticism,* and *Philosophic Abstracts.*

associations, not affiliated with the national organization, have appeared in great numbers in recent years. Further specialization and spread of activities are indicated by the formation of the Association for Symbolic Logic, the Philosophy of Science Association, the International Phenomenological Society, the Charles S. Peirce Society, the American Society for Esthetics, the American Catholic Philosophy Association, and others.

As every good doctor knows, however, a large heart is not always a good heart. What, then, happened to American philosophy during these years, which will partially explain this rapid growth? Still applying an external criterion we may say, I think, that philosophy was compelled by the pressure of circumstances to play a role in the educational drama which was being staged in the colleges and universities during these years. This was the period of the first experiments in "general education," and of the discovery of the blessed word "integration." In this movement philosophy was destined to play a distinctive role. As one of the "liberal" studies it had its part to play along with literature, religion, music, and art in the make-up of the new general humanities courses which were established for the purpose of breaking down departmental boundaries and overcoming the high degree of specialization and fragmentation characteristic of much higher education of the period. But philosophy has always been more than just one of the humanities; it has sought that *Weltanschauung* which is itself the goal of the integrative process. Thus philosophy was often selected by educators as the most effective device for achieving the unification which the old curricula lacked, and which even the new program, if the courses were merely "survey" rather than truly "general," failed to provide. This meant that philosophy was called upon to integrate the humanities, to unify the physical sciences, to organize the biological sciences, to interrelate the social sciences, and even, as at the University of Chicago, to integrate the resulting integrations.

The result was that philosophy, or, to be more exact, philosophers, underwent something of a transformation. It would be somewhat indiscreet to say that they had to become educated. But they did have to become educated in something besides philosophy. They had to acquire sufficient familiarity with the other humanities to enable them to participate intelligently in cooperative courses in which these other disciplines were represented, and they were further obliged, in their integrative roles, to learn enough about all the subjects entering into the general curriculum to discuss their common philosophical presuppositions and to fit them into the total picture of the educational program. Philosophy thus ceased to be pure and isolated, and it took root in the soil of value appreciation, social problems, and scientific methodology. Some educators even went so far as to suggest that there should no longer be any general philosophers in departments of philosophy; instead there should be only philosophers of art in departments of art, social philosophers in departments of sociology, and philosophers of science in departments of physics and of mathematics.

Where this movement will lead, no one can say. So far as the present scene is concerned one can affirm only that philosophical department lines are being obliterated, and that philosophers are being drawn, if not into the market place, at least into the other classrooms of the colleges and universities. At the University of Chicago, for example, there are more technically trained philosophers engaged in the teaching of general education in the College than are to be found in the department of philosophy. Many graduate students, realizing this tendency, are demanding that doctorate work be modified so as to provide the broader training which will prepare them for the new kind of teaching. Some universities in the country openly recommend that doctorate students in philosophy prepare themselves for this study by taking a master's degree in some non-philosophical field. On the other side there is the same reaching out for philosophy on the part of those with more specialized training. Scientists are becoming increasingly interested in the logical and metaphysical presuppositions of their subjects, social scientists are more and more concerned with problems of methodology, and the advocates of the liberal arts are beginning to see their disciplines as intimately related to problems of value and problems of the philosophy of language.

What I have been saying thus far is that philosophy has increased in stature and has made many friends. This is not to say, however, that it has developed or changed character. Is there any evidence for this? In fact, is there any evidence that American philosophy, either in this period or in its longer history, has had an individuality which can be described and distinguished from other national philosophies in anything but geographical terms?

A fairly definite answer, negative in character, has been given to this question in recent years by H. W. Schneider. After a scholarly and competent study of American philosophy from its beginnings, he confesses his inability to tell what it "stands for." He finds that it possesses no central content or dominant note. There is no definable direction or movement but only a vitality—a "vague yet tangible energy which it exerts when it is faced with new ideas. When a new idea comes to us we project it, semi-consciously, against one historical perspective after another to discover how and where the idea can best be used and assimilated."[3] Our heritage is simply the many ways we have of reacting to the novel.

Another authority, R. B. Perry, writing at the very beginning of the period we are considering, suggests an answer which, while somewhat more positive than Schneider's, leaves much to be desired on the part of those who are seeking a peculiarly American philosophy. That which is indigenous to our culture, he suggests, is something expressible in terms of individualism, experimentalism, meliorism, and democracy. Dewey and James, though educated under the influence of the Anglo-German idealistic tradition, were not persuaded by it. Rather than compromising with the Absolute, they reacted against it and gave us the "priceless boon of an Absoluteless world."[4] Such an attitude, he goes on to say, gave American philosophy its three distinctive characteristics — its pluralism, its democracy and humanity, and its faith.

This is certainly not a metaphysics in the traditional sense of the term, and it is hardly more than an intense moral enthusiasm. But if American philosophy never had a distinctive point of view it cannot have had such a character during the period under consideration; that which has no character cannot change or develop.

Perhaps, however, the criteria which we have been employing are still, in a sense, external rather than intrinsic. Presumably the proper way to determine what happened to American philosophy during this period is to turn to the writings of the outstanding authorities in the field. But at this point one runs against a serious difficulty. Clearly no comprehensive survey of the total writings in philosophy over even so short a time is possible in a limited space. Nor can a truly *representative* selection be made, since it is bound to reflect the interests and prejudices of the one who is making the choices. How, then, can a more impartial procedure be followed?

One method suggests itself immediately. A significant event which occurred early in this period was the establishment of the Carus Lectures by the family of Dr. Paul Carus as a memorial to this eminent scholar who was editor of the *Open Court* and the *Monist,* and who himself

---

3. H. W. Schneider, *History of American Philosophy* (New York, Columbia University Press, 1936), p. ix.
4. R. B. Perry, *The Present Conflict of Ideals* (New York, Longmans, Green and Co., 1922), p. 536.

wrote extensively in the field of philosophy. These lectures, originally
scheduled to be given biennially, are presented in each case by an
individual selected by a committee of the Divisions of the American
Philosophical Association as the most eminent American philosopher.
The themes of the lectures are not prescribed, and the recipient of the
honor is free to present his mature and considered conclusions on what
he deems to be the important issues of philosophy. An examination of
the subject matter of these lectures, therefore, over the period under
consideration provides a sketch of the topics about which the most
distinguished philosophers, selected by their peers, have been thinking
and writing. Unfortunately the fourth and fifth of the series have never
been published, though the topics indicate roughly the area within which
they fall. The list[5] is as follows:

     I. *Experience and Nature,* by John Dewey, 1925.
    II. *The Revolt Against Dualism,* by A. O. Lovejoy, 1930.
   III. *The Philosophy of the Present,* by G. H. Mead, 1932.
   IV. *The Great Visions of Philosophy,* by W. P. Montague, 1933.
    V. *Toward a Perspective Realism,* by E. B. McGilvary, 1939.
   VI. *The Meaning of Human History,* by M. R. Cohen, 1947.
  VII. *An Analysis of Knowledge and Valuation,* by C. I. Lewis,
       1946.

Brief reference may be made to the published items in this list.

Dewey directs his attention to an attempted redefinition of "experience." He wants to be an empiricist, but he objects strenuously to the
subjectivistic interpretation of experience which compels one to begin by
arbitrarily selecting some limited area of this realm and neglecting the
rest. Empiricism, properly speaking, "signifies beginning back of any
science, with experience in its gross and macroscopic traits."[6] One of the
great errors of philosophy is the overemphasis on *knowing,* to the more
or less complete neglect of *having* and *doing.* This has led the philosopher to retire into a world of timeless absolutes, rather than to immerse
himself in the concrete world of everyday life. Lovejoy, insisting that
epistemology *is* an important subject in spite of the fact that many philosophers consider it unprofitable and repugnant, argues that dualism is
not only the natural belief of the common man but the one solution to
the epistemological problem which does not lead to insurmountable diffi-

---

    5. The topics and dates of numbers IV and V are those of the lectures. The remaining
items are given in the form of published titles and publication dates. The publisher in
each case is Open Court, formerly of Chicago, now of LaSalle, Illinois.
    6. *Loc. cit.,* p. 6.

culties. All other forms of realism, he insists, lead to contradictions either of the implications of realism itself or of admitted facts. Mead, who died before he could revise his lectures for publication, and who employed a somewhat unfortunate literary style, deals not with present-day philosophy, as the title of his lectures might lead one to believe, but with the world as centered in any present. Past and future are to be understood in terms of the present, and the past undergoes change as new data, in terms of which it is to be understood, are disclosed in the present. The pragmatic, functional point of view is assumed throughout, and the dominating idea is the attempt to make the concept of sociality into a natural category. Cohen's lectures are a consideration of the philosophy of history—a topic which, according to the author, had been generally neglected by American philosophers. The book propounds no philosophy of history as such but deals with the aims, methods, and assumptions of historical study with special reference to the metaphysical categories used and to the various theories of the nature of historical change. Lewis presents a naturalistic theory of value and in the attempt to show that values can be studied empirically, he finds it necessary to analyze carefully empirical knowledge in general. Such knowledge, contrary to the claim of the skeptic, is admitted to be possible, though the three kinds of empirical truth—statements of what is presently given, statements involving prediction of further possible experiences, and statements asserting an objective state of affairs—make different claims to knowledge and are differently verified.

A second method of throwing light on the course of American philosophy during these years is available. The period is characterized by the publication of a large number of cooperative studies in philosophy.[7] Perhaps the most representative of these was the one entitled *Contem-*

---

7. In addition to the strictly American studies to be mentioned later in the essay there were several international projects in which American philosophers participated. Among these were *Philosophy Today,* edited by E. L. Schaub (Chicago, Open Court Publishing Co., 1928), and *Twentieth Century Philosophy,* edited by D. D. Runes (New York, Philosophical Library, 1943). The series entitled "Library of Living Philosophers," edited by Paul Schilpp, and published by Northwestern University, Evanston, has contained noteworthy contributions to American philosophy; among those published are volumes on Dewey (1939), Santayana (1940), and Whitehead (1941). In addition there were departmental studies, such as the *University of California Publications in Philosophy,* which issued several volumes during this period, and *Essays in Philosophy,* edited by T. V. Smith, and containing the contributions of a number of Chicago graduates in philosophy (Chicago, University of Chicago Press, 1929). Several cooperative honorary and memorial volumes were also published, such as *Essays in Honor of John Dewey* (New York, 1929), and *Freedom and Experience,* essays presented to H. M. Kallen, edited by Sidney Hook and M. R. Konvitz (Ithaca, New York, Cornell University Press, 1947).

porary American Philosophy.[8] This two-volume work consisted of a series of personal statements by a group of American philosophers who were selected because of their eminence in the field. They were chosen by popular vote of the members of the American Philosophical Association as the philosophers most entitled to this recognition. Each contributor was requested to "state his principal philosophic beliefs, the reasons for supporting them, and the manner in which he reached them."[9]

An examination of these volumes serves only to substantiate the claims of Schneider and Perry. As personal statements of formative influences they are very illuminating, and as clear-cut expressions of philosophical points of view which certain of the writers had already presented in less adequate form in other places they are gratifying. But together they form no pattern and make up no picture. All kinds and shades of philosophical position are represented, and no one viewpoint dominates the scene. The only conclusion one can draw is that Perry erred by understatement; American philosophers believe so firmly in pluralism that no two of them accept the same philosophy.

To be sure, if one is willing to accept philosophical labels at their face value, and if one employs a somewhat artificial classificatory scheme, some pattern is detectable. Out-and-out materialists are conspicuously lacking. W. P. Montague is willing to call himself an animistic materialist, though this is to be equated in his understanding with cosmological spiritualism.[10] Skepticism has in Theodore De Laguna its only representative, though J. Loewenberg calls his position "problematic realism," which, he insists, ends in the conviction that "reality is full of surds."[11] Dewey is the only pragmatist, though even he does not so characterize himself in this essay. The conceptual pragmatism of C. I. Lewis[12] has little in common with the position of Dewey. Ethics is represented in the moral idealism of G. H. Palmer, which he identifies with theism, and in the naturalistic view of W. G. Everett. J. H. Tufts avoids considerations of the metaphysics of ethics and argues that moral problems should be tied down to earth by the active participation of the philosopher in civic affairs. Only one, C. J. Ducasse, concerns himself specifically with the question of philosophic method; he develops the

8. Edited by G. P. Adams and W. P. Montague, 2 vols. (New York, The Macmillan Co., 1930).
9. *Loc. cit.*, Vol. I, p. 9.
10. *Loc. cit.*, Vol. II, p. 158.
11. *Ibid.*, Vol. I, pp. 56-7.
12. See also his *Mind and the World Order* (New York, Scribners, 1939).

point of view later argued in his *Philosophy as a Science*[13] that the methods of philosophy and of science are the same, philosophy being occupied wholly with the examination of the meaning of appraisals. Others, not directing their attention to the problem of method in particular, insist that their positions are empirically founded, and there is some justification for the impression that professed rationalists are a rarity in American philosophy. The majority of the contributors place themselves on one side or the other of the idealism-realism controversary. In terms of numbers the representatives of the two schools are about equal, though the variety of forms of idealism is much greater than in the case of realism. Of the former, two (M. W. Calkins and Warner Fite) identify themselves with the personalists; of the three whose idealistic positions suggest absolutism (G. W. Cunningham, J. A. Leighton, and W. E. Hocking) only the first is willing to accept the characterization, and he insists that the word should not be written with a capital letter.[14] H. B. Alexander accepts a Platonic idealism; D. H. Parker calls his position "empirical idealism"; C. A. Strong defends panpsychism; and G. P. Adams acknowledges idealism only in the sense that it involves the "belief that there are meanings embedded within experience and that their nature may be apprehended by thought."[15] There is somewhat more unity among the realists if one makes an exception of the logical realism of M. R. Cohen and the naturalism of R. W. Sellars and George Santayana. The other realists base their views primarily on the epistemological problem. R. B. Perry directs his arguments against subjectivism. Durant Drake, A. O. Lovejoy, J. B. Pratt, and C. A. Strong, all in the group of critical realists who contributed to a cooperative volume in 1920,[16] place their emphasis on the transcendence or intention of ideas and thus accept a representative theory of perception.

Just five years later another cooperative study[17] was published. From the point of view of giving a unified conception of what was happening in American philosophy at the time, this is even less satisfactory than the

---

13. New York, Oskar Piest, 1941.

14. *Loc. cit.,* Vol. I., p.268.

15. *Ibid.,* Vol. I, pp. 68-9.

16. *Essays in Critical Realism,* by Durant Drake and others (New York, The Macmillan Co., 1920).

17. *American Philosophy Today and Tomorrow,* edited by H. M. Kallen and Sidney Hook (New York, Lee Furman, 1935). The contributors were chosen in this case not by popular vote but by the editors. They were, in general, the younger men and were confined to those who had not at the time presented their philosophical self-portraits elsewhere. The principle of selection was somewhat broader than in the case of the earlier study, and allowed for the inclusion of several individuals who were not technical philosophers in the strict sense.

earlier one. The pluralism of outlooks is even more pronounced. Heavier emphasis is placed on value theory, and on social and political ethics. Naturalism has gained adherents. There is a new concern for the common man and his predicament, and the responsibilities of the philosopher in this area are called to attention.

One is tempted to say that in terms of generalizations concerning American philosophy during this period this is all that can be said. But a careful examination of this latter volume discloses an interesting fact which, by itself, might easily escape notice. However, a survey of other writings, particularly of the last decade of the period, serves to bring it into clear perspective. Indeed, if one were forced to make a single generalization about recent trends in American philosophy, on the grounds that no enterprise can remain stagnant over even so short a period, he might well call attention to this one fact.

I have in mind the increasing self-consciousness of American philosophers and philosophy. Philosophers are talking less philosophy and more about philosophy. The subject has always, of course, been self-critical; its very nature demands that presuppositions and assumptions never remain long unexamined. But this critical examination of foundations has been until recently to a large extent theoretical and unrelated to the role which philosophy is playing and ought to play. It has been really not an examination of philosophy but simply more philosophy. Today, however, philosophers are beginning to ask themselves what they are doing in teaching and preaching this subject, and they are asking what the subject is and what it can contribute to the life of modern man.

Evidence for this change in attitude, once the suggestion has been made that it is really taking place, is to be found in a number of areas. The outstanding example is the very significant study, unique in American philosophy, entitled *Philosophy in American Education*.[18] This book, again a cooperative study, represents the conclusions of five of the most eminent American philosophers concerning what philosophy is, how it should be taught, and what it can contribute to the education of American youth. While the views expressed are those of the writers of the volume, the circumstances surrounding the gathering of the material are highly significant. The five individuals, selected again by popular vote of the members of the American Philosophical Association, and operating under a grant from the Rockefeller Foundation, traveled about the country,

18. By Brand Blandshard, C. J. Ducasse, C. W. Hendel, A. E. Murphy, and Max Otto (New York, Harper and Brothers, 1945).

talked with individual philosophers, and held seven two-day symposia in as many geographical localities to which were invited those philosophers in the areas who had indicated in their writings a common concern for and interest in the problem of the role of philosophy in contemporary education. Discussion at these sessions was completely unrestricted so far as points of view were concerned; non-philosophers as well as philosophers were invited to participate; and the interchange of ideas was, at least so far as concerned my own experience, never dull. There is every reason to believe that the authors of the book tried conscientiously to reflect the views presented by the participants, and many direct quotations from them are included in the final document. The conclusions of the book are impossible to summarize in a limited space. There is not so much agreement as one would hope to find, though this in no way detracts from the value of the study. For our purposes the significant fact is that such a study was made, and that it was made in this particular manner. It provided both the stimulus and the opportunity for philosophers to take stock of themselves and their work, to pool their resources, and to tabulate their assets and liabilities.

Other evidence of the trend toward self-evaluation may be found in the increased attention on the part of Americans to American philosophy itself. While, as we have already seen, no distinctive characteristics of such a national philosophy may be disclosed, nevertheless the question whether there are such characteristics is being repeatedly asked. More specifically, the history of American philosophy is emerging as a legitimate subject for study, and the number of new courses in this field together with the growing literature[19] suggests that American philosophers are becoming increasingly aware that they have something distinctive to offer to the world, even though they are not in a position to say, with any unanimity of outlook, exactly what this is.[20]

---

19. In addition to the book by Schneider, already mentioned, the following should be cited: *Philosophical Ideas in the United States*, by H. G. Townsend (New York, American Book Co., 1934); *Philosophy in America from the Puritans to James*, by P. R. Anderson and M. H. Fisch (New York, Appleton, 1939); and *The Development of American Philosophy*, by W. G. Muelder and Laurence Sears (Boston, Houghton Mifflin, 1940).

20. Further evidence may be found by noting the number of programs of the American Philosophical Association which in recent years have been devoted to symposia on philosophy and education, philosophy and democracy, and philosophy and the world crisis. In addition, attention should be called to the "Conferences on Science, Philosophy, and Religion in Their Relation to the Democratic Way of Life," held at intervals in New York City, and to the "Hazen Conferences," which have recently emphasized problems lying on the borderline between philosophy and religion.

II

Turning away from generalities we may now ask whether there is any more particular and precise evidence of the state of American philosophy during this period. Realizing that objectivity on this matter is almost impossible to achieve, I shall state dogmatically what in terms of specific movements, specific individuals, and specific fields of activity seem to me to be the outstanding features of the recent period of philosophical thought in this country. The movements are pragmatism, idealism, and naturalism; the individuals are Whitehead and Peirce; and the areas are the philosophy of science and the theory of value.

The first movement to which reference should be made is pragmatism. To the average European, and, indeed, to the average American who is not a technical philosopher, pragmatism would seem to have been the outstanding movement in the philosophy of this country not only in recent years but in the entire course of its history. The reasons for this attitude are easy to understand. The European, whose vision is somewhat warped by distance and whose estimate of us is determined largely by the fact that we have had the money and industrial efficiency necessary to the winning of two wars, has naturally tended to think of us as the most practical of all people. For him this means that in the early stages of our history we were too busy with pioneering to occupy ourselves with cultural values, and now that we have the necessary leisure we are no longer concerned with such — a view which easily becomes identified with a popular version of pragmatism. The non-philosophical American sees pragmatism largely in terms of its influences on education; and since these forces are still at work, he readily thinks of pragmatism as the dominant movement in current philosophy.

Any truth which there is in this contention must be faced by the commonly held opinion of specialists in philosophy that pragmatism is no longer a significant movement in our country. As early as 1930, for example, Boodin expressed himself on the issue. "Pragmatism is now dead, and it is not seemly to speak ill of the dead. No one seems to want to own it now, except writers of French doctors' theses. . . Long live pragmatism."[21] This is, no doubt, an attitude which is somewhat more extreme than most philosophers would be willing to take even today. To be sure, when Boodin was writing, James and Peirce had both died; but Dewey was, and still is, very much alive, and, what is more important, Peirce's most significant writings had not yet been published. Even

---

21. *Contemporary American Philosophy,* Vol. I, pp. 140-1.

in the early thirties, however, the term was gradually disappearing from philosophical literature, and most serious-minded philosophers already had made up their minds that they were either pragmatists for reasons which were too obvious to acknowledge, or not pragmatists for reasons which had been so often expressed that pragmatists had had ample time to reply to the arguments if they had been willing or able.

There is, I think, a safe compromise between these two positions. Pragmatism has disappeared as a distinct movement in American philosophy, but the significant truths of pragmatism, and there are many, have been absorbed by other points of view for which they have had certain natural affinities. Pragmatism began in eclecticism and ended in dispersal, as all eclecticisms must since they lack an essential integrating principle. The evidence for this seems to be fairly widespread and conclusive. Dewey, as we shall see later, has been adopted by the naturalists. S. C. Pepper[22] has applied pragmatism to a contextualistic metaphysics; Sidney Hook[23] has absorbed it in his dialectical materialism; Charles Morris[24] has incorporated it into a general theory of signs, insisting that one "dimension" of a sign is the pragmatic one. Even the logical positivists, who will be considered in greater detail later, have, in the spirit of pragmatism, turned away from speculative metaphysics, have recognized that language has an emotive function, and would be willing in the end, I think, to admit that their own investigation into the nature of signs and sign-functioning has an ultimate practical value in the elimination of obscurity and in the final advancement of science. Indeed, some of those who disavow pragmatism have themselves adopted a position which suggests that strong pragmatic influences have played upon them. For example, A. E. Murphy, although admitting that he has never considered pragmatism to be even plausible,[25] has, in his "objective relativism," not only hit upon one of those fortunate phrases which (like R. B. Perry's "ego-centric predicament," Santayana's "animal faith," and Whitehead's "fallacy of misplaced concreteness") captivate the philosophic mind, but characterized what seems to be the essential goal of pragmatism, *viz.*, the consideration of all things functionally, and the objective description of the laws according to which things are thus relative. The most conclusive bit of evidence, however, lies in the fact that pragmatism has never been a unified movement. Lovejoy's now famous article,

22. *World Hypotheses* (Berkeley, University of California Press, 1942).
23. *American Philosophy Today and Tomorrow*, pp. 205-25.
24. *General Theory of Signs*, (Chicago, University of Chicago Press, 1938).
25. *American Philosophy Today and Tomorrow*, p. 362.

"The Thirteen Pragmatisms,"[26] called attention in a pointed manner to this fact. One could hardly expect a movement with so many independent strands to survive for a very long time.

In a similar vein there are many who would claim that idealism has suffered a decline in recent years—eclipsed, perhaps, by naturalism. The evidence for this is far from conclusive. To be sure, the cooperative study in idealism[27] was published sixteen years ago while that in naturalism[28] is only four years old, and several of those who contributed to the former volume have already retired from teaching. Thus it is easy to think of the latter movement as having the vigor and promise that are lacking in the former. But an argument on such insecure grounds as these could be countered by an equally superficial claim that as age indicates wisdom so idealism represents a more mature outlook which many naturalists may be expected to adopt when their experience has been properly rounded out. Furthermore, in terms of contemporary periodical literature the naturalists seem to be more active than the idealists. But again one cannot overlook the fact that a comprehensive and systematic study of idealism[29] has appeared in recent years which has no parallel among the writings of the naturalists. Add to these the facts that the moral idealists are still strong in our midst, the personalists are represented in large numbers, and Whitehead can in many respects be considered an idealist,[30] and one comes out with the somewhat lame conclusion that it is only absolute idealism, never too significant in American thought, which seems to be on the wane.

At any rate one cannot adequately characterize the period without calling attention to the cooperative study in idealism mentioned above. Some of the articles in this volume are essentially historical in character, and the one by G. W. Cunningham, which is an excellent analysis of the meaning situation, does not necessarily commit one to the idealistic position. W. E. Hocking and J. E. Boodin are the only absolutists in the group. J. A. Leighton and E. S. Brightman argue for a pluralistic idealism, emphasizing the reality of the individual rather than of any social whole in which selves are merged. Considerations of value constitute the dominant theme of the volume. W. E. Urban, R. A. Tsanoff,

26. *Journal of Philosophy,* Vol. V, Nos. 1, 2 (Jan. 2, 16, 1908).
27. *Contemporary Idealism in America,* edited by Clifford Barrett (New York, The Macmillan Co., 1932).
28. *Naturalism and the Human Spirit,* edited by Y. H. Krikorian (New York, Columbia University Press, 1944).
29. *Nature of Thought,* by Brand Blanshard, 2 vols. (London, Allen & Unwin, 1939).
30. R. F. A. Hoernlé argues this convincingly in *Contemporary Idealism in America,* chap. xii.

and C. W. Hendel all argue along independent though compatible lines that the pursuit of values becomes meaningless unless they have some cosmic status. "Of these values most modern thinkers are quite ready to say that they are *there* in some sense. With the exception of a few whose notions of being and existence still move within the circle of the ideas of scientific positivism, there are none for whom values are merely subjective states."[31]

While it seems safe to say that naturalism is today a dominant philosophy in America, such an assertion carries with it no implication of a general adherence among naturalists to a specific point of view. There is great variety in the interpretations of this word, and even among those most willing to use it there is the frank admission, as in the case of J. H. Randall, Jr., that naturalism is "not so much a system or body of doctrine as an attitude and temper; it is essentially a philosophic method and a program."[32]   Most of those connected with the movement are willing to admit that it arose out of the earlier nineteenth century materialism, and that it still has much in common with this point of view. The strong influence of Santayana[33] is granted by all its adherents. But it has attempted, as Dewey clearly indicates,[34] to rid "matter" of its base significance. Paralleling this it has reacted vigorously against supernaturalism, which seems to have contaminated thought. Hence the contenders claim that their task is also to rid "spirit" of its otherworldliness. The arguments here are simple and convincing. If belief rests on a supernatural source of knowledge, both science and morality are impossible. S. P. Lamprecht is the only contributor to the cooperative volume who ventures to give a definition of the term. It means for him "a philosophical position, empirical in method, that regards everything that exists or occurs to be conditioned in its existence or occurrence by causal factors within one all-encompassing system of nature, however 'spiritual' or purposeful or rational some of these things and events may in their functions and value prove to be."[35]   The most controversial issue among the naturalists is, perhaps, that of "levels" or "emergents," and centers about the question whether "mind" can be "reduced" to "life," and "life" to "matter." In general the naturalists are anti-reductionists.

---

31. Urban, *loc. cit.,* p. 128.
32. *Naturalism and the Human Spirit,* p. 324.
33. *Life of Reason,* 5 vols., 1905-6; *Scepticism and Animal Faith,* 1923; *Realm of Essence,* 1927; *Realm of Matter,* 1930; *Realm of Truth,* 1938; *Realm of Spirit,* 1940; all published by Scribners, New York.
34. *Naturalism and the Human Spirit,* pp. 1-16.
35. *Ibid.,* p. 18.

Our problem is somewhat easier when we pass from movements to individuals — easier, that is, once the problem of selection has been solved. This is a difficult matter and one which I have attempted to handle, as I have already said, by admitting that my principle of selection is more or less completely arbitrary. Why Whitehead and Peirce should be chosen and others neglected must remain unexplained. To be sure, it is always better to select a man who has already died, for he acquires a certain immortality, strange to say, by the mere act of dying; but this is hardly a sound season for my selection. As for the other important figures in the period, I can only hope that the remaining essays in this volume will do them proper justice.

Some will claim, and with a certain amount of reason, that Whitehead is not truly an American philosopher. In terms of birth, of course, he was not; perhaps also in terms of residence, since he did not come to this country until he was 63. But measured by his influence during his twelve years at Harvard and after his retirement, he is entitled to first consideration among American philosophers. Whatever one may say about the obscurity of his writings, he has left his mark on all schools of philosophy — idealists and realists, intellectualists and intuitionists, rationalists and empiricists — and he has occupied a position which is almost unique in American philosophy in the way in which he has influenced views of such non-philosophical groups as scientists, theologians, and educators. Although his early studies were in logic and mathematics, his later writings were directed largely against the quantitative, "paving-block" theory of the universe according to which it was considered to be made up of hard, instantaneous, independent lumps of matter. A more adequate theory, he insists, is one which considers process and inter-relatedness to be the fundamental concepts. "In the place of the Aristotelian notion of the procession of forms, it has substituted the notion of forms of process."[36] Matter has been eliminated as a basic metaphysical category and the concept of event has taken its place. All events are sensitive to the existence of all others, the relationship being a kind of feeling. Thus life, the organism, with its three essential characteristics of self-enjoyment by appropriation, creative activity, and aim, i. e., its entertainment of the purely ideal as directive of the creative process, is the pattern for understanding nature.

C. S. Peirce, again, might rightly be denied mention in this essay, for

---

36. *Modes of Thought* (New York, The Macmillan Co., 1938), p. 192.

he died in 1914. But the posthumous publication of his collected works[37] brought him to the attention of the philosophical world and gave him the fame that was denied him in life. The many-sided character of his position has enabled him to exert influence in a number of philosophical channels. Though he is commonly known for his essay, "How To Make Our Ideas Clear,"[38] which is justly considered to have been the first clear-cut formulation of the thesis of pragmatism, his writings extend over the fields of metaphysics, logic, and theory of signs. His discussion of the categories is unfortunately couched in a terminology which is somewhat awkward; the three basic notions are "firstness" or quality, "secondness" or reaction, and "thirdness" or representation. These notions are tied in with his theory of signs, much of the terminology of which has now become an accepted part of the vocabulary of general semantics. His tychism, or theory of objective chance, has provided the anti-mechanists with a battery of arguments against the deterministic position which dominated thought during the nineteenth century.

Turning to the consideration of areas of study in which there has been significant progress during the last quarter-century, the field which has been characterized in this essay as the "philosophy of science" is, properly speaking, much more extensive than the label indicates. The phrase has here been used to designate all studies pertaining to symbolic logic and general theory of signs, and is meant to cover the major investigations of the logical positivists and of all those connected with the unity of science movement. The interrelations of these many studies make any consideration of them in independence of one another quite impossible.

While the philosophy of science was not in any sense a type of investigation which was novel or peculiar to this period, it did achieve for the first time a certain formulation and organization of its problems which had been previously lacking. I may modestly claim some small part in this activity since my *Introduction to the Philosophy of Science*[39] was, I believe, the first attempt to do this in a systematic manner in America. The movement has gained momentum, and the discipline is now recognized as an established one, courses in the subject being given in most of the large colleges and universities of the country. The attempt is made to look upon science much as science looks upon nature, and to examine critically its method, its presuppositions, and its broader impli-

---

37. *Collected Works*, 6 vols., edited by Charles Hartshorne and Paul Weiss (Cambridge, Harvard University Press, 1931-35).
38. *Popular Science Monthly*, 1878.
39. New York, The Macmillan Co., 1937.

cations for religion, society, politics, education, and general philosophy. A highly specialized branch of this study, symbolic logic and the philosophy of mathematics, developed rapidly during this period, and now has an extensive literature.[40]

Stemming from this same movement, there has been a greatly increased interest in the philosophy of language, semantics, and the general theory of signs. In many cases this interest has been strongest among teachers of English, of journalism, and of speech, and among psychologists and psychiatrists, who have been mainly concerned with language as a device for communication and with its possible role in the treatment of psychological abnormalities. Philosophers, on the other hand, have undertaken an analysis of signs in general, of which language is a special class, with reference to an attempted definition of "sign," a consideration of the possible modes or dimensions of meaning, and an endeavor to understand symbolic logic, art, science, moral behavior, and religion as special modes of sign-functioning.

Within the same general area logical positivism and the unity of science movement deserve mention. The logical positivists, who now seem to prefer to be called "logical empiricists," are those who stem from the *Wiener Kreis*—a group of men who organized in Vienna to discuss the broad area of problems lying between science and philosophy. Many of this group have come to the United States and have been active in continuing the movement and gaining further adherents. In its early stages their view was characterized by an anti-metaphysical attitude which antagonized many philosophers, but in its later developments a somewhat more generous criterion of meaningfulness has been admitted which prevents the too ready characterization of all metaphysical propositions as nonsense. Many of this school, together with others not identifiable with the group, have participated in the writing of the *International Encyclopedia of Unified Science*,[41] which is an attempt to interrelate the special sciences by bringing to light common methods and common presuppositions, and by establishing, so far as this is possible, a common vocabulary. To date only parts of the first and second volumes of this contemplated twenty volume work have been published.

The other area within which significant advances have been made in recent years, the theory of value, is, like the philosophy of science, not a new study. The publication of Urban's *Valuation, Its Nature and*

---

40. Books have appeared by Carnap, Quine, Tarski, Reichenbach, Lewis and Langford, and others.

41. Chicago, University of Chicago Press, 1938.

Laws,[42] though it antedates the period we are considering, was one of the first contributions to the field in this country. In this work the term, "axiology," was introduced,[43] and it is now preferred by many for the designation of the problems within this area. During the last twenty-five years an imposing list of books on the theory of value has been published,[44] and the number of articles in philosophical journals has indicated an even wider interest in the subject. In spite of the apparent progress in the solution of the problem, however, Dewey, in an article entitled "Some Questions About Value"[45] acknowledged his discouragement with the headway which was being made, and suggested that attention should be directed to the determination of the questions or issues fundamentally involved. As a preliminary listing he proposed the following: "I. What connection is there, if any, between an attitude that will be called prizing or holding dear and desiring, liking, interest, enjoying, etc.? II. Irrespective of which of the above-named attitudes is taken to be primary, is it by itself a *sufficient* condition for the existence of values? . . . III. Whatever the answer to the second question, is there anything in the nature of appraisal, evaluation, as judgment or/and proposition, that marks them off, with respect to their logical or their scientific status, from other propositions or judgments? . . . IV. Is the scientific method of inquiry, in its broad sense, applicable in determination of judgments and/or propositions in the way of valuations or appraisals?" Using these questions as a basis, a group of American philosophers is now engaged in the preparation of a cooperative volume which is designed to clarify, if not to answer them. This should do much to unify the consideration in this area and to indicate any progress which has been made in the last two decades.

III

In conclusion reference may be made to certain tendencies which are minor, perhaps, in character, and may be of no great significance in the total picture of American philosophy during this period. On the other hand they may prove, in the next few years, to have indicated significant trends.

Perhaps the most important of these is the apparent decline of interest in epistemology, using this term in its narrower sense. To be sure, this

---

42. New York, The Macmillan Co., 1909.
43. *Contemporary American Philosophy,* Vol. II, p. 361, footnote.
44. Selected items are given in the bibliography.
45. *Journal of Philosophy,* Vol. XLI, No. 17 (Aug. 17, 1944).

may be nothing more than the natural trough which could be expected to follow the crest of the huge epistemological wave which swept American philosophy in the earlier years of the century. During this period two cooperative volumes, *New Realism*[46] and the study in critical realism already mentioned in this essay, appeared, and there was much supplementary periodical literature. Since that time, however, interest seems to have waned. The main exceptions are the contributions of Lovejoy and McGilvary to the Carus Lectures, and some of the writings on naturalism listed in the bibliography. Many American philosophers have felt that concern with such issues was essentially a waste of time (Boodin calls it "the philosophical disease, psychologitis"),[47] but there has always been a certain group, whose number now seems to be decreasing, who considered that problems of this kind were basic to philosophy. Perhaps the most significant evidence of the decline is the fact that *Preface to Philosophy*,[48] a cooperative textbook in introductory philosophy prepared for use in the armed forces in the second war, contains no mention of this problem — a point which is striking since the subjectivism-objectivism controversy, whatever philosophers themselves have tended to think about it, has always been one of the most effective topics for stimulating student interest in the subject. Coincident, however, with the lessened interest in the problem of perception and the status of perceived objects, there is a much greater enthusiasm for the broader problems of method, well illustrated by Part I of Montague's *Ways of Knowing*.[49] This has also taken the general form of an interest in the methods of the natural and of the social sciences, and particularly in the possibility of the successful use of the scientific method in the study of values.

Finally, on the positive side, though here the evidence is still far from conclusive, there is an awakening of interest in the problem of the role of philosophy in the international situation. This is not by any means a new concern,[50] but it has been greatly stimulated by the recent war and particularly by the formation of UNESCO, which has as one of its acknowledged tasks the elimination of conflicts through increased under-

---

46. Holt and others (New York, The Macmillan Co., 1912).
47. Quoted by Schneider, *op. cit.*, p. 491.
48. By W. E. Hocking, Brand Blanshard, C. W. Hendel, and J. H. Randall, Jr. (New York, The Macmillan Co., 1946).
49. New York, The Macmillan Co., 1925.
50. Several good books in this area have already appeared. Among these are one by Hocking (*The Spirit of World Politics*, New York, The Macmillan Co., 1932) and three by R. B. Perry (*On All Fronts*, New York, Vanguard Press, 1941; *Our Side is Right*, Cambridge, Harvard University Press, 1942; and *One World in the Making*, New York, A. A. Wyn and Co., 1945).

standing of opposing cultural ideologies. One indication of this growing interest is the wide reception which has been given to F. S. C. Northrop's *Meeting of the East and West.*[51] Whatever one may say of the merits of this book it has encouraged many people, not otherwise disposed, to think about the problem of cultural conflicts. UNESCO is now defining its philosophy and formulating concrete projects for study,[52] and the new *Fédération Internationale des Sociétés de Philosophie,* organized at the Tenth International Congress of Philosophy in the summer of 1948, provides the means by which these projects may be administered. A few years ago there was appointed in the Eastern Division of the American Philosophical Association a Committee on International Cultural Cooperation, and plans are under way for nationalizing and enlarging this committee. In view of these events there is every reason to believe that the outstanding character of American philosophy in the next twenty-five years may be the concern for world understanding and the contribution which philosophy can make to this important issue.

SELECTED BIBLIOGRAPHY

CARUS LECTURES:

Dewey, John. *Experience and Nature.* Chicago, Open Court Publishing Co., 1926.

Lovejoy, A. O. *The Revolt Against Dualism.* Chicago, Open Court Publishing Co., 1930.

Mead, G. H. *The Philosophy of the Present.* Chicago, Open Court Publishing Co., 1932.

Cohen, M. R. *The Meaning of Human History.* LaSalle, Ill., Open Court Publishing Co., 1947.

Lewis, C. I. *An Analysis of Knowledge and Valuation.* LaSalle, Ill., Open Court Publishing Co., 1946.

COOPERATIVE STUDIES:

Adams, G. P., and Montague, W. P., editors. *Contemporary American Philosophy,* 2 vols. New York, The Macmillan Co., 1930.

Barrett, Clifford, editor. *Contemporary Idealism in America.* New York, The Macmillan Co., 1932.

---

51. New York, The Macmillan Co., 1946.
52. "A Philosophy for UNESCO," by Richard McKeon, *Philosophy and Phenomenological Research,* Vol. VIII, No. 4 (June, 1948).

Kallen, H. M., and Hook, Sidney, editors. *American Philosophy Today and Tomorrow*. New York, Lee Furman, 1935.

Farber, M., editor. *Philosophical Essays in Memory of Edmund Husserl*. Cambridge, Harvard University Press, 1940.

Krikorian, Y. H., editor. *Naturalism and the Human Spirit*. New York, Columbia University Press, 1944.

PRAGMATISM:

Hook, Sidney. *The Metaphysics of Pragmatism*. Chicago, Open Court Publishing Co., 1927.

Dewey, John. *The Quest for Certainity*. New York, Minton, Balch Co., 1929.

——————. *Art as Experience*. New York, Minton, Balch Co., 1934.

——————. *A Common Faith*. London, Oxford University Press, 1934.

——————. *Logic, the Theory of Inquiry*. New York, Henry Holt and Co., 1938.

IDEALISM:

Boodin, J. E. *Cosmic Evolution*. New York, The Macmillan Co., 1925.

Brightman, E. S. *A Philosophy of Ideals*. New York, Henry Holt and Co., 1928.

Urban, W. M. *The Intelligible World:Metaphysics and Value*. New York, The Macmillan Co., 1929.

Cunningham, G. W. *The Idealistic Argument in Recent British and American Philosophy*. New York, Appleton-Century Co., 1933.

Blanshard, Brand. *The Nature of Thought,* 2 vols. London, Allen and Unwin, 1939.

NATURALISM:

Sellars, R. W. *Evolutionary Naturalism*. Chicago, Open Court Publishing Co., 1922.

Drake, Durant. *Mind and Its Place in Nature*. New York, The Macmillan Co., 1925.

Sellars, R. W. *Philosophy of Physical Realism*. New York, The Macmillan Co., 1932.

Woodbridge, F. J. E. *Nature and Mind*. New York, Columbia University Press, 1937.

Pratt, J. B. *Naturalism*. New York, Oxford University Press, 1939.

Woodbridge, F. J. E. *An Essay on Nature*. New York, Columbia University Press, 1940.

A. N. WHITEHEAD:

Science and the Modern World. New York, The Macmillan Co., 1925.
Process and Reality. New York, The Macmillan Co., 1929.
Adventures of Ideas. New York, The Macmillan Co., 1933.
Modes of Thought. New York, The Macmillan Co., 1938.
Essays in Science and Philosophy. New York, Philosophical Library, 1947.

C. S. PEIRCE:

Chance, Love and Logic, edited by M. R. Cohen. New York, Harcourt, Brace and Co., 1925.
Collected Papers, edited by Charles Hartshorne and Paul Weiss, 5 vols. Cambridge, Harvard University Press, 1931-35.

PHILOSOPHY OF SCIENCE:

Carnap, Rudolf. *The Unity of Science*. London, Kegan Paul, Trench, Trubner, and Co., 1934.
——————. *Philosophy and Logical Syntax*. London, Kegan Paul Trench, Trubner, and Co., 1934.
Weinberg, Julius. *An Examination of Logical Positivism*. London, Kegan Paul, Trench, Trubner, and Co., 1936.
Benjamin, A. C. *Introduction to the Philosophy of Science*. New York, The Macmillan Co., 1937.
Neurath, Otto, ed. *International Encyclopedia of Unified Science*. Chicago, University of Chicago Press, 1938.
Morris, Charles. *Signs, Language, and Behavior*. New York, Prentice-Hall, Inc., 1946.
Werkmeister, W. H. *The Basis and Structure of Knowledge*. New York, Harper and Brothers, 1948.

THEORY OF VALUE:

Perry, R. B. *General Theory of Value*. New York, Longmans, Green, and Co., 1926.
Parker, D. H. *Human Values*. New York, Harper and Brothers, 1931.
Dewey, John. *Theory of Valuation*. Chicago, University of Chicago Press, 1939.

Lepley, Ray. *Verifiability of Value.* New York, Columbia University
    Press, 1944.
Pepper, S. C. *Digest of Purposive Values.* Berkeley, University of Calif-
    ornia Press, 1947.

THE HISTORY OF
PHILOSOPHY

George Boas [*]

It may seem surprising that in a country where the relations between philosophy, politics, education, and religion have been particularly intimate, there should have been so little interest in the history of philosophy. But that is only one of the many puzzles which confront the man who would try to understand the growth of civilization in the United States. For whereas jurists from Marshall to Holmes seem to have been impelled to indicate, though sometimes too briefly, the philosophic standpoint from which they made their decisions, the scientists on the whole seem to have been singularly uninterested in the problems of scientific method or of epistemology. Again the history of education in this country shows a steady awareness of the necessity of a philosophic basis for a pedagogical program; the history of art and of criticism shows almost none. If Americans from the start had been philosophic conservatives, the problem of how their ideas arose would naturally never have occurred to them. For they would have felt that their ideas had always been held by everyone, or at least all intelligent human beings. But even before the days of Jonathan Edwards, Americans who wrote books were radicals, innovators, schismatics, revolutionaries. An interest in the history of philosophy might have served to justify their new ideas, if only as the final discovery of a truth which for long ages had remained hidden. For it is one of the most familiar devices of the innovator to point out how after centuries of obscurantism the truth has finally burst forth in his brain.

But though the works of Stanley and Brucker were in existence before 1750 and were very well known in Europe, and that of Tennemann was completed before 1819, they do not seem to have been read in this country. None of these names occur in the index to the *Commonplace*

---

[*] Born in 1891. Studied at Brown, Harvard, and Columbia; Ph.D. University of California, 1917. Professor of the History of Philosophy, Johns Hopkins University. Author of *French Philosophies of the Romantic Period* (1925), *The Happy Beast in French Thought of the Seventeenth Century* (1933), *Essays in Primitivism and Related Ideas in the Middle Ages* (1948).

Book of Jefferson, who of all Americans might have been expected to read them, nor is either mentioned, so far as we have been able to discover, in the works of Emerson who had even stronger reason for exploring their contents. Curiously enough this lack of interest was not attributable to any dislike of books about the past. Two of the most popular books in the United States in the early years of our independence were Condorcet's *Esquisse* and Volney's *Ruins*. *The Decline and Fall,* again, was so widely read that by 1836 Harpers was publishing the fifth American edition.

Whatever the reason, it was not until the 1830's that sufficient interest was manifested in philosophy's past to warrant the publication of a history. The first to appear, as far as we know, was a translation of Cousin's introduction to the history of philosophy, made by H. G. Linberg in 1832 and published in Boston where the eclectic philosophy had an extraordinary vogue. In 1838 there appeared the first historical sketch written by an American, a work entitled *The Progress of Philosophy,* by the Maryland lawyer, Samuel Tyler. This work, written by a Baconian was an apology for the inductive method as understood by its author. It had the same weakness that so many other histories of ideas have had, the weakness that lies in a confusion between a history of what men actually have believed and that which they ought to have believed if only they had agreed with the historian. This weakness appeared also in the *Epitome of the History of Philosophy,* translated in 1842 by C. S. Henry, Cousin's disciple. With the sub-title, "Being the work adopted by the University of France for instruction in the colleges and high schools," it was a document which could be used to combat the transcendental heresy in those fields where the young American might be exposed to it. By the middle of the nineteenth century a series of historical works had begun to appear. Schwegler's *Umriss* (1856), McCosh's *The Scottish Philosophy . . . from Hutcheson to Hamilton* (1874), Dabney's *Sensualistic Philosophy of the XIXth Century Considered* (1875) appear to be the first three in this series. In 1876 Ueberweg's history had been translated by G. S. Morris and published with additions by Noah Porter, and the same year saw the appearance of what might be called the first general history of philosophy by an American, that by Joseph Haven, a member of the Scottish School.

But meanwhile there had risen in Saint Louis that extraordinary group of writers known as the Saint Louis Hegelians. From 1867 to 1893 W. T. Harris published and edited the *Journal of Speculative Philosophy* which, because of the industry and eloquence of its writers, if not because of the intrinsic merit of its articles, did more than any other one publication to stimulate an enthusiasm for German idealism. For though *The Dial,* the organ of the Concord Transcendentalists, had brought to the public of the Eastern seaboard ideas which were similar to those of the Hegelians in some ways, its metaphysics was unsystematic and its style that of dilettantes, not that of scholars. Hegel by 1867 had been dead for over thirty years, so that the articles which appeared in the *Journal* might be termed historical at least in the sense that they were dealing with the past. But they were also historical in Hegel's peculiar sense, in that they situated whatever notions they might be expounding in a given moment in the dialectical history of the Spirit. Those American philosophers who read and believed in the articles of the Journal must have been numerous, for it took only another generation for American philosophy as taught in colleges—and what other American philosophy was there?—to become almost entirely Hegelian or Neo-Hegelian. It was thus no longer possible for any student of the subject to escape this influence. By the end of the century one was either an Hegelian or some form of evolutionary naturalist, though here and there were found certain individuals who called themselves Personalists. The influence of the Personalists upon the historiography of philosophy was to all intents and purposes *nil;* the evolutionary naturalists were looked upon as Positivists were looked upon by Cousin's Regiment. It was the Hegelians who predominated. At Cornell under Creighton, at Johns Hopkins and Michigan under Morris, one of whose most distinguished pupils was John Dewey, at Harvard under Royce, at Yale under Porter and then Ladd, students were indoctrinated with German idealism in such a persuasive manner that any other species of philosophizing was made to seem to them somewhat naive, if not worse. It was inevitable that a school which believed in the appearance of the Absolute in intellectual history should encourage the study of the past. But on the whole little was done to re-read the philosophers of the past, to edit their writings, or to reinterpret their ideas. To this very day, for that matter, the text-books in the history of philosophy follow the general outline of Hegel's *History* even when they omit Hegel's reason for that outline.

In the 1890's were published two works whose influence, even if one judge only by the numbers of their editions, must have outweighed that of any other historical studies. One was Tuft's translation of Windelband's history of philosophy (1893), the other Royce's *Spirit of Modern Philosophy* (1892). We do not agree either with the method of historiography or with the interpretation of doctrine which these two books illustrate, but enough people have agreed with both to set a fashion in intellectual history which still obtains. That fashion consists (1) in breaking the history of philosophy into periods, which (2) are dominated by a certain "spirit," and (3) are arranged in accordance with the prescriptions of the Hegelian dialectic, so that (4) those conflicts of ideas which are as characteristic of a time as harmony of thought are minimized, if mentioned at all, and (5) each man, as well as each period, must be interpreted as "really" a member of a philosophic school, the name of which ends in "ism," with the result that (6) a distinction is made between the profound thinkers who built elaborate systems and the shallow thinkers who often took a limited problem and attempted to settle it before moving on to grander constructions. The erudition of both Windelband and Royce was of course very great and it would be the height of presumption to accuse them of superficiality. But the philosophic prejudices of both men were compulsive in forming their judgements and one of their prejudices was precisely to form judgements.

Since Windelband is not an American historian except in translation,[1] we shall confine ourselves here to Royce's *Spirit of Modern Philosophy*. This work originated in a series of lectures delivered before philosophic amateurs and repeated several times. The object of the series was, as its author says, twofold. On the one hand, it dealt "not so much with the minuter details as with the connections, the linkages, the general growths." On the other hand, it was "constructive as well as expository." That a series of authors has a "general growth," is not at all self-evident, and the general growth might be interpreted in at least two ways: (1) that as was the case with the so-called British Empiricists, successive thinkers accepted the conclusions of their immediate predecessors and drew new implications out of them, or (2) that there was a kind of logical entelechy in a philosophic tradition which was realized step by step. It was the latter which directed Royce's thinking as it had Hegel's. The entelechy was, it is not surprising to learn, Royce's own philosophy. But what is surprising is his thought that by showing its steady emergence in history gives it a firmer basis than what he called "the dialectical fashion" could give it. Other philosophers, primarily Aristotle, had used the history of philosophy to show that their predecessor had been mistaken, but who before the Hegelians had assumed, for it was an assumption, that history had a direction and that the direction was Truth?

It is not clear from Royce's text whether he meant that the truth, as

---

1. And since I have expressed my opinion about his method in some detail elsewhere— see *Naturalism and the Human Spirit,* ed. by Y. Krikorian (New York, 1944), pp. 135 ff.

in Hegel, transcended the individual philosophies of the past and was being uncovered step by step as had been maintained by Philo, the Montanists, and Lessing, to mention only three different proponents of such a theory, or whether he thought that, for reasons which he does not state, each thinker discovered some truth and that his successors by grasping it could gradually build up a more inclusive truth. The development of Euclidean geometry would be an illustration of the former situation. Omitting for purpose of discussion the question of the relevancy of geometry to fact, it could be easily shown that at different times individuals discovered proofs of new theorems and that body of theorems which had been demonstrated was all that one meant by the science. Thus it has been maintained that God revealed certain truths to the Jews, more truths to the Christians, and final truths to the Joachites. An illustration of the second situation might be, but one cannot be sure, the development of Newtonian physics in which physical law became more general, being modified in order to describe more phenomena. Just what Royce meant cannot be settled, for like other members of his school, he believed in something called "synthesis" which was quite different from what he disdained above all else, "mere eclecticism." Now synthesis, as all readers of this essay already know, was not the collecting of a group of true propositions and the rephrasing of them by means of a unified vocabulary. On the contrary, a synthetic philosophy, in the Hegelian if not in the Spencerian sense, included contradictory propositions. How this was possible has never, as far as we know, been satisfactorily explained, and indeed in the United States people have largely given up the attempt to explain it. It seems at this date almost incredible that anyone should have believed in the possibility of history's producing a series of inconsistent propositions whose inconsistency did not prevent their being "coherent." But incredible or not, such was the case.

In spite of Royce's methodological weakness, he had a shrewd sense of historical fact. For instance, he refused to begin his modern philosophy with the Cartesian *cogito* for, as he quite correctly said, Descartes "was himself best known to his contemporaries, not for his theory of knowledge, but for his physical and metaphysical system." It was therefore the opinion of one's contemporaries which determined the nature of a period for though Royce's absolutism could be traced back to Descartes, as some idealists still trace their philosophy to the *cogito,* to do so would be to select from the Cartesian corpus a doctrine which did not seem of paramount importance at the time it was pronounced. Modern philosophy was that philosophy in which Royce believed. The only philosopher of the seventeenth century who could be called an absolutist was of course Spinoza and it was therefore with Spinoza that he began. But oddly enough in the very paragraph in which he announces his selection of Spinoza and the reasons for it he also says, "The seventeenth century was not on the whole a period of subjectivism, but the very reverse." This being so, why did he not start his history of modern philosophy with the reverse of subjectivism? The answer clearly is that to produce the synthesis of past doctrines into present doctrines, as it is exhibited in history, one must first decide what present doctrines are the pre-eminent doctrines of our time and, second, look in the past for something which might seem to foreshadow them. It is probably true in the seventeenth century no one saw any thing in the *Ethics* resembling post-Kantian idealism. Indeed it was not until the early nineteenth century that certain German romanticists began to see in Spinoza one of their forerunners. The historian is thus confronted at the outset of his task by the necessity of asking himself what his main problem is, whether it is that of showing how present ideas emerged out of the past or that of showing in general what the past believed in. These would appear to the writer of these lines to be two different problems, not to be reconciled nor reduced to one.

Royce, however, was in no doubt about this question. He knew the truth and he knew that some of his contemporaries were in error. His problem was not to show the history of error but that of truth. But his metaphysical theory led him to believe that no one was either completely right nor completely wrong. He must show in his history how truth gradually emerged from error. He therefore divided modern history into three periods, to which he gave in chronological order the names of "naturalistic," "humanistic," "idealistic." The first was chiefly concerned with the external world of nature, the second began to turn its attention to the inner world, the third synthesized the inner and the outer worlds in philosophy as man's dual nature is synthesized in man's life. Our own period, said Royce, quoting Ibsen's *Emperor and Galilean,* is that in which "Caesar shall become a spiritual, God an earthly ruler," in which nature and spirit shall be fused into one. Few sentences could better illustrate the profound dislike of multiplicity nor the unhappy vanity of prophecy than this.

Royce's book continued to be the outstanding work produced by an American philosopher until the influence of A. O. Lovejoy began to make itself felt. Lovejoy's contributions to the history of ideas were made in form of separate articles which began to appear as early as 1904. His interests have been as broad as they are numerous. He has contributed to the history of Greek philosophy, of evolutionism, Kantianism, romanticism, pragmaticism, naturalism, to cite only those themes which appear most frequently in his bibliography. His book, *The Great Chain of Being,* his studies of primitivism in its various forms, have succeeded in exhibiting to scholars fields of research which had been so neglected that they never occurred in the traditional histories. The complex of ideas which has been named "primitivism," though closely allied with another theme of equal importance, man's appraisal of man, appears in one form or another in literature, painting, ethics, politics, religion, and education, and yet awaited the twentieth century until it found its historians. In reading Lovejoy's books and essays, it must have struck the attention of more than one scholar that the "persistent problems of philosophy" had been selected out of the totality of problems simply through the inertia of custom and that the word "philosophy" covered a number of problems which seldom got into the histories at all.

But Lovejoy's contribution was not simply the discovery of new topics of research. He has a technique of his own which was novel when first utilized and which, though attempts have been made by students of literary history to adopt it, has not had its full effect upon historians of philosophy. This technique can best be found expressed and exemplified in his recently published *Essays in the History of Ideas.* [2] In the preface to that volume he points out the following "*general* or frequently recurring phenomena in the history of ideas." 1. "The presence and influence of the same presuppositions or other operative 'ideas' in very diverse provinces of thought and different periods." The best illustration of this is the occurrence of "nature," "the natural," and terms derivative from them as normative terms. 2. "The role of semantic transitions and confusions, of shifts and ambiguities in the meanings of terms, in the history of thought and of taste." He himself gives as an illustration of these shiftings and confusions the semantic history of the word "romantic," a history which he has done so much to clarify. 3. "The internal tensions or waverings of the mind of almost every individual writer . . . arising from conflicting ideas or incongruous propensities of feeling or taste, to which . . . he is susceptible." By the tendency which historians have to unify and to reconcile these waverings, authors are made to stand for a set of ideas which in reality they did not stand for and thus to overlook what to Lovejoy has been "precisely the most interesting

---

2. A collection of articles which had originally appeared in various periodicals from 1916 to the present.

and most noteworthy fact" about them, namely the influence upon them of diverse and even conflicting ideas and "the dim emergence in [their] thinking of new ideas destined to be seized upon and made much of by [their] successors."

Lovejoy has thus invited historians' attention, both by exhortation and by example, to the diversity of the thoughts which orient a man's philosophy and also to the complex influence of both thought and what, for want of a better term, must be called feeling. The sentences in which philosophers express their theories are so phrased that they seem purely descriptive, but as a matter of fact, it turns out that their apparently descriptive terms are often also normative. Thus such words as *nature, unity, eternal,* and since the nineteenth century, *variety, creative, spontaneous,* are eulogistic, *unnatural, multiple, temporal* and so on, pejorative. For instance when an ancient writer points out that a certain practice is in accordance with nature, he is usually praising it as well as describing it. So, after the theories of evolutionism began to influence a wide public, it became better to be creative than not to be creative, to be dynamic rather than static. The question of why one of these alternatives was better than the other was seldom, if ever, raised, for there seemed to be a tacit assumption in the minds of many metaphysicians that whatever "reality" might be, it must be good. That we are living in a world which is thoroughly evil and hostile to the realization of human ideals has occurred to few occidental thinkers and even those who seem to have entertained that possibility, like Schopenhauser, provided an escape from this world into another more real and hence better.

The influence of Lovejoy is at the present time greater than that of Royce, for if one use these names to indicate tendencies in historiography, there appears to be a greater willingness on the part of Americans to write down what they discover and not to read into their authors what they "must have meant." The great weakness of the idealistic historian was a preconconceived idea of the course of intellectual history according to which every man stands for or expresses a moment in the revelation of *The Idea.* There is no doubt that this technique has a kind of sublimity about it which makes the history of philosophy a moving panorama in which there is a goal and a grand design. Thus one can point out that Plato and Aristotle were items in the *praeparatio evangelium,* in spite of the fact that the writers of the Gospels had never heard of either of them. Or again, that because Hume aroused Kant from his dogmatic slumbers, and Rousseau in all probability pointed the way which the aroused sleeper might profitably take, Hume and Rousseau stand for two opposing

views which were destined to be reconciled in Kant. Such arrangements
of history can of course only be made after the facts. No contemporary
of Hume or Rousseau could have known the use to which Kant was to
put them, for if he had, he would have written the first two *Critiques.*

Such playful reading of texts could have done little harm in itself
but on the contrary much good, if it had limited itself to discovering the
anticipation of later views in earlier thinkers. It is certainly one of the
tasks of history to point out just such details. The real harm came from
the selective reading not only of individual authors, but of whole periods.
It is, for instance, next to impossible to fit French philosophies after Rousseau into any such scheme. And hence, as far as American manuals are
concerned, the French philosophers are noticeably absent.[3] It is curious
to find that few if any histories of philosophy written for the use of American undergraduates mention such people as Maine de Biran, Cournot,
Renouvier, or, to take a man whose influence was greater than his subtlety but nevertheless very great, Cousin. The whole French tradition
of the philosophy of science, to take another striking example, is usually
passed over in silence. No mention is made of the intimate relation between French philosophy and French literature and science and educational theory. Many of the French philosophers from the time of the
Encyclopedists to our own day have attempted to solve, or at least to
analyze, the problems which their daily lives presented. Since these
problems were not always identical with those which would arise from
a reading of Kant or Descartes, the men who occupied themselves with
them seem to have been considered unworthy of a place in a history of
philosophy which would not hesitate to include the names of a Geulincx
or a Wolff.

One of the problems confronting the historian is that of exegesis, and
their publications should be included the more compendious works of
late Paul Shorey and his students. Thanks to their studies our knowledge
of Plato and of Platonism has been greatly increased. In the series of
their publications should be included the more compendious works of
Harold Cherniss which should have led scholars to reconsider the Aristotelian interpretation of the Pre-Socratics, as well as of Plato himself. By
a meticulous study of the Aristotelian texts, Cherniss showed to the
satisfaction of some readers how anachronistic they were when they attempted to give an historical survey of the former and how unreliable.
The last chapter of *Aristotle's Criticism of Pre-Socratic Philosophy* sketches

---

3. The present writer, for instance, when he included them in a textbook, was harshly
criticized for wasting the students' time on unimportant thinkers.

a reconstruction of the Pre-Socratics which might well serve as prolego-menon for any future historian of philosophy. His second major work, *Aristotle's Criticism of Plato and the Academy,* has at the time of writing not been completed, only the first volume having been printed. But if one may judge from this much of the book, it too will reveal a Plato who has been disfigured by his disciple and who can be better understood, as might have been guessed, by a direct reading of the *Dialogues.*

One should also indicate in this connection the influence of F. J. E. Woodbridge of Columbia. Woodbridge's written work was not bulky. Aside from a few articles and his book, *The Son of Apollo,* there is little in print to show his imaginative insight or even his erudition. But the scholars whom he influenced are numerous and productive and his teach-ing inevitably traversed the lines of the university "departments." The place he will be given in future histories of American philosophy will no doubt be smaller than he deserves, unless his pupils, like those of Socrates perpetuate his teaching. Interestingly enough, some of them have joined with the associates of Lovejoy in what seems to the writer of this essay to be one of the most important developments in intellectual history, the publication of the *Journal of the History of Ideas.* What *Isis* and the bulletins of the *Institute of the History of Medicine* of the Johns Hopkins University have done for science, this journal has attempted to do for ideas in general. Having enlisted the abilities of such scholars as Marjorie Hope Nicolson, J. H. Randall, Chinard, Philip P. Wiener, and P. O. Kristeller as editors, it has enjoyed the collaboration of the most skillful and erudite of our historians. Its tables of contents are a revela-tion of what historical scholarship can do when it refuses to limit itself to the fields traditionally called "literature," "art," "politics," "economics," "philosophy," and the like. The articles which it has published are vivid proof that an idea traverses many fields, a thesis of Lovejoy, and that a term usually thought of as primarily philosophical may in fact have echoes in science, the arts, politics, or indeed wherever the human mind is at work. The cross-fertlization of human ideas is of special interest to philosophers since it gives us new information on the effect of ideas on life in general. For though limitations have to be set up when a man proceeds to solve a problem, limitations beyond which he will deliberately and arbitrarily refuse to go, yet the relevance of his ideas may and usually will spread well beyond these limitations. A standard example of this is the inter-relations between Claude Bernard, Zola, and Courbet. But one could just as fruitfully take any esthetic manifesto issued in France dur-ing the nineteenth or twentieth century and see in it the ingression of doctrines which originated in fields so remote from the esthetic that their sponsors would have been amazed by the use to which they had been put. What for instance is there in the original program of Freud which would justify surrealism? One might on the contrary have prophesied that a Freudian esthetic would be more like that which was preached by Schopenhauer and that an art *au service de la révolution* was an inherent absurdity. Again, the *mechanophila* of a painter like Leger might be justified by the predominance of the machine in twentieth century life. But on the other hand, one might as easily maintain that although we are dependent on machines for our industry, our play, and our warfare, the arts might very well take as their task the liberation of the human spirit from their domination. As a final example, it is certain that when Neo-classicism first appeared in the eighteenth century, it had no political overtones, that during the French Revolution, largely because of the prestiege of David, it began to take them on, and that finally in the School of Ingres it took on quite different ones. But this will be known by abandoning the idea of isolated doctrines pertinent solely to one field of interest and by looking for that interplay of ideas, feelings, tastes, which constitute the living heart of reflection.

There have been, moreover, certain ideas, habitually entertained by philosophers which have seldom been incorporated into the histories. The newer historians, here again thanks largely to Lovejoy, have been attempting to restore them to their rightful place. The field which is known as philosophic anthropology, for instance, might seem to be of primary importance for such interests as ethics and political philosophy, and yet one would look in vain for it in the histories written in the United States. Yet the differentia of man is a cardinal element in Plato and Aristotle; it determines the thinking of all the Christian philosophers; and though it has lost much of its interest for our contemporaries, it orients their thinking nevertheless. Any doctrine which implies that man should change his behavior must, in order to be effective, indicate the limits within which such changes are possible, must have as clear an idea as is attainable of what distinguishes human behavior from non-human, whether angelic or animal.

Man's appraisal of man is a second problem whose history might have been expected to occupy a certain place in histories of philosophy. For from Hesiod to our own day, philosophers have had a very intense preoccupation with man's value. Here Lovejoy and his collaborators and colleagues have made their contribution and the series of works on primitivism and related ideas which have come from their research are testimony to the constant attention which philosophers have given to this question. For the legend of the Golden Age and the story of the Garden of Eden have been more influential than any two other themes in causing men to reflect upon their civilization, the values which they and their contemporaries have been seeking to realize, and to accept or reject the societies in which they were living. The Christian contempt for the world is paralleled by the pagan's self-sufficiency, though the motivation behind the two drives would seem to be far from identical, for the pagan had nothing in his tradition which would give him the motive of penance.

But the most surprising omission in histories of philosophy is that of what has been called the *protophilosophies*. Before a man can begin to think, he must have a set of premises, basic metaphors, syntactical rules, and so on, to guide him and give structure to his inferences. He must have some notion, more or less clear, of what he is trying to prove before he can set out to prove it. Interferences do not emerge automatically from premises. The rise of new problems, the retention of old, the development of a new technique of thinking, of those moulds of thought which produce such astonishing novelties in philosophy, should all be studied if a genuine history of philosophy is ever to be written.[4] To take but one example, where can one find the story of the rise and spread of the hierarchical method of thought? We know that there are adumbrations of a logical hierarchy of classes in Aristotle, possibly—though only possibly—in Plato, but the enormous extension of this technique from logic to value-theory in general, including politics and morals, is something whose history has yet to be written.

The question arises, as a matter of fact, whether there is any utility in attempting a general history of philosophy. From one point of view one could introduce the study of philosophy as a whole by a history of the meaning of the term itself, of its almost universal denotation in the early days, of its gradual narrowing down to denote a few disciplines like those of metaphysics and logic, and finally in our own times its shift from meaning a subject matter to meaning a method. Such a history if worked out in detail, would of course be a useful and indeed a novel work. But as the term is generally used by historians, it covers a field of inquiry so wide, that no one man could do it justice. It is moreover, plausible that there is no necessary connection between such disciplines as metaphysics and esthetics, between ethics and politics, whatever historical connections may have existed. Would it not be more profitable to take up

---

4. Obviously "genuine" can only mean "of interest to me."

the separate problems one by one and study their history instead of assuming a necessary linkage between them and calling the collection "philosophy?" The profit would reside in the information which we should have of the actual workings of the human mind. We should be given the material for real self-criticism, for it is only by seeing in detail the assumptions on which a set of beliefs rests that one can completely evaluate the system. Most philosophers can be credited with the ability of reasoning consistently. It is the assertions which they hold to be self-evident that require scrutiny and which when scrutinized turn into conventions which might be established by custom, which might have a pragmatic value, which might harmonize with such a science as, for example, Newtonian physics, but which would have to be revised to harmonize with that of Einstein.

It may, to be sure, be denied by those philosophers who believe in the perennial philosophy that profound changes in the ways of thinking are possible. It is our opinion that they are not only possible, but they have occurred within the limits of recorded western philosophy. We should maintain that the rise of statistical thinking is such a change and that the as yet undeveloped logic of events is another. But this paper is no place to discuss such moot points and we shall be satisfied with having raised the question. In any case, the only way to discover whether there has been such a change is to study the protophilosophies of the philosophers of the past.

This consideration brings us to our final question. Is it possible to write the history of philosophy from a philosophically neutral standpoint? Before this question is answered, it would appear reasonable to answer the following questions:

1. What is the relation of ideas to their subject matter?

2. What is the relation of philosophical ideas to non-philosophical?

3. What is the relation of philosophical ideas to what can best be called "action?"

These three questions would seem to us to be fundamental to the more inclusive problem of why men change their minds. For if they are answered, we shall know what part the biographical factor, the socio-economic factor have to play in the formation of philosophies. But besides these three questions there are others which will determine the kind of history which we shall write.

4. Is the historian to consider time as purely phenomenal or is he to consider it as irreducible to anything else?

5. Upon what principle of selection shall the historian choose those philosophers to whom he will devote much space? Shall it be their influence upon others, their breadth of interest, their originality, their critical power?

6. In selecting those parts of a given philosopher's writings which are to figure in a history, should one choose those which seemed of importance to his contemporaries or those which became of interest after his death?

These are but a few of the problems which confront one who would attempt to write a general history of philosophy and they must be added to those which have been raised earlier in this paper. It does not seem feasible to us to answer them in such a fashion that one will satisfy everyone, for none of them can be answered without previously taking a definite philosophic position. One is involved in epistemological considerations before one begins. And who would be rash enough to assert that his particular epistemological theory would prove satisfactory to even a small fraction of his colleagues? The histories of the Hegelians have become so familiar to us in America that their mode of exposition, their principle of selection, their formulation of problems, their grouping of philosophers into periods and schools, seem the natural and sound technique to follow. But it requires only a minimum of reflection to see clearly that we have substituted habit for necessity or have perhaps followed the easiest way rather than the most fruitful.

SELECTED BIBLIOGRAPHY

(This list gives only books, not articles, and, with the exception of the earlier period, only those books which in the opinion of the compiler had a certain influence. Translations are not included.)

Tyler, S. *The Progress of Philosophy*. Philadelphia, J. B. Lippincott and Co., 1838.

McCosh, James. *The Scottish Philosophy, Biographical, Expository, Critical, from Hutcheson to Hamilton*. New York, R. Carter and Brothers, 1874.

Dabney, R. L. *Sensualistic Philosophy of the Nineteenth Century Considered*. New York, 1875.

Frothingham, O. B. *Transcendentalism in New England*. New York, G. P. Putnam's Sons, 1876.

Haven, Joseph. *A History of Philosophy, Ancient and Modern*. New York, Sheldon and Co., 1876.

Price, E. K. *Some Phases of Modern Philosophy*. Philadelphia, 1878..

Rand, Benjamin. *Tables of Philosophy*. Cambridge, 1882.

Holland, F. M. *The Rise of Intellectual Liberty from Thales to Copernicus*. New York, Henry Holt and Co., 1885.

Burt, B. C. *A Brief History of Greek Philosophy*. Boston, Ginn and Co., 1889.

Burt, B. C. *A History of Modern Philosophy*. Chicago, A. C. McClurg and Co., 1892.

Royce, Josiah. *The Spirit of Modern Philosophy*. Boston and New York, Houghton, Mifflin and Co., 1892.

Osborn, H. F. *From the Greeks to Darwin*. New York and London, The Macmillon Co., 1894.

White, Andrew D. *History of the Warfare between Science and Theology*. New York, D. Appleton and Co., 1896.

Clodd, Edward. *Pioneers of Evolution from Thales to Huxley*. New York, 1897.

Jones, A. L. *Early American Philosophers*. New York, The Macmillan Co., 1898.

Rogers, A. K. *Student's History of Philosophy*. New York and London, The Macmillan Co., 1901.

Albee, E. *History of English Utilitarianism*. London, Sonnenschein and Co.; New York, The Macmillan Co., 1902.

Turner, W. *History of Philosophy*. Boston and London, Ginn and Co., 1903.

Shorey, Paul. *The Unity of Plato's Thought*. Chicago, University of Chicago Press, 1903.

Riley, I. W. *American Philosophy; the Early Schools*. New York, Dodd Mead, and Co. 1907.

Perrier, J. L. *The Revival of Scholastic Philosophy*. New York, The Columbia University Press, 1909.

Hibben, J. G. *The Philosophy of the Enlightenment*. New York, Charles Scribner's Sons, 1910.

Taylor, H. O. *The Mediaeval Mind*. London, The Macmillan Co., 1911.

Fuller, B. A. G. *The Problem of Evil in Plotinus*. England, Cambridge University Press, 1912.

Thilly, F. *History of Philosophy*. New York, Henry Holt and Co., 1914.

Marvin, W. T. *History of European Philosophy*. New York, The Macmillan Co., 1917.

Robinson, J. H. *The Mind in the Making*. New York and London, Harper and Brothers, 1921.

Rogers, A. K. *English and American Philosophy since 1800*. New York, The Macmillan Co., 1922.

Randall, J. H., Jr. *The Making of the Modern Mind*. Boston and New York, Houghton, Mifflin Co., 1926.

Parrington, V. L. *Main Currents of American Thought*. New York, Harcourt, Brace and Co., 1927.

Schneider, H. W. *The Puritan Mind*. New York, Henry Holt and Co., 1930.

Lovejoy, A. O., and Boas, G. *A Documentary History of Primitivism and Related Ideas*. Baltimore, Johns Hopkins Press, 1935.

Lovejoy, A. O. *The Great Chain of Being*. Cambridge, Harvard University Press, 1936.

Ekirch, A. A., Jr. *The Idea of Progress in America, 1815-1860*. New York, Columbia University Press, 1944.

Schneider, H. W. *A History of American Philosophy*. New York, Columbia University Press, 1946.

Lovejoy, A. O. *Essays in the History of Ideas*. Baltimore, Johns Hopkins Press, 1948.

IDEALISM IN AMERICA

H. G. Townsend*

A philosophical vocabulary is notoriously lacking in precision. As yet no remedy has been discovered. If a technical or quasi-scientific language is invented, it narrows the range of discourse to an esoteric few who eventually find that they have little or nothing to say even to each other. The other alternative is to use the common language of history and literature and thus court the disaster of vagueness. Every writer has to use to the best of his ability a more or less intelligent compromise between these two extremes. Perhaps no common philosophical term has been more abused than "idealism." It has had a long history and has been defined in so many contexts that it must of necessity be defined again and again. The popular use of the term is especially misleading. More often than not it is taken as a synonym for any ill-grounded hypothesis which appears to common sense to have in it more of hope than it does of observation. Idealism is, however, widely used in a less objectionable manner in conversation and literature to mean that beyond the objects of common experience there is to be discovered a world of meanings, relations, and objects not immediately presented to the senses. This use of the word has at its heart the sound discernment that idealism as a philosophy is deeply concerned with the humanistic problems of value, history, civilization, education, religion, etc.

In the more restricted language of philosophers idealism is a theory of the nature of being and knowing. Specifically it is the theory that the universe is some sort of an intelligible order and that insofar as men discover that order, they truly know. To whatever degree human knowledge is fragmentary, confused, contradictory, to that extent it is presumed to be unreliable. The value theory of idealism is more or less congruent with its logic and metaphysics. In such a definition an effort is made to find the common denominator rather than to enumerate the fractions.

---

* Born in 1885. Ph.D., Cornell University, 1913. He was the senior member of the department of philosophy in the University of Oregon, where he taught from 1926 to the time of his death in December 1948. He was the author of *Philosophical Ideas in the United States* (1934) and of periodical papers on philosophical topics. He did extensive work on the philosophy of Jonathan Edwards, and prepared a book for publication on *The Philosophy of Jonathan Edwards as found in his Private Notebooks.*

There are, of course, many fractions. Perhaps the most conspicuous of them all is the one that divides the ancient tradition of Platonism from the modern idealism of Descartes, Locke, Berkeley, and Hume. For the one ideas are discussed in the context of physics, astronomy, and mathematics, for the other ideas belong to the shadow world of dreams, images, impressions, and emotions, i.e., they are *mental phenomena*. The two are variously mixed in modern literature and hence idealism is often confused with solipsism or some other subjectivism. The proper name for this is probably "mentalism"—the theory that the mind is shut off from an objective world by an impenetrable screen of mental phenomena.

Jean-Paul Sartre has by indirection provided a very good definition of idealism in his definition of his own currently popular philosophy called "existentialism." He says, what all the "existentialists" have in common "c'est simplement le fait qu'ils estiment que l'existence précède l'essence, ou, si vous voulez, qu'il faut partir de la subjectivité." (*L'existentialisme est un humanisme*, p. 17.) For idealism it is essence which is logically prior to existence. This is a neat and fruitful definition of idealism. To one who has made the elementary distinction between temporal and logical priority Sartre's definition of his own philosophy is luminous and by the same token it should, by contrast, clarify the fundamental meaning of idealism. For the idealist, if anything whatsoever is given, it is an index of some reality beyond itself which the mind grasps, if at all, by processes of mediation. We might say, therefore, nothing given is essential rather than, with Santayana, that nothing given exists. (*Scepticism and Animal Faith*, chap. vii.) The context of Santayana's remark is a Cartesian-Lockean mentalism. The supposition of idealism on the contrary is that beyond any given object or event presented to our subjective perceptions there is an objective realm of essence to which the ostensible given is but indicative and subsidiary. The immediate is a sign and token of the mediate.

Because idealism is a recondite philosophy it suffers more distortion in popular interpretation than some others. Nevertheless, there is something in ordinary human experience to keep it alive and make it attractive to men generation after generation. It was a deep root of our colonial inheritance in the form of Christian Platonism. Practical Yankees were quite as idealistic as they were practical. There is no good ground for supposing that one of these traits is arrayed against the other. In fact the energies of men are marshalled and directed by the assumption, whether conscious or unconscious, that there is a structured realm of entities and values inclusive of the flux of man's joys and sorrows, and by reference to which they are significant.

New England transcendentalism was a resurgence of Platonism in the dress of Kant's newer fashion. But it was also a good example of the modern mixture of idealism and mentalism and did much to produce in America the confusion in the public mind of the one with the other.

A half-century after Emerson there were two leading exponents of American idealism: William James, the psychologist, and Josiah Royce, the logician. The fact that they were so intimately associated as colleagues at Harvard University sharpened the differences between them and tended to obscure the fact that they were both in the idealistic tradition. Their differences and their agreements are equally instructive, although scholars have given insufficient attention to the latter and have overemphasized the former. James took the mentalistic turn and developed the Lockean theme that ideas are whatever the mind makes its objects when it thinks. The *cul-de-sacs* of his epistemology multiplied until, as Locke had discovered that "the extent of our knowledge comes not only short of the reality of things, but even of the extent of our own ideas" (*Essay,* Bk. IV, Ch. 3), so James found himself shut off from the world and nature. How James sought escape from this predicament is no part of the present story. Royce did not find himself in the predicament because he had followed the older tradition of idealism by assuming, not that ideas are the objects of knowledge, but that they are signs within nature leading to the true object of knowledge, which is nature itself.

Idealism has been persistent in American philosophy though by no means always fashionable. Some fifty years ago, or about the turn of the century, it was definitely in the ascendent but, perhaps for that very reason, it underwent some very sharp criticism during the next two or three decades. The so-called revolt against idealistic philosophy came somewhat later here than in Europe but was similar in origin and followed the same general direction. First there was the spreading distrust of the idealist's ambition to see the universe in a single perspective. The influence of the empirical methods of science made a telling invasion into any complacent metaphysics. Many idealists had become complacent. They had come to rest in the conviction that the ultimate nature of things was an integrated system of intelligible relations and seemed to forget that this was a postulate rather than a demonstration. This complacency was compared, unfavorably, with natural science, with its diligent accumulation of detailed knowledge, its apparent modesty, its emphasis upon the tentative, the problematic, and the probable. This phase of the "revolt" was usually called "realistic" and it was implied that the idealists were "unrealistic." When idealists had found their voice, the answer was that realism is a game which all can play. In the perspective of history realism is in fact the search for, and confidence of finding, universal "reals" beyond particular instances; hence, said the idealists, it is we who are the realists and you who are the nominalists. Moreover, does it not appear that the modesty of science does in fact express a trust in the same principle of intelligibility to which the idealist appeals? What, for example, is "probability" without the supposition that there is a quasi-mathematical system as the standard of interpretation? There is no probable and no improbable in a world in which there is no order.

The second aspect of the "revolt" went under the name of pragmatism. Like its companion, "the new realisms," it was rooted in nineteenth century natural science but now specifically in biology. It was a resolution to think through the problems of philosophy in the spirit of the new discoveries made by Charles Darwin. It was a philosophy of the organism. Its dominant categories were "adjustment," "adaptation," "struggle," "hunger," "desire," "will." Its theory of knowledge and, beyond that, its theory of nature followed these assumptions.

When Royce died in 1916 he was the acknowledged spokesman for idealism in America. This does not mean that he was blindly followed by a company of disciples but only that his published expression of idealism was a fairly comprehensive doctrine in modern American idiom. He was authentically American and authentically idealistic. He had not only fairly faced the issues raised by the Darwinian biology but he had gone beyond to a competent handling of the more fundamental problems posed by the new mathematics. It was this which distinguished him amongst us. A generation only slightly younger than Royce continued in the same mood. In 1930 two volumes called *Contemporary American Philosophy, Personal Statements* were published. There were sixteen contributors to the first volume, ten of whom would be recognized as within the idealistic tradition; and practically all of them were much influenced, directly, by the work of Royce. In the second volume, however, the contributors were, by and large, younger, and of the eighteen perhaps three or four would be called idealists while the others were consciously nonidealistic. However slight the significance of these facts may be, they do provide a concrete symbol of a gradual recession of idealism in American philosophy of which every observer had been aware.

In 1932 a volume of essays entitled *Contemporary Idealism in Amer-*

ica appeared; it included interpretations by eleven individuals. Among them was R. F. Alfred Hoernlé, who was sufficiently identified with American scholarship by the fact that he had spent several years of teaching in our universities. The title of his essay, "The Revival of Idealism in the United States," is significant because it recognized that idealism here was finally on the defensive. He emphasized the importance of the work of A. N. Whitehead, but perhaps the underlying theme of his contribution was "What is living and what is dead in idealism."

Throughout its history idealism has been employed with the problem of mind and has frequently been called a philosophy of "spirit." But it is not on that account to be identified too closely with psychology, especially with the modern psychology as the empirical science of mental phenomena. It can no more be reduced to psychology in this sense than physics can be reduced to psychology. In both cases the object is paramount, however much its discussion involves subjective states of mind. The philosopher, like the physical scientist, addresses his inquiry to a *de facto* objective world. J. E. Creighton said somewhere that once and for all there is a world and we are in it. This must be the posture of any intelligent inquiry. Even when the mind becomes its own object the problem is still the nature of the object.

The incubus of British empiricism has plagued idealism throughout its modern history and at times has seemed about to transform it into romantic dreaming. For this reason many recent American idealists have insisted that they are *objective* idealists. Although the immediate historical context makes such a claim intelligible, it is misleading if it suggests that in fact in the longer perspective of history idealism as a philosophy may be either subjective or objective. In that long perspective it is unmistakably objective. The "ego-centric predicament," whatever it may be, is no more an embarrassment to the idealist than it is to anybody else. The objective world to which he looks presents not only private conscious phenomena but public action and communication as well. An objective idealist, then, is an idealist who finds it temporarily necessary to explain that, although idealism is interested in the mind and spirit of man, it is not taking refuge from the world in the dark chambers of the private self.

In the idealistic literature between the two World Wars was a significant book by George P. Adams, *Idealism and the Modern Age.* "Idealism," he says, "is the philosophy of solidarity, of possession, of the mind's knowledge of, and participation in, Reality" (p. 140). This quotation illustrates the tenor of the entire work — its insistence that idealism postulates an objective order by reference to which all questions of knowledge or value must be formulated and answered. This is the living heart of idealism, ancient and modern. Whatever minor twigs or branches may die, the root and trunk live on.

No insistence upon the dominant interest of idealism in a thoroughly objective world should be allowed to obscure the fundamental difference between idealism and naturalism. There is a latent dualism in the idealistic position. The philosophical problem differs from the scientific one. The philosophical problem is not only concerning nature or concerning the mind as a part of nature but concerning the mind *and* nature. This is, in short, the problem of how knowledge is possible. Following the spirit rather than the letter of Kant's question, Royce asks, "How is error possible?" The question may be put in a variety of ways without greatly altering its tantalizing paradox. It we study a natural science as if it had no past and no future, the sense of paradox may never develop. But this surely is a highly incredible supposition. *De facto* knowledge raises *de jure* considerations. There is no denying that a man may for a time innocently accept a belief or that he may continue indefinitely to act upon it; but such a trust is inherently unstable in the flux of experience and certainly implies something beyond itself as the condition of its credibility.

One of the distinguishing marks of idealism is therefore its treatment of the realm of mind. For it mental phenomena occur in a realm distinguishable from the realm of nature. But as nature in its entirety can hardly be a mere sum of natural objects, so the idealist insists that mental phenomena do not actually comprise or constitute the realm of mind. Mental phenomena, either severally or collectively, point beyond themselves not merely to other mental phenomena but to a texture of meanings and relations of which the *de facto* sensations, memories, emotions, and ideas are exploratory instruments or, perhaps more specifically, "signs." Mind therefore connotes, for the idealist, a realm of being.

The realm of mind is that in which *dialectic* acquires its distinctive and strict meaning. The word dialectic is frequently employed as a synonym for what psychologists call "rationalization." This is most emphatically not what the tradition of idealism in its use of the phrase "dialectical method" has intended. The dialectical method is a slightly pretentious name for rational inference. Rationalization is one thing and rational inference is quite another. The realm of mind is the realm of rational inference. Within that context there is a necessary distinction between immediate and mediate experience. What we see is not precisely what we discover. The activity of our minds is the process by which the immediately given in experience is transformed into that which is implied by experience. A thoughtful interpretation of data is not a datum.

The individual minds of men belong to the realm of mind in a way not wholly unlike that in which individual bodies belong to a physical realm. In neither case are the properties of the individual to be carelessly attributed to the realm of being to which they belong. In both cases there is this difference between the individual and the realm — the one is the given while the other is the implied. Realms of being are not data, at least in the usual and primary sense in which an observation is called a datum. They are systems of interpretation employed by the active intelligence in its effort to discover meaning. The rising and setting sun when observed evoke a cosmology which by no stretch of the imagination can be supposed to have the properties of the sun. It is not a sun but is hardly on that account to be dismissed from our consideration. It does not belong to the physical realm because it does not have the properties of bodies, but it does belong to a realm of meanings because it has the properties of an implicative system. Cosmologies along with histories, systems of government, art, and religion are integral aspects of what idealists call the realm of mind. They distinguish it from the physical realm because the relationships discoverable here are not such as those discovered in physics. In the physical realm bodies have certain relations to one another such as position, size, and number. In the realm of mind, however, it appears that the observed relations are very inadequately described by those categories. In general the categories appropriate to the realm of mind are categories of interpretation involving the use of signs, and of bodies only insofar as they are signs. Minds use, understand, modify, value, or otherwise interpret objects; they communicate with, love, hate, fear, emulate, cooperate with and resist other minds.

Perhaps no one in recent time has more adequately expressed this fundamental idealistic view than Professor George P. Adams. In his book, *Man and Metaphysics* (pp. 74-75), we read:

A small low-pressure area in the South Pacific is born, migrates eastward as it grows and gathers momentum and, in a few days, bursts with full-fledged fury over the entire Pacific area, and there thins out and loses itself in the encompassing atmosphere. Here is an individual episode in nature, compacted of moving air masses, temperature changes, condensations of vapor, and electrical disturbances, all presenting a pattern of events in space-time. But these moving energy transactions find no resonance in any experiences lived through by cloud and air. They do evoke experiences of hardship, suffering, and heroic toil in the workers who must keep trains running and the mountain passes open. The imaginative mind of a novelist, catching a sense of the human drama, will depict the course of the

storm as if it, too, were a drama. He personifies the storm, naming it
Maria. But the ingredients of the storm possess and live through no experiences as do the minds of men.

    Contrast this with another migration. Masses of men, women, and
children migrate westward from the arid dust bowl of Oklahoma. Here is a
human storm. The economist or social scientist will now play the role of
the meteorologist with respect to this social migration. Here are economic
pressures, "lows" and "highs," a massive disequilibrium the stresses and
strains of which cause upheaval and dislocations. But what a wealth of
meaning is here over and above any observed or inferred events and behavior!
Here are hopes and frustrations, anxieties and fears, retrospective memories
and prospective longings, things precarious and insecure. Not one of these
nouns or adjectives, or the meanings they denote, is applicable to cloud masses
or movements, as viewed within the perspective of the observer. The novelist
who depicts this human situation has no need of imagining it to be a drama
or tragedy. That is what it actually is, because it is compacted of human experiences and actions consciously lived through. There is no meaning nor
are there any values in moving air masses. There are motions in space and
time, and redistributions of energy. The moving masses of men hold and
incapsulate meanings and values, because here are minds, centers of conscious life and experience. Here, alone, are there any values, and meanings as well.

    Because of the emphasis which idealists have placed upon the dis-
tinguishing features of mind, idealism has often been closely associated
with certain religious doctrines, particularly with theistic doctrines such
as those of Christianity. And there is no denying the fact that idealism
has a more sustained interest in religion than do certain other types of
philosophical theory. It is deeply interested in religion because religion is
a pervasive human trait and provides many chapters in history. There
are strands of it in art and science and indeed in whatever other aspects
of culture anyone may choose to consider. So much is clear. Nevertheless, much confusion has arisen over the precise and detailed relation between idealism and Christianity.

    There is need of an elementary distinction between religion on the
one hand and theology or philosophy on the other. For good or for ill
philosophy is not a religion, for somewhat the same reason that a treatise
on human anatomy, physiology, and dietetics is not health. Philosophy
is primarily an intellectual or theoretical enterprise, while religion is
primarily a set of convictions, moral practices, habits, and forms of worship. This is not to argue that the two are unrelated but only that clear
thinking about them requires discrimination. As for theology, it is,
strictly speaking, a theoretical speculation concerning the nature of God
and hence a legitimate segment of philosophy.

    Christian theology is dominantly theistic, which for the philosopher
simply means that throughout its history the Christian religion has taught
that God is a person. The history of dogma is replete with the intricate
exposition of this central teaching. Idealists may or may not be theists.

Many idealistic writers sedulously avoid theology while others have their interest centered in that field. Of the latter one has only to recall the names of George Berkeley and the American philosopher and theologian, Jonathan Edwards. For Edwards "beings which have knowledge and consciousness are the only proper and real and substantial beings, inasmuch as the being of other things is only by these" (*Of Being*). With this as a foundation he was of course convinced that God is a being with "knowledge and consciousness."

Quite a number of contemporary idealists in America belong to this Christian tradition. Josiah Royce came very close to it in his conception of a self-representative system and even closer in his final book, *The Problem of Christianity*. A vigorous group of writers call themselves "personalists" to indicate that they subscribe to this doctrine. They trace their lineage back at least as far as the teaching of Borden P. Bowne, who was an older contemporary of Royce and James.

On the other hand, the so-called critical or objective idealists distrust the personalistic and theistic tendencies in philosophy. Though they are as convinced as their fellows that there is a realm of mind demanding its own appropriate categories, they are by no means ready to suppose that minds are "the only proper and real and substantial beings." An objective world order may be capacious enough to embrace a realm of mind along with a realm of matter or any number of other realms. They can entertain the theory that the universe is some kind of an intelligible order without supposing that it is a mind or that it is presided over by a personal God. They are closer to the Platonic tradition in philosophy than they are to the Augustinian. In some sense or other all categories may be categories of the mind, and yet it may not follow that mind has swallowed up the world. The abstract demonstration that objects appear only in the presence of subjects can hardly convince us that there were no objects until man came into existence. This is to confuse temporal with logical order.

It is neither possible nor appropriate to explore the arguments on either side of this debate but it is apparent that the objective idealists are seeking to reconcile an idealistic philosophy with the evolutionary hypothesis that the minds of men and animals have actually appeared long after the processes of nature had found expression in a physical and mechanical world. Emergent evolution is one theory advanced to account for the late appearance of mental phenomena, human history, and value. It is unwarranted to say that idealism must be identified with some kind of theistic doctrine.

The writing of Samuel Alexander, especially in his great work, *Space, Time, and Deity,* is an impressive attempt at evolutionary naturalism. Though he is usually considered a "realist," there is no feature of his philosophy which is essentially discordant with the central theme of idealism.

One of the most persistent idealistic doctrines is that of "levels of being." In one form or another it appears in all stages of the history of idealism from Plato to Bradley. The several categories need not be supposed to be on all fours with each other. A hierarchy of the categories may be supposed such that the later include and pass beyond the earlier and simpler ones. This theory, though often associated with Hegel, has both earlier and later expression in idealistic literature. In American philosophy excellent examples are found in C. S. Peirce and Royce—in Peirce the doctrine of "firstness, secondness, and thirdness," in Royce the doctrine of a "self-representative" system and the emergence of "interpretation and the use of signs."

In choosing to make meaning and the realm of mind its central theme, idealism must, I think, finally rest its claim to acceptance on its theory of value. A naturalistic theory tends to conceive value as a transitory phenomenon directly connected with man's life and subject to his mortality. Its fragile blossom is not deep-rooted in nature. In fact nothing is good or bad, beautiful or ugly, true or false, but our thinking makes it so. An idealistic theory must take issue with such a view at all points. In philosophy, of course, taking issue does not mean opposing an absolute "No" to an equally absolute "Yes." Many distinctions must be made.

Perhaps the fundamental distinction is between the existence and the apprehension of value. The idealist not only can agree that apprehended values are transitory, precarious, and imperfect; he insists upon it. But, in keeping with his conception of philosophy, he is bound to add that the significance of such affirmations is to be sought beyond them—in what they imply concerning the nature and structure of the universe within which they occur. Once and for all there is a world and we are in it. What does our limited experience of that world tell us about its nature and being? How could there be failure to achieve the good in a world in which there is in fact no good to be achieved? How can one mistake the direction when there is no direction? Such questions are often dismissed as formal; but the entire idealistic hypothesis is formal, problematical, even paradoxical.

Humanistic studies are *ipso facto* studies in meaning and interpretation. Religious phenomena, the education of the mind, the struggles of history, the expenditure of moral energies of the present moment are presumed to need and to have some rational interpretation beyond their immediate givenness. Certainly the apprehension of values is a transitory phenomenon but is it impertinent to draw a distinction between the values apprehended and the apprehension of them? The question, as idealists see it, is not: do human joys and sorrows wax and wane, do our desires and the satisfactions of them come and go? It is rather: granting that all these things are tragically so, what does it signify?

Instances from the history of philosophy are often cited of rather extreme answers to that question. It has been said that values have some kind of transempirical residence beyond the reach of time where they abide in untroubled, changeless being. Some interpretations even attribute such a doctrine to Plato. But it does not appear that this view is necessarily entailed by the idealistic hypothesis. As a matter of fact, the more characteristic position of idealism is one which seeks a middle course between the abstract extremes of temporalism and nontemporalism. It is the very genius of idealism to search for a reconciliation of abstract extremes. It can never be a question of time *or* eternity but rather of time *and* eternity. Plato's cryptic dictum that time is the moving image of eternity is still to be taken seriously.

Contemporary idealists in America certainly do not pursue their study of values as if time and history were not involved. Their common doctrine is that value judgements, or *experiences* if anyone prefers that term, require validation by reference to an objective state of affairs in essentially the same manner that "factual" propositions require it. Errors are as evident and obtrusive in moral and esthetic experience as they are in any other. There are degrees of moral maturity as there are degrees of knowledge in intellectual maturity. How is error possible? This is an appropriate and imperative question in both realms of discourse. When the idealist insists upon the objective nature of value, he means that values within our experience necessarily imply somthing beyond our experience. It is that which he calls "objective." And it is that which he supposes has a nature and structure of its own, not wholly unintelligible or wholly beyond the reach of our minds.

Idealistic literature is, to be sure, studded with the phrase "eternal values." If a reader insists on taking that phrase out of the context of idealism and giving to it a meaning which idealism could not approve, it can be refuted by the simple device of pointing to any fading beauty or diminishing good. But if he will first see what idealists since Plato have to say of time and eternity, he will not be so ready to conclude that because values are brief they are not eternal. For the idealist the "eternal" is neither long continued or soon over; it is the significance of time not its duration. Here, as often in the course of idealistic exposition, there is a note of paradox. The idealist is not easily cornered by the "either-or" predicaments; for he thinks that human experience and the world in which it occurs are at bottom "this *and* that" rather than "this *or* that." Are goods temporal *or* eternal? If the idealist is asked the question, he replies with a question: Why not both? Is this evading the issue or is it insight into the true nature of things?

I suppose idealism has many purple passages of dogma, but its sustained mood is the mood of critical inquiry and openmindedness. Its logic is the logic of question and answer rather than the logic of naked truth and falsity. Propositions do not stand alone but stand or fall together. And so, probably, the ultimate dogma of the idealist is that the truth is the whole truth, the good is the final good, and the beauty is the ultimate beauty. But this sort of a dogma is more hypothesis than conclusion. It is once, proposition; twice, method; thrice, faith.

In these respects, the "dogma" is the mirror image of what we call scientific inquiry. At least the casual interpretation of natural science is that it is first of all propositional or factual, secondly methodological, lastly and if at all, hypothetical. The idealist, on the contrary, considers the "factual" result of scientific inquiry in functional relation to questions propounded and methods employed by our minds. The casual interpretation of science gets its plausibility in short views and staccato moments in the history of science, whereas the idealistic interpretation must depend upon the long views and the continuing dialectic of human knowledge.

Idealism has sometimes been erroneously identified with a zeal for social and political reform. It is of course true that some reformers are philosophical idealists; but it is equally true that some conservatives are philosophical idealists. It is not difficult to see how each may find support in idealism. Whether one is conservative or radical in his political opinions probably depends more on biological than on philosophical considerations. To take the long view of politics does not necessarily convince a man that he must act to set the world right, though it may of course have that effect. Whether it does or not depends upon the man more than it does on his philosophy. The fever of reform may be viewed as the necessary means by which the kingdom of Heaven is brought to earth; but the repose of the soul of the saint may equally spring from the idealistic doctrine that the real world is an intelligible order.

SELECTED BIBLIOGRAPHY

Adams, George P. *Idealism and the Modern Age.* New Haven, Yale University Press, 1919.

——————. *Man and Metaphysics.* New York, Columbia University Press, 1948.

Barrett, Clifford, *et al. Contemporary Idealism in America.* New York, The Macmillan Co., 1932.

Blanshard, Brand, *The Nature of Thought,* 2 vols. New York, The Macmillan Co., 1940.

Brightman, Edgar S. *Nature and Values.* Nashville, Tenn., Abingdon-Cokesbury Press, 1945.

Cohen, Morris R. *Reason and Nature.* New York, Harcourt, Brace and Co., 1931.

Cunningham, G. W. *The Idealistic Argument in Recent British and American Philosophy.* New York and London, The Century Co., 1933.

Hoernlé, R. F. A. *Idealism as a Philosophy.* New York, George H. Doran, 1927.

Urban, Wilbur M. *The Intelligible World; Metaphysics and Value.* New York, The Macmillan Co., 1929.

DESCRIPTIVE PHILOSOPHY AND THE NATURE OF HUMAN EXISTENCE

*Marvin Farber**

I

R ecent and current philosophy in the United States reflect the aim to serve the ideals of a strict scientific procedure, although there is also ample evidence of the influence of practical motives, going all the way to irrationalism. Perhaps the greatest achievement in American philosophy is seen in the field of logical inquiry. The attempt to construe philosophy as logic was vitiated by excessive narrowness in the version of logic. In any case, the traditional functions of philosophy included the task of clarifying ultimate or basic ideas; of synthesis, with the aim to achieve the best possible world view at a given time; and of the formulation of a philosophy of values. It is only by an artificial restriction to a methodology excluding such functions, aided by a limited test of meaning, that some philosophical writers were able to exclude all reference to reality and values.

The prestige of science has nowhere been greater than in the United States, and it has made its impression on philosophy. The philosophical expression is often one-sided, as seen in the emphasis upon physics, biology, psychology, or any one of the social sciences. What purports to be a rigorous scientific philosophy may thus take a single science as its model; or it may be an attempt at a synthesis, which is inevitably limited by the writer's specialized equipment, if not by his motives.

This is also seen in the case of philosophies which are allegedly descriptive. The great success of descriptive procedures in the special

* Born in 1901. B.S., 1922, Ph.D. 1925, Harvard University. As a travelling fellow of Harvard University, studied with Husserl and his group in Freiburg. Professor of philosophy and chairman of the department, University of Buffalo. Guggenheim Fellow, 1945-46. President of the International Phenomenological Society and editor of the quarterly journal, *Philosophy and Phenomenological Research,* since 1940. Author of works listed in the bibliography, and of numerous contributions to philosophical publications.

sciences, the immense prestige of statistical devices and of scientific methods of observation, with all their safeguards, have made the ideal of a descriptive philosophy appear to be the last word in philosophical rigor. But there has been no general agreement concerning the nature of experience and its significance for philosophy, due primarily to "standpoint" affiliations and implicit assumptions. Thus Royce's analysis of experience was undertaken within the frame of his idealistic philosophy.

On the other hand, there is a tradition of philosophy of experience in America, with Charles S. Peirce, William James, John Dewey, C. J. Ducasse, and C. I. Lewis among its prominent representatives. If phenomenology is taken to mean the same as "descriptive philosophy of experience," it is necessary to acknowledge the fact that it has had an independent American history, quite apart from the recent influence of Husserl. In the present account, it will only be possible to refer to Peirce as an early representative of phenomenology.

Peirce was important in more than one respect: a noted logical investigator, he also contributed the first impetus to pragmatism; and he also preceded Husserl in his sketch of "phaneroscopy" or phenomenology. But Peirce's reflections on phaneroscopy did not get beyond the broad outlines, and he did not go very far in integrating that realm with the other departments of philosophy. What he did do, however, is penetrating and suggestive, and merits the attention of the methodologist in philosophy.

Peirce's phaneroscopy resembles the earlier Husserl of the *Logical Investigations,* and not the later transcendental-idealistic Husserl. In terms of Husserlian phenomenology, Peirce is a "pre-reductionist" who is concerned with delimiting a descriptive field of experience. There is no reduction to an individual's conscious experience; he begins with an intersubjective realm, with a society of knowers who are to report their findings. Although he aims to have an account of appearances, of the way things "seem" to one "before" and apart from all theory, he does not provide a well-defined technique for instituting that procedure.

Briefly, Peirce's conception of phaneroscopy is as follows:[1] It is the first division of philosophy and is defined as the description of the *phaneron;* and by the latter is meant "the collective total of all that is in any way or in any sense present to the mind, quite regardless of whether

---

1. Cf. *Collected Papers of Charles Sanders Peirce,* edited by Charles Hartshorne and Paul Weiss, Vol. I (Cambridge, Harvard University Press, 1931), pp. 141 ff.; and James Feibleman, *An Introduction to Peirce's Philosophy* (New York, 1946).

it corresponds to any real thing or not." He has no doubt that those features of the phaneron that he has found in his mind are present at all times and to all minds. The *formal* elements of the phaneron have alone concerned Peirce. He recognizes that there is another series of elements imperfectly represented by Hegel's Categories but acknowledges that he had been unable to give a satisfactory account of them.

The term "idea" had been used by English philosophers in a sense similar to "phaneron," but in addition to objecting to their restricting the meaning, Peirce wishes to exclude the psychological connotations of the term.

The program of phaneroscopy is clearly indicated by Peirce as follows: "What I term *phaneroscopy* is that study which, supported by the direct observation of phanerons and generalizing its observations, signalizes several broad classes of phanerons; describes the features of each; shows that, although they are so inextricably mixed together that no one can be isolated, yet it is manifest that their characters are quite disparate; then proves, beyond question, that a certain very short list comprises all of these broadest categories of phanerons that are; and finally proceeds to the laborious and difficult task of enumerating the principal subdivisions of these categories."

Ruled out is the question of how far the phanerons correspond to any realities; and all speculation as to relations between its categories and physiological facts; and all hypothetical explanations are avoided. The appearances are simply scrutinized; and it is left to the reader to repeat the author's observations for himself, and thus to decide whether the author's account of the appearances is correct or not.

William James's philosophy of experience — his conception of "radical empiricism"— in American philosophy, and Shadworth Hodgson's sketch of a subjective procedure for a philosophy of reflection, in British philosophy, also have much in common with Husserl's early phenomenology. The same may be said of Dewey's philosophy of experience, which provides for the analysis of experience into its simplest elements, and also for the conceptual reconstruction of all structures. Dewey did not propose to treat experience as disengaged from its natural setting; there is no thought of "pure experience" or "pure forms" in complete separation from the causal order of the natural world. Thus Dewey wrote: "To see the organism *in* nature, the nervous system in the organism, the brain in the nervous system, the cortex in the brain, is the answer to the problems which haunt philosophy. And when thus seen they will be seen to be *in*, not as marbles are in a box but as events are in history, in a moving, growing, never finished process."[2]

II

The influence of Edmund Husserl, Max Scheler, and other European phenomenologists has been mainly felt in the United States since the 1920s. Husserl had been previously reported on in American periodicals.[3] The first comprehensive attempt to expound Husserl's phenomenology was contributed by the present writer in a monograph entitled *Phenomenology as a Method and as a Philosophical Discipline*.[4] Husserl's later system of transcendental phenomenology, and his attempt to found a "first philosophy" which is "valid once and for all time" are the central theme of this monograph. In the years following its appearance there were occasional publications on phenomenology, but no organized discussion.[5] Upon the death of Husserl in 1938, a group of his former students and friends, both native Americans and refugees, planned a volume of commemorative essays.[6] These essays are mainly expository in character, but some dissenting criticism is contained in the volume. Thus, Wild repeats the well-known charge, so often voiced in Germany, that Husserl, after his critical rejection of psychologism in the first volume of his *Logical Investigations*, had lapsed back into it in his later writings; and McGill, adopting a materialistic approach to phenomenology, points out his reasons for rejecting phenomenological idealism as a philosophy.

Simultaneous with the planning of this volume, the International Phenomenological Society was founded on December 26, 1939, at a meet-

---

2. Cf. *Experience and Nature* (Chicago, 1925), p. 295.
3. Cf. A. R. Chandler, "Husserl's Program of Philosophical Reform," *Philosophical Review*, Vol. XXVI (1917). In Chandler's account, however, Husserl's descriptive analyses are not granted the same level accorded to James. Cf. also Henry Lanz, "The New Phenomenology," *The Monist*. Vol. XXXIV (1924).
4. University of Buffalo Studies in Philosophy, 1928.
5. Cf. J. S. Bixler, "German Phenomenology and its Implications for Religion," *Journal of Religion*, Vol. IX (1929); Street Fulton, "Husserl's Significance for the Theory of Truth," *The Monist*, Vol. XLV (1935); A. D. Osborn, *The Philosophy of Edmund Husserl* (New York, 1934); E. P. Welch, *Edmund Husserl's Phenomenology* (Los Angeles, The University of Southern California Press, 1939); Marvin Farber, "A Review of Recent Phenomenological Literature," *Journal of Philosophy*, Vol. XXVII (1930), and "Husserl's *Méditations cartésiennes*," *Philosophical Review*, Vol. XLIV (1935).
6. *Philosophical Essays in Memory of Edmund Husserl* (Cambridge, 1940), edited by M. Farber, with essays by Dorion Cairns, Marvin Farber, Aron Gurwitsch, Charles Harts-horne, W. E. Hocking, Gerhart Husserl, L. O. Kattsoff, Felix Kaufmann, Fritz Kaufmann, Jacob Klein, Helmut Kuhn, V. J. McGill, Alfred Schuetz, Herbert Spiegelberg, Hermann Weyl, John Wild, and a hitherto unpublished manuscript by E. Husserl.

ing held in the New School for Social Research, in New York City. At the foundation meeting the aim of the new organization was stated as being "to further the understanding, development, and application of phenomenological inquiry as inaugurated by Edmund Husserl." National divisions were to be organized wherever possible, meetings planned for the discussion of phenomenological problems, and plans for the prompt publication of a journal were approved. Despite the initial declaration of the purpose of the Society, its program as well as the policy of its journal were conceived more broadly from the outset. The philosophy of Edmund Husserl was to be the *point of departure,* a point of view strongly endorsed by Husserl's former research assistants, Eugen Fink and Ludwig Landgrebe, in preliminary communications. The new publication retained the title of Husserl's famous *Jahrbuch für Philosophie und Phänomenologische Forschung,* which had come to an end with the accession to power of the Nazis. It was firmly resolved that there was to be no spirit of a "school" or sect. The decision to honor Husserl's memory and to attempt to continue his positive achievements did not in any way imply a restriction to his philosophy. The papers and symposia presented at early meetings of the Phenomenological Society were concerned mainly with phenomenological themes, but there was always an effort to facilitate the interplay between phenomenology and other disciplines and movements. The relationship between phenomenology and psychology has been a recurrent theme. The central interest of the publication is in philosophy as a descriptive discipline, which includes the epistemological and philosophical studies of scholars who are far removed from transcendental phenomenology as a universal philosophy, but who nevertheless have much in common with its descriptive program. The journal is also hospitable to the entire field of philosophical scholarship in all countries, and distinguished symposia on Meaning and Truth, Probability, Materialism, and Educational Philosophy have helped to realize the aim to serve philosophy as a whole. In this way it has not been necessary to debate the question of the range and varieties of description, which is at present still in need of scholarly exploration and is not ready for a formal solution for the purposes of a journalistic policy.

In its actual practice it is the spirit of William James which characterizes the publication. A *modus vivendi* in the United States could hardly have been secured otherwise. An opposition to "schools" in the traditional sense, and a spirit of readiness to offer ideas and findings for their further independent use by scholars in all fields and traditions, are

indeed typical both of Husserl and James. If Husserl came to avoid discussion with representatives of other movements, it was largely because
of his own absorbing plans for work. But it is the freer and easier
manner of James in his practical relations with others — students and
fellow scholars — which is meant here, and which is more suitable for a
publication than the stern and, in effect, isolationist policy of the *Jahrbuch,* which could not hope to get a general hearing in our time.

It is not implied that Husserl would ever have vouched for every
statement in his own *Jahrbuch.* As a matter of fact, there is good reason
to suppose that he unqualifiedly endorsed only his own contributions to
that organ. That was certainly the case after the appearance of the sixth
volume, as the present writer knows from personal conversation with him
at the time. Husserl always stood alone; he always endeavored to make
further progress and never failed to change, mercilessly criticizing his
past efforts and scorning those who failed to participate in what he characteristically called "the development."

III

That an organization of phenomenologists could not proceed along
strict Husserlian lines, or along Husserlian lines alone, must be evident
to anyone who knows both the background of the movement and the
state of philosophy in our time. In addition to the need for various types
of procedure in philosophy, there is the complicating circumstance of the
diverse elements in the larger phenomenological movement. Max Scheler,
the most interesting of the early collaborators of Husserl, has had a widespread influence far beyond the limits of descriptive philosophy, all the
way from religious and social thought to the Nazi ideology.[7] Much of
Scheler's work and influence could hardly survive critical inspection, but
it must be reckoned with practically. Of the early phenomenologists,
Pfänder and Geiger exercised the greatest influence, next to Scheler, of
course, and their students are among those contributing actively at the
present time, especially in the interests of a "realistic" descriptive philosophy.

The most conspicuous development in phenomenology after the First
World War was due to Martin Heidegger, who became Husserl's suc-
cessor in Freiburg. It was Heidegger's crowning glory, after Hitler's rise

----

7. Cf. the "Symposium on the Significance of Max Scheler" in *Philosophy and
Phenomenological Research,* Vol. II.

to power, to join the Nazi Party while rector of Freiburg University.[8] Heidegger has been credited with freeing recent philosophy from the limits of subjectivism to which Husserl had restricted it, by means of a "philosophy of (human) existence." Only a largely uninformed person could entertain such a notion seriously. For one thing, Husserl himself tried to allow for the world of culture and human existence, in his way, although his subjectivistic approach to philosophy was admittedly a sadly inadequate way. But there were others, in the past, and in philosophical movements *other* than phenomenology and existentialism, who saw the problems of human existence in their fullness, and with clarity. It is sufficient to refer to the recognition of man's real place in nature in the broad evolutionary movement, and to the dynamic philosophy of man in the literature of historical materialism. It is quaint, even amusing, to hear the tall claims made for Heidegger's originality in recognizing "the problem of existence." For Heidegger, the interpretation of human existence is a "preparation" or means to answer the question concerning the "meaning of being." Thus his theoretical objective was a "fundamental ontology," rather than "philosophical anthropology." Like Husserl, Heidegger had in mind the general plan of a philosophical preparation for the special sciences with their variously circumscribed regions of being. Although Heidegger made the basic phenomenon "I am in a world" to be his starting point, instead of Husserl's absolute or pure consciousness, it is also true that Husserl operated with a "pre-given life-world" in his later period.

The aim of submitting the structural whole of human existence to a systematic analysis is a worthy program for the philosopher. Its value depends, however, upon the selection of significant features of human existence as manifested in its actual cultural and natural setting, and also upon the mode of expression that is employed. In both respects Heidegger errs grievously, for he has succeeded in avoiding the pressing problems of human existence as they have appeared historically—the concrete conflicts between slaves and slaveholders, serfs and feudal lords, workers and capitalists, and the numerous concrete problems and tensions of our existing socio-economic system; and the terminology he has so studiously devised has enabled him to conceal whatever insights he has attained. "Human existence" is not an undifferentiated thing, or essence;

---

8. It may also be recalled that Oskar Becker, who had been for years a close student of Husserl as well as Heidegger, chided Husserl with having published his *Méditations cartésiennes* in the French language in 1929, calling it "a tragic symbol." Later on, Becker fell in line with the Nazi "blood and earth" doctrine.

it must be considered as human existence in a slave economy, or in a capitalist economy; and, again, as human existence in the form of a worker, or of an employer of labor. Furthermore, the *attitudes* toward human existence which we have are historically and socially conditioned. To ignore such considerations is to condemn one's studies of human existence to a limited group of experiences purporting to transcend actual historical conditions. But even a careful selection of types of experience, such as the consciousness of death, may not entirely disregard the actual cultural setting. "Man in general" is of far less interest to us than types of historical men. Such types are to be characterized, not as essences, not by making generic statements, but by painstaking descriptive studies involving statistical methods and all the resources of causal methods, to which numerous special sciences contribute. Not a single essential ("generic") determination could be declared, which might not in fact be refuted. If characteristics *a, b,* and *c* are "essential" to man, what shall we think of a "man" not having one of them, or having them in a form somewhat different from the declared characteristics? The consciousness of finitude will not be found to impress all men alike, just as the awareness of change is seen to depress some and exhilarate others.

Such characteristic utterances as "Man is man only on the basis of the existence in him," the untranslatable statement "Im Sein des Seienden geschieht das Nichten des Nichts," and the expression "a pre-ontological understanding of being" are typical. One writer in America, struggling with Heidegger's language, found it necessary to resort to the "English" equivalent "it shalling be." Heidegger finds it necessary to deduce that the world is "essentially related to existence," which he accomplishes in a teleological manner: the world is "that for the sake of which existence exists"—namely, in the state of "being lost"—out of which the drive for independence leads. It would be better for all concerned, were he to restrict himself to the ineffable. Were it not for his extensive influence in Germany, and the surprising hold he has taken on philosophy in so many countries, including France and Latin America, there would be little profit in emphasizing this point. The critique of Heidegger is at the same time a critique of many philosophers who have found inspiration and support in his efforts.[9] His philosophy agrees basically with the tradition of the "philosophy of life" and serves to advance irrationalism

---

9 Cf. Guenther Stern's critique of Heidegger, and Herbert Marcuse's critical analysis of Sartre's *L'être et le néant,* in *Philosophy and Phenomenological Research,* Vol. VII (March, 1947); and Alfred Schuetz's article, "Sartre's Theory of the Alter Ego," same journal, Vol. IX (December, 1948). Cf. also Marjorie Grene, *Dreadful Freedom: A Critique of Existentialism* (Chicago, 1948).

as a general tendency. The evil effects of the undermining of confidence in reason in Nazi Germany are now well known.[10]

Apart from the existentialists, who frequently also appear in phenomenological clothing, there is quite a diversity of elements in the broader phenomenological movement. Husserl himself passed through various stages, from psychologism (he accepted, to begin with, a psychologistic foundation of logic and mathematics) to "neutralism," and then to transcendental idealism. Reflecting in part his stages of development, there were "realistic" and idealistic phenomenologists, religious and non-religious members of the movement, rationalists and fideists, conservatives and radicals (a comparison with the left-wing and right-wing Hegelians is suggested). The mystical elements could only be swept away by the descriptive procedure, and yet they persisted through the years. The early phenomenological movement thus anticipated the present movement in point of the diversity of its members.

IV

The possibility of coherently presenting Husserl's own attempt at a scientific construction of philosophy is a tribute to his clarity of thought, whether or not one agrees with his metaphysics. In agreement with the tradition of rationalism, Husserl conceived philosophy as a rigorous science in which every proposition is established by means of adequate insight and evidence. He protested in his essay on "Philosophy as a Rigorous Science" [11] against the procedure of traditional philosophers in setting up finished systems like so many full-grown Minervas emerging from the heads of men of creative genius, only to be stored up in the quiet museum of history. The ideal of a descriptively founded philosophy may be held up as a final definition of what we would like to achieve if we adopt the scientific ideal in philosophy. This is not to say, however, that Husserl's own method of descriptive analysis within the limits of what he called "transcendental subjectivity" was adequate for all philosophical purposes, for it was not.

A non-idealistic reader beginning with Husserl's argument for idealism would probably pay no more attention to his work. All American readers who are familiar with the realistic reaction against idealism are prepared to challenge Husserl's departure from a strictly delimited descriptive procedure in order to instate idealism as a general philosophy.

10. This thesis has been strikingly set forth by Professor Georg Lukács.
11. *Logos*, Vol. I (1911).

Despite the heavy technical apparatus involved, the attempt conforms to the traditional defense ot idealism.

Various ways of defending an idealistic philosophy have been adopted. At times it is simply propounded as an article of faith; at other times, the fight is carried to the enemy (philosophy as determined by the sciences), and the incompleteness of science is held up as a reason for abandoning materialism or naturalism in favor of a principle of spirit. The positive motive of appealing to "ultimate" values is also prominent. It is a very rare occurrence for an idealist to regard the principle of spirit as a hypothesis, subject to all the logical requirements of a principle of explanation. Much more frequent is the attempt to provide grounds for idealism which go back to Berkeley's use of the cardinal principle of idealism (*viz.*, that being depends upon being known).

Berkeley's argument, as advanced in his *Principles of Human Knowledge,* is really a pathetic example of bad reasoning from any point of view. His aim was clear: he wished to refute materialism and irreligion, his critique of abstractions being designed to undermine the concept of matter itself. In order to prove his thesis that *"esse is percipi,"* he had to restrict reality to a relationship with a knower; and he could only make progress in his argument by confusing qualities and "ideas." His argument can be rendered in the following six propositions: (1) All known objects are related to a knower; (2) Only ideas are known (qualities are called ideas); (3) Being depends upon being known; (4) We do not, and cannot know that which is not known; (5) There is no being that is not known; (6) Therefore, all being is in the mind ("ideas" are in the mind). The vagueness and ambiguity of concepts such as "relatedness," "dependence," and what it means to be "known" help to secure the illicit conclusion.

Royce's offer of a reward to anyone who could produce an object that is not known shows how the Berkeleyan vagueness persisted in philosophy. Royce, whose scholarly attainments made him for many years a leader of American idealism, did not have to pay the reward. The tenuous nature of the "known" protected him adequately. Surely no philosophical consequences could follow from such an amusing gesture. A discerning person would point out the different kinds of "knowing," directly and indirectly, and would not fail to recognize the facts established by organized knowledge as well as the truths of common sense. Most important of these facts, for the present discussion, is man's late arrival in cosmic history, so that there was a time (presumably an infinite time) when there was no "knowing" at all. Also important and pertinent is the fact that man is a cultural, historical product. Hence it is indeed quaint to assert that the knower conditions reality, or that reality depends upon being known. It is hard to understand how idealists, who are compelled to derive their sustenance from the earth, can persuade themselves that the earth depends upon their "knowing" it. The appeal to an absolute mind is the pathetic element in the argument; it is a plea of confession and avoidance.

The opposition to the idealistic theses may be expressed in the following counter-theses: (1) Natural existence is independent of knowing; (2) Knowing is itself a kind of existence; (3) Qualities are objective; (4) "Ideas" of qualities are "subjective"; (5) There is no evidence for a "mind," or spiritual substance, great or small. It is now a fairly common attitude in American philosophy to treat concepts of "spirit," "absolute mind," or "absolute self" as hypotheses requiring not only satisfactory definition, but confirmation and justification. They are regarded widely as not being different in this respect from the concept of the ether in physics, and they tend to suffer the same fate.

When Husserl forsakes his originally conceived methodological device for questioning all beliefs and judgments for their evidence in direct experience, and proceeds to argue (as he does in his *Formale und Transzendentale Logik,* for example) that objects are only conceivable in a subjective context, he is no better off basically than Berkeley. He is really exploiting the "ego-centric predicament," and is guilty of the fallacy of "definition by initial predication," as Ralph Perry has called it. [12] It is unwarranted to maintain that objects can only *be* in the context in which they happen to be examined or experienced. Following the analysis by Perry and his realistic contemporaries, all arguments for idealism making use of the "ego-centric predicament" are post-mortem efforts. Nothing metaphysical follows from the sterile fact that all objects of knowledge are related to knowers; and the cardinal principle of idealism remains an unjustified dogma. Husserl himself once denied that there is such a "predicament," but went on to assert that it is a condition of "essential relatedness"—i.e., an object without a knowing subject is "unthinkable." If the appeal to conceivability is construed subjectively, one encounters a relativistic impasse at once, for no concept could be more tenuous, with freedom of judgment on the part of each individual. If, on the other hand, the appeal is to objective considerations, they should be adduced. To date they have not appeared, notwithstanding the claim to "apodictic grounds of essence."

---

12. Cf. R. B. Perry, *Present Philosophical Tendencies* (New York, 1919), for his critical analysis of idealism.

Neither idealistic phenomenology nor existentialism could long survive on the American scene, assuming that they could get a significant foothold. With the systematic arguments for idealism exploded in the period of the First World War,[13] the defenders of idealism could only argue from the incompleteness, or the inadequacy, of the sciences, and for a philosophy which could provide the ultimate values of religion. Unfortunately, idealists have sometimes derived support from scientists of recognized standing, so that observers are entertained by the doubtful spectacle of men ignorant of science deriving support from scientists deficient in philosophy, especially in general logic. (The noted physicist Millikan is an outstanding example.) Such performances are effectively met, but by no means stopped, by logical criticism, as amply shown by articles and reviews in the various American philosophical journals.

Similarly, existentialism founders on the solid achievements of the sciences, social as well as natural. Their prestige in America is so great that there is no room in respectable circles for self-styled oracles mouthing general statements about man—his anxiety, his "forlornness," or his "thrownness," whether theological or supposedly natural.

V

The recent Kierkegaard renaissance[14] in America might seem to give evidence of receptiveness to existentialism. It does indeed signify something: it indicates the growing awareness of the inadequacy of idealism and its philosophy of man, and the vain hope of finding an effective substitute outside the domain of science. A few references will be revealing.

In his *Concept of Dread* Kierkegaard states that if ethics must include sin, its ideality is lost.[15] Again, he imparts his observation to readers, that "the fact that woman is more sensuous than man is shown at once by her bodily organism"; and, further, that "woman is more in dread than man," being more sensuous.[16] The women in Kierkegaard's field of vision are presumably thus constituted "essentially." How baseless such "essential determinations" really are, is seen when we reflect upon

---

13. Cf. *The New Realism* (New York, 1912), essays by E. B. Holt, W. T. Marvin, W. P. Montague, R. B. Perry, W. B. Pitkin, and E. G. Spaulding; also E. G. Spaulding, *The New Rationalism* (New York, 1918), and W. P. Montague, *Ways of Knowing* (New York, 1925).

14. Cf. the translations of Kierkegaard's works, published by the Princeton University Press.

15. Lowrie translation (Princeton, 1944), pp. 16 f.

16. *Ibid.,* pp. 58 f.

the inferior status of women through the centuries, as a sufficient reason for developing certain traits (not necessarily sensuous!); and upon the way in which women change when given equal opportunities. It is apparent that Kierkegaard indulges in commonplace opinions, and that he brings his observations and knowledge, such as it is, into conformity with his articles of faith.

Kierkegaard has had only a moderate amount of historical influence. His influence on the existentialists, especially on Heidegger, is well known, as well as his historical significance as a minor critic of Hegel. He was far less important than Feuerbach in that respect, as well as in his theological criticism. His writings are for the most part not distinguished, so far as their philosophical content is concerned. Extensive reading is required, in order to find a single philosophical thought that may be referred to as such.

Although the history of philosophy unavoidably marches past every thinker, and he later appears uncritical or lacking in various respects, truly great thinkers nevertheless preserve their stature, and it is always rewarding to return to their texts. That cannot be said for Kierkegaard. He was not a fruitful thinker in his time, and our present scientific perspective cannot alter this judgment. The onward march of ideas after Hegel proceeded in four main directions: (1) the post-Hegelian development, via Feuerbach, to Marx and Engels; (2) the Darwinian-evolutionary trend; (3) the renewed development of a descriptive philosophy of experience, in which Brentano and Husserl figured prominently; (4) the development of logic and logical analysis in the various departments of philosophy. Kierkegaard does not fit into any one of these trends. The most that can be said for his significance is that he influenced a decadent tendency in the wake of Husserl's teaching.

The talk of "human existence" in a non-naturalistic setting (strictly speaking, in an idealistic setting, as is the case with existentialism) is misleading and presumptuous. There is a limit to permissible usage: having a locus in space and time, and being *physically real,* are necessary conditions for "existence." "Attitude toward existence" should not be confused with existence itself. As for dealing with "attitudes toward existence," and in particular one's own existence, that may be done in different ways: (a) with the "natural attitude," on the ground of the natural world and on the given culture level; (b) with the attitude of "pure" or completely "critical" reflection, with "inner" description; or (c) with the balanced complete method of reflection, which makes use of (b) and all other procedures, including causal analysis. Thus, for (c), one does not forget the cardinal truth that a man is a product of his cultural group and a part of the independent order of nature. Any philosophical procedure which does violence to these basic facts stands convicted of falsity and barrenness in fact.

In what sense can we speak of a "problem" of existence? There are problems, rather than a single problem, and some are perennial, others unique or merely historical. Kierkegaard finds death to be of paramount importance; and so does Heidegger. Hence "dread," "anxiety," and "care" become titles for the most deepseated features of experience. In the context of theology that is understandable, and a coherent picture can be worked out, in accordance with the well-known other-worldly tradition. But *secular* anxiety or care is another matter, and we do not hesitate to describe an excessive preoccupation with the prospect of death as abnormal, perhaps seriously pathological, and as morally harmful at best, in view of the obligations everyone must have toward the living, including himself. The basic problems of existence, properly construed, are problems of food, shelter, clothing, companionship, health, cultural achievement, and, as conditioning all of these, problems of economic relationships. It is not only death that is combatted, as an evil faced by all humanity. There is a host of problems encountered in the normal process of living, and death is a factor in many of them. That is the case in illness, or in the various sciences which contribute toward lengthening the span of human life. There is really no limit to the span of life which could not conceivably be passed by scientific achievement. With respect to the present level of knowledge, we must indeed reckon with the certain prospect of decline and death, and our life-plans must be formed with that fact in view. But it does not follow that life must always be so limited in extent, or that it must be limited at all. Pessimism is not justifiable here, any more than it is with regard to the prospects of the earth, which was condemned to a scientific death in the nineteenth century, but was happily granted a reprieve in recent scientific speculation. Neither is it necessarily true that life, as life, engenders death, as Hegel and so many others have believed. Change is universal, but that is another matter. Without denying the grave importance of the anticipation of death, it should be emphasized that it does not outweigh and may not displace the normal, daily interests of our lives. What are the consequences which are drawn from the over-emphasis of the death-motive? There are theological consequences, as in the case of Kierkegaard, who is able to rest on faith; or a "tragic" view of man, a kind of "heroic" man, whose heroism consists in feeling and pretense, as in the case of Heidegger. In short, the death-motive as portrayed by the existentialists is a means of defeating the claims and needs of existence, of depreciating and disregarding the normal needs of living beings. It is part and parcel of a philosophy of renunciation of human existence. In a word: the "philosophy of existence" is not properly concerned with existence. No amount of talk about the attitudes of human beings toward their own status in existence will justify the failure to take account of the real needs and interests which the special sciences have so abundantly illuminated in the last century.

VI

In view of the untenable arguments for Husserl's idealism, the present writer long ago found it necessary to divest the phenomenological procedure of all idealistic entanglements. It then became one important procedure among others for philosophical purposes. By stressing the principle of the cooperation of methods, the alleged uniqueness and transnatural character of the phenomenological procedure was denied. The fact that Husserl, Scheler, and their associates were aligned against the philosophy based upon the natural sciences is reflected in the literature of phenomenology, and even in the very mode of expression employed. Thus, although allowing that the "natural attitude," or "natural view of the world," has its rights, it was found necessary to suspend (provisionally, one would suppose, and, indeed, insist) all its "assumptions" in order to examine them for their evidence in terms of the experience of an individual knower. This is all very good for the purposes of a critical method. One should be aided in distinguishing facts from assumptions, and immediate evidences from constructions, if the procedure is properly executed.[17] Unfortunately, however, this is not entirely the case, due to ulterior metaphysical motives, as revealed by the tendency to speak disparagingly of the natural view of the world as "naive," in contrast to the "radical" point of view of pure reflection. It is often forgotten that the facts of the "natural view" are basic and incapable of being "suspended," and that the entire point of the procedure of "pure reflection" is to suspend *judgments* provisionally. Thus a relatively autonomous realm is delimited for purposes of inquiry—the realm of experiences with their "intended" objectivities as such. The *natural* facts that man lives in a

---

17. Cf.   M. Farber, *The Foundation of Phenomenology* (Cambridge, 1943), for a detailed account of the phenomenological method, its misunderstanding, and abuses.

world infinitely extended in time and space, that there are other people independent of himself, and that although man makes his cultural world, every individual man is causally conditioned by cultural forces—such facts should not be referred to as "assumptions." Furthermore, it is again a basic "natural" fact that value judgments differ at different times and places and that they are conditioned by prevailing social interests, as well as by the more constant biological interests. The full appreciation of such basic facts would prevent philosophers from accepting extravagant metaphysical views, or from utter emptiness, when they retire to the realm of "pure" thought. How Husserl himself erred in this respect is evident to all who have examined his phenomenological studies. His retirement to "pure immanence"; his delineation of the realm of "transcendental subjectivity," at first taken as a methodological expedient, in order to make "radical reflection" possible, and then reified or frozen into a metaphysical domain; and his location of all genuinely philosophical problems within the "reduced" realm of pure experience (extruding all judgments of transcendent realities)—these are themes prominently featured in his *Ideas, Cartesian Meditations,* and other writings. The phenomenological method was most successful and fruitful in the philosophy of logic and in descriptive psychology, and most vulnerable in the philosophy of history,[18] where it is essential to bear in mind the real events of history, as antecedent to and independent of the conscious experiences of any individual knower. The tradition in which Husserl chose to move derived from Kant and the post-Kantians, as well as the more recent "philosophy of life." Thus it can be understood why an acute method, perhaps the most exacting device and effort for reflective observation ever formulated, became subordinate to an extravagant speculative philosophy, becoming lost in effect.

VII

For Kant, a method is "transcendental" if it is concerned not so much with *objects* as with our method of knowing objects. William James made essentially the same distinction, with his customary lucidity, in his *Principles of Psychology.* The terminology used in phenomenology can by no means be defended in its entirety. Numerous pretentious and misleading terms should be replaced, including "transcendental," "a priori," "constitutive," "pure," "eidetic intuition," etc. Thus there are members of the

---

18. Cf. *Philosophy for the Future,* edited by R. W. Sellars, V. J. McGill, and M. Farber (New York, 1949), for the present writer's discussion of this quite infelicitous phase of Husserl's work, in his essay on "Experience and Subjectivism."

phenomenological movement who really believe that the world itself is "constituted" in "absolute consciousness." Nevertheless, when clearly defined and strictly controlled, the methodological technique will be recognized as continuing and extending already recognized procedures.

A philosophy of experience must be thoroughly reflective; nothing may be left unexamined. For philosophical understanding, everything must be placed in question, including the philosophical method itself. How is it possible to achieve that end? A simple reflective inspection of experience is not enough; the reflection must be so thoroughgoing that every assumed element or construction in experience is questioned. The phenomenological suspension (or "epoché") is instituted for that purpose, as a primary condition of all philosophical analysis. All beliefs concerning existence are "suspended" to begin with; but that does not mean the "denial" or "discarding" of the world,[19] unless the method has been fundamentally misconstrued. In order to reflect "purely," the phenomenologist undertakes to become a "non-participating observer" of the process of experience. In actual fact, however, he may not be as "non-participating" as may be suggested, because for most phenomenologists, as well as for most philosophers in general, the existing social relations appear to be a finality. Inequalities and class distinctions are not apt to be "questioned." In any case, the suspension of beliefs (or "positings") is intended to be universal, and must apply not only to the real world and other knowers, but to the various systems of knowledge as well. If the aim is to ascertain how far we can proceed by means of direct inspection ("intuition") of experience, the smallest possible residuum of the process of suspension must constitute the starting point. This turns out to be the perceptual experiences of an individual knower.

Having "reduced" the data of philosophy to "pure consciousness" in the sense of "experiencings," and having thus defined the framework for philosophical analysis, the problem then becomes the constructive ("constitutive") one of accounting for the "origin" of the various structures of ordered experience and knowledge on that basis. The contributions of the mind on the various levels of experience are examined. It turns out that a vast amount of descriptive work remains to be done, despite the partial achievements of past philosophers and the numerous descriptive studies of Husserl himself. Nothing less than the cooperative efforts of generations of investigators will be sufficient to lay the desired firm foundation

---

19. This interpretation is found, e.g., in W. Köhler's *The Place of Values in a World of Facts* (New York, 1938).

for a descriptive philosophy, which in one sense will always remain an ideal.

The phenomenological procedure also involves the restriction to essence, or essential relations and structures. Although much has been said about the concept of essence in the past, and Santayana, in recent philosophy, has given it great prominence,[20] Husserl was the first to begin to do justice to it systematically, as a matter of method.[21] Essences are not to be hypostatized as metaphysical entities in a Platonic heaven; nor are they to be treated after the fashion of nominalism. It is a matter of common experience that general facts are "seen."

Both types of "reduction," involving the "suspension" of beliefs and the restriction to essential structures, are familiar to philosophers, although Husserl's language may not be used. Without the use and recognition of universals, no scientific knowledge is possible. A pure phenomenology of experience, which is to serve as a theory of science, must do justice to the importance of universals, and, as scientific itself in a primary sense, it has a special interest in restricting itself to essential structures—whereby it is not at all implied that particular events are not of interest to the scientist, or, for that matter, to the analyst of experience. Furthermore, every science illustrates a partial "epoché" or "suspension"— it "places in question" a certain number of concepts and principles. Ethics provides a good illustration; for how could one hope to make any progress in ethical thinking if he did not first of all perform an *epoché?* It may then be seen that the universal *epoché* of phenomenology is really a necessary condition not only for philosophical investigation, but for effective cooperation among philosophers. General agreement among philosophers is only to be valued if it is achieved on logically defensible grounds, where a rational solution is possible. *Per se,* it may be pointless, or even absurd, if there are conflicting interests among irreconcilable groups. But even under relatively favorable social conditions, philosophers may never hope to come to any agreement if they retain unexamined or unjustified assumptions, and are prompted by unclarified motives. This is true on a national scale, and all the more so internationally. The severe criteria of phenomenology in a strict sense, requiring that all items of knowledge be tested before the bar of immediate experience, represents one stage of philosophical inquiry which philosophers must strive to realize if they

---

20. Cf. G. Santayana, *Scepticism and Animal Faith* (New York, 1923), *The Realm of Essence* (New York, 1927), and *The Philosophy of Santayana*, edited by P. Schilpp (Evanston and Chicago, 1940).

21. Cf. Husserl's formulation of his "method of variation," in his *Erfahrung und Urteil* (Prague, 1939, and Hamburg, 1948).

are not forever to continue with "school" alignments and with issues which are never solved, but are at best forgotten for a time.

Certainly phenomenological description may be abused, as statistical methods may be abused, to "prove" almost anything. "Intuition" may be construed by some in a mystical manner, as "ecstasy," or it may be called "the heuristic principle of aristocracy" (Scheler). In appropriating descriptions of human attitudes "existentially," it may be forgotten that the procedures of philosophy may not be substituted for the causal analyses and descriptions of the positive, special sciences, with all their critical requirements, and also that they may not do justice to the findings of "natural" experience. As represented by phenomenology in its strict sense, the relentless, systematic examination of assumptions of all kinds can only exercise a freeing influence on the mind, and that is a necessary condition of all philosophy worthy of the name. An *epoché* must be performed with respect to all "standpoints" and traditionally accepted views, and the descriptive test of "seeing" must be regarded as final.

The method of Husserlian phenomenology is subjectivistic, and therein lies its merit as well as its limitation. An "objectivistic," developmental approach to philosophy is also incomplete in "questioning" experience and knowledge, i. e., as usually applied. The necessity and importance of the developmental approach to philosophy, with its "longitudinal" view of experience and the "continuum of inquiry" (to use the language of Peirce and Dewey), will not be challenged. It is indispensable. But it is also not in conflict with the subjectivistic, "cross-sectional" view of phenomenology. Both types of approach have their own proper questions, and appropriate methods have been devised to answer them. As methodological devices and orientations, they should cooperate, rather than conflict.

Nevertheless, it must be emphasized that it is not a matter for arbitrary decision as to which type of procedure is primary. So far as the world of actual existence is concerned, the truth of the "longitudinal" view is primary — namely, that there really is a field of existence not only independent of knowing, but antedating all knowing.[22] The "cross-sectional" view can never be regarded as primary except in an artificial sense, for purposes of clarification in a region of inquiry which is considered in isolation from real existence.

___

22. V. I. Lenin is entirely correct in stressing this point in his *Materialism and Empirio-Criticism* (New York, 1927), for it has far-reaching importance in heading off idealism as a general philosophy.

In order to achieve complete objectivity, and to understand the conditions acting upon the stream of experiences which are simply taken as a finality by the phenomenologist, it is necessary to "project" or view the thinker in his position in natural and social history. It is necessary to consider his interests, and to ascertain whether they influence his motivation and thought as an investigator. This is not to object to a thinker being led by his interests, for he may perhaps be justified. The point is, to make an explicit avowal of that fact, rather than to claim "neutrality" with respect to social questions while tacitly falling in line with one group — usually the dominant group in society.

The naturalistic reflection which is "radicalized" and added to in pure reflection must in turn be supplemented by the inspection of social-historical significance. The other alternative would be to rest in "pure subjectivity" with the aid of an absolute consciousness that is removed from all problems of matters of fact. The procedure of pure reflection is a stage in the complete process of reflection. It is sufficient for one dimension of problems — to contribute to the clarification of basic concepts in terms of direct experience — and is therefore an important auxiliary method. But it should not be used beyond its proper range of application. The ideal of using one method of procedure would only be possible if all problems were of one type. A never-ending plurality of methods is the response to the great diversity of problems. Taking care not to disparage the so-called "naive" theorizing of the naturalistic methods, and recognizing the need for a plurality of procedures, phenomenology may take its proper place in the total organization of constructive scholarship.

VIII

It is fair to ask, finally, whether anything at all would be lost by the formulation of a program for phenomenology on the basis of a naturalistic or materialistic theory of reality. Why the requirement of "purity" for philosophy as a whole? It can only mean the aim to outflank naturalism and materialism by setting up a "radical" procedure which "questions" all beliefs and all knowledge on the basis of another tacit theory of thought and reality. There are certainly assumptions in the use of the purportedly descriptive procedure of "pure" phenomenology. Although this was admitted by Husserl, they were consigned by him to another order of assumptions, in accordance with his general habit of separating the "pure" from the "natural." It would be the merest escapism to "retire to immanence," to the ideal realm of essences, while ignoring the urgent problems on the social scene.   When a pure mathematician develops theories without any apparent concern with physical problems, there is ample justification, for his results may find application.   Moreover, it would never occur to him, *qua* mathematician, to confuse his type of conceptual analysis with the real physical world.   Such a strange confusion is reserved for philosophers.

Reflective experience must also be a real activity, and the findings of such inquiry face the same tests as any other type of inquiry.   The descriptive investigator may be wrong, even though he deals with essential structures.   There is no guarantee of avoiding error in the subjective realm, any more than there is in the objective realm.   Furthermore, if the uniformity of nature must be assumed in any sense for objective inquiry, it must also have its subjective counterpart, as applied to general structures and "ideal" relations.   "Sameness" must be assumed; it can never be proved by any act of observation, whether it be natural or "eidetic."   The ego, or trinity of egos in the later development of phenomenology,[23] are dubious constructions at best, well suited to connect with the reality-building egos or selves of the tradition of idealism, and leading to a peculiar kind of transnatural agnosticism.   The primacy of the "inner" over the "outer" realm is also maintained as a principle going back to St. Augustine and Descartes.   The "method of doubt" precedes the phenomenological *epoché*.   It is still widely supposed that self-knowledge is "certain," so that there is a great advantage in the subjective procedure.   Inspection shows, however, that the entire attempt is nugatory, if certainty is the ideal.   If certainty means "indubitability without contradiction," it cannot be shown that the realm of thought as a whole is indubitable.   Granting that a present experience, the "now," is certain, the "now" has already become "not now" and a new "now" has taken its place.   Unless absolute reliance be placed upon the memory, one can only be certain of the present, passing experience, so that a solipsism of the present moment is all that results.   The principle of the primacy of the self is as much a dogma as a spiritual ego, whether individual or general, empirical or transcendental in character.   It seems appropriate that this idealistic dogma be snatched from the phenomenological movement by exponents of the philosophy of existence, all the more so since Heidegger himself attached so much importance to "nothing" (in his *What is Metaphysics?*).

Entirely different is the requirement that a scientific philosophy at-

---

23. Cf. M. Farber, *The Foundation of Phenomenology*, pp. 543 ff., for a critique of this phase of Husserl's thought.

tempt to do full justice to the complexities introduced into experience by knowers. All the structural-analytical studies of scholars, whether idealistic or non-idealistic, must be considered. Thus there is no reason why a naturalistic or materialistic philosophy [24] cannot do full justice to all phases of experience, from the perceptual level to "pure" reflection, and beyond that to the complete process of reflection which includes the consideration of the reflecting knower in his historical and social relations. In the total structure of philosophy, the theory of reality is fundamental, and is not to be subordinated to the theory of knowledge. Hence the knowledge of facts established by the special sciences cannot be upset by more or less clever epistemological arguments which detach the mind from its natural setting and then proceed to impose a falsifying view of reality on that basis.

* * *

Description is the ideal procedure in all types of inquiry, but it cannot always be achieved. Explanatory devices must also be utilized, and there are other types of reasoning and inquiry which are not descriptive in character. Thus the insistence upon a subjectivistic descriptive procedure is a twofold error: description cannot be a sufficient method; and subjectivistic description is merely one of the types of descriptive inquiry. The complete inspection of human experience is an ideal, and is always beset by obstacles. It requires not only the analysis of experience by an individual knower, but also the consideration of the place of the knower in reality, and above all in the social world. This balanced, or logically weighted, point of view is so well supported by scientific scholarship that it is not likely that an effete subjectivism or an idealism masquerading as a philosophy of human existence will gain much headway in America. If philosophy is to earn its way honestly it must at all times conform to the relevant achievements of the special sciences, and never fail to observe the canons of logic.

SELECTED BIBLIOGRAPHY

Farber, M., editor. *Philosophical Essays in Memory of Edmund Husserl.* Cambridge, Harvard University Press, 1940.

Farber, M. *The Foundation of Phenomenology. Ibid.,* 1943.

---

24. It is not necessary to distinguish the two tendencies in the present essay. Historically, naturalism has been a more conciliatory view, even though it was intended to be based directly upon the sciences, emphasizing either their methods or their subject matter. It has been cautious to the point of agnosticism. Materialism, on the other hand, has been uncompromising in its role as a philosophy of science. Care must be taken in characterizing materialism, however, in view of its mechanistic and dialectical varieties.

Philosophy and Phenomenological Research, an international quarterly journal, published by the University of Buffalo since its founding in 1940.

Sellars, R. W., McGill, V. J., and Farber, M., editors. *Philosophy for the Future.* New York, The Macmillan Co., 1949.

Perry, R. B. *Present Philosophical Tendencies.* New York, Longmans, Green, and Co., 1919.

Ducasse, C. J. "Objectivity, Objective Reference, and Perception." *Philosophy and Phenomenological Research,* Vol. II, 1941.

Feibleman, J. *An Introduction to Peirce's Philosophy.* New York, Harper and Brothers, 1946.

Runes, D., editor. *Twentieth Century Philosophy.* New York, Philosophical Library, 1943.

Grene, M. *Dreadful Freedom: A Critique of Existentialism.* Chicago, University of Chicago Press, 1948.

THE GIVEN AND
PERCEPTUAL KNOWLEDGE

*Charles A. Baylis**

hilosophers in the United States, like their colleagues elsewhere, are very much interested in that whole aspect of epistemology which is concerned with the philosophical problems of perception. That there is in some sense both perceptual knowledge and perceptual error is commonly agreed but the analyses offered of their nature are numerous and varied. Underlying these diverse theories, however, is widespread agreement about the facts to be interpreted. It is generally accepted, for example, that some perceptual experiences are veridical, some illusory, and some hallucinatory. There is even considerable agreement in practice as to which are which. The empirically verifiable facts of the relativity of perception and of the "mechanism" of perception are commonly accepted as something of which any adequate theory must take account.

As long as the statement is made in general terms, there might also be agreement that in veridical perception the perceiver is immediately aware of something, the given, which through its relationship to perceptual objects such as tables, trees, and turkeys, gives him knowledge about those objects. At this point, however, uniformity gives way to diversity. There is wide disagreement as to the nature of the given, as to the nature of its relation to perceptual objects, and as to the nature of those objects.

Though in part this variety is indigenous, philosophical discussion in the United States of the problems of perception has been much influenced by the works on the topic of such English writers as Russell, Moore, Broad, and Price. It is impossible to give anything like an adequate account of American thought in this field without reference to English developments.

One characteristic division of opinion that dates back to the realist

* Born in 1902. Ph.D., Harvard, 1926. Formerly a member of the department of philosophy at Brown University. Professor of philosophy and chairman of the department at the University of Maryland. Author, in collaboration with A. A. Bennett, of *Formal Logic* (1939), and contributor of numerous articles in philosophical journals.

revolt against idealism, shortly after the turn of the century, and that has had considerable influence ever since, is the split between new realism and critical realism. In a cooperative volume,[1] published in 1912, six American philosophers, E. B. Holt, W. T. Marvin, W. P. Montague, R. B. Perry, W. B. Pitkin, and E. G. Spaulding, announced their adoption of a presentative rather than a representative theory of perceptual knowledge, their acceptance of an epistemological monism rather than an epistemological dualism. They held that idealism, with all its "mistakes" was due in large part to the representative character of the classical forms of realism, as found for example in Descartes and Locke. We should get away, they said, from the older realistic notion of thinking of the mind as a sort of a camera in which there are images which sometimes copy the outer reality, and think of it rather on the analogy, if we must have an analogy, of a searchlight. Tulips, for example, when they are perceived, come within the rays of the mind's searchlight. They are illuminated by the mind's awareness. They stand revealed *before* the mind—not *in* it—and the mind is then directly acquainted with them. When the perceiver's attention turns elsewhere, the tulips remain just as they were when they were observed save that they no longer are observed. Being perceived or being sensed is an external relation into which material objects such as tulips may enter but from which they may withdraw unscathed.

Not long thereafter seven other American philosophers, Durant Drake, A. O. Lovejoy, J. B. Pratt, A. K. Rogers, G. Santayana, R. W. Sellars, and C. A. Strong, replied in a joint volume,[2] charging that the new realism should really be called naive realism, because it neglected almost completely the problem of error. What, for example, they asked, is the nature and ontological status of the object a new realist would say he is directly aware of when light which started 1000 years ago from a distant star which has since exploded falls on his retina? And even if the real star has not been destroyed during the passage of the light, it is certainly at a place different from that at which the seen star appears to be. The new realists are perhaps right, they admitted, in pointing out the crudeness of the camera analogy, but they are clearly wrong, the critical realists urged, in suggesting that that there can be a relation of identity between the real external star and the visual star-like datum of which a percipient is immediately aware. Rather, what we are directly aware of, the critical realists urge, is never a material object itself, but rather

---

1. *The New Realism.*
2. *Essays in Critical Realism.*

certain data which are either essences or instances of essences. In cases of veridical perception some of these essences are also embodied in the material object. We can in this way have literal knowledge of some of the primary qualities of material objects. But even in veridical perception, other essences with which or with instances of which we are directly acquainted, for example, those corresponding to secondary qualities, are not embodied in the material object. Our acquaintance with them can at most give us symbolic knowledge of other primary qualities of the object. For example, our awareness of redness, or of an instance of redness, can inform us that the object we are perceiving has certain causal characteristics, such as the ability to reflect light waves of a certain frequency and to absorb light rays of other frequencies. In no case, however, are we aware of a material object directly. Such immediate knowledge is only of essences, or their instances. This alternative calls attention to a point in which critical realists disagreed. Lovejoy, Pratt, and Sellars held that in cases of veridical perception the perceiver is directly aware of particular mental existents which are instances of the same essences as those exemplified in the perceived object. Drake, Rogers, Santayana, and Strong on the other hand, held that the perceiver is directly aware of universal essences themselves and that in veridical perception the very essence of which the perceiver is aware is itself embodied in the perceived object.

Russell's neo-realism, as expressed in his *Our Knowledge of the External World* and in *Mysticism and Logic,* succeeded in obviating most of the standard critical realist objections to a presentative view by emphasizing that the direct items of awareness are *aspects* of objects rather than objects, and that objects themselves are classes of aspects, a few of which are perceived, but most of which are unperceived. Thus in the case of the star, from which light started earthward 1000 years ago but which is now extinct, we are aware not of the extinct star itself but of one aspect of the real star, that aspect of it which can be seen from the earth 1000 years later. Russell's view in turn seemed to have difficulties of its own and was modified by later writers. Many variations of neo-realism developed, among them the "multiple location" theory of Whitehead, the "objective relativism" of A. E. Murphy, and others.

Arthur O. Lovejoy, in his Carus Lecture book, *The Revolt Against Dualism,* marshalled the arguments of critical realists in an organized and slashing attack on the positions of the early new realists and on the modified positions of later advocates of a presentational view. He closed his lectures by reaffirming the position of critical realism. "There are, in short, changes in certain physical structures (perceptual objects, intervening medium, and sentient organism) which generate existents (sensa) that are not physical in the sense in which those structures are; and these non-physical particulars are indispensible means to any knowledge of physical realities" (p. 319).

One of the most recent and most influential views of the nature of perceptual knowledge is that of C. I. Lewis, stated in his *Mind and the World-Order,* and elaborated and developed in his Carus Lecture book, *An Analysis of Knowledge and Valuation.* He describes the elements of the given as "qualia" and says of them that they are universal in the sense that they can be repeated but are particular in the sense that they are sharply to be distinguished from concepts which always imply more than can be verified in any single experience.[3] He asserts that the whole meaning of statements about perceptual objects can in theory be expressed by a series of statements of the general form, "If S be given and act A be initiated, then in all probability E will follow," where 'S', 'A', and 'E' each refers to some recognizable item of direct experience.[4] For example, the statement, "There is a doorknob a few feet in front of me," is equivalent to an indefinitely large, perhaps infinite, series of statements such as, "If a doorknobish visual appearance be given, and a complex of kinaesthetic sensations of walking be initiated, then a round, hard tactile sensation will in all probability occur."

One view not mentioned above and not discussed later is that of extreme behaviorism. This view seems not so much false as irrelevant. It provides an answer to a different question, not to the one here treated of the nature of the given and of its relation to perceptual objects and the manner in which it gives us knowledge of them. It may well be that corresponding to each element of the given there is some characteristic modification of the nervous system. But the present state of neurology helps very little in understanding perception. The situation seems to be analogous to that which exists with regard to our knowledge of neuroses. Though each neurosis may have its physiological counterpart, we are at present able to discover and treat neuroses much better through the "mental" approaches of psychiatry and psychoanalysis than through the careful scrutiny of neurons.

The main development of this paper is systematic rather than descriptive or critical. Though the views noted above are typical, they do not

---

3. *Mind and the World-Order*, pp. 123 ff.
4. "Professor Chisholm and Empiricism," *The Journal of Philosophy,* Vol. XLV, No. 19 (Sept. 9, 1948), p. 517.

by any means exhaust the many variations of recent epistemological theories of perception. And of the views mentioned, criticism will be incidental to the main line of the discussion rather than a principal concern. Our attention will turn first to a consideration of the nature of the immediately given element in experience and secondly to an examination of the way in which this enables us to obtain perceptual knowledge of such objects as doorknobs, tennis balls, and stone walls. We limit our discussion to knowledge of such macroscopic material objects and do not consider the further problem of our knowledge of the kinds of objects modern physicists talk about such as electrons. We shall call the former "material objects," and restrict the term "physical objects" to the elements revealed or suggested by physical analysis. We omit also specific consideration of the problem of substance as applied to material objects. What is said can be interpreted in one way by those who hold a material object to be a complex of characteristics at a space-time locus, and in another by those who regard a material object as a substance having characteristics and generating space-time characters by its relations to other material substances.

The main contentions of the paper are two: (1) If we seek to determine the nature of the given by empirical examination rather than by prescriptive definition, we shall find it very much richer than is ordinarily supposed and consequently a much more adequate basis for knowledge about perceptual objects. (2) To obtain such knowledge we need transcend the given only by means of the ordinary processes of extrapolation and induction. One of the most important elements in such "transcendence" is the knowledge that we sometimes obtain of what Lewis has called "natural" or "real" connections, of connections which are empirically necessary.

One reason that the problem of "the transcendence of the given in our knowledge of perceptual objects" has seemed so difficult is that the given has often been defined in such a way that it cannot have the characters it would need to have if it were to provide literal knowledge of an object. Thus to define the given as necessarily private and objects as necessarily public makes it necessary that the given be transcended or in some sense *aufgehoben* before it can yield objective knowledge. Similarly, to limit the existence of the given by definition to those brief intervals when it is being sensed, and the characteristics of the given to those that are actually noticed, makes it hard to understand how such a narrowly limited given could yield us knowledge of a material object which exists though not observed and which has many characters which remain un-noticed.

Would it not be a more fruitful approach to limit the given as little as possible by definition, leaving as many problems about its nature open for empirical investigation and solution as we can? For insofar as questions are answered by stipulative definition, no knowledge results save knowledge of our linguistic habits or intentions. Thus, in the language of one who defines a sense-datum as existing only while it is sensed, it is self-contradictory to speak of an unsensed sense-datum. But may not even one who adheres to this convention agree that there may be other aspects of that which is immediately given which may continue to exist unchanged even when it is no longer given? To be sure, what is meant by "the given" must be identified in some way, but it seems desirable to keep its defining characteristics to a minimum and, if possible, leave open for empirical determination such questions as: "Can it exist when not given?" "Can it have charasteristics which though given for notice are not noticed?" "Can it have a third spatial dimension?" "Can it have a back side?" "Can certain repeated features of it exist in a definite number without that number being noticed?" and "Can it have characters other than those it is declared to have?" As Price puts it, "Only inspection of sense-data themselves can tell us what qualities and relations they actually have; and if it follows from some theory that they ought to have other ones, so much the worse for the theory."[5] Indeed, some of these questions just raised are exactly the sort which Gestaltists or phenomenologists try to answer with the aid of carefully controlled experiments. We want to use our definition to identify unequivocally the subject of our inquiry, but we want to avoid assigning to the subject by definition any characters not required for such identification.

C. I. Lewis has made an attempt to do this in his account of the given as that in experience to which no element of interpretation by the mind has been added, the brute fact element of experience which cannot be altered by mental activity alone.[6] Sense-data, he says, are perhaps the most common species of the given. And they in turn are analyzable into ultimate elements which he calls "qualia." This account of Lewis's is a step in the right direction. He seeks to assign by definition as few characteristics as possible to the given. But even so he goes too far. In order to avoid confounding the given with any element of interpretation

---

5. H. H. Price, *Perception*, p. 242. Compare also R. M. Chisholm, "The Problem of the Speckled Hen," *Mind*, N.S., Vol. LI, No. 204, pp. 368-373.
6. *Mind and the World-Order*, chap. ii.

he makes it ineffable. He remarks, for example that to describe the shape that is given, when, as we ordinarily say, we look at a penny from an angle, as "elliptical," is just as much of an interpretation as to describe the penny itself as "round."[7] But this seems to mean that the given has no mentionable characters at all; it is recognizable but not describable.

An objection of quite a different sort to his account is that the criteria of givenness which he specifies are neither necessary nor sufficient. "These are," he says, "first, its specific sensuous or feeling-character, and second, that the mode of thought can neither create nor alter it — that it remains unaffected by any change of mental attitude or interest. It is the second of these criteria which is definitive; the first alone is not sufficient . . ."[8] It seems doubtful, however, that this second requirement holds of any experienced content. Thus, if images are included among the given, we seem able both to create — or at least to recall — them and to modify them by acts of will. Whether our mental attitudes affect our sensory data or not appears at least an empirical question, and the evidence of Freudian clinical reports and of psycho-somatic medicine indicates that they do. In any case, as long as there is doubt about the matter, we shall do well to specify the given in such a way as to leave open for further investigation the question of whether or not this content is alterable by our mental attitudes.

Lewis's account may be said to be an attempt to describe the given in terms of psychological priority. It is that, he seems to say, which is first in consciousness in the sense of being unmodified by any form of mental activity. It is the psychologically pristine or virginal, uncontaminated by the mental activities of interpretation or judgment. Quite a different line is taken by those who seek in the given that which is epistemologically prior, the "hard data" of Russell, the core of certainty on which probable knowledge is based. According to this sort of view, the given can be described in statements which, if no merely linguistic error has been made, are incorrigible. But such efforts have always met with considerable skepticism. When we say that the given has certain characteristics, may we not sometimes be in non-verbal error? We may perhaps know with certainty that a colored patch of which we are directly aware is reddish, but it may have such a borderline color that we may err if we say that it is scarlet rather than crimson. This may be no mere verbal error, for we may use the correct terms for the concepts we have in mind. There may even be no lack of clarity or distinctness in our

---

7. *Ibid.*, p. 62.
8. *Ibid.*, p. 66.

color concepts which we signify by "scarlet" and by "crimson." But we may still err in comparing our color datum with the conceptual schema—to use Lewis's phrase — which we use as a criterion.

A better meaning, for our purposes, to give the term, "the given," is what William James would have called "the content of our specious present." It is the content of an act of awareness, or — if the existence of such acts be doubted — the object of a stroke of attention. We may be aware of it for a short duration of time, i. e., throughout a specious present; we may be aware of it, James notes, more or less "vividly," or "dimly," or "focally," or "marginally," providing, as he warns, that these terms are taken as signifying degrees of attention or awareness and are not confused either with the vividness or dimness of a sensation or with the focus and margin of a sensory field. For we can be acutely aware of a very faint sound, and focally conscious of a dim light in the margin of vision. The given in this sense is the sort of thing that non-behavioristic psychologists have investigated with the aid of a tachistoscope. There are many empirical questions about it as yet unsolved, but we do at least have a good deal of relatively well-confirmed empirical knowledge about it.

We know that we seldom observe the simple qualities which Lewis calls "qualia" existing in isolation. Neither redness nor roundness, for example, is likely to occur alone. To put it conservatively, most of the colors we observe have some shape and most of the shapes that we observe have some color. Further, even if we restrict ourselves for this example to the visual field, we often find a number of colored shapes spatially and otherwise related in some pattern or other. What is visually given is often quite complex and it is only by abstraction that we single out a single colored patch or a particular color for special attention. And if we wish to describe accurately all that is sensorily given at any one time we shall usually find that it includes tactile, auditory, kinesthetic, interoceptive, and proprioceptive data as well as other varieties. When our attention is focused on some one of these, the rest fall into the margin of awareness; but the focus of our awareness can be redirected to others as we wish. Sometimes the focus of awareness is itself broad as when we are aware of the variety of color data before us.

Included in what is given are data other than those of sense, for example, the feelings and emotions of which we are immediately conscious. We appear also to be directly aware of certain relations. Sometimes these relate data in the same sensory field as when we observe one colored patch above and to the right of another, or as when we observe color similarities or dissimilarities. But apparently, also, we can and do notice relations between data of different kinds. Can we not, for example, be directly aware of the difference between the color of orange and the odor of orange? Any nonbehavioristic psychologist could add to this list indefinitely, but perhaps enough has been said to indicate the richness, the variety, and the complexity of that which is given in immediate awareness.

There are other types of entities which the given probably includes, but they are more controversial and we need not insist on them here. It seems likely, for example, that we can sometimes be directly aware of the absence of all data of a certain kind. For instance, in judging correctly that there are exactly three colored patches before us, do we not have to notice that there is no other? Again, it may well be, as many would maintain, that we can be directly acquainted with concepts or universals and with propositions. But even without insisting on these borderline cases, it is clear that much more is given in immediate awareness than is suggested by the way in which such terms as "sense-data" and "qualia" are often used.

To avoid misunderstanding due to such disparate use of terms, it may be desirably to clarify the terminology of this paper. Let us agree, for the discussion at hand, on the following usages: Anything of which we are immediately aware is "given." All that we are immediately aware of in any one stroke of attention is "the given" during that specious present. We leave open the possibility that what is given may exist even when it is not given. Within the given we can distinguish between the sensorily given and the non-sensorily given. Within the sensorily given we can identify the data of any one sense field, by criteria such as those suggested by Price.[9] Any group of data within the given which appear to constitute a particular, such as a round red patch or a cold hard expanse, we can call a "sensum," using that term in such a way that it does not follow from its meaning that what is signified either does or does not cease to exist when it ceases being sensed. And we can use Lewis's term, "quale," stripped of its suggestion of ineffability, for any single distinguishable characteristic of any sensum, such as a color quality, a shape quality, and so on.

Can the given or any of its components have qualities other than, but compatible with, those which are noted? It seems to be possible to alter our degree of attention on given sensa. Whether this occurs through

---

9. *Op. cit.*, pp. 234-5.

a change of attention within one specious present or results from the overlapping of specious presents is hard to decide, but in any case it seems well established that we can concentrate on the same group of sensa and shift our focal attention from one to another. Thus, while noticing that the content of one's awareness remains the same, one can give greater attention than before to an aspect previously present but neglected. If one's attention is first focused on the color of the dots in one's visual content, one may notice that they are numerous without noticing their exact number. But then one can attend to their numerousness and notice that exactly the same dots are five in number. One can be sure that they are the same because they have been continuously observed throughout the shift of attention. Similarly, closer attention can reveal in an unchanged sense-field similarities or dissimilarities or a pattern not at first noticed.

Discussion as to whether in such a situation one is observing different data or the same data seems futile, disagreement being due to differing choices of subject matter. What one *notices* is different in the two cases; different sense-data have been noticed. But if one describes the given, as has been done above, as that content of experience which is before one to be noticed, then sensa may correctly be said to remain the same though in successive parts of the specious present different aspects of them are noticed. All that is sometimes required to make them noticeable is a change in attention, not a change in the content there to be attended to.

Even if more detailed discrimination or attention to neglected sensa requires more than one specious present, one often has good grounds for believing that the sensa of the two specious presents are qualitatively and numerically exactly alike. Within one of them, the observer has simply discriminated or noticed that which was also present in the other but unnoticed. How can we tell that this detail was there though unnoticed? In this way: There are degrees of attention, varying from acute to vanishingly weak. By noticing that a certain characteristic, say the three-ness of some dots, remains unchanged though one's attention to this characteristic becomes less and less, one gains knowledge of a series and one can extrapolate beyond this series from the vanishingly weak to the barely vanished.

An apparently more difficult question is the query: Can the given have characteristics which are incompatible with those it appears to have? Can a colored patch be red though it is seen as gray, be scarlet though it is seen as crimson? Can an observed shape that departs only slightly from the square be seen as square? Perhaps a better approach to the problem is obtained through putting the question in this form: Is it possible to make mistakes about the given, and if so of what kind?

We must of course accept the analytical propositions that what is observed is observed, that what is noticed is noticed. But it does not follow from such propositions that our judgment about what is given, and our statements about it are incorrigible. A mistake in one's choice of a word is always possible, either through ignorance or through a verbal slip. And, as noted earlier, some mistakes in judgment about the given seem possible. Even the simplest judgment about it will describe the given or some part of it as being an instance of some concept. But it seems possible, even in simple cases to make mistakes and to think wrongly that a certain element of the given exemplifies a certain concept. Such a gross mistake as judging that a red sensum is gray, seems unlikely, but it seems possible that one might, either through insufficient acquaintance with the two concepts involved, or through insufficient attention to the given, judge a scarlet patch to be crimson or vice-versa. Similarly, though it seems highly unlikely that one would judge a round patch to be square, it seems possible that through careless attention one·might judge a given rectangular patch, only slighter longer than it is wide, to be square.

Part of the difficulty of this question seems to be due to the ambiguity of the form in which it is often put, *e.g.,* "Can a given scarlet patch *be seen* as crimson?" Because of the application of the law of identity, what one is aware of when one's content is a scarlet patch, is of course a scarlet patch. In that sense of "see" one does not see it as crimson. But one may misjudge it to be crimson, and in that sense "see" it as crimson. Once this distinction is made, little difficulty remains. One can be mistaken in predicating a certain characteristic of that which is immediately given. And one can be mistaken in formulating even a correct judgment. But one cannot be directly aware of what is not there to be an object for awareness, though one need not notice or be aware of all that is there as an object for awareness.

Are sensa ever three-dimensional, ever solid? Price urges that they have sensible depth.[10] Ayer states flatly that ". . . the visual sense-field is sensibly three-dimensional."[11] C. D. Broad quotes with approval the contention of Marc-Wogau that often when we look at, say, the moon,

---

10. *Op. cit.,* p. 218.
11. A. J. Ayer, *The Foundations of Empirical Knowledge,* p. 246.

our visual prehensum, i.e., the object of our immediate awareness, is convex rather than flat. He adds that it seems to him defensible, though he would hesitate to say that it is correct, to hold that a cricket ball may be "prehended as *part* of the *outer surface* of a three-dimensional object of *some form or other;* which may be either closed or open on the side invisible to the observer; which, if closed, may be either hollow or filled with matter; and which, even if it be open, or closed and hollow, has a certain finite thickness, and therefore a *hind*-surface or an *inner* surface of some kind or other as well as a front-surface or outer surface." [12] The detailed study of how much is given in our perception of three-dimensionality is a task for experimental psychology. But it is significant that such careful students of sense-data as Broad and Marc-Wogau regard it as possible or probable, respectively, that what is given in visual perception has thickness, and therefore an inner surface of some kind and shape.

Enough has perhaps now been said about the given to indicate that it can provide a sufficient basis for our knowledge of physical objects. Indeed we find within it entities which are complex enough to be called "minimal objects." Sensa may, and usually do, have characters they are not noticed as having. Even as given they endure for a finite though short period of time. Some sensa have thickness as well as length and breadth. With minimal objects of this sort there seems to be reasonable hope of using inductive procedures to go from knowledge of them to knowledge of more enduring and more perceptual objects.

How this can be done in detail is a long story, but one method of doing it is suggested by the careful work of Price. To outline his procedure very briefly, he distinguished certain sensa as "nuclear." They are those sensa which are "perfectly constructible and perfectly stereoscopic." [13] These nuclear data can, by the "Method of Progressive Adjunction," be combined into a nuclear solid. [14] Through application of the "Principle of Specific Detail" and imagination, these nuclear solids can be rectified into "Standard Solids." [15] Standard Solids have location in objective space, and together with their "physical occupants" constitute material objects. [16]

Price's work, though invaluable in many respects, involves two complications, which, in view of the account presented here as to the

12. *Mind*, N.S., Vol. LVI (April, 1947), pp. 108-9.
13. *Op. cit.*, p. 222.
14. *Ibid.*, p. 242.
15. *Ibid.*, p. 227.
16. *Ibid.*, pp. 246, 301.

nature of the given, seem unnecessary. (1) He is led to deny that sensa are public or have position in objective space, although he holds the *families* of sensa which constitute Standard Solids are public and do have such spatial position. (2) Because he denies causal characteristics to sensa he is led to suppose that material objects must be constituted not alone by a family of sensa but also by a "physical occupant" which is the substance or at least the entity which has the causal characteristics which belong to the perceptual object. But each of these difficulties can be avoided.

(1) The principal reason that Price advances for his view that sensa have no location in the objective space of Standard Solids is his belief that no sensum has thickness. But this, as we have seen, seems to be an error. He admits that some sensa have sensible depth, and Ayer and Broad and Marc-Wogau concur in the judgment that some sensa are three-dimensional. It is hard to see why, therefore, save perhaps for the lingering influence of physiological theories about retinal images, these visual sensa should be denied to have the characteristics of three-dimensionality and thickness which they are observed to have. As Price himself says, "If it follows from some theory that they ought to have other ones, so much the worse for the theory." [17]

If nuclear sensa are three-dimensional there seems no good reason why they cannot be literally part of the surface of a Standard Solid, and be related in the objective space of Standard Solids to the other sensa which constitute the other surfaces of this solid and to the sensa which are the surfaces of other Solids.

This consideration in turn influences our answer to the related questions: Can some sensa exist unsensed? Are some sensa public? The reasons for giving negative answers to both questions seem to be the result either of unnecessarily limiting prescriptive definitions or of unverified and unneeded theories about the genesis of sensa. We have already considered the former; let us turn to the latter.

We need not repeat the mass of detailed evidence, evidence showing a variation of sensa "of objects" with variations in sensa "of the intervening medium" and in somatic sensa and perhaps in the attitudinal or emotional elements of the personality to be found in the given. These concomitant variations are generally accepted as facts. The question about them is rather whether they must be accounted for on a causal

17. *Ibid.*, p. 242.

theory or whether the selective theory that Price discusses so carefully [18] is not satisfactory. Can it not be our *sensing* of the sensa which is conditioned by these environmental, physiological, and perhaps psychological factors, rather than the *existence* of these sensa? Price rejects the selective theory principally on the basis that, though possible, it would leave us no ground in any case for distinguishing between selection and causation. But he himself, following Kant, carefully provides a means for distinguishing in a series of sensa between a succession which is merely subjective and ɔne which is objective.[19] He uses the criteria he there develops for distinguishing between those sensa which though not being sensed are really capable of being sensed—if only a standard observer were present— and those conceivable sensa which have no such possibility of being sensed. But exactly the same criteria can be used to distinguish unsensed though existent sensa from unsensed and nonexistent sensa. It seems a reasonable view on the basis of the distinctions which Price himself advances, therefore, to discriminate between "wild" sensa, which are somatically or otherwise *caused* and which endure only briefly and privately, from nuclear sensa which are not so caused but whose observation is conditioned by such factors as, for example, the physiology and actions of an observer. These nuclear sensa may very well exist unsensed.

This being true of nuclear sensa, and it also being the case that such sensa have position in the objective space of Standard Solids, there is no reason why they cannot be regarded as public. Precisely the same stereoscopic sensum which is the surface of such a Solid may be observed now by one observer, now by another. Perhaps, if Price's theory about the observability of sensa that are qualitatively alike by observers with different points of view be correct, precisely the same nuclear sensum, the same both qualitatively and numerically, can be observed simultaneously by two or more observers.

(2) Price's view that material objects must be constituted jointly by a physical occupant and a family of sensa rests on his attempt to account for the causal characteristics which we judge such perceptual objects to have. He holds, correctly enough, that these cannot properly be predicated of the space or space-time location of the family of sensa, since causal properties, though manifested at a location are not the result of the location. For it remains always the same though occupied at different times by different families of sensa associated with different sets of

---

18. *Ibid.,* chap. ii.
19. *Ibid.,* pp. 260-268.

causal properties. He holds also that the causal properties associated with any one family of sensa cannot correctly be ascribed to this family itself, since, he says, neither an individual sensum nor a family of sensa can itself have causal properties.

Price's reason for denying that a family of sensa can have causal properties are based on his view that sensa exist only when they are being sensed.[20] Hence, he holds that, at any given time, most of the members of a family of sensa do not exist; they are only obtainable. A causal property, such as the relative impenetrability of a wall, may be manifested throughout the area occupied by the wall, by, for example, the wall's resistance to the ground and to the surrounding air. But only the sensa constituting certain members of the family, namely those constitutive of one surface of the wall, may be observed, or perhaps no members of the family may be sensed. Hence it would be false to say, he concludes, that the causal properties are properties of a family for most of the members of that family do not exist. He is led then to suppose that there is a physical occupant of the region manifesting the wall-like impenetrability, and that it is this physical occupant which has the causal properties. He admits that this physical occupant must also have certain intrinsic, i.e., non-relational properities but he declares them to be unknowable.[21] The material object, he concludes, is a conjunct of this unknowable physical occupant and the family of sensa coincident with it.[22]

But this whole conception of a mysterious physical occupant becomes unnecessary once it is realized that sensa may, and nuclear sensa often do, continue to exist unsensed. If such is the case the Standard Solid has that kind of continuity and unity that Price says are required of anything which has causal characteristics. Consequently, a great simplification of his proposals is possible.

Price's rejection of the possibility of individual sensa serving as causes seems to be based also on his view that they come into being at the time they are sensed and cease to be at the moment they are no longer sensed. Thus he says that when crossing a street, it is not a loud honk-like sensum that causes one to jump, but rather the sensing of that sensum. If he were urging only that events rather than things are causes, we could perhaps agree with him. It may indeed be better to say that the occurrence of a sensum or a change in a sensum causes the occurrence of another or a change in another. But we would insist that sensa can come

20. *Ibid.*, pp. 289-291.
21. *Ibid.*, p. 294.
22. *Ibid.*, p. 293.

into being, change, and cease to be, all without these events being sensed. If this is so, then it seems reasonable to suppose that some such sensa events may stand in causal relations to others.

There has been a pronounced trend in recent American philosophy to regard causation, whether among sensa or perceptual objects, as a prime example of empirically necessary connections. At about the same time, C. I. Lewis in his Carus lectures,[23] and R. M. Chisholm,[24] and Nelson Goodman[25] in articles, urged that some of the empirical connections we wish to describe cannot be expressed in the indicative mood, but require for their adequate expression a contrary to fact conditional statement and the subjunctive mood. Lewis's discussion is most complete, and significantly so, because the topic is so directly relevant to his central contention that perceptual judgments can be expressed in a series of "If . . . then" statements about the relations of sensa. These "if . . . then" relations are, he argues, neither relations of material implication, formal implication, nor strict implication—which last would make them analytic —but rather a distinct species. Hume referred to them as "necessary connections of matters of fact." Lewis suggests calling them "real connections." He gives as an example, "If Clarence Lewis were to jump from the second floor window, he would be hurt." He points out that we believe the relationship thus expressed holds even though we expect the antecedent never to be fulfilled. All three writers note that we are able to, and constantly do, distinguish between "accidental" universal connections, such as all the chairs in this room being made of wood and all crows being black, and "empirically necessary" universal connections, such as increased tidal movements when the moon is either full or dark.

Unfortunately, neither Lewis nor the other writers have done much more than baptize this hitherto largely unnoticed relation. This is itself a noteworthy advance, but there remains the still more important task first of describing in positive terms what the nature of the relation is, rather than merely noting what it is not, and second of telling us how we can discover cases of it and increase the probability of our knowledge of them. Lewis proposes elsewhere in his book only the knowledge of frequencies as a basis for probable knowledge. But this will not do here, for we often have such knowledge in the case of merely "accidental" con-

23. *An Analysis of Knowledge and Valuation*, chap. viii.
24. "The Contrary to Fact Conditional," Mind, N.S., Vol. LV (1946), pp. 289-307.
25. "The Problem of Counterfactual Conditionals," *The Journal of Philosophy*, Vol. XLIV (1947), pp. 113-128.

nections. There must be something which enables us to distinguish such cases from the empirically necessary ones.

I suggest that one distinctive feature of our knowledge of real connections is the applicability of Mill's methods of Agreement, Difference, or Concomitant Variations, or of modifications or combinations of these, or of other somewhat similar types of method. Thus in the case of every chair in the room being made of wood, we know even without trying it, that we could apply Mill's methods and ruin the generalization by bringing in a steel chair. In the case of the black crows we believe that the color determinant in the genes could be varied without varying any of the determinants of those characteristics in terms of which crows are defined. We may be wrong, but we shall know this only if we find by application of methods such as Mill's that there is a necessary connection between the color characteristic and the defining characteristic.

We are, I think, just at the threshhold of the discovery of better methods for confirming hypotheses as to the existence of empirically necessary connections. When they are added to our arsenal of weapons for attack on the problem of perceptual knowledge, we should be able to know much more clearly than we do now, the grounds for our passing from acquaintance with some sensa to perceptual knowledge, and for our refusal to make such a transition when confronted by other sensa.

SELECTED BIBLIOGRAPHY

BOOKS:

Ayer, A. J. *The Foundations of Empirical Knowledge*. New York, The Macmillan Co., 1940.

Broad, C. D. *The Mind and Its Place in Nature*. London, Kegan Paul, Trench, Trubner and Co., 1925.

Drake, Durant; Lovejoy, A.D.; Pratt J. B.; Rogers, A. K.; Santayana, G.; Sellars, R. W.; and Strong, C. A. *Essays in Critical Realism*. London, Macmillan Co., 1921.

Holt, E. B.; Marvin, W. T.; Montague, W. P.; Perry, R. B.; Pitkin, W. B.; and Spaulding, E. G. *The New Realism*. New York, The Macmillan Co., 1912.

Laird, John. *A Study in Realism*. London and New York, Cambridge University Press, 1920.

Lewis, C. I. *Mind and the World-Order*. New York, Charles Scribner's Sons, 1929.

——————. *An Analysis of Knowledge and Valuation,* The Paul Carus Lectures, Seventh Series, 1945. La Salle, Ill., Open Court Publishing Co., 1946.

Lovejoy, A. O. *The Revolt Against Dualism.* LaSalle, Ill., Open Court Publishing Co., 1930.

Moore, G. E. *Philosophical Studies.* London, Kegan Paul, Trench, Trubner and Co., 1922.

Russell, B. *Our Knowledge of the External World,* lectures 3 and 4. Chicago, Open Court Publishing Co., 1914.

——————. *Mysticism and Logic.* New York, Longmans, Green, and Co., 1918.

Price, H. H. *Perception.* New York, Robert M. McBride and Co., 1933.

Whitehead, A. N. *Science and the Modern World.* New York, The Macmillan Co., 1925.

ARTICLES:

Broad, C. D. Review of "Professor Marc-Wogau's Theorie der Sinnesdaten," *Mind,* N. S., Vol. LVI, January and April, 1947, pp. 1-30; 97-131.

Chisholm, R. M. "The Problem of the Speckled Hen," *Mind,* N. S. Vol. LI, No. 204. pp. 368-73.

——————. "The Contrary to Fact Conditional," *Mind,* N. S. Vol. LV, pp. 289-307.

Ducasse, C. J. "Objectivity, Objective Reference, and Perception," *Philosophy and Phenomenological Research,* September, 1947, pp. 43-78.

Goodman, Nelson. "The Problem of Counterfactual Conditions," *The Journal of Philosophy,* Vol. XLIV, 1947, pp. 113-128.

Lewis C. I. "Professor Chisholm and Empiricism," *The Journal of Philosophy,* Vol. XLV, No. 19, 1948, pp. 517-524.

Moore, G. E. "A Defense of Common Sense," in *Contemporary British Philosophy,* Second Series, edited by J. H. Muirhead. London, Allen and Unwin, 1925, pp. 193-223.

——————. "The Nature of Sensible Appearances," Part III of a Symposium. *Aristotelian Society,* Supplementary Vol. VI, 1926, pp. 179-189.

Murphy, A. E. "Ideas and Nature," in *University of California Studies in Philosophy,* Berkeley, 1926.

—————. "Substance and Substantive," in *University of California Studies in Philosophy,* Berkeley, 1927.

—————. "Objective Relativism in Dewey and Whitehead," *Philosophical Review,* Vol. XXXVI, 1927, pp. 121-144.

CRITICAL REALISM AND MODERN MATERIALISM

Roy Wood Sellars *

For the purpose of this book which is the promotion of a better understanding, on the part of French and American thinkers, of trends of thought in the two countries, it may be simplest to sketch a general outline of my own position, indicating, in passing, its setting in American philosophy. Where possible I shall, likewise point to possible continuities with French eighteenth-century thought, such as that which appeared in the writings of Cabanis and De Tracy and which affected Thomas Cooper, and even John Adams. Let me confess that I have always been an admirer of the blending of science and philosophy in eighteenth-century thought.

There is this historical thread of continuity in the acceptance of the scientific view of man and the universe in which he finds himself. But the idealogues were quickly pushed to one side in France; and the materialistic naturalism of Cooper did not secure much of a hearing in the United States. Since then, the theory of evolution and the tremendous growth of the biological and the social sciences, as well as the series of revolutions in physics, itself, have introduced new possibilities and given plasticity to empirical thought. In general, these changes are manifested in terms of such principles as those of emergence and levels. I would also point to the increasing emphasis upon symbols in connection with thought, something which takes us away from sensations and images *per se*. Concepts and symbols are functional.

The materialism I represent stresses, then, emergent novelty as against the kind of reductionism associated with classical, mechanical principles. It seeks to do justice to levels of causality in nature and thus to treat human personality·and its associated categories empirically and with respect. In a certain sense, therefore, it recognizes the past motivations of idealism and Kantianism while arguing that historical idealism took the easy way

* Born in 1880. Ph.D., University of Michigan, 1908. Professor of philosophy at the University of Michigan. President of the American Philosophical Association, 1923. Author of works cited in bibliography, and of many articles in philosophical publications.

of breaking with physical realism and with naturalism. In this regard, did not dualism, Kantian phenomenalism, and idealism all represent a temporary strategy for which the time is now past? Even if this is the case—as I think it is—there remain technical problems to be cleared up. The gateway here is epistemology. That is the reason for my stress upon critical realism. It represented an empirical realism which broke through subjectivism and phenomenalism to nature.

The period in which I matured is best characterized as one influenced by (1) a reaction against Anglo-American idealism and by (2) an expansion of the sciences. The growth of biology and psychology under the guidance of the theory of evolution was particularly important. This led to a stress upon genetic considerations. Fortunately, this emphasis was in some measure moderated by the rise of mathematical logic and an interest in analysis. Something of an equilibrium between the genetic outlook and the analytic established itself. The cultural atmosphere became increasingly secular. All this was to point ultimately to a humanistic perspective.

The implication of this cultural situation was not positivism in the technical sense of that term, for Anglo-American traditions were colored by a concern for theory of knowledge and metaphysics. It was philosophy after the grand manner with its feeling for basic questions which sought to come to terms with science.

It was fairly evident that the Kantian gambit was outmoded. That as we saw it, reflected a wrong premise in epistemology to the effect that to know is to construct what is known. And the reaction against idealism had made a fairly direct form of realism more promising. Moreover, Kantianism was tied in too intimately with the Newtonian view of the world.

In this situation, the path my own thinking took still seems to me the promising one. It was that of realism in epistemology and of an evolutionary, materialistic naturalism in metaphysics. At one and the same time, I explored the possibilities of a new form of empirical realism and of a rejection of traditional forms of dualism with respect to the mind-body problem. And I soon found these two explorations supporting one another. May not consciousness be intrinsic to brain-patterns as these are activated? What is the nature and reach of objective knowing? In this fashion—and quite logically, I think—realism was becoming a door to an evolutionary way of handling the mind-body problem. I thought much in terms of organization.

I suppose philosophy has always moved in terms of puzzles of a large sort. That is certainly true of Aristotle and of Kant. In this sense, it represents what, in the jargon of today, might be called a *meta*-level. There are knowledge-claims in our experience—but what is knowledge? No particular science investigates it, even though the various sciences may throw light upon its conditions. Suppose we look at human knowledge-claims. The older empiricism had become so entangled in the causal, or transmission, approach that it could think only of sensations and images. And yet do we not know through, and by means of, these, taken up into the context of referential designations and concepts? I certainly seem to myself to be looking at this typewriter and not at my sensations *qua* sensations. Response, meanings, an awareness of extra-bodily externality, the category of thinghood, all play their part. And so the critical realists began to stress reference, action, symbols, as empirically discoverable in the perceptual act. The causal approach did not do justice to perception. There was stimulation, of course; but that was just in initiation. Much was added in the way of direct response, conceptual interpretation, an awareness of objectivity. Why not, then, analyze perceptual judgment and statements? In so doing, one would still be empirical. Thus American critical realism was born. In the essay contributed to the *Essays in Critical Realism,* I emphasized knowledge and its categories.

Now this was not neo-Kantianism because it was strictly *physical realism*. It was gnostic and not agnostic. It did not speak of things-in-themselves but of things. And, what was more, it regarded the knower as the organic self. Here it was more in line with Hobbes as against Descartes. Do you need a mental substance for the cogito? In our ordinary language is not the *I* the organic speaker? The same question can be asked about Kant's *I think*. In perception the percipient is clearly organic. Perhaps it is because the cortex in verbal symbolism does not always call up organic resonance to a marked degree that this illusion of incorporeality so easily arises. Symbols may involve cortical patterns and be engaged in thought without that feeling of motor attitude and sense of preparatory response so characteristic of the *set* of perception. Thus the cortex may have misled a culture with a predisposition to spiritualism and dualism. In the light of recent work on the brain, that temptation is lessening. After all, language took the place of gesticulation with the hands, leaving them free for business. But we shall have more to say about all this in connection with the mind-body problem.

There was, I believe, a certain inevitability about this direction of philosophical development in the United States. Idealism and Kantianism had been able to hold the fort against Spencerian materialism—I leave out, of course, Spencer's gesture to the Unknowable and the Unconditioned—by emphasizing mind and experience. But now, in the realistic movement, the physical world was being recognized as basic and not phenomenal or mental. Yet there still remained the job of naturalizing mind. Today psychology is doing this fairly well. But there still remains an aporia, a puzzle. In what sense is mind, or intelligence, a physical category emergent upon life? And what is the nature of the *inness* of consciousness to the brain? Neo-materialism has subtle clarifications to make. It must use epistemology to clarify our double knowledge of the functioning brain. We can have external, descriptive knowledge about the brain; and it may be that, in consciousness, each one is *participating* in the thalamic-cortical operations of the brain. Linguistic and philosophical distinctions must aid the actual movement of science in these matters.

To make a long story short, pragmatism and realism challenged idealism in the United States. And they, themselves, began to interact upon one another. For a long time now, John Dewey has called himself a realist, though his realism is less epistemological in character than that of the new realists and the critical realists. Having given up idealism, he gradually dropped back upon the human organism and its *transactions*. And so he moved to evolutionary naturalism, much as I had done. In fact, he and his followers have finally come to adopt the label of non-reductive materialism. All of which I welcome since I had arrived at this decision by 1916 in my book *Critical Realism*. I still think, however, that certain epistemological distinctions are of value in clarifying our complex conception of the integral unity of mind, body, and consciousness. But, as I have already promised, I shall touch upon this *aporia* more systematically later.

Thus far, I have been more concerned with opening up a perspective in American thought than with points of detail. In what follows I shall explain the direct form of realism which I defend, then pass to metaphysics, that is, to ontology and cosmology, and, finally, consider axiology or value. While these main divisions of philosophy are distinguishable and while each requires relevant analyses, they, of course, should finally fit into each other and throw light upon one another. In the conclusion, I shall try, very briefly, to draw these main divisions together. Valuing and knowing must be shown to be natural operations of human beings within the evolutionary diversified universe. This is, if you will, a quite pluralistic, empirical way of looking at valuing and knowing.

I

First of all, then, to an attempt to clarify the principles of critical realism.

In place of traditional empiricism, largely reflecting the preconceptions of the time, the realists tended to start with an analysis of actual perceptual experiences with their designations and meanings. It was realized that perceiving is a thick experience, dominated by attitudes of response, the arousal of concepts, the felt awareness of the body of the percipient over against what he is concerned with. In short, it reflects a high level of organic and minded activity and not merely the effect of a stimulus. Of course, this fact is manifested in the linguistic expression of perception as well as in overt behavior. Thus I am aware of myself as looking at this typewriter whose keys I am at present pounding. And I say that I "see" this typewriter-sort of thing. That is, I am visually aware of it. But what does this expression mean? Essentially that my designative concern with it is dominated by the visual appearance. I look at it *through* the visual appearance. It, like my concepts, are means of referential awareness.

Now the point of all this is that referential awareness is a complex achievement, *sui generis,* which must be studied in the light of its conditions and its claims. There is no need to be mystical about it. There is not some entity, called the mind, which bodily gets outside the organism and spiritually touches the thing with which the minded organism is concerned. Rather is there an awareness of extra-bodily referring and intent, and awareness guided by the embodiment of the self in the organism. The objectivity of reference and meaning at the level of perception is tied in with organic action and passion. The *I* is the self, the concrete human being.

The categories of objective knowing must be seen in this context to be understood. Action, social intercourse, symbolism are, all of them, of this level. The flaw, then, in early empiricism was its neglect of the perceptual experience and its concentration upon the one moment of causal, transmissive stimulation. No wonder subjectivism was the consequence, especially while the soul-mind theory was in the ascendancy. Now I am not going to deny the possibility of a reflexive introspection of experiencing, as such, in all its complexity. This is sometimes called knowledge of acquaintance. But it would be vicious to make this shift of attention and interest negate our actual objective concern and cognitive claims.

While both the new realism and critical realism were, intentionally, forms of *direct realism,* the new realism, dominated by James's famous essay, *Does Consciousness Exist?* with its appeal to contexts, by the vogue of the phrase, external relations, and by the fear of the pitfalls of representative realism, sought its direct realism in a kind of searchlight view. The external world is, for it, open to an apprehension of an unmediated sort. Things are as they seem. Perceiving is apprehending. As Perry put it, the idea is the thing and the thing is the idea. This was called epistemological monism and panobjectivism. In England, it dominated the outlook of S. Alexander. The difficulty was, of course, to understand error and illusion.

I want it to be quite clear that critical realism, as I understood it, was a form of direct realism but that it thought of this directness in terms of designative, responsive directness which used sensory data and concepts as factors in its objective concern. Perceiving was an activity of a minded organism in which response, the use of sensory data and symbols, the awareness of the felt body in its commerce with the things around it, all played their part. Now the thing to do was to analyze perceptual judgments in an empirical way and then to go to modern biology and psychology, the better to understand what processes sustained them. Obviously, we were far from Cartesian and Lockian conceptions.

Now it has always been my contention that the critical realist was a direct realist, or epistemological monist, in the sense that perceptual cognition involved a pointing, or direct reference, to the thing, or event, *made* the object of cognition by the concerned, designative activity of the organic knower. But such direct, objective designation did not mean that the object was *literally* open to inspection, that it entered consciousness in the way James and the new realist assumed. It merely meant that we sensuously symbolized what we were dealing with and that we could check up on the fact by walking to the thing and taking hold of it, if necessary. But the descriptions added, under the guidance of sensory data and accrued concepts, always needed verification, though it was to be assumed that sensory data gave an *appearance* of the object, that is, that it in some measure disclosed the object. And yet this premise, founded on the very guidance-use of sensory data by the working organism in the know-how of animals, could be studied in the light of criteria, such as control of nature, coherent cognitive systems, increasing insight, power of prediction. In other words, the human knower could *confirm* the essential trustworthiness of his point of departure, given to him by organic perception itself. And that gives us the correct conception of what epistemology is. It is a study of human knowing as to its claims, its mechanism, its conditions, and its reach. And its results must fit into scientific knowledge. But it is *philosophical* in that knowing is *sui generis,* even though a natural achievement.

But I cannot linger upon epistemology, fascinating as the subject is. I shall merely make a few additional, general remarks. First, by its very logic, the new realism tended to be scornful of substance or continuant bodies with dispositional properties. It was a transformation of radical empiricism. The critical realist, because of his stress upon reference and the body, could explore matter and bodies. Second, the critical realist could avoid mystical ideas of the so-called cognitive relation and deny that there was anything involved but selective pointing and designation, the sort of thing, at the elementary level of perceiving, carried by gesture and demonstrative, like *this* and *that.* Though language has an organic base in the brain, it is functionally symbolic and, in a sense, super-organic and tied in with objective, social understanding. In this regard, it is different from sensations and images and has the same context as action. It represents an emergent, cultural level. In other words, designative and symbolic reference and conceptual predication must replace mystical notions of an internal subject-object relation, so dear to idealism. Third, I am decidely skeptical of Santayana's *essence.* Sensory discriminations and concepts in the setting of referential awareness can carry cognition. Ultimately, it is a question of the confirmation of statements in accordance with scientific method. Such confirmed statements formulate *facts about* things and events in the context of categorial meanings. As I see it, a fact is a cognitive disclosure to the effect that a thing or event is so-and-so.

The theory of truth implied is logically obvious. To say that a statement is true is to say (1) that it has been tested and (2) that it gives knowledge about its referent in terms of facts. Such a theory of truth is a revision of the correspondence tradition in terms of a direct realism. The testing is logical and methodical. And agreement is a verified implication. *Since we know,* the statement must correspond.

So far as I can see, the logical empiricists (or positivists) can have no essential objection to this analysis. It is unfortunate that they neglected epistemology and metaphysics; but they seem to have done so in ignorance of realistic and naturalistic developments in the United States. Curiously enough, England developed realism but fought shy of naturalism. Bertrand Russell is, of course, sympathetic with naturalism and materialism but never escaped from Hume. That is, he never clearly enough distinguished between sensing and perceiving. I mean that he never adequately supplemented the causal approach to perception with the responsive, objective activity which sets the percipient over against the perceived something which appears in meanings and language.

It is only fair to say that Thomism is realistic; but it never allowed itself to reanalyze the distinction between form and matter and retained an antiquated conception of reason. I have tried to show that the broader, empirical term is *intelligence,* working through the operational development of concepts under strict control of observation and action. Thomism never underwent the *agony* of modern philosophy with its false starts, its plunge into subjectivism, Kantian machinery, romanticism, and idealism. But it paid a price for this escape. It found it hard to understand the more functional view of mind and the logic of scientific method.

We have already paid our respects to Kant. The point is that he did not reanalyze perceiving to give it objective reference but took sensations and added to them innate forms. To know is to construct. But, given a better epistemology and a more genetic view of the categories, there is much in his analysis that can be taken up into a critical realism. Yet ordinary neo-Kantianism gives one something super-organic with no suitable foundation in the human knower. Only an analysis of perceptual cognition in the light of its causal and responsive, operational conditions which we have outlined *can put knowing into the world.*

Now I have treated epistemology at this great length, comparatively speaking, because it has, rightly or wrongly, seemed to me that French philosophy has not wrestled with it to the same extent that English and American philosophy has. We could never forget Locke, Berkeley, and Hume. For instance, Bergson, in *Matter and Memory,* makes some passing references to Berkeley and images at a time when the major energy in England and the United States was devoted to the refutation of Berkeley, Germany exercised too much of a fascination. I suspect it still does in existentialism.

II

I pass now to ontology and cosmology, that is, to metaphysics.

Being a physical realist and skeptical, as an evolutionist would be, of Cartesian dualism, I was early pushed on to challenge what is usually called the reductive, or dead-level, view of nature. Could not mind, like life, be taken in a functional sense as a high-level, *physical category?*

Suppose we use the term of the biologist, C. Judson Herrick, and speak of mentation. Now this, of course, is what the comparative psychologists are doing. Mind, as substance, does not mean anything to them. How to conceive *consciousness* still remains a problem, in the handling of which epistemology, I think, aids. How *existentially penetrative* is our external knowledge of brain-activity? Are, to use *Gestalt* terminology, psychical contents in some sense isomorphic with brain events? Are they "in" the brain in an existential sense? That was the position I explained in *Critical Realism* in 1916 and in articles going back to 1907. Bertrand Russell has recently been advocating the same notion. Let us recall that, for critical realism, external knowledge is factual and not intuitively penetrative. It builds on the disclosures mediated by sensory data and concepts. But surely, physical processes must have *existential content* or thickness of being. They cannot, to use Whitehead's expression, be vacuous. Therefore, there is nothing in our factual knowledge which excludes what I have called, in default of a better expression, a qualitative dimension. This does not signify panpsychism. That is the other extreme to old-fashioned materialism.

Now the theory of emergent levels with novel properties implied a rejection of both the Thomistic theory of causality, as agency from above, and dead-level, atomistic mechanicalism. It postulated what I call *integrative causality,* the forming of wholes, the effective reality of organization. Of course, *time* would be a feature of such active wholes. It would be physiological, functional time, adjustment, pattern-forming, and functioning. As we pass from the microscopic to the macroscopic, temporal units change. It takes a long time for a person to make a moral decision, while an electron jumps almost instantaneously. Integrative patterns rest upon included patterns. But I can only hint at the categorial problems of evolution. The whole-part relation needs thorough analysis.

If, then, organization, levels in nature, and functional wholeness were to be taken seriously — as the theory of evolution seemed to demand — then the idea of operational unity, or togetherness, must needs be explored. In what sense, for instance, is an atom *other than* its constituent particles as these are thought of in isolation from one another? In what sense is a molecule other than an external addition of two atoms? In what sense is a living thing other than a sum, or aggregation, of what it can be broken down into? There were, no doubt, additive properties but other properties were, on the face of it, novel or emergent and apparently went with organization and functional wholeness.

Such reflection on what may be called functional unities in nature was exploratory and tried to avoid anything of the nature of mysticism. I, myself, was convinced that what I called *integrative causality* was at work, that is, that unified wholes with a degree of capacity for self-maintenance could arise in nature under favoring conditions. This would signify some measure of action-as-a-whole. It was this action-as-a-whole which should be correlated with emergent properties. Any part, taken by itself and studied in isolation, would involve some measure of disregard of the total context. In this sense it would be an *isolate*.

Obviously, philosophy could do only a preliminary piece of analysis. It could challenge preconceptions by emphasizing the whole range of things from the human to the inorganic. It could move in imagination from the lowest level to the highest and back again in a quite empirical and undogmatic fashion. And the more naturalistically it was inclined, the more would it be skeptical of the final adequacy of principles built upon a concentration upon additive, molar properties alone, as Newtonianism was in the main. All the sciences should be heard from before the final synthesis was in order. What philosophy could do was to make suggestions as to demands which, on the face of human experience, had to be met either by explaining or by inexorable explaining away. And it had to be made very certain that the supposed inexorable explaining away was inexorable in the light of verifiable principles. It seemed to me that the tradition of reduction to isolates and their simple, mechanical relations was not as inevitable as had been assumed. Did not evolution mean the cumulative effect of integrative causality in bringing about functional, self-maintaining wholes?

One of the characteristics about wholes is that their pattern of action involves a temporal as well as a spatial dimension. This stage here prepares the way for that stage there. In this fashion, there are inner controls and conditions, a differentiated, moving equilibrium. Now, as I see it, all this is empirical; and I should expect that the sciences from physics to psychology would increasingly work out the categories demanded by the facts. And there are many indications that various developments in science are moving away from old principles to new and more flexible ones. Flat reductionism now seems *a priori* and dogmatic. If integrative organization goes on in nature under favoring conditions of free energy, genuine novelty of process and procedure can take place. And this implies the ontological import of biological and social history on this planet of ours. As to the universe as a whole, that is quite another matter. Solar systems may, in a certain sense, be episodic and local. Whether astrophysics and astronomy can work out principles for the universe as a whole remains to be seen. I suppose that all materialistic naturalists regard the universe as intrinsically eternal.

The theory of emergence and levels arose in the United States and England practically simultaneously. It is particularly associated with the names of S. Alexander and Lloyd Morgan in England and with Spaulding and, in its naturalistic form, with myself in the United States. It seemed to me to imply the importance of organization and, with it, levels of causality. I tried to give it a completely naturalistic setting. In this it differed, I take it, from certain aspects of Bergson's creative evolutionism. That is, there was about it less of neo-Platonism and vitalism. It has already been pointed out that the epistemological preparation in terms of *physical realism* was important. Yet there is an ingredient of naturalism in Bergson.

III

Since I have taken the side of Hobbes against Descartes in a rejection of a mental substance, I should like to call attention to the impact of the thinking of Cabanis and De Tracy upon the United States in the time of Jefferson. As is well known, they explored the domain of organic sensations and voluntary movements, an area which had been neglected by Condillac. In philosophy all this represented a shift from the more analytic to the exploratory and empirical. Locke, it will be recalled, was often thought of as having a materialistic implication. Hobbes could never be completely forgotten.

In this country Thomas Cooper moved to an explicit materialism with the denial of soul. Not far from him was Priestley with his doctrine of the homogeneity of mind and matter. Wrote Cooper: "We have not the slightest proof of any kind that ideas can arise or exist independently of corporeal organization." And then, continuing in the spirit of Cabanis, he points to the growth of a human being from infancy under the influence of nature and society. But genetic psychology, as we know it, was still in the future.

For the sake of the historical setting, let me introduce Jefferson. In a letter dated from Monticello, the fourteenth of March, 1820, Jefferson discusses these theories. "Mr. Locke, you know, *and other materialists* have charged with blasphemy the spiritualists who have denied the Creator the power of endowing certain forms of matter with the faculty of thought. These, however, are speculations and subtleties in which, for my own part, I have little indulged myself . . . Were it necessary, however, to form an opinion, I confess I should, with Mr. Locke, prefer swallowing one incomprehensible rather than two."

This association of materialism with Lockianism is evident in Emerson as he turns toward idealism. In the essay, *The Transcendentalist,* he contrasts the two philosophies. "The materialist insists on fact, on history, on the force of circumstances and the animal wants of man; the idealist on the power of Thought and Will, on inspiration, on miracle, on individual culture." Like Theodore Parker, he demands objective validity for moral intuitions. How can materialism justify such a demand? Leaving out capitals, it is evident that materialism must handle value-judgements and be prepared to justify them. I have been accustomed to speak of *verifying* factual statements and of *justifying* normative ones.

In France, Maine de Biran became the father of French spiritualism in a somewhat analogous way. Starting from the ideologists he moved in the direction of dualism by means of his marked introspective capacity. How can this realm of will and feeling be brought into the compass of the organism?

It must not be forgotten, however, that neither Descartes nor Maine de Biran felt satisfied with a dualistic treatment of the mind-body puzzle. Professor Jean Wahl has brought out this fact in his recent book, *The Philosopher's Way.* For that matter, neither were Plato and Aristotle too happy about it. The active reason was Aristotle's only way of escape. The burden of proof would seem to be upon dualism.

The physical realist, in the light of modern science, seeks to begin with the concrete human being. We are not only sensitive but active and responsive. If we emphasize the thalamus and the cortex we must see them as agencies in emotional, volitional, intelligent conduct. We have already noted that perceiving is designative, directed and interpretative. In this sense, mentation is as concerned with the environment as is life, itself, which it aids. Gesture and language grow up together. As we have pointed out, epistemological categories must be studied in the light of this context and in terms of actual judgments of perception.

But the critical realist admits the *existential privacy* of the current of consciousness, or experiencing, as it arises in connection with minded conduct. How shall we think it ontologically? Let us remember that we are concerned not merely with sensations and images but with all that is actually experienced, with all that we have in some measure by *knowledge of acquaintance.* We can take this knowledge in terms of introspection, or more naively, as the Gestaltists do. As I see it, *thought about* is experienced but not the referant of that thought. Concepts display themselves in language and conduct.

The experiential status of concepts apart from language is a difficult, psychological question, tied in with abstraction and generalization. The forebrain seems to be crucial for this higher level, though it has been found that areas around the visual projection in the brain are important for the significant use made of the visual sensations. But, as I see it, the philosopher is concerned with the basic questions involved. How are we to *think* this existential *inness* of sensations with respect to brain events?

First of all, it is important to bear in mind the point that perceptual knowledge of the brain and the more abstract scientific knowledge developed upon it, as a base, do not represent an *intuition* of the brain event. It is not a literal participation in the very functioning of the area of the brain observed. We are not on the inside of the brain studied. What we get are facts about it. Such knowledge is knowledge and should not be belittled. But to know a thing is not to be it. It is a disclosure of facts about it, facts of size, composition, structure, pattern, etc. All of which is a very wonderful achievement.

However, in a sensation we seem to be participating in a brain event, to be on the inside existentially.

Now those who had a feeling for this unique situation and did not have an adequate epistemology often spoke of the double-aspect theory. But the term *aspect* is metaphorical. Epistemologically, it is better to speak of a "double knowledge." On the one hand, we have objective knowledge mediated by sensory data, which represents the cognitive use of sensations. Such data are taken up into references and concepts and play their part in empirical statements. But, underlying knowledge-claims of this sort, are the mediating factors. These are studied in introspection. They are then objects of what can best be called intuition. Now we are on the percipient pole of perceiving, reflexively examined.

The situation is specific, just as human knowing is. Both sensation and the total process of experiencing which contains it are *natural isolates* within the brain activity. It would seem, however, that the various kinds of sensations have a degree of localization as yet best worked out for visual sensations. A visual sensation is "in" the visual area, not as one physical thing is in another, but as one kind of event can be in a more inclusive kind of event. And the significant point is that the sensation is a *quale* whose context and background cannot be given as it is given. It is sensed as taken up in the complex act of awareness. How the sensation is sustained by, and one with, the action-pattern of the area cannot be intuited, as the sensation, itself, is intuited. But we can well believe that we have here a seamless unity. Thus, a sensation is, I am convinced, one with a brain activity and not something separate. It is, if you will, an expression, isomorphic with the activated brain event. But further knowledge of this unity can be gained chiefly by finding correlations between external knowledge of the neural event and the intuitions of subjects. Such investigation must be left to psychologist and neurologist.

There are, of course, language complexities. Our ordinary language is dominated by perception and action. Thus it is objective and easily social. But man has been able to symbolize the realm of the subjective within the social I-thing which each one of us is. Such references are introduced by the phrase "I have." Thus, I have a "feeling of pain," a "color sensation," etc. These symbols are public but refer to the intra-organic, to that which cannot be perceived as things are perceived. Rather to that which only the person having them can intuit. But because people can communicate about objective, common referents, they have little difficulty in adding symbols of that which can be intuited within the intra-organic. The private thus becomes symbolically public, always with the addition of such phrases as "I have or experience" or "You have or experience."

The neo-materialist holds it essential to do full justice to mental operations and to personality. And in all this he is rather commonsensical, regarding it as unlikely that certain broad distinctions which stand out in human thought should not be valid. Since his outlook is not reductionist, he considers it his primary task to further clarification and to develop heuristic principles. The growth of the psychosomatic perspective, which regards the human organism as the unit, illustrates the trend in modern materialism.

Traditional empiricism tended to confuse introspective acquaintance with its flow of psychical data with self-knowledge. Realistic empiricism does not. Reflexive self-knowledge involves judgments about tendencies, capacities, and dispositions. All this concerns verifiable knowledge about the self as a continuant. It would seem that the object of both external knowledge and reflexive self-knowledge is the same concrete human being. And this is the basic reason why the pronoun *I* is both public and personal in import. My self-knowledge develops within a social and public frame.

While, then, self-knowledge is mediated by intra-organic sensations, feelings, and words, it is important to realize that these are given a categorial setting of substantiality, that is, of organic selfhood. At the linguistic level, this is symbolized by the *cogito* of Descartes and the "I think" of Kant. But the neo-materialist, somewhat like the Aristotelian, takes the *I* to symbolize the self-conscious, human organism. The modern challenge against dualism was, as we saw, issued by Hobbes. But we are better prepared today to analyze the situation. The main point is that there is no good reason to begin with a disembodied self or mind. Nor, for that matter, with a body alien to the self. When I look out through my eyes and "see" an object, that means that I am coordinately aware of myself and of the external thing I am designating and interpreting. Awareness, here, is referential in both directions.

This sense of agency which we have, as percipients and doers, is lifted to a higher level and internalized in thought and moral decision. Yet there is no break with the organism. There is, simply internal rehearsal. But it would seem that cortical activity does not carry with it the same sense of localization that is involved in the mechanism of sensory projection. That is, we do not feel our brain to be busy in thought in the same sense as we feel our arms to be busy in action. Our knowledge about the existential location of consciousness *in* the brain is gained indirectly. But all this means is that consciousness does not locate itself. How could it? And why should it? There is no sensori-motor circuit for cortical action. I do not move my brain in thinking as I move a muscle.

There are, then, two points about modern materialism which I desire to make clear as possible. First, sensory data are emergent *qualia* which are "natural isolates" within an active, cortical matrix whose totality we cannot intuit. What corresponds to these *qualia* is an activation of pattern. Epistemology is important here. We must realize that knowledge, as against experiencing, involves a complex referential and interpretative process and that the object is never intuited. Thus, the brain is never intuited from outside. Perception is not existentially penetrative. It is, at the most, cognitively descriptive. This situation should not surprise us. Why should not nature have a qualitative content? And here, alone, are we on the inside of nature. But I see no reason to generalize to panpsychism, particularly not to the idealistic variety which rejects matter.

The second point concerns the complex identity of cerebral and mental processes.

The majority of opponents of neo-materialism build on classical physics. They argue that the kind of interpretative awareness which we can introspect involves a unique togetherness which is alien to even cortical processes. But is this not a case of dogmatism? Certainly, modern neurology is far more open-minded. The brain seems to function as a differentiated whole with activated patterns expressive of accumulated dispositions. And we have noted that referential self-knowledge tends to use much the same categories. That is, self and mind are less event-terms than substantival, dispositional, and operational, terms. The complex identity of cerebral and mental processes is a theory based upon the belief that the categories of self-knowledge harmonize with the categories of cerebral action and upon the principle that, in experienced awareness, the subject is participating in mind-brain activity. The burden of proof would appear to rest upon the denial of this identity.

IV

Let us observe how this framework enables us to escape epiphenomenalism. It does so by (1) not defining the brain as alien to consciousness and by (2) identifying mental and cerebral operations, this identity being achieved by the common reference of self-knowledge and objective, scientific knowledge.

But if we escape epiphenomenalism we must do justice to the categories of the self, such as freedom and choice. Modern materialism takes this responsibility.

What, then, is freedom? It is the *power* to handle problems confronting the self with the resources at its command. It is another term for intelligent agency. Now I would make much of the notion of levels of causality, a notion opposed to reductive ideas. An organism has a certain autonomy or causal internality. And man is particularly gifted in resources by means of his intelligence. There are, then, degrees of capacity within freedom as relative autonomy.

It is obvious that freedom is opposed to external constraint; and at the human level, it has a more positive and complex meaning. It symbolizes the more or less realizable ideal of the intelligent and rational handling of critical, moral problems by the self. As such, it is opposed both to external constraint and to the denial of the significance of intelligence. The neo-materialist flatly takes the stand for the reality of intelligence as both neural and mental. In self-knowledge we are aware of ourselves as solving problems and living up to norms. In the use of the term, norm, I am anticipating axiology.

But such freedom as rational capacity still meets with the ultimate question of free-will. As I see it, free-will signifies the reality of choice and time as features of agency at the human level. A choice does not express a blind freedom of indifference but decision upon awareness of alternative lines of action. But could I have done otherwise? Yes; the self could have decided otherwise if it had known other facts or if its activated values had been different. The point is that the self is a changing continuant and decisions are temporal actions. Free-will is, to the materialist, meaningful as a term for agential decision within a locus of relative autonomy. A decision is an event and has its existential context. It can however, be challenged and even reversed. This signifies that the self is a continuant inclusive of its decisions. Only if decision is not regarded as an expression of the self do we have mythological free-will. There are, of course, emotive meanings connected with all these terms.

One final point in ontology as against Thomism. The materialist sees no realistic reason to accept the *esse* of supernaturalistic creationism. In the first place, existence is, *logically,* a property of applicable concepts. In the second place, existing things are not unions of forms and existence. Existing things are just concrete things. And we, ourselves, are instances of felt and known existence. That is, we are immersed in existence. And the whole mechanism of knowledge presupposes existence in the *concrete.* I doubt that neo-Thomism does justice to the concreteness of existence by breaking it up in the traditional Platonic-Aristotelian fashion and adding *esse.* The materialist's conception of self-organizing matter has always constituted a protest against the dualism of "form and matter." And, immersed in being, he sees no empirical reason to doubt the conservation of the *resources* of being, any more than the neo-Thomist doubts the maintenance of the resources of a God.

V

Let us now turn briefly to axiology. Modern materialism is humanistic and takes values and valuation seriously as expressions of the dynamics of personality. Their primitive roots are in desire and aversion. But these can be lifted to the rational level. Hobbes and Spinoza began this *relational* theory of valuation. It develops within the realistic framework given by cognitive awareness.

Valuation is as objective in import as cognition but is differently concerned. In cognition the aim is to gain facts about objects; in valuation the concern is with their *bearing* upon the agent or group of agents. All this is relational and reflexive. While knowledge can help to mediate valuation, the base of the latter is the self. It is too often forgotten that self-knowledge includes awareness of the hormic, or agential, nature of the self. In valuation, this tendency to activity is illuminated by guiding knowledge of things, events, and consequences. At the symbolic level, man is able to correlate himself *as an agent* with his environment.

Now it has been my custom to speak of value judgments as *justifiable* and factual judgements as *verifiable*. In both cases the appeal, befor acceptance, is to investigation. Value judgments are not private even though they are personal. To be socially justified, they must do justice to whatever is relevant. Moral judgements, for instance, involve other selves within an estimation of consequences.

Values are *in* the world because man is a sensitive agent in the world. How far down the scale of being, something akin to valuing goes it is hard to say. But to look at the universe in terms of the inorganic sciences alone is unempirical. The modern materialist is a pluralist in all these matters. What is significant for man is the proliferation of values within cultures. One of the main problems of social philosophy is that of the rational justification of institutions in terms of moral values.

So much for the general perspective of a humanistic materialism.

VI

And so we come to the conclusion. I have concerned myself only with general principles. It will be noted that I see promise in a realistic empiricism which escapes the many false starts in modern philosophy, such as Humianism and Kantianism. In the realistic framework, so given, science and philosophy can cooperate. Idealism had good intentions and sought to counter the reductionism of nineteenth-century science. But, technically, its epistemology was poor.

Philosophy concerns itself, in the main, with general puzzles about epistemological and ontological categories. The Aristotelian tradition was fairly sound but it needs far more overhauling logically, epistemically and ontologically than neo-Thomists are willing to admit. The logical positivists made the mistake of ignoring epistemology and ontology. They were analytic enthusiasts with a Mach-Hume outlook. The modern materialist finds he has much in common with the Dewey type of pragmatism. But to speak of the *transactions* between the organism and its environment does not set aside the responsibility for a clear epistemology and ontology. It is my belief that critical realism gives an essential opening gambit. But it is a realism of guided reference and tested concepts in accordance with scientific method.

SELECTED BIBLIOGRAPHY

Sellers, R. W., McGill, V. J., and Farber, M., editors, *Philosophy for the Future*. New York, The Macmillan Co., 1949.

Sellers, R. W. *Critical Realism*. Chicago, Rand, McNally and Co., 1916.

————. *The Next Step in Religion*. New York, The Macmillan Co., 1918.

Sellers, R. W., and others. *Essays in Critical Realism*. London, The Macmillan Co., 1920.

Sellers, R. W. *Evolutionary Naturalism*. Chicago, Open Court Publishing Co., 1922.

————. *The Philosophy of Physical Realism*. New York, The Macmillan Co., 1932.

Chinard, G. *Jefferson et les idéologues*. Paris, Presses Universitaires de France, 1925.

Cooper, Thomas. *A View of the Metaphysical and Physiological Argument in Favor of Materialism*. Philadelphia, 1823.

Harlow, Victor. *Bibliography and Genetic Study of American Realism*. Oklahoma City, Harlow Publishing Co., 1931.

Holt, E. B., and others. *The New Realism*. New York, The Macmillan Co., 1912.

Pratt, James Bissett. *Matter and Spirit*. New York, The Macmillan Co., 1922.

Santayana, George. *The Realm of Matter*. London, Constable and Co., Ltd., 1930.

Strong, Charles Augustus. *The Origin of Consciousness*. New York, The Macmillan Co., 1923.

THE PLACE OF
JOHN DEWEY IN MODERN
THOUGHT

Sidney Hook*

I

There are many paradoxes connected with the philosophy of John Dewey who at the age of ninety still continues an active intellectual life. For the purposes of exposition to an audience unfamiliar with his doctrines, the most striking of the paradoxes is the relative disparity between the influence he has exerted upon the professional philosophers on the one hand, and the nonphilosophic public of professionals upon the other. For good or for evil, no American philosopher has affected so vitally the doctrines and thought ways of jurists, sociologists, psychologists, educators, and a whole miscellany of investigators and practitioners on the borderlines of the separate disciplines. And yet professional philosophers themselves have remained largely mystified and puzzled by Dewey's philosophy.

Discounting the conventional politeness which accompanies birthday celebrations, and disregarding those philosophers who have come into direct relation with Dewey as his students or students of his students, we find that Dewey's influence has really been negligible on professional philosophers. On the continent he is but a name. As far as the philosophers of Great Britian are concerned, he might just as well have written in an unknown foreign tongue. And the striking fact about the type of criticism passed upon Dewey by American philosophers as well as about Dewey's own answers to this criticism, is that it has not varied in essentials for the last forty years. Now when incisive critical minds like Bertrand Russell or Morris R. Cohen either admit that they do not under-

* Born in 1902. Ph.D., Columbia University, 1927. Guggenheim Fellow, 1928-29. Professor of philosophy and chairman of the department of philosophy, New York University. Author of *The Metaphysics of Pragmatism* (1927), *From Hegel to Marx* (1936), *John Dewey: An Intellectual Portrait* (1939), *Reason, Social Myths and Democracy* (1940), *The Hero in History* (1943), *Education for Modern Man* (1946).

stand Dewey, except on matters where they think he is clearly wrong, or are charged with persistent and continuous misunderstanding, there must be some central difficulty in their approach to Dewey's philosophy. It is not a question of some ordinary misconception but of something basic. It seems to me that this basic difficulty can be traced to John Dewey's radical departure from certain traditional concepts of experience which almost all of his philosophic critics have in common. In their criticisms they always translate what he says about experience into their own conceptions, conceptions that have been framed in terms of mentalistic psychology, and naturally find Dewey either obscure or preposterous. Reflective nonprofessional individuals, however, have the advantage over the technical philosophers in approaching Dewey's meaning in that they take experience more nearly in the sense that Dewey gives it, and test what he says in terms of the "experiences" in which they are actively engaged.

We turn first therefore to a statement of Dewey's theory of experience. For purposes of exposition it may be helpful to indicate the three generic influences which Dewey himself explicitly acknowledges to have been important in helping him formulate his position. They are *historical, experimental,* and *biological.*

The historical influence manifests itself in the emergence of a culture in which man appears primarily as an actor or doer to whom the world presents a series of challenges to be mastered, not by withdrawal, resignation, or preparation for salvation, but by reflective action. No matter how we characterize the modern age, it is marked by an emphasis upon control rather than pure contemplation, upon the extension and enrichment of human horizons in *this* world to a point that transcends anything to be found at any time anywhere else. The causes of this new attitude of man in and toward the world are irrelevant to our present purpose. The fact is that the kinds, nature, and degree of human experiences, for good or for evil, in war, economics, exploration, and science, have resulted in changing the face of the earth, the fabric of social systems, and the very texture of personal relations. This is the first source of Dewey's theory of experience.

The second flows from the realization of the pervasive significance of one of the chief conditions of control, *viz.,* the place and use of instruments, of which the organs of man's body are a part. Through instruments men intervene in natural processes and actually modify—in the most literal sense of the word—natural qualities and relations. These instruments are as natural as that which they affect, and become the source of novelties as objective as anything else in the cosmic scene. Further, instruments, more obviously than ever before, enter into the processes of knowledge-getting. Hypotheses themselves, which thinkers of the past had interpreted either as *a priori* rational truths or residual summaries of the effects of the world on our senses elaborated by the mind, are now justified by their instrumental efficacy in turning up new knowledge. Scientific laws are ultimately "instrumentalities for control of individualized situations." The symbols of scientific discourse do not mirror the structure of things but are devised for purposes of inquiry.

The third and perhaps the decisive influence in Dewey's theory of experience, is the rise of modern biology and biological psychology after the time of John Stuart Mill. As Dewey interprets the findings of modern biology and psychology, they challenge the assumptions of every traditional school of philosophy about the nature of mind and experience. The traditional philosophy assumed either that mind was a substance whose essential nature was independent of the body and environment or regarded it merely as an introspectively experienced function of bodily or environmental changes. The nature of these changes was communicated by sensations that carried knowledge-bearing reports of the world we live in. The mind's activity was exhausted in combining these sensations into images, perceptions, and conceptions. As Dewey reads biology and psychology, to be alive means to be a kicking, reacting, struggling creature whose responses to the environment are always selective. Living behavior which is *mental* is a selective response to things in the environment as *signs* of other things. Sensations, images, desires, hopes are not distinct mental entities, even though we use nouns to designate them. They are qualities by which we characterize some distinctive phase or nodal point in the process of action and interaction between society, the individual organism, and the physical world. For Dewey this conception of mind is not a resolution to use a word in a strange and unfamiliar sense. It is justified by current usage in which mind refers to the activity of "minding" and by the evidence of the manifold continuities between man and nature. Whatever else beliefs and inferences are, they are implicit habits of an acculturated organism.

Dewey frames his general theory of experience in the light of these influences and assumptions. The very language he uses about experience cannot be understood without reference to them.

I shall now try to state some of the chief characters of experience as Dewey interprets it, explain his central doctrines in terms of it, show

how the appearance of paradox arises in his formulation and disappears when we analyze the experience which Dewey thinks justifies his doctrines as opposed to others.

Experience, according to Dewey, is an affair of interaction between a live thing and an environment. He sometimes speaks of it as a process of doing and undergoing, or more simply as a "transaction." Action always presupposes something acted upon. Therefore the process of experience is not an act of total creation; and at one stroke both the God of Bishop Berkeley and the God of Genesis are ruled out of the process of genuine creation. Although experience does not create the things acted upon in the course of experience, the course of experience in specific ways modifies the thing experienced. The modification is the result of the reciprocal influence of the original powers of things upon our actions, and the directive impact of our actions upon the original powers of things. *"Everything experienced is in part made what it is because there enters into it a way of experiencing something."* This is usually granted as far as ordinary modes of experience are concerned like making a fire, or eating, or painting, or loving, or skating. The objects involved are experienced in different ways and this means that different procedures are adapted to them and different consequences ensue.

Now the process of inquiring or knowing for Dewey is a mode of experience, also. As a mode of experience there are two distinct things that Dewey says about it which are relevant for our purpose. And it is of the utmost importance that these two things be not confused. The first is that knowing is a mode of experience which intervenes between *other* modes of experience that are *not* cognitive. Although knowledge when it is secured has tremendous significance, actually or potentially, for other forms of experience, it arises as a secondary result when some affective or practical mode of experience has been interrupted by a difficulty or a *problem*. When the difficulty or problem has been resolved, the mode of experience, practical or esthetic, whose disruption had set the context for thinking, has been enriched by a new meaning or significance. That cognition, as a mode of experience, whenever it takes place, is intermediate between noncognitive modes of experience, is a fact. That the habit of cognition *should be cultivated* as a way of meeting difficulties in other modes of experience is a recommendation, a proposal. This is the first point about knowing as an experience.

The second point concerns the nature of the knowing experience itself considered no longer in relation to other experiences but in terms of what is done when we get valid knowledge. The whole of Dewey's logic is a theory directed to explaining this point, *viz.,* what goes on when inquiry terminates in the warranted assertion that defines knowledge. Dewey claims that inquiry is a process of behavior by which an existential problematic situation is transformed by certain operations and experiments upon symbols and things; and that these operations at some point literally modify existing things.

This conception of logic is the key to Dewey's theories of meaning and truth. According to him the intent of a term, or of any statement, is to be construed from the behavioral procedures by which it is introduced into inquiry, and is indissoluble from the controlling context of the problem or situation which provokes inquiry. A statement is true if the actual consequences of the action taken to modify the conditions that generate the problem, are such that they realize the validly predicted consequences. This is what Dewey means when he says that thinking which eventuates in knowledge is *practical, and this is all that he means by practical in this connection.*

No misunderstanding of Dewey has been more widespread; and although Dewey is often to blame for many *other* misconceptions about his philosophy, on this *particular* point, misunderstandings on the part of his critics seem almost willful. Thinking is *practical* not because it is useful or because it makes us happy, wealthy, or healthy. It is practical because, like all forms of experience, it is a form of doing, and as distinct from other forms of experience, a mode of doing which employs symbols to direct its operation. Truth or falsity has nothing to do with the practical effects of "believing" anything; dying, for example, may be sometimes sufficient evidence for the truth of the belief that "this substance is poisonous." The truth *may* make us free: if it does not, it is not any less true. Truth or falsity is concerned with the conditions and operations which must be fulfilled in order to warrant or justify "the believing" of anything.

But, can we ever know what the antecedent conditions of knowledge are, if it is true that "everything experienced is in part made what it is because there enters into it a way of experiencing something?" Yes, if the object of our inquiry *is* some specific antecedent condition of knowledge, say the kind of world which existed before man appeared or before life appeared. Warranted assertion about what the world *then* was depends, however, upon the consequences of what we *now* do to some aspect of the *present* world. This means that some aspect of the present world is modified by a series of controlled operations and experiments whose outcome gives us the evidence for statements made about events and conditions whose occurrence antedated all human experience. If this be called anthropocentrism or anthropomorphism, it is a *methodological* anthropocentrism, not a cosmological one. Methodological anthropocentrism is but a generalization of the fact that science is a human enterprise, a systematic process by which one bit of nature finds out about other bits of nature. Existence and experience are not synonymous; experience is a kind of existence which by affecting other existences, enables us at the same time to discover their nature.

Dewey's notion of truth is a correspondence theory in which, however, the traditional terms of "idea," "object," and "corresponds" differ from the meanings given them in the representative theory of knowledge. An idea is not an object of thought, nor is it an image or representation of an object. It is a directive to act in a certain way so as to uncover observational data bearing on the problematic situation which provoked reflection. It has a representative office which points to the future whose deliverances will confirm its validity. It "corresponds" with the facts in the sense that it fits them, makes subsequent experiences of them relevant and coherent, and contributes to reordering the situation so that knowledge is achieved.

Dewey has often expressed his regret that the term "pragmatism" has been affixed to his theories of meaning and thruth. Insofar as he uses the term, he intends it to mean nothing but the logic of scientific method in its widest sense. In this sense it is not to be identified with specific methods of inquiry in special fields, nor only with disciplines in which the measurement of extensive magnitudes is possible. It is to be identified with the basic pattern of hypothesis, deduction, controlled experiment, and / or observation which is always illustrated whenever we make warranted assertions. The contrast between common sense and science is therefore illegitimate because, among other reasons, the procedures of science, although more exact and refinded, are continuous with some of the procedures of common sense.

Dewey maintains that his theory of experience accounts for certain objective features of scientific inquiry more adequately than any other theory.

(a) The first of these features is the existence and nature of *problems,* which are always the point of departure and controlling context of significant inquiry. Dewey somewhere remarks it is puzzling that philosophers who are professionally engaged in the discussion of problems of knowledge, should be so very incurious about the very existence and nature of problems. According to him, problems arise out of disharmonies which result from the objective processes of interaction between an organism and an environment. They cannot be dissociated from specific situations. A problem is *au fond* a problematic situation. Genuine problems are *not* merely private; i.e., they are not something that exists only in the mind of a subject who is outside the object. If this were the case, *both* doubt and knowledge would be private states of mind of a subject. There would be no connection between what is called mind and the world of events which most philosophers take to be the objective reference of knowledge. We couldn't explain why problems arise, how they are solved, and what constitutes a solution. Skepticism about the existence of anything but our own private states of minds would result. According to Dewey any theory of mind or knowledge which makes a mystery of the fact that there *are* problems whose resolution, by controlled action and experiment, has been the motor force of all science, must be rejected as inadequate. If we are going to have mysteries let us keep the number to a minimum.

(b)   The second feature of scientific method which Dewey claims to account for is that of all human enterprises it is the one in which we communicate with each other more freely and accurately than in any other. There is no scientific knowledge which is incommunicable. Norman Campbell goes so far as to define science as the study of those judgments which affect action concerning which universal agreement can be obtained. Communication of any kind between human beings involves reference to an environment, which their action, at least in part, makes common. On the conventional theory of mentalistic psychology, communication is an intuition or guess about the meanings of other minds, *if* there are other minds, and about the structure of the world, *if* there is a world. Mysteries multiply, not one is solved, not even by the assumption of states of mind introspectively observable by the "normal" person. For Dewey, we communicate with materials and language initially supplied by society; but in communicating with other men it is ultimately with and through natural operations that we are enabled to integrate our behavior in a common pattern. "To understand is to anticipate together, is to make a cross reference which when acted upon, brings about a partaking in a common, inclusive undertaking."

(c)   The most important feature of scientific inquiry which Dewey's theory explains is the simple fact that such thinking makes a difference to the world. Our recognition of this fact is testified to, not only by the obvious effects, good or bad, of invention and discovery in our world, but by most of the justifications and exhortations to people to think soundly. I do not believe that it would be an exaggeration to say that this universally agreed upon feature of scientific thinking is unintelligible from the point of view of classical or traditional philosophy except by making the assumption absolute idealism does, that the events and stuff of experience are at bottom ideal, an assumption which takes us away from the primary subject matter of concrete inquiries and for which no plausible evidence can be offered but only a highly intricate dialectic. It is the recognition, e.g., that thought *is* practical (not necessarily useful) which is one of the basic premises of Santayana's *Life of Reason;* it is the failure to explain how on his theory of experience, thought *can* be practical which accounts, in part, for Santayana's flight to the *Realm of the Spirit.* Nor must we permit the glib distinction between pure logic and applied logic, pure thought and applied thought, to pass as a solution or answer. For the question is not whether logic or thought *can* be applied but *how* can it be applied on the basis of distinctions which imply absolute separations between the mind and the world, in some formulations, and form and matter, in others.

Dewey's theory may be invalid but at least it attempts to come to grips with the problem. Thinking counts in the world because ideas are plans of *action* in respect to things and symbols; in the course of the operations guided by symbols, existential subject matter at some point is literally transformed, and the problematic situation objectively resolved. The distinction between the existential and nonexistential, the formal and material, observations and inference, are recognized but only in terms of their functional role in the process of inquiry. Again I must 'insist that this view of thinking is not a consequence of an arbitrary resolution to use the term "thought" in some special sense but is presented as more adequate than any rival theory in explaining what is actually done, without benefit of philosophical doctrine, in the fields of science and common sense when we successfully cope with genuine problems.

I think that it is now clear why, despite the opacity and dullness of so much of his writing, Dewey's general ideas concerning experience and knowledge have had such great influence upon nonphilosophical professional thinkers who concern themselves with concrete problems. (This influence of course is not an argument for their validity.) For his theories account for the existence of problems, the facts of communication, and the actual triumphs of mastery and control over subject matter instead of making mysteries of them.

I should like now to show how the most paradoxical feature of

Dewey's thought flows naturally from these considerations, *viz.,* his belief that situations transformed in the course of an inquiry constitute knowledge in its *preeminent sense.* Bridges, tunnels, buildings, cities, observatories, orchards, ships, are for Dewey illustrations of knowledge in a more final sense than the formulas we use to construct them. At first this sounds shocking but when we reflect that problems are the starting point of inquiry, and the transformed problematic situation the end of inquiry, we can see that the specific achievements of inquiry are ultimately the tests of the general conceptual instruments, of the universal formulas and laws, which we use to get relevant and certified results in particular cases; just as analagously physical tools receive their test of adequacy in the course of working with them. For Dewey the world is not inherently reasonable or unreasonable; but aspects of it become or are made reasonable (not good or bad) by that human activity or mode of experience which we call inquiry. All intelligent inquiry about existential matters as a process of finding out is also a process of construction and reconstruction.

Leaving aside the question of the validity of the details of Dewey's theory of experience (which is of course the decisive question) the intent of the theory is clear. It is a culmination of the movement which developed in Western culture with the rise of experimental science from its lowly origins in the industrial arts and common everyday uses to the forefront of concern with the most general motions of things. As we all know, experimental science did not come into existence at one bound nor without difficulties. It was compelled to struggle for its very right to a hearing against two hostile intellectual traditions—one drawn from the speculative metaphysics of antiquity, the other from the revealed religion of the medieval church. It was natural for scientists to state and justify their findings in terms of the metaphysical and theological traditions in which they were originally nurtured and which had been formulated previously to explain the ways of God or the Universe at Large to men.

Experimental science justified itself by its *works,* not by its intelligibility in terms of the earlier traditions. Despite the constant war waged by religious and philosophic orthodoxy against science, scientists marched on from one triumph to another until by the end of the nineteenth century, the position of the physical sciences was unassailable. But part of the price paid for this victory was addiction by scientists and popularizers of science, to a mode of speech and a set of assumptions which were not rooted in their own experimental procedures in achieving conclusions that were fruitful and rigorous, but which were derived from an inherited tradition. The consequences, as Dewey sees it, has been the generation of artificial problems and a failure to appreciate the potentialities of scientific method for cultural life.

What Dewey means by artifical problems are problems whose assumptions are such that no solution is possible which does not contradict one or another of the initial assumptions. It is a question in the first instance not of misuse of language but rather of mistaken, or unverifiable, or unnecessary assumptions of fact on the basis of which the problem appears. For Dewey most of these assumptions are expressions of dualism, where dualism is defined not as the recognition of duality in any context, but as the denial of some experiential continuity between whatever is recognized as dual or plural. Dewey's work in philosophy may be characterized as a systematic attempt to transcend the great dualisms which men have inherited from the dominant religious and metaphysical traditions—e.g., the dualism between nature and life, body and mind, matter and form, sensation and reason, action and standards. There is an oft quoted passage from Dewey which explicitly states this opposition to dualism: "To see the organism *in* nature, the nervous system *in* the organism, the brain *in* the nervous system, the cortex *in* the brain is the answer to the problems which haunt philosophy. And when thus seen they will be seen to be *in,* not as marbles are in a box, but as events are in history, in a moving, growing, never finished process." Some critics have interpreted this and similar passages as if it denied that we can make legitimate distinctions, and since Dewey like everybody else makes all sorts of distinctions, e.g., between symbols and things, observations and deduction, he is charged with gross inconsistency. But the nub of the question is not whether we recognize distinctions but their status and interpretation. In opposing dualism, Dewey denies that distinctions correspond to any ontological separations or that they refer to transempirical entities; and offers proof by analysis that any interpretation based on such assumption of separation is untenable.

Dewey's personal motivation in attempting to undermine dualism is moral. This moral bias arises from his discovery that many current inhuman and obscurantist practices are fortified by appeal to dualistic metaphysics. The *truth* of this connection between philosophical rationalization and social malpractice and the validity of his argument against what he designates as rationalizations, do not, of course, depend

upon the character of his motivation. One does not have to be a reform-
er to see that many of our doctrines of responsibility and social organization presuppose a dualistic theory of mind and body according to which
what human beings do, and what we should expect them to do, is independent of natural and social causes, conditions, and circumstances.

II

The logic of scientific inquiry for Dewey is not a self-contained process carried on by pure minds but an activity which by its nature presupposes a physical and social world of which man is a part. What this
world is like can be truly known only by the tested methods of inquiry.
And Dewey's *experimental naturalism* differs from all other varieties of
materialism and naturalism in that it refuses to go beyond the evidence
warranted by the methods and results of science. Man is part of nature
and subject in all his actions to the conditions of material determination.
"Matter" for Dewey is not a special stuff or substance but "the subject
matter of the physical sciences" whose spatio-temporal *changes* affect the
nature and history of everything which exists. The "laws of matter" are
descriptions of the patterns of events used for purposes of prediction and
control. This position does not forbid anything to exist for which there
is evidence in experience and reason—whether Gods, electrons, or fairies—
provided that from the assumption of their existence we can predict something of a determinate kind which we did not know before. That is why
we may legitimately believe in the existence of electrons and not in
fairies or Gods.

Natural though man be, he differs from other things as an organism,
and from other organisms as a human being. These differences are just
as genuine as his similarities. As distinct from a stone, man breathes,
fears, loves, and makes a selective response to his environment. As distinct from other organisms, he responds selectively through the use of
symbols to the future as if it were already present. Man is a symbol using
animal who lives in a community whose history is transmitted through
culture.

Experimental naturalism is never guilty of materialistic "reductionism"; the view which *identifies* the meaning of qualities and relations
with the physical conditions of their emergence. It rejects all views
which assert that "consciousness is nothing but neural energy" or that
the esthetic qualities of a sunset are "merely" a collocation of particles of
vapor illuminated by light rays. For it, nothing is *nothing-but;* and noth-

ing is *merely* one thing and not anything else. Dewey holds that it is a contingent fact, and not a logically necessary one, that all qualities and events in human experience depend upon the organization of a material system in space and time, and that their emergence, development, and disappearance are determined by changes in such organization. It therefore becomes impossible to deny meaningfully the existence of any qualities and events, no matter how exquisite, whose existence has been empirically confirmed. Qualities of the human spirit are to be explored— not denied, ignored, or hypostatized.

In consequence, Dewey's naturalism recognizes the genuineness of all the varied qualities of experience in different contexts and on every level. It does not exaggerate the degree of interconnectedness in the world, and accepts the discontinuities and pluralisms of experience as something given, but at the same time as something that may be taken to be overcome. It rejects both logical atomism and the one great concrete universal of absolute idealism as alike incompatible with the method and consequences of science. It does not make of man a stranger in a hostile void as some older forms of materialism do. Admitting that he is limited by the determinations of the past and the compulsions of the present, it also recognizes the openness of man's future and his moral responsibility for those future possibilities which his intelligence and courage succeed or fail in actualizing.

So far we have been discussing Dewey's general theory of experience as it bears upon his specific conceptions about that form of experience which we call controlled reflection, inquiry, or science. What Dewey says about it can be tested directly and indirectly in the same way we test any theory of scientific knowledge without wondering overmuch whether or not the inquiry concerning the validity of the theory falls in the domain of logic, science, or the special science of psychology.

III

We now come to Dewey's conception of philosophy. Philosophy is practical but not in the same sense as knowledge or science. Science, as we have seen, is practical only in the sense that it involves existential modification, but philosophy is practical in that it is "an organized attitude of outlook, interpretation, and construction"—in short, it has a *moral* interpretation and function. According to Dewey whatever else philosophy has been, *insofar as it can be distinguished from science and formal logical analysis,* it has *always* had a moral function, usually one of criticism, rationalization, or edification. Dewey's conception of what philosophy is might be rejected by a different reading of the history of philosophy. What I shall discuss, therefore, is not Dewey's conception of philosophy *überhaupt* but *his* specific conception of philosophy which he presents in the form of a proposal. This proposal is that we should use the reliable methods and results of scientific or cognitive experience as a basis for "criticism of current beliefs and institutions involving value considerations." *Philosophy is to be the current quest for wisdom.*

What does such a proposal mean? Why does Dewey make it? What grounds does he offer for accepting it?

Such a proposal means, if it is to have any point at all, that we must explicitly recognize the continuity between our cognitive experience and our other modes of experience. This follows not only from Dewey's general theory of experience but is confirmed by the observable fact that our judgments of evaluation *are* affected by the presence or absence of knowledge. Dewey makes his proposal about the task of philosophy because he believes that only if the same general pattern of inquiry, employed to settle issues of fact, is extended to issues of value, can we reach sufficient agreement on what should be done in the concrete situations of personal and social life. The grounds he offers, aside from the fact that the only alternative methods of resolving differences, like force, authority, revelation, intuition, have demonstrably failed, consist of (1) the clearing away of the theoretical difficulties which have been raised against the possibility of an experiential ethics, and (2) a sketch of the method of inquiry which in *principle* would enable us to determine what is "better" in any ethical situation.

(1) In clearing away the theoretical difficulties raised against the possibility of an experiential ethics, Dewey is compelled to fight on two fronts. On the one hand, he argues against the attempt made by some metaphysical materialists and positivists to deny the existence of value *judgments* altogether. On the other, he argues against the position of the Platonic idealists and apriorists who maintain that standards of evaluation cannot be of the same order as the natural events evaluated. On both fronts, Dewey's theory of experience is crucial for his argument. He shows, for example, that the attempt to analyze value expressions by interpreting them as ejaculatory manifestations of feeling or emotion ignores the empirical facts that such expressions function to redirect conduct in much the same way that judgments of nonvalue fact do, and that a meaningful manifestation of feeling depends upon signs which function like linguistic symbols or propositions. On the other hand; the

belief that we can resort to a principle or standard of evaluation, called eternal which is transcendental to experience, not only gainsays what we know of biology and psychology but cannot explain how we can make *this world* better or worse than it is, an assumption involved in every moral action. In passing, let us note that Dewey, in his criticism of the emotive theory of value expressions, has stood for a "physicalism" both more radical and commonsensical than that of many logical empiricists; but whereas for the logical empiricists "physicalism" is a purely *logical* thesis, a convenient device to get a universal language, for Dewey it is a demand, whose reasonableness is certified by the history of scientific inquiry, that scientific statements take form which permits us to test them by designating certain objective procedures leading to differential determinate consequences, to the end that a common structure of knowledge about all sorts of facts, including value facts, results.

(2) Dewey maintains that the same pattern of inquiry which justifies us in making warranted assertions about nonmoral situations holds for the different subject matter of moral situations. The good or more accurately, "the better" of a particular situation, is to be found in that specific reconstruction of affairs which removes the initial difficulty. The initial difficulty arises from conflicts between the needs and interests of men and the social rules which regulate their expression. Need and interest are not unobservable states of mind but are qualities of behavior, biological and social. Standards and ideals, old or new, are brought to bear on the situation like hypotheses. They, too, are plans of action. Whether or not they enable us by controlling or modifying the relevant features of the situation, i.e., either the environmental factors or the self, to enstate "the good" or "better," is subject to verification. Given a situation of conflict, born of needs, desires, or lacks, given also a set of ends or standards that offer directions to courses of conduct designed, as means, to fulfill these needs, desires, or lacks; then the adequacy of any of the given ends or of new ones to the situation in hand can *in principle* be settled with scientific objectivity. If Dewey's theory of inquiry explains how we can make the world more reasonable, his theory of valuation explains how we can make it better.

There is a standing difficulty in Dewey's ethical theory to which critics are wont to recur. If moral ideals are to function like hypotheses and to be judged by the consequences to which they lead, must we not already know in advance what *are* good consequences if our analysis or experiment is to be significant? If we do, then Dewey's argument is circular; if we do not, Dewey, apparently has no theory of the good. The answer is that we approach an ethical situation with a whole series of *assumptions* as to what are goods—health, friendship, kindness, justice, security, adventure, just as we approach any other problem of inquiry with a whole store of principles and information we assume to be valid. But where there is a *problem* to be solved, these goods or values can no more be assumed to be *finally* valid than, in conducting an inquiry into fact, the information we bring to its resolution can be regarded as absolutely final and certain. No *one* value is supreme in all problematic situations, none is above the necessity of pointing to consequent goods or values in case its own presumptive validity is questioned. For it is obvious that we do not actually understand what our ends and values are as plans of action, before we have inquired into the probable consequences of carrying them out in practice; that we criticize ends by the means designed to realize them; and that there are no ends above or beyond criticism. The poignant fact is that the goods of this world are not always in harmony with each other. One good conflicts with another, safety with zest, loyalty with truth, kindness with justice. It is not often that problems are so much alike that we can resolve the conflict of goods in the same way. Hence, although we use the values and standards that have emerged out of previous deliberations as guiding principles of action, of themselves they can never determine the unique good of *this* particular situation, or even whether the exigencies of this situation will not compel us to abandon them, i.e., *to reformulate* standards. True, without some standards we should no more know how to find out what we should do, than we could begin a scientific inquiry into any matter of fact without some knowledge assumed to be valid. But there is something *more* always present, or the possibility of something more, which controls the relevance, the manner, and the degree of their application. The good of any situation in which the problem arises as to what *should* be done is something discovered as a result of reflective inquiry, and the objective changes produced in the course of that inquiry. There is no such thing, on this view, as the Good in the large, any more than there is Truth in the large. Faced by a problem in which we have to evaluate conflicting evaluations, in *principle* an answer is always possible which is objectively more adequate than all other alternatives which profess to be directed to the same problem. But there are always other problems some of which can be generated by demanding that our directing values show their credentials. The process may be unending, but it does not involve an infinite regress if we remember we are not called upon to solve all problems at once.

Formulated in another way, it may be said that Dewey is concerned with a theory of "reasonable goods" and not with a theory of "immediate goods." The latter require no theory. They are the desireds, the enjoyeds, about which no question of knowledge can be raised so long as they are had in their immediacy. The question of what constitutes a "reasonable good" arises only "when enjoyment ceases to be a datum and becomes a problem."

It follows from Dewey's ethical theory that the only effective way in which the world can be made better is through the modification of the complex of institutional patterns in society. It follows also that the most grandiose social philosophies are to be tested by the cumulative consequences of their day-by-day practices, not by their verbal professions. These aspects of Dewey's philosophy are so obvious that I need not dwell upon them. But their intent throws light from another quarter upon Dewey's place in modern thought.

The break-up of the medieval synthesis marked a decline in the influence and power of authority both in the field of knowledge and of social organization. In the field of natural knowledge the authority of the church and state was replaced by the authority of scientific method. Scientific workers throughout the world constituted a community which permitted the widest freedom to individuals, irrespective of race, sex, religion, and nationality, to initiate theories and experiments subject only to the voluntarily assumed discipline of a common method. This method, which vouchsafed no dogmas and culminated in no certainties, resulted in increasing control and community of agreement. Whatever disagreements occurred contributed to further progress in scientific knowledge. Quite the contrary is the case, in the field of society. No authority has arisen, except in totalitarian countries, to replace the authority of the medieval church-state. Perhaps it would be more accurate to say that the latter has been replaced by conflicting authorities, all appealing to different absolutes, and recognizing no method of negotiating difference, except fraud, force, and, at best, uneasy opportunist compromise. In contradistinction to these tendencies, and to the cry from many quarters today for a new unifying metaphysical faith to meet the crisis of man and society, John Dewey's social philosophy expresses the frank avowal of the desirability and possibility of substituting for the lost authority of a previous age, the authority of scientific method.

This proposal is simple and revolutionary, to many—preposterously so. But before it is condemned as a pathetic survival of a hopelessly lost cause, several things should be borne in mind. First of all, it is a proposal not a prediction that the proposal will be accepted. As a proposal, it should be evaluated in the light of its alternatives, i.e., of the consequences to the world of adopting any of its rivals or substitutes. Secondly, reliance upon scientific method does not necessarily mean pitting our loyalty to a set of pallid abstractions against the fervent faiths that are burning up the world. For the point of the method is that it yields conclusions only to the extent that it is acted upon. This action is attended by risks, to be sure, but it is more than compensated for by the assurances that we are more likely to achieve what we want by this form of action than by other forms. Fervent faith, toughness, and courage can be enlisted in behalf of the method and conclusion of scientific method just as much as in behalf of blind, searing fanaticism. Thirdly, although such scientific action can only solve problems one at a time, and each one piecemeal, for it recognizes no total solutions, the problems may encompass action on a large scale, political and industrial. Finally, the use of scientific method in social and personal affairs, although humane, is not a sentimental committal to sweetness and light. Force is not the opposite of intelligence; it may be necessary to use it in the interests of intelligence to safeguard the conditions which makes its continuous use possible. But the intelligent use of force will always seek to enstate the conditions which will make the further resort to force unnecessary to settle differences.

In elaborating the conception of a society in which the ways of authority are set by scientific method, Dewey is somewhat in the same predicament as Plato although for different reasons. Plato maintained that the good society could not function properly without genuine philosophers as rulers; but he also maintained that, with the possible exception of himself, the genuine philosopher could not be produced outside of the good society. Dewey maintains that the good society is one that employs the method of organized intelligence for planning in behalf of economic security and personal freedom. At the same time the employment of the method is contingent upon the removal of the existing institutional obstacles to the use of intelligence, and to a larger consensus of willingness to be guided by intelligence than now obtains. For Dewey this means only that we make a beginning wherever we are. Whatever changes are necessary must be such as to give institutional force to the methods of intelligence. This involves political action in the largest sense of the term, action which must exemplify the method of intelligence even as it works to clear the field for the extended use of intelligence.

Dewey has been reproached for his failure at this point to work out successful *techniques* of political action in order to win a free field for truly experimental social policies. Failed here he undoubtedly has. But despite his deep interest and active participation in all sorts of liberal political movements, Dewey never set himself up as a politician. New Dealers have often invoked his philosophy but rarely received his blessings. We do not judge a man's theory of science by his personal capacity to perform successful experiments. Why should the recognition that certain political steps are required to achieve an end, make it incumbent upon Dewey personally to work out these steps? This is everybody's problem, not merely his.

I think it is more legitimate to attribute a deeper failure to Dewey's philosophy than a personal political inability to compete on the same plane with Roosevelt, Churchill, Hitler, and Stalin. That failure might be described as a systematic overoptimism about human *willingness* to follow the lead of intelligence; and an allied failure to appreciate the consequences upon the perspective of liberal action of hostile political movements which use scientific techniques to acquire power, in order to prevent more ruthlessly than ever before in history, scientific criticisms of social ends and goals. The first defect arises from the fact that Dewey's social philosophy looks to a kind of impersonalized intelligence to mould institutions without asking questions about the carriers of that intelligence, their class origins and loyalties. In other words Dewey has given more weight to the rare occasions in which liberated intelligence modifies social institutions than he has to the much more frequent occasion in which "intelligence" is merely the harnessed power to keep things moving in their institutional grooves. Sometimes he has not distinguished carefully enough between an objective morality and a universal morality. The limits of the latter depend upon the extent to which interests can be shared.

The second difficulty arises from the consequences on democratic institutions and practices, as we have known them in the past, of measures that are necessary to combat scientific antidemocratic movements. If we permit scientific antidemocratic movements to go unchecked, democracy is finished at the hands of its enemies without and within; if we check them effectively, we may have to use means which threaten to distort our democratic ends.

Dewey meets this dilemma with a shift in his social philosophy during late years which has gone unnoticed, but which brings it into explicit consonance with his earlier educational theory. Until recently the chief burden of his social writings has been that individual and personal attitudes reflect institutional patterns; today he reminds us that it is just as true to say that "they are expressions, projections, and extensions of habitually dominant personal attitudes."

This means that even though we grant the indispensability of institutional changes, yes, even their inescapability, insofar as they are considered as a set of mechanical rules and arrangements, they cannot offer safeguards against the possibility of their being abused. Take any social reform you are interested in. Ask yourself whether if the institutional changes envisaged by it were realized, the human relationships regulated by them would therewith be automatically guaranteed to be satisfactory. Suppose property were socialized and the customary forms of exploitation were eliminated. Would that mean that you could be sure that new, and even more horrible varieties of exploitation, would not arise under different forms, as is the case in the Soviet Union and recently in Hitler's Germany? After all, institutions express behavioral relationships between men, and function through and with men. When we speak with awe about the state or the government, ultimately we are speaking as Mosca reminds us, about government clerks and officials. There are some things which they cannot do, there are no things which they *must* do. Insofar as social arrangements and institutions entrust human beings with the power to regulate the sensitive relationships between men, can they, by and large, function on a higher level than the individuals who sit at the strategic controls?

Dewey's answer is that they cannot, that social ideals are moral ideals, too, and that therefore these ideals must be expressed in our personal attitudes and character, as we seek to establish the effective objective conditions of morality. Whatever the world of tomorrow is, it depends to a large extent upon the personal attitudes and characters of the men and women who make that world. That is why the basic and unending task of the formation of attitudes is assigned by Dewey to the schools. At this point Dewey reestablishes contact with older ethical traditions in which whatever else moral decisions are, they are personal; but he transcends them in his view that content of these decisions always has social bearings and that therefore intelligent moral decisions involve some form of social action.

These considerations help explain the rich cluster of meanings which the term democracy has in Dewey's philosophy. From one point of view democracy is not a form of government but a way of personal life. It is a way of life "controlled by working faith in the possibilities of human nature . . . (more specifically) by faith in the capacity of human beings

for intelligent judgment and action if proper conditions are furnished."
It is a way of life in which continued education becomes the basis of all
other institutions. Democracy as a set of *political* institutions justifies
itself as the best generic procedure available to achieve the shared meanings, the common activities, the cultivation of harmonious differences
which mark the nature of growth of democracy as a way of personal life.
It is in this conception of growth, open to every member of society, that
Dewey combines in his own way the perenially attractive ethical ideals
of Hellenism and Christianity but always in terms of concrete, contemporary, social options.

"... the test of all institutions of adult life is their effect in furthering
continuous education. Government, business, art, religion, all social institutions have a meaning, a purpose. That purpose is to set free and to
develop the capacities of human individuals without respect to race, sex,
class, or economic status. And this is all one with saying that the test
of their values is the extent to which they educate every individual into
the full stature of his possibility. Democracy has many meanings but if it
has a moral meaning, it is found in resolving that the supreme test of all
political institutions and industrial arrangements shall be the contribution
they make to the all-around growth of every individual of society."

This enables us to fix the last point of Dewey's place in modern
thought. It is obvious that in different ways all existing societies are
moving towards a common economic pattern in the production and
distribution of goods and services. The old order of separation between
economics and government is gone beyond recall. One of Dewey's merits
is that even before 1929, he recognized a drift toward the "United States
Incorporated." Since that time his social philosophy has been of a democratically socialist character. Dewey's ideas represent the aspiration of a
free people to retain and develop its libertarian traditions in a world
profoundly different from the world of Washington or Jefferson or
Lincoln. Quite literally, Dewey's place in modern thought will depend
upon whether the coming age will witness the strangulation of individual
patterns of life by totalitarian controls, in the interests of mechanical
efficiency or a power-drunk elite, or whether the administration of things
will be operated in the interests of free individuals. If the first alternative is realized, even if Dewey's books escape the flames, his philosophy
will be remembered only as a brave symbol of a lost cause; if the second
alternative is realized, Dewey's thought will receive a new development.
It is quite appropriate that Dewey should be regarded as philosophic

enemy Number One by the Soviet regime, and its minions everywhere, because of his forthright opposition to its rule of total cultural terror.

The statement that we have a choice between only two generic alternatives in the cultural pattern of the future society, is for Dewey not prophecy but scientifically grounded prediction. Those who think that the *status quo,* or the economic tradition and practice of yesterday, is a third viable alternative to totalitarianism are profoundly mistaken. The successful, genuine democratic alternative to totalitarianism is still in the making, it is something to be achieved. It constitutes a challenge to *intelligence.* The stakes are so high that the challenge may well engage our hopes, our courage, and our very life. Dewey's philosophy may be regarded as a huge judgment of practice which by bringing into play intelligent energy and action may significantly contribute to the outcome.

SELECTED BIBLIOGRAPHY

MAJOR WORKS OF JOHN DEWEY:

>   *Essays in Experimental Logic.* Chicago, University of Chicago Press, 1919.
>   *Experience and Nature.* Chicago, London, Open Court Publishing Co., 1923.
>   *Logic, the Theory of Inquiry.* New York, Henry Holt and Co., 1939.
>   *Problems of Men.* New York, Philosophical Library, 1947.
>   *Democracy and Education.* New York, The Macmillan Co., 1916.
>   *Human Nature and Conduct.* New York, Henry Holt and Co., 1920.
>   *Art as Experience.* New York, Minton, Balch Co., 1935.
>   *Freedom and Culture.* New York, G. P. Putnam's Sons, 1940.

CONTRIBUTIONS TO EXPERIMENTAL NATURALISM

>   Dewey, Nagel, *et al.* Articles in *Naturalism and the Human Spirit.* New York, Columbia University Press, 1945.
>   Dewey, Nagel, and Hook. Articles in the *Journal of Philosophy,* 1945-47.
>   Boas, George. *Our New Ways of Thinking.* New York, London, Harper and Brothers, 1933.
>   Hook, Sidney. *Metaphysics of Pragmatism.* Chicago, London, Open Court Publishing Co., 1929.
>   Hook, Sidney. *John Dewey.* New York, John Day Co., 1939.

PHILOSOPHY OF SCIENCE
IN AMERICA

*Victor F. Lenzen**

I

Contemporary philosophy of science in America exemplifies the philosophical standpoint of logical empiricism. Science is conceived to be an activity of discovering, recording, and organizing empirical phenomena; organization is recognized as a logical achievement which is accomplished especially through the concepts of mathematics. The logico-empiricistic philosophy of science has been created against a background of idealism in metaphysics; scientists, epistemologists, and logicians have cooperated in its development. Important methods of approach have been through criticism of physics, analysis of meaning, and independent creative work in logic. These modes of philosophical activity have their roots in the early period of the American Republic.

During the colonial period, American thought was guided by the Cambridge Platonists, whose influence on science is represented by the theological and absolutistic concepts in Newton's philosophy of physical theory. Later, during the middle of the eighteenth century Benjamin Franklin (1706-1709), America's first creative scientist, whose achievements and illumination of thought won the friendship of France for the new nation, exhibited critical insight into the nature of physical theory. Franklin was an ingenious experimenter and a creator of theoretical ideas as well. In descriptions of his electrical experiments he recognized the hypothetical and tentative character of theoretical explanation. For example, after describing experiments [1] which led to the conclusion: "That the clouds of a thunder-gust are most commonly in a

---

* Born in 1890. Ph. D., Harvard University, 1916. Professor of Physics, University of California. President, Pacific Division American Philosophical Association, 1944. Author of *The Nature of Physical Theory* (1931), *Procedures of Empirical Science* (1938), *The Figure of Dionysos on the Siphnian Frieze* (1946); contributor to scientific and philosophical publications.
1. Franklin, *Experiments and Observations on Electricity,* edited by I. B. Cohen (Cambridge, Harvard University Press, 1941), p. 271.

negative state of electricity, but sometimes in a positive state," he said, "But tho' the light gained from these experiments makes no alteration in the practice, it makes a considerable one in the theory. And now we as much need an hypothesis to explain by what means the clouds become negatively, as before to show how they become positively electrified. I cannot forbear venturing some few conjectures on this occasion: They are what occur to me at present, and though future discoveries should prove them not wholly right, yet they may in the meantime be of some use, by stirring up the curious to make more experiments, and occasion more exact disquisitions." Franklin then outlined his one fluid theory of electricity. On another occasion he expressed dissatisfaction with the Newtonian theory that light consists of particles which are continually driven off from the sun's surface. Franklin wrote,[2] "May not all the phenomena of light be more conveniently solved, by supposing universal space filled with a subtile elastic fluid, which, when at rest, is not visible, but whose vibrations affect that fine sense in the eye, as those of air do the grosser organs of the ear?" The use of the term convenient in characterizing a physical hypothesis shows that Franklin had some of the insight of Henri Poincaré who expounded the fundamental role of conventions in physical science. From the preceding quotations it seems evident that Franklin anticipated in general terms the contemporary conception of physical theory as founded on tentative hypotheses which serve to correlate as simply as possible the results of experiments and to predict new experiments.

The analysis of meaning, which plays a major role in contemporary American philosophy, had an able exponent during the first half of the nineteenth century. During this period idealism under the name of transcendentalism occupied a significant place in American thought. In sharp contrast to such vague and mystical speculations, Albert Bryan Johnson (1786-1867), whose background was British empiricism, set forth the empirical reference of all meaningful discourse in a *Treatise on Language*. The *Treatise,* first published in 1836, was an expanded and revised edition of an earlier work, published in 1828. Johnson's work was neglected until recently, when interest in semantics, which has been stimulated by the introduction into America of positivism of the Vienna Circle, led to the critical study and republication of Johnson's *Treatise.*[3] In anticipation of later doctrines, Johnson declared that the external universe may be divided into sights, sounds, tastes, feels, and smells; the

---

2. *Ibid.,* p. 325.
3. Edited by David Rynin. (Berkeley, University of California Press, 1947).

words of a language name these sensible existences. He asserted that names become so identified and confounded with the external existences, that we cannot discover the subordination which language bears to the realities, but continually impute to nature limitations, ambiguities, and properties which truly belong to language alone. Distance is a unity in language but is two distinct phenomena: a sight and a feel. Table, though a unity in language, is two existences, the sight table and the feel table. In anticipation of the operational theory of physical concepts, Johnson maintained that the language in which an experiment is announced must be interpreted by the experiment. An account of the resolution of white light into a spectrum by a prism and the recombination of the constituents, has as its signification only the experiment. Theoretical agents are to be distinguished from sensible agents. The pressure of the atmosphere, as a theoretical agent which enables us to methodize numerous phenomena which are exhibited by the air pump and barometer, is a fabrication of man and is to be distinguished from pressure as a feel. The word atom is the name of a sight and a feel, and Johnson declared, "When I say atoms exist which cannot be seen or felt, I divest the word of signification." [4] According to Johnson, a theory is a human contrivance by which we artificially associate sensible realities, and by familiar processes account for their production. Theories are useful, for we are acquainted with no mode of creating a science, except by embodying facts in a theory. Furthermore, new facts are occasionally developed by experiments which are deducible from a theory.

The empirical and operational point of view of Johnson did not win adherence in a period of American history which was molded largely by absolute idealism. In the latter half of the nineteenth century, however, there began a reaction against idealism and metaphysics in general. The positivism of Auguste Comte received growing recognition, indeed, to the extent that it became an object of attack by idealists. J. B. Stallo (1823-1885), who originally expounded "Naturphilosophie," criticized absolutism and expounded a physical relativism in *The Concepts and Theories of Modern Physics* (1882). The antimetaphysical point of view of Ernst Mach became known through translations into English of his history of mechanics and other works. Karl Pearson's *Grammar of Science* (1892) aroused considerable interest in America. The critical work of Henri Poincaré became known through articles in a journal *The Monist*, edited by Paul Carus. Early in the twentieth century was published a translation of three works of Poincaré under the title *Foundations of Science*

---

4. *Ibid.*, p. 98.

(1913). By the beginning of this century the revolt against absolute idealism found expression in the radical empiricism and pragmatism of William James and in the instrumentalism of John Dewey. Thus was created a basic constituent in contemporary American philosophy of science, a philosophy which may be characterized as based on logical empiricism.

The word logical in the preceding sentence indicates that a third root in American philosophy of science is logic. Charles S. Peirce (1839-1914) was educated in the idealism of Kant and of the post-Kantians, but by virtue of mathematical and scientific training he created new theories in logic and theory of knowledge. In 1870 Peirce created a logic of relatives, and in other ways contributed to the development of symbolic logic. Peirce formulated the experimental criterion of meaning which became the basis of pragmatism and instrumentalism. He stated, "If one can define accurately all the conceivable experimental phenomena which the affirmation or denial of a concept could imply, one will have therein a complete definition of the concept." [5] Peirce also contributed to inductive logic. He described induction as a procedure of determining the properties of a collection by inference from the properties of fair samples. In 1883 was published under the editorship of Peirce, *Studies in Logic,* which included his own "Logic of Induction" and contributions by collaborators at Johns Hopkins University.

The logical tradition founded by Peirce was continued by Josiah Royce (1855-1916). Royce contributed an original monograph [6] "The Relation of the Principles of Logic to the Foundations of Geometry," expounded his conception of logic as the science of order in "Principles of Logic," [7] and especially expounded Peirce's theory of induction. In a significant paper "The Mechanical, the Historical and the Statistical," Royce predicted that the canonical form of future scientific theory would be statistical. [8] By his own contributions and those of his students Royce did much to create philosophy of science as a definite field in America. A colleague of Royce, the mathematician E. V. Huntington, made notable contributions to the field of postulates for mathematical systems. The pioneer work of Peirce, Royce, and Huntington laid the foundation for the strong school of mathematical logic in America. As we shall see, the

---

5. Quoted by John Dewey, "The Development of American Pragmatism," in *Twentieth Century Philosophy,* edited by D. Runes. (New York, The Philosophical Library, 1943).

6. *Trans. of the American Mathematical Society,* Vol. VI, (1905), pp. 353-415.

7. Ruge's *Encyclopedia of the Philosophical Sciences,* Vol. I, (London, The Macmillan Co., 1913).

8. *Science, N. S.,* Vol. XXXIX (1914), pp. 551 ff. Royce also wrote the introduction to Poincaré, *Foundations of Science* (1913).

logical' movement finally combined with the empirical one to form logical empiricism.

II

Philosophical activities in the United States expanded after World War I and new influences arose in philosophy of science. A great impetus was given to this field when A. N. Whitehead, the English logician, assumed a professorship in America. Prior to his departure from England Whitehead had invented the method of extensive abstraction and had applied it in works on natural knowledge. The method was subjected to criticism in America,[9] but Whitehead stimulated interest in the place of science in modern culture. In his Lowell Lectures, *Science and the Modern World* (1925), he reviewed the basic ideas of classical physical science and set forth the requirement of revision in the light of the theory of relativity and the quantum theory.[10] The classical physics which was based on the synthesis of the seventeenth century presupposed the "fallacy of simple location." Instead of treating natural things in isolation, Whitehead declared that the concept of organism should be made fundamental in science. He then constructed a speculative metaphysics which was published under the title *Process and Reality* (1929)[11] This work introduced a metaphysical element into the consideration of science antithetic to the instrumentalism which had become characteristic of American thought. The concept of organism as the basis of science has had influence in biology. Thus R. S. Lillie has recently published a philosophical work on biology which reveals the continuing influence of Whitehead.[12] All aspects of the philosophy of Whitehead have been discussed critically in a volume *The Philosophy of Alfred North Whitehead,* edited by Paul Arthur Schilpp.[13]

Whitehead did not accept Einstein's theory of gravitation as based upon a space-time of variable curvature. He retained homogenous space-time and set up an alternative law of gravitation. F. S. C. Northrop has been an interpreter of Whitehead. In *Science and First Principles* (1931), Northrop expounded a macroscopic atomic theory, the purpose of which

9. V. F. Lenzen, "Scientific Ideas and Experience," in *University of California Publ. in Philosophy,* Vol. VIII (1926), pp. 175-189. Ernest Nagel, "Russell's Philosophy of Science," in *The Philosophy of Bertrand Russell,* edited by Paul Arthur Schilpp (Northwestern University, 1944).
10. New York, The Macmillan Co.
11. New York, The Macmillan Co.; Cambridge University Press.
12. *General Biology and Philosophy of Organism* (Chicago, University of Chicago Press, 1945).
13. Northwestern University, 1941.

was to reconcile Whitehead's demand for homogeneity and Einstein's requirement of variability of space-time.[14] Recently Northrop has published a work of wide scope *The Logic of the Sciences and of the Humanities* (1947).[15] He conceives logic broadly to include forms of knowing in the sciences proper and in religion and art as well. According to Northrop, the deductive science of the Western World operates with concepts by postulation, whereas the philosophy of the Eastern World operates with concepts by intuition. In Northrop's philosophy the Oriental method of intuition, or immediate apprehension, is treated as falling under logic. This intimately relates logic to art, to culture, and to the humanities generally. Since logic is conceived so comprehensively, there is no single scientific method. The particular problem of a specific field determines the appropriate scientific method. A science may pass through different stages of development. The method of empiricism, which characterizes natural science in Northrop's second stage of inquiry, is correlated with the method of impressionistic art and with problems of value in the humanities. The logic of one field in a particular stage is identical with the logic of another field in an appropriate stage of development. A problem to which Northrop gives special attention is that of an adequate method for the normative sciences.

Northrop's broad conception of scientific method is expressed in his doctrine of the basic importance of philosophy of science for ideals of culture. He asserts, "That philosophy of the good for the social sciences and the humanities is a publicly valid one which is also the philosophy of the experimentally verified theory of the natural sciences."[16] Guided by an ideal of comprehensive thought in the manner of Whitehead, Northrop has constructed a philosophy of science which recognizes both the role of intuition and theoretical construction and thereby provides a basis for a world civilization in which the East and the West may exist in complementary harmony.

Whitehead's analysis of the origins of modern science was followed by other historical studies. In *Metaphysical Foundations of Modern Physical Science* (1927), E. A. Burtt presented evidence for the thesis that the metaphysical ideas of Pythagoras and Plato inspired the creation of modern astronomy and physics by Copernicus, Kepler, Galileo, and Newton.[17] Interest in the metaphysical elements in science was furthered

---

14. New York, The Macmillan Co., 1931.
15. New York, The Macmillan Co.
16. *Ibid.,* p. 361.
17. London, Kegan Paul, Trench, Trubner and Co.; New York, Harcourt, Brace and Company.

through the translation into English of Émile Meyerson's *Identité et realité* by the American Kate Loewenberg (1930).[18] In opposition to the metaphysical emphasis, E. W. Strong in *Procedures and Metaphysics* (1936) declared that the basis for early modern science was the mathematical operations of Archimedes, Euclid, and other Greek mathematicians.[19] Subsequent to the publication in England in 1931 of B. Hessen's essay *The Social and Economic Roots of Newton's "Principia,"* there appeared various studies on the influence of social and technological problems on the development of science. R. K. Merton made a study of such influences during the seventeenth century in England.[20] Later, Edgar Zilsel demonstrated that the practices of craftsmen furnished the techniques of experiment for the founders of modern science.[21] In a synoptic paper "Science and Social Context," which utilized the results of earlier studies, V. F. Lenzen sought to assign due credit to disinterestedness in the pursuit of knowledge as well as environmental factors.[22] Studies of the period prior to the rise of modern science were made by Lynn White, Jr. He utilized valuable results of historical research in France in his account of the development of medieval technology;[23] in a subsequent paper he correlated the development of naturalism in art with a growing interest in the natural environment.[24] The use of historical material for philosophical purposes was set forth by E. A. Singer, Jr., who expounded a logico-historical method for the study of the dialectical development of ideas.[25] It may be added that the history of science, which is of genuine service to the philosopher, was fostered by the editorial work of George Sarton, who founded the periodical *Isis* in Belgium and then edited it in the United States. The *Journal of the History of Ideas* further provided a medium of publication for historical studies which are an essential element in the philosophical analysis of ideas with which man seeks to comprehend nature as well as himself. Recently, James B. Conant in lectures *On Understanding Science* has argued that the best method to expound the strategy and tactics of science to laymen is through historical examples.[26]

18. London, George Allen and Unwin.
19. Berkeley, University of California Press.
20. "Science, Technology and Society in Seventeenth Century England," *Osiris*, Vol. IV (1938), pp. 360-632.
21. "The Origins of William Gilbert's Scientific Method," *Journal of the History of Ideas*, Vol. II (1941), pp. 1-32.
22. *U. C. Publ. in Philosophy*, Vol. XXIII (1942), pp. 3-26.
23. "Technology and Invention in the Middle Ages," *Speculum*, Vol. XV (1940), pp. 141-59.
24. "Natural Science and Naturalistic Art in the Middle Ages," *American Historical Review*, Vol. LII (1947), pp. 421-35.
25. *Philosophy of Science*, Vol. I (1934), pp. 271-295.
26. Yale University Press, 1947.

While metaphysical factors in science were emphasized by Whitehead and Burtt, and historical studies were pursued avidly, the dominant philosophical point of view in America during the decade after World War I was pragmatism. Under the name of instrumentalism John Dewey expounded a logic, according to which scientific method is the procedure by which creative intelligence solves the contradictions which are presented in experience. In *Creative Intelligence* (1917),[27] a cooperative volume by John Dewey and others, the pragmatic method was applied to various fields of knowledge. Of special interest are the essay on mathematics by H. C. Brown and the essay, "Scientific Method and the Individual Thinker," by G. H. Mead.

A notable contribution to the pragmatic point of view was the *Logic of Modern Physics* (1927), by P. W. Bridgman.[28] In this book he introduced the expression operational theory of physical concepts, in order to describe the doctrine that the meaning of physical concepts resides in the methods by which those concepts are found applicable to the physical world. Bridgman's demand that the concept of a physical quantity be defined by a description of the mental and physical operations by which values of the quantity are determined, exerted a great influence on other sciences. Especially have psychologists sought to define in terms of operations the concepts employed in their science. The point of view of a large group of psychologists is exemplified in the book, *Purposive Behavior in Animals and Men* (1932), by E. C. Tolman.[29] In his system of psychology mental processes are conceived to be intervening variables, or behavior-determinants, between stimuli and responses of the organism. The types of determinant are to be discovered by behavior experiments; the determinants are pragmatically conceived, objective variables the concepts of which can be altered and changed as proves most useful. The operational point of view and its application to psychology has been expounded in a monograph, "Psychology and the Science of Science" (1939), by S. S. Stevens.[30] The operational point of view is employed by B. F. Skinner in *The Behavior of Organisms* (1938),[31] and by C. C. Pratt in *The Logic of Modern Psychology* (1939).[32] An issue of the *Psychological Review* in 1945 was devoted to a symposium entitled "Operationism in Psychology."[33]

---

27. New York, Henry Holt and Co.
28. New York, The Macmillan Co.
29. New York, Century Co., 1932.
30. *Psychological Bulletin,* Vol. XXXVI, pp. 221-263.
31. New York, Appleton-Century Co.
32. New York, The Macmillan Co.
33. Vol. LII, pp. 241-294.

While the general philosophical and psychological journals provided media of publication for philosophy of science, as the references in this essay indicate, discussion of the foregoing problems was facilitated by the establishment in 1934 of the journal, *Philosophy of Science*, under the editorship of the late W. M. Malisoff.

III

Bridgman's *Logic of Modern Physics* was the first of a series of studies in physics by physicists which warrant special consideration. The program of Bridgman was to extend to all physics the method of analysis which had led to the reconstruction of the concepts of space and time through the special theory of relativity. This reconstruction by Einstein was based upon the doctrine that concepts for the description of phenomena have significance only if the method of testing their applicability can be specified. The meaning of the concept of a physical quantity resides in the operations by which values of the quantity are found by measurement. Some critics interpreted the operational theory as placing too much emphasis upon physical manipulations, so that Bridgman's criterion of meaning was held to be too narrow. This criticism was unjustified, for Bridgman explicitly recognized the role of mental as well as physical operations. W. F. G. Swann has discussed the meaning of physical concepts so as to place emphasis upon mental operations.[34] According to him, the truth of a theory of mathematical physics consists in the fact that it is possible to assign numbers such that, if specified mathematical operations are performed on the fundamental equations, the results can be confirmed by measurement.

While Bridgman emphasized the operational basis of physics, a subsequent work by V. F. Lenzen, *The Nature of Physical Theory*, was devoted primarily to the logical structure of physical theory as a relatively finished product.[35] Lenzen acknowledged the correlation of physical concepts to the operations by which the concepts are applied to the physical world, but he was primarily concerned to exhibit physics as consisting of deductive systems based on principles. He sought to set forth the fundamental principles of a theory and to determine their epistemological status, that is, to determine whether principles should be interpreted as definitions or as empirical generalizations. The aim was to expound the systematic structure of physical theory in the light of postulational methods as well as its relation to experience. This task was undertaken

---

34. *Reviews of Modern Physics*, Vol. II (1930), p. 286.
35. New York, John Wiley, 1931.

against a background of study of the works of Pierre Duhem and Henri Poincaré.

In view of the uncompleted state of theoretical physics and lack of unity in the foundations, an inductive method of exposition was adopted. Physical description presupposes definitions which are required in order to interpret the results of experiments. The acknowledgment of definitions of concepts as the basis of description testifies to the *a priori* in physical theory in conformity to ideas set forth by C. I. Lewis in *Mind and the World Order* (1929).[36] Upon definitions of concepts of physical quantities, functional relations can be established by experience between the quantitative properties of physical phenomena. The generalizations from experience may then be transformed into more general definitions of the concepts which occur therein. Thus in building a system of science one initially constructs primitive concepts by abstraction from the data given in experience, and then establishes relations between the concepts, which relations then serve to define more precisely defined concepts. An empirical generalization which was initially founded on primitive concepts becomes transformed into an implicit definition of the concepts which it involves. The question, are fundamental principles *a posteriori* or *a priori,* is answered so as to recognize the claims of both. The exposition of physical theory by the procedure of exhibiting the successive stages of empirical generalization and definition has been called the method of successive definition. By this method is shown the genesis in experience of the conventions of Henri Poincaré.

A particular example of the method of successive definition is the discussion of Archimedes's restricted principle of the lever: If to each end of a lever of equal arms are attached equal weights, the lever remains horizontal. This principle has been characterized as a self-evident axiom in Archimedes's theory of the lever; from it Archimedes deduced a general principle which holds for levers of unequal arms. Ernst Mach argued that the restricted principle was a generalization from experience. The method of successive definition yields the following analysis: Initially the weight of a body may be considered a force which is measured by balancing it with muscular exertion through the hand. Two bodies judged equal in weight by this method would then be found to maintain an equal arm lever in equilibrium, at least approximately. The lever with equal arms in the form of a balance is used in experimental physics to test the

---

36. New York, Scribner's. The latest book by Lewis is *An Analysis of Knowledge and Valuation,* The Paul Carus Foundation Lectures VII (Lasalle, Open Court Publishing Co., 1946).

equality in weight of a body to a standard of weight. Such employment of the balance presupposes the principle of the lever as a definition. The empirical basis for the definition is the following: If two bodies have been found equal in weight by the balance, they have been judged equal by muscular exertion. More significantly, if two bodies have been found equal by one balance they have been found equal by other balances, regardless of kind of material, size, position, and time. On account of such experimental results, the definition of equality in weight which is based upon the restricted principle of the lever is useful.

The entire structure of classical physics may be built conceptually by the method of successive definition. Thus the spatial properties of configurations of solid bodies are defined to the first approximation, at least, by the propositions of Euclidean geometry; the theory of clocks defines the structure of time; the laws of classical mechanics define concepts of momentum, mass, and force; the laws of electromagnetism define concepts of the electromagnetic field; the laws of thermodynamics define the concepts of internal energy and entropy; the principle of the constancy of the velocity of light defines time in the special theory of relativity; in Eddington's interpretation of the general theory of relativity, Einstein's law of gravitation defines matter. The principles of quantum theory set limits to the applicability of the classical concepts as defined by classical physics. Thus Lenzen's mode of expounding physical theory interprets concepts as instruments which arise from experience and then serve *a priori* for the interpretation of new experience. A further analysis of this concept of the *a priori* has been presented by Arthur Pap in his dissertation *The A Priori in Physical Theory* (1945).[37]

A treatise on physics which also embodies philosophical analysis is *Foundations of Physics* (1936), by R. B. Lindsay and H. Margenau.[38]

Questions of metaphysical interpretation of physical theory have been considered. Lenzen sought to remain neutral with respect to idealistic or realistic theories of the ontological status of the objects in the physical universe of discourse . In *Procedures of Empirical Science* (1938), he stated that the physical existence of molecules, atoms, electrons, radiation, and other elements of physical reality is equivalent to the existence of the physical properties of perceptible bodies.[39] If a colloidal particle exists in the sense of realism, then so does the molecule which is conceived to interact with it in conformity to physical principles. If a zinc sulphide screen

37. New York, King's Crown Press.
38. New York, John Wiley.
39. *International Encyclopedia of Unified Science,* Vol. I, No. 5.

exists, then so does the alpha particle which is conceived to excite the screen to scintillate. But if the objects of perception are interpreted as fictions, or constructs, such will be the status of microphysical constituents of reality also.

The metaphysical problem has been discussed quite explicitly by Henry Margenau. His views are presented in "Metaphysical Elements in Physics" (1941).[40] By metaphysics he means the study of the role of perceptions and infra-sensible elements of our experience. The totality of perceptions he calls sensed nature, or just nature. The words energy, charge, field strength, electron, photon signify infra-perceptible elements of physical theory and are called constructs of physical explanation. Constructs serve to explain nature. Margenau defines the realm of physical reality to include nature plus all constructs which occur in physical theories held valid at present.

A very sophisticated interpretation of physical concepts repeatedly has been expounded by W. F. G. Swann. His views are represented in "The Relation of Theory to Experiment in Physics" (1941).[41] Swann points out that hardly any of the quantities which occur in physics are measured directly. In general, one measures the magnitudes of quantities such as positions and velocities of electrons in classical dynamics by assuming some equations in which these quantities occur, solving the equations to predict the values of some measurable quantities and then determining the unknowns so as to fit the facts. Swann contends that particles ultimately will be unnecessary and that the only role of particles is one of convenience. Swann has stated that the experimentalist of former times usually was a materialist, but the modern theorist is likely to become a mathematical spiritualist. He is, however, a pseudo-spiritualist, for his ghosts are of his own creation and serve only the purpose of giving the semblance of life to the picture of nature which he possesses and which, in the last analysis, is a creation of his own mind.

IV

We have seen that problems of meaning were brought into the center of philosophical discussion, especially in the fields of physics and psychology, by Bridgman's operational theory. This interest was furthered by the work of C. I. Lewis, *Mind and the World Order* (1929), and by the introduction into America of the doctrines of the Vienna Circle. The

40. *Reviews of Modern Physics*, Vol. XIII, No. 3 (1941).
41. *Ibid.*

basis of the latter doctrines was well known in America through Bertrand Russell's translation of Wittgenstein's *Tractatus Logico-Philosophicus* (1922).[42] But interest in the thesis that philosophy is essentially clarification of meaning was given great impetus through the teaching of Moritz Schlick in America during the summer of 1929 and the academic year 1931-1932. Indeed, a student of Schlick, David Rynin, later edited Johnson's *Treatise on Language* which anticipated on American soil some of the Viennese doctrines a century earlier. In 1931 A. E. Blumberg and H. Feigl expounded the views of the Vienna Circle in the *Journal of Philosophy* under the name logical positivism.[43] The name was intended to indicate that the methods of mathematical logic were applied to the empiricistic and antimetaphysical analysis of knowledge of Ernst Mach. Schlick preferred the name consistent empiricism, but the enduring influence in America of the positive philosophy of Auguste Comte is shown by the fact that the term positivism became current. The doctrines of the Vienna Circle were also developed in America by a former member, Rudolf Carnap. Later, Philipp Frank assumed residence in America. Under the title, *Between Physics and Philosophy,* were published translations of his interpretations of the doctrines of Ernst Mach and also his criticisms of metaphysical views founded on the theories of relativity and of quanta.[44] Recently Frank has published a scientific biography of Einstein (1947) which is especially valuable for its philosophical analysis.[45]

The decade which ended in World War II was characterized by discussions in philosophy of science which centered about logical positivism. Since the task of philosophy was declared to be clarification of meaning, the heart of the positivistic doctrine was the criterion of meaning: The meaning of a sentence resides in the procedure by which it could be confirmed or disconfirmed. Charles W. Morris especially contributed to the attainment of precision of discussion. In his monograph *Logical Positivism, Pragmatism, and Scientific Method,* he sought to unite the movements of European and American origin and proposed the name logical empiricism.[46] Morris described the program of logical empiricism in terms of a division in the theory of signs, or Semiotic. He distinguished three sets of relations of signs. The relation of signs to the objects to which signs are applicable was called the semantical dimension of semio-

42. New York, Harcourt, Brace and Co.
43. *Journal of Philosophy,* Vol. XXVIII, pp. 281-296.
44. Harvard University Press, 1941.
45. New York, A. Knopf.
46. *Actualités scientifiques et industrielles* (Paris, 1937). Also, Charles Morris, *Signs, Language and Behavior* (New York, Prentice-Hall, 1946).

sis; the study of this dimension is Semantics. The relation of signs to interpreters was called the pragmatical dimension and its study is Pragmatics. The formal relation of signs was called the syntactical dimension and its study is Syntactics. Carnap has published *The Logical Syntax of Language* (1937) [47] and also *Introduction to Semantics* (1942). [48] Also worthy of note is the paper "The Semantical Conception of Truth, and the Foundations of Semantics" by Alfred Tarski. [49]

The positivistic, or empiricistic, movement proclaimed as an aim the creation of unity of science by demonstrating that all scientific terms are reducible to the language of physics. At International Congresses for the Unity of Science there was planned an *International Encyclopedia of Unified Science,* with the late Otto Neurath as editor-in-chief, and Charles Morris and Rudolf Carnap as associate editors. Numbers constituting volumes one and two, *Foundations of the Unity of Science,* began to be published in 1938 by the Chicago University Press. Among numbers by authors in America are *Foundations of the Theory of Signs,* by Charles W. Morris; *Foundations of Logic and Mathematics,* by Rudolf Carnap; *Procedures of Empirical Science,* by V. F. Lenzen; *Principles of the Theory of Probability,* by Ernest Nagel; *Foundations of Physics,* by Philipp Frank.

The plan of the *Encyclopedia* was to establish unity in science. This was interpreted as a problem in the logic of science, not of ontology. The logical relations among terms of different parts of the language of science were based upon reducibility which has been analyzed by Carnap. [50] If a specific term is such that the conditions for its application in the language of science can be formulated with the help of some other terms, the formulation is called a reduction statement of the first term in terms of the other ones, and the first is said to be reducible to the others. A definition is the simplest form of reduction statement. Example of definition of 'ox': x is an ox is equivalent to x is a quadruped, etc. A reduction statement sometimes can be formulated only in conditional form. Thus, a reduction statement for the term electric charge may be the following: If a light body is placed near x at the time t, then: x has an electric charge at time t is equivalent to the light body is attracted by x at t.

The physical thing-language is the language that we use in speaking

47. New York, Harcourt, Brace and Co.
48. Harvard University Press.
49. *Philosophy and Phenomenological Research,* Vol. IV (1944), pp. 341-376.
50. "Testability and Meaning," *Philosophy of Science,* Vol. III (1936), pp. 419-471; Vol. IV (1937), pp. 1-40. Also *Logical Foundations of the Unity of Science, Encyclopedia,* No. 1.

about the properties of the observable inorganic things surrounding us. The thesis of physicalism is that the terms of the thing-language, and even the narrower class of observable thing-predicates, furnishes a sufficient basis for the whole language of science. In particular, it is asserted that psychological terms are analogous to those physical terms which are introduced by reduction statements of the conditional form. Terms of both kinds designate a state characterized by the disposition to certain reactions. The unity of the language of science does not, however, imply the unity of laws. According to Carnap, it is not possible in the present state of development of science to derive biological laws from physical ones. There is at present no unity of laws.

In an attempt to extend physical concepts to biological processes, F. S. C. Northrop and his colleague H. S. Burr have applied field concepts of physics, such as the concept of electromagnetic field, in order to explain the organization of living things. [51] The electro-dynamic theory of life which has been formulated by these thinkers goes beyond the present claims of physicalism. By contrast, W. H. Werkmeister apparently expects that the concepts of biology will prove to be more general than those of physics. [52] He has noted that in physical science new theories may include older theories as limiting cases; for example, relativistic mechanics includes classical mechanics. Now biological processes have physico-chemical constituents, but are more complex than the latter. Hence one may expect that the laws of biology, when adequately formulated, will reduce to the laws of physics in the limit. The relation between vital and mechanical phenomena has been studied by E. A. Singer, Jr., by the logico-historical dialectical method. [53] He reconciles the opposition between mechanism and vitalism by the view that a system may be mechanical from one point of view, but simultaneously it may possess membership in the organic realm.

The positivistic conception of science did call forth statements in opposition. Hans Reichenbach was in agreement with the program to analyze science logically, but he favored a realistic theory of knowledge. [54] A realistic position was also taken by A. G. Ramsperger in *Philosophies of Science* (1942). [55] The Catholic philosopher Fulton J. Sheen in *Philosophy of Science* (1934) argued that relativism of measure does not affect

51. References in *Logic of the Sciences and Humanities*, p. 234.
52. *A Philosophy of Science* (New York, Harper and Brothers, 1940).
53. *Op. cit.*
54. *Experience and Prediction* (Chicago, University of Chicago Press, 1938).
55. New York, F. S. Crofts and Co., 1942.

the absoluteness of reality which is independent of mind.[56] In "Physics and Reality" (1936), Einstein constructed the system of physics upon a foundation of sensible experiences, but he has repeatedly acknowledged the existence of a realm beyond experience.[57] In an essay on Bertrand Russell's theory of knowledge, Einstein maintained that there is value in the concept of an independent reality.[58] The logician Everett Nelson has argued that the metaphysical concept of substance is necessary for science.[59]

In a systematic work, *The Logical Structure of Science* (1936), A. C. Benjamin has sought to achieve the rapprochement of opposing views.[60] His critical positivism starts with the given, and he distinguishes between things which are clearly given and obvious and things which are obscurely given and conjectural. According to Benjamin, it is the task of science and philosophy to symbolize the total realm of the given, through discovery of relations connecting the clearly given with the obscurely given. The doctrine of Benjamin is positivistic in its insistence that one should begin with the clearly given, but it is antiposivistic in its insistence that one should not give to obscurely given constructions an unreal status.

Logical empiricism has created a new outlook in the theory of induction, one which has been expressed by H. Feigl in "The Logical Character of the Principle of Induction."[61] He distinguishes between the meaning and validity of induction, and asserts that the principle of induction is a principle of procedure. Current theories of induction are based upon a theory of probability. Reichenbach, whose views are expressed in *Experience and Prediction,* declares that the aim of induction is to find series of events which occur with frequencies that converge toward a limit. The prediction of a single event is a posit and has the form of a wager, the weight of which is determined by the frequency within the corresponding class. Another application of the frequency theory of probability has been made by C. West Churchman, who in *Theory of Experimental Inference* (1948) expounds an "Experimentalism" which is a generalization of statistical methods.[62] Donald Williams in *The Ground of Induction* (1947) offers a definition of probability in terms of truth frequencies similar to Laplace's classical conception of probability.[63] Williams's analytic proof of the validity of induction consists in pointing out that

56. Milwaukee, Bruce Publishing Co.
57. *Journal of the Franklin Institute*, Vol. CCXXI, No. 3.
58. In *The Philosophy of Bertrand Russell*, edited by Paul Arthur Schilpp.
59. *Philosophical Review*, Vol. LVI (1947), pp. 491-509.
60. London, Kegan Paul, Trench, Trubner and Co.
61. *Philosophy of Science*, Vol. I (1934), pp. 20-29.
62. The Macmillan Co., 1948.
63. Harvard University Press, 1947.

an inductive inference from the composition of a sample to the approximate composition of its population has a high degree of probability. In contrast to the doctrines just cited, Carnap distinguishes two meanings of the term probability: (1) a logical concept of probability as a logical relation between sentences, or propositions; (2) an empirical concept of probability as a relative frequency.[64] Carnap has outlined an inductive logic based on the concept of degree of confirmation as a logical relation between sentences.[65] He has further stated that an entirely different question is the validity of the proposed system of inductive logic.

V

The interpretation of quantum mechanics has created special logical and ontological problems which have been discussed in America. According to the logical investigations of Garrett Birkhoff and J. von Neumann, the principle of indeterminacy requires a modification of logic.[66] Along with the concept of simultaneous observability there is introduced its negation, nonsimultaneous observability. The distributive law is declared to be the one which fails in quantum mechanics, and Birkhoff and Neumann have proposed a set of postulates which includes a suitable modification of the distributive law.

Of interest has been the construction of a three-valued logic for quantum mechanics. A multiple-valued logic was constructed by the American logician, E. L. Post, in 1921,[67] and such logics have been developed especially by Polish mathematicians. Paulette Février created a three-valued logic for quantum mechanics in 1937.[68] The outstanding American contribution to this field is the logic of Hans Reichenbach which he has expounded in *Philosophic Foundations of Quantum Mechanics* (1944).[69]

Reichenbach's procedure is to restrict the interpretation of quantum mechanics so that causal anomalies are obviated. An interpretation re-

---

64. *Philosophy and Phenomenological Research*, Vol. V (1945), pp. 513-532.

65. *Philosophy of Science*, Vol. XIII (1945), pp. 72-87. Definitions of degree of confirmation have also been given by Olaf Helmer and Paul Oppenheim in *Journal of Symbolic Logic*, Vol. X (1945), pp. 25-60; and by C. G. Hempel and Paul Oppenheim in *Philosophy of Science*, Vol. XII (1945), pp. 98-115.

66. *New Theories in Physics* (Paris, International Institute of Intellectual Co-operation, 1939), pp. 32-38.

67. *American Journal of Mathematics*, Vol. XLIII (1921), p. 163.

68. *Comptes rendus de l'Academie des Sciences*, T.204 (Paris, 1937).

69. University of California Press. Reichenbach's work has been reviewed critically by C. G. Hempel, *Journal of Symbolic Logic*, Vol. X (1945), pp. 97-100; Ernest Nagel, *Journal of Philosophy*, Vol. XLII (1945), pp. 437-444; V. F. Lenzen, *Philosophy and Phenomenological Research*, Vol. VI, pp. 478-486. Reichenbach's reply to the latter review is in the same issue, pp. 487-492.

duces physical processes to the behavior of a model, for example, a corpuscular or wave model. Reichenbach's discussion is based on a distinction
between phenomena and interphenomena. Phenomena are exemplified
by coincidences between electrons and are described as observable in a
broad sense. Interphenomena are the unobservable processes between coincidences, such as the movement of an electron, or of a light ray from its
source to a collision with matter. On the basis of the distinction just
made, Reichenbach distinguishes between exhaustive and restrictive interpretations. An exhaustive interpretation characterizes interphenomena
in terms of the behavior of corpuscles or waves, and the detailed application of either results in causal anomalies. A restrictive interpretation attributed to Bohr and Heisenberg is based on the rule that only statements
about measured entities are admissible; statements about unmeasured
entities, or interphenomena, are called meaningless. Reichenbach's restrictive interpretation calls statements about unmeasured entities indeterminate and gives them a status in three-valued logic.

The logic of classical physics is constructed in terms of two truth
values, truth and falsehood. Reichenbach introduces an intermediate
truth value, indeterminacy, and coordinates this truth value to the group
of statements which in the Bohr-Heisenberg interpretation are called
meaningless. The operations of three-valued logic can be considered as
generalizations of two-valued logic. In Reichenbach's three-valued logic
there are three kinds of negation: cyclical negation, $\frown A$; diametrical
negation, $-A$; complete negation, $\overline{A}$. The order of truth values running
from the highest value to the lowest value is T, I, F. Cyclical negation
shifts a truth value to the next lower one, except that the lowest is shifted
to the highest value. Diametrical negation reverses T and F, but leaves
I unchanged. Complete negation shifts a truth value to the higher one
of the other two. Disjunction and conjunction correspond to the homony-
mous operations of two-valued logic. The truth value of disjunction is
given by the higher one of the truth values of elementary propositions;
that of conjunction by the lower one. Three kinds of implication are defined: Standard implication, $A \supset B$, leads from three truth values of the
elementary propositions to three truth values of the operation; Alternative
implication, $A \rightarrow B$, leads from three truth values to the values T and F
only; Quasi-implication does not satisfy all the requirements which are
usually made for implication.

The foregoing logical scheme may be exemplified by the definition
of complementarity. The assertion $\frown A$ states that A is false. That B is
indeterminate is expressed by $\frown\frown B$. Two statements are called com-

plementary if they satisfy the relation $A \lor {\sim} A \rightarrow {\sim}{\sim}B$. This can be read: If A is true or false, B is indeterminate. Let U be an abbreviation for the statement, the first entity has the value u; and let V be an abbreviation for, the second entity has the value v. Then the rule of complementarity of quantum mechanics can be stated as follows: If u and v are noncommutative entities, then $U v {\sim} U \rightarrow {\sim}{\sim} V$.

The logical problems of quantum mechanics suggest ontological problems. The problem of reality was raised by Einstein, Podolsky, and Rosen in "Can Quantum Mechanical Description of Physical Reality Be Considered Complete?" (1935).[70] These authors, EPR, in language which contrasts with that of logical empiricism, declare that consideration of a physical theory must distinguish between objective reality, which is independent of any theory, and the physical concepts with which the theory operates. These concepts are intended to correspond to the objective reality, and by means of these concepts we picture this reality to ourselves. EPR require of a theory that it be correct and complete. The following requirement for a complete theory is deemed to be necessary: every element of the physical reality must have a counterpart in the physical theory. The test of completeness requires a criterion of the elements of physical reality. EPR offer the following criterion as reasonable: If, without in any way disturbing a system, we can predict with certainty (probability equal to unity) the value of a physical quantity, then there exists an element of physical reality corresponding to this physical quantity.

The foregoing discussion is background for the question whether or not the wave function which symbolizes the state of a system contains a complete description of the physical reality of the system in the state to which it corresponds. EPR argue that the assumption that the wave function does provide a complete description leads to a contradiction. They suppose that there are two systems which interact during an interval of time and then cease to do so. After the interaction we can measure the position of one system and then infer that of the other, or we can measure the momentum of the first and then infer that of the second. Since at the time of measurement the two systems no longer interact, no real change can take place in the second system in consequence of something done to the first. Thus it is possible to assign position or momentum to the same reality (the second system after interaction with the first). Thus the assumption that the wave function gives a complete description leads to the result that position and momentum can have

---

70. *Physical Review,* Vol. XLVIII (1935), p. 777.

simultaneous reality, since the value of either can be predicted with certainty without disturbing the second system. But this contradicts the quantum mechanical principle that when momentum is known, coordinate of position is not predictable and therefore has no physical reality. EPR state that one would not arrive at their conclusion, if one held that two or more quantities can be regarded as simultaneous elements of reality only when they can be measured or predicted simultaneously. This would make reality of position and momentum depend upon the process of measurement carried out on the first system, a measurement which does not disturb the second system in any way. EPR hold that no reasonable definition of reality could be expected to permit this. They conclude that quantum mechanics does not provide a complete description of reality.

The foregoing discussion called forth a reply by Niels Bohr in the *Physical Review*.[71] He explained that the reality of a quantity is relative to the process of measurement. Preparation for measurement of position requires a fixed frame and for the measurement of momentum a mobile collision body. These preparations for measurement of conjugate quantities exclude each other. The significance of the concept of a quantity pertaining to the second system is relative to the preparation for measurement which may be carried out only on the first system. As Bohr has declared, the classical concept of physical reality as independent of modes of observation is abandoned for atomic realities in quantum mechanics.

The physicist Kemble in "Operational Reasoning, Reality, and Quantum Mechanics" (1938) has concluded concerning the problem of reality that the province of the physicist is not the study of the external world, but the study of a portion of the inner world of experience.[72] Hence there is no reason why the constructs introduced need correspond to objective realities. According to Kemble, and perhaps most students of the subject would concur, an analysis of the relationship between the world of experience and the world of quantum theory indicates that no such correspondence does in fact exist.

---

71. Vol. XLVIII (1935), p. 696.
72. *Journal of the Franklin Institute*, Vol. CCXXIII (1938), pp. 263-275.

PROBABILITY, INDUCTION,
AND THE PROVIDENT MAN

Donald Cary Williams[*]

There was little of importance or originality in American philosophical writing until late in the nineteenth century. Most of it was second-hand and second-rate, epiphenomenal on European thought. Yet from the first founding of the English colonies, there appeared a pattern in the American selections and amendments of old-world ideas which reveals a philosophic mood of considerable distinction and coherence. This is epitomized in the ideal of the provident man, the self-reliant and responsible individual, finding his own way and striking his own bargain with God, nature, and his fellows.

The American has been a portent to the world, for better or for worse, because he was the only modern or Cartesian man. In other lands, the great revolutions of science, Protestantism, liberalism, and capitalism have been agitations of an environment already furnished with the accumulations of ancient and medieval economies. Of America, however, they are the native atmosphere, and all have nurtured the provident and individualist ideal. At the knees of science, the American was taught to take for granted the Cartesian lesson that every generation rebuilds the house of knowledge by the cooperative competition of individuals encouraged to speculate and experiment without limit. He far exceeds Descartes, however, in that he leaves nothing beyond reach of individual enterprise. An inveterate Protestant in religion, he affirms the right of private judgement and of reaching his own conception of and contact with the Supreme Power. A liberal in his very bones, he knows, because he has seen them made, that societies are artificial combinations engineered by private citizens for their own ends. He is a democrat, not because of a romantic faith in the equality of human endowment or desert, but because individuals are the ultimate units, entitled to equal opportunity to show their stuff, and because republican institutions, with free discussion and the

* Born in 1899. Ph.D., Harvard University, 1928. Professor of philosophy and chairman of the department, Harvard University. Guggenheim Fellowship for research in realistic epistemology, 1938. Author of various essays in the theory of empirical knowledge in American and European journals, and *The Ground of Induction* (see bibliography).

ballot, are the pioneering and experimental way to approach the right. He is a capitalist because he believes that freedom of contract, the competitive market, and investment enterprise will bring prosperity as surely as free scientific enterprise yields truth and free political enterprise yields justice.

The metaphysical root of self-reliance is a reliance on nature to be amenable to intelligence and effort. Nature does not have its own purposes, friendly or unfriendly, as prescientific philosophies averred, but an inanimate and automatic integrity, without mystery or perversity. Protestantism has often been irrationalist and fatalist, but the Calvinism of the American Puritans—English, Scotch, German, Dutch, and French—was tinctured by Platonic cosmology and the logic of capitalist initiative, and it agreed with the Cartesian and deistic philosophy, sanctifying the causal order of nature as the embodiment of God's covenant with the provident man. As other philosophies came to America—Scotch realism or German idealism—they experienced a sea-change to the service of this principle.

In morals, the result is a rational rigorism. By the easygoing and arbitrary codes of noncommercial, nonscientific, and non-Protestant communities, most behavior is morally indifferent. For the man who holds himself responsible for his own acts in the inexorable framework of the causal order, however, the comfortable neutral zone between what is definitely wrong and what is definitely obligatory is narrowed to vanishing. The essence of righteousness is incessantly to foresee, prepare, and prevent, to fit means to ends with patience and courage, and to check the lazy or lascivious impulses of the moment in order to drive the best possible bargain with the cosmos in the long run. The only reward of virtue which the provident man asks of God or the government is that he shall reap where he has sown. Profligacy, self-indulgence, idleness, unchastity, estheticism, monasticism are improvident violations of the causal covenant, and are properly requited with ruin.

If the order of nature were knowable with certainty, the ethics of enterprise would have only the single dimension, the steadfastness which undertakes a present sacrifice for a recompense which is remotely future. Then knowledge itself, however, could hardly be a business for individual initiative, but would best be left to a few expert authorities. In fact, the order of nature is knowable only partially and probably. The second dimension of enterprise is then the boldness which will incur sacrifice for the sake of a recompense which not only is remotely future but is only probable. The enterprising and provident man must labor and wait, but also he must serenely accept risk—necessary and calculated risk, to be sure, but real risk still. Since knowledge is then tentative and cumulative, it is everybody's responsibility. The epistemology of provident individualism, under every disguise the conviction of most Americans, is an empirical realism which depicts inquiry as an ordered freedom, inviting every idiosyncrasy of experiment and hypothesis, but checked and channeled by an indifferent and exact logic, on the one side, and the data of observation on the other, to converge toward a forever imperfect but ever more adequate fit with the facts. This is equally the principle of science, of democracy, of economic capitalism—and of the God-seeking of a hundred enterprising Protestant sects.

The philosophy of thrift and initiative is not lovely, but it is very sane, powerful, peaceful, and productive. Insofar as it is dissolved, the America which the rest of the world has variously despised and admired will degenerate to just one more flatulent empire. There are no practical grounds for its enervation. Scientific inquiry and technology, business enterprise, and republican government have surpassed the most extravagant hopes of their founders. Yet today the provident man is the target of more criticism than the older America aimed at the devil. The very success of the provident system, in solving the problems which *can* be solved, transferred to it the blame for the haunting and incurable discontents which are part of the color of life itself. With the passing of the frontier and the rise of finance, cartels, and labor unionism, success was less patently associated with an intelligent and industrious application to the causes of things. The delicate and the disappointed combined to promote insurance schemes, welfare taxes, and socialistic measures which further divorced economic causes from their normal effects, leveling out risk and reward, and pooling the results of abstinence and industry with those of greed and sloth. The name "liberalism," which once stood for the philosophy of the free and enterprising individual, is given by a new intelligentsia to a diametrically opposite doctrine of collectivism.

During the last century, an immense immigration from Catholic Europe, steeped in an ancient and authoritarian ideology fundamentally hostile to Puritanism, science, and capitalism, built a broad popular basis for the cult of improvidence. During the last fifteen years, thousands of able and assertive refugees, thinkers and teachers fleeing from tyranny or poverty in Europe, have discoursed a babel of unsympathetic doctrine such as no nation ever had to accommodate before. Meantime, the bohemian intellectuals,[1] rootless writers and talkers of whatever origin, congregated in the big cities and universities, have cultivated a precious disdain for the common American life which Franklin, Jefferson, Emerson, and Mark Twain were content to share and celebrate. Most of the literary figures whom Europe regards as typically American in this century are enemies of the ancestral ideal. Jack London and Upton Sinclair are tumultuous socialists. Sinclair Lewis, Ernest Hemingway, and John Steinbeck venomously caricature the life of dutifulness and industry, and the last two at least, glorify the indolent, the drunken, and the feckless revolutionaries who dream of a Schlaraffenland where the mills of God grind corn and gravel and pods of wind to the same meal. Even the movies and the magazines, once devoted to stories of how hard work, foresight, and self-denial bring wealth, honor, and love, have learned to portray the provident man worsted by the amiable vagrant and wastrel.

It would be a mistake to suppose that these literary campaigns have yet fundamentally changed the national fibre: the ruthless, and perhaps needless, closing down of civilian production for the fighting of the recent war would have gratified the sternest Puritan. Implemented by serious philosophical criticism, however, the attack on the provident man can eventually turn the scale. In technical philosophy, the worldliness and Promethean *hybris* of the provident ideal have always earned it the enmity of those who love fate, mystery, hierarchy, submission and tradition. The new and dangerous attack, however, is launched against its epistemological base, the theory of empiricism. The attack comes from a bizarre alliance of two main parties, to be called, in the frank terminology of the eighteenth century which shaped the provident ideal, the "superstitious" and the "skeptical." The superstitious enemies are those, such as the neo-scholastics and the romantic spiritualists, who would soar beyond the method of observation and hypothesis and the world of technological fact, to assert a nonexperimental insight and an absolute reality which transcends and discredits the maxims of the provident life. The skeptical enemies are the positivists, who in the very citadel of the philosophy of science, contemn the logic of providence and argue that the scientific intelligence is incapable of valid discovery of the causal order and the future. Alone, the superstitious philosophies were no match

---

1. Frederick Watkins, *The Political Tradition of the West* (Harvard University Press, 1948), writes well of the destructive role of the new class of "bohemian intellectuals" in all Western countries. (I shall hereafter refer in footnotes to the relevant literature only when a specific passage is cited, but there is a brief classified bibliography at the end of the essay.)

for the scientific world-view. Alone, the positivists would be nearly harmless, because, in spite of their theoretical skepticism of empirical inquiry or provident action, most of them would remain loyal to it in practice. Superstition inevitably, however, surges into the vacuum which skepticism created. Thomists joyfully profit by the positivists' emasculation of their scientific rival. Positivists turn from philosophy to such empty and improvident studies as esthetics and the analysis of analysis, or are catastrophically converted to scholasticism, existentialism, or the mystic historicism of Toynbee or Marx.

Nothing happening in American thought, therefore, is more momentous than the philosophical controversy over the foundations of empirical knowledge and the validity of inference from causes to effects. Although it is impossible here to report the whole of the debate, we can observe the four theories of inductive inference which seem most likely to decide the fate of scientific philosophy and the provident man—the positivistic, the pragmatic, the organicist, and the logical.

Current positivism in America is a revival of David Hume, improved a bit by modern logic, and little affected by Comte. The first of its principles is that a statement has meaning only so far as it is empirically confirmable. This is no detriment to the ideal of the provident man, although I think it is false. The second principle, however, which consorts very strangely with the first, is that empirical confirmation is not a rationally valid process; and this turns providence and science into wanton faith and preference. Hume pointed out (let us recall) that our belief that drenching a fire with water will cause it to go out—a typical piece of providence—cannot be established with the intuitive certainty of a mathematical truth, because there is no contradiction in the idea of a drenched fire which keeps on burning. We must then, he said, acquire the belief from experience; we have observed many drenched fires to be extinguished, and we expect that other drenched fires will be extinguished too. This is an inductive inference, of the form: *All MQ is P; hence all M is P* (or anyhow, *the next M is P*). Psychologically says Hume, this inference is perfectly intelligible—it is a result of habit, an animal propensity to believe, which he rather invidiously calls "probability." Logically, however, it is invalid. There is no more demonstrative connection between the fact that past fires have gone out when drenched and the conclusion that future fires will do likewise, than there is between the drenching of any one fire and its extinction. There is no contradiction in the supposition of the contrary.

The heirs of Hume who teach in America today include the logical positivists (led by scholars from Berlin, Vienna, and Prague), the 'therapeutic positivists' trained by Wittgenstein and Moore at Cambridge University, and the behaviorists and operationalists, whose doctrines are indigenous to American psychology and physics, respectively. The new positivism appears to surpass Hume's nihilism by denying to induction even the title of "probability," but this is because it redefines that word by the socalled 'frequency theory of probability.' On this theory, to say that there is a probability of one-half that a child will be a boy is to predict that in an infinitely long series of births the relative frequency of boys will converge toward .5. It is explicitly impossible then to assign a probability to the conclusions of inductions because the only way of knowing any probability is to observe the relative frequency which characterizes the beginning of a series and to assume that it characterizes the rest, and to do this is already to presuppose the principle of induction. Some positivists therefore confess—too rashly, perhaps—that the frequency theory has nothing to do with rational credibility, but concerns only certain conventions for summarizing the statistics of mass phenomena. The only credibility, at any rate, which an induction can have is 'credibility' in the literal sense—propensity to be believed, the result of Hume's 'custom acting on the imagination,' or of what Santayana calls "animal faith."[2] Like Hume, nevertheless, the positivists practice and recommend a strict adherence to the rules of scientific induction, and many devote themselves assiduously to defining exactly and systematically the illogical 'logic' of science, that is, the methods and assumptions by which 'the scientists of our culture circle' do in fact choose one conclusion in preference to another.

Some positivists carelessly excuse this partiality for scientific induction with the plea that it has always been very successful. This argument is flagrantly circular, since it uses the inductive method itself, and it is not improved by the reminders of some that it does not claim to be demonstrative but only to give probability. Some positivists, again, declare that the inductive method is valid by definition; it is one of the processes which we *mean* by "valid" or "rational," the other being the deductive procedure. Unless there can be shown some fundamental continuity and identity of principle between deductive and inductive 'validity,'

---

2. David Hume, *A Treatise of Human Nature,* edited by Selby-Bigge (Oxford, the Clarendon Press, 1896, etc.), Book I, p. 103; George Santayana, *Scepticism and Animal Faith* (New York, Charles Scribner's Sons, 1923), and *Realms of Being* (same, 1942; see especially p. 303).

however, this is only verbalism, and leaves the preference for the rules of induction a pure decision, the *Blutgefühl* of the scientific *Volksgenossen*.

Pragmatism and the several philosophies called "critical naturalism" endeavor to improve on plain positivism by infusions of vitalism and voluntarism. The maxim that 'life solves the problems which logic leaves,' and John Dewey's reiteration that problem-solving is a continuous and purposeful interaction of organism and environment, are only a loose elaboration of Hume's doctrine of animal faith, and throw no light on its efficacy. More amusing but not more helpful is the extreme pragmatic doctrine that inquiry fulfills its own prophecies by manufacturing their objects, carving facts out of the raw *hyle* of experience, 'inventing' scientific entities, and 'constructing' world models. Even the most thorough pragmatist must concede that there is a hard residue of fact which we must predict without being able to create it, and this residue is just the fulcrum on which providence must act.

Much more moderate and more impressive is the reconciliation of the demands of logic and of life by Clarence Lewis and Hans Reichenbach. Since life is impossible except as we anticipate and prepare for future experience, they argue, in order to justify the inductive method of anticipation we need not show that it is actually a good method but only that it is the best method—that no other method could be better. Both take as fundamental the key conception of the frequency theory of probability, the limiting frequency with which a character, such as whiteness, occurs in an endless random series of a certain kind of observation, of swans, let us say. The inductive process to be justified is the one by which, having observed the frequency within part of such a series, we infer that the frequency in the whole series converges on a similar value.

Reichenbach calls the limiting frequency of white in the total series of swan observations the 'probability' of white among swans. He will not let us speak of this as the 'probability' that any one swan will be white; but we can call it the 'weight' of the 'posit' that a specified swan is white. Our inductive inference, however, does not even have a 'weight.' It is a 'blind posit,' so blind that Reichenbach will not admit that a posit founded on many or well-chosen instances is better than a posit founded on few or ill-chosen instances, except after we have established a second-level 'probability' and 'weight' by observing long series of whole inductions in which those which are based on more numerous or better chosen instances are more often correct than the others. His justification of the inductive rule is, in brief, that we cannot predict at all unless there is a limiting frequency of the predicted character in the 'reference class' which we are considering; and if there is such a limiting frequency, either it is altogether undiscoverable, or it will be discoverable by the inductive rule. A person might conceivably make true predictions by clairvoyance or palm reading, but in that case, he argues, the success of such a method, or such a person, must be apparent by the inductive rule also.

Lewis uses the word "probability" not for the actual limiting frequency of the predicted or 'quaesitum' character in the reference class or series but for the best or most reliable estimate of that frequency, and he permits us to speak of 'the probability' that some member of the series (some one swan, for example) will have the quaesitum character (white). A reliable estimate is a 'posit' (in Reichenbach's term) which is based on the observation of part of the series, but it is not a blind posit—it is one which conforms to such rules of scientific procedure as that the sample must be large, must be qualitatively homogeneous with the rest of the series, and must remain statistically homogeneous when divided into subsets. These rules or reliability are intuitively plausible and are in fact used by the scientists of our culture circle, but to justify them Lewis presumably must appeal, like Reichenbach, to second-order inductions about inductions.

His vindication of the whole procedure is again that we cannot live without predicting, and we cannot predict unless we can predict in this way; but he goes further in a Kantian direction. He sometimes suggests that the mind can actually in some degree impose order on its objects. More often he assterts the milder doctrine that regularity is the presupposition of all possible experience. A consistent failure of induction or memory, therefore, would mean a disorder tantamount to annihilation of the empirical cosmos.

The theories of Lewis and Reichenbach are landmarks in modern philosophy of knowledge. Yet the judicious reader may doubt if they have so much as shown that induction is the *only* method which could truly predict, and if they have, whether the forlorn hope they offer is an appreciable improvement on sheer fiat and animal faith. Certainly it is incommensurate with both the feeling of assurance and the degree of success with which we make inductions. The Kantianism of Lewis is especially interesting, and especially controversial. If it proved that experience will continue uniform, it must still meet the argument of Charles Peirce, R. M. Eaton, and J. Nicod, that even a uniformity principle much stronger than Kant's can tell me no more than that lightning, for example, is regularly connected with something, and this gives no *logical* support to the conclusion that lightning is regularly connected with the thunder which I have happened to find accompanying it.[3] But Lewis really promises no uniformity at all, but only that there must be uniformity or nothing. A Job's comforter, instead of giving us ground for expecting induction to work, he tells us that if it does not the world will end.

While epistemological pragmatists eke out logical analysis in behalf of induction by appeal to vitality and organization in the conscious *subject* of induction, some kindred but more metaphysical philosophers eke it out by appeal to a vitality or organization in the *object* of induction—in the universe at large. These include metaphysical pragmatists, teaching what Stephen Pepper calls "contextualism," the few Hegelians still extant, and, most explicit, the late Alfred North Whitehead and his philosophy of organism. They all find the root of Hume's puzzle in his atomistic account of the world, and they reply that the relations among things and events are more intimate and active, more vital and organic, than Hume confessed. Briefly to illustrate this philosophy, let us confine ourselves to the several proposals of Whitehead.

The least remarkable of his contributions is the notion of cosmic epochs, which compares the universe to a living body, growing through stages (epochs) with different characteristic patterns of regular habits of action and reaction.[4] So far, he only repeats a mitigated principle of uniformity in cosmogonic dress, which suffers from the two defects, first, that no general principle of uniformity can guarantee the continuation of any particular uniformity which we may be trying to confirm; and second, that the principle of uniformity itself must wait on induction to be confirmed.

Whitehead acknowledges that his cardinal principle must be 'some doctrine of internal relations'[5] to show that events 'intrinsically refer' to one another.[6] Hume and Kant, like most philosophers before and since, erred by taking as primitive the clear and distinct perceptions which occur in the mode of presentational immediacy: 'sense-data such as colors, sounds, tastes, smells, temperature feelings.'[7] 'This special

---

3. *Collected Papers of Charles Sanders Peirce,* edited by Hartshorne and Weiss (Harvard University Press, 1932), Vol. II, pp. 58, 489-90; R. M. Eaton, *General Logic* (New York, Charles Scribner's Sons, 1931), pp. 539-542; J. Nicod, *Le problème logique de l'induction* (Paris, Libraire Félix Alcan, 1923), pp. 26 ff.
4. *Process and Reality,* pp. 53, 148, 310-11, 313; *Adventures of Ideas,* pp. 142-43. (The works of Whitehead here cited are described more fully in the bibliography below.)
5. *Adventures of Ideas,* p.144.
6. *Science and the Modern World,* p. 75.
7. *Process and Reality,* pp. 257 and 263.

mode of functioning essentially exhibits percepts as *here, now, immediate,* and *discrete,'* betraying no internal connections with one another and nothing of their origins.[8] Perception in the mode of causal efficacy, on the other hand, is 'our general sense of existence, as one item among others, in an efficacious actual world.'[9] It is 'the experience dominating the primitive living organisms, which have a sense for the fate from which they have emerged and for the fate toward which they go.'[10] We thus massively feel our present to be the product of the immediate past and the producer of the future.[11] We perceive one event *making* another.[12]

This feeling of causal efficacy is not the mere habit of expectation which Hume describes as the 'natural relation' of causation. It is immediate awareness of a real connection of facts, which Whitehead further explains by his doctrine of prehension, concrescence, and 'objective immortality.' Nothing is self-enclosed, cut off, or isolated; nothing has 'simple location.'[13] 'One actual existent repeats itself in another actual existent';[14] indeed, 'in a sense, everything pervades the whole world', and every actual entity is present in every other.[15] The past and the future are truly immanent in the present.[16]

How literally to take this philosophy of coalesence is a moot question. Perhaps Whitehead is asserting no more than the fluidity, activity, and continuity of nature which have been taught by James and Bergson, by John Dewey, and by the physics of energy fields. If so, I think, with Professor Wesley Robson, that he has not answered Hume. No matter how fluid the world, we can speak about it, or wish to predict it, only as we can somehow identify and distinguish its strands and strains. In a fluid and interfused world, this is more difficult, but their concomitance remains a blank fact, not knowable except by inductive observation of the sort which Hume exposed. On a stronger interpretation of Whitehead, however, he rejects the very principle of identity, that everything is what it is and not another thing. The then and the now, the here and the there, this and that, mingle their being in such mysterious wise that the one can be read off from the other. The operation of the firing mechanism of the gun and the explosion of the charge are not two distinguish-

---

8. *Adventures of Ideas,* pp. 232, 251.
9. *Process and Reality,* p. 271; *Symbolism,* p. 55.
10. *Symbolism,* p. 44.
11. *Adventures of Ideas,* pp. 246-47.
12. *Process and Reality,* p. 266.
13. *Process,* p. 208; *Science,* pp. 72-75, 81; *Symbolism,* p. 38.
14. *Process,* p. 211.
15. *Process,* pp. 42, 53, 79.
16. *Adventures,* pp. 246, 250.

able affairs at all, but are members one of the other, and tomorrow's sunrise is literally present today. This would do the job all right; but with due diffidence, and with all allowance for a grand new categorial system, I cannot convince myself that it is not contradictory both of reason and of experience.

Intermediate between the hopelessly weak and the preposterously strong interpretations of Whitehead's philosophy of organism, there is a more promising version analogous to the idealistic notion of the concrete universal and systematic implication. On this doctrine, the primordial relation which governs all entities is the kind of ultimate fitness or organic harmony by which certain musical chords, for instance, are said to 'call for' certain resolutions. Thus Whitehead uses the word "conformation" to describe the relation of cause and effect,[17] and affirms that in addition to the statistical basis of probability there is basis in a principle of 'intensive relevance' and 'preferential adaptations,' 'an intrinsic suitability of some definite outcome from a presupposed situation.'[18]

That there exists much systematic harmony and conformation is hardly deniable. Very obscure, however, are the questions exactly wherein this harmony consists, how far it extends, and what is the justification of our confidence in it. The idealists tried to prove it *a priori* but succeeded only by confusing the idea of coherence (which is required for the principle of harmony) with the infinitely weaker idea of consistency (which is all that logic will yield). Most plausible is that the incidence of harmony must itself be ascertained by induction. But even though we were sure *a priori* that there is perfect harmony in the world (whatever that may mean), it could not validate many of our causal inferences, because the details of most causal connections are not exposed to us. Nobody directly intuits, for example, the connection between lightning and thunder, which, however perfectly organic it be *in rerum natura,* must accordingly remain *to us* a blank concomitance of experiences.

The fourth, the logical, proposal for closing the inductive gap and salving the ideal of the provident man, enlists no magical *élan* and does not sacrifice his individuality by binding him in the fabric of holism. It can accept Hume's account of the psychological mechanisms by which we in fact proceed from the inductive premise to its conclusion, but it objects that Hume overlooked or fallaciously denied the crucial *logical* connection which underlies and justifies the animal habit, as the principles of arith-

---

17. *Symbolism,* pp. 41, 46; *Process,* p. 364.
18. *Process,* pp. 306, 315.

metic underlie the mathematician's habits. This logical connection is not demonstrative certainty, to be sure, but a *probability* which is analogous to deductive entailment but of less degree.

The most flourishing philosophical science in the United States is mathematical or symbolic logic, not a rival to traditional logic but a consummation of it in a vastly more complete and systematic format. By all parties it is sharply distinguished, as an *a priori* and formal science, from ordinary empirical or inductive studies, being variously called "necessary," "analytic," "tautological," and "syntactical." If "probability" can be defined in the terms of this logic without departing from our best intuitions of the subject, and if a very high degree of such probability can be proved to be conferred on an inductive conclusion by its premises, then induction, and the ideal of the provident man, would be 'rationally justified' in the most exact sense which these words can bear. This is the end which Rudolf Carnap is attempting in a promised two-volume work whose theses have been partially set forth in single essays, and which I have pursued, along a somewhat different line, in *The Ground of Induction*.

Carnap develops his account of probability from the *Spielraum* theory of Wittgenstein and Waismann, which antedates the positivistic stampede to the frequency theory.[19] He takes as fundamental the notion of what, as a semanticist, he calls "state-descriptions" but what a cosmologist would call "possible states of the universe." Probability is defined as a ratio between the numbers of the state-descriptions compatible with a premise and with its conclusion. The concept is awkward, and Carnap's full account is not yet available. Essentially, however, he depends on the counting of alternatives in much the same way as Laplace's classic description of probability, which requires the ratio between the numbers of 'favorable cases' and 'possible cases'; and his results seem virtually to agree with Laplace's calculus. My own precedure is simpler, taking its start from what Charles Peirce called "the statistical syllogism."[20] In relation to the premises, for example, that 50 per cent of American voters in 1948 cast their ballots for Harry Truman, and that Ruth Chapman is an American voter (and given no other relevant information), there is a probability of .50 that Ruth Chapman voted for Truman. Putting *"a"* for any individual and *"M"* and *"P"* for classes,

---

19.   Ludwig Wittgenstein, *Tractatus Logico-Philosophicus* (New York, Harcourt, Brace and Co., 1922), p. 111 (but Wittgenstein denied validity to inductive inference, pp. 109, 181); F. Waismann, "Logische Analyse des Wahrscheinlichkeitsbegriffs," *Erkenntnis*, Vol. I (1930-31), pp. 288-48.
20.   Peirce, *op. cit.,* pp. 433 ff.

and *"m/n"* for a fractional number between 0 and 1, inclusive, we can state the principle generally: Given that m/n of M is P, and that a is M, there is a probability m/n that a is P. This obviously accords with common sense and also with Laplace's principle (relieved of the inscrutable requirement that the 'cases' be equally probable), while the syllogistic form shows how probabilities thus yielded are degrees of logical credibility intermediate between strict entailment and inconsistency. When the fraction m/n is 1, we have the strictly entailed conclusion of the ancient categorical syllogism: If *all* men are mortal and Socrates is a man, then it is certain that Socrates is mortal. When the fraction is 0, we have the opposite extreme of impossibility: If *no* man is perfect, and Stalin is a man, it is altogether precluded that Stalin is perfect. When the fraction is equal to 1/2, the rational credibility of the conclusion is halfway between certainty and impossibility—it is 'an even bet'—and so forth.

It remains to show that the conclusion of an induction has a high degree of this kind of probability. The inductive problem as the logician conceives it is one of *sampling*. When we make an induction, the conclusion which we seek to establish concerns the statistical composition of a population X with respect to a character (or class) Y, where X may be any class whatever, either a series of observations or (more often) a pre-existent aggregate like the apples in a truck-load. Thus we want to know, for example, what is the relative number of wormy apples in a truck-load—whether all of them are wormy, or three-fourths, or one-third, and so on. Our premise must be a statement of the relative number (.3, let us say) of wormy apples in an observed sample, or subclass, of the load, XQ. Animal faith and good sense tell us that very likely the proportion of wormy apples in the whole shipment is approximately the same as in the sample, to wit, .3. Logically, we justify them as follows.

The sample or subclass XQ is one of a vast multitude of subclasses, or possible samples, all of the same size or number as XQ, which are logically included in the whole population X. Some of these subclasses must contain instances of the character Y in the same, or nearly the same, proportion as does the population itself. We know the size of XQ, and if we knew the size and composition of X, we could calculate exactly how many of those 'representative' subclasses there are. Of course, we do not yet know the composition of X; but even so, we know *a priori* that, no matter what the size and composition of X, if XQ is fairly large, the great majority of the subclasses must be representative (within some small margin of approximation). This is a law of arithmetic, deducible from the theory of combinations, which is deducible from the logic of classes. By Bernoulli's theorem and the law of error, furthermore, we can deduce approximately how great a majority of the subclasses of any size, say *s,* must be statistically similar to their population, within any assignable margin of approximation. Specifically, at least 95 out of 100 of them will vary from the true composition of the population by no more than $\frac{1}{\sqrt{s}}$

Suppose, then, that our sample contains 400 apples. Applying the above formula and employing the statistical syllogism, we infer: Since at least .95 of the subclasses of 400 members each which exist in the load of apples do not differ from the population (the whole load), with respect to the proportion of worminess, by more than 5 per cent; and since our sample is a subclass of 400 members, there follows with a probability of at least .95 that it does not differ from the population by more than 5 per cent. Examining the sample, now, and finding, for instance, that 30 per cent of its apples are wormy, we infer by ordinary logic and arithmetic that there is a probability of at least .95 that between 25 and 35 per cent of the total load of apples are wormy. If we want a higher probability or a more exact approximation, we have only to enlarge the sample. Special knowledge about the conditions of this particular sampling may suggest that the indicated probability is too high or too low, but if it does so, it is only by reason of other and previous inductions, about the success of different sorts of sampling, which must be validated by the same logic. On this basis, I think, the whole structure of scientific methodology may be systematized and justified, and the provident man vindicated.

Carnap's theory of probability would yield much the same result, but he prefers a different procedure, nearly the same as the classical method of Bayes, Laplace, Jevons, and Nicod, which treats induction as a problem in inverse probability. That is, he considers the various possible compositions of the population (from .00 to 1.00) as contrary hypotheses to account for the observed composition of the sample. For each such possible population composition there can be calculated the direct probability that it would yield a sample of the observed sort. If, now, we assume that all population compositions are antecedently equally likely, we can calculate, by Bayes's theorem, the 'inverse' probability, given the observed sample, of any one of the hypotheses about the population composition, and especially the probability of the hypothesis that the composition of the population is approximately the same as that we have found in the sample. Unfortunately, however, the assumption of equally probable population compositions seems to be not only without justification but productive of serious paradoxes.

Carnap's scheme can be translated into our terms as follows. He supposes that the population investigated (the load of apples, for example) is one of a great number of populations or loads exemplifying all possible statistical compositions with respect to the investigated property (worminess), each possible composition being exemplified once and only once. We now calculate how many subclasses like our sample (namely, 400 apples of which 120 are wormy) are included in each of these diverse populations, and how many are included in the whole array of populations. The probability that the population with the observed composition (it is .3) is the one from which the sample actually came, is then equal to the ratio between the number of such subclasses which are included in *that* population and the total number of such subclasses in the whole array of populations. This is a satisfactory result—but the fact that it is a satisfactory result is the one reason which Carnap can give for making the remarkable assumption of an array of nicely varied populations on which it is all based, for these, as Peirce said, 'are not and cannot, in the nature of things, be statistical facts.'[21] Whether he can give a better justification may appear in his further publications.

Philosophically, the two theories of the logical probability of induction are very similar. Each is individualistic, finding in the sheer numerical distinctness of particular things the bond by which we infer from one sector of the universe to another. Each justifies induction, and the sane prudence which is based on inductive conclusions, by means of concept of credibility defined in terms of *taking chances*. Each affirms the ultimate rationality, in any situation, of making that decision which has the most chances in its favor, in spite of the fact that not only is there no guarantee that any one such choice will be successful — there is no guarantee that any series of such choices will be generally successful.

The main critical attack on the logical theories is directed to this acceptance of *real risk*. On our logical theory, the proposition that most of the possible samples which are included in a population must be similar to the population is *ipso facto* a good, though not absolutely conclusive, reason for believing that the particular sample I draw is one of those which are similar to it. The critic, however, influenced by the frequency

---

21. *Op. cit.*, p. 498. Peirce believed that the inverse method 'has set back civilization and has corrupted ideals' (p. 58)! My account of induction owes much to Peirce, who seems sometimes to have held the same view, although he generally submits to the frequency theory.

theory of probability, declares that this is irrelevant unless I am *sure* that I shall in the long run actually *select* matching samples in this preponderant proportion. The difference here is fundamental, keyed to the very textures of different minds, and certainly cannot be resolved at once. We can observe, however, that the guarantee which the critic demands concerning a whole future history is in principle impossible, and would lead to grotesque paradox if it occurred; and that the demand itself is an interesting commentary on the decay of enterprise.

The logical theory grounds the principle of calculated risk and leaves the provident man to try his luck within an objective framework which is guaranteed to be predominantly favorable to him. The residual risk, which calls for what we earlier described as the second dimension of enterprise, is the fact that his luck *may* turn out persistently better or worse than the logical probability. The frequency theorist resents and rejects the ideas of risk and enterprise together. He does not require a dead certainty of an advantageous return on every investment, but he does require a dead certainty of a net total advantage from his whole life's program of investments. Otherwise, he declares, he sees no *reason* for believing or acting at all, and if his animal nature would allow, he would quit. His philosophy is the epistemological apotheosis of the insurance policy and the socialistic pool. But it is one socialistic ideal which demonstrably cannot be realized.

SELECTED BIBLIOGRAPHY

ON PURITANISM AND THE PROVIDENT SPIRIT:

Miller, Perry. *The New England Mind*. New York, The Macmillan Co., 1939.

Perry, Ralph Barton. *Puritanism and Democracy*. New York, The Vanguard Press, 1944.

THEORIES OF PROBABILITY AND INDUCTION:

Wright, von G. H. "The Logical Problem of Induction." *Acta Philosophica Fennica,* Fasc. 3, 1941. (Exhaustively reviewed and supplemented by C. D. Broad, *Mind,* Vol. LIII, 1944, pp. 1-24, 97-119, 193-214.)

Nagel, Ernest. *Principles of the Theory of Probability, International Encyclopedia of Unified Science,* Vol. I, No. 6. Chicago, University of Chicago Press, 1939.

Lalande, André. *Les théories de l'induction et de l'expérimentation*. Paris, Boivin et Cie., 1929.

POSITIVISM AND THE FREQUENCY THEORY:

Bridgman, P. W. *The Nature of Physical Theory*. Princeton, Princeton University Press, 1936.

Mises, von R. *Probability, Statistics, and Truth*. New York, The Macmillan Co., 1939.

"A Symposium on Probability," *Philosophy and Phenomenological Research*. Part I, by Donald Williams, Ernest Nagel, Hans Reichenbach, and Rudolf Carnap; Vol. V, 1945, pp. 449-532. Part II, Henry Margenau, *Gustav Bergmann, R. v. Mises, Felix Kaufmann,* Donald Williams; Vol. VI, 1945, pp. 11-86. Part III, Carnap, Kaufmann, v. Mises, Nagel, Williams; Vol. VI, 1946, pp. 590-622 (A general discussion of the frequency theory and positivism, which were vigorously defended by the persons whose names are printed in italics, more moderately by Nagel, Reichenbach, and Margenau. Articles by Carnap marked "*" below are parts of this symposium.)

POSITIVISTIC ANALYSES OF SCIENTIFIC INFERENCE:

Churchman, C. West. *Theory of Experimental Inference*. New York, The Macmillan Co., 1948.

Hempel, Carl G. and Oppenheim, Paul. "Studies in the Logic of Explanation," *Philosophy of Science,* Vol. XV, 1948, pp. 135-75. (This has an extended bibliography of related works by the same and other authors.)

Kaufmann, Felix. *Methodology of the Social Sciences*. London, New York, and Toronto, Oxford University Press, 1944.

Neyman, J. *Lectures and Conferences on Mathematical Statistics*. Washington, Graduate School of the U. S. Department of Agriculture, 1938.

JUSTIFICATIONS OF INDUCTION BY INDUCTION AND BY DEFINITION:

Black, Max. "The Justification of Induction," *Proceedings of the Tenth International Congress of Philosophy*. 1948, pp. 57-59.

Feigl, Herbert. "The Logical Character of the Principle of Induction," *Philosophy of Science,* Vol. I, 1934, pp. 20-29.

Will, Frederick L. "Is There a Problem of Induction?" *Journal of Philosophy*. Vol. XXXIX, 1942, pp. 505-513.

————. "Will the Future Be Like the Past?" *Mind,* Vol. LVI, 1947, pp. 332-347.

CRITICAL NATURALISM AND PRAGMATISM:

Krikorian, Y. H. *Naturalism and the Human Spirit*. New York, Columbia University Press, 1944.

Dewey, John. *Logic, the Theory of Inquiry*. New York, Henry Holt and Co., 1938.

Lewis, Clarence I. *An Analysis of Knowledge and Valuation*. La Salle, Ill., Open Court Publishing Co., 1946. (Especially Chaps. IX-XI.)

Reichenbach, Hans. "Les fondements logiques du calcul des probabilités," *Annales de l'institut H. Poincaré,* tome 7, Paris, 1937, pp. 267-348.

——————. *Experience and Prediction*. Chicago, University of Chicago Press, 1938. (Especially Chap. V.)

——————. "On the Justification of Induction," *Journal of Philosophy,* Vol. XXXVII, 1940, pp. 97-103.

——————. *The Theory of Probability*. Berkeley and Los Angeles, University of California Press, 1949. (A revision and translation of *Wahrscheinlichkeitslehre,* Leiden, A. W. Sijthoff, 1935.)

Nelson, Everett J. "Professor Reichenbach on Induction," *Journal of Philosophy,* Vol. XXXIII, 1936, pp. 577-580.

Creed, Isabel P. "The Justification of the Habit of Induction," *Journal of Philosophy,* Vol. XXXVII, 1940, pp. 85-97.

ORGANICISM:

Pepper, Stephen C. *World Hypotheses*. Berkeley and Los Angeles, University of California Press, 1942.

Blanshard, Brand. *The Nature of Thought*. New York, The Macmillan Co., 1940. (Especially Vol. II, Chaps. XXIII and XXXII.)

Whitehead, A. N. *Science and the Modern World*. New York, The Macmillan Co., 1926.

——————. *Symbolism, Its Meaning and Effect*. New York, The Macmillan Co., 1927.

——————. *Process and Reality*. New York, The Macmillan Co., 1929.

——————. *Adventures in Ideas*. New York, The Macmillan Co., 1933.

Robson, J. Wesley. "Whitehead's Answer to Hume," *Journal of Philosophy,* Vol. XXXVIII, 1941, pp. 85-95.

Gross, Mason W. "Whitehead's Answer to Hume," the same, pp. 95-102.

LOGICAL THEORIES OF INDUCTION:

Kemble, E. C. "The Probability Concept," *Philosophy of Science,* Vol. VIII, 1941, pp. 204-232.

Carnap, Rudolf. *"The Two Concepts of Probability," *Philosophy and Phenomenological Research,* Vol. V, 1945, pp. 513-532.

——————. "On Inductive Logic," *Philosophy of Science,* Vol. XII, 1945, pp. 72-97.

——————. *"Remarks on Induction and Truth," *Philosophy and Phenomenological Research,* Vol. VI, 1946, pp. 590-602.

——————. "On the Application of Inductive Logic," *Philosophy and Phenomenological Research,* Vol. VIII, 1947, pp. 133-47.

——————. "Probability as a Guide in Life," *Journal of Philosophy,* Vol. XLIV, 1947, pp. 141-48.

——————. *Probability and Induction.* (To be published, in two volumes, by the University of Chicago Press.)

Williams, Donald. *The Ground of Induction.* Cambridge, Harvard University Press, 1947.

Nagel, Ernest. (Review of the foregoing), *Journal of Philosophy,* Vol. XLIV, 1947, pp. 685-693.

ATTRIBUTE AND CLASS

Frederic Brenton Fitch[*]

The role played by symbolic logic is coming to be increasingly important in contemporary American philosophy. The effect of this trend will possibly be to give rise to new types of philosophy as radically different from the philosophies of the past one hundred years as symbolic logic itself is different from the narrow and inadequate logic of Aristotle, or from the ambiguous "logic" of such writers as Hegel and Bradley.

Symbolic logic is a relatively new science, having first arisen, in anything like its modern form, in the writings of George Boole around the middle of the nineteenth century. Naturally it meets with strong opposition from those who do not have the technical training to understand it, and from those who feel that, though science has made great advances by use of mathematics, no analogous advance, by similar use of exact methods, is to be expected in philosophy. There is also the mistaken supposition that value concepts (e.g., those of ethics and esthetics) cannot be handled by symbolic logic and that all use of symbolic logic indicates a return to a hopeless materialism and skepticism. Quite the reverse is actually the case. The only way that mankind can develop an ethics and a philosophy commensurate with its achievement in building the atomic bomb is to make full use of symbolic logic in criticizing and correcting the past systems of ethics and philosophy and in constructing new and better ones. To do anything less than this is very much like trying to do research in modern physics while using the old Roman arithmetic that lacked even the number zero. Symbolic logic provides us with as exact a technique for dealing with qualitative and quantitative concepts as modern mathematics provides for dealing only with mathematical concepts.

Very extensive research is now being done in symbolic logic. The present essay is designed to assume little or no familiarity with this field on the part of the reader, but there will be numerous references to

* Born in 1908. Ph.D., Yale University, 1934. Guggenheim Fellow, 1945-46. Member of the faculty of Yale University since 1936. Consulting editor of the *Journal of Symbolic Logic,* and author of numerous articles in that and other journals. Co-author with C. L. Hull, C. I. Hovland, and others, of *Mathematico-Deductive Theory of Rote Learning* (1940).

technical articles, and some familiarity with symbolic logic would no doubt be helpful to the reader. The topics discussed will be some which are of interest to both philosophers and symbolic logicians and which arise in regions of thought where the first important impacts of symbolic logic on philosophy are being felt. More specifically, this essay will be concerned with the nature of attributes and classes. If it is felt that many basic philosophical and logical questions about attributes and classes are not even raised, the answer has to be that space permits a discussion of only a few crucial aspects of the problem. But in any case the relevance of this topic to traditional philosophical controversies about the nature of universals should be apparent.

The views expressed below are very largely my own, but some indication is given of their relationship to views of other American logicians. The first part of the essay introduces the doctrine that classes are attributes of a special sort. The desirability of regarding equivalent classes as identical is then considered at some length, and various relevant logical problems are discussed. The latter part of the essay contains a brief presentation and a suggested revision of C. I. Lewis's theory of meaning.

*   *   *   *

Corresponding to every attribute there is a class. The correspondence is such that, if a class C corresponds to an attribute A, then it is logically necessary that every member of C have the attribute A and that everything having the attribute A be a member of C. One class may correspond to several attributes, but more than one class cannot correspond to an attribute. In fact, if two attributes are logically equivalent in the sense that it is a necessity of logic that they apply to exactly the same things, then only one class corresponds to these two attributes.

Classes themselves may be regarded as being attributes of a special sort. Thus if a class C is treated as being an attribute, to say that x is a member of C is interpreted as meaning that x has the attribute C. Conversely, to say that x is a member of the attribute A may be interpreted as meaning that x has the attribute A, so that the notion of "membership" may be used in connection with all attributes, and not merely in connection with those that are classes. In the following discussions it will be assumed that classes are being treated as attributes in the way just indicated. Classes will sometimes be called "class-attributes."

Now to every attribute there corresponds a unique class-attribute such that it is logically necessary that the attribute and the class-attribute have the same members. Furthermore, if two attributes are logically equivalent (whether or not one or both of them is a class-attribute), the same class-attribute must correspond to them both. This is simply restating the first paragrph in the new terminology.

It will be assumed that no class-attribute corresponds to another class-attribute. Hence the class-attribute corresponding to a given class-attribute C must be C itself.

Suppose that we consider a system of logic that deals with attributes but not with classes, and suppose that this system contains a "well-ordering" postulate or theorem according to which all the entities of the system are arranged into a serial order in such a way that among all the entities having some given attribute there is always one that precedes all the others in the ordering. Such an entity may be said to be the "first" member of the given attribute. Suppose also that logically equivalent attributes always have the same first member. Suppose, finally, that the system of logic is capable of dealing with attributes of attributes, and in particular with the attribute of being logically equivalent to a given attribute A. Then there must be a "first" attribute among all those attributes that have the attribute of being logically equivalent to a given attribute A. Let the "class-attribute corresponding to A" be, by definition, this first attribute. It can be shown that class-attributes, when specified in this way, have all the characteristics that were assigned to them previously. Thus, in a system of logic of the requisite kind, the concept of "class" (or "class-attribute") is definable in terms of well-ordering and of logical equivalence of attributes.

An alternative method for defining classes would be to proceed as before but use "material equivalence of attributes" in place of "logical equivalence of attributes." (Two attributes are materially equivalent if they in fact apply to exactly the same things. They are logically equivalent if it is logically necessary that they apply to the same things.) Classes would then be only materially equivalent to their corresponding attributes, instead of logically equivalent to them in all cases. The notions of "attribute" and "material equivalence of attributes" are handled in most systems of logic with much claim to adequacy, and results due to Gödel[1] indicate that in various standard systems of logic the well-ordering principle can be added without introducing any inconsistency not already present. This alternative method is therefore available in most standard systems of logic. The original method, which is here regarded as preferable to the alternative method, is available in any system which can deal

---

1. K. Gödel [16]. References in square brackets are to the bibliography.

with the notions of "attribute" and "logical equivalence of attributes," provided that the well-ordering principle is present or may be added. Such systems must be able to deal with "logical necessity," at least if "logical equivalence of attributes" is to be definable, and so they must be modal systems.[2]

If classes are defined in terms of logical equivalence rather than material equivalence, then class-attributes that are logically equivalent must be identical with each other, because the same class-attribute must correspond to each of them and hence (since they are themselves class-attributes) be identical with each of them. The principle is thus obtained that classes that are logically equivalent to each other are identical with each other. This might called "the restricted axiom of extensionality for classes," since the unrestricted or usual axiom of extensionality for classes asserts that classes that are materially equivalent to each other are identical with each other. This unrestricted form of the axiom is obtained if classes are defined by use of material equivalence in place of logical equivalence. According to the unrestricted form of the axiom, classes that happen to have the same members are identical. According to the restricted form of the axiom, classes that of logical necessity have the same members are identical.

The unrestricted axiom of extensionality for classes is objectionable in modal logic. This can be seen as follows:[3] Suppose that it is an accidental fact of evolution that just the same entities have the attribute of being men and the attribute of being featherless bipeds. Then, by the unrestricted axiom of extensionality for classes, the class of men is identical with the class of featherless bipeds, because these classes are materially equivalent. Hence whatever is true of the class of featherless bipeds must also be true of the class of men. For example, it is true of the class of featherless bipeds that it is, by logical necessity, identical with the class of featherless bipeds. But if the class of men is by logical necessity identical with the class of featherless bipeds, then surely it cannot be an

2. This method of defining classes could be used, for example, in Ruth Barcan's systems S2² and S4² if a well-ordering principle is added. See footnote 10 below.

3. See the *Journal of Symbolic Logic*, Vol. VIII (1934), pp. 45-47, where Alonzo Church reviews W. V. Quine, "Notes on Existence and Necessity" (*Journal of Philosophy*, Vol. XL [1943], pp. 113-127). Church gives essentially the example given here. Quine raises similiar problems in his article. Problems of this sort go back at least to G. Frege, "Uber Sinn und Bedeutung," *Zeitschrift Phil. u. phil. Krit.*, N. S. Vol. C (1892), pp. 25-50. (An English translation of the latter by Max Black may be found in the *Philosophical Review*, Vol. LVII [1948], pp. 109-230.) See also R. Carnap, *Meaning and Necessity* [9], pp. 133-144.

accidental fact of evolution that the same entities have the attribute of being men and the attribute of being featherless bipeds.

One way to attempt to overcome this difficulty would be by maintaining that the previous sentence involves a *non sequitur*. This position would amount to holding that two classes could, of logical necessity, be identical with each other (and hence not really two), while the attributes to which they correspond are only accidentally equivalent. In fact the alternative method for defining classes leads to just this result. But then there is the further unsatisfactory conclusion that in general a class would be only materially equivalent to the attributes it corresponds to. Thus the class of men would be only materially equivalent to the attribute of being a man, instead of being logically equivalent to it. This seems quite odd.

The most satisfactory way of avoiding these difficulties therefore seems to be to employ the restricted axiom of extensionality for classes and to use the original method for defining classes instead of the alternative method. The class of men and the class of featherless bipeds could then be regarded as distinct from each other, though possessing the same members. The difference between them would not be one of membership, but rather it would be a difference of the same sort as that between two distinct, materially equivalent attributes. More specifically, the class of featherless bipeds would have the attribute of being necessarily identical with the class of featherless bipeds, while the class of men would not have the attribute of being necessarily identical with the class of featherless bipeds.

A still stronger unrestricted axiom of extensionality, and one that wipes out all distinction between classes and attributes, is the unrestricted axiom of extensionality for attributes. This axiom asserts that attributes that are materially equivalent are identical. Quine perhaps holds to the axiom in this form, for example, in his *System of Logistic* [22]. He and Goodman object to "platonism" on the ground that formal expressions are regarded by the "platonist" as classes of their own occurrences, so that those expressions which have never been written (and never will be written) are empty classes and hence identical with each other.[4] The answer to this objection is that the indicated identification does indeed result if the unrestricted axiom of extensionality for attributes is employed; but that if the unrestricted axiom of extensionality for classes is employed instead, then formal expressions can be treated as being attributes of their

---

4. Nelson Goodman and W. V. Quine, "Steps toward a Constructive Nominalism," *Journal of Symbolic Logic,* Vol. XII (1947), pp. 105-122, esp. bot. of p. 121.

occurrences, while if this latter axiom is replaced by the still weaker re-stricted axiom of extensionality for classes, formal expressions can, after all, be treated as classes of their occurrences without identifying all non-occurring expressions with each other.

It is to be noted that use of this weakest extensionality axiom leads to the result that though there may be many empty classes, there is only one null class (necessarily empty class).[5] Mathematics and empirical science may not require any axiom of extensionality at all,[6] but if they do, this weakest one should be sufficient.

The notion of "truth-value" may be regarded as bearing very much the same relation to the notion of "proposition" that "class" bears to "attri-bute."[7] Truth-values will here be treated as being propositions of a special kind. We assume that a truth-value corresponds to every proposition, that if two propositions are logically equivalent, the same truth-value corres-ponds to each of them, that a proposition and its truth-value are logically equivalent, that only one truth-value corresponds to a given proposition, and that no truth-value corresponds to a different truth-value. From these assumptions can be obtained what might be called "the restricted axiom of extensionality for truth-values": Truth-values that are logically equiva-lent are identical.

If, with respect to some fixed well-ordering, the truth-value of a proposition is defined as being the first proposition logically equivalent to the given proposition, then truth-values, as thus defined, are seen to have the properties outlined in the previous paragraph.

The unrestricted axiom of extensionality for truth-values asserts that materially equivalent truth-values are identical. (Two propositions are materially equivalent if they are both true or both false.) An objection can be raised against this axiom similar to that raised against the unre-stricted axiom of extensionality for classes. For example, the two proposi-tions, "Some roses are yellow," and "5=5," have respective truth-values which we will designate by the letters 'X' and 'Y.' Now since the two propositions are both true, their truth values X and Y must also be true, and by the unrestricted axiom of extensionality for truth-values X=Y. Now Y has the attribute of being, by logical necessity, identical with Y; and since X=Y, it is clear that X also has the attribute of being, by logical necessity, identical with Y. Furthermore, just as Y has the attribute of

---

5. For discussion of null and empty classes see A. A. Bennett and C. A. Baylis, *Formal Logic* [2], pp. 102-107.

6. See Carnap, *loc. cit.*, pp. 115-117.

7. See Carnap, *loc. cit.*, pp. 26-27; also Frege, *loc. cit.*, pp. 33-36.

being logically equivalent to Y, so also X must have the attribute of being logically equivalent to Y. If propositions are assumed to be logically equivalent to their truth-values, it then follows that the proposition, "Some roses are yellow," must be logically equivalent to the proposition, "5=5," since the truth-values of these two propositions have been shown to be logically equivalent to each other. But if "Some roses are yellow" is logically equivalent to the logically necessary proposition "5=5," then "Some roses are yellow" must itself be logically necessary. One way of avoiding this conclusion is to refuse to assume that propositions are logically equivalent to their truth-values. But then to be consistent it would be necessary also to refuse to assume that it is logically necessary that those and only those things having some given attribute are members of the class corresponding to that attribute. Thus it would not be assumed that there is any logical necessity that those and only those things that have the attribute of being men also belong to the class of men. A better method for avoiding the difficulty is to use the restricted form of the axiom in place of the unrestricted form. Then there would be no need to assume that X is identical with Y.

Carnap [9] would object to the above argument on the ground that identity in his sense does not guarantee intersubstitutability of the identified entities in all contexts, and that in particular the substitution of X for Y at certain stages of the above argument are not permissible, even granting X=Y. But this objection seems to mean only that Carnap does not employ any genuine identity relation at all. What he treats as "identity" is merely a sort of equivalence that falls short of full identity.

Another objection to the above argument might be that it involves a fallacy because, in a similar way, any true identity could be shown to be a logically necessary identity. But it seems to be a perfectly sound position to hold that every true identity is logically necessary. This is simply the view that an entity is never identical with anything but itself, and that, of logical necessity, it is identical with itself.

For example, consider the often-discussed statement, "Scott is the author of *Waverly*."[8] It might be contended that this is a true statement of identity, though contingently true rather than true by logical necessity. Now there are at least two different ways of analyzing the above statement. (1) The phrase, "the author of *Waverly*," may be regarded as just another name for Scott. In this case the statement could just as well have been expressed as "Scott is Scott," and there is no reason for not

---

8. See B. Russell, "On Denoting," *Mind*, N. S. Vol. XIV (1905), pp. 479-493.

regarding it as a truth of logic. But this is an unsatisfactory interpretation because the statement seems to convey an empirical fact rather than a mere truth of logic. (2) The phrase, "the author of *Waverly*," may be regarded as being a descriptive phrase in the sense of Bertrand Russell's theory of descriptions, which is set forth in elaborate detail in Whitehead and Russell's *Principia Mathematica*. The statement, "Scott is the author of *Waverly*," is then analyzed as meaning that one and only one person wrote *Waverly* and that he is identical with Scott. Thus the statement is not a mere identity from this viewpoint, and so can be true without being true by logical necessity.

Church[9] would contend that still a third alternative is tenable: (3) The phrase, "the author of *Waverly*," is not to be treated as a proper name merely, nor is it to be regarded as a descriptive phrase in Russell's sense; but it is to be thought of as having a "denotation" (namely, the individual who in fact wrote *Waverly*), and as having a "sense" (namely, the meaning of the phrase). On this view, the word "Scott" and the phrase, "the author of *Waverly*," have the same denotation (Scott himself), but differ in sense or meaning. This position of Church is derived from Frege and has important merits, but it seems designed to support the contention that there may be purely contingent identities. The system of modal logic developed by Ruth Barcan[10] suggests that the simplest view is that no identities should be regarded as merely contingent and that identified entities should be everywhere intersubstitutable. (Indeed, no entity is correctly identifiable with any entity but itself, so permission of substitution of this sort is trivial anyway.) Furthermore, if entities X and Y have been identified with each other, it seems reasonable to suppose that the *names* of X and Y should also be everywhere intersubstitutable where they are being used as names. According to Church's view, on the other hand, two names of the same thing might differ in sense and so not be intersubstitutable.

---

9. *Loc. cit.*

10. Ruth Barcan, "The Identity of Individuals in a "Strict Functional Calculus of Order," *Journal of Symbolic Logic,* Vol. XII (1947), pp. 12-15. (See *Errata* in Vol. XIII.) Quine in his review of this paper, *ibid.,* pp. 95-96, emphasizes the fact that Miss Barcan's system S2^2 contains two kinds of identity, a weak identity and a strong identity, such that a general substitutivity theorem can be proved with respect to the strong identity but not with respect to the weak identity. He thinks that this situation supports his view that modal logic must resort to something like Carnap's "individual concepts" ([9], pp. 41, 180 f.); but actually what is indicated is merely a logical inadequacy or incompleteness in S2^2. This inadequacy is not present in Miss Barcan's system S4^2, and there the two kinds of identity are in all respects equivalent. The inadequacy in S2^2 can be overcome by assuming that $\Box$A is an axiom of S2^2 whenever A is, where the square symbol is the modal operation expressing *logical necessity.*

This discussion of identity is well illustrated by the problem about the Morning Star and the Evening Star. Let us grant that the Morning Star is identical with the Evening Star, so that they have all the same attributes.[11] Since the Morning Star is necessarily identical with the Morning Star, it must be the case that the Evening Star also has the attribute of being necessarily identical with the Morning Star. Hence we cannot assume that they merely *happen* to be identical without concluding that they must necessarily be identical, in the sense that their identity is a truth of logic rather than merely of astronomy. Quine regards this problem as indicating that modal logic must be rejected or at least severely restricted. But A. F. Smullyan[12] has shown that there is no real difficulty if the phrase "the Morning Star" and "the Evening Star" are regarded either as proper names or as descriptive phrases in Russell's sense. His argument is essentially the same as that given above in discussing the phrase, "the author of *Waverly*." If one chooses to assume Church's third alternative, then Smullyan's solution does not apply and serious complications have to be faced.

The position of Carnap bears some resemblance to that of Church. Carnap[13] would assume that the phrase, "the Morning Star," has an "individual concept" as its "intension" (like Church's "sense") and has the planet Venus as its "extension" (like Church's "denotation"). Carnap avoids difficulties like that of the Morning Star and Evening Star by omitting any genuine relation of identity from his system, as has already been noted.[14]

Smullyan, incidentally, accepts the unrestricted axiom of extensionality for classes. This gives rise to difficulties along the lines already discussed. Instead of using the restricted form of the axiom to avoid these difficulties, Smullyan assumes, in effect, that classes are only materially equivalent to their corresponding attributes rather than logically equivalent to them.

In dealing with relations a distinction can be made which is analogous to that between class and attribute. We may speak of "extensional" relations as playing the same role with respect to relations in general

11. See Frege, *loc. cit.*, p. 27, and Quine, "The Problem of Interpreting Modal Logic." *Journal of Symbolic Logic*, Vol. XII (1947), pp. 43-48.

12. *Journal of Symbolic Logic*, Vol. XII (1947), pp. 139-141, where Smullyan reviews Quine's paper, "The Problem of Interpreting Modal Logic." See also, by Smullyan, "Modality and Description," *ibid.*, Vol. XIII (1948), pp. 31-37, and the review of the latter by Ruth Barcan, *ibid.*, pp. 149-150.

13. *Loc. cit.*, p. 165.

14. Smullyan, in his review of Quine, calls attention to Carnap's abandonment of identity.

that classes (class-attributes) play with respect to attributes in general. (Classes or class-attributes might have been called "extensional" attributes.) An extensional relation corresponds to each relation in essentially the same way that a class-attribute corresponds to each attribute. In order to avoid the difficulties connected with identity, a restricted axiom of extensionality for extensional relations can be assumed. Whether the relations considered are two-termed or of higher degree, the same technique applies. If relations are treated as being attributes of ordered couples, then extensional relations would be classes of ordered couples.

Quine seems to wish to regard all "non-extensional" aspects of logic (those connected with modality, belief, knowledge, etc.) as being aspects which are to be understood primarily in terms of syntax, that is, nominalistically.[15] He holds that the theory of quantification in modal logic must be subjected to severe limitations, partly because of problems like that of the Morning Star and Evening Star, as already indicated, and partly also because if a syntactical approach to modal logic is employed, as he thinks it should be, then quantification can be explained only in terms of substituting constants for variables. The trouble is, he points out, that there is only a denumerable infinity of such constants, while the variables of quantification are intuitively to be thought of an ranging over a non-denumerable infinity of entities. This is perhaps an objection to be met by modal logicians who accept as valid Cantor's proof of the existence of non-denumerable infinities, but I would hold to a universe that is only denumerably infinite and reject Cantor's argument.[16]

The most ambitious attempt to develop a completely nominalistic account of logic has been made by Goodman and Quine.[17] They reject attributes, classes, relations, and propositions, and assume only individuals. This is an interesting and enterprising program, but the details of their method seem in some ways very artificial. Also there is the difficulty (if it is a difficulty) that no way is provided in their nominalist language for them to state their fundamental position or to say that they do not assume any universals. To make such statements they have to resort to some natural language like English that does seem to deal with universals.

One consideration that caused Goodman and Quine to seek to dis-

---

15. See his *Notes on Existence and Necessity, The Problem of Interpreting Modal Logic*, and (with Goodman) *Steps toward a Constructive Nominalism* (all previously referred to).

16. In my paper, "An Extension of Basic Logic," *Journal of Symbolic Logic*, Vol. XIII (1948), pp. 95-106.

17. *Loc. cit.*

pense with universals altogether is the fact that the theory of classes and attributes tends to give rise to the well-known paradoxes, such as the Russell paradox, the Richard paradox,[18] and many others similar to these. Goodman and Quine felt that the usual methods for avoiding these paradoxes seem so unnatural as to make it preferable not to assume classes and attributes at all.

Among these methods is the use of a "theory of types."[19] Another method is due to Zermelo[20] and has been further developed by von Neumann.[21] Theories of types seem to be open to serious philosophical objections and to be semantically unstatable except by violation of their own principles.[22] Neither the simple theory of types nor the Zermelo method provides, of itself, any guarantee of consistency[23] or protection against the semantical paradoxes, though they both seem to provide protection against the ordinary mathematical paradoxes such as the Russell paradox and the paradox of the greatest cardinal number. Yet these methods are both widely used.[24]

Quine has obtained the main advantage of the simple theory of types by use of a notational technique which he calls "stratification."[25]

---

18. See A. N. Whitehead and B. Russell, *Principia Mathematica*, Vol. I (Cambridge University Press, 1910), esp. chap. ii, sec. viii of the Introduction.

19. For example that of Whitehead and Russell, *loc. cit.* See also Quine [23].

20. E. Zermelo, "Untersuchungen über die Grundlagen der Mengenlehre," *Math. Annalen*, Vol. LXV (1908), pp. 261-281.

21. J. von Neumann, "Eine Axiomatisierung der Mengenlehre," *Jour. r. angew. Math.*, Vol. CLIV (1925), pp. 219-240. A similar method is used by Quine [24] and by Gödel [16].

22. F. B. Fitch, "Self-Reference in Philosophy," *Mind*, n. s. Vol. LV (1946), pp. 64-73. See also, *ibid.*, Vol. LVI (1947), p. 184. A similar point is made by Weiss, *ibid.*, Vol. XXXVII (1928), pp. 338-348, and by Henry Winthrop, "Metalypsis and Paradox in the Concept of Metalanguage," *Philosophical Review*, Vol. LIV. (1945), pp. 607-610.

23. Except that if the axiom of infinity is omitted in dealing with the simple theory of types, then a consistency proof can be given as by G. Gentzen in "Die Widerspruchsfreiheit der Stufenlogik," *Math. Zeitschrift*, Vol. XLI (1936), pp. 357-366.

24. The simple theory of types, for example, is used by K. Gödel in his paper "Über formal unentscheidbare Sätze der Principia Mathematica und verwandter Systeme," *Monatsh. Math. Phys.*, Vol., XXXVIII (1931), pp. 173-198. Gödel here uses an unrestricted axiom of extensionality for classes. He does not distinguish between classes and attributes. This paper contains Gödel's famous theorem on incompleteness and bears a close relationship to A. Tarski, "Der Wahrheitsbegriff in den formalisierten Sprachen," *Studia Philosophica*, Vol. I (1936), pp. 438-460. See also, A. Church, "A Formulation of the Simple Theory of Types." *Journal of Symbolic Logic*, Vol. V (1940), pp. 56-68. Church distinguishes in his system between attributes (propositional functions) and classes. He assumes what amounts to an unrestricted axiom of extensionality for classes but not for attributes. He mentions the possibility of employing an unrestricted axiom of extensionality for propositions. This, he says (p. 61), would make possible the identification of classes with propositional functions. Quine in his *System of Logistic* [22] employs the simple theory of types together with an unrestricted axiom of extensionality for classes and relations. He in effect identifies attributes with classes, but he claims not to identify propositions with truth-values.

25. W. V. Quine, "New Foundations for Mathematical Logic," *American Mathematical Monthly*, Vol. XLIV (1937), pp. 70-80.

This method is much more economical than the simple theory of types, but the question of its consistency is still unanswered.[26]

Another theory of types is the ramified theory of types.[27] It is stronger and more complex than the simple theory of types. It provides protection against all the standard paradoxes, including the semantical paradoxes, and makes possible a proof of consistency even in the presence of the axiom of infinity.[28] This theory of types is so strong, however, as to place unwanted restrictions on some fundamental parts of mathematics.[29] Russell and Whitehead, in the first edition of *Principia Mathematica,* proposed to weaken the effect of these restrictions by the "axiom of reducibility." Although this latter axiom has not been proved to be consistent with the axiom of infinity, still it weakens the restrictions just enough so that classical mathematics can be developed without apparently losing protection against the usual mathematical and semantical paradoxes.[30] The simple theory of types, Quine's method of stratification, and the Zermelo method all are less satisfactory methods since they seem to offer no protection against the semantical paradoxes. The method of the first edition of *Principia Mathematica* offers a maximum protection with a minimum mathematical loss. This method, unfortunately, was nevertheless repudiated in the second edition of *Principia Mathematica* (but, it is said, without Whitehead's actual consent), and the simple

---

26. See J. B. Rosser, "On the Consistency of Quine's New Foundations for Mathematical Logic," *Journal of Symbolic Logic,* Vol. IV (1939), pp. 15-24.

27. This is the theory of types employed in the first edition of Whitehead and Russell's *Principia Mathematica.*

28. F. B. Fitch, "The Consistency of the Ramified Principia." *Journal of Symbolic Logic,* Vol. III, (1938), pp. 140-149. The system proved consistent is essentially that of the first edition of Whitehead and Russell's *Principle Mathematica,* but without the axiom of reducibility and with the addition of axioms of infinity and choice and an unrestricted axiom of extensionality for classes and relations. Attributes are not distinguished from classes.

29. See F. P. Ramsey, *The Foundations of Mathematics* [26], pp. 29 and 63-64. (In line 13, p. 64, by "sum" is meant "logical sum.") See also H. Weyl, "Uber die neue Grundlagenkrise in der Mathematik," Math. Zietschrift, Vol. X (1921), pp. 39-79. The consistent system of logic of my paper, "An Extension of Basic Logic," *loc. cit.,* is capable of handling in a fairly general way the mathematical method of "Dedekindian section." (See bottom of p. 105 and top of p. 106 of the paper.) It is just this method of Dedekindian section which cannot be validated in the ramified theory of types unless the axiom of reducibility is used, as Ramsey points out.

30. See Ramsey, *loc. cit.,* pp. 28-29. His argument for rejecting the axiom of reducibility (p. 57) seems to me far from convincing. (I would reject the whole theory of types, but for other reasons.) Also unconvincing to me is his view (p. 77) that the semantical paradoxes can be attributed to psychological and epistemological ambiguities of more or less the usual sort, so that no drastic logical device, such as the ramified theory of types or a reformulation of basic logical principles, is required for avoiding them.

theory of types was in effect introduced, together with an unrestricted axiom of extensionality for classes.

In a recent paper I have proposed a method for avoiding all the paradoxes without sacrificing as much of mathematics as is done if the ramified theory of types is used without the axiom of reducibility.[31] No theory of types is involved. The essential technique could be described by saying that the system is so constructed that the principle of excluded middle is not satisfied by every entity with which the system is concerned. Propositions may then be regarded, by definition, as being those entities that do satisfy the principle of excluded middle. Hence it may still be said that all propositions satisfy the principle of excluded middle. Expressions which have the form of seeming to express propositions that lead to paradoxes usually do not in this system express propositions at all, but rather refer to entities that cannot be shown to satisfy the principle of excluded middle, or if they do express propositions, the propositions do not lead to paradoxes after all. The system indeed is demonstrably consistent. It deals with attributes and relations and can apparently without loss of consistency be extended to handle classes and extensional relations, and to include a restricted axiom of extensionality for classes and relations. The modal concepts of logical necessity and logical possibility can also be incorporated into it. It seems to be adequate for the more fundamental parts of mathematical analysis, though Cantor's proof of non-denumerability fails to hold. In fact an axiom to the effect that all classes are denumerable can be added without destroying the validity of the consistency proof.

In connection with any discussion of class and attribute, mention should be made of the views of C. I. Lewis, who is well known as a philosopher and as a modal logician[32]. In his recent book, *An Analysis of Knowledge and Valuation* [19], he presents a general account of the meanings of "terms." (The word "red," for example, is a term.) He distinguishes (p. 39) between (1) the *denotation* of a term, (2) the *comprehension* of a term, (3) the *signification* of a term, and (4) the *intension* (or *connotation*) of a term. The third of these, the signification, seems especially important, since the other three can apparently be defined in terms of it fairly directly. The signification of a term is an attribute, such that the term correctly applies to those and only those things having the attribute. Lewis makes a distinction between "actual" things and

---

31. "An Extension of Basic Logic," *loc. cit.*
32. *Symbolic Logic* [20]. See also the doctoral dissertation of Miss Ruth Barcan, Yale University, 1946.

"possible" things. (Presumably every actual thing is possible, but not *vice versa*.) His four "modes of meaning" can be described as follows, letting an attribute S be the signification of a term T:

(1) The denotation of T is the class of actual things having the attribute S.

(2) The comprehension of T is the class (or, in his words, "classification") of all possible things that have (or would have) the attribute S.

(3) The signification of T is S itself, that is, the attribute that those and only those things have to which T may be correctly applied.

(4) The intension (or connotation) of T is the class (or, in Lewis's words, "conjunction") of terms each of which can be correctly applied to anything to which T can be correctly applied. (Lewis feels that if the intension were called a "class" of terms instead of a "conjunction" of terms, then it would be wrongly suggested that a term haveing zero connotation has the empty class of terms as its connotation (p. 45). But connotation has to be defined in such a way that terms of zero connotation connote no terms at all or else in such a way that they connote only tautologous terms, since they are themselves tautologous terms.)

Lewis is not altogether consistent in his discussion of signification, for (on p. 43) he says that the term "man" signifies animality and that animality is included in the signification of the term "man". This is not consistent with the statement he makes on p. 39 that the signification of a term is a property whose presence indicates that the term applies and whose absence indicates that the term does not apply. The property animality does not indicate that the term "man" applies. Hence Lewis is wrong in saying that the term "man" signifies animality. To avoid this confusion, we can distinguish between "intension" and "connotation" in such a way that "connotation" is still allowed to mean the same thing that "intension" and "connotation" both mean for Lewis, while "intension" is so defined that the intension of a term T is said to be the class of all attributes signified by terms connoted by T. Thus intension would refer to attributes, while connotation would refer to the terms signifying those attributes. It would then be correct to say that the term "man" connotes the term "animality," and that the attribute animality belongs to the intension of the term "man." The intension of the term "man" would consist of all the attributes that an entity must have if it has the attribute of being a man.

It is possible and probably desirable to reject Lewis's distinction between "actual" and "possible" entities, while still retaining a distinction between propositions that are true ("actually true") and those that are "possible" ("self-consistent") whether or not they are true.[33] Furthermore this would still allow us to keep various modal distinctions between attributes. Thus the attribute of being "possibly red" is the attribute that an entity A has if and only if the proposition, "A is red," is possibly true. From this standpoint it is possible to rewrite Lewis's four modes of meaning as the following five modes of meaning, distinguishing between intension and connotation. We let S be the attribute which is the signification of a term T.

(1)   The denotation of T is the class of entities that have the attribute S (or have had or will have the attribute S).

(2)   The comprehension of T is the class of all attributes which entities can have only if they have the attribute S. Thus an attribute belongs to the comprehension of T if and only if the having of that attribute logically necessitates the having of the attribute S. (We can define what might be called the "proper comprehension" of T as being the comprehension of T without all self-inconsistent attributes.)

(3)   The signification of T is S (that is, the attribute whose presence is the necessary and sufficient condition for T to be correctly applicable.)

(4)   The intension of T is the class of attributes that entities must have that have the attribute S. (We can define what might be called the "proper intension" of T as being the intension of T without tautologous attributes.)

(5)   The connotation of T is the class of terms whose significations belong to the intension of T, in other words, the class of terms that must be applicable to anything to which T is applicable. (We can define what might be called the "proper connotation" of T as being the connotation of T without tautologous terms.)

For example, let T be the term "typewriter." Then the denotation of T is the class of all (past, present, and future) typewriters. The comprehension of T is the class of all attributes that entities cannot have without being typewriters. Thus the attribute of being a thousand-keyed typewriter is an attribute belonging to the comprehension of T, regardless of whether or not anything ever has this attribute. (If we follow Lewis's own procedure we would say instead that every "possible" thousand-keyed typewriter belongs to the comprehension of T, regardless of whether or not such typewriters are "actual" as well as merely "possible." This way

33. See W. V. Quine, "On What There Is," *Review of Metaphysics*, Vol. II (1948), pp. 21-38.

of speaking, and the theory of "possibles" that it suggests, is here rejected.) The signification of T is the attribute of being a typewriter. The intension of T is the class of attributes which entities must have if they are typewriters. Thus the attribute of being either a typewriter or a printing press is an attribute that belongs to the intension of T. Finally, an example of a term belonging to the connotation of T is the term "type-using."

It can be seen that the comprehension and intension are inverses of each other in the following respect: The intension of a term consists of logically necessary ("tautologous") attributes (and the signification itself is tautologous) if and only if the comprehension consists of all attributes; while the comprehension consists of logically impossible (self-inconsistent) attributes (and the signification itself is self-inconsistent) if and only if the intension consists of all attributes.

In the case of adjectival terms, it seems adequate to regard *the* meaning of the term as being the attribute which Lewis calls the "signification," since the other modes of meaning are definable in terms of signification. It can be assumed that different adjectival terms always have different significations. If two different adjectival terms are synonymous, then their respective significations are logically equivalent attributes, but not exactly the same attribute. Thus two tautologous adjectival terms need not be said to have exactly the same signification, though the signification of each is a tautologous attribute and though these two tautologous attributes are, as they must be, logically equivalent to each other.

Lewis's own theory of synonymity is very complex. Part of his difficulty seems to arise from supposing that in some way two synonymous terms must have the *same* meaning as each other, while all that is really required is that they have logically equivalent meanings. To identify such logically equivalent meanings with each other is to employ, without clear need or justification, some sort of axiom of extensionality.

The simpler view suggested above (according to which the meaning of an adjectival term is its signification in Lewis's sense) can be extended by analogy to other sorts of terms and expressions. The meaning of a relational term may be taken to be a relation, the meaning of a class term to be a class, the meaning of a sentence to be a proposition, and, in general, the meaning of the name of an entity to be that entity. Descriptive phrases (like the phrase, "the author of *Waverly*") are meaningful in the sense that they involve terms that have meanings and in the sense that they are parts of sentences that have meanings. But I am inclined to follow Russell in his analysis of the use of these phrases and in his supposition that as isolated phrases they have no meaning of the sort we have been discussing. The reason for this was explained earlier in the discussion of the problem of the Morning Star and the Evening Star and similar problems.

In the case of relational terms, class terms, and sentences, it is possible to define denotation, comprehension, intension, and connotation, in terms of meaning (signification) by proceeding analogously to the case for adjectival terms. Thus the denotation of a sentence would be its truth-value, the comprehension of a sentence would be the class of propositions that logically imply the proposition expressed by the sentence, and the intension of a sentence would be the class of propositions logically implied by the proposition expressed by the sentence. In the case of a class term, the meaning (signification) would be the class itself (recalling that classes are here regarded as attributes of a special kind), and so would the denotation. In the case of the name of an individual, however, it seems unwarranted to speak of comprehension, intension, and connotation, unless we are referring to the name of the unit class having that individual as its only member. We may regard both the denotation and the meaning (signification) of the name of an individual as being that individual itself.

SELECTED BIBLIOGRAPHY

Ambrose, A., and Lazerowitz, M. *Fundamentals of Symbolic Logic.* New York, Rinehart and Co., 1948. [1]

Bennett, A. A., and Baylis, C. A. *Formal Logic.* New York, Prentice-Hall, Inc., 1939. [2]

Black, M. *The Nature of Mathematics.* New York, Harcourt, Brace and Co., 1933. (London, Kegan Paul, Trench, Trubner and Co., 1933). [3]

—————. *Critical Thinking.* New York, Prentice-Hall, Inc., 1946. [4]

Carnap, R. *The Logical Syntax of Language.* New York, Harcourt, Brace and Co., 1937. [5]

—————. *Foundations of Logic and Mathematics.* (Vol. I, No. 3 of *The International Encyclopedia of Unified Science*). Chicago, University of Chicago Press, 1939. [6]

—————. *Introduction to Semantics.* Cambridge, Harvard University Press, 1942. [7]

—————. *Formalization of Logic.* Cambridge, Harvard University Press, 1942. [8]

————. *Meaning and Necessity.* Chicago, University of Chicago
    Press, 1947. [9]

Church, A. *Elementary Topics in Mathematical Logic.* Brooklyn, Galois
    Institute of Mathematics, Long Island University, 1940-41.
    Mimeographed. [10]

————. *The Calculi of Lambda-Conversion.* Princeton, Princeton
    University Press, 1942. [11]

————. *Introduction to Mathematical Logic,* Part I. Princeton,
    Princeton University Press, 1944. [12]

Cohen, M. R., and Nagel, E. *An Introduction to Logic and Scientific
    Method.* New York, Harcourt, Brace and Co., 1934. [13]

Cooley, J. C. *A Primer of Formal Logic.* New York, The Macmillan Co.,
    1942. [14]

Eaton, R. M. *General Logic.* New York, Charles Scribner's Son, 1931. [15]

Gödel, K. *The Consistency of the Axiom of Choice and of the Generalized
    Continuum-Hypothesis with the Axioms of Set Theory.*
    Princeton, Princeton University Press, 1940. [16]

Kattsoff, L. O. *A Philosophy of Mathematics.* Ames, Iowa, Iowa State
    College Press, 1948. [17]

Langer, S. K. *An Introduction to Symbolic Logic.* Boston, Houghton
    Mifflin Co., 1937. [18]

Lewis, C. I. *An Analysis of Knowledge and Valuation.* La Salle, Ill.,
    Open Court Publishing Co., 1946. [19]

Lewis, C. I., and Langford, C. H. *Symbolic Logic.* New York, Century
    Co., 1932. [20]

Post, E. L. *The Two-Valued Iterative Systems of Mathematical Logic.*
    Princeton, Princeton University Press, 1941. [21]

Quine, W. V. *A System of Logistic.* Cambridge, Harvard University Press,
    1934. [22]

————. *Mathematical Logic.* Cambridge, Harvard University Press,
    1940. (Second printing, 1947.) [23]

————. *Elementary Logic.* Boston, Ginn and Co., 1941. [24]

————. *O sentido da nova logica.* Sao Paulo, Brazil, Biblioteca de
    Ciencias Sociais, Livraria Martins Editora, 1944. [25]

Ramsey, F. P. *The Foundations of Mathematics.* New York, Harcourt,
    Brace and Co., 1931. (London, Kegan Paul, Trench, Trub-
    ner and Co., 1931.) [26]

Reichenbach, H. *Elements of Symbolic Logic.* New York, The Macmillan
    Co., 1940. (London, Allen and Unwin, 1940.) [27]

Tarski, A. *Introduction to Logic*. New York, Oxford University Press, 1941. [28]

Ushenko, A. *The Problems of Logic*. Princeton, Princeton University Press, 1941. (London, Allen and Unwin, 1941.) [29]

Woodger, J. H. *The Technique of Theory Construction* (Vol. II, No. 5 of *The International Encyclopedia of Unified Science*). Chicago, University of Chicago Press, 1939. [30]

BASIC ISSUES IN LOGICAL POSITIVISM

*Felix Kaufmann**

I

In one of Rudolf Carnap's early writings [1] the issue between realists and idealists concerning the reality of the physical world is discussed with the end-in-view of showing the spuriousness of metaphysical problems. Carnap introduces two geographers—one a realist, the other an idealist—who embark upon a joint expedition to Africa, in order to find out whether a mountain, purported to be located in a certain region of this continent, is only legendary, or actually exists. Regardless of their conflicting philosophical views, the two geographers are supposed to arrive at the same answer to this question, and if they affirm the existence of the mountain, to agree also on its shape, height, and other features. Consensus ends, however, when it comes to the metaphysical interpretation of the results obtained. Then the realist will insist on the existence of the mountain independent of any perceiving mind, whereas the idealist will take the opposite stand. But neither of the two explorers will be able to indicate any experience by which the correctness of his own interpretation could be established. Hence, Carnap concludes, the sentences expressing the two (apparently) conflicting metaphysical doctrines are pseudo-sentences, and the issue dividing the two geographers is a pseudo-issue. This argument applies to metaphysical sentences in general. They are meaningless, because they are not susceptible of verification.

Ludwig Wittgenstein had a few years earlier succinctly formulated this view in his *Tractatus Logico-Philosophicus*.[2] The meaning of a

* Born in 1895. LL.D. and Ph.D., University of Vienna. Formerly teacher of philosophy of law at University of Vienna. Was a permanent member of the Vienna Circle (1924-1936), though he did not subscribe to the tenets of logical positivism. His philosophical development has been strongly influenced by Edmund Husserl's phenomenology. Professor of philosophy in the Graduate Faculty of the New School for Social Research, until his death December 23, 1949. Author of *Methodology of the Social Sciences* (1944).
1. *Scheinprobleme in der Philosophie. Das Fremdpsychische und der Realismusstreit* (Berlin, 1928).
2. London, 1922.

sentence, he pointed out, is determined by its truth-conditions. "To understand a proposition means to know what is the case, if it is true" (*Tract.* 4.024). Accordingly, we can dispose of metaphysics by laying bare the pitfalls of language which are responsible for the illusion that metaphysics makes sense. "Most propositions and questions, that have been written about philosophical matters are not false, but senseless. We cannot, therefore, answer questions of this kind at all, but only state their senselessness. Most questions and propositions of the philosophers result from the fact that we do not understand the logic of our language.

"(They are of the same kind as the question whether the Good is more or less identical than the Beautiful).

"And so it is not to be wondered at that the deepest problems of philosophy are really *no* problems" (*Tract.* 4.003).

"All philosophy is 'Critique of language' (but not at all in Mauthner's sense). Russell's merit is to have shown that the apparent logical form of the proposition need not be its real form" (*Tract.* 4.0031).

Virtually all members of the Vienna Circle—the birthplace of the logical positivist doctrine—agreed in maintaining that the sentences quoted above contain, in a nutshell, a sound program for philosophical analysis; but opinion was divided as to whether Wittgenstein's approach toward an execution of this program was adequate.

Moritz Schlick and Friedrich Waismann endorsed Wittgenstein's approach almost without reservation, whereas Rudolf Carnap, Hans Hahn, Otto Neurath, and other members of the group raised serious objections. In retrospect, it has become more and more clear to me that a good many time-honored philosophical issues, which had been dismissed by the members of the Vienna Circle as pseudo-problems, were implicit in these discussions. That this could happen was due to the fact that the positivists' criticism had disposed only of some objectionable *formulations* of these problems, but had failed to penetrate to their cores.

The point may be briefly illustrated by reference to the above-mentioned issue between realists and idealists. This issue seems to be a pseudo-problem when presented in the usual formulation. Carnap is right in declaring that the two sentences, "The physical world is real" and "The physical world is not real," do not assert facts. This implies that we cannot ask which one of the two (alleged) assertions ought to be accepted. But this "critique of language" does not settle the crucial issue; it merely suggests a reformulation. The underlying genuine problem is that of clarifying the meaning of "physical reality." This term, it is agreed, should be defined in conformity with its use, which seems to imply that the definition ought to be congruous with the procedures by which we confirm assertions of the existence of a physical object, or the occurence of a physical event, of a certain kind. This consideration leads to the idealist thesis that "physical reality" is to be defined in terms of "experience" or "knowledge."

But realists will contest the adequacy of any definition of this kind. They may advance the argument that "physical experience" implies "physical existence," because experience is experience of existence. Or they may make the point that the conceptions of physical inquiry as a collective enterprise and of intersubjective physical knowledge imply the idea of an identical physical object, capable of being experienced by different people and at different times. They may also submit that *actual* experiences can be had only by *existing* psycho-physical beings, so that "existence" is essentially prior to "experience." Such arguments and counter-arguments cannot be dismissed as "meaningless."

It is thus seen that the problem of clarifying the relation between "experience" and "reality" is not disposed of by discarding inadequate formulations of this problem as pseudo-sentences. The kindred problem of the relation between "knowledge" and "truth" was indeed to become one of the major issues in logical positivism. This issue, in turn, was complicated by interpretation of "logical truth" in terms of "language." This interpretation leads to the questions: Are the standards of criticism of a given language extra-linguistic, and hence extra-logical, and, if this is the case, how are these standards established? Different answers to these questions indicate conflicting epistemological views, which are, in most cases, easily identifiable with traditional doctrinal positions.

The preceding remarks will aid us in appraising the strictures raised in the Vienna Circle against some of Wittgenstein's basic points, and also in understanding later trends in logical positivism. These trends, of which Carnap's works during the past fifteen years are representative, were indeed largely anticipated by the arguments advanced within that group in its discussion of the *Tractatus*.

Wittgenstein sets out to determine the criteria of a logically adequate language. To be logically adequate, he declares, a language has to be isomorphous (structurally identical) with reality. The fulfillment, or nonfulfillment, of this condition can be *shown*, but it cannot be stated in language. Wittgenstein proclaims the general principle: "What *can* be shown *cannot* be said" (*Tract.* 4.1212).

This basic tenet of his doctrine was attacked on the ground that we cannot compare propositions with reality, but only with other propositions. This amounts to the rejection of correspondence theories of truth, as proposed by realists. But it is worth mentioning that even Bertrand Russell, who advocates a correspondence theory of truth, was reluctant to endorse the principle laid down by Wittgenstein. He comments on this point in his Introduction to the *Tractatus*:

"What causes hesitation is the fact that, after all, Mr. Wittgenstein manages to say a good deal about what cannot be said, thus suggesting to the sceptical reader that possibly there may be some loophole through a hierarchy of languages, or by some other exit." [3] Russell suggests "that every language has, as Mr. Wittgenstein says, a structure concerning which, *in the language* nothing can be said, but that there may be another language dealing with the structure of the first language, and having itself a new structure, and that to this hierarchy of languages there may be no limit." [4]

This suggestion, which was in tune not only with Russell's theory of types, but also with Hilbert's distinction between mathematics and meta-mathematics, fell on fertile ground. It may well be regarded as an anticipation of Tarski's *semantical theory of truth*.

Another basic tenet of Wittgenstein's doctrine that was thoroughly discussed in the Vienna Circle, is his theory of *atomic* and *molecular* propositions, which interprets all propositions as *truth-functions* of atomic (elementary) propositions.

The chief objections raised against this theory were (a) that one cannot establish the truth of any atomic proposition, and (b) that Wittgenstein's view does not properly account for the meaning of *general* propositions, such as physical laws.

It was the sensationalist position, which is basic for Wittgenstein's theory, that became the main target of criticism. This position is in line with David Hume's doctrine, as elaborated by British empiricists like Bertrand Russell, and by continental empiricists like Ernst Mach. "Immediately given" sense data are taken to be the building blocks of knowledge, and a logically adequate language is supposed to reveal the structure of the process which leads from the initial data to the mental constructs of scientific objects.

This "atomistic" view had been attacked not only by neo-Kantian

3. *Loc. cit.*, p. 22.
4. *Loc. cit.*, p. 23.

and neo-Hegelian philosophers, but also by behaviorists and pragmatists. Under the influence of behaviorist doctrines, the reaction against Wittgenstein's atomism took the form of strictures against the psychological basis of his doctrine. The point was made that psychological terms should be reduced to biological and, ultimately, to physical terms. This "physicalist" trend in logical positivism was chiefly advocated by Otto Neurath and, in the early thirties, strongly endorsed by Carnap and C. G. Hempel. Physicalism in its most radical form maintains that all scientific concepts are reducible to physical concepts, and that all scientific laws—biological, psychological, sociological laws—are derivable from physical laws. The Unity of Science Movement, started by Neurath, aimed at establishing a unification of the sciences *under the hegemony of physics*.

But Neurath's physicalism was modified by its combination with a *conventionalist* view, which bears some resemblance to William James's *pluralism*. According to this position, which had been developed by Carnap even in his first major work,[5] we must not regard either the psychological or the physical language as fundamental in an *absolute* sense. In selecting one of these languages as the language of science, we are guided by considerations of convenience rather than by *a priori* principles.

This conventionalist approach had a strong bearing on Carnap's criticism of Wittgenstein's view that all propositions in a logically perfect language are either atomic propositions or molecular propositions— in other words, that all propositions are truth-functions of atomic propositions, where "truth-function" is understood in the strict sense, which excludes the use of *general operators*. According to this position, which is akin to J. S. Mill's view, that all inference is from particulars to particulars, we must conceive of scientific laws not as propositions. but rather as rules for the formation of propositions. The fact that this tenet of Wittgenstein's doctrine is inconsonant with the established use of the word "proposition," which does include laws, made many members of the Vienna Circle reluctant to accept Wittgenstein's molecular language, and the implied identification of "meaning" and "truth-conditions." In their attempts toward amending Wittgenstein's criterion of meaningfulness, they reflected upon the requirements that such a criterion should fulfill, and these reflections were apt to strengthen the conventionalist trend in logical positivism.

Karl Popper in his *Logik der Forschung*[6] insists that the criterion of meaningfulness *(Abgrenzungskriterium)* is introduced by a methodo-

---

5. *Der logische Aufbau der Welt* (Berlin, Schlachtensee, 1928).
6. Vienna, 1934.

logical resolution, based upon considerations of convenience. He proposes to make *falsifiability* rather than verifiability the criterion of meaningfulness, and to establish singular existential sentences, describing inter-
subjectively observable events, as basic sentences. Thereby general sentences become meaningful, because they can be falsified by demonstrating
their incompatibility with basic sentences. The decisive objection raised
against this criterion was that it allows for genuine sentences (namely,
general sentences) the negation of which would have to be regarded as
devoid of meaning.

Problems of the theory of probability were brought into focus by
considering the falsifiability (uncertainty) of every statement of fact.
Hans Reichenbach, who was the leader of a philosophical discussion
group in Berlin, which kept in close contact with the Vienna Circle, came
to the conclusion that the logic of science should be based upon the
statistical concept of probability. The traditional two-valued logic was
to be replaced by an infinite-valued probability logic, with all real numbers between 0 and 1 as possible values. He develops this idea in his
Wahrscheinlichkeitslehre.[7] Reichenbach holds that *all* differences in degrees of certainty (credibility, confirmation) can be interpreted in numerical terms, and he contrasts, accordingly, his own view as the *"Identity*
conception" of probability with the *"diversity* conceptions" held by most
other workers in this field, among whom J. M. Keynes[8] occupies a prominent place.

Keynes defends the view that the word "probable" stands for an intensive magnitude, and that we cannot, in all instances, establish a statistical interpretation of its meaning by assigning a numerical value to the
probability relation between the proposition to be appraised and the propositions which represent the evidence available for it. This applies likewise to propositions stating the probability of a fact, such as "It is probable
on the evidence that Caesar visited Britain" and to propositions stating
the probability of a theory, such as "On the evidence available to Clerk
Maxwell, the wave theory of light is more probable than the corpuscular
theory of light."

The question whether Reichenbach's theory of probability, or rather
an interpretation of probability resembling that of Keynes, should be
accepted has been thoroughly discussed by logical positivists for many
years. Most of them, including Carnap, reject Reichenbach's identity
conception of probability. But Reichenbach's attempt to make the notion

---

7. Leiden, 1935; cf. also *Experience and Prediction*, (Chicago, 1938).
8. *Treatise on Probability*, (London, 1921).

of probability the cornerstone of the logic of science, had a strong impact on Carnap's later writings. This idea has indeed dominated his interpretations of scientific procedure, since he delivered his Harvard lectures on "Testability and Meaning" [9] in 1935.

We shall deal with these remarkable lectures in some detail, for they contain a methodological program which was promoted by Carnap himself and a number of his disciples in subsequent publications. The lectures represent a concise account of his philosophical position at the time he left Europe for the United States.

II

In "Testability and Meaning" Carnap tries to weave into a coherent pattern the different strains of thought to which we referred, by proposing the "most liberal form of language," that is, the broadest possible criteria of meaningfulness. He admits, in contrast to Wittgenstein, generalized sentences of any degree of complexity. A sentence of this language may contain any number of universal operators (all) and existential operators (some). In other words, the formal characteristics of this language are those of an extended functional calculus. The criterion of meaningfulness (for synthetic propositions) in this language is not *complete* confirmability, but rather confirmability *to a certain degree*. We cannot, strictly speaking, verify a law, "but we can test it by testing its single instances, that is, the particular sentences which we derive from the law and from other sentences established previously. If in the continued series of such testing experiments no negative instance is found but the number of positive instances increases then our confidence in the law will grow step by step. Thus, instead of verification, we may speak here of gradually increasing *confirmation* of the law.[10]

Accordingly, the "Principle of Empiricism," introduced by Carnap, reads: "Every synthetic proposition must be confirmable." [11] This principle is offered as a proposal rather than as an assertion.

We cannot properly appraise the significance of "Testability and Meaning," unless we bear constantly in mind that Carnap attempts in these lectures to pave the way for a synthesis of the different empiricist

---

9. *Philosophy of Science*, Vol. III, No. 4 (Oct. 1936), pp. 420-471; Vol. IV, No. 1 (Jan., 1937), pp. 1-40.
10. *Loc. cit.*, p. 425. Carnap distinguishes between the requirement of confirmability and the stricter requirement of testability. "We shall call a sentence *testable*, if we know a method of testing for it; and we call it *confirmable* if we know under what conditions the sentence would be confirmed." (*Loc. cit.*, p. 420).
11. *Loc. cit.*, p. 34.

doctrines. The belief in the possibility of such a synthesis was shared by most members of the Vienna Circle and by many empiricists all over the world. We have already mentioned the Unity of Science Movement that was to bring about cooperation among all philosophical groups that espoused a "scientific world view." The underlying idea was that there could not be irreconcilable differences among philosophers who reject the conception of philosophy as a body of eternal truths beyond the scope of scientific inquiry, and who are united in regarding the clarification of scientific method as their chief objective. The logical positivists take it for granted that there is, on the whole, agreement among scientists on the principles of scientific method, despite some indications to the contrary offered by spirited methodological controversies. Hence, it was argued, competent interpretations of scientific method must be consonant in essentials. Apparent incongruities of interpretations are frequently due to the use of different "languages" and can be eliminated by a unified symbolism. With this end in view, Carnap constructs a system of symbols, which, he thinks, could be accepted by all empiricists.

Two essential features of this language have already been noted, namely (a) that it admits the extended functional calculus, and (b) that *confirmability to a certain degree* (rather than verifiability) is made the standard of meaningfulness. Another important property of this language is that new terms may be introduced into it in two different ways, namely, by *definition* or by *reduction*.

The idea underlying Carnap's *theory of reduction* is readily understood. The meanings of sentences and the words of which they consist are determined by the pertinent rules of confirmation and disconfirmation. "We know the meaning (*designatum*) of a term if we know under what conditions we are permitted to apply it in a concrete case and under what conditions not." [12] But these conditions may be altered as science proceeds, and each change would involve a redefinition of terms, which is inconvenient. To overcome this predicament Carnap introduces terms by a merely partial determination of their meaning, that is, by stipulating *some* conditions under which the terms may be applied, and *some* conditions under which they cannot be applied. This is done by incorporating into his language sets of pairs of universal sentences which he calls "reduction pairs." One of the two sentences of a reduction pair establishes a case of applicability, the other one, a case of nonapplicability of the

---

12. "Logical Foundations of the Unity of Science," *International Encyclopedia of Unified Science*, Vol. I, No. 1 (Chicago, 1936), p. 49. This paper contains another account of the theory of reduction.

term. When new connotations accrue to a term in the course of scientific inquiry, new reduction pairs can be added, and thus a more precise determination of its meaning attained. In considering whether a term should be introduced by definition or by reduction, the logician of science will have to assess the actual state of inquiry.

"If the situation is such that we wish to fix . . . the new term once for all, then a definition is the appropriate form. On the other hand, if we wish to determine the meaning of the term at the present time for some cases only, leaving its future determination for other cases to decisions which we intend to make step by step, on the basis of empirical knowledge which we expect to obtain in the future, then the method of reduction is the appropriate one rather than that of definition."[13] This implies that the introduction of a term in one way rather than the other is a matter of convention. It is not determined by *a priori* principles. Nor is there, according to Carnap, a principle *a priori* that would determine what kind of sentences ought to be introduced as atomic sentences, and what kind of predicates as primitive predicates. This again is a matter of convention.

We are now confronted with the question whether Carnap's position is indeed apt to serve as a rallying point for all empiricist doctrines. I shall approach this question by comparing Carnap's and Wittgenstein's views concerning an adequate language of science.

Carnap suggests, as has been pointed out, that the restrictions imposed by Wittgenstein upon such a language be liberalized by (a) recognizing that we are free to select the kind of propositions which are to be introduced as atomic, (b) admitting generalized sentences of maximum complexity, and (c) replacing complete verifiability by confirmability to a certain degree as the criterion of meaningfulness. He accordingly conceives of his own theory as a generalization of Wittgenstein's theory.

But this view cannot bear closer examination. The two theories are indeed diametrically opposed in some of their basic tenets. Wittgenstein links the notion of atomic propositions to that of elementary truths, and constructs a language which is meant to vindicate the point that empirical knowledge of any degree of complexity has its source in the data of immediate experience. Carnap had leaned toward this view at an earlier stage of his philosophical development, but he had abandoned it by the time he wrote "Testability and Meaning." He had, then, realized that the idea of immediate experience as *the* source of factual knowledge is incompatible with the standards of empirical procedure. In other words,

---

13. "Testability and Meaning," *loc. cit.,* p. 449.

he had shifted from an atomistic interpretation of knowledge, as proposed by Wittgenstein, to a contextualistic interpretation. His rejection of Wittgenstein's view that the atomicity, or nonatomicity, of a proposition can be intuitively grasped must be appraised in the light of this fact.

Similar considerations apply to his substitution of confirmability to a certain degree for verifiability as the standard of meaningfulness. Wittgenstein's view that all statements of fact are truth-functions of atomic propositions, and that therefore comprehension of the truth-conditions of a proposition is implied in the comprehension of its meaning, is indissolubly linked to his theory of immediate experience. Carnap's criterion of meaning, on the other hand, is a corollary to his contextualistic view. Hence we must not interpret Carnap's criterion as a generalization of Wittgenstein's criterion.

Turning to a comparison between Wittenstein's molecular language and Carnap's generalized language, we may indeed say that the latter is wider than the former, because it comprises the molecular language and contains additional signs. But we have to consider Wittgenstein's claim that only a molecular language fulfills the requirement of isomorphy with the world. This leads to the conclusion that Carnap's and Wittgenstein's approaches are irreconcilable in this respect as well. Hence we must not take it for granted that the two philosophers agree on the task of philosophy when they declare that philosophy is critique of language. Such a declaration takes on a different sense according to whether one adopts an intuitionist theory of meaning or a conventionalist theory of meaning. Wittgenstein criticizes a given language (symbolism) by pointing out that it is not isomorphous with the world; Carnap's criticism seeks to establish the fact that the rejected language is inconvenient for the pursuit of scientific inquiry. This difference bears even on the rejection of metaphysical sentences as meaningless. Meaningfulness, according to Carnap's view, is relative to the established rules of a given language, that is, to conventions; but this view is not shared by Wittgenstein.

The incongruity of Carnap's and Wittgenstein's theories has been obscured by the fact that both philosophers are animated by a "geometrical spirit," and that they were both substantially influenced by Frege's and Russell's philosophies of mathematics. But Wittgenstein's position is much more akin to Russell's epistemology than is Carnap's position, notwithstanding Wittgenstein's criticism of some basic tenets of Russell's doctrine. If Carnap's work is to be linked to that of a great logician of science of the two preceding generations, then it will be to Henri

Poincaré's work rather than Russell's. And the genealogy of Russell's doctrine leads us back to David Hume, whereas Poincaré's view may well be interpreted as a modified Kantianism. Thus one might be tempted to conclude: *Plus ça change, plus c'est la même chose.* The philosophical problems of old have not disappeared; they are only dressed in a new garb. But in making such a statement one should bear in mind that the garb does make a difference for a philosophical issue. Logical positivism has made significant contributions to philosophy by stripping traditional epistemological issues of their outmoded garbs, so that their true shapes became visible.

I shall now briefly indicate my own views on the controversial points. It seems to me that Wittgenstein is fundamentally right in regarding what may be called "intuitive insight" as the basis of a "critique of language." However, I would not describe these intuitions in terms of a comparison between the structure of language and the structure of the world, but rather as the outcome of a process of a clarification of meanings. This difference might seem to be irrelevant, but it is not. The system of meanings corresponds to *"any possible* world," whereas Wittgenstein's formulation suggests a comparison of language with the real world *qua* real. Rational intuition is thus being linked to immediate sensory experience, and truth of atomic propositions is held to be ascertainable by immediate experience. This sensationalist interpretation of truth and knowledge is, in my view untenable, and I agree with Carnap in rejecting it. But I cannot accept Carnap's interpretation of meaningfulness in terms of confirmability, nor his conception of a partial determination of meaning by reduction-pairs. (This point will be discussed in the following section.)

As to the requirement of universal and existential operators in a logically adequate language, I hold that they are needed. It does not seem to me that Wittgenstein has succeeded in eliminating them. A logically adequate language has, in my view, the form of a *functional calculus of first order.* The introduction of an *extended* functional calculus, as proposed by Carnap, may be technically convenient, but it is not structurally adequate.[14]

As regards the notion of *probability,* I agree with Carnap and with the majority of logical positivists in rejecting Reichenbach's unity conception of probability with its interpretation of "degree of confirmation" in statistical terms. But their proposed distinction between *two* concepts

---

14. Cf. Kaufmann, *Das Unendliche in der Mathematik und seine Ausschaltung* (Vienna, 1930).

of probability does not dispose of another ambiguity in the use of the word "probable."

It is customary in modern as well as in ancient philosophy to contrast factual knowledge as (merely) probable with "absolutely certain" rational knowledge, and to regard rational certainty as an ideal of empirical science which can be more and more closely approximated, but never attained. Though this idea emerged in the doctrinal climate of rationalism, it has been adopted by many empiricist philosophers. There is little doubt that it underlies Carnap's as well as Reichenbach's conceptions of factual knowledge and their attempts toward a unified theory of deductive and inductive logic. But this notion of probability, which marks the distinction between empirical knowledge in general and rational knowledge, must not be confounded with the concepts of "degree of confirmation" and "statistical probability," which refer to distinctions *within* the domain of empirical science. I have developed this point at greater length in a discussion with Carnap to which I shall refer below. [15]

Carnap's conception of "probability" is intertwined with his interpretation of the relation between "knowledge" and "truth"; that is, with his treatment of a fundamental issue in the doctrinal struggle between realists and idealists. The basic problems that divide nominalists and conceptual realists, or empiricists and rationalists, are likewise alive in Carnap's more recent writings.

We shall now discuss the bearing of some of these problems on an appraisal of the development of logical positivism in the United States during the past twelve years.

III

It is one of the chief problems of epistemology to determine the relation between rational knowledge, as represented by deductive logic and pure mathematics, and factual knowledge (knowledge of existence). Extreme rationalists claim that some questions of existence can be answered by an analysis of the "nature" or "essence" of the objects concerned. More moderate rationalists do not endorse this view, and, accordingly, draw a sharp dividing line between perfect (absolutely certain, indubitable) knowledge of essences, and imperfect (merely probable, dubitable) knowledge of existence.

All doctrines which are usually classified as "empiricist" agree in rejecting *extreme* rationalism. They subscribe to the verdict pronounced by

---

15. See footnote 17.

David Hume in the concluding chapter of his *Inquiry*: "Whatever *is* may *not be*. No negation of a fact can involve a contradiction. The non-existence of any being, without exception, is as clear and distinct an idea as its existence. The proposition, which affirms it not to be, however false, is no less conceivable and intelligible, than that which affirms it to be." "If we reason *a priori* anything may appear able to produce any-thing. The falling of a pebble may, for aught we know, extinguish the sun; or the wish of a man control the planets in their orbits. It is only ex-perience which teaches us the nature and bounds of cause and effect, and enables us to infer the existence of one object from that of another."

Empiricists are, however, divided over the issue whether logic and mathematics are autonomous or "dependent upon" experience, that is, sense perception and/or self-perception. J. S. Mill holds the latter view, and claims that the principles of logic and mathematics are generaliza-tions from experience; but his arguments, like those of many earlier em-piricists, are vitiated by the *genetic fallacy*.

Mill's view has been opposed by logical positivists, who defend — up to a certain point—the autonomy of logic and mathematics. But the question of determining the extent and precise character of this autonomy has always been one of their major problems. In their approach to this problem they were influenced by the nominalistic tradition, as trans-mitted by David Hume. Universals are, according to this view, a product of language; and logical and mathematical reasoning, which deals ex-clusively with universals, is, therefore, analysis of language. Such an analysis, they point out, is not concerned with existing things *qua* existing, or with actual events *qua* actual, but rather with conventions which regulate the use of signs. The analysis is, accordingly, independent of per-ceptual experiences that are required for the attainment of factual knowl-edge.

Recognition of the fact that conventions concerning linguistic signs are, like any other conventions, man-made, is supposed by them to remove the vexing problems of knowledge *a priori* in logic and mathematics. Truth by convention, while exempt from testing, seems still to be indis-solubly connected with human experience. And the interpretation of pure thought in terms of language seems to permit, moreover, the elimi-nation of time-honored metaphysical problems, related to the notion of *substantia cogitans*. The calculization of logic and mathematics is sup-posed to lend further support to this interpretation.

But the ejected problems enter through another door as soon as we try to make explicit the principles which guide us in establishing those conventions. This door is thrown wide open by the distinction between "good syntax" and "bad syntax," which has to be made, in one way or another, by every logician who embarks upon a "critique of language." Similar considerations apply to an appraisal of semantical rules. It is clear that standards for the evaluation of conventions must not be taken to be conventions of the same type. They are, in a well-determined sense, extralinguistic, though they may be formulated in a *metalanguage*.

But how are these standards established? Carnap suggests that they are established by experience, but his "Principle of Empiricism" which traces "meaningfulness" back to "confirmability," does not settle the issue, because "confirmability" presupposes "meaningfulness." In confirming the assertion "There is a blue spot on the ceiling of this room," we presuppose the "givenness" of this assertion, and hence, the "givenness" of the meanings of all terms contained in it. On the other hand, it can hardly be denied that such concepts as "blue" are somehow "derived from" percepts.

Some philosophers, for instance, Russell and Pepper, say that such terms are introduced by "ostensive definitions," but this is a misleading expression. It is safe to say that the problems raised by these two apparently irreconcilable views concerning the relation between "meaning" and "experience" have ben in the center of philosophical speculation ever since the days of Plato, and that they are at the core of the most persistent doctrinal controversies between rationalists and empiricists, and between conceptual realists and nominalists. Edmund Husserl's distinction between *formal logic,* where objective meanings are presupposed, and *transcendental logic,* where different levels of objectivation are to be discerned, offers a clue to a reformulation of this problem. We are led to realize, on the one hand, that the postulate of the objectivity of meanings, which underlies deductive logic (and, *a fortiori,* the logic of science) precludes a reduction of "meaning" to "experience"; and, on the other hand, that this postulate is relative to only one level of clarification.

But be this as it may, it will hardly be contested by any logician that we need not refer to the standards of confirmation for two propositions p_1 and p_2 in demonstrating that p_1 entails p_2, or that any other internal relation between p_1 and p_2 obtains. This being admitted, it should be recognized as well that a reduction of "meaning" to "confirmation" does not square with the sense in which "meaning" is used in deductive logic.

These and other considerations lead us to a distinction between *"prop-*

osition" as a basic concept of deductive logic and "*assertion*" as a basic concept of the logic of science. A proposition describes a *possible* state of affairs; to assert this proposition is to claim the *actuality* (existence) of such a state of affairs. Standards of confirmation are then seen to refer to assertions *qua* assertions: they do not refer to propositions as such. Recognition of this distinction is incompatible with the acceptance of Carnap's theory of reduction pairs, and of his subsequent attempts to establish a unified theory of deduction and induction.

Problems of the logic of science, of which inductive logic is an integral part, are quite different in structure from problems of deductive logic in the strict sense. I have criticized Carnap's view concerning the relation between induction and deduction in another context,[16] and shall confine myself here to a restatement of some essential points, which will include a brief outline of my conception of the logic of science.

Let p_m and p_n be two propositions, and P_m and P_n the corresponding assertions of p_m and p_n, respectively. Then let K be the *body of knowledge*, that is, the set of scientifically established assertions at the given time. To deduce p_n from p_m is to demonstrate that p_m entails p_n. The *result* of the deduction is therefore "p_m entails p_n."

The result, on the other hand, of what is usually called an inductive inference from p_m to p_n reads: "P_n may be incorporated into K." This conclusion is derived from the two premises: "If P_m belongs to K, then P_n may be incorporated into K," and "P_m belongs to K." The first premise is a rule of inference; the second states the fulfillment of the conditions stipulated by this rule. The conclusion is an appraisal of a *scientific decision*, that is, of the decision to change the status of an assertion with respect to the body of knowledge. Inductive logic is, accordingly, in contrast to deductive logic, intrinsically related to a *scientific situation*, that is, to a given stage of scientific inquiry.

This applies to the logic of science in general. Scientific procedure is, from the logician's point of view, a series of changes in the body of knowledge, which take place in conformity with given rules of procedure. Such changes may consist either in the incorporation of an assertion into the body of knowledge, or in the elimination of an assertion from this body. The logic of science deals, in the first place, with questions concerning the *correctness* of such changes, that is, their conformity with presupposed rules of scientific procedure (standards of verification or invalidation). This involves the explicit formulation of these rules, which is

_____

16. Symposium on Probability, see next footnote.

obtained by *clarification of the actually applied standards of scientific criticism*. The rules differ widely for different fields of inquiry, and they are liable to be altered as inquiry proceeds. But there are some invariant structural properties of the system of rules, which determine the meaning of *"scientific procedure in general."* We may call them *"scientific principles."* Listed below are some of these principles:

1. The rules must preclude the simultaneous presence of two contrary or contradictory assertions in the body of knowledge.

2. Conditions for the incorporation of any assertion into the body of knowledge must be established by the rules.

3. Conditions for the elimination of any assertion from the body of knowledge must be established by the rules.

4. Changes in the body of knowledge must be substantially (though not exclusively) determined by results of observations.

Principles like these are the backbone of a general methodology (logic of science). They must be clearly distinguished from the principles of deductive logic in the strict sense.

The first principle listed is a case in point. It is usually identified with the *principle of contradiction* in deductive logic, which is frequently presented in the formulation: "No proposition is both true and false." But the principle of contradiction, as actually applied in deductive logic, is, together with the principle of excluded middle, simply an explication of the meaning of "negation." It does not imply any reference to the rules of empirical procedure. We must therefore distinguish it clearly from the first principle listed. I have done this by calling the latter *"procedural correlate of the principle of contradiction."*

A similar relation obtains between the *principle of excluded middle* in deductive logic and the second principle listed. Let us call the incorporation of assertion P into the body of knowledge, in conformity with the rules, *"verification of P,"* and the incorporation of its negation (non P) in conformity with the rules the *"falsification of P."* Then we may formulate the second principle as follows: *"Any given* assertion P must be verifiable and falsifiable." (To say, "All assertions must be verifiable and falsifiable" would be a pleonasm, since "falsification of P" has been defined as "verification of non P").

This principle is hardly ever distinguished from the principle of excluded middle in deductive logic, which is taken to read: "Every proposition is either true or false." But this principle too is simply explicative of the meaning of "negation"; it does not imply any reference to rules of procedure. We shall therefore distinguish it from our second principle by calling the latter *"the procedural correlate of the principle of excluded middle."* This principle may be combined with the third principle, which I have called the "principle of permanent control," in stating: "Every scientific decision must be reversible." It is readily seen that this principle is quite different from any principle in deductive logic.

These observations indicate the general task of establishing an autonomous (formal) logic of science, by making explicit the structure of the network of procedural rules. This task involves an analysis of such concepts as "verification," "invalidation," "falsification," "confirmation in different degrees," "evidence," "problem," "solution," "explanation." This analysis corresponds in a sense to the one performed in deductive logic of such terms as "and," "or," "if-then," "all," "some." But this is not to say that the two types of analysis are coordinated. Deductive logic is "prior to" the logic of science in the sense that the concepts of deductive logic are implicit in the logic of science, but not conversely.

The relation between deductive logic and the logic of science has been obscured by ambiguous conceptions of "truth." Both deductive logic, inasmuch as it deals with statements of fact, and the logic of science, are supposed to be concerned with factual truth or falsity conceived as nontemporal properties of propositions. Deductive logic, it is held, examines the *formal* conditions of truth, whereas the logic of science examines the *material* conditions of truth.

But closer analysis reveals that the notion of nontemporal factual truth has no place in deductive logic. It is almost generally recognized that intensional logic (which does not employ the notion of truth) is apt to cover all problems of deductive logic. The fact that many logicians prefer, for technical reasons, extensional logic, which does operate with the notion of truth, is epistemologically irrelevant. The crucial epistemological question is whether deductive logic presupposes a general notion of truth which comprises rational truth and factual truth; and this question must be answered in the negative by anyone who admits that intensional logic is capable of describing adequately all internal relations between concepts and between propositions.

This conclusion is of great significance for the logic of science, because it bears upon the interpretation of "scientific knowledge." We are here confronted with the following problem: Recognition of the principle of permanent control, which is acknowledged by virtually all philosophers as a principle of scientific procedure, is incompatible with a conception of scientific inquiry as a progress toward perfect knowledge of truth, where "truth" is supposed to be logically independent of, and logically prior to "knowledge." For it does not make sense to interpret an assertion *P* established today, and an assertion *non P* which may be established tomorrow, as different approximations to perfect knowledge of the selfsame truth.

This becomes even more clear when we consider that "perfect (empirical) knowledge" is a contradiction. We have indeed, by accepting the principle of permanent control, ruled out the possibility of perfect (indubitable) knowledge. This is tantamount to saying that the notion of nontemporal factual truth is "transcendent." But such a conclusion seems to be unacceptable, as long as this notion is held to be implicit in deductive logic, and therefore presupposed in the logic of science.

I have dealt with this predicament in a series of papers to which Carnap replied.[17] He grants in his rejoinder to the last of these papers that the notion of truth "is not *necessary* either in deductive or in inductive logic since the basic concepts of these two fields (logical implication and degree of confirmation respectively) can be defined without referring to truth."[18] But he holds that the concept of truth is often useful, and that no cogent objections can be raised against its use. Referring to some examples taken from extensional logic, Carnap remarks: "Kaufmann prefers to avoid the concept of truth in all these cases in order to preserve the conceptual purity of deductive logic. There is no objection against this procedure. On the other hand, there does not seem any compelling reason for requiring others to follow the same ascetic procedure if they find the use of the concept of truth convenient."[19] However, the question of usefulness (convenience) of the introduction of a symbol is not the point at issue; what is at issue is, rather, the meaningfulness of the notion of truth, as conceived by Carnap.

I stated in may first paper[20] that this notion is meaningless in the

---

17. The papers are listed below. CI: "The Two Concepts of Probability," *Philosophy and Phenomenological Research*, Vol. V, No. 4 (1945), pp. 512-532; CII: "Remarks on Induction and Truth," *ibid.*, Vol. VI, No. 4 (1946) pp. 590-602; CIII: "Rejoinder to Mr. Kaufmann's Reply," *ibid.*, Vol. VI, No. 4 (1946), pp. 609-611; CIV: "Reply to Felix Kaufmann," *ibid.*, Vol. IX, No. 2 (1948), pp. 300-304; KI: "Scientific Procedure and Probability," *ibid.*, Vol. VI, No. 1 (1945), pp. 47-66; KII: "On the Nature of Inductive Inference," *ibid.*, Vol. VI, No. 4 (1946), pp. 602-609; KIII: "Rudolf Carnap's Analysis of 'Truth'," *ibid.*, Vol. IX, No. 2 (1948), pp. 294-299. Cf. also, chaps. ii-vii of my *Methodology of the Social Sciences* (New York, Oxford University Press, 1944).
18. C IV, pp. 302 f.
19. C IV, p. 303.
20. K I, p. 60.

sense in which the term "meaningless" is used by logical positivists. In contesting this view Carnap introduces, for the sake of illustration, the sentences:[21] (1) "The substance in this vessel is alcohol." (2) "The sentence 'the substance in this vessel is alcohol' is true." He then argues as follows: "Now the decisive point for our whole problem is this: the sentences (1) and (2) are logically equivalent; in other words, they entail each other; they are merely different formulations for the same factual content; nobody may accept the one and reject the other; if used as communications, both sentences convey the same information though in different form. The difference in form is indeed important; the two sentences belong to two quite different parts of the language. (In my terminology (1) belongs to the object part of the language, (2) to its meta-part, and, more specifically, to its semantical part.) This difference in form, however, does not prevent their logical equivalence."

Referring to this argument in C IV, Carnap writes: "As the repeatedly emphasized equivalence of the sentences (2) and (1) makes clear, the truth of a sentence means simply that the facts are as described in the sentence, whether anybody knows it or not. The question as to how we are to find out whether the facts are as described is a different matter; this question is to be answered by stating criteria of confirmation."[22]

These remarks bring the crucial point into focus. It should be noted first that Carnap's term "sentence" stands for what we have called "assertion." When he declares that a sentence is true if the facts are as described in the sentence, he means to say that an assertion is called 'true,' if it is in conformity with reality. This raises the persistent issue between realists and idealists concerning things-in-themselves. This issue is not squarely faced by pointing out that things are what they are regardless of whether anybody knows it or not. The problem is rather whether "existence" (and particularly "physical existence") may be introduced as a transcendent concept, or whether it has to be defined in terms of possible experience.

Carnap's argument throughout our discussion hinges upon his adoption of the *realist* view. He never tires of reaffirming this position, most pointedly, perhaps, in the defense of his theory of induction. *But it seems to me that his realism is irreconcilable with his empiricism.* The view that criteria of confirmation are required only for the determination of the meaning of "knowledge," but not for the determination of the meaning of "truth," is incompatible with the empiricist position in general,

---

21. C II, pp. 598 f. Cf. also C IV, pp. 300ff.
22. *Loc. cit.*, p. 302.

and with the position of the logical positivists in particular. This becomes obvious as soon as we realize that claiming the independence of "truth" from any standards of confirmation is tantamount to claiming the independence of "existence" from "possible experience." It is this point that I wanted to stress in declaring that his notion of truth is meaningless in the sense in which the term "meaningless" is used by logical positivists.

Carnap's treatment of this problem has been impaired by his interpretation of logic and philosophy as analysis of language. In the twenties and early thirties he had shared Wittgenstein's view that all legitimate philosophical problems are problems of the *syntax* of language.. This position was systematically developed in one of his major works. [23] But a few years after the publication of this book, he adopted a broader conception of a philosophical critique of language by endorsing C. W. Morris's general theory of signs (semiotic). [24] Morris calls the process in which something functions as a sign "semiosis" and distinguishes three "dimensions" of semiosis, and their respective studies. Syntactics deals with the formal relations of signs to one another; semantics analyzes the relations of signs to the objects to which the signs are applicable; pragmatics is concerned with the relation of signs to interpreters. Semiotic is supposed by Morris and Carnap to be capable of absorbing all legitimate philosophical problems.

Carnap's own work during the past ten years has been almost exclusively devoted to semantics. He interprets his attempts toward clarifying the meanings of "truth," "knowledge," "probability" as semantical analyses, and joins Alfred Tarski and other prominent workers in the field of mathematical logic in regarding truth and falsity as properties of *sentences* ("linguistic entities").

It seems to me that this view is untenable. I submit that the expression "true sentence" is as objectionable as the expression "odd numeral."

But if we grant this, then we find ourselves confronted with the question of how one can account for the fact that so many eminent logicians and mathematicians should insist upon interpreting logic as analysis of language, where "language" is taken to consist of physical marks. We have already mentioned some trends of thought which are in tune with such an interpretation, but these trends themselves ought to be more

---

23. *Logische Syntax der Sprache* (Vienna, 1934; revised English edition, New York, 1937).
24. Cf., C. W. Morris, "Foundations of a Theory of Signs," *International Encyclopedia of Unified Science*, Vol. I, No. 2 (1938); and R. Carnap, "Foundations of Logic and Mathematics," *ibid.*, Vol. I, No. 3 (1939).

thoroughly explored. I shall here refer to but one point which seems to have been conducive to the endorsement of the nominalist view by many modern logicians, namely, the failure to distinguish properly between the meaning of "logical" in "logical relations" and in "logical procedure." Logical relations are extralinguistic in a sense in which logical procedure is not. It is not correct to say, " 'Triangularity' logically implies 'two-dimensionality' *in English.*" [25]

But logical procedure cannot be characterized without referring to a given symbolism. (This point was driven home by the calculization of logic and mathematics). In distinguishing, for example, between a rigorous and a nonrigorous demonstration of a mathematical theorem, we have to make explicit the transformation rules which refer to given kinds of marks and configurations of marks (formulae). [26]

Concepts like "deducibility" or "demonstrability" are therefore relative to a given language (symbolism), but "entailment," "contrariety," "contradictoriness" are not.[27] The truth-functions in extensional logic are completely determined by internal relations between propositions and hence likewise extralinguistic.

Carnap has been gradually emancipating himself from nominalism, but he still endorses the semantical theory of truth. His unqualified rejection of nominalism would augur well for the further development of logical positivism.

SELECTED BIBLIOGRAPHY

Ayer, A. J. *Language, Truth and Logic.* Oxford University Press, 1936; second edition, London, Gollanz, 1946.

———. *The Foundations of Empirical Knowledge.* New York, The Macmillan Co., 1940.

Bergmann, G. "Sense Data, Linguistic Conventions and Existence." *Philosophy of Science,* Vol. XIV, 1947.

Black, M. *The Nature of Mathematics.* New York, Harcourt, Brace and Co., 1933.

———. "The Semantic Definition of Truth." *Analysis,* 1948.

25. But Carnap presents as an example of an elementary statement in deductive logic "i L - implies j (in E)." And he adds: "('L-implication' means logical implication or entailment. E is here either the English language or a semantical language system based on English.)" C II, p. 593.

26. It should be noted that the marks and formulae of an uninterpreted calculus are not completely devoid of meaning. They stand for different kinds of identities and diversities which are specified when the calculus is interpreted.

27. Kurt Gödel's famous "incompleteness theorem" reveals the importance of this distinction.

Carnap, R. *Meaning and Necessity*. Chicago, University of Chicago
    Press, 1947.
Feigl, H. "Logical Empiricism," in *Twentieth Century Philosophy*. D.
    Runes, editor, New York, Philosophical Library, 1943.
Feigl, H. and Sellars, W. S. *Readings in Philosophical Analysis*. New
    York, Appleton-Century-Crofts, Inc., 1949.
Frank, P. *Das Kausalgesetz und seine Grenzen*. Vienna, Springer, 1932.
————. *Between Physics and Philosophy*. Cambridge, Harvard Uni-
    versity Press, 1941.
Hempel, C. "The Logical Positivist's Theory of Truth." *Analysis*, 1935.
————. "Studies in the Logic of Confirmation." *Mind*, Vol. LIV,
    1945.
Hempel, C. and Oppenheim, P. "Studies in the Logic of Explanation."
    Philosophy of Science, Vol. XV, 1948.
Gödel, K. "Russell's Mathematical Logic," in *The Philosophy of Ber-
    trand Russell. The Library of Living Philosophers*, Vol.
    V, edited by P. A. Schilpp, Evanston, 1944.
Kaplan, E. "Definition and Specification of Meaning." *Journal of Philo-
    sophy*, Vol. XLIII, 1946.
Kaufmann, F. *Methodenlehre der Sozialwissenschaften*. Vienna, Spring-
    er, 1936. (Spanish trans. *Metodología de las Ciencias
    Sociales*. Mexico, D. F., Fondo de Cultura Economica,
    1946.)
————. "Phenomenology and Logical Empiricism," in *Philosophi-
    cal Essays in Memory of Edmund Husserl*, edited by
    Marvin Farber. Cambridge, Harvard University Press,
    1940.
————. "Symposium on Meaning and Truth." *Philosophy and
    Phenomenological Research*, 1943-44.
————. "Problems of Philosophical Education," in *Freedom and
    Experience: Essays presented to Horace M. Kallen*, edited
    by Sidney Hook and Milton R. Konvitz. Ithaca, Cornell
    University Press, 1947.
Langford, C. H. see Lewis, C. I.
Lenzen, V. F. "Experience and Convention." *Erkenntis*, Vol. VII, 1938.
Lewis, C. I. *An Analysis of Knowledge and Valuation*. LaSalle, Ill.,
    Open Court Publishing Co., 1946.
Lewis, C. I. and Langford, C. H. *Symbolic Logic*. New York, The Cen-
    tury Co., 1932.
Menger, K. "The New Logic." *Philosophy of Science*, Vol. IV, 1937.

Mises, R. von. *Kleines Lehrbuch des Positivismus.* The Hague, W. P. van Stockum and Zoon; Chicago, University of Chicago Press, 1939.

—————. *Probability, Statistics and Truth.* New York, The Macmillan Co., 1939.

—————. "Symposium on Probability." *Philosophy and Phenomenological Research,* 1945-46.

Morris, C. W. *Signs, Language, and Behavior.* New York, Prentice-Hall, 1946.

Nagel, E. "Principles of the Theory of Probability." *International Encyclopedia of Unified Science,* Vol. 1, No. 6. Chicago, University of Chicago Press, 1939.

—————. "Symposium on Meaning and Truth." *Philosophy and Phenomenological Research,* 1943-44.

—————. "Symposium on Probability." *Philosophy and Phenomenological Research,* 1945-46.

—————. "Logic without Ontology," in *Naturalism and the Human Spirit,* edited by Yervant H. Krikorian, New York, Columbia University Press, 1944.

Neurath, O. *Le développement du Cercle de Vienne et l'avenir de l'empiricisme logique.* Paris, Hermann, 1935.

—————. "Unified Science as Encyclopedic Integration," in *Encyclopedia of Unified Science,* Vol. I, No. 1. Chicago, University of Chicago Press, 1938.

—————. "Foundations of Social Science," *ibid.,* Vol. II, No. 2.

Ogden, C. K. and Richards, I. A. *The Meaning of Meaning,* fifth edition. New York, Harcourt, Brace and Co., 1940.

Oppenheim, P. see Hempel, C.

Pap. A. *The A Priori in Physical Theory.* New York, Kings Crown Press, 1946.

Popper, K. R. "What is Dialectic?" *Mind,* Vol. XLIX, 1940.

—————. "Why are the Calculuses of Logic and Mathematics Applicable to Reality?" *Arist. Suppl.* Vol. XX, 1946.

Quine, W. V. "Truth by Convention," in *Philosophical Essays for A. N. Whitehead,* edited by Otis H. Lee. New York, Longmans, Green, and Co., 1936.

—————. "Universals." *Journal of Symbolic Logic,* Vol. XII, 1947.

Reichenbach, H. *Symbolic Logic.* New York, The Macmillan Co., 1947.

—————. "Symposium on Probability." *Philosophy and Phenomenological Research,* 1945-46.

Russell, B. *An Inquiry into Meaning and Truth.* New York, W. W. Norton and Co., 1940.

Schlick, M. *Allgemeine Erkenntnislehre,* second edition. Berlin, Springer, 1935.

——————. *Gesammelte Aufsaetze.* Vienna, Gerold and Co., 1938.

Sellars, W. S. "Epistemology and the New Way of Words." *Journal of Philosophy,* Vol. XLIV, 1944.

——————. see also Feigl, H.

Stevenson, C. L. *Ethics and Language.* New Haven, Yale University Press, 1944.

Tarski, A. *Der Wahrheitsbegriff in den formalisierten Sprachen.* Commentatorium Societatis Philosophicae Polonorum Studia Philosophica, Leopoli, 1935.

——————. "Symposium on Meaning and Truth." *Philosophy and Phenomenological Research,* 1943-44.

Waismann, F. "The Relevance of Psychology to Logic." *Arist. Suppl.,* Vol. XV, 1936.

——————. "Verifiability." *Ibid.,* Vol. XIX, 1945.

Weinberg, J. R. *An Examination of Logical Positivism.* New York, Harcourt, Brace and Co., 1936.

Wick, A. W. *Metaphysics and the New Logic.* Chicago, University of Chicago Press, 1942.

Wisdom, J. "Metaphysics and Verification." *Mind,* Vol. XLVII, 1938.

Williams, D. C. *The Ground of Induction.* Cambridge, Harvard University Press, 1947.

——————. "Symposium on Probability." *Philosophy and Phenomenological Research,* 1945-46.

SOME TRENDS IN AMERICAN NATURALISTIC ETHICS

Abraham Edel*

Three fairly distinct periods can be noted in twentieth century
American naturalistic ethics. The first stage is an expansive one:
emphasis falls on giving a go-ahead signal to men in the pursuit of
happiness, the development and expression of their interests.
Then comes a sharp development of arbitrary relativism: the possibility
of ultimate disagreement looms as the central fact of ethical theory, and
in this outlook even where men's interests come together the contingency
of the coincidence overshadows the fact of community. Now scientists
and philosophers are beginning to search for a theoretical basis for an all-
human ethics. These periods can be read from the very inner texture of
the ethical theories that successively dominated the scene, and to read
them off is the aim of this paper.

When one looks at the general setting of American life and problems,
one is hardly surprised to find that naturalistic ethical theory took this
particular course. For it reflected clearly the major movement of twentieth century American historical development. American life prior to
the first World War, and even after it, was thoroughly expansive both in
material development and general spirit. The tremendous growth of
technology generated and increasingly satisfied fresh needs. A growing
population found increasing opportunities for success. In the intellectual
arena, a liberal capitalism that saw the League of Nations as a step to the
end of war and traced economic individualism and political democracy as
the outcome of human evolution might foresee steep ascents ahead, but
no serious downgrade. This hope of intelligent social harmony and grow-

* Born in 1908. Ph.D., Columbia University, 1934. Assistant Professor of Philosophy,
College of the City of New York. Visiting lecturer, University of California 1947-48; Guggenheim Fellow, 1944-45. Author of *Aristotle's Theory of the Infinite* (1934), *The Theory
and Practice of Philosophy* (1946); contributor to *The Philosophy of G. E. Moore*, ed. P. A.
Schlipp (1942), *Naturalism and the Human Spirit*, ed. Y. H. Krikorian (1944), and various articles, principally in *The Journal of Philosophy*.

ing satisfaction was succeeded by depression, mass unemployment, open class conflicts, the rise of fascism, war, the frustration of vast multitudes. In the climate of opinion, the conflict of irrational power became the prevailing theme; democracy seemed convicted of inefficiency and reason was declared helpless in principle. The intensity of the conflict that ensued in World War II made inroads on this outlook. Full employment, vast increase in productive power, combined with the necessities of energetic action, the unmasking of Nazi barbarity, and the devastation of modern war, to underscore the common human needs for global peace and greater global productivity as minimal bases for any special goals.

I

The first phase may be illustrated from the leading theories of Ralph Barton Perry and John Dewey. The keynote of Perry's ethics is harmonious human happiness, that of Dewey's is the growth of effective intelligence. Both are characterized by emphasis on individualism, growth, equalitarianism, the growth and integration of interests or preferences into a system achieving a maximum fulfillment. Both refuse to accept a sharp theoretical separation of value and fact. Perry uses the language of interests, Dewey that of preferences, ends-in-view; but both seek to ground whatever terms they use in a psychology that is more than introspective. Perry's individualism has tended to be more atomic than Dewey's. But both, in very different ways, give expression to the expansive mood in their very formulation of ethical concepts and methods. George Santayana, the third outstanding figure in American naturalistic ethics of the early twentieth century, while sharing the naturalistic basis, differs sharply with this fundamental value-attitude. His *Life of Reason* (1905-6) embodies the values of the classical outlook, heightened consciousness rather than dynamic expansion. Harmony in his ethics has therefore quite a different tone from what it has in Perry's and Dewey's. Since their outlook has been typical and more influential in the context we are considering, discussion of Santayana's work is here sacrificed.

Perry's ethical structure shows its foundations most clearly in *The Moral Economy* (1909). The title indicates the controlling model which permeates the work and, in effect, provides the categories of the structure. Morality is defined as "simply an observance of the laws of provident living" (p. 1). In this "unavoidable business of living" morality "offers the most competent advice as to how to proceed with an enterprise" (p. 2). The elaboration of this theme shows clearly that the model is not any enterprise but the specific one of the growing business enterprise of the early twentieth century. In fact many of the concepts have a direct business parallel, and the analogy in attitudes is explicit. The "venerable institutions" of government, education, metaphysics, morality, "yield a steady return" (p. 3). Morality is regarded almost as the basic articles of incorporation for the business of living; it represents "what is virtually undertaken by all parties to the adventure of life." Hence "moral liability" applies to every man (p. 8), presumably constituting a standing expense in the accounting.

Individualism appears in the initial definitions. "The mark of life is partiality for itself" (p. 10); "an *interest,* or unit of life, is essentially an organization which consistently acts for its own preservation" (p. 11). Goodness is fulfillment of interest or desire. Yet no interest operates alone. It recognizes other interests "as parts of its environment" and "as partners in the general enterprise of life." The moral idea is evolved as *"interest allies itself with interest in order to be free-handed and powerful* against the common hereditary enemy, the heavy inertia and the incessant wear of the cosmos. Through morality a plurality of interests becomes an *economy, or community of interests"* (p. 13). No interest, however humble, is excluded from this economy. "In pleasure and pain life records its gains and losses . . ."(p. 17). Morality is related to life as simply a later phase of the one development. The role of competition in forcing life up the scale is recognized, but it is equally asserted that progress involves the steady elimination of competition (p. 24).

Equalitarianism extends to individual interests. One simple interest is not more good than another any more than one inch is longer than another (p. 56). The higher interest is simply the more inclusive one, as two good books are better than one good book because there is more of goodness in them. This equalitarianism is used to reject egoism (pp. 60 f.), and issues in the principle of good will: "the goodness of action must be determined with reference to nothing less than the totality of all affected interests" (p. 67). But business must have an eye out to expansion: "One's moral account cannot be made up without a provision for entries that have yet to be made. Such a provision will take the form of a purpose to grow, an ardent spirit of liberality, an eagerness for novelty" (p. 68).

The emphasis on expansion and growth having precluded as "wantonness or willful carelessness" any deliberate preference for a short merry life (p. 55), the good may now be defined with full scope: "The good is fulfilled desire; the moral good the fulfillment of a universal economy, embracing all desires, actual and possible, and providing for them as liberally as their mutual relations permit" (p. 72). An action is accordingly judged "first in respect of immediate return of fulfillment; second, in respect of its bearing on all residual interests. Every good action will be both profitable and safe; both self-sustaining and also serviceable to the whole" (p. 75). Thus other interests correct the inherent impetus of each interest to excess. Various virtues are interpreted in terms of this whole framework of interacting interests. But there is no standing still: "Nature will not permit life to keep what it has unless it gains more" (p. 131). In fact, there has been explicit delineation of the way in which a gradual corporate structure of interests is developed from specific reciprocity.[1] The never-ending vista of organized growth is underscored by the tone of the analysis in the chapter on art (chap. v). Although the esthetic interest is recognized to be "one of the safest of investments" (p. 192), there is a genuine fear of its arresting quality, evidenced in Perry's criticism of Pater's "Not the fruit of experience, but experience itself, is the end" (p. 196).

An easy optimism is likewise fundamental to this early structure of Perry's. The human field is so ordered that morality has a natural quality. "Morality is simply the forced choice between suicide and abundant life" (p. 14). That is why egoism can be so lightly dismissed, and why the enlightened pursuit of any interest, like the enlightened management of any business enterprise, leads to the common welfare. For example, "An industrial corporation, in order to overreach its competitors, is compelled to adjust its intricate functions with incredible nicety, to utilize byproducts, and even to introduce old-age pensions for the promotion of morale among its employees" (p. 25).

I have dwelt on Perry's early work because it seems to me to provide the key to his ethical structure. The economic model almost disappears in his great book, *General Theory of Value* (1926), but at many points at which it is forgotten the residual structure has raised problems for wide philosophical criticism; once it is remembered the underlying values at least are clear. Perry's traditional liberal individualism is manifest throughout. It appears at the beginning in the insistence that value characterizes *any* object of *any* interest, without qualification of either object or interest (e.g., by limitation to *ultimate* aim or *rational interest*). It is

---

1. Pp. 78 f. See the table on p. 81.

more explicit toward the end of the book, when love is exalted and described as "an interested support of another's preexisting and independently existing interest" (p. 677). Similarly, moral judgments are definitely assigned to the organization of interests, not their internal critique (pp. 136-37).

One also looks in vain, in the book, for the role of what traditional ethics called "intrinsic good" or "worth while in itself." For Perry has given interest itself an inner teleological structure. As a consequence he assimilates liking or enjoyment to desiring, treating the former as a "recurrent interest" directed to holding the object through time, the futurist or maintaining aspect being the source of value. His discussion of this question begins with the assertion that "there is no more fundamental notion in our whole field of discourse than that which assigns a greater value to objects of aspiration than to objects already achieved" (p. 242), and ends with the tie-up of interest and success: "Success, in other words, is a process and not a state. Interest is always alive and looking forward" (p. 251). Now while this may be a psychological theory of what goes on in interested responses — in which case it must reckon more intimately with the objection that satisfaction over a given period is concerned predominantly with what happens in that period — the whole discussion makes sense at once if we see it is a formulation of what Perry values in the interest situation. For then it simply carries on the stress on the propulsive or expansive character of interest as developed in his earlier book with an eye on economic life. Indeed, the happy man is described in *General Theory of Value* as one all of whose interests are prosperous (p. 293).

Perry's writings on social philosophy make even more explicit the values contained in his ethical theory. He stands out as perhaps the most consistent philosophical exponent in recent times of a social policy that takes seriously as a basis of social evaluation the traditional promises of a liberal capitalism and insists on their performance. In book after book he has proposed the creed of harmonious happiness as the common basis of action for different religions, economic systems, philosophical outlooks. For example, in a paper on "Catholicism and Modern Liberalism," [2] he urged that special groups distinguish between esoteric doctrines for their own adherents and the common goal of harmonious happiness embedded in their traditions. And in facing the question of American Soviet relations, he urged that the war alliance should not be regarded as a tempor-

---

2. Published in *Proceedings of the American Catholic Philosophical Association*, Vol. XIX: *Philosophy in Post-War Reconstruction*, 1943.

ary expediency.[3] Not merely the two countries, but even the two philosophies of communism and American democracy have a sufficient community of values to act as a basis for united work toward peace and progress. For both "justify themselves by the same standard, namely, the maximum satisfaction of human needs and wants by inventive enterprise and widening distribution. Both systems profess the same desire to raise the level of the masses of the people and to get rid not only of poverty, disease, and ignorance, but of unfairness, parasitic privilege, and wage slavery. Both seek the freedom of the individual, while differing in the tyrannies they fear."[4]

In short, the expansive values of an ethic molded in the light of business enterprise in the early twentieth century are readily applied by Perry to a world all set to embark—if men will allow it—on unified global expansion. This democratic and equalitarian goal of traditional liberalism (which Perry also sees as contained in the Christian tradition), rather than the "free enterprise" of its capitalism, constitutes his critical basis of evaluation.

John Dewey has, in a quite different way, been the American spokesman for a dynamic ethics, an ethics grounded in existence and exalting expansive process. From the very beginning he has resolutely refused to separate value and fact, seeing both transcendental and emotive interpretations of value as opposite faces of the same coin. In the first number of the *International Journal of Ethics* he wrote: "The 'ought' always rises from and falls back into the 'is' . . . the 'ought' is itself an 'is,' — the 'is' of action."[5] Already in his early *Outlines of a Critical Theory of Ethics* (1891), attacking ready-made rules, fixed goals and ideals, he asserted that "good consists in the freeing of impulse, of appetite, of desire, of power, by enabling them to flow in the channel of a unified and full end . . ." (pp. 154-55). The outcome is that "morality is a life of *aspiration,* and of faith; there is required constant willingness to give up past goods as the good, and to press on to new ends; not because past achievements are bad, but because, being good, they have created a situation which demands larger and more intricately related achievements. This willingness is aspiration and it implies *faith"* (p. 213).

The fundamental message is precisely the same thirty years later, in his philosophical manifesto, *Reconstruction in Philosophy* (1920). "Not perfection as a final goal, but the ever-enduring process of perfecting,

---

3. *Our side is Right* (Harvard University Press, 1942), chap. v.
4. *Ibid.,* p. 108.
5. "Moral Theory and Practice," *International Journal of Ethics* (1891), p. 198.

maturing, refining is the aim in living . . . Growth itself is the only moral 'end' " (p. 177). And, even more pointedly: "Happiness is not, however, a bare possession; it is not a fixed attainment. Such a happiness is either the unworthy selfishness which moralists have so bitterly condemned, or it is, even if labeled bliss, an insipid tedium, a millenium of ease in relief from all struggle and labor. It could satisfy only the most delicate of mollycoddles. Happiness is found only in success; but success means succeeding, getting forward, moving in advance." (p. 179).

The psychological foundations of Dewey's ethical theory are to be found in his *Human Nature and Conduct* (1922). The theory itself is most formally worked out in the middle part of Dewey and Tufts's *Ethics* (revised edition, 1932). The picture presented is that of man as a plastic being with practically no specifically determinate instincts. The latter constitute at most pivots for reorganization of habits and institutions when these are overly frustrating. The individual, fashioned by social and cultural forces upon which he in turn reacts, finds himself in a continual stream of problem situations. These situations are already structured physically and socially, and include the claims of others that arise naturally and press upon the individual. Ends-in-view are goals set up to resolve a situation and to release impulse; they are, says Dewey, like targets a man sets up to shoot at. The criteria for their evaluation are thus inherent in the situations, and to articulate them is, in effect, to provide a method for resolving problems.

The conceptual counterpart of ends is the *good*. The interlocking claims of a group are organized under the idea of *right,* but their content is judged by the degree to which they further the goods of individual human beings constituting the group. *Standards* are the bases of criticism and approbation. In terms of the interaction of these ethical elements — always *in mediis rebus*—an interpretation is given to the customary equipment and problems of ethical theory. Thus egoism, so far from constituting a purely theoretical issue, emerges as the problem of special character to be refashioned. Freedom, instead of being an inherent spiritual endowment, becomes a mark of well-integrated and intelligent choice. Responsibility is prospective rather than retrospective, exercised on beings capable of change and molding under added incentives.

Dewey's analyses of all these elements in ethical theory converge on a methodological emphasis, an exaltation of scientific method as intelligence. The ends or goods are always in flux and to be constantly evaluated. There are no fixed ends, and the distinction between means and ends is merely a relative one. Moral rules are always tools of analysis for individual situations, never even scientific results to be automatically applied. Standards turn out to comprise the character-traits requisite for intelligent action (for example, whole-heartedness, sympathy, impartiality); any more specific virtues themselves require constant evaluation. Intelligence thus joins expansive process as a dominant value in Dewey's ethics. It is enshrined by Dewey's whole philosophy which gives a primacy to method over results.

The theoretical consequences of this valuation are clearest in Dewey's own *Theory of Valuation*.[6] Here he formulates the problem as a search for unique valuation-propositions, and equates them with *appraisal* propositions in which things are appraised as serviceable means. Mere assertions of liking or enjoyment are rejected as candidates, largely on the psychological theory that if these notions be taken seriously as involving expenditure of energy, even *prizing* carries one into consideration of conditions and consequences: "valuations in the sense of prizing and caring for occur only when it is necessary to bring something into existence which is lacking, or to conserve in existence something which is menaced by outward conditions . . ."[7] Dewey is thus deliberately opposing the separation of ends (prizing) from means (appraising), whether ends be construed in the older fashion of fixed natural forms or the more recent fashion of simple likings and dislikings or emotional expressions. The upshot of identifying valuation-propositions as appraisals is the unrestricted applicability of scientific intelligence to so-called ends as well as to merely techncal means.

Opponents of Dewey's conception can, however, easily reverse his argument. If I appraise the end E1 (having a car to ride around in) by the means M (overtime work to earn the money required) and the consequences C (cost of upkeep, diversion of attention from other activities), can I not be said more justly to be balancing various goods implied in M and C (leisure, other goals attainable for same expenditure and attention) against the goods of using a car? Why not then describe the ethical process as ultimately one of direct preference among ends?[8] Decision between these opposing conceptions of the ethical process may rest on the adequacy of their respective psychological assumptions. But there is obviously also a clash of value-attitudes involved. Dewey is not simply analyzing a process but also imparting to it a character dictated by his

---

6. In *International Encyclopedia of Unified Science,* Vol. II, No. 4 (1939).
7. *Theory of Valuation,* p. 14.
8. C. I. Lewis's account of prizing and the immediately valuable in his *An Analysis of Knowledge and Valuation,* chap. xiii, is a good illustration of an analysis at the opposite pole from Dewey's. See below, part III.

own dominant values — expansive process and universal applicability of scientific intelligence.

These values also stand out in Dewey's application of his outlook to educational and social theory. His writings on education, so widely known and influential, gave an impetus to progressive methods by centering on the individual child and the process of growth. His social theory has been guided by the view that "The general adoption of the scientific attitude in human affairs would mean nothing less than a revolutionary change in morals, religion, politics, and industry." [9] He has therefore fought against those who deny the need for change, and, increasingly in recent years, against the Marxians who affirm the class struggle. The latter he equates with the denial of the use of freed intelligence, on the assumption that "the only alternatives to dependence upon intelligence are either drift and casual improvisation, or the use of force stimulated by unintelligent emotion and fanatical dogmatism..." [10] Why these are the only alternatives is not clear, especially as Dewey recognizes that conservatives need not advocate the use of force but just employ it since it is built into the procedures of existing society. The role which he assigns to liberalism, with its ideas of liberty, individuality, and freed intelligence is that of mediation and adjustment in social transition. But he by-passes the question whether intelligence will be powerful enough in fact or have sufficient support to mediate present social transitions. Since Dewey himself takes a socialized economy to be the means of free individual development, this question of fact ought to have a central place. His issue with the Marxists is clearly the empirical one whether fundamental social transitions mediated by intelligence are possible and under what conditions organization capable of exercising force is required. By regarding his opponent as advocating violence as a substitute for intelligence, not as its support against existent or threatened coercion, Dewey is constantly grappling with a man of straw. When he faces the problem of fact his answer is simply a hope or faith: "I for one do not believe that Americans living in the tradition of Jefferson and Lincoln will weaken and give up without a whole-hearted effort to make democracy a living reality. This, I repeat, involves organization." [11]

A more basic attitude underlying Dewey's conviction is perhaps to be found in the wider role that he gives intelligence in human history. He regards the rise of scientific method and the technology based upon it as

---

9. *Individualism Old and New* (1930), p. 155.
10. *Liberalism and Social Action* (1935), p. 51.
11. *Ibid.*, p. 92.

the genuinely active force in bringing about social change, and interprets technology as organized intelligence in action.[12] Apparently, then, it is the march of organized intelligence on earth that lies at the base of Dewey's confidence in the continued efficacy of liberalism. Whether the outlook stems from an early Hegelianism with Reason or Social Mind naturalized as intelligence embedded in technology, or whether it more directly reflects the confidence of an expanding industrial society, may be left to historians of Dewey's thought to determine in detail. But the outlook has enabled him to avoid facing the problem of ultimate conflict in values as well as that of social conflict. And it has had the unfortunate effect on the philosophical scene that a generation faced with this as a central problem has taken Dewey's failure to meet the issue to be equivalent to the failure of a rational or scientific approach to ethical theory.

II

Beginning in the twenties and swelling into a chorus in the thirties is the movement of ethical theory that I have characterized as *arbitrary relativism*. It saw more or less clearly that the kind of optimistic expansive outlook which took for granted a democratic equalitarianism represented a *set of values* not a necessary or inherent character of ethical theory. It learned the lesson from the rise of Nazism, if it had not before, that the various ethical theories constituted, in effect, moral outlooks from one or another perspective. Nietzsche had proclaimed this as his discovery; Marx and Engels previously had argued that ethical theories expressed class values. The failure of basic agreement sufficient to preserve the peace both between and within societies seemed to spell the failure of a reasonable or scientific ethic which gave one answer for all men.

Numerous theoretical influences played into the stream. The ethical realism of men like G. E. Moore, with its sharp separation of value and fact, the positivist treatment of ethical judgments as simply expression of emotion, behaviorist psychology with the lesson that a man's values are conditioned, comparative ethnology with its portrayal of alternative values culturally standardized—all had their effect in American thought.

Arbitrary relativism had a multiple potential in actual feeling. On the one hand it tended to trivialize values—put them all on a par with matters of taste. To prefer Nazi values to democratic values was like preferring port to sherry. On the other hand, the very element of ar-

---

12. *Ibid.*, pp. 73-74, 81-82.

bitrariness showed the possibility of ultimate conflict, and a man thus realized he might have to fight for his ways even though the best he could say for them were that they were his.

The periodical literature of the thirties in America reflects concern with the relativistic base of morality. For example, in the very year that Hitler took power in Germany (after three years of depression in America), two attempts were even made to *found* morality on the fact of arbitrary choice. The titles almost tell the story: "The Arbitrary as Basis for Rational Morality" by Charner M. Perry [13] and "Ethics as Pure Postulate" by Donald C. Williams. [14] "Morality," says Charner Perry, *"has as its basis, in other words, an arbitrary, underived commitment to certain of the possible guiding principles and purposes.* Faced with an assortment of a number of possible selves, one must make a choice." [15] Williams likewise underscored the act of subscription or pure postulation at the base of judgments of the good, and the futility of looking endlessly for reasons: "the realm of values is characterized by encounters between ultimate sets of postulates, of resolves, or of will-attitudes." [16] And of the ultimate acts, he says: "It may be that at this blank last moment there is no room for the operation of anything but blind causes or blind caprice, so that the ethical philosopher can only watch the happening of these fiats, as the scientist watches the happening of eclipses or cyclones, and can chronicle and classify them with natural piety. On the other hand, it is conceivable that this moment provides for the exercise of some strange and unanalyzable creativity, and that the ethical philosopher can claim for himself the duty of presiding at the choice which creates." [17]

Both Williams and Charner Perry seek to build morality on this ultimate arbitrariness. Williams points to existing community of postulates given homogeneity of culture, and to methods of persuasion; Perry relies on compromise and the historical background of the ideals and principles embodied in the group, regarding tradition and precedent as "the ultimate source of moral premises in social discussion and the court of final appeal in the determination of rights, duties, and obligations."

The basic points in such analyses—that any chain of arguments rests on premises, that without specifically value premises there can be no value conclusions (i.e., complete value impartiality makes value decision impossible)—seem clear enough simply as questions of logic. Why were

13. *International Journal of Ethics*, Vol. XLIII, No. 2 (Jan., 1933).
14. *Philosophical Review*, Vol. XLVII, No. 4 (July, 1933).
15. C. Perry, *op. cit.*, p. 138.
16. Williams, *op. cit.*, p. 402.
17. *Ibid.*, pp. 410-411.

they so exciting? Why did they seem to overthrow the hopes of traditional morality? The tone with which they were, and have since then
been advocated is very much like that with which Hume approached the
subjectivization of necessity. Were they suggesting that the demands of
traditional ethics were *logically* impossible? Or did the assertion and
acceptance of the arbitrary as the basis of morals carry the emotional tone
of the battles that were shaping up all over the globe?

One might have hoped that, attention being fastened on the act of
commitment, there would follow careful psychological analysis of the
act itself, as a basis for a more scientific ethics. But nothing of the sort
happened on the philosophical scene. Naturalistic ethical analyses continued to draw their inspiration from the procedure of scientific *method*
rather than the scope of scientific *results*. In the later thirties ethical inquiry increasingly turned to problems of language and the form of expression, and naturalistic ethical theory threatened to become a branch of
applied semantics. The direct stimulus for this came from the positivistic
analyses of both the Cambridge and Vienna schools. The earlier positivist view that cognitive propositions about the world were in principle
translatable into sensation statements left ethical judgments no alternative but to be *expressive*. A. J. Ayer's *Language, Truth, and Logic* (1936),
and R. Carnap's *Philosophy and Logical Syntax* (1935), gave classical
formulations of this view.[18] Perhaps the most systematized development
of this trend in America is found in the writing of Charles L. Stevenson.

Stevenson's views went through a significant transition. In an earlier
article entitled, "The Emotive Meaning of Ethical Terms,"[19] he offered
a dominantly emotive interpretation. He stipulated that the "vital"
sense of "good" must be such that we are able sensibly to disagree about
whether something is good, that a person recognizing something to be
good must acquire a stronger tendency to act in its favor than he otherwise would have had, and that the goodness of anything must not be
verifiable only by the use of scientific method, lest ethics be simply psychology. The major use of ethical judgment was taken to be "not to
indicate facts, but to *create an influence*. Instead of merely describing
people's interests, they *change* or *intensify* them. They *recommend* an
interest in an object, rather than state the interest that already exists."[20]
Ethical terms are thus used less to communicate beliefs than to give vent
to feelings and incite other people.

---

18. Ayer, pp. 149-170; Carnap, pp. 22-26.
19. *Mind*, New Series Vol. XLVI (1937), pp. 14-31.
20. *Ibid.*, pp. 18-19.

In his book, *Ethics and Language* (1944), Stevenson moved somewhat away from a purely emotive theory. A fundamental ethical judgment such as "This is good" was given both a descriptive and an expressive function. A rough model interpreting such a judgment is "I approve of this; do so as well." Ethical disagreement arises in virtue of the emotive part, involving contrary mutual influence or incitement. The descriptive element depicts subjective attitude held by the speaker. In the sections of the book devoted primarily to language, Stevenson formulated emotive meaning as one type of psychological or pragmatic meaning. His critics [21] have urged that the emotive element is external to the content of the ethical judgment, just as the attitude of the scientist (hope, confidence, conviction) is external to the content of his scientific judgment. But Stevenson is bound by the three premises of his earlier article, especially that ethics should not become directly scientific. The farthest he goes is to allow that, even apart from the use of scientific method in dealing with means, disagreement in attitude is to some extent *rooted* in disagreement in belief, in the sense that the former can sometimes be reconciled by reconciling the latter. But he denies that this is universtally so, and the contingency of disagreement in attitude keeps its ultimate place. At the same time he examines with great care the types of relations of means and ends (chap. viii), showing, against the traditional view that agreement on ends is primary, that one can have ample agreement on action without agreement on ends.

Stevenson formulates clearly what he calls the "persuasive" role of many definitions of ethical terms, thus recognizing that central valuations are imported into the initial definitions in theories such as those of Perry and Dewey. But he fails to recognize that even where he thinks he is engaging in "neutral analysis" he is doing the same thing. His initial models, for example, set the ethical scene as one in which individuals with identifying attitudes which may or may not agree seek to influence one another. Hence this initial contingency limits the applicability of scientific method. Dewey sets the scene by identifying valuation propositions as appraisal propositions so as to give unrestricted scope to scientific method. Charner Perry, in the article cited above,[22] in spite of his insistence on the arbitrary as basic, declared that when there was failure of basis for agreement there could be only force or passive resistance, but that might did not make right. This implies a definition of the ethical situation as one in

---

21. See especially Henry D. Aiken's review in *The Journal of Philosophy*, Vol. XLII, No. 17, pp. 455-470 (Aug. 16, 1945); also, John Dewey, "Ethical Subject Matter and Language," *The Journal of Philosophy* 42,26:701-718 (Dec. 20, 1945).
22. Charner Perry, *op. cit.*, p. 143.

which people sharing some values seek to determine others. Now all these different settings of the scene for ethical inquiry are in the same boat as far as expressing values or being "persuasive" is concerned. Max Black suggests such a point in a recent paper, in commenting on Stevenson's analysis: [23] "A way of speaking about 'emotive meaning' which focuses attention upon the irrational aspects of ethical communication, and leaves ethical issues to be resolved by the interplay of generated emotive influence seems not merely inconvenient but almost mischievous. A reversal of emphasis, made possible by a fuller recognition of the informative aspect of utterances, however charged with feeling, may encourage some, perhaps, to search further for a basis of *rational* agreement on ethical questions."

This criticism, strong as it is, still ties the question to problems of analysis of language. Stevenson's answer [24] seems to conclude that the fundamental questions here are not linguistic: "My methodological conclusions center less on my conception of meaning than on my conceptions of agreement and disagreement. If the solution of normative issues requires agreement in attitude, if the relation between attitudes and beliefs is causal and possibly subject to individual differences, and if rational methods can effect agreement in attitude only through the indirect means of altering beliefs, then the essential features of my analysis remain intact." All these essential features are, however, clearly propositions about human psychology, not conclusions of a specialized discipline of analysis. Whether they constitute a sound basis for an ethical methodology would seem to rest less on the study of the use of language than on the *results* of the human sciences. In the long run it is possible that the whole ethical formulation of arbitrary relativism may stand out as primarily a value-expression — the extreme form of the traditional ideal of liberal individualism, that all obligation has its source solely in the will-acts of isolated individuals acting upon one another.

If all fundamental ethical formulations already embody valuations, and if the valuations of arbitrary relativism bear the mark of the world problems of the last two decades, we can see in turn that the conflicts of World War II, the genuine jeopardy of human survival in another war, the mass killings of Nazi brutality, have all added their weight to the demand for a common-human ethic and a wider role for rationality. If American naturalism learned during its arbitrary relativist phase that

---

23. "A Symposium on Emotive Meaning," *The Philosophical Review* (March, 1948), p. 126.
24. *Ibid.,* p. 142.

expansiveness is a value, not a natural law or an ethical fact, that harmony and equality are something to be fought for and achieved rather than an inherent order of morality, that there is a contingent existential basis to human life and feeling, it can now look more realistically for the degree of actual community of interest in mankind, psychologically and historically. And it need no longer equate the picture of human nature obtained by individual introspection into feelings and attitudes under special social and cultural conditions with the inevitable structure of human nature.

III

In the current American scene, C. I. Lewis has attempted to avoid both transcendentalism and skepticism by seeing valuations as a type of empirical cognition. Prizings and disprizings refer ultimately to a quality of the presently given: "the only thing intrinsically valuable — valuable for its own sake — is a goodness immediately found or findable and unmistakable when disclosed; all values of any other sort, including all values attributable to objects, are extrinsic, and valued for the sake of their possible contribution to such realizations of the immediately good." [25] Lewis does not regard this as subjectivism, since any inquiry about valuations is "directed upon facts as obdurate and compelling as those which must determine the correctness of any other kind of knowledge." [26]

On such a basis, Lewis builds up the concept of a life good on the whole, which "can be contemplated only by some imaginative or synthetic envisagement of its on-the-whole quality." [27] This is used as the criterion for evaluation of experienced values, and is also involved in the fundamental ethical imperative which is final and universal: "Be consistent, in valuation and in thought and action"; "Be concerned about yourself in future and on the whole." [28] And he adds: "It requires no reason; being itself the expression of that which is the root of all reason; that in the absence of which there could be no reason of any sort or for anything." This imperative rules the realm of obligation and makes it fundamentally different from that of value.

The status of this imperative is not clear. Lewis has first insisted that "To repudiate normative significances and imperatives in general, would

---

25. *An Analysis of Knowledge and Valuation*, Paul Carus Lectures 1945 (published 1946), p. 397.
26. *Ibid.*, p. 407; cf., p. 458 f.
27. *Ibid.* p. 483.
28. *Ibid.*, p. 481.

be to dissolve away all seriousness of action and intent, leaving only an undirected floating down the stream of time." [29] To repudiate concern for any future is to contradict oneself, *not logically but pragmatically,* since anyone following this as a maxim would be taking himself seriously. The fundamental imperative seems therefore to be analytic of the desire for serious action. But Lewis refuses to regard man's acceptance of serious action in the form of a rational end or ideal of the good life as a psychological datum, although his discussion of it suggests it has a psychological basis. [30] If this is the case, and if the argument is not resting on a Kantian nonnaturalistic ethical assumption, the imperative can only be taken to express the content of a fundamental value. But if this is so, alternative values are possible subjects for election, and the question is whether *in fact* men do elect them under special or typical human conditions and find value in their election. [31] Yet Lewis does not touch this question, and instead concludes the book with the view that "value-determinations are not sufficient by themselves for any solution of ethical problems, in general or in particular." [32] Thus the empirical approach proclaimed for values in order to achieve objectivity is denied to ethics at the crucial point.

The outcome of the criticism of Lewis here suggested is therefore the same as that offered of Stevenson above. The question of the role of science in ethics is not advanced much by setting up a language or formulating concepts for ethical inquiry in such a way as to make a common-human ethic either utterly contingent by definition or necessary by definition. If such questions are to be answerable, they will have to be formulated as empirical, not merely logical or methodological problems; consequently the answer one way or another will come from the *results* of the biological, psychological, social, and historical sciences.

This search for bases for a common-human ethic characterizes many scientists in America today, in all these fields. It is not a unified enterprise, but the materials available for it on many fronts merit the most serious philosophical attention. On the whole, they seem to me to be advancing the enterprise along five main (somewhat overlapping) directions: 1. They carry out the search for agreed-on or common values and

---

29. *Ibid.,* p. 481.
30. *Ibid.,* pp. 483-84.
31. Lewis simply refuses to argue with an alternative, e.g., Bentham's principle of propinquity or remoteness, which Lewis interprets as that we should be less concerned about the future according as it is more remote, apart from the question of probabilities of occurrences (p. 493).
32. *Ibid.,* p. 554.

explore their implications. 2. They restore objectivity to the value phenomenon by exhibiting it as a proper object of scientific inquiry, thus helping remove all metaphysical imputations of subjectivity. 3. They develop concepts and techniques which may make it possible to criticize preferences of an individual, no matter how strongly held by him on introspection. 4. They point toward an empirical interpretation of happiness. 5. They relate values to social and historical contexts of human life. Such directions of inquiry do not predetermine the actuality of a common-human ethic, but they make possible progress toward the solution of the question.

Biologists generally start with the admitted value of survival and group perpetuation. This sometimes gives them a social perspective at the outset; often, however, this has been balanced by the older assumptions of trans-group conflict in the predatory interpretations of evolutionary development. Perhaps the major effort of American biological writing on ethics has gone into offering evidence for the right to take a naturalistic rather than a supernaturalistic approach to human life and conduct, and thus for relating rather than separating value and fact. Sometimes the attempt is made to put the weight of a long development behind a pattern of life. As one biologist expressed it, in discussing perfection: "if certain clear trends be recognizable in the whole course of evolution, certain colored threads which can be traced through the patterned tapestry of life history, then those individuals are the most perfect of their kind which are furthest in the indicated direction. Here, then, would be a criterion for good and bad, better or worse, which is not absolute or normative but which has the total weight of the living past behind it."[33] The attempt has also been made, especially in the light of problems of war and social conflict, to provide a biological basis for a harmony ethics. Thus Chauncey D. Leake states as an operative natural principle that "The probability of survival of a relationship between individual humans or groups of humans increases with the extent to which that relationship is mutually satisfying."[34] Such formulations are still insufficiently precise. One cannot be sure that there is an independent scientific test for satisfaction, apart from survival, nor that the principle will do more than give biological sanction to relationships that in fact are perpetuated. Leake recognized the possibility that the harmony ethics as he interprets it may lead to a

---

33. R. W. Gerard, "A Biological Basis for Ethics," *Philosophy of Science*, Vol. IX (1942), p. 105.
34. "Ethicogenesis," The Philosophical Society of Texas, Proceedings 1944 (published 1945), p. 31.

status quo, but relies on the expectation that human beings are not likely to be satisfied indefinitely under any circumstances.[35]

Biological contributions to naturalistic ethics are likely to gain in importance because of the central role of survival in contemporary problems of possible atomic war. In developing biological bases for ethics, however, care should be taken not to repeat the old errors of simple equation of value with developing pattern, of ignoring the possibility of novel qualitative change, or of attempting to derive an ethics from the materials of biology alone.

Psychologists likewise have turned self-consciously to the ethical problems of our time, and contributions have been offered by a variety of schools.

The Gestalt school has concentrated on restoring objectivity to the value phenomenon. Wolfgang Köhler, for example, in *The Place of Value in a World of Facts* (1938), elaborates the concept of "requiredness" as a qualitative feature of the phenomenological field in value situations. The Gestalt hope is that careful study of the field may do for values the same kind of job that was so successfully carried out for perception. And it is no doubt that the case that such inquiries have challenged the traditional relativist assumption that for any given structure of phenomenological field opposing values may in fact be found to adhere to it. But even if it should prove that there is no internal relativity in the field, there still remain problems of changes within the field over time, control over changes, different fields for different persons, bases of comparative evaluation, and so forth. Up to the present, the results of Gestalt inquiry seem to me to alter the form, not the substance of the relativity that is attacked.

In several psychological approaches today we find formulations which transcend the limits imposed by arbitrary relativism. The latter starts and stops with the individual's preferences: if the opponent in an ethical disagreement does not feel himself convinced that he is wrong, it is meaningless to declare him wrong, and no scientific investigation could possibly show him to be wrong. The psychological formulations here referred to attempt to develop a mode of criticism applicable in such cases, through a theory of human nature and personality development. The trend is the same both where it appears in behaviorist schools, applying the lessons of animal psychology, and in psychiatric and psychoanalytic schools. Its essence is to develop empirical criteria for evaluating preferences to see

---

35. *Ibid.,* p. 34.

whether they express "genuine" aims or are some type of frustration response.

Edward C. Tolman makes such an attempt in his "Motivation, Learning and Adjustment." [36] His general psychological framework is one of drives, biological and social; the individual is driven to seek satiation and avoid sufferance, and these states have intrinsic value and disvalue. In reacting to obstacles and difficulties, frustration mechanisms are employed, such as fixation, phantasy, suppression, and regression. Behavior which is of such character does not represent the individual's true values.

While this appartus, if successful, gives some meaning to the idea of a scientific ethics, its consideration is apparently limited to the individual's satisfaction of needs, and leaves open the question of one man's or group's complete satisfaction of needs at another's expense. In his *Drives Toward War* (1942), Tolman does offer the hypothesis that "only when man's total psychology is understood and all his absolutely necessary psychological needs are allowed balanced satisfaction will a society permitting relatively universal individual happiness and welfare be achieved and war abolished." [37] But it is not clear how the transition from individual to group, and group to world can be achieved purely in the terms of individual psychology. The same problem emerges as central in Stephen C. Pepper's *A Digest of Purposive Values* (1947), which develops Tolman's scheme into a general basis for value theory. Pepper is compelled to make a sharp contrast between individualistic and group-survival ethics. These are not unified, but left in separate contexts, survival ethics taking over only where individualistic ethics fails.

There is, of course, no guarantee in the mere use of such psychological concepts that the result will be a basis for a *common-human* ethic. *A priori,* aggression against one's fellowmen might turn out to be a basic drive. Tolman's thesis is that it is a frustration mechanism. This is an increasingly widely-held thesis among psychologists. For example, Gordon W. Allport states it in its full international implications: [38] "When President Roosevelt enunciated the Four Freedoms he was speaking of certain common intentions of the human race. An important feature of his historic formulation lies in his assumption that *all* men, in *all* cultures, intend (that is, long for) freedom from want, freedom from fear, freedom of speech and of worship. Note how this assumption contrasts with the

---

36. Proceedings of the American Philosophical Society, Vol. LXXXIV, No. 4 (June, 1941).
37. P. 5.
38. "Scientific Models and Human Morals," *Psychological Review,* Vol. LIV, No. 4 (July, 1947), p. 188.

prevailing creed of modern social science. Cultural relativity, really a doctrine of stimulus-expectancy, has laid such a heavy hand upon us that we have overlooked the possibility of universal intentions. Yet unless Roosevelt's bold assumption is found justified, we can scarcely hope to find a psychological basis for effective world organization."

Allport believes "the ruthless pursuit of personal and national power to be a result of the frustration of basically affiliative intentions." He lists "security, affection, and an affiliative and comprehending relation to the surounding world" as wants of the child, and conceivably also of most adults.

The most important bases for such ethical conclusions on psychological grounds are to be found in psychoanalytic theory, with its well-defined picture of human nature and personality development. Erich Fromm's recent *Man For Himself* (1947) is a serious attempt to trace the ethical implications of psychoanalytic theory. It supports the view that aggression is fundamentally frustration reaction, [39] and takes initial steps toward an empirical identification of happiness by distinguishing in such human feelings and relations as love, loyalty, etc., those forms which are productive from those pseudoforms which express anxiety dependence.

Among the social sciences, anthropology has increasingly contributed materials for ethical analysis. In the thirties, in opposition to racist claims of inherent superiority, it stressed the diversity of culture patterns and the cultural basis of value acts. While this reenforced the dominant ethical relativism, it also carried the general historical lesson that there are similar needs and problems which all peoples have faced, expressed, and solved in different ways. Today there is some tendency in anthropological writings to seek bases for cross-cultural evaluation. For example, Ruth Benedict, whose *Patterns of Culture* (1934) conveyed the earlier lessons of cultural diversity and the need for tolerance, more recently sought to find at least negative criteria of mental health in judgments across cultural lines. [40] How self-confident such criticism has already become in anthropological analysis may be seen from the following conclusion of a field study in one group of American Indians: "The picture of Dakota child personality which emerges from the tests is one of weakness of natural drives and spontaneity resulting from repressive forces set in action early in the

---

39. As against Karl A. Menninger's *Man Against Himself* (1938). Menninger holds to the Freudian view of the death instinct. His impressive marshalling of data can logically, so far as I can see, fit either view.
40. "Some Comparative Data on Culture and Personality with Reference to the Promotion of Mental Health," publication No. 9 of The American Association for the Advancement of Science, pp. 245-249.

child's life. This paucity of impulse and emotion appears to blight the creativity, imagination, and fantasy that are normal in a healthy mental life and to prohibit wholesome relationships with other people. Dakota child personality seems crippled and negative, as if it rejected life. The unfriendly environment, which offers so little opportunity or satisfaction, retards the growth of personality, and prevents it from becoming positive, rich, and mature. Life is lived on the defensive." [41]

Among historical schools, Marxian materialism has long attempted to ground ethical theory in socio-historical context so as to offer a basis for comparative evaluation. In recent American ethics, Howard Selsam has expounded this point of view in his *Socialism and Ethics* (1943). The Marxian analysis of history as the growth of freedom, in the sense of collective knowledge and control aiming at the satisfaction of basic human needs for all mankind, provides a measure for the aims and activities of succeeding classes; for it sees such aims as implicit in human striving even where actual conduct represents the social analogue of frustration mechanisms. Since aims are set in the *specific* socio-historical context of the mode of production and the economic, political and cultural relations clustering around it, there is a specific character to the criteria constituting the touchstone of progress in a given period. Hence concreteness is added to the psychological lists of general human needs. Since the present social struggle is seen as moving toward the abolition of classes, and a world of increasing material abundance as the forces of production are fully unleashed, the ethics of the proletariat is seen as representing and growing into an all-human ethic in an increasingly unified globe.

In this survey of bases for a common-human ethic that have been offered in various scientific and historical analyses, I have presented the ethical implications for the most part without special evaluation or critique. To carry this out would be a long and detailed task, here clearly out of place. But enough has been said, I hope, to indicate that the actual *results* of scientific investigations do have a bearing on the formulation of and answer to ethical questions; that a common-human ethic, so much demanded today, cannot be created or destroyed by logical fiat or methodological analysis alone; that the mere fact that value conclusions require value premises shows simply that ethical inquiry begins and revolves in the middle of things, but does not reveal what is to be the complexion of things.

---

41. *Warriors Without Weapons,* A Study of the Society and Personality Development of the Pine Ridge Sioux, by Gordon Macgregor, with the collaboration of Royal B. Hassrick and Wm. E. Henry (University of Chicago Press, 1946), p. 209.

Although twentieth century American naturalistic ethics has remained in line with the major modern movement of secularization of human life and value, and although it has kept fairly close to the ground, it has not self-consciously geared itself to serve the needs of men in time and place. It has tended rather to look upon itself as discovering ethical *truth,* or as performing *the correct analysis* of ethical ideas. And, of course, insofar as an ethical theory carries an implicit picture of human nature, it is resting on scientific propositions whose truth and scope determine in part the theory's adequacy; and insofar as an ethical theory presents a conceptual network for doing a specified job, one analysis may be more refined and systematic than another. But the suggestion I have made over and above these, in tracing some developments of the past half century, is that in its very inner texture as theory, naturalistic ethics has reflected the development of human needs and problems; and that therefore by becoming more self-conscious it can do more thoroughly the job it has been doing in a partial way. This thesis has been illustrated above rather even than argued, much less demonstrated. But if it is true, naturalistic ethics would do well to take present-day fundamental global needs — peace, increased world productivity, concrete freedom for the submerged masses of the world — and use them as actual bases for the selection of theoretical ethical formulations. And if to this it adds constant attentiveness to the results of the sciences as well as logical refinement, the resulting theory may remain metaphysically relative or arbitrary, but its selection over its opposite will be as arbitrary as the choice of health over sickness, realistic appraisal over neurotic anxiety, life over death. In this sense, perhaps, Perry saw far ahead when he made morality "simply the forced choice between suicide and abundant life."

SELECTED BIBLIOGRAPHY

Dewey, John, and Tufts, James H. *Ethics (revised edition), Part II.* New York, Henry Holt and Co., 1932.

Dewey, John. *Human Nature and Conduct.* New York, Henry Holt and Co., 1922.

——————. "Theory of Valuation," *International Encyclopedia of Unified Science,* Vol. II, No. 4., University of Chicago Press, 1939.

Edel, Abraham. "Coordinates of Criticism in Ethical Theory," *Philosophy and Phenomenological Research,* Vol. VII, No. 4, June, 1947, pp. 543-577.

Fromm, Erich. *Man For Himself, An Inquiry into the Psychology of Ethics.* New York, Rinehart and Co., Inc., 1947.

Köhler, Wolfgang. *The Place of Value in a World of Facts.* New York, Liveright Publishing Corp., 1938.

Lepley, Ray. *Verifiability of Value.* New York, Columbia University Press, 1944.

Lewis, Clarence Irving. *An Analysis of Knowledge and Valuation*, Book III. La Salle, Ill., Open Court Publishing Co., 1946.

Pepper, Stephen C. *A Digest of Purposive Values.* Berkeley, University of California Press, 1947.

Perry, Charner M. "The Arbitrary as Basis for Rational Morality," *International Journal of Ethics,* Vol. XLIII, January, 1933, No. 2.

Perry, Ralph Barton. *The Moral Economy.* New York, Charles Scribner's Sons, 1909.

——————. *General Theory of Value.* New York, Longmans, Green and Co., 1926.

Santayana, George. *The Life of Reason.* New York, Charles Scribner's Sons, 1905-6.

Selsam, Howard. *Socialism and Ethics.* New York, International Publishers, 1943.

Stevenson, Charles L. *Ethics and Language.* New Haven, Yale University Press, 1944.

Williams, Donald C. "Ethics as Pure Postulate," *Philosophical Review,* Vol. XLVII, July, 1933, No. 4, pp. 399-411.

MATERIAL POSSESSIONS
AND THOMISTIC ETHICS

*Vernon J. Bourke**

Thomistic philosophy in America still lags behind European Thomism. This is less evident in speculative thinking than in the approach to practical problems. Significant contributions have been made by American scholars, in the area of Thomistic epistemology, psychology, and metaphysics. With the recent development of several centers of research in medieval studies, both in the United States and Canada, the history of St. Thomas's thought is now being studied in a scholarly manner on this side of the Atlantic. However, though America is probably regarded in many other parts of the world as the home of a practical-minded people, it can hardly be claimed that much work has been done by American Thomists on the problems of ethical, social, or political philosophy. That is not to say that there is a lack of interest in these questions, or that the work already done is of negligible value.

The fact is that American Thomism is a comparatively young movement. Many of its leading writers and teachers are European scholars who, perhaps, hesitate to handle questions of practical import because they necessarily require a background of familiarity with American customs and circumstances of life, difficult for a newcomer to acquire. There is also, no doubt, a certain unwillingness to become involved in controversies of a practical character, because of the danger that any criticism of existing conditions or practices may be misunderstood. It is far easier to be daring and critical in the speculative order than in the practical. There is a tendency of the general reading public to regard any new or different type of thought, if it be practical, as an attack upon the established order of things. Yet, it is the function of the philosopher to criticize

* Born in 1907. Ph.D., Pontifical Institute of Mediaeval Studies, University of Toronto, Professor of philosophy, St. Louis University. President of the American Catholic Association of Philosophy, 1948; member of the American Mediaeval Academy and of the American Philosophical Society. Associate editor of *The Modern Schoolman*. Author of *Augustine's Quest of Wisdom, Thomistic Bibliography* (1920-1940), *Syllabus on Ethical Problems*, and *Saint Thomas and the Greek Moralists*.

life, and to suggest better ways of living. *Sapientis est ordinare,* must apply to more than theoretical problems.

For this reason, and because of its intrinsic interest, the topic for this paper has been chosen from the field of practical philosophy.

THE PROBLEM OF MATERIAL POSSESSIONS

Consider a group of men and women shipwrecked on a previously uninhabited island. Suppose the island affords food, materials from which clothing may be made, locations suitable for shelter. What would be the best way for these people to arrange for the distribution and use of these things?

Suppose one of these people were to find the only source of good drinking water on the island. What are his rights in regard to this spring? What are the rights of the whole group to the use of this water?

This imaginary example intentionally simplifies the problem. Such simplification has some advantages. We may consider ourselves as emotionally disinterested spectators, judging the claims and conduct of the islanders from the point of view of what is right and best. Reasonably to make such judgments, we must already be in possession of some standards of moral value. We must have formed some views on human life and what is generally good for man. To say, for instance, that the discoverer of the spring is entitled to keep all the water in his possession and exclude the others from its use, if he is strong enough to enforce his claim, is not an initial moral judgment. This conclusion implies a previous general position, either consciously or unconsciously adopted. Such a judgment may be based on the notion that "might is right," or that "possession is nine-tenths of the law," or some other prior principle. Even to say that our problem might be solved by depending on the moral instincts, or feelings, of a normal person placed in these conditions, is to presuppose a general theory of moral judgment which has been already adopted. To take such a general theory as given, as not open for examination, is not to proceed in a philosophical manner. One might start with the law-as-given, or with a certain religious faith-as-given, or with the assertion of what "science teaches" as something-given, or with some other absolute initial position. The point is that every attempt to face a particular moral problem, even a pragmatic approach which professes to do without absolute standards, does imply some initial point of view which is adopted, with full awareness in some cases, with sub-rational faith in others. The conclusions reached from such a point of view are only as good as the starting point permits.

To postulate our starting point and promise to verify this initial position from the conclusions which we reach as we go along, is not to avoid this difficulty. Many sets of moral postulates may be adopted which can be logically related to practical conclusions, after the conclusions have been made. If, at any point in the process, we endeavor to give more than logical validity to such postulates, we must revert to some absolutely given position on which our demonstration will depend. If we deny this, we have adopted the absolute view that logic, with sufficiently consistent development, becomes a philosophy of real and moral value. This is, then, to adopt a general theory of value, a meta-morality.

The moral philosopher should be conscious, then, of what he takes as his general interpretation of what is good for man in his life. Thomistic ethics has such a position in that initial part of its development which is usually called general ethics, or ethical theory. It takes some time to present such a theory of moral values. That is not possible in a brief paper. For that reason, some references are given in the appended bibliography to books which explain the general theory of Thomistic morality. What we can do here is to summarize this theory. Obviously, the truly philosophic part of such a position is omitted in summary. What we are doing is something like giving the gist of Euclid's theorems, without the reasoning which accompanies and justifies them geometrically.

THE THEORETICAL BASIS OF THOMISTIC ETHICS

What is taken as a starting point, in Thomistic ethics, is a certain metaphysical interpretation of the human being in his concrete setting, in a real universe. Man is viewed as a substantial agent capable of freely choosing to do, or to refrain from doing, certain real actions. These are called human acts; they do not include all the acts of man but only those which have the quality of voluntariness. To be voluntary, an act must issue from the agent himself, be at least partially under the control of his intellect, and powered, as it were, by his own will.

Moreover, man is taken as a being having a definite kind of nature, with a definite set of functions which characterize this nature. As a species of animal, man is regarded as having a final cause, or end, which is manifested by his specific capacities. What man is best equipped to do, in comparison with other species of beings, is to think rationally. The peak of such action is not the process of discursive reasoning but the flash of understanding, the quick contemplation of truth, with which reasoning begins and finishes. It is not thought that intellectual contemplation can be achieved in any high degree of perfection, during this earthly life. Though Thomists do not pretend that the beatific vision of God in heaven is a fact demonstrable from reasoning founded on natural experience, they find some evidence in the tenth book of Aristotle's *Nicomachean Ethics* (and more clearly in the *Eudemian Ethics,* 1249b20) that a philosopher may see the possibility of the vision of a Perfect Being, as an ultimate end for man.

This does not mean that each individual man will actually attain this end. It is an end of the species, which may be attained by any member of the human species who lives in keeping with the highest potentialities of his specific powers. If we consider the end of the apple tree to be the production of apples, this does not mean that all such trees will do it. But an individual tree is good and perfect, to the extent that it does produce apples. It fails as a member of its species, to the extent that it produces imperfect, or no apples.

All of this theory is frankly teleological. The only known way to judge the goodness of a function is to determine its purpose and then decide whether it is achieving this end. We may substitute other terms and ask whether the agent is useful, whether a given action "works," whether action contributes to this or that — but the thought implied in a value judgment seems to be, overtly or covertly, teleological.

To say that man's moral end is to achieve happiness by as perfect an act of understanding as is possible, is based, of course, on an acceptance of human freedom and immortality, together with an acceptance of the existence of God as a Supreme Object of knowledge. These are Kant's postulates. They are not regarded as postulates by Thomists, but as conclusions demonstrated in speculative reasoning about the nature of reality.

The determination of the moral goodness or evil of a given human act requires more than the foregoing theory. Acts done for the sake of the ultimate end are regarded as morally good; other voluntary acts are morally bad. It is not easy to distinguish the acts which belong in either category, when we deal with the individual action. The ordinary moral agent, the non-ethician, can only be expected to do as well as the circumstances of his intellectual development permit. The ethician never tries to judge the moral value of individual human actions, and then incorporate them into his science as ultimate conclusions. It is the work of ethics to go as far as is possible in determining the value of definite types of human action. So, the ethician must discover some means of applying the theory of the end of man to less general and more practical questions. This is done in Thomistic ethics by distinguishing between those broad types of action which are always suitable to a rational agent, and those which are not. Such suitability is determined by a rational consideration of the specific capacities of man in relation to the ultimate end. Thus, the act of telling a lie (defined as: speaking in contradiction to what one thinks to be true, with the formal intention of doing so) may be judged unfitting to a human being. Notice that this can be made into a moral rule, because lying is defined in a strict sense, so as to exclude cases of conveying an untruth without actually intending to do so. It is possible to work out a set of general rules of moral behavior in this way. These are the primary principles of the natural moral law. Less universal rules, including more of the concrete circumstances of human life, can be stated. These derivative rules of the moral law have moral validity as long as the circumstances in them remain approximately the same. But such conditions may change, and so, the more removed are one's moral rules from the primary principles of moral law, the more necessary is it to know the actual circumstances surrounding the proposed action. The alteration of one important circumstance may change the reasonableness of doing, or omitting, a proposed action. So, it is not possible to plot an ideal moral life ahead of time.

A concrete decision about an individual moral problem is called the act of conscience. This decision must be made by the individual agent who has done, or proposes to do, the action. It is not an act of science but of prudence. The ethician does not perform acts of conscience for any other agents than himself. No good Thomistic ethician would venture a judgment as to whether President Truman was morally right or wrong in deciding to use the atomic bomb against the Japanese people. All that can be done, in regard to such a moral problem, is to offer a judgment of what *in general,* under given circumstances, would be right or wrong. Science, even practical science, cannot go beyond universal conclusions.

It is regrettable that the foregoing has had to be stated in a categorical manner. It may give rise to the understandable reaction, that Thomism is a dogmatism, rather than a philosophy. In one sense, it is a dogmatism. It does endeavor to reach some conclusions which are true and right. These conclusions, when formulated to the best of one's ability, are held to be true and are taught as true. Until recently, this has been the practice of the great philosophers of history. Thomism is not a dogmatism, however, in the sense that it tries to impose infrarational beliefs upon its adherents. The starting point of Thomistic philosophy is not supernatural faith but natural experience. That a man's religious beliefs influence his understanding of things is admitted. But so do his other beliefs. An atheist may, consciously or unconsciously, be just as much affected in his thinking, by his atheism, as a theist is by his theism. It is no doubt better to be conscious of such influences and to endeavor to understand one's beliefs. "Faith seeking understanding," is not an unreasonable motto.

In the context of this theory, let us now examine the moral problem of material possessions.

ST. THOMAS'S TEACHING ON THE RIGHTS, TO USE, AND TO MANAGE THINGS

This historical section of his paper is included for two reasons. There is some general misunderstanding among students of Thomism as to the precise position which St. Thomas took on this problem. Perhaps because of a strong tendency of some Catholic thinkers to defend the institution of private possessions, and also because of the well-known Catholic opposition to modern Communism, it is rather generally thought that a Thomist must defend private ownership at all costs, and must utterly reject any suggestion of communal theory in regard to possessions. This is not wholly true. The second reason, for a brief exposition of St. Thomas's teaching, is to indicate to non-Thomists the attitude which a modern student of Thomism may take in regard to the original thought of St. Thomas. It will become evident that it is not maintained that St. Thomas has solved all our modern problems. He lived under different circumstances from those of the present. He is not an infallible authority, to be followed at all costs. But before deciding whether he has anything to contribute to the discussion, it is necessary to examine what he did think.

Fundamental in St. Thomas's handling of the problem is the distinction of two quite different moral rights. First and most important, is the *right to use* material things. Man is not an angel; he has a body which must be fed and clothed and protected. He cannot long continue his proper existence on earth, unless he makes use of things for these purposes. Such use is natural to man in his genus. All animals unhesitatingly take over food and other things from their environment for their use. Such use is a necessary and natural means of life; every man is morally entitled to satisfy his material needs by using material things.[1] This is not to be confused with the right to own things. One may occupy, and thus use, a house without being its owner. In fact, both the terms "ownership" and "property" may well be avoided in the initial stages of discussion, for they suggest a private holding of things to the exclusion of other persons.

The other right, in relation to material things, is called in Latin: *potestas procurandi et dispensandi*.[2] Literally, this means the power to acquire and dispose of things. It is roughly equivalent to the modern economist's notion of management. Apart from consumptive use, there is a group of actions which man may perform in regard to material things: he may obtain them from nature, work upon them to make them more suitable for human use, hold them over a period of time, dispose of them by exchange, sale, gift, and in other ways. For convenience, let us just call this the *right to manage* things.

Now, while the right to manage things is chronologically prior to the right to use them, this does not necessarily mean that it enjoys moral precedence. This statement contains the essence of the Thomistic position. It is absolutely necessary to a good life upon earth that each human being exercise the right to use material things. You must eat in order to live. On the other hand, it is not absolutely necessary for each human being to exercise the right to manage things. Some people may live, and even live well, without holding anything as their own. We shall see that St. Thomas considers three possible forms of "management" and eventually decides that one form is best for most men. The point now to be observed is that there is only one way of exercising the right to use, and that is incumbent upon all men. It is for this reason that St. Thomas suggests that the right to use things is common to all human beings. As he expresses it: "The other thing which pertains to man in relation to exterior things is the use of them. And, in regard to this, man should not hold exterior things as private (*ut proprias*) but as common (*ut communes*), in order that one may easily share them with others in need."[3]

To put this very bluntly, it means that if a starving man has no other way of getting food, and if he asks a farmer for a melon, the farmer is morally obliged to give it to him, provided the melon is not immediately needed for consumption by the farmer and his family. Moreover, if the

1. *Summa Theologica* II-II, q. 66, a. 1, c; *Summa contra Gentiles* III, c. 22 ad fin.
2. *Dicendum quod circa rem exteriorem duo competunt homini. Quorum unum est potestas procurandi et dispensandi.* S.T. II-II, q. 66, a. 2, c. init.
3. *Ibid.*

farmer refuses to share his excess goods, the starving man is morally right in taking the melon and eating it.[4] Morally then, the right to use is more natural, more basic, than the right to manage things.

If we say that it is necessary to get, to have, some things before we can use them, it may be admitted that the notion of possession is not entirely separable from that of use. But possession is not identical with private ownership. What must be recognized is the common right of all men to use material things. This is not incompatible with private management of material things, provided the right to hold things as private possessions is not taken to exclude others, who are in need, from their use. As St. Thomas puts it: "the rich man does not act immorally, if, in taking over possession of a thing which was common from the start, he also share it with others."[5]

Historically, three ways of handling the management of things have been tried by men: (i) private and individual possessions; (ii) communal possessions; and (iii) mendicancy. In the first case, one person obtains some material things, perhaps improves them by his labor, manages their use and distribution by his own efforts. In the second case, a group of human beings (usually conceived to be larger than the family) exercises these functions as a corporate unit. The third possibility is obviously not open to all people but some men may choose to do nothing about acquiring and managing things, depending simply on the gifts of others as a means of getting the things which they must use.

While at least some men in any age may get along by following any one of these three systems of possession (the third amounts to a form of minimal possession), the question that is asked by St. Thomas is: which of these is the most reasonable for the majority of men to practice? It should be recalled that the mendicant Orders in the Catholic Church were originally groups of men living a religious life and supporting themselves by begging. Gradually these religious groups turned to a special form of communal possession. St. Thomas Aquinas lived his mature life under a system of community possession; he owned no private possessions. When he discussed these possibilities, he knew them as real methods of living and managing things.

His decision is that the most reasonable method is that of private

---

4. Such taking of goods in the possession of another is not regarded as an act of theft; one may even take over things held by another to help a third person who is in extreme need. *S.T.* II-II, q. 66, a. 7, ad 2m, et ad 3m; cf. A.D. Sertillanges, *La philosophie morale de s. Thomas d'Aquin* (Paris, Aubier, 1946), pp. 185-186.
5. *S.T.* II-II, q. 66, a. 2, ad 2m.

possession and management of material things. A life of poverty is a fine thing, when voluntarily adopted by the individual for some special motive. Forced poverty is the source of much trouble.[6] This leaves the choice between private and communal management. St. Thomas makes it clear that, to his mind, the natural moral law in its primary principles enjoins neither communal nor private possession. "According to natural law, there is no distinction of possessions, but rather according to human agreement and this pertains to the positive law."[7] Previously, he had pointed out that some things are natural to man in two senses. Some actions, such as the union of male and female for the production of off-spring, or the feeding of the young by their parents, are suited to human nature in a primary sense. Even brute animals grasp these things and practice them without deliberation. Other things are natural in a de-rivative sense; they follow from a reasonable consideration of possible ways of acting, in relation to the rational nature of man. By this kind of reasonable deliberation it is possible to understand that private possession is natural, in a secondary sense, to man. St. Thomas uses the example of property to illustrate this general distinction between that which is natural to man, as it is to all animals, and that which is natural to man because human beings may use their reason to reach a reasonable agreement. He suggests that, if we consider *this field* in relation to *this individual man,* there is nothing in either to indicate that this field should belong to this man. But, if we make a reasonable examination of the possibilities of this man to cultivate and use this field, then we may conclude that he is entitled to be its private owner.[8]

Three reasons are suggested for the conclusion that private possession is the best system for most people to follow. First of all, a man is more careful and conscientious in procuring things which will belong to him privately than he is in managing public, or common, possessions. Secondly, private possession is more orderly; confusion arises where everyone is look-ing after everything. Finally, there is less opportunity for quarrels under a system of private possessions; disputes frequently arise where property

---

6. *Contra Impugnates Dei cultum et religionem* c. 6, *ad primum* (ed. Mandonnet, *Opuscula Omnia,* Paris, 1927, IV, 85): *sicut divitiae non sunt in culpa, sed divitiarum abusus, ita mendicitas sive paupertas non est in culpa, sed paupertatis abusus, quando scilicet aliquis paupertatem invitus et impatienter sustinet; tunc enim desiderio divitiarum in multa peccata quandoque incidit.*

7. *S.T.* II-II, q. 66, a. 2, ad primum.

8. *S.T.* II-II, q. 57, a. 3, c; the meaning of a reasonable agreement of men (*con-dictum*) is discussed in the preceding article (2, c).

is undivided and held in common.[9] These reasons are considered sufficient; they do not make St. Thomas an eager proponent of the system
of private possessions. He simply says that it is "licit" (*licitum est*) for
a man to possess things privately. It is not opposed to the natural law
(*proprietas possessionum non est contra jus naturale.*)[10]

We should remember that this right of private possession, or management, is strictly limited by the common right to use. The person who
undertakes to hold and manage large possessions is also undertaking the
problem of seeing that they will be properly used to satisfy the reasonable
needs of himself and others. A rich man is not required by Thomistic
ethics to go all over the world trying to find people whom he may help.
He is strictly required to give of his excess goods (and not out of charity
alone, but as a matter of strict justice) to those who are in need in his
immediate vicinity. With modern systems of communication and monetary exchange, this position would seem to make it difficult for a person
to retain a large fortune and do what is morally right.

USURY AND THE RIGHT TO USE

An excellent illustration of the Thomistic attitude to the right to
use of possessions is found in the medieval teaching on usury. A brief
consideration of this doctrine may cast some light on the general theory,
as well as the poorly understood notion of usury. It will be observed that
the term *usury* is etymologically related to the word *use*. The only primary use for money, that the medieval man knew, was to spend it. Merely to put it away somewhere and keep it was not regarded as a form of
use. Of course, coins have various secondary uses, such as bodily adorn-
ment, but these do not stem from the fact that coins are money but from
other attributes which they possess.[11]

Now under these conditions, if one man had some extra money and
another man needed some, a loan of accommodation might be made.
This was usually done among friends. The man who had no present
use for the money simply allowed someone else to use it, with the understanding that the sum would be returned in full later. The lender was
really giving up nothing, for he was not using the money himself. When
the loan was repaid, he was in just the same position as he would have

---

9. *S.T.* II-II, q. 66, a. 2, c. Somewhat the same reasoning is found in Aristotle's
Politics II, 4, 1263a21. The last reason is connected with a very old principle of common
law: that common property should be divided wherever possible.
10. *Ibid. ad primum.*
11. *Quaest. Disp. de Malo* q. XIV, a. 4, c. et ad 15m.

been, had he kept the money all the time. To try to charge a fee, or interest, on such an accommodation, was considered immoral. It was regarded as an attempt to get something for nothing. It was called usury, because it was an attempt to charge for a use which was not given up.[12] This is precisely an example of how moral circumstances change, and with them some secondary rules of ethics must change. It is not that the original rule becomes false; rather, the real conditions which it embodies are modified and, with this modification, the rule itself may lose its original application.

In the modern world, money seems to have acquired a new primary use. In the form of capital it appears to become an instrument of production and distribution. Investment is a modern use which was not open to the ordinary man in the middle ages. Even St. Thomas could grant that a man is entitled to some compensation when he risks losing his possessions.[13] Hence, in the present world, a loan (even between friends) can involve the loss of the moderate interest which comes from leaving extra money in a bank. There is no reason to suppose that St. Thomas would consider it immoral to accept a moderate amount of interest on a business loan. It is still unreasonable to take excessive interest, and that is what is called usury by modern Thomists.

THE CONCEPT OF COMMON USE AND COMMUNISM

A possible reaction to the Thomistic theory of possession for common use is that it is nothing but communism. What is the good in being industrious, thrifty, a good manager, if one is expected to give of one's excess goods to any persons who are in need? The answer would seem to be: this moral theory is quite different from communism and also from *laissez faire* capitalism.

The Catholic attitude toward communism is much too complicated to be expressed briefly.[14] We may note two great points of difference. If we take communism, not as an ideal theory (on which basis it is very difficult to find a positive program for which it stands) but as the world view of a large segment of mankind today, many of whom insist that

---

12. *S.T.* II-II, q. 78, a. 1-4; *Quaest. Quodlibetales* III, q. 7, a. 19, c. For a broader treatment of the whole medieval attitude toward money and loans, consult: Bede Jarrett, *Social Theories of the Middle Ages* (Westminster, Md., Newman, 1942), pp. 150-180.

13   See the discussion of the danger of a business man losing goods in transport: *S.T.* II-II, q. 77, a. 4, ad 2m. Consult also the four articles on usury, in the next question, 78.

14.   For a philosophical appraisal of communism see: C. J. McFadden, *The Metaphysical Foundations of Dialectical Materialism* (Washington, Cath. U. Press, 1938); J. Lafarge, "The Philosophical Basis of Communism," *Proc. Amer. Cath. Philos. Assoc.*, Vol. IX (1933) pp. 47-62.

the economic ideal of a real communism will not be reached in any country for many years yet, then we can say that it is much more than an economic program. Apart from their views on property holding, communists have an outlook on human life which is very largely antithetic to Thomism. The majority of vocal communists seem to reject the existence of God, the spirituality and immortality of the human soul, the dignity of the individual person. If they grant any moral freedom to the individual man, it is of a very restricted character. Their interpretation of the course of human history, the conclusions of natural science, the social institutions of men, excludes many of the things considered true and right in Thomism. This is not, perhaps, applicable to all communists—but the general trend of actual communism seems to be atheistic, antispiritualistic and deterministic. Thomistic philosophers oppose communism for more than merely economic reasons.

Secondly, in the purely economic area, Thomism is wedded neither to communism nor to capitalism. A Thomist is interested chiefly in the moral implications of any system of economics. Extreme forms of capitalism have obvious defects.[15] Despite its other-worldly attitude toward moral and social problems, Thomism is definitely concerned about providing every human being with the necessary means to work out his earthly life in a manner suited to the dignity of a human person.[16] The successful capitalist does not seem to share this concern. Nevertheless, capitalism does leave some personal freedom, even to those who are economically depressed; communism appears to be directed toward an exaltation of the material values of the group and an annihilation of the worth of the individual man. In an economy of material abundance, to which communist theorists point as a sort of Marxian heaven, most any kind of system will work. Under present conditions and those of the predictable future, modern man has the choice between forced poverty under communism or free enterprise (with the possibility of individual failure or success) under capitalism. There is no question that the second option is the better. Capitalism and the whole practice of private possessing can be abused. There is good promise, however, that it could be well used by men who are properly concerned about the moral and social welfare of their neighbors.

---

15. Cf. J. A. Ryan, "The Philosophy of Capitalism," *Proc. Amer. Cath. Philos. Assoc.,* Vol. IX (1933), pp. 35-46; V. Michel, *St. Thomas and Today. Comments on the Economic Views of Aquinas* (St. Paul, Minn., Wanderer Press, 1935).
16. This theme has been very well developed by Jacques Maritain in several works, the most recent being: *The Person and the Common Good* (N.Y., Scribner's, 1947).

The heart of the Thomistic theory of possessions lies not in the details of arrangements for the acquisition and distribution of things but in the original distinction of the right to use from the right to manage things. There is no "official" system of economics, dogmatically imposed on Catholics, which Thomists wish to foist upon an unsuspecting world. Nor is there any Catholic political movement working toward such an end. Thomists would like to convince the average man, by appealing to his reason, that the improvement of his condition in human society on earth depends on the perfecting of the moral character of the individual man. It all reduces to the proposition that no society can be good unless the members who constitute it are good.

The moral perfection of the individual person requires not only the internal development of prudence and temperance and fortitude, it also demands the outward-looking virtue of justice. To will the good for other men, as one naturally does for oneself, is a most difficult habit to acquire. Yet it would seem to be the only basis for good social life. The willingness to share earthly possessions with others who are in need is but one application of the social virtue of justice. Fundamental to all this is the conception that all men have an equal right to use material things. This is the right which is most natural.

Placing the other, less natural right, to acquire and manage things privately, above the right to use, is responsible for many of the evils of modern economic and social life. Private possession for common use is not offered as a fool-proof system which will immediately bring about ideal social conditions. For it to work properly, most men must be morally good people. Thomism is optimistic about this possibility, holding that there is much goodness left in mankind, that most men want to do what is right. If this confidence is misplaced, then no theory of possessions will do any practical good.

SELECTED BIBLIOGRAPHY

I. GENERAL EXPOSITIONS OF THOMISTIC ETHICS

St. Thomas Aquinas. *Summa Theologica,* Ottawa (Collège Dominicain) Vol. III: 1941, xlviii pp.—2412 cols.— 28 pp.; *Summa contra Gentiles,* Romae (Ed. Leonina manualis: Desclée Herder) 1934, vi-581 pp.; *In X Libros Ethicorum Aristotelis ad Nicomachum,* cura A. M. Pirotta, Taurini

(Marietti) xxiv-747 pp.; *Contra Impugnantes Dei cultum et religionem*, ed Mandonnet (*Opuscula Omnia*) Paris, 1927, IV, 1-195.

St. Thomas Aquinas (English translation), *The Summa Theologica*, literally transl. by the English Dominicans, London (Burns-Oates) 2nd rev. ed. 1912-1936, 22 vols.; *The Summa contra Gentiles*, transl. by the Eng. Dom., London (Burns-Oates) 1928-1929, 5 vols.; Pegis, A.C., *Basic writings of St. Thomas Aquinas*, N.Y. (Random House) 1944, Vol. I: liii-1097 pp., vol. II: xxxi-1179 pp.; Phelan, G. B., *St Thomas Aquinas, On the Governance of Rulers*, Toronto (St. Michael's College), 1935, 143 pp.

Bourke, V. J. *Syllabus in Ethical Theory*. St. Louis, St. Louis University Press, 1946.

Deploige, S. *The Conflict Between Ethics and Sociology*, transl. by C. C. Miltner. St. Louis, Herder, 1938.

Gilson, E. *S. Thomas d'Aquin* (*Les moralistes chrétiens*). Paris, Gabalda, 1930. (*Moral Life and Moral Values*, transl. by L. Ward, St. Louis, Herder, 1931.)

Grabmann, M. "Das Naturrecht der Scholastik von Gratian bis Thomas von Aquin." *Archif f. Rechts- und Wirtschafts-Philosophie*, Vol. XVI, 1922-23, pp. 12-53.

Lottin, O. *Le droit naturel chez s. Thomas d'Aquin et ses prédécesseurs*, Bruges, Beyaert, 1932.

Sertillanges, A.D. *La philosophie morale de s. Thomas d'Aquin*, Paris, Nouv. éd., Aubier, 1946.

Wittmann, M. *Die Ethik des hl. Thomas von Aquin*, München, Hueber, 1933.

II. STUDIES OF THE PROBLEM OF MATERIAL POSSESSIONS

Brucculeri, A. "La funzione sociale della proprietà," *Civiltà Cattolicà*. 1936, pp. 112-126.

Brunet, R. "La propriété privée chez s. Thomas," *Nouv. Rev. Théol.*, 1934, pp. 914-927; pp. 1022-1041.

Cordovani, M. "Il diritto di proprietà in S. Tommaso d'Aquino," *Economia*, Vol. XL, 1937, pp. 117-119.

Henry, J. "Thomisme et propriété privée," *Collect. Mechlin.* Malines, Vol. XVIII. 1932, pp. 119-123.

Jarrett, Bede. *Social Theories of the Middle Ages, 1206-1500*, second printing. Westminster Md., Newman, 1942.

Lafarge, J. "The Philosophical Basis of Communism," *Proc. Amer. Cath. Philos. Assoc.,* Vol. IX, 1933, pp. 47-62.

Malone, J. D. "Is the Rich Man Obligated to Feed the Poor?" *Dominicana,* Vol. XVII, 1932, pp. 119-123.

Maritain, J. "Personality, Property and Communism," *Univ. of Toronto Quarterly,* Vol. III, 1934, pp. 167-184.

—————. *The Person and the Common Good,* New York, Scribner's Sons, 1947.

Michel, V. *St. Thomas and Today. Comments on the Economic Views of Aquinas,* St. Paul, Minn., Wanderer Press, 1935.

Missiaen, B. "De economische gedachte narr S. Thomas, en het moderne kapitalisme," S. Thomas van Aquin, *Bijdragen over zijn lijd, zijn leer* . . . Bruxelles, Standard Boekhandel, 1927, pp. 109-113.

Perez Garcia, J. *De principiis functionis socialis proprietatis privatae apud D. Thomam Aquinatem.* Fribourg, Suisse, 1924 (Univ. Dissert.).

Renard, R. G. et Trotabas, L. *La fonction sociale de la propriété privée.* Paris, Sirey, 1930.

Riedl, C., "The Social Theory of St. Thomas Aquinas," *Proc. Amer. Cath. Philos. Assoc.* Vol IX, 1933, pp. 24-34.

Ryan, J. A. "The Economic Philosophy of St. Thomas," *Essays in Thomism,* ed. R. Brennan. New York, Sheed & Ward, 1942.

—————. "The Philosophy of Capitalism," *Proc. Amer. Cath. Philos.* Vol. IX, 1933, pp. 35-46.

Spicq, C., "Comment construire un traité thomiste de la propriété?" *Bulletin Thomiste,* Vol. VIII, 1931, 62*-68*.

—————. "Note de lexicographie philosophique médiévale, (*Potestas procurandi et dispensandi, S.T.,* II-II, q. 66, a. 2)," *Rev. des Sc. Philos. et Théol.,* Vol. XXIII, 1934, pp. 82-93.

Tawney, R. H. *Religion and the Rise of Capitalism.* (Holland Memorial Lect. 1922), Harmondsworth, Penguin, 1938.

PHILOSOPHY OF RELIGION IN THE UNITED STATES IN THE TWENTIETH CENTURY

*Daniel Sommer Robinson**

I. THE STATE OF AFFAIRS AT THE DAWN OF THE TWENTIETH CENTURY

In 1895 a notable symposium was held at the Philosophical Union of the University of California (Berkeley). The participants were Professors Josiah Royce (1855-1916), Joseph Le Conte (1823-1901), G. H. Howison (1834-1917), and Sidney E. Mezes (1863-1931); and the general theme under consideration was *The Conception of God.* When the book containing the original contributions of these distinguished philosophers was published in 1897 it bore the subtitle, "A philosophical discussion concerning the nature of the divine idea as a demonstrable reality," and it also included a long supplementary essay by Professor Royce entitled, "The Absolute and the Individual," in which he amplified his position and replied to his critics. The importance of this supplementary essay is indicated by the facts that it restates the author's earlier argument of *The Religious Aspects of Philosophy,* and contains the germ of his well-known Gifford Lectures, *The World and the Individual* (2 vols., 1901), as well as that of his significant later works, *The Philosophy of Loyalty* (1908), *The Sources of Religious Insight* (1912), and *The Problems of Christianity* (2 vols., 1913).

An introduction by Professor Howison, who was also the editor of the book, not only contains an excellent summary of the discussions, but succinctly states the status of the philosophy of religion at the end of the nineteenth century. He pointed out that attempts to establish religion

---

* Born in 1888. Ph.D. Harvard University, 1917. Professor and Director of the School of Philosophy, University of Southern California, Los Angeles. President of the Western Division American Philosophical Association, 1942-1944. During both World Wars he served as a chaplain in the United States Navy. His most recent book is *The Principles of Conduct — An Introduction to Theoretical and Applied Ethics* (1949).

on a rational foundation had been on the defensive during the last half of the century as a result of the influence of the doctrines of the Unconditioned of Sir William Hamilton, and of the Unknowable of Herbert Spencer, and of the atheistic positivism of Auguste Comte. All of these doctrines were strongly reinforced by Darwin's proofs of biological evolution. Their popularity made necessary a reconstruction of theological conceptions to bring them into accord with the new ideas of evolution. This reconstruction took the form of the doctrine of an Immanent God. Although it was definitely built upon Kantian and Hegelian foundations, this doctrine was quite original and thoroughly modern. Hence it became the chief reliance of those thinkers who refused to surrender to those agnosticisms that were based upon the theory of evolution. Now the significant fact is that this idealistic philosophy of religion was dominant among most Protestant groups at the end of the nineteenth century. Under the leadership of John Fiske evolutionism and idealism united in spreading the doctrine that there exists one and only one Immanent Spirit.

All the contributors to the symposium at Berkeley accepted a personal God as real, and they were all united in holding that there is a close correlation among three basic concepts that are common to philosophy and religion, namely, God, freedom, and immortality. In his introduction Howison explains that all the participants agree that neither of these three concepts can be properly interpreted without using statements of each of the other two. Quoting his own words: *"No God except with human Selves free and immortal in some sense, in some degree or other;* and so, likewise, *mutatis mutandis,* of Freedom and of Immortality" (p. xiv). Now it must be admitted that this is an extensive and significant agreement, and that it is sufficient to justify the inclusion of all of these philosophers under the common name of idealists. Moreover, some other prominent thinkers of that period, who were not participants in this famous symposium, are correctly classified as idealists. These include especially Borden Parker Bowne (1847-1910), a first-rate thinker and founder of personalism in the United States, and William Torrey Harris (1835-1909), leading representative of the Hegelian St. Louis School of Philosophy, and U. S. Commissioner of Education. We are, therefore, justified in concluding that idealism dominated the thinking of the majority of leading philosophers who contributed to the philosophy of religion in the United States at the dawn of the twentieth century.

Nevertheless, there were profound differences among these philosophers with respect to their interpretations of the meaning of the three basic concepts—God, Freedom, and Immortality, and these differences came to sharp expression in the symposium. Royce defended a doctrine of *monistic and absolutistic personalism*. Here is his succinct statement of this doctrine: "The Divine Will is simply *that aspect of the Absolute which is expressed in the concrete and differential individuality of the world*. Hereby the world appears, not as a barely abstract world of pure ideas, but as a world of manifested individuals, known in the unity of the one transcendent moment of the Absolute Experience, but there known as a discrete and clearly contrasted collection of beings, whose presence everywhere expresses, amid all the wealth of meaning which the whole embodies, an element of transcendent Freedom" (pp. 202 f.).

Howison advocated *pluralistic personalism*. He sharply criticized Royce for merging individual persons in a single rational and free World-Will, and insisted that his argument contains a mystical and an antiethical tendency. Accordingly, Howison clearly formulates his own conception in this excellent statement: ". . . the human consciousness is seen to have, in its total unity, the all-encompassing form of a CONSCIENCE—that Complete Reason, of a truly infinite sphere, in which the primal self-consciousness of the creature *actively* posits the Ideal which is its real world of being. In this complete reason, or Conscience, the single spirit sees itself as indeed a *person*—a self-active member of a manifold *system* of persons, all alike self-active in the inclusive unit of their being; all independent *centres of origination,* so far as *efficient* causation is concerned; all moving from 'within,' i.e., each from its own *thought,* and harmonized in a society of accordant free-agents, not by any efficient causation, but by the operation of what has been called, since Aristotle, *final* causation—the attraction of an Ideal Vision, the vision of that CITY OF GOD which they constitute, and in which, reciprocally, they have their being. . ." (pp. 91 f.).

Le Conte upheld a special form of pluralism which is called evolutional idealism. This he clearly stated in a summary of his position: "I assume, then, the immanence of Deity in Nature. Furthermore, . . . I regard *physical* and *chemical* forces, or the forces of dead Nature, as a portion of the omnipresent Divine Energy in a *diffused, unindividuated state,* and therefore *not self-active* but having its phenomena determined directly by the Divine Energy. Individuation of this Energy, i.e., self-activity, begins, as I suppose, with Life, and proceeds, *pari passu* with organization of matter, to complete itself as a Moral Person in man. . . . On this view, spirit—which is a spark of Divine Energy—is a potential in dead Nature, a germ in plants, a quickened embryo in animals, and comes to birth into a higher world of spirit-life in man. Self consciousness—from which flows all that is distinctive of man—is the sign of birth into the spiritual world. Thus an effluence from the Divine Person flows downward into Nature to rise again by evolution to recognition of, and communion with, its own Source" (pp. 76 f.).

The twentieth century opened with idealistic philosophy of religion dominant in the United States. But it had a triune form. One group of philosophers followed Royce's absolutistic personalism, another followed the pluralistic personalism of Howison, and another followed the evolutional idealism of Le Conte. Today, as we approach the middle of the twentieth century, each of these three forms of idealistic philosophy of religion is still vigorously advocated. We shall discuss these contemporary types later, after expounding another highly significant trend which began near the end of the nineteenth century. (See section IV below.)

II. THE INFLUENCE OF WILLIAM JAMES

William James (1842-1910) first published his now classical lecture entitled, "The Will to Believe," in the *New World* in June, 1896, and included it in the volume, *The Will to Believe and Other Essays,* the first edition of which appeared in February, 1897. His Gifford Lectures appeared in 1902 under the title, *The Varieties of Religious Experience.* These two contributions of one who is now generally recognized as among the ablest and most seminal of American philosophers definitely mark the beginnings of the reaction against the dominance of idealism in the philosophy of religion which has characterized the first half of the twentieth century. James succeeded in shifting the emphasis from a rationalistic and speculative metaphysical method to an empirical approach to the basic problems of the philosophy of religion. In fact he originated the empirical psychological method of dealing with these problems.

a. *The Shift of Emphasis.*

Recognizing that there is an outer husk of verbal symbols and of "innocent over-belief" in every man's religious experience, James insisted upon turning inward to the real kernel of this experience, which he claimed was affective and volitional rather than rational. Here is a key passage which clearly states the shift of emphasis from rationalism to empiricism: "What religion reports, you must remember, always purports to be a fact of experience: The divine is actually present, religion says, and between it and ourselves relations of give and take are actual. If definite perceptions of fact like this cannot stand upon their own feet, surely abstract reasoning cannot give them the support they are in need of. Conceptual processes can class facts, define them, interpret them; but they do not produce them, nor can they reproduce their individuality. . . . In all sad sincerity, I think we must conclude that the attempt to demonstrate by purely intellectual processes the truth of the deliverances of direct religious experience is absolutely hopeless" (*The Varieties of Religious Experience,* p. 454). James argues that the philosophy of religion performs a purely secondary function and never can prove that religious beliefs are true. Whether they are true must be decided by the individual believer whose religious experiences they interpret.

It is this principle which explains James's conception of a genuine option in his lecture on *The Will to Believe*. Since religious beliefs make a difference in one's attitude toward the future, they are genuine options and consequently the believer has a moral right to consider them to be true rather than to reject them as fallacious. In so doing, he is interpreting his own inner religious insight which is itself nonintellectual and nonrational, and deeply rooted in our "passional nature." By this phrase, James means all that influences one's action and belief that is not definitely intellectual, and this includes one's hopes and fears, one's temperament and basic likes and dislikes, one's deepest valuations. In making a sharp separation between reason and passional nature, James is able to shift the emphasis from metaphysical arguments to prove the existence of God, the possibility of freedom, and the hope of immortality to practical attitudes of acting as though these beliefs are true.

James does not seem to have realized the faultiness of this analysis of a human self. It is true that any ultimate philosophical interpretation of the relation of the self to the universe rests back upon an act of faith. It has to be accepted as true rather than proven to be true. However, this acceptance is not wholly irrational, nor can our "passional nature" be set in sharp opposition to our intellectual activity. The self is essentially a unity, it is not dyadic in its essence. Every normal individual is a self-conscious person, not a split personality. But whether we agree with him or not, James shifted the emphasis from the rational to the affective-volitional elements in religious experience, and by so doing, he initiated a reaction against the idealistic interpretation of religious experience.

b. The Empirical Psychological Method.

In the *Varieties of Religious Experience,* James's purpose was to seek and to discover "the unique nature of religious experience which is ultimately conclusive in respect to the judgment as to what religion in general is." To accomplish this purpose he selected from a rich store of autobiographical and first hand reports of religious people those that were most unique and original, and he classified these into types. He called this the empirical method to differentiate it from the rationalistic method of idealists. In using the word empirical he was not altogether clear since he also spoke of an empirical philosophy as well as an empircal psychological method. This empirical philosophy was his version of *pragmatism.* Undoubtedly, he meant that the study of religion should be confined to the analysis of inner religious experience of those individuals who are deeply religious. Accordingly, he used numerous pious persons to discover the different types of individual religious experience, dealing specially with conversion and counter-conversion, prayer and meditation, and the contrast between the religion of the healthy-minded and that of those he called sick souls.

Obviously a major defect in such a method is its neglect of the religious community which results from its exclusive emphasis upon the inner religious life of devout individuals. Royce pointed this out in the preface of his *Problems of Christianity,* and especially emphasized the fact that his own method stood in sharp contrast to that of James on this important issue. This contrast between the religious experience of individuals and social religious experience as exemplified in the Church is crucial for a philosophy of religion. Royce wrote: "James supposed that the religious experience of a church must needs be 'conventional,' and consequently must be lacking in depth and in sincerity. This, to my mind, was a profound and momentous error in the whole religious philosophy of our greatest American master in the study of the psychology of religious experience. All experience must be *at least* individual experience; but unless it is *also social* experience, and unless the whole religious community which is in question unites to share it, this experience is but as sounding brass, and as a tinkling cymbal" (Vol. I, p. xv). On this point Royce is unquestionably right.

James's empirical psychological method is open to two opposite interpretations in another respect. Can we hold to the distinction between outer and inner experience, between sensory experience of the natural realm, which is objective, and self-awareness of those elements which James said constitutes our passional nature which is subjective? According to one interpretation the empirical psychological method is primarily concerned with outer experience, and the entire conception of inner experience is seriously questioned. According to the other interpretation, religion has practically no interest in sensory experience of the outer world, but is almost exclusively concerned with those inner longings and deeper aspirations of the soul which point to a relationship of man to a nonspatial and nontemporal spiritual world. (See the section on mysticism below.) James undoubtedly intended that the empirical psychological method should be understood in this latter sense, but many of his followers insisted that it would necessarily involve the complete abandonment of the distinction between inner and outer experience and the consequent reduction of inner to outer experince, or at least, the denial that it has any cognitive significance whatsoever.

James H. Leuba (1868-1946) is a leading representative of this reduction. He drew the conclusion that religious beliefs are illusions because there are no outer sensory experinces which can be used to verify them. In his book *A Psychological Study of Religion, Its Origin, Function and Future* (1912), Leuba developed an American form of illusionism which is far more rigid than the classic form of illusionism which was formulated in Germany by Ludwig Feuerbach more than a century ago.

James B. Pratt's (1875-1944) application of the Jamesian method is much the same as James's own use of it. In his important book, *The Religious Consciousness,* Pratt elaborated James's conception of different types of religious experience, worked out a valuable contrast between the subjective form of worship represented by Protestant church services and the objective form represented by the Catholic Mass, and insisted upon the reality of the Determiner of Destiny as a basis for any adequate understanding of the nature of religious experience. The fact that the method of James has been given these two opposite interpretations by his own followers is a clue to the understanding of the master's influence upon religious thinking. He did not found a school, but he has profoundly affected all the major trends of religious thinking in the United States.

Thus at the opening of the twentieth century two opposed interpretations of religion were defended by American philosophers. The idealistic school stressed the rationalistic approach, and the pragmatic school stressed the empirical psychological method. There were three chief types of idealism, absolutistic personalism represented by Josiah Royce, pluralistic personalism represented by G. H. Howison and Borden Parker Bowne, and evolutionary theism represented by Joseph Le Conte. James's emphasis on the empirical psychological method had resulted in two opposed interpretations of this method, a positive interpretation in which religious experience was assumed to imply the objective reality of a nonhuman divine spirit, and a negative or illusionistic theory in which religious experience was held to be purely subjective and the reality of an objective divine spirit was denied. The former of these interpretations was undoubtedly the position of William James.

III.   THE EMPIRICAL DEVELOPMENT

We are now prepared to trace the progressive development of the empirical school which has had a remarkable growth in the United States since James initiated the psychological method of studying religion. Three distinct movements constitute this empirical trend in American philosophy of religion. These are A. *Naturalistic Humanism,* B. *Empirical Religious Realism,* and C. *Mysticism.*

a.   Naturalistic Humanism.

This movement arose at the University of Chicago under the influence of the special form of pragmatism developed by Professors John Dewey (1859-) and George H. Mead (1863-1931). It was strongly influenced by the positivism of Auguste Comte, the evolutionism of Herbert Spencer, and the humanitarianism of John Stuart Mill. But it was also indebted to the Hegelian philosophy in that the evolutionary logic of Hegel was given a temporalistic interpretation by these thinkers, and was identified with the biological evolution of living organisms up to the highest level of human society, thoroughly organized by reflective thinking under the guidance of the method successfully applied in the experimental sciences. It was the hope of the pragmatists that the social sciences could become as completely effective as the mathematical and physical sciences, and that this process of gradually transforming social institutions by the application to them of the methods of the empirical sciences would result in an increasingly better social order. Consequently the philosophy of religion of representatives of this school stressed the ideal of a more perfect human society as an adequate substitute for the conception of God. On this view religion is not an illusion, but many of the doctrines and forms of worship of traditional religion are wholly antiquated. Religion must keep pace with the gradual transformation that is going on in all social institutions. Religious leaders through their practical activities can help to bring about the adjustment of people to the new social order that is coming into existence as the result of the growth of modern knowledge.

Edward Scribner Ames's (1870-) two important treatises on religion well represent this naturalistic humanism. In his early work, entitled *Psychology of Religious Experience* (1910), Ames gave a social interpretation of prayer and other unique expressions of religious worship and came to the conclusion that the "other" involved in them is a "social other" because its nature is determined by the level of social life attained by a given group and by the general social pattern of such a group. In *Religion* (1929), Ames carried this conception still further. He there formulates this definition: "Religion . . . is the cherishing of values felt to be most vital to man's life and blessedness, by means of ceremonial dramatization, expressive symbols, and doctrinal beliefs. These values and their representations change with the economic and cultural life. In the more primitive levels they were embedded in routine custom and cult lore. In the metaphysical Middle Ages they were rationalized in impressive systems of though and elaborate rituals. Today the most advanced societies are absorbed in the values of scientific knowledge, of universal human welfare, and in search for the means of control by which these may be made imaginatively dynamic and inspiring" (p. 32). Ames's other books are entitled *The Divinity of Christ* (1911), *The Higher Individualism* (1915), *The New Orthodoxy* (1918).

Scientific naturalistic humanism is quite widespread in the United States today. Many liberal Protestant clergymen have completely abandoned a theistic interpretation of the universe in favor of this humanistic conception. Man working with his fellow man in creative achievements that result in the improvement of the social order is the only creator these humanists recognize. This earthly existence is the only reality we can ever know. Other-worldliness and eternality are outmoded conceptions that belong to the social pattern of a static and mechanical society. They are completely out of place in the dynamic and progressive society which dominates the people of the twentieth century.

Another leading representative of this position is Professor Henry N. Wieman (1884-). It comes to expression in all of his writings, but especially in his most recent book, *The Source of Human Good* (1946). Wieman, like some other naturalists, offers three different interpretations of the conception of God or "the source of human good." Sometimes he writes as if God is the ideal of a human society to be created in the future in which the maximum of value will be realizable by all its members. Again he identifies God with the creative human activities now going on that are contributing to the realization of such an ideal future society. Finally he looks upon the natural forces that are being utilized in these human functionings as a kind of deity. Wieman expressly denies that God is "mind" or "personality." He conceives God to be the temporal process of growth which perpetually renews human institutions and cultures.

Wieman is strongly under the influence of John Dewey and of Alfred N. Whitehead (1861-1947). Dewey's lectures, entitled *A Common Faith* (1934), is an important contribution to scientific naturalistic humanism, and is the only book in which he deals at any length with problems of the philosophy of religion. Whitehead's seminal work, *Religion in the Making,* as well as his more metaphysical writings, have deeply impressed Wieman. However, Whitehead is not properly classified as a naturalistic humanist, since he incorporates a generous ingredient of Platonism into his philosophy of religion. Being an Englishman who taught at Harvard University for a decade, his writings fall outside the scope of this essay.

b. Religious Realism.

Religious realism is the name that has been given to a unique philosophy of religion which has been developed primarily by Professor D. C. Macintosh (1877-1948), of Yale University. In an autobiographical article he tells of a mild conversion experience which he had at the age of ten, and of a pronounced and vivid "assurance" experience when he was fourteen. Concerning the latter he made this interesting comment: "I firmly believe that no event of my life has been so fundamentally determinative in the Christian direction as this experience." After serving as a mission pastor in Western Canada, Macintosh became a graduate student at the University of Chicago, where he came under the influence of Professor G. B. Foster (1858-1918) and the Dewey-Mead type of pragmatism. Before that time he was an admirer of Hegelian idealism as represented by T. H. Green and Josiah Royce. Some of his works are: *The Problem of Knowledge* (1915), *Theology as an Empirical Science* (1919), *Reasonableness of Christianity* (1925), *Social Religion* (1939), *The Problem of Religious Knowledge* (1940), and *Personal Religion* (1942).

Impressed with the importance of the problem of religious knowledge, Macintosh worked out an involved and complicated general theory of knowledge which he called *"representational pragmatism"* and *"critical monistic epistemological realism."* Briefly stated, this means that an idea is held to be identical with its object to some degree at the moment of perception. In working out this theory, Macintosh took over the term intuition from Bergson and used it in three senses. (i) Intuition is the discovery of suitable working hypothesis in scientific investigation. (ii) It is the sure awareness of the truth of a scientifically verified hypothesis. (iii) It is the grasping of "ideal values" in religious perception. Immediate experiences of appreciations are "divine values" if and when they are valid ends for all persons everywhere and at anytime. Examples are rationality, truth, goodness, and beauty. The religious object, God, is held to be the reality that makes possible the emergence of divine values. Macintosh writes: "In the complex of divine processes we intuit, perceive, or apprehend the presence and activity of a divine factor. Empirical awareness of this divinely functioning reality we may call religious perception or religio-empirical intuition." (*The Problem of Religious Knowledge*, p. 165). Macintosh holds that prayer is a complete surrender of the self to God —"a *right* turning to Supreme Reality for the realization of Supreme Value" (*Personal Religion*, p. 195). In this way he builds an empirical theology on our intuitions of intrinsic values. God is held to be real because of man's intuitive appreciations of and aspirations to possess the highest values. Thus valuational analysis is made the foundation of philosophy of religion.

In his emphasis on "common sense" Macintosh is close to the Scottish realists, who were ably represented in the United States by James Macintosh (1811-1895). Being professor of systematic theology at the Yale Divinity School for many years, and the author of a number of important books and monographs, Professor Macintosh has profoundly influenced the thinking of a large number of American liberal Protestant leaders, who now hold prominent positions in churches, colleges, and universities.

c. *Mysticism*.

From the very beginning, philosophy of religion in the United States has contained a strong mystical ingredient. In his valuable historical survey, *Philosophical Ideas in the United States*, Professor H. G. Townsend has pointed out that in the colonial period Jonathan Edwards advanced a unique doctrine of *divine light* that was similar to and yet quite distinct from the idea of the *inner light* of the Quaker, John Woolman. According to the Quaker doctrine, God directly communicates with each devout worshipper at a given particular moment of perplexity when he is in special need of providential guidance; but Edwards taught that a divine and supranatural light illumines the worshipper's mind and its object at all times, just as the sun illumines the visible world. This divine light of the soul does not add any specific elements to our knowledge, but it transforms the understanding of those who experience it. Only those who love and completely surrender themselves to God have this experience.

This dual interpretation of mystical religious experience has continued to our own day. During the nineteenth Century, under the influence of Quakers and many other consecrated Christian thinkers, Protestants have been taught in the various churches to believe in and rely upon divine guidance in the practical affairs of life. We find in the religious poems of John Greenleaf Whittier this conception of guidance by an inner light of the soul through which one receives direct communication from God in hours of difficulty and perplexity. He wrote:

> The soul itself its awful witness is,
> Say not in evil doing, "No one sees,"
> And so offend the conscious One within,
> Whose ear can hear the silences of sin
> Ere they find voice, whose eyes unsleeping see
> The secret notions of iniquity.
>
> Nor in thy folly say, "I am alone,"
> For, seated in thy heart, as on a throne,
> The ancient Judge and Witness liveth still,
> To note thy act and thought; and as thy ill
> Or good goes from thee, far beyond thy reach,
> The solemn Doomsman's seal is set on each.

Thus, according to this interpretation of the mystical religious experience God is within the central core of every soul and no man is ever alone.

The other idea is that the God within every soul is an all-inclusive supersensible being who is the source and ground of all that is, and whose inmost essence is incommunicable. Thus Ralph Waldo Emerson writes in his oft-quoted "Brahma:"

> They reckon ill who leave me out;
> When me they fly, I am the wings;
> I am the doubter and the doubt
> And I the hymn the Brahmin sings.

In "Threnody" he writes:

> . . . . *What is excellent,*
> *As God lives, is permanent.*

And he also has written in this marvelous poem this fine passage:

> The pure shall see by their own will,
> Which overflowing love shall fill,
> 'Tis not within the force of fate
> The fate-conjoined to separate.
> But thou, my votary, weepest thou?
> I gave thee sight—where is it now?
> I taught thy heart beyond the reach
> Of ritual, bible, or of speech;
> Wrote in thy mind's transparent table,
> As far as the incommunicable;
> Taught thee each private sign to raise
> Lit by the supersolar blaze.

During the twentieth century the mystical conception of religious experience has been especially advocated and defended in the writings of Rufus M. Jones (1863-1948), Quaker Philosopher and friend of Baron von Hugel: *Fundamental Ends of Life* (1924), *New Studies in Mystical*

Religion (1928), and *Pathways to the Reality of God* (1931). In the preface to *Fundamental Ends of Life,* he wrote: "I am calling in this book for a deeper consideration of the interior life within us, and I am quite confident that there are presented here some real clues and hints which point us to the spiritual source of Life and to those deeper forces that will heal us of our grievous wounds." He defines mysticism as "A direct way of vital intercourse and correspondence between man and God," and he makes this claim: "when the powers of the mind are fused and unified, overbrimmed and vitalized by intense mystical concentration and unification, the whole interior self becomes an immensely heightened organ of spiritual apprehension in correspondence with the real world to which it belongs" (*Pathways to the Reality of God,* pp. 23 and 41). The mystic, he says, "is a person who has cultivated with more strenuous care and discipline than others have done, the native homing passion of the soul for the Beyond, and has creatively developed the outreach of his nature in the God-direction" (*New Studies in Mystical Religion,* p. 15). Jones was such a mystic himself, and his influence on philosophy of religion in the United States has been considerable and still continues. However, he acknowledged his indebtedness to his Quaker traditions, to Emerson, and to Royce; and our selection of him as the leading representative of the mystical interpretation of religious experience brings us back to the idealistic philosophy of religion with which we began this discussion.

IV. THE IDEALISTIC PHILOSOPHY OF RELIGION OF THE TWENTIETH CENTURY

In section I, it was pointed out that the twentieth century opened with three different forms of idealism: (i) *absolutistic personalism* represented by Josiah Royce, (ii) *pluralistic personalism* represented by G. H. Howison and Borden P. Bowne, and (iii) *evolutional idealism* represented by Joseph Le Conte. Throughout the first half of the century these three schools have continued to flourish. Today evolutional idealism is ably defended and uniquely interpreted by John Elof Boodin. The personalists have as their advocates Bishop Francis J. McConnell (1871-), Professor Edgar S. Brightman (1884-), A. C. Knudson (1873-), Ralph Tyler Flewelling (1871-), and many others. Absolutistic personalism is most ably upheld by Professor William Ernest Hocking (1873-), Brand Blanshard (1892-), and others.

a. Boodin's Evolutional Idealism.

John Elof Boodin (1869-) was a student of William James and Josiah Royce at Harvard at the turn of the nineteenth century (1899-1900).

Although he acknowledged Royce as his master, his doctoral thesis developed a unique critique of the conception of time of absolute idealism. Later he complicated his own theory of time into an interpretation of evolutionary processes as guided by an eternal cosmic spirit. (See *Truth and Reality* (1911); *Cosmic Evolution* (1925); *God and Creation:* Volume I, *Three Interpretations of the Universe,* and Volume II, *God, a Cosmic Philosophy of Religion* (1934); and *Religion of Tomorrow* (1934).

Boodin especially emphasized the fact that there have been many evolutionary processes in the natural world and he believes that there are likely to be many more. Each such process has its own history—it begins and ends, or will eventually end. In the unfolding of these processes divine creativity is at work. This activity of the divine spirit produces various interacting systems that are also creative. Boodin suggests that the lowest of these systems may be the realm of chemical elements, including isotopes, electrons, and protons, and the physico-chemical laws which express their motions. A higher creative system is constituted by light and magnetism—the electro-magnetic field which prevades the whole physical cosmos. Higher still is the socio-mental field of human, animal and plant life.

Now, using the reality of these systems as a factual basis, Boodin infers that there must be one of all-inclusive context or field within which these other three, and any others there may be, have their being. That all-inclusive context is creative spirit or God, viewed as a cosmic energizing activity that is at once temporal and eternal. He writes: "God is the spiritual field in which everything lives and moves and has its being—the field which guides the cosmic process, though the parts must adapt themselves to the structure of this field in their own way, according to their own relativity in their moving finite frames of reference. God is the soul of the whole, suffusing it with meaning, making possible the advance of nature—the emergence of new levels as matter is prepared to advance. In this enveloping, pervasive spiritual medium, worlds of matter float like islands." Further on he adds this comment: "God's creative activity comprises space and time on a cosmic scale. It furnishes the pattern of the passing events of history, eternally interpentrating, incarnating itself as the material makes it possible" (*God,* Vol II, pp. 34 f.). Boodin thinks that the "spirit of God is intrinsically eternal," but he admits that "God is the greatest of all mysteries," and that he is ultimately ineffable in his essence.

Having thus established the reality of God as the guiding spirit of the natural processes of cosmic evolution, Boodin has no hesitation in affirming that the souls of men are capable of free creative activity, thus sharing with God the production of durable values. In this participation in the divine creativity men share God's eternality, and this is their immortality. Quoting Walt Whitman, he writes: "Let us venture

All, all for immortality,
Love, like the light, silently wrapping all,

And Eternity is not mere duration, but that which is noble and significant" (*God,* Vol. II, p. 225).

Although there is no evidence that Boodin was a reader of the writings of Joseph Le Conte, it is obvious that both thinkers shared the philosophy of evolutional idealism. (See the exposition of Le Conte's view, end of section I above.)

b. *Brightman's Pluralistic Personalism.*

Edgar Sheffield Brightman is today the leading philosophical disciple of Borden Parker Bowne, who shared with Howison the defense of pluralistic personalism at the beginning of the twentieth century. Brightman now serves as professor, holding the Bowne Chair of Philosophy at Boston University where he formerly studied as a graduate student during the first decade of the century. For some time he was a follower of Josiah Royce, and then came under the spell of the empiricism of William James. He finally learned from Bowne a philosophy which contained the truth of what both Royce and James proclaimed, without their errors.

Brightman accepts the basic principle of pluralistic personalism that the term "reality" has no meaning except "in, of, or for persons." Differently expressed this basic principle means that there are no realities in any sense of that word in any context from which persons are entirely excluded. It follows from this principle that the universe is ultimately a realm of persons, and that any beings that are lower in the hierarchy of realities than persons exist only "in, of, or for persons." If one could conceive of all persons being completely obliterated, including the conceiver of this fatality, the universe would thereby pass into nothingness.

On this general presupposition of pluralistic personalism Brightman argues that each person is a "primary datum" to himself. Hence he often refers to the datum-self to designate the original noninferential element in experience. Scientific knowledge of the natural world, and religious knowledge of the spiritual world are both constructions which result from rational reflection upon the experience of this primary datum and other experiences which flow from this original experience. But one must not think that this primary datum is experienced only once. It is continuously present in experience with every intellectual act of interpretation. Consequently sense awareness is an abstraction from the whole of experience, and reason is itself a function of experience conceived as a whole. In fact he defines experince as "a movement toward rational totality." In this respect Brightman declares himself to be in complete sympathy with Hegel. He writes: "Hegel has led me to see that true rationalism is simply the principle of confronting every part of experience with our view of the whole, while true empiricism is the principle of accepting only that view of the whole which is honestly built up by observation of the acceptable parts of experience" (*The Christian Century,* Vol. LVI, 1939, p. 276).

Brightman thinks that Hegel's error is to be found in his considering persons to be transmuted into an impersonal or superpersonal social absolute spirit. He insists that such a conception is purely speculative whereas a personalistic conception of God is entirely consistent with religious experiences. These are: (i) a unique sense of dependence upon the underlying *ground* (Bowne's term) of the universe, (ii) worship and prayer, (iii) the consciousness of divine guidance, (iv) submissiveness to nonhuman cosmic purposes, and (v) our experience that the permanence of intrinsic values depends upon powers beyond our human abilities. When such experiences are given a genuine objective interpretation by the assertion of the existence of God, they become genuinely meaningful; but when they are regarded as essentially illusory, they lose their significance. Consequently the hypothesis that a conscious and purposeful Supreme Person is the "ground" of the universe is verified by the fact that it is essential to the validation of our deepest value experiences, which include essential religious experiences.

Where Brightman breaks with the earlier personalists is in his advocacy of the doctrine of a finite or limited God. He thinks that this is required to deal adequately with the problem of evil. By taking this position he has aroused considerable controversy within the personalistic camp. Brightman also minimized the eternal and magnified the temporal in his philosophy of religion, whereas the founders of personalism in the United States reversed this emphasis. His chief writings are: *Religious Values* (1925), *A Philosophy of Ideals* (1928), *The Problem of God* (1930), *The Finding of God* (1931), *Is God a Person?* (1932), *Moral Laws* (1933), *Personality and Religion* (1934), *The Spiritual Life* (1942).

Brightman has a large following among liberal Christian leaders throughout the United States. His writings are essential to an understanding of American personalism, as are also the writings of Ralph Tyler Flewelling (see *Creative Personality* (1926) and various articles in *The Personalist*, Vols. I-XXIX, of which he is editor), Bishop Francis J. McConnell (see *Is God Limited?* (1924), *Borden Parker Bowne*, with full bibliography (1929)), and Professor A. C. Knudson, whose *Philosophy of Personalism* (1927), is a good general study of the movement.

c. Hocking and Absolutistic Personalism.

William Ernest Hocking (1873-), a student of Royce and James at Harvard University and later Alford Professor of Philosophy there, is generally recognized today as the leading representative of absolutistic personalism in the United States. More than any other American philosopher he has succeeded in synthesizing the empirical and the rational elements in religious thinking. In labeling his own theory he refers to it as "realism," "myticism," and "idealism." Interpreting the first of these terms he calls his position "realism of social experience" and "social realism," and concerning the name idealism he insists that he holds a "realism of the Absolute, not far moved from Absolute idealism." He also says that his view is "a transfigured naturalism."

Hocking's *opus magnum* is entitled, *The Meaning of God in Human Experience* (1912), and the title suggests that God performs a special function in our experiences which will be explained presently. Since that monumental and now classic volume appeared, Hocking has published a number of other important works dealing in whole or in large part with the philosophy of religion. Among these should be mentioned: *Human Nature and its Remaking* (1918, new and revised edition 1923), *The Self—Its Body and Freedom* (1938), *Lasting Elements of Individualism* (1937), *Thoughts on Death and Life* (1937), *Living Religions and a World Faith* (1940), and *Science and the Idea of God* (1944). He was Gifford Lecturer at the University of Glasgow 1937-1939, and Hibbert Lecturer at Oxford and Cambridge Universities in 1938. Hocking has contributed numerous valuable articles to philosophical and religious journals. The philosophy of religion, metaphysically interpreted, has always been a field of major interest and concern to him. Being a first-rate thinker, gifted with a penetrating and original mind, his contributions to American philosophy of religion stand out as the most substantial that have been produced during the first half of the twentieth century.

The best approach to an understanding of Hocking's unique contribution to liberal philosophy of religion is through his solution of the problem of how we know other minds. His doctoral thesis at Harvard

University dealt with this problem, and it contains the germs of the *Meaning of God in Human Experience*. Hocking went back to Fichte, who was the first philosopher seriously to raise the question of how we know other minds, and used that author's moral idealism as a foundation upon which he constructed an original religious metaphysics.

Each experiencer, Hocking contends, is continually confronted with two kinds of active outer realities — other experiencers who are like himself and who are in communication with him, and physical objects which beat in upon him in unnumbered and innumerable coercive sensory stimuli. At first the experiencer, misled by common sense realism, imagines that these two outer realms of being are entirely different, and he builds up complicated categories of physical nature and of social life on this unjustifiable assumption. But further reflection, coupled with intuitive insight, reveals another reality beyond physical nature and beyond the separate minds of our fellows, and we eventually discover that this transcendent but environing reality is a Being who can and does communicate with us. Hence that ultimate reality is Other Mind or God. Hocking concludes that this knowledge of Other Mind or God which all men possess, at least potentially, is the true explanation of how we know the minds of our fellows. If we think of this supreme Other Mind as the Absolute Personal God we will comprehend why this position is called absolutistic personalism in contrast with pluralistic personalism. Like Emerson, Hocking thinks that God is the spiritual supersolar blaze of light who gives us eyes to see, ears to hear, and minds to communicate with our fellows. This is the meaning of God in human experience that our relationship to him makes possible both the development of self-consciousness and of social consciousness, neither of which is capable of independent reality.

In this short essay it is not possible to expound in any detail the elaborate arguments Hocking uses to establish this basic thesis. However, it is possible to state briefly his reconstruction of the classic ontological argument, which he considers to be far superior to the cosmological and teleological arguments for the existence of God. He writes: "I have preferred to state the argument not thus: I have an idea of God, therefore God exists. But rather thus: I have an idea of God, therefore I have an experience of God . . . Insofar as reality dwells in Self, or Other Mind, or Nature, an ontological argument may be stated in proof of their existence. . . . The object of certain knowledge has this threefold structure, Self, Nature, and Other Mind; and God the appropriate object of ontological proof, includes these three" (*The Meaning of God in Human Experience,* pp. 314 f.).

God must be real because we have an experience of him in knowing the minds of our fellows. Brightman starts with the self as the primary datum. Hocking starts with God as the all-inclusive Being who unites self, other minds, and nature in a communal spiritual reality that is ineffable by the inductive method which yields valid scientific knowledge, but is known, in part at least, in the mystical experiences of saints and seers. Therefore, God is metaphysically real even though his essence surpasses our powers of comprehension.

<h3 style="text-align:center">V.   ORTHODOXY AND NEO-ORTHODOXY</h3>

So far we have been expounding various liberal American philosophies of religion that have flourished in the twentieth century. We have to acknowledge that we could not cover them all, and we regret that we have been compelled to omit such important thinkers as Professors Edwin E. Aubrey (1896-), Edwin A. Burtt (1892-), Walter M. Horton (1895-), Radoslav A. Tsanoff, (1887-), and others. Some of their books are listed in the selected bibliography below. But it is now necessary to give brief consideration to the nonliberal and antimodernistic thinkers whose views are today attracting attention and winning a large following among clergymen and intellectual laymen.

Orthodox Protestant theology is ably represented in the United States by a number of dogmatic theologians who consider their doctrines to be interpretations of direct revelations of God in the Scriptures of the Old and New Testaments. An outstanding defender of this position is Dr. Rufus W. Weaver (1870-). In his book entitled, *The Revolt Against God; The Conflict between Culture and Christianity* (1944), he deals with various types of world-mind, for example, apostolic, Gentile, Hellenistic, theological, sacerdotal, scientific, *et cetera.* His apologetic consists in showing the inadequacy of each and every special kind of world-mind except the Christian, interpreted in the orthodox Protestant sense.

The so-called neo-orthodoxy is considerably less hostile to modern culture, and frankly accepts the results of liberal Biblical scholarship, as well as the established findings of the empirical sciences. Nevertheless it vigorously attacks all liberal forms of the philosophy of religion, and charges them with failing to deal adequately with the crucial practical problems of Western culture, and especially criticises them for not meeting the crisis which generated the two world wars, with their consequent destructiveness and spread of materialistic communism.

The most outstanding American representative of neo-orthodoxy is Professor Reinhold Niebuhr (1892-). He began his career as an author with the book, *Does Civilization Need Religion?* (1927). This was followed by these notable publications: *Leaves from the Notebook of a Tamed Cynic* (1929); *Moral Man and Immoral Society* (1932); *Reflections on the End of an Era* (1934); *An Interpretation of Christian Ethics* (1935); *Beyond Tragedy* (1937); *Christianity and Power Politics* (1940); the Gifford Lectures entitled, *The Nature and Destiny of Man* (Vol. I, 1941, Vol. II, 1943); and *The Children of Light and the Children of Darkness* (1944).

Niebuhr's philosophy of religion is built around and with the concepts of faith, sin, freedom, and anxiety, in their varied relations to God. Man's freedom causes him to attempt to surpass his definitely limited powers and this is sin. Anxiety arises from having committed this sin, and it is itself a kind of continuous condition of temptation which leads to more and more wrong doing. Consequently man, who was created good, becomes sinful by overexercising his will to power, and by surrendering to the drive of insatiable ambition. Faith in God and submission to God is the only avenue of escape from this intolerable flying propeller of misdeeds. The "ideological taint" consists of man's effort to hide his own ignorance by pretending to know a great deal more than he really knows.

Niebuhr accepts the word personality as a serviceable analogical concept, but he recognizes that the term is anthropomorphic when applied to God. He holds that the "self-disclosure of God in Christ" is "the revelation of the atonement . . . the revelation of the mercy of God in its relation to the justice of God." And then he treats this revelation as belonging to history and as clarifying history of its confusions and contradictions, thereby giving it a meaning that is constantly threatened with meaninglessness. He concludes: "Revelation does not remain in contradiction to human culture and human knowledge. By completing the incompletness, clarifying the obscurities, and correcting the falsifications of human knowledge, it become true wisdom to 'them that are called'" (*The Nature and Destiny of Man,* Vol. II, p. 67). This passage gives a fair idea of the weight of emphasis that is placed on divine revelation by neo-orthodoxy.

This philosophy of religion presents the paradox of an anti-intellectual attack on metaphysics in behalf of an irrational metaphysics which has completely lost confidence in the capacity of human intelligence to discover the truth. Hence neo-orthodoxy is the religious counterpart of atheistic metaphysical existentialism. Niebuhr stands in the same relation to Hocking in the twentieth century in which Kierkegaard stood to Hegel in the nineteenth century. However, there is no denying that neo-orthodoxy has revitalized Protestantism in the United States. Perhaps its chief value is to be found in its catharsis function.

VI. AN EXPOSITION AND CRITIQUE OF THE WIEMAN-MELAND CLASSIFICATION OF AMERICAN PHILOSOPHIES OF RELIGION

In 1936 Professors Henry Nelson Wieman and Bernard Eugene Meland published an interesting book entitled, *American Philosophies of Religion*. Both of the authors being naturalistic humanists, the book is strongly biased in favor of this interpretation of the philosophy of religion. Bias is shown by the fact that the major emphasis of the book is on the various forms of naturalism, and also by the way in which the authors minimize the importance of the idealistic tradition in favor of the supranaturalistic and the romantic traditions. Thus they give the impression that idealistic philosophy of religion is the least important trend in America, whereas we have shown conclusively that it was at the beginning, and still is in the middle of the twentieth century, the *philosophical* conception of the nature and significance of religious experience that is dominant in the United States. The following classification of American philosophies of religion is based on Professors Wieman's and Meland's book.

I. SUPRANATURALISM

A. *Traditional Supranaturalism*
Leading representatives: Machen, Mullen, Patton

B. *Neo-Supranaturalism*
Tillich, Pauck, Richards, Reinhold and Richard Niebuhr, Lewis, Cell

II. ROMANTICISM

A. *Ethical Intuitionists 1st group*
(Philosophical Group)
King, Foster, McGiffert, Macintosh, John Bennett, Lyman

B. *Ethical Intuitionists 2nd group*
(Theological group)
Horton, Brown

C. *Esthetic Naturalists*
Alexander, Brownell, Santayana

II. IDEALISM

A. *Absolute Idealism*
Royce, Hocking, Urban, Leighton, Adams, Cunningham

B. *Mysticism*
Rufus M. Jones, C. A. Bennett

C. *Personalism*
Brightman, Knudson, Flewelling, McConnell

III. NATURALISM

A. *Evolutionary Theism*
Boodin, Montague, Calhoun, Wright

B. *Cosmic Theism*
Whitehead, Northrop, Conger, Noble, Overstreet

C. *Religious Humanists*
Leuba, Dean Martin, Otto, Sellars, Haydon, Lippmann

D. *Humanistic Theism*
Ames, Dewey, Shailer, Matthews, G. Birney Smith

Note that there are nineteen naturalists, not counting the two authors, twelve idealists, eleven romanticists, and ten supranaturalists named in this classification. This makes a total of forty nonidealists to twelve idealists. However, several other names are mentioned by the authors so that this ratio is not especially significant.

We may note in passing that Boodin, Whitehead, Northrop, Conger, and Alexander are all Platonists at heart, and consequently none of them are genuine naturalists, and that fact removes five of the most important members of the naturalists groups. Professor Wieman's effort to interpret Whitehead as a John Dewey type of naturalist must be branded as a complete failure. It should also be mentioned that there are several important idealists who are not even mentioned by the authors.

Since idealism and supranaturalism are both discussed in much fewer pages than romanticism and naturalism, and the last group of romanticists are called esthetic naturalists, the authors of *American Philosophies of Religion* create the impression that naturalism is the virile and progressive movement in the philosophy of religion, and that idealism is conservative and reactionary and akin to orthodox supranaturalism. But the truth is that idealism is much closer to romanticism, which the authors admit is of Ritschlian origin and is especially rooted in the philosophy of religion of Schleiermacher. Taken together, idealism and romanticism represent the center over against the extreme left position of naturalism and the extreme right doctrines of supranaturalism. They constitute the genuine liberalism of American Protestant philosophy of religion. Hocking and his followers, Brightman and other personalists, and the followers of Macintosh are the authentic voices of genuine liberalism in American philosophy of religion today. The other movements are important, and they are making significant contributions to the interpretation of religious experience, but they are essentially tangental and peripheral to the majestic central core of American religious philosophy. This is the author's considered opinion and conclusion.

SELECTED BIBLIOGRAPHY

In addition to the books mentioned in the text of the essay the following works are especially informative and helpful.

ANTHOLOGIES AND COLLECTIVE VOLUMES

Adams, G. P., and Montague, Wm. P., editors *Contemporary American Philosophy,* 2 vols. New York, The Macmillan Co., 1930.

Anderson, Paul R., and Fisch, Max H. *Philosophy in America—From the Puritans to James.* New York, Appleton-Century Co. 1939.

Anderson Wm. K. *Protestantism—A Symposium.* Nashville, Tenn., Methodist Book Company, 1944.

Barrett, Clifford, editor. *Contemporary Idealism in America.* New York, The Macmillan Co., 1932.

Bixby, J. S., Calhoun, R. L., and Niebuhr, H. R. *The Nature of Religious Experience.* New York, Harper and Brothers, 1937.

Dewey, John, essays in honor of. *The Philosopher of the Common Man.* New York, G. P. Putnam's Sons, 1940.

Ferm, Vergilius T. A., editor. *Contemporary American Theology.* New York, Round Table Press, Vol. 1, 1932; Vol. II, 1933.

——————. *Encylopedia of Religion.* New York, Philosophical Library, 1945.

Macintosh, D. C., editor. *Religious Realism.* New York, The Macmillan Co., 1931.

Muelder, Walter E., and Sears, Laurence. *The Development of American Philosophy.* Boston, Houghton Mifflin Co., 1940.

Schaub, Edward L., editor. *Philosophy Today.* LaSalle, Ill., Open Court Publishing Co., 1928.

INDIVIDUAL AUTHORS

Alexander, Hartley B. *Truth and the Faith—An Interpretation of Christianity.* New York, Henry Holt and Co., 1929.

Aubrey, Edwin Ewart. *Present Theological Tendencies.* New York, Harper and Brothers, 1936.

Bennett, Charles A. *A Philosophical Study of Mysticism.* New Haven, Yale Press, 1923.

——————. *The Dilemma of Religious Knowledge.* New Haven, Yale Press, 1931.

Bennett, John C. *Christian Realism.* New York, Charles Scribner's Sons, 1941.

Bertocci, Peter Anthony. *The Empirical Argument for God in Late British Thought.* Cambridge, Harvard Press, 1938.

Bixler, Julius S. *Religion in the Philosophy of William James.* Boston, Marshall Jones and Co., 1926.

——————. *Religion for Free Minds.* New York, Harper Brothers, 1939.

—————. *Conversation with an Unrepentant Liberal.* New Haven, Yale Press, 1946.

Blanshard, Brand. *The Nature of Thought.* 2 vols. London, George Allen and Unwin, Ltd., 1939.

Bowne, Borden P. *Philosophy of Theism.* New York, Harper and Brothers, 1887.

—————. *The Immanence of God.* Boston, Houghton Mifflin Co., 1905.

—————. *Personalism.* Boston, Houghton Mifflin Co., 1908.

Burtt, Edwin A. *Types of Religious Philosophy.* New York, Harper and Brothers, 1939.

Buckham, John Wright, and Stratton, George M., editors. *G. Holmes Howison, Philosopher and Teacher.* A selection of His Writings with a Biographical Sketch. Berkeley, University of California Press, 1934.

Calhoun, Robert L. *God and the Common Life.* New York, Charles Scribner's Sons, 1935.

Fosdick, Harry E. *As I See Religion.* New York, Harper and Brothers, 1932.

—————. *On Being a Real Person.* New York, Harper and Brothers, 1943.

Haydon A. Eustace. *The Quest of the Ages.* New York, Harper and Brothers, 1929.

—————. *Man's Search for the Good Life.* New York, Harper and Brothers, 1937.

Horton, Walter M. *Theism and the Modern Mood.* New York, Harper Brothers, 1930.

—————. *God.* New York, Association Press, 1937.

Leighton, Joseph A. *Religion and the Mind of Today.* New York, Appleton-Century Co., 1924.

Martin, James Alfred, Jr. *Empirical Philosophies of Religion.* New York, King's Crown Press, 1945.

Moore, John M. *Theories of Religious Experience.* New York, Round Table Press, 1945.

Rall, Harris F. *The Meaning of God.* Nashville, Tenn., Cokesburg Press, 1925.

—————. *Christianity — An Enquiry into its Nature and Truth.* New York, Charles Scribner's Sons, 1940.

Sellars, Roy Wood. *The Next Step in Religion.* New York, The Macmillan Co., 1918.

——————. *Religion Coming of Age*. New York, The Macmillan Co., 1928.

Tsanoff, Radoslav A. *The Problem of Immortality—Studies in Personality and Value*. New York, The Macmillan Co., 1924.

——————. *The Nature of Evil*. New York, The Macmillan Co., 1931.

——————. *Religious Crossroads*. New York, E. P. Dutton Co., 1942.

Urban, Wilbur M. *The Intelligible World—Metaphysics and Value*. New York, The Macmillan Co., 1929.

——————. *Language and Reality*. London, George Allen and Unwin, Ltd., 1939.

PRESENT TENDENCIES IN AMERICAN ESTHETICS

Thomas Munro[*]

1. INTERNATIONALISM.

DURING the past decade, even under war conditions, there has been a notable growth of interest in esthetics in the United States. One indication of this is the establishment in 1941 of the *Journal of Aesthetics,* and of the American Society for Aesthetics in the following year. College courses and published articles in the field are increasing in numbers. But unsettled conditions, at home and abroad, are slowing the advance. High printing costs obstruct the publication of scholarly books and magazines, and college students are under strong pressure to study practical, vocational subjects.

In spite of these obstacles, leaders in various countries are reviving communication, and making esthetics once more an international subject. Important publications in each country are noted elsewhere, and international meetings are again being held. A new generation of American scholars is taking an active part in the revival of esthetics on a world scale. Cooperation is especially active between the American and French groups, now that the latter has revived its own *Société d'esthétique,* and begun publication of its *Revue d'esthétique.*

The past leadership of Germany in esthetics has been outstanding, from the first recognition of the subject as a branch of philosophy in the early eighteenth century, down almost to 1939. It was ably carried on by such contemporary figures as Max Dessoir, Emil Utitz, and Richard Müller-Freienfels, in the rich pages of the *Zeitschrift für Ästhetik und allgemeine Kunstwissenschaft,* and in an output of books and articles on the subject which overshadowed that of all other countries put together. A series of international congresses on esthetics was held in Germany and France, with one in Paris in 1937. Since the recent war, the leadership

---

* Born in 1897. Ph.D., Columbia University, 1920. Formerly Lecturer in Philosophy at Columbia University, and professor of philosophy at Rutgers University. Curator of Education, Cleveland Museum of Art; professor of art and chairman of the Division of Art, Western Reserve University. Editor of the *Journal of Aesthetics and Art Criticism.*

has passed to France and the United States. There has been little activity in philosophical esthetics in the British Isles since World War II, in spite of some excellent work in collateral fields.

In the United States, the subject is still at a rudimentary stage of development, by comparison with prewar Germany and with other branches of philosophy in America.[1] We have produced some important writings on the philosophy of art from Emerson to Dewey, but with little continuity in research or discussion. No American university has taught it long and steadily, so as to build up a cumulative tradition of interest and achievement. It is usually taught, if at all, as an advanced elective course in the philosophy department; less often in the fine arts, music, English, or psychology department, by some teacher who happens to be interested in theory. But it is seldom regarded as necessary, even in a liberal, humanistic curriculum.

Isolationism is slowly giving way to extensive cooperation in esthetics and related fields. But American writers still tend to quote chiefly from other Americans, while the English quote English sources, the French quote French ones, and the Germans those in their own language. Reading books on esthetics from any of these countries, one is led to imagine a separate line of succession there, owing little to outside influence; its own writers always leading the way. This is partly due to national pride; partly to lack of facilities for quick translation and exchange of ideas.

Complacent isolationism exists also in each specialized branch of scholarship in the arts. The literary critics have their own little cliques for mutual admiration and quotation, each discussing the other's latest essay as if it were vastly important and original, requiring only one or two small corrections. Each new generation of sophisticated critics, many of them unfamiliar with philosophical esthetics, revives in slightly altered wording, the ancient perennial problems and arguments about criteria of value, as if they had discovered something radically new.

In science, a new demonstration or discovery is quickly made common property, and used as a starting point by later scientists. In esthetics and criticism, one cannot hope that yesterday's conclusions will be accepted as final. But there is unnecessary waste of effort and lack of cumulative progress, when important work in each generation is almost ignored by

---

1. T. Munro, "Aesthetics and Philosophy in American Colleges," *Journal of Aesthetics,* Vol. IV, No. 3 (March, 1946), pp. 180-186.

the next,[2] and its unfinished researches dropped in the scramble to appear up-to-date and to quote only the newest, most fashionable authorities.

Recent French and German writings on esthetics and related subjects have been little read in the United States. Even the long and productive career of Charles Lalo in Paris has been little discussed, and his younger colleagues, such as Souriau, Bayer, and Rudrauf, were almost unkown here until after World War II. A reading knowledge of French and German has been none too common among our college graduates and artists. The influence of German esthetics has reached us largely by way of foreign intermediaries. From Coleridge to Bosanquet and Carritt, we have received from England thinned-out versions of German transcendentalism as applied to esthetics. Ainslie's translation in 1909 of Croce's *Aesthetics,* an Italian adaptation of Hegelianism, has influenced our intellectuals more than the vigorous Hegel himself has done. Its pompous obscurantism toward naturalistic esthetics has done much to discourage and delay the latter's rise in this country. In the late nineteenth century, aspiring young American philosophers went to German universities if they could, but after 1900 the stream of pilgrims gradually tapered off to the vanishing point. In consequence, contemporary German philosophers were less read here, although the German classics, especially Kant and Schopenhauer, were still studied in translation. Only a few highly publicized writers, such as Freud, Jung, and Spengler, had much direct influence. Only a few young Americans went to Germany or Austria to study art history.

Hitler's rise to power in the early thirties sent to the United States, as previous waves of oppression in Europe had done, a flood of German-speaking scholars in exile. The result has been a new stream of influence from recent German, Austrian, and Swiss esthetics, art history, psychology, musicology, and art education. Comparatively little of the great mass of valuable German writings in these fields, especially during the twenties, has yet been translated. (Wölfflin's *Principles of Art History* appeared in English in 1932; hardly any of the writings of Dessoir, Utitz, Müller-Freienfels, or other contemporary German estheticians have yet been translated.) Much American work in these fields is still done in blithe ignorance of the fact that European scholars have gone over the same ground, and could save us a good deal of trouble. But a large number of German scholars are now publishing in English, and teaching in our universities. The present growth of esthetics in America is being greatly

2. For example, R. G. Moulton's *The Modern Study of Literature* (Chicago, 1915), Univ. of Chicago Press.

stimulated by this influx of learned *émigrés,* especially in the history of the arts. They bring us, not only their own individual talents and ideas, but a delayed appreciation of the advances made in German-speaking countries since 1918, in all the fields contributing to esthetics.

More fundamentally, however, the American development has been a slow maturing of certain tendencies within American culture itself, which parallel to some extent those of Europe. We are the heirs of the long British tradition in the philosophy and psychology of art. It has been, on the whole, one of naturalism and empiricism from Bacon and Hobbes[3] to Santayana; one of evolution, democracy, and liberalism from Herbert Spencer to John Dewey. Adverse theorists have attempted to discredit this tradition by identifying it with a few outworn ideas, such as Schiller's "play theory" of art, and with a narrow, sensual type of hedonism. These survivals of romanticism, and of the aristocratic conception of art as intended for leisurely enjoyment, are not essential to the British naturalistic, evolutionary tradition in esthetics. Its lasting value has been along other lines: for example, in leading to recent psychological and ethnological studies of art in various cultures.

Working in this philosophical tradition, the author of the present chapter proposed in 1928 [4] a scientific, descriptive, naturalistic approach to esthetics; one which would be broadly experimental and empirical, but not limited to quantitative measurements; utilizing the insights of art criticism and philosophy as hypotheses, but deriving objective data from two main sources—the analysis and history of form in the arts, and psychological studies of the production, appreciation, and teaching of the arts. A descriptive, relativistic approach to esthetic valuation and value standards was also outlined. The analysis of form was broadly conceived, not as limited to the mere skeleton or external shell of the work of art, but as covering the organization of suggested meanings, emotions, and other components. In 1928, the time was not yet ripe for concerted action along such lines in the United States; it had to wait another fourteen years.

Individual writers had attempted, throughout the late nineteenth and early twentieth centuries, to establish esthetics as an important subject in American scholarship. William Knight's *Philosophy of the Beautiful,* a history of esthetics published by a Scottish writer in 1891-93, found much of interest in American writings on the subject from 1815 down to Ladd, Scott, Gayley, and the youthful John Dewey. Santayana's *Sense of Beauty*

    3. C. D. Thorpe, *The Aesthetic Theory of Thomas Hobbes* (Ann Arbor, Mich., 1940), Univ. of Michigan Press.
    4. T. Munro, *Scientific Method in Aesthetics* (New York, Norton, 1928).

was a notable step toward a naturalistic, psychological orientation in 1896; it still retains considerable vitality. Max Dessoir presented a forward-looking paper on the "science of art" and its problems in St. Louis in 1904.[5] It has been almost completely ignored. Hugo Münsterberg made valiant efforts, in the early 1900's to introduce German ideas on the psychology and teaching of art. They came to grief in 1914. Each similar attempt has suffered a setback, in part through wars and depressions, in part because conditions had not yet produced a widespread intellectual need for esthetics in this country. That need is now arising because of the recent growth of art and art education in America.

Before long, the history of esthetics will have to be completely re-written, from a much more cosmopolitan point of view. It will have to include a great deal of important art criticism and esthetic psychology, hitherto ignored in histories of esthetics, which has recently been assembled in anthologies and histories of criticism. Instead of following a single line of apostolic succession from Plato through Kant and Hegel to Croce and Bosanquet, it will have to consider much wise theorizing about the arts from China, India, Japan, the Near East, Russia, and other cultures besides our own. Knight's *Philosophy of the Beautiful,* in 1891, was much more international in scope than either of the two large histories of esthetics which have appeared in English since then. It contained chapters on the beginnings of esthetics in prehistoric and Egyptian culture; on the classical and medieval periods; and on modern esthetics in Germany, France, Italy, Holland, Britian, America, Russia, and Denmark. By contrast, Bosanquet's *History of Aesthetic,* which appeared in London in 1892 and has been scarcely altered since, is narrow and biased, ignoring not only American contributions but almost everything outside the German transcendentalist tradition which Bosanquet admired. Dull and stodgy in treatment, it persistently omits the vital, stimulating, and colorful aspects of its subject matter, the discerning comments of great writers on art and artists, to plod through the endless course of pedantic speculation about the nature of Beauty. For the past five decades, it has served as a wet blanket, to dampen the interest of students in esthetics.

In view of all that had happened since 1892, there was even less excuse in 1939 for Gilbert and Kuhn's *History of Esthetics* to continue ignoring American contributions to the field. Strongly German and anti-

---

5. M. Dessoir, "The Fundamental Questions of Aesthetics," tr. by Ethel Puffer, *Congress of Arts and Science, Universal Exposition, St. Louis, 1904* (Boston, Houghton, Mifflin, 1905), pp. 434-447. See also his "Aesthetics and the Philosophy of Art in Contemporary Germany," *Monist,* Vol. XXXVI (1926), pp. 299-310.

scientific in bias, it condescendingly dismisses not only American but French and British writings, especially in the evolutionary, naturalistic tradition, with a few completely inadequate sentences. Santayana and Dewey together are given a total of four lines (p. 554). Prall gets six words as a mere follower of the German formalists. Lalo, DeWitt Parker, Dessoir, Basch, and Delacroix are disposed of together in four and a half lines (p. 554). Dessoir and the whole "general science of art" movement receive another four lines on page 527. Utitz and Müller-Freienfels are not mentioned. Thus even German writers unsympathetic to the authors' point of view are neglected, in spite of world-wide recognition elsewhere. Obviously, the history of esthetics has still to be written, with due consideration of different schools of thought, and of different national contributions.

In spite of obstacles, esthetics as a whole is steadily becoming more international in scope. It has never been pervaded by narrow chauvinism or blindly worshipful patriotism. Its leaders have been on the whole, philosophers with a broadly humanistic attitude. The few exceptions, as in certain Nazi pronouncements on art, are taken seriously only as examples of political propaganda. But one could easily cite examples of leading art historians and philosophers of history, whose racial and national pride has led them to exaggerate the importance of their own cultural background. If they were Germans, it has led them to regard all Gothic culture, or all modern Western, "Faustian" culture, as somehow peculiarly German in spirit. There have been French and Italian scholars, so dazzled by the wealth and beauty of their own culture, with its roots in the classical past, as to ignore or minimize others. Such bias can produce a distorted view of art history and world civilization, in which one's own spiritual ancestors are constantly brought to the center of the stage.

All esthetic theory before the late nineteenth century was cramped and distorted by ignorance of exotic and primitive styles of art. It was based, as in Winckelmann, largely on the late Greek and Roman traditions in sculpture, vase-painting, and architecture, and on the Renaissance styles which carried them on. Even the art of advanced oriental civilization was regarded, as by Hegel, condescendingly and superficially. Theories of the ideal and beautiful in art were founded mainly on late Greek principles of naturalistic representation, balance, and proportion. Gothic art was imitated at times, but had little effect on esthetic theory. With only a single great tradition in art before one's eyes, one could easily erect it into an absolute norm of all that was good and beautiful; one could interpret all art history as a process of groping ascent from the "crude ugliness" of tribal and archaic art to the pinnacle of neo-classic refinement.

The enlargement of cultural horizons in the late nineteenth and twentieth centuries has produced a revolutionary effect on recent esthetics, making it not only international but intercultural in scope. The data for its generalizations are coming to be drawn from the artistic products and experiences of all peoples. We are rapidly losing the complacent assumption that Western styles of art are necessarily the best in all respects. In interpreting these data—for example, the significance of a Hindu statue—we are learning not to judge everything through modern Western eyes, but to understand what the statue meant to the culture which made it. One effect, inevitably, is to make esthetic theory more *relativistic*. It seems more and more unreasonable to appraise the tremendous variety of styles by any one simple rule or fixed standard. More and more styles of art, which do not conform to strict neo-classical rules, are becoming accepted by critics, historians, art museums, and the public. It seems increasingly evident that each great historic style of art, however strange and repellent it may seem at first to untrained Western eyes, had its functions and values—perhaps its own type of beauty—in its own cultural setting. Perhaps all these types of esthetic value can be reduced to some one formula; if so, it will have to be an extremely broad and flexible one. For the present, there is more interest in observing and describing the infinite variety of ways in which art can be produced, used, regarded, and evaluated in different cultures.

2. SPECIALIZATION AND SYNTHESIS.

The recent growth of interest in esthetics is partly due to a widespread belief, among teachers and students of the arts, that specialization has gone too far.[6] Esthetics is traditionally supposed to give a comprehensive, philosophical interpretation of the arts; hence persons from all walks of life are turning to it for enlightenment. Philosophers, they assume, ought to have something profoundly illuminating to say on this as on other matters.

Unfortunately, these flattering expectations are too often disappointed. There has always been, and still is, a great gulf between philosophical esthetics and the arts themselves. A person may study the former for years in an American philosophy department, without having to examine

6. L. Balet, "The History of Art of the Future," *Journal of Aesthetics* (Fall, 1941), pp. 42-62. E. Winternitz, "Overspecialization and Art Education," *Ass'n. of American Colleges Bulletin*, Vol. XXVIII, No. 2 (May, 1942), pp. 276-282.

a single work of art. As in Europe, esthetics here has usually emphasized highly general problems concerning the nature of art, beauty, and esthetic value. Esthetics of this narrow, traditional sort has always failed to interest many college students, or to satisfy the inquiring layman. They find in it, not a unifying approach to the arts, but another highly specialized little subject, off in a corner by itself, devoted to endless debate over small technicalities.

To be sure, there is room in esthetics for intensive research as well as for general syntheses. But the latter are most urgently needed at present, in liberal education and by the general public. They are needed especially in the English-speaking countries, because of the extreme pluralism and disunity of our intellectual life. Reacting against grandiose esthetic systems of the German type, we have gone to the opposite extreme, avoiding even that minimum of broadly systematic thinking which is essential to a rational world view, and which has been philosophy's distinctive contribution in the past. In a period of rapid cultural change and mixture, when science is discovering particular facts at unparalleled speed, there is urgent need for the large-scale, organizing phase of philosophic thinking. Much that passes for philosophy today, and that is written by professional philosophers, does not deserve the name because of its minute specialization. It should be classed rather as science or historical scholarship. There is need for intensive, semantic researches on the meanings of "beauty," but these are not a substitute for the vitally needed, comprehensive interpretation of the arts.

In the twentieth century, Santayana is the only American philosopher who has produced any approach to a full-scale philosophic system with a place for the arts, and he has written little about them since *Reason in Art* appeared in 1905. Literature is the only art about which he has written with assurance. Dewey, our other front-rank philosopher, has consciously avoided system-building. In *Experience and Nature* and *Art as Experience,* his far-ranging commentary on human life was extended, late in life, to deal with the esthetic realm. Most of his comments on the arts are abstract and general. In the present generation we have produced no comprehensive examination of the arts which is comparable in scope to G. F. Raymond's huge series on comparative esthetics, written at Princeton during the nineties. Obsolete in many respects today, it still sets an example as a large-scale application of theory to copious illustrations from the arts. T. M. Greene's substantial volume on *The Arts and the Art of Criticism* is the only recent attempt in America at a large-scale, philosophical survey of the arts. It deserves to be emulated, from different philosophical points of view.

A number of recent American books have undertaken to present a comprehensive survey of the arts. Almost all have been on the level of introductory college textbooks or popular outlines for the general reader. Some adopt the historical approach, some that of appreciation and criticism, some that of psychology, some that of esthetic theory. They help to satisfy educational needs, and to build a larger public for esthetics. Simple language is not necessarily a bar to good thinking, and some of these popular books contain fresh, enlightening interpretations. But they are under great pressure from publishers to be brief, entertaining, and untechnical, to avoid long analyses and erudite allusions. Hence, they are often superficial and misleading, confirming the specialist's prejudice against any attempt to deal with art extensively. There is little present sale in America for long thorough treatises on esthetic theory, on the level of advanced scholarship, analogous to those produced in Germany during the past two hundred years.

There are many intermediate stages between extreme specialization on one hand, and grandiose, all-embracing system on the other. Synthetic and sometimes philosophic thinking can be done on a much smaller scale, as when a historian uses insight from both psychology and economics to explain what happened in fifteenth century Florence; or when the archeologist asks help from geology, chemistry, and botany in determining the date of a neolithic burial. Intellectual synthesis may consist in linking a single change in musical style with a contemporary change in painting or poetry, or with a social or religious movement. Some philosophers use a significant, key idea of the time to link together and explain phenomena from widely distant fields. In the nineteenth century, "evolution" was such a key idea, and much of the world's best philosophizing on art and other matters was linked up with it. It served to stimulate and suggest inquiry in every subject. Today, no single concept holds so central a place in our thinking, but certainly that of symbols and symbolism is near the focus. As Susanne K. Langer [7] has pointed out, it has important bearings in contemporary logic, semantics, language, psychology, religion and ritual, visual art, literature, music, and ethics. Thinkers in fields as remote as psychoanalysis, ethnology and the history of Renaissance (as in the Warburg Institute researches) find themselves organizing their discoveries in terms of symbols and meanings—individual and cultural,

7. S. K. Langer, *Philosophy in a New Key, a Study in the Symbolism of Reason, Rite and Art* (Cambridge, Mass., Harvard Univ., 1942).

conscious and unconscious, words and concrete images. Philosophical synthesis can be exercised with such new tools, on a moderate scale: e.g., by combining the insight of psychoanalysis and art history or literary scholarship on the symbolism of a single work of art, such as *Hamlet* or *Ulysses,* Dürer's *Melancolia* or Goya's *Foolish Fury.*[8] Such cooperation is welcomed, not by esthetics alone, but by each cooperating specialist. The psychoanalyst today looks to the arts as a rich source of data for understanding the human mind, but he cannot exploit it without some help from experts in the field of art.

Every job of synthesis well done has far-reaching repercussions. For example, it was mentioned above that recent art and art criticism had shown a tendency to specialize on "pure form"—i.e., on the visual or auditory aspects of painting, music, or poetry—and to disparage "sentimental associations." This was a fruitful temporary line of experimentation. But now, we are discovering that art can have a wealth of other, unsuspected meanings, of many different kinds. This in turn affects the kind of art produced. Surrealists and other modernists are trying to exploit such meanings (e.g., unconscious, dream symbolism) as a source of interest and emotional power.

3. THE JOINING OF SEVERAL STREAMS OF THOUGHT IN PRESENT ESTHETICS.

There has been a marked change in American esthetics in recent years. It is branching out vigorously, to include more study of the arts themselves, as well as of theories about them. It is now commonly conceived as the subject which seeks to understand and explain the arts and related types of behavior and experience in a broadly theoretical way, with as much use of scientific method as the data will permit. It has not abandoned the traditional, philosophical approach, emphasizing beauty and value; but it also takes in what Dessoir and his associates called *allgemeine Kunstwissenschaft,* or general science of art.[9] This comprises the more fundamental, broadly comparative and philosophical areas of *Kunstwissenschaft,* or scholarly research in the arts. Esthetics covers also the more philosophical areas of art criticism, of the psychology of art, of the sociology and ethnology of art, and of all other subjects touching upon the arts and related types of behavior and experience. Each of these contributory subjects has other areas, less general and fundamental in import —for example, ordinary journalistic criticism of day-to-day theatrical

---

8. F. S. Wight, "The Revulsions of Goya: Subconscious Communications in the Etchings," *Journal of Aesthetics,* Vol. V, No. 1 (Sept., 1946), pp. 1-28.

9. C. J. Ducasse, "Aesthetics and the Aesthetic Activities," *Journal of Aesthetics,* Vol. V, No. 3 (March, 1947), pp. 165-177.

performances—which are more remote from esthetics. The outer boundaries of esthetics are indefinite, but its central core consists of theoretical
studies which select, coordinate, and interpret relevant facts and hypotheses
from all sources, about works of art and those who make, perform, and
use them.

Esthetics in the narrow sense, as theory of beauty. Through a series
of technical discussions in eighteenth and early nineteenth century philosophy, the word "esthetics" came into use, derived from the Greek word
for perception. Originally referring to sensuous knowledge, it came to
signify a branch of philosophy concerned with beauty, especially in the
fine arts, but also in nature. In the works of some philosophers, "esthetics" covered a wide field, identical with "philosophy of art"; that is,
it included a consideration of the particular arts. Hegel made his cover
a philosophy of art history. On the whole, the tendency was to narrow
"esthetics" down to the single problem of beauty and esthetic value; to
the question of whether judgements of value and claims to superior taste
in art have any objective basis, or rest on mere personal preference;
also to the relations between esthetic value and moral value.

*So-called "experimental esthetics"; the laboratory or psychometric
approach to the psychology of beauty and esthetic preference.* This branch
of esthetics has also been largely concerned with the nature of beauty,
sensory pleasantness, and esthetic evaluation. But its methods have been
descriptive, factual, empirical, and quantitative. As a rule, it does not
make or defend evaluative judgements about art, but observes and describes certain external aspects of evaluation. Psychometric esthetics (a
more exact term than "experimental") follows the lead of Fechner, whose
Vorschule der Aesthetik in 1876 helped bring about the experimental
approach to general psychology. It emphasizes statistical studies of
esthetic preference, especially of what kinds of visible shape, proportion,
and color combination are considered most beautiful or pleasing by the
greatest number of persons. The objects to be judged are usually not
complete works of art, but simple geometrical figures, arrangements of
dots or strips of color, etc. Hence this approach is, in its own way, almost
as abstract as the philosophical theories of beauty. Supposedly, Fechner's
approach was "from below," or from empirical data; but in practice it
has paid little attention to the complex types of form which are actually
encountered in art and nature. Its data consists rather in certain be-
havioristic responses, expressions or preference by the persons tested.

In the early twentieth century, Fechner's approach was actively pursued in the United States, by Witmer and others. It has weakened in recent years. In experimental psychology, now a huge, diversified science, quantitative researches are still occasionally done on problems related to art and esthetic preference.[10] Such work will be considered later on, as a contribution of psychology to modern esthetics. The psychometric approach is only one small element in this contribution.

Kunstwissenschaft; science or knowledge of art. This consists largely in historical studies of the visual arts. It includes such related subjects as determining the authenticity, date, and provenance of a work of art. It differs from "philosophy of art" not only in being thus restricted, but in being more neutrally descriptive in aim; it seeks to ascertain the facts, rather than to appraise them. As distinguished from the earlier art history and from art criticism, it aims at objectivity and generalization, describing stylistic traits as facts without assuming that one style is better. Much of it has been minutely specialized art history, devoted to ascertaining and recording particular facts, such as the date and origin of a certain work of art. There is no clear distinction between *Kunstwissenchaft* and *Kunstgeschichte,* and many scholars in art prefer the latter name.[11] Scientific methods can be used, of course, in discovering particular facts, as well as general principles. At times, *Kunstwissenschaft* rises toward theory in generalizing on the stylistic traits of certain periods in art, such as the differences between Greek, Byzantine, Renaissance, and Baroque architecture.

A leader in this movement was Conrad Fiedler (1841-1895). Says L. Venturi, "He renounced reflections on the beautiful to occupy himself only with art, and in that way he is founder of the science of art, distinct from esthetics."[12] Riegl and Wölfflin carried on this approach, the latter's "principles of art history" being widely influential. Wölfflin, in Venturi's opinion, lacks "the comprehensive universality which is the greatest glory of Riegl." But both are philosophic in scope. They com-

---

10. H. S. Langfeld, "Aesthetics, Experimental," *Encyclopaedia Britannica,* 14th edition. P. R. Farnsworth, "Aesthetics, Psychology of," in *Encyclopedia of Psychology* (New York, Philosophical Library, 1946). Cf. Chandler, *Beauty and Human Nature* (New York, Appleton-Century, 1934). R. M. Ogden, *The Psychology of Art* (New York, Scribners, 1938.)

11. The *Reportorium für Kunstwissenschaft* began publication in 1876 in Stuttgart, under the editorship of Franz Schestag, a Vienna museum curator, as an outgrowth of the first congress on *Kunstwissenschaft,* held in Vienna in 1873. Its pages have been devoted more to specialized history than to theory.

12. L. Venturi, *History of Art Criticism* (New York, Dutton, 1936), p. 278 f. Taine had previously proclaimed a scientific approach to art: see his *Philosophy of Art* (New York, Holt, 1875), but had not avoided evaluation. (Venturi, *op. cit.,* p. 229.)

bine intensive historical knowledge with the power to compare and generalize widely and deeply.

Allgemeine Kunstwissenschaft; general science of art. Much *Kunstwissenschaft,* as we have just seen, is highly specialized and remote from esthetic theory. But it provides another source of data; hence the possibility of another kind of esthetics "from below," rising into general theory from concrete works of art and historical knowledge about them; not (as Fechner's approach) from statistics about preference.

It is a long way, as to degree of generality, from the details of art history to philosophical esthetics. Hence, Max Dessoir believed, there was need for an intermediate real of *allgemeine,* or general *Kunstwissenschaft.*[13] It should continue to be scientific, objective, and descriptive, not indulging in dogmatic appraisal or value speculation about beauty. It should be concerned with all the arts, including music and literature, and with comparison between the arts; not with the visual arts alone.

There was much discussion in Germany as to whether "esthetics" and "general science of art" should be considered one subject, or two allied ones. Dessoir and his friends chose the latter alternative, assuming that the traditional, narrow definition of esthetics as philosophy of beauty was too firmly fixed to be altered. That definition was too narrow to cover all the newer, more descriptive studies of the arts and esthetic experience. Hence the other name must be added, to cover them.

The current tendency in France and America is away from Dessoir's double title and toward including both subjects under the single name "esthetics." The very fact that esthetics as a subject has been so undeveloped in America has prevented its name from acquiring the definite meaning, restricted to the philosophy of beauty, which Dessoir and his friends found obstructive. It is correspondingly easier, for those who now seek to establish it as an important subject in American higher education, to give the word "esthetics" the newer, broader interpretation. Only a few American writers[14] have sought to preserve the sharp distinction between esthetic and the science or philosophy of art. Of course, if we could start with a clean slate, it would not be hard to find a better name than "esthetics," with its many confusing associations. But it is fairly well established in the broader sense, and a new name would be hard to substitute.

---

13. Dessoir, M., *Aesthetik und allgemeine Kunstwissenschaft,* (Stuttgart, Enke, 1906, 1923); *Beiträge zur allgemeinen Kunstwissenschaft* (Stuttgart, 1929).

14. E. *g.,* H. Kuhn on "Philosophy of Art" and D. H. Parker on "Aesthetics," in *Encyclopedia of the Arts* (New York, Philosophical Library, 1946), pp. 741, 14.

It would be going too far to give the Germans full credit for *Kunst-wissenschaft,* or for the scientific, naturalistic approach to esthetics. French, English, and American scholars during the past seventy-five years have done a tremendous amount of objective research in the history of all the arts, and in the description of styles, which parallels the *Kunstwissenschaft* movement in Germany. The French have their own scientific tradition in esthetics, stemming largely from Comte and Taine. They have their own cultural historians and analysts of style, such as Mâle in the medieval, and Grousset in the oriental field. To name only one English example, Banister Fletcher's monumental *History of Architecture on the Comparative Method* first appeared in 1896. It gives a comparative analysis of the Gothic, Classic, and Renaissance styles in regard to general plans, walls, openings, roofs, columns, mouldings, and ornament, with many concrete examples and a discussion of geographical, geological, climatic, religious, social, and historical influences on style. Works of this type qualify as *allgemeine Kunstwissenschaft,* and as esthetics in the broad present sense, whether or not their authors so labelled them. But in the English-speaking world, such studies within a single art have not been linked up systematically with analogous studies in other arts, or with philosophic esthetics. This is true of many important British studies in special fields related to esthetics, such as those of Frazer in cultural anthropology and folklore, of Tovey on music analysis, and Herbert Read on contemporary visual arts. The ingredients for scientific esthetics are present, but more synthesis is needed. The time is overdue for bringing these ingredients together, first of all through a large-scale program of bibliographies, translations, critical summaries, and publication in different languages; second, through more thoroughly integrated, original syntheses.

4. DEVELOPMENT OF THE PREREQUISITE FOR SCIENTIFIC ESTHETICS.

To an extent not commonly realized, the necessary tools and materials for scientific esthetics have been developed since 1900. Let us briefly summarize three groups of them.

In the first place, a sufficient amount and variety of *works of art* are now available, to allow generalization about the arts of mankind on a broad scale. For the first time, we now have a fair sampling of the chief art products, of all the principal civilizations, nationalities, and stages of developments. There are still large gaps in our knowledge, but we can see world art as a whole in a way impossible as late as 1900. This applies to the visual arts, where our data for comparison include a much wider sampling of oriental, archaic, and primitive arts.[15]   This is due in part to archeological excavation; in part exploration, travel, commerce, museum techniques, and improved methods of reproduction, as in color-prints and casts.   It applies to world literature, where improved translations and new editions are now available on a much greater scale.   It applies to music, where new phonograph and sound-film recordings are bringing us exotic music such as that of India, Java, and the African tribes, as well as much unfamiliar European music of the Baroque, Renaissance, and Middle Ages.[16]

In the second place, the *social sciences* have cooperated to document these works of art for us historically and culturally: to help us understand them by seeing them, not merely as museum exhibits, but in their cultural setting.   They show us the status and functions of art and artists in various times and places. Anthropology and ethnology are showing us the meaning of primitive and oriental arts, in relation to the entire culture-pattern in which they were produced, including religious, social, economic, moral, technological, and other factors.   Slowly, this approach is being extended to the complex and diversified higher civilizations of East and West.[17]

In the third place, recent *psychology* has given us a general, naturalistic description of human nature; of its physiological basis, its animal origin, its inborn mechanisms, powers and processes of learning; its cycle of growth and senescence in personality and mental abilities.   We are given an account of such basic functions as visual and auditory perception. Psychoanalysis and depth psychology have explored the life of fantasy in its conscious and unconscious levels; the nature of emotion and motivation.   All these have a direct, obvious bearing on the arts.   The processes and mechanisms involved in the creation and appreciation of art are now seen to be, not fundamentally unique or separate, but special applications of those which occur in all other main realms of human activity.   Before scientific psychology had given us this general framework of human nature, it was impossible for esthetics to lift itself, by its own bootstraps, into an understanding of art.

In terms of psychology, we can now approach the analysis of esthetic form in a new and searching way.   A painting or statue is not only a

---

15. F. Boas, *Primitive Art* (Cambridge, Mass., Harvard Univ. Press, 1927). R. Linton and P. S. Wingert, *Arts of the South Seas* (New York, Museum of Modern Art, 1946).
16. E. g., the phonograph albums *Musik des Orients, African Native Music,* and *L'Anthologie Sonore;* this last with program notes by Curt Sachs.
17. R. Benedict, *Patterns of Culture* (Boston, Houghton Mifflin, 1934); *The Chrysanthemum and the Sword* (Boston, Houghton Mifflin, 1946).

physical form, a configuration of molecules; a sonata is not only a succession of sound-waves. Each is also an esthetic form: a stimulus to apperception, which includes the apprehending of complex configurations of presented sensory details and of suggested meaning. Suggested meanings become comparatively objective (or intersubjective) when culturally established, as in the cross as a symbol of Christianity. A work of art also stimulates emotional, conative, and evaluative responses, which are important for study in esthetic psychology, but which are highly variable from person to person and moment to moment. Hence it is usually advisable to exclude the observer's affective responses from a description of the form of a work of art. Even the apprehension of its meaning or suggestive factor is dependent partly on the observer's previous experience and education. Its powers of stimulation are determined to a large extent by the culture pattern within which the work of art is experienced. A work of art is a vehicle for preserving and transmitting individual and social experience culturally. When the work of art is produced in one culture, and is exported or preserved for observation by another culture, its meanings are certain to change. Thus the description of a work of art in regard to its powers of suggestion requires reference to one or more cultural backgrounds. The analysis of form also involves a study of the sensory and other psychological ingredients in artistic form, such as line, color, pitch, and rhythm. It involves a study of the ways in which these ingredients are combined in various arts and mediums to produce the countless variety of individual works of art, and of historic styles. The descriptive analysis of form and style, along this and similar lines, is some times called the "morphology of art," or "esthetic morphology."[18]

Philosophical esthetics has been slow to accept the contributions of recent psychology. Its attempts at a psychology of art have clung to metaphysical abstractions, of little relevance in explaining actual works of art. There has been a long series of attempts to formulate one simple principle for explaining esthetic phenomena, from "the sense of beauty" to "expression" and "empathy." Some, like "wish-fulfillment," have been taken from other branches of psychology, in a detached way, without assimilation of the related materials—in this case, psychoanalytic. The psychology of art in the United States has been too narrowly devoted to

---

18. D. H. Parker, *The Analysis of Art*, (New Haven, Conn., Yale Univ., 1926), chap. ii. F. Lehel, *Morphologie comparée des arts* (Paris, 1930). T. *Munro*, "Form in the Arts: an Outline for Descriptive Analysis," *Journal of Aesthetics*, Vol. II, No. 8 (Fall, 1943), pp. 5-26; "Style in the Arts: A Method of Stylistic Analysis," *Journal of Aesthetics*, Vol. V, No. 2 (Dec., 1946), pp. 128-159. H. Hungerland, "Problems of Descriptive Analysis in the Visual Arts," *Journal of Aesthetics*, Vol. IV, No. 1 (Sept., 1945), pp. 20-25.

psychometric experiments and specious "tests of art ability;" too remote from contact with works of art. The extreme behaviorism of much American psychology has made us timid about other approaches, especially the introspective. There are promising signs of increasing rapprochement between psychology, esthetics, and the arts; one after another, approaches such as Gestalt, personality diagnosis, and the psychology of learning are applied to esthetic problems.[19]

With the aid of psychoanalysis and individual psychology, we are now in a position to explore systematically the types of personality found in the world of art, the personalities of artists, and their relation to the kind of art produced; the symbolic meanings of art as an expression of the artist's partly unconscious desires and conflicts;[20] the relation between taste and personality; the factors determining preference in art; the ways in which art is experienced, used, and evaluated by persons of different age-levels, sexes, and personality types, of different social, educational, economic, religious, and racial groups. Special attention is being given to the art produced and preferred by children of different ages and sexes, in different mediums; to the development of art abilities and individual types of expression, as related to general mental and emotional growth, health, and maladjustment. Methods of education in the arts are being revised in the light of a fuller understanding of child psychology, the factors making for creative imagination, and the value of it to the child.

Semantics, with its study of words and other signs and meanings, involves an application of psychology and logic to a certain kind of cultural mechanism for the communication and recording of thought. It overlaps esthetic psychology, especially in the study of literature, of signs, symbols, and meanings in all arts, and of art criticism and evaluation expressed in words.[21]

General psychology has much to learn from a study of esthetic data. Its account of human nature is sadly incomplete while it neglects those

19. M. Schoen, "Aesthetic Experience in the Light of Current Psychology" *Journal of Aesthetics,* (Spring, 1941), pp. 23-33. N. C. Meier, *Art in Human Affairs,* (New York, McGraw-Hill, 1942). T. Munro, "Methods in the Psychology of Art," *Journal of Aesthetics,* Vol. VI, No. 3 (March, 1948), pp. 225-235.

20. J. Weiss, "A Psychological Theory of Formal Beauty," *Psychoanalytic Quarterly,* Vol. XVI, (1947). H. B. Lee, "The Cultural Lag in Aesthetics," *Journal of Aesthetics,* Vol. VI, No. 2, (Dec., 1947), pp. 120-139.

21. C. Morris, *Signs, Language, and Behavior,* (New York, Prentice-Hall, 1946). "Aesthetics and the Theory of Signs," *Journal of Unified Science,* Vol. VIII, (1939), pp. 131-150. M. W. Hess, "Symbolic Logic and Aesthetics," *Journal of Philosophy,* Vol. XXXVII, (1940), pp. 579-581. I. P. Creed, "Iconic Signs and Expressiveness," *Journal of Aesthetics,* Vol. III, No. 11-12, pp. 5-14. C. Amyx, "The Iconic Sign in Aesthetics," *Journal of Aesthetics,* Vol. VI, No. 1 (Sept., 1947), pp. 54-60.

forms of thought and construction in which human nature expresses itself on civilized levels. Indeed, many of its ideas about "basic human nature," put forward as true of all mankind, have been derived from too limited a sampling of human beings; mostly from modern Western urban culture. Its dilemma has been, that in examining thought on a high level of complex, rational, and imaginative development, is necessarily moves away from those levels on which generalizations can be made about all human beings, or even all humans of a certain age, sex, and personality type. It enters a realm where the patterns of thought, feeling, and behavior differ tremendously in different cultures and periods of history. To find psychological principles with any approach to universal validity on this level, we must first compare a great many cultures, and trait-complexes within them.

This leads directly to the comparative analysis of styles in art; to their interpretation, not only as kinds of art product, but as evidences of how people think, feel, imagine, and act in a certain place, time, and cultural setting. One of the new psychological approaches which is most promising for esthetics is that of *cultural psychology,* or the psychology of different cultural groups. In the works of Benedict, Kardiner, Linton, Mead,[22] and others, it involves a combination of psychology and psychoanalysis with anthropology and ethnology. Building upon the suggestive hypotheses of Freud's *Totem and Taboo,* but often differing with Freud on special points (e.g., the universality of the Oedipus complex), and building also on fresh data gathered in the field, they provide illuminating theories of the different types of basic personality involved in different culture-patterns. Little has been done so far to interpret the art products of these different peoples in the light of deeper understanding of their psychic structure; but that is the obvious next step, from the standpoint of esthetics.

Important contributions to esthetics are being made, in America, as elsewhere, by logic, mathematics,[23] the physical and biological sciences; but space is lacking here to discuss them.

---

22. A. Kardiner, and others, *The Psychological Frontiers of Society,* (New York, Columbia Univ. Press, 1945). R. Linton, *The Cultural Background of Personality* (New York, Appleton-Century, 1945). G. Bateson, and J. Mead, *Balinese Character* (New York, New York Academy of Sciences, 1942).

23. G. D. Birkhoff, *Aesthetic Measure* (Harvard Press, 1933). J. Schillinger, *The Mathematical Basis of the Arts* (New York, Philosophical Library, 1948).

5. SUMMARY OF CURRENT TRENDS.

The following tendencies appear to be ascendant in American esthetics, though by no means completely victorious:

(a) An *international and intercultural* outlook, rather than a narrowly nationalistic one; a human, world outlook, rather than a purely occidental one; a selective synthesis of attitudes toward art from many different cultures. This parallels and supplements the current eclectic wave in the arts themselves, with much selective borrowing, revival, and adaptation from exotic and primitive styles, and different degrees of success in thoroughly integrating them.

(b) An *enlargement* of the scope of esthetics to include, besides the traditional problems of esthetic value, all theoretical studies of the arts and related types of experience and behavior. Thus it includes the more general, philosophical areas in a number of different scientific approaches to these phenomena: especially these of psychology, the history of the arts and of culture, sociology, and anthropology.

(c) As a phase of this enlargement, a *shift of emphasis away from the traditional concepts* of beauty, ugliness, the sublime, taste, and pleasure, which dominated esthetics up to recent years. These words occur much less frequently in contemporary discussion. There is no other small set of concepts to take their place, but a much wider range, to cope with the diverse phenomena of art and behavior toward art. As to art, there is much discussion of the varieties of form and style and of factors in them, such as design, representation, and symbolism. The psychology of art (esthetic psychology) is no longer limited to "the sense of beauty," "good taste," and the "esthetic attitude" in a narrow sense (e.g. implying complete disinterestedness). It studies a great variety of responses to art, of ways of experiencing and using it, all of which are in a broad sense esthetic phenomena; also many ways of producing and performing it— there is no one, uniform "creative process." To understand the processes involved in art, esthetic psychology has to study them in other manifestations also: e.g. to study fantasy in dreams and neurotic symptoms as well as in art. But it emphasizes the ways in which human nature manifests itself in art.

(d) Greater interest in the *cultural* and *social* aspects of art, along with sustained interest in the artist as an individual personality. Art is

---

24. F. S. C. Northrop, *The Meeting of East and West* (New York, Macmillan, 1946). J. Remenyi, "Nationalism, Internationalism, and Universality in Literature," *Journal of Aesthetics* (Sept., 1946), pp. 44-49.

regarded more as a social manifestation than as a product of isolated, individual genius or supernatural inspiration. Both artist and work of art are linked up with recurrent psychological and cultural trends, instead of being placed on a high pedestal as completely unique and inexplicable. Art is also a social problem and responsibility; for best use and development in the interest of general welfare.[25]

(e)   Greater interest in the *utilitarian, instrumental, functional* aspects of art, along with sustained interest in the more distinctively esthetic ones, which are experienced in direct perception.   Abandonment of the sharp antithesis between esthetic and practical, fine and useful art; recognition that both types are constantly mingled.   Abandonment of the aristocratic assumption that purely fine and esthetic art and experience are essentially superior.[26]   At the same time, there is a growing belief that American culture has overemphasized the narrowly practical, and needs to develop the esthetic and intellectual phases of its culture.

(f)   A democratic attitude, regarding art as for the benefit of all who are capable of making, using, or enjoying it; a disposition to extend its benefits and opportunities as widely as possible, and to allow considerable freedom of experience in it.   Such freedom is limited by precarious economic support for many kinds of art; also by moral codes which are still strict in sexual matters, though relaxing; also by pressures from various racial and religious groups to prevent artistic expressions offensive to them.   This applies especially to mass media such as film and radio.   Otherwise, there is no strong tendency to limit the production of art to that which all can understand and enjoy, or to make it directly subservient to the state, as in totalitarian regimes.   The activity and influence of government in art remain slight, having declined again since the wave of government sponsorship for art projects during the depression.   One of the distinctive features of American art is its almost wholly private sponsorship, by individuals or corporations; the lack of assistance or attempted control by political or ecclesiastical agencies.   This is reflected in esthetic theories of the autonomy of art, its right to complete freedom of individual expression, as opposed to the belief in its subordination to church or state; and to an emphasis on its religious, moral, or civic responsibility. The doctrine of "art for art's sake" remains strong in practice though

---

25. As in the books of John Dewey and Lewis Mumford (see Bibliography).   Also, for example, C. W. Condit, "Modern Architecture: a New Technical-Aesthetic Synthesis," *Journal of Aesthetics*, Vol. VI, No. 2 (Dec., 1947), pp. 45-54.   P. Zucker, "The Role of Architecture in Future Civilization," *Journal of Aesthetics*, Vol. III, No. 9-10, pp. 30-38.

26. J. Dewey, *Art as Experience* (New York, Minton, 1934).

often attacked by American theorists; art being still popularly regarded as a superficial frill or means of entertainment.

(g) *Relativism* in standards of value, as against the two opposite extremes of absolutism and anarchy.[27] This implies a belief that there is no single rule or standard for determining the worth of a work of art under any and all conditions; there is no metaphysical or religious basis for believing that any specific standards of good art are inherent in the nature of the universe. There is no particular kind of art which is best from every point of view; there is no one right way to produce, perform, or experience art; there are many good ways, each with different values. On the other hand, esthetic value is not to be dismissed as purely subjective and individual. Evaluation is both an individual and a social process, based in part on our common physical nature, in part on diverse and changing conditions, needs, and functions, in relation to which works of art are given different values at different times.[28]

(h) Increasing emphasis on the *descriptive, fact-finding* approach, as contrasted with the former normative, evaluative emphasis. However, evaluation remains one of the major concerns of esthetic theory. Many evaluative problems are now being approached from a descriptive standpoint.[29] "Description" and "facts" in esthetics are not limited to superficial, isolated details; as in all science, they include interpretation and explanation, through discovery of underlying tendencies, recurrent patterns in phenomena, and causal relationships.

(i) *Empiricism,* in a broad sense, rather than *a priori* rationalism or mysticism. The basing of inferences on observation through the senses and by introspection; on experience, individual and collective, rather than on deduction from first principles regarded as self-evident or as revealed by supernatural authority. This does not imply any of the special psychological and epistemological theories which have been as-

---

27. John Dewey, *Theory of Valuation* (Chicago, Ill., Univ. of Chicago Press [Reprint from *International Encyclopedia of Unified Science,* Vol. II, No. 4], 1939, 1943).

28. George Santayana, in a letter to the author from Rome, recalling the latter's enthusiasm for primitive Negro sculpture, added *"There* is a theme for your Society to investigate philosophically and scientifically. I am glad that you are approaching the vast subject of the arts from that side, rather than from that of precepts and taste. The philosophers have written a good deal of vague stuff about the beautiful and the critics a good deal of accidental partisan stuff about right and wrong in art. If you will only discover why and when people develop such arts and such tastes, you will be putting things on a sounder basis." (*Journal of Aesthetics,* Vol. IV, No. 2 [Dec., 1945], p. 131.)

29. F. P. Chambers, *Cycles of Taste* (Cambridge, Mass., Harvard Univ. Press, 1928). *The History of Taste* (New York, Columbia Univ. Press, 1932). B. S. Allen, *Tides in English Taste* (Harvard Univ. Press, 1937). L. L. Schücking, *The Sociology of Literary Taste* (London, Kegan Paul, Trench, Trubner, 1944.)

sociated with empiricism in the past, especially in British eighteenth century philosophy. It does not imply extreme associationism or behaviorism, or the limiting of data to what can be directly sensed and measured.

(j) *Naturalism,* in a broad sense opposed to esthetic theories stressing supernaturalism, transcendentalism, mysticism, pantheism, metaphysical idealism or dualism. The belief that works of art and experiences connected with them, like other human activities, are phenomena of nature, continuous with those examined in the physical and biological sciences, and arising out of them through evolution; different in degree of complexity, variability and other respects, but involving no fundamental difference in kind which would make esthetic phenomena permanently inaccessible to scientific, empirical investigation.

SELECTED BIBLIOGRAPHY

Art in American Life and Education (40th Yearbook of the National Society for the Study of Education), Bloomington, Ill., Public School Publishing Co., 1941.

Boas, G. *A Primer for Critics.* Baltimore, Johns Hopkins Press, 1937.

Chandler, A. R. *Beauty and Human Nature.* New York, Appleton-Century, 1934.

Coomaraswamy, Ananda K. *The Transformation of Nature in Art.* Cambridge, Harvard University Press, 1934.

Dewey, John. *Art as Experience.* New York, Minton, Balch Co., 1934.

Ducasse, C. J. *Art, the Critics, and You.* New York, Piest, 1945.

Giedion, S. *Space, Time and Architecture.* Cambridge, Harvard Press, 1941.

Gilbert, K. E., and Kuhn, H. *A History of Esthetics.* New York, The Macmillan Co., 1939.

Greene, T. M. *The Arts and the Art of Criticism.* Princeton, Princeton University Press, 1940.

Kroeber, A. L. *Configurations of Culture Growth.* Berkeley, University of California Press, 1944.

Heyl, B. C. *New Bearings in Esthetics and Art Criticism: a Study in Semantics and Evaluation.* New Haven, Yale University, 1943.

Kallen, H. M. *Art and Freedom.* New York, Duell, Sloan, and Pearce, 1942.

Leichtentritt, Hugo. *Music, History, and Ideas.* Cambridge, Harvard University Press, 1938.

McMahon, A. P. *Preface to an American Philosophy of Art.* Chicago, University of Chicago Press, 1945.

Morris, B. *The Aesthetic Process.* Evanston, Ill., Northwestern University, 1943.

Mumford, L. *The Condition of Man.* New York, Harcourt, Brace and Co., 1944.

——————. *The Culture of Cities.* New York, Harcourt, Brace and Co., 1938.

——————. *Technics and Civilization.* New York, Harcourt, Brace and Co., 1934.

Munro, T. (ed.). *The Future of Aesthetics: a Symposium on Possible Ways of Advancing Theoretical Studies of the Arts and Related Types of Experience.* Cleveland, Cleveland Museum of Art, 1942. Reviewed by J. Alford, *Art Bulletin* (Sept., 1945).

Munro, T. (ed.). *Scientific Method in Aesthetics.* New York, W. W. Norton and Co., 1928.

Nahm, M. C. *Aesthetic Experience and Its Presuppositions.* New York, Harper and Brothers, 1946.

Pepper, S. *The Basis of Criticism in the Arts.* Cambridge, Harvard University Press, 1945.

Prall, D. W. *Aesthetic Analysis.* New York, Thomas Y. Crowell Co., 1936.

Runes, D., and Schrickel, H. G. (eds.). *Encyclopedia of the Arts.* New York, Philosophical Library, 1946. Articles: Aesthetic Inquiry; Aesthetics; Artist, Psychology of; Art Tests; Beauty; Children's Art; Form; Philosophy of Art; Psychology of Art; Sociology of Art; Style; Taste.

Sachs, C. *The Commonwealth of Art.* New York, W. W. Norton and Co., 1946.

Schoen, M. (ed.). *The Enjoyment of the Arts.* New York, Philosophical Library, 1944.

Sorokin, Pitirim A. *Social and Cultural Dynamics,* Vol. I: *Fluctuation of Forms of Art.* New York, American Book Co., 1937.

Torossian, A. *A Guide to Aesthetics.* Stanford, Calif., Stanford University Press, 1937.

THE MAIN TREND OF
SOCIAL PHILOSOPHY
IN AMERICA

*V. J. McGill**

INTRODUCTION

Alexis de Tocqueville could see, even 108 years ago, that democracy in America was committed to progress and individualism. Its dynamism he traced to the spirit of the people, the lack of orders and feudal restraints, and the vast untapped resources of the continent. The impact of the frontier was pointed out by Hegel, and was later to be described at length by the historian, F. J. Turner.

American resilience and expansiveness was expressed by Emerson. While praising great men as the *raison d'être* of life, he is quick to add that there is no such thing as masses or common men. "True art is only possible on the conviction that every talent has its apotheosis somewhere. . . Each is uneasy until he has produced his private ray into the concave sphere, and beheld his talent also in its last nobility and exaltation." [1] William James's famous essay, "The Energies of Men," was also typical. As a rule, he concluded, *"men habitually use only a small part of the powers which they actually possess and which they might use under appropriate conditions."* [2] The teeming wealth of the rivers and fields and of the people of the country is always the theme of Walt Whitman. For example:

Fecund America—today
Thou art all over set in births and joys!
Thou groan'st with riches, thy wealth clothes thee as a swathing garment,
Thou laughest loud with ache of great possessions, . . .

The great American novelist Herman Melville thought self-love had gone

* Born in 1897. Ph.D., Harvard University, 1925. Studied under Sheldon Fellowship (Harvard University) 1925-26, at Cambridge and Freiburg. Associate Professor of psychology and philosophy, Hunter College. Author of biographical studies of Strindberg and Schopenhauer and of a book of philosophical-literary essays, and of various articles on philosophy and psychology. An editor of *Science and Society,* and Secretary-Treasurer, International Phenomenological Society.

1. Ralph Waldo Emerson, "Uses of Great Men" in *Representative Men* (New York, Thomast Y. Crowell & Co.), p. 29.
2. *Essays on Faith and Morals* (New York, Longmans Green & Co., 1943).

too far. He derided his countrymen for their boastful pride in their new world, yet was himself under its spell.

But momentous economic changes had been under way since the Civil War, which were to temper this optimism, reorient individualism, and transform the vaunted self-reliance into patterns of interdependence and collective action. The rapid growth of technology, which greatly increased the productive proficiency of the nation, was accompanied by an even more rapid concentration of economic power. The Western farmers were at the mercy of the railroads and the "money power" of the East. Corporations, which had been given the rights of persons under the Fourteenth Amendment, became increasingly imperious. Trusts and monopolies, pools and holding companies, drained off the advantages of improved technology and organization. Reinvestment was needed to support the expanding economy, but the waste and human suffering involved, led, as is well known, to widespread discontent and agitation, and to political action to secure a more equitable distribution of the national wealth. The ominous regularity of booms and depressions, and the gradual closing of the American frontier increased popular unrest. The deference of the Supreme Court and State legislatures to the economic interests of the corporations could only add fuel to the resentment.

In 1883, where our brief account of social philosophy in America begins, the Supreme Court had already (1877) approved regulation of railroad rates by the states. In 1886, however, it restricted such regulation to interstate commerce. In 1894, similarly, when counsel emphasized the socialistic character of the proposed graduated income tax, the Supreme Court reversed itself, and found the tax unconstitutional.[3] Such reversals reflected the high tensions and divisions of the time. The farmers organized in the Grangers and Farm Alliance, and soon swept up in the populist current, had made their bid for power; and the misguided free silver issue was to focus popular discontent.

The struggle, altered of course by the preponderance of industrial workers, and by many other factors, was to continue. It forms the background of the present discussion of social philosophy. Philosophers, psychologists, and social scientists were faced with increasingly complex problems resulting from the haphazard growth of American economy, and were obliged to work out theories to explain, to cushion the impact, or to redirect the process.

---

3. See, for example, Arthur C. Millspaugh, *Democracy, Efficiency, Stability, An Appraisal of American Government* (Wash., D.C., the Brookings Institution, 1942), pp. 93-4.

WARD'S MELIORISM

A number of leading ideas characteristic of American social thought are to be found in the writings of Lester Frank Ward (1841-1913). His first main book, *Dynamic Sociology* (1883), written when he was still an obscure government scientist, was a systematic and original work, laying the basis for a new science. By the turn of the century he had been named with Comte and Spencer, as a founder of modern sociology. Although greatly influenced by Spencer, Ward was one of the first and most effective opponents of Social Darwinism, and his polemics against that doctrine in the heyday of its influence, probably had much to do with its decline.

Social and organic evolution are radically different, Ward argued, "since in the latter it is the environment that transforms the organism, while in the former, man transforms the environment." Organic evolution, operating through natural selection and the survival of the fittest, is incredibly slow and wasteful, whereas human progress, which "has been accomplished mainly through the exercise of the directive agent (intelligence) in changing the motion of physical bodies so that ... they are made to pour into the channels of human advantage," [4] is distinguished by purpose, economy, and rapid adjustment. Practical intelligence is the main lever of human history. Though men have usually worked at cross purposes in the past, and so cancelled out their intended effects, progress in the future can be achieved by collective action based upon universal education and social planning. If human intelligence is to become really effective, competition in many sectors must give way to cooperation. Social legislation and the role of government must be greatly extended. In combatting Spencer's view that *laissez-faire* is part of the immutable and beneficent order of nature, so that government regulation is necessarily unavailing or disruptive, Ward pointed out that in Europe government regulation of industries and trade, and state ownership of railroads and utilities were, even in the eighties, increasing at a rapid rate. The Cobden Club and other free-trade societies might continue to distribute their pamphlets, while Spencer thundered his warnings. The trend to socialization was unmistakedly clear even in 1881.[5] Indeed the evils of competition, its wastefulness, cruelty, and inefficiency, and especially its tendency to foster monopoly, demanded state ownership and controls no matter what the Spencerians might think about it.

---

4. *Pure Sociology* (New York, 1903, 1925), p. 544.
5. Richard Hofstadter, *Social Darwinism in American Thought* (Philadelphia, 1944), p. 56.

Ward, however, was no socialist, and was singularly unaffected by Marxist theory. The socialization he advocated provided equal opportunity but also recognized the actual inequalities of men and insisted on rewards for special merit. That this was consistent with socialism Ward did not see. Though he found a measure of truth in the great man theory of history, his main contention was that men are formed by their environment which they in turn can refashion to their purposes. Even the most backward and degraded peoples have vast potentialities which are submerged by unfavorable conditions. The worker or city slum dweller, he wrote, is a peer to the most distinguished eugenicist in everything but privilege. Coupled with this reliance upon the potentialities of the masses of people was a sympathy with the struggles of the working class for better standards of life. What was needed for progress was universal education and the application of science and statistics to legislation.

Ward's environmentalism gave him confidence in progress, not only material but also spiritual. "Material civilization," he wrote, "is essentially moralizing."[6] It lays the foundation for real liberty, i.e., liberty to *act,* as contrasted with mere freedom to will. "The alleged liberty of man to will whatever he may will," Ward contended, "is one of nature's great delusions, and only worthy of serious refutation because the practical effect of a belief in it is to deprive men of their real liberty, and to subject the masses to the domination of the few."[7] Though Ward's ideas were not always acceptable to his contemporaries, the trend of history has borne him out. Spencerism is now a thing of the past, and the illusions of *laissez-faire* lie exposed. Meliorism, the capacity of man to transform the economic and cultural environment; Progress, as a goal to be reached by the spread of education and enlightenment, and by scientific lawmaking; Strong Government, as an instrument increasingly needed to regulate industry and trade, and to control monopolies; Social Legislation, as an essential means to happiness—these ideas, in spite of cross currents of doubt and hesitation, have been adopted into the American tradition.

OUR PECUNIARY CIVILIZATION

On many issues Lester Ward and Thorstein Veblen stood close together, and each respected the other's work. The basic conflict that

6. *Op. cit.,* p. 454.
7. *Dynamic Sociology* (New York, 1883, 1897, 1926), Vol. II, p. 232.

Veblen discovered in our culture, the conflict between business and industry, had already been described by Ward in 1883, and Veblen acknowledged his indebtedness. By 1903, Ward, in turn, had been influenced by Veblen. Veblen, he wrote, "has shown how the mere maintenance of caste requires gratuitous and ostentatious waste of property, . . ." [8] The leisure class achieves its "predatory" purpose at first by force, but increasingly by deception. "The idea of the essential inferiority of the subject class must be steadily kept in the minds of that class," Ward wrote. Thus many subterfuges had to be adopted ". . . and even at the present time, those artificial inequalities which enable the prosperous classes to thrive at the expense of the proletariat, . . . are chiefly maintained through the systematic deception of the latter, . . ." [9]

The capacity for deception is of great importance, Ward held. It has enabled man to survive and to exploit other animals. In our society, however, it becomes the foundation of business, taking the form of "shrewdness" which is usually regarded as upright and proper, within limits. Deception also abounds in politics. Behind the politician stand the "vested interests" which dictate to the press and form public opinion. Deception also explains the role assigned to upper-class women. Ward, the ardent feminist, agreed that such women often "represent what Mr. Veblen calls 'vicarious leisure' and 'vicarious consumption,' devoting their lives to 'reputable futility'." [10]

Commenting on another favorite theme of Veblen, Ward remarked that it is natural that the leisure class should manifest the "instinct of sportsmanship," just as the industrial classes display the "instinct of workmanship," since all men must derive their satisfaction from the normal exercise of the faculties. If men's obligatory work had been less monotonous and degrading, effort would not have come to be regarded as evil.

The area of agreement between the two thinkers was considerable. Both explained human institutions as adaptations, as products often delayed, of material and social conditions, and both emphasized economic factors in history. On the other hand, Veblen explicitly rejected Ward's pragmatism, contending that attention is directed, not only by meliorative, practical, or ethical interests, but also, especially in the higher ranges of intelligence, by an "idle curiosity." [11] It is this idle curiosity which ac-

---

8. *Pure Sociology, op. cit.,* p 278.
9. *Ibid.,* p. 486.
10. *Ibid.,* p. 363.
11. Thorstein Veblen, *The Place of Science in Modern Civilization* (New York, 1923), pp. 7, 19.

counts for science. Veblen also rejected Ward's hedonistic psychology in favor of a dynamic theory of motivation, and preferred to talk of instincts and propensities. The instinct theory was a step in advance; but it was soon outmoded in the United States, by the results and implications of learning experiments, and was replaced by the theory of drives or needs.

Veblen's insistence that economics should fall in line with the biological sciences and adopt an evolutionary standpoint was iconoclastic. He charged that the classical economists, instead of describing causal relations, projected standards and norms into the economic process which were not observable, but only conformed to their own ideal of the way things should go. Economic laws were formulated for this "normal," or "natural" state of affairs, and features of the process which failed to conform, became "abnormal cases due to ·disturbing causes." [12] The ideal of classical and neo-classical economists, and even marginalists, was not discovery of causal relations but "ceremonial adequacy."

A real evolutionary economics, on the contrary, "must be the theory of a process of cultural growth as determined by the economic interest, a theory of a cumulative sequence of economic institutions stated in terms of the process itself." [13] Veblen's espousal of the empirical study of institutions provided the inspiration and set the stage for the important school of institutionalists, and is sometimes regarded as his greatest contribution to American thought. But his avowed followers, having shed his radicalism, are often bound to him only by their devotion to factual study and quantitative methods. Two of the most prominent institutionalists, Wesley C. Mitchell and Walton Hamilton, however, may have somewhat closer links with the master. For example, Mitchell in his protracted study of business cycles, treats depression, not as an abnormality due to disturbing causes, but as a phenomenon arising from "the process itself," while Hamilton in his brilliant study of monopoly displays much of Veblen's breadth, irony, and radical animus. There is no disputing the value of the immense array of factual and quantitative studies of institutional forms which have been produced by economists in universities, or under government auspices in Washington. They are sometimes regarded as the chief pride and distinction of American economics.

At a time when the railroad boom and the Granger movement were in full swing, and Western farmers were reacting to the pressure of business and financial interests of the East, Veblen's exposure of the pretenses

---

12. *Ibid.*, pp. 65, 67.
13. *Ibid.*, p. 77.

of business, in contrast to its real motives, was immensely clarifying. His main theme, the conflict between business and industry, has already been mentioned. The conflict comes about because business aims, not at serviceability to the community, but only at serviceability to the owner, and under the price system the prospect of pecuniary gain induces the owners "to inhibit, curtail, or misdirect industry, and so to turn the community's technological proficiency to the community's detriment." [14]

Since business aims prevail in our civilization there is no proportion between remuneration and service rendered,[15] though the myth is widely disseminated that the business man's gain is the gain of all. Banking, investment, advertising, competitive selling, and other forms of competition, are unproductive, Veblen argues, and must be paid for out of the earnings of the real producers, the engineers, technicians, managers, and skilled workers. Since business aims prevail, and the "business of United States is business," education, communications, and government itself tend to become subservient not to the community, but to pecuniary interests. "Representative government means, chiefly, representation of business interests." [16] With the advancing strength of corporations, these invasions of community life, become proportionately more serious.

In the past the discrepancy between business and industrial needs of the community was not nearly as great as at present. With the modern extension of the credit system, the increase of absentee ownership, and the growth of trust and monopoly, the gulf has widened. Capitalization of a business no longer bears any relation to the value of the physical plant or its productive capacity, but being determined by the income the ambitious owner expects it to yield, is usually inflated. The contradiction, Veblen argues, is inherent in pecuniary economy. For example, the growth of technology, which serves the community, distresses the owner, since it tends to reduce capital values. As a result, technological change is often shelved at the community's expense.

The basic contradiction, according to Veblen, is the discrepancy between capitalization and earning capacity. In "normal" times there is a constant tendency toward "inflation of capitalization and a large extension of credit, which normally ends in a period of liquidation." [17] The depression which follows is characterized by a shrinkage of earning capacity. The significant thing about Veblen's theory of boom and depression is

14. *Ibid.*, p. 359.
15. Thorstein Veblen, *The Theory of Business Enterprise* (New York, 1919), pp. 63-4.
16. *Ibid.*, p. 286.
17. *Ibid.*, p. 249.

his insistence that they are business phenomena having nothing to do with the productive process as such. It follows that if the management of the economy could be shifted from businessmen to engineers and technicians, the problem would disappear; and conversely, so long as business is at the helm, crises and depressions are inevitable. They are in fact becoming worse, Veblen argues. The periodicity of depression and inflation (every 12 years) has not been proved and Veblen sees rather a descending spiral, with crises becoming ever more frequent and severe.[18]

Veblen offers no plausible solution and has almost nothing to say of current political issues. He likes to imagine the social management in the hands of the engineers, but his silence regarding the role of unskilled workers and of the general population in such an order, exposed it to suspicion. The short-lived technocratic movement in the United States, which drew its inspiration from Veblen, was rightly criticized not only for its inaccuracies but also for its undemocratic preconception. At most, the movement served to popularize the knowledge that American productive power is greater than usually supposed, capable of servicing the consumer needs of the entire population. The exact figures and documentation, however, were to be supplied by sober statistical studies, such as those of the Brookings Institution.

While Veblen could sometimes envisage an industrial republic under the rational management of engineers, he believed that business habits and values were too deeply ingrained and popular to permit any such outcome in the near future. Underestimating the strength of organized labor and other resistance forces, he seems to have thought that business controls, myth-making, and coercion would increasingly impose status and conformity on the entire population, in spite of a continued lowering of living standards.[19] Whereas Ward's outlook had been robust and confident, Veblen's view of the future was typically vague, cynical, or pessimistic. He rejected not only business civilization, but also the socialist alternative, and had no viable third possibility to offer.

Although Veblen took account of the ensuing economic developments better than any other American economist of the time, he neglected the rising trade union movement altogether. Perhaps the greatest figure in the American trade union history was Eugene V. Debs. In 1894 Debs's American Railroad Union won a big victory over the Great Northern Railroad. In a subsequent strike in Illinois, the Union was completely

---

18. *Ibid.*, pp. 245 f.
19. See, for example, *Absentee Ownership* (New York, 1923), pp. 416 f., and 445.

smashed, and Debs himself was sent to jail, but only after a sweeping
Federal injunction had been issued, and United States troops dispatched
to the troubled area. Veblen might have seen in such events the burgeoning of a new force in American history, but their significance escaped him.
Debs, who joined the socialists in 1901, and five times ran for President of
the United States, is also important for his efforts to link socialism with
the American trade union movement, and for his insistence that both
economic and political action are necessary. His contemporary, Daniel
De Leon, also emphasized the importance of combining economic and
political action, and formulated the principle of industrial unionism.
Political action, though it could not alone secure basic reforms, would
prepare the ground for socialism, which he held to be the only solution.
Socialism as he conceived it, was to be made possible by a great industrial
organization of the workers (whom Veblen had left out of account), and
their representatives were to constitute the government of the future.

Veblen's relation to Marx is often regarded as a mystery. The economist, Erich Roll, has suggested that Marx was the real institutionalist because he devoted his efforts to an analysis of the structure and function
of economic institutions, whereas Veblen was always more concerned
with psychological motives and therefore remained on the level of what
Marxists call, the superstructure. Veblen's theory of crises and depression,
though it bears a strong resemblence to the Marxian theory, is sketchy,
unburdened by economic details. One of the few systematic books presenting the Marxist position in this country was written by the labor
lawyer, Louis B. Boudin (*The Theoretical System of Karl Marx in the
Light of Recent Criticism*, 1918). Paul M. Sweezey, in a much later
work (*The Nature of Capitalist Development*, 1942) has characterized
Boudin's conception of crisis and depression as an oversimplified underconsumption theory. The Marxian theory, he says, is more complex, involving underconsumption, overproduction, disproportion, and other factors. The same book essays to answer the kind of criticism Veblen directs
against the Marxian labor theory of value.

THE INDIVIDUAL AND SOCIETY

All leading American social thinkers since the first World War have
accepted democracy without question. The people is understood to be
sovereign, though interpretations differ. For example, is it the separate
individuals who enter into the hypothetical social compact as Hobbes and
Locke had held, or the people as a whole, as Rousseau had assumed?

Does each separate individual confer sovereignty, or the group? Professor Perry has shown that the distinction has made some difference in American history. For example, some justified the secession of the Southern States in the Civil War in terms of an *individual,* others in terms of a *social,* contract. If each citizen is a party to the compact no change in the settlement would be justified without universal consent. This interpretation seemed to make change almost impossible, but it had its appeal to individualist thinkers. Professor Perry rejects Rousseau's view. "In thinking of a collective will as absorbing and superseding individuals, and as being in its solidarity the ultimate source of sovereignty (Rousseau) was thinking the thoughts of Spinoza, or Hegel, rather than those of the Enlightenment." He was "either a backslider or a prophet ahead of his time." [20]

For Perry, on the contrary, it is the individual who has sovereignty to confer, not the people, not even the vast majority. "There is no profounder misunderstanding of democracy than to suppose that it means the rule of the majority." The majority is not *better* than the minority, and its good (or pleasure) is not greater than that of the minority, because the goods of individuals are unique and incomparable, hence nonadditive. "The purpose of the state is not the happiness of the majority of its members, but of all. . ." [21] Happiness is individual as is also choice. The actual conflict of wills cannot be resolved by Rousseau's "general will." Like other metaphysical inventions, this merely "gives reality to an ideal which is contrary to fact." [22]

How does Perry reconcile his extreme individualism with the fact that majorities, within the restriction of the bill of rights, do rule in a democracy—that majority rule is regarded as the essence of democracy? Intent upon upholding the finality of the individual, who is not to be overruled by any show of hands or counting of heads, Perry reduces the majority to a mere political device. "Since unanimity is usually impossible," he says, "the decision to abide by the vote of the majority provides a way out of what otherwise would be an impasse." [23] Perry's argument implies that the decision to abide by the will of a minority, even a very small minority, would have been morally just as sound and defensible.

Now a great many social thinkers admit Perry's main premises but not his conclusion. They would admit that the individual is final in

20. Ralph Barton Perry, *Puritanism and Democracy* (New York, Vanguard Press, 1944), p. 172.
21. *Ibid.,* p. 490.
22. *Ibid.*
23. *Ibid.,* p. 491.

the sense that he is the only seat of hopes and values, will, and choice, but would point out that if progress is to occur, individuals and minorities must obviously be overruled and outvoted. This does not mean that majorities are always right, but that they are more apt to be right, at least about broad questions affecting public interests, than minorities are. Most philosophers would also say that the uniqueness of values does not prevent their being added. Thus it is *better* to save the lives of many children than to save only a few, though each child's life and happiness is unique and irreplaceable. In the same way, the prosperity of a majority is *better* than that of a minority, and also a closer approach to Perry's ideal of universal prosperity. But Perry clearly recognizes the summation of values in an earlier book.[24]

Yet Perry's view of the finality of the individual, though seldom stated so explicitly, seems to be assumed by much of current discussion in which democracy is practically equated with the preservation of individual and minority rights. That such an emphasis now serves the interest of privileged classes can hardly be denied. Exclusive concern for the minority which opposes the majority also involves injustice to other minorities, for the majority itself is nothing but a set of minorities with certain common aims. Though obvious, this is often forgotten. Minorities composing a majority, such as, for example, unskilled laborers and poor farmers, deserve at least as much consideration as the more articulate and prosperous minorities.

The liberalism which arose as a champion of the rights of opposition minorities, has either turned conservative, or revamped its position. One prominent American liberal, for example, has spoken of "the socialization of liberalism." "The liberalism that began by glorifying freedom of speech, thought, religion and association in terms of absolute individual rights has learned at last to speak the language of social welfare." [25] Professor Perry himself is aware that it is social welfare, rather than natural rights, which justifies social policy. The aim of government is not only the protection of life, property, and other formal rights, he contends, but the full realization of the potentialities of every individual. Perry's justification of social progress, even if it is achieved against the wishes of some individuals and minorities, is the principle of equality, namely: There is no moral ground for denying to one individual or group what is grant-

---

24. *General Theory of Value* (New York, 1926), p. 647. Here the principle of "inclusiveness" implies that the value of a policy depends on how many favor it. In the present book (*op. cit.*, pp. 49, 632), the principle is still regarded as basic, but now it implies that policies must exclude no legitimate interest.

25. Morris R. Cohen, *The Meaning of Human History* (LaSalle, Illinois, 1947), p. 271.

ed to others. But does not this principle conflict with Perry's former conclusion that majorities have no moral right to outvote and overrule a
minority? If the third of a nation which is ill-housed, ill clothed, and ill-fed
has a moral claim to goods which the rest of the population enjoy, does
not a majority have a moral right to overrule minority interests in order to
achieve this end?

The conclusion seems to be that majorities are, by right, more authoritative and, in the long run wiser, than minorities. Since they embrace
more minorities within them, they exclude more injustice to minorities.
Professor Perry's chivalrous concern for the welfare of every individual
is better served by majority rule than by minorities. A further assurance
could be provided by current proposals for the extension of the bill of
rights. Besides the formal rights granted by the United States Constitution, there are other material rights which were proposed, for example,
by the late President Roosevelt, some of which have already been written
into the constitutions of other countries. Roosevelt proposed for example:
"The right to a useful and remunerative job. . ., the right to earn enough
to provide adequate food and clothing and recreation . . . the right of
every family to a decent home, adequate medical care, . . . protection from
economic fears. . . and unemployment. . . the right of every businessman
to. . . freedom from unfair competition and domination by monopolies," [26]
and so on. It is important to recognize rights in this nonlegal sense,
as Professor Perry has pointed out, since in the past, standpatters have so
often denied that rights exist merely because they are not contained in
current constitutions and statutes. Rights exist as moral convictions, he
argues, even before they are guaranteed, for otherwise the state would
have nothing to guarantee.[27]

John Dewey is also a leading American individualist, but no one has
more persistently attacked the atomic individualism of the eighteenth
century.

"Popular franchise and majority rule," he wrote, "afforded the
imagination a picture of individuals in their untrammeled individual
sovereignty making the state. To adherents and opponents alike it presented a spectacle of a pulverizing of established associations into the
desires and intentions of atomic individuals. The forces, springing from
combination and institutional organization which controlled below the
surface the acts which formally issued from individuals, went unnoted." [28]

26. Cited by Georges Gurvitch, *The Bill of Rights* (New York, 1946), p. 152.
27. *Ibid.,* p. 440.
28. John Dewey, *The Public and its Problems* (New York, 1927), p. 101.

These underlying forces for Dewey, as for Ward and Veblen, were preponderantly economic. He describes the changing economic conditions which laid the foundations of democracy, and the transformation of face-to-face relations in the modern community by the growth of technology and vast impersonal economic organizations. What has resulted is a failure of effective communication. "The Great Society created by steam and electricity may be a society, but it is no community." [29]

A community, as something more than a society, exists "wherever there is conjoint activity whose consequences are appreciated as good by all singular persons who take part in it, and where the realization of the good is such as to effect an energetic desire and effort to sustain it in being just because it is a good shared by all . . ." [30] The amount of free communication and cooperative action in any society is a measure of the degree of its democracy. Democracy is not an alternative to other principles of human association, "It is the idea of community itself."

This statement of the social ideal would be acceptable to most social philosophers in this country, except that some would specify more concretely such obvious desiderata as proper housing and medical care. The question is how the goal is to be attained. Economic facts, i.e., raw materials, technology, and human resources, according to Dewey, set the conditions of action—define the possibilities. They do not fully determine the actual consequences, because economic agencies "have a different outcome in the degree in which knowledge of consequences is equitably distributed, and action is animated by an informed and lively sense of a shared interest." [31] Economic determinists forget that foreknowledge of economic consequences, when coupled with common interests, and cooperative action, can change or nullify these consequences. Men are not chained by "natural" economic laws, nor by biological necessities, nor by *a priori* certainties of any kind, but can cooperate in setting up new conditions for action. Social needs and circumstances explain the differences in concrete behavior far better than do biological facts. Human adaptation is a social process, and ideas are instruments. Social doctrines were invented to ward off ill or to serve some pragmatic need. "But often their very adaptation to immediate circumstances unfitted them pragmatically to meet more enduring and more extensive needs. They lived to cumber the political ground, obstructing progress all the more so because they were . . . held not as hypotheses with which to direct social experimen-

29. *Ibid.,* p. 98.
30. *Ibid.,* 149.
31. *Ibid.,* p. 150.

tation but as final truths, dogmas. No wonder they call urgently for revision and displacement." [32] What is needed to release human potentialities is an unremitting application of experimental tests. Democracy is now the general belief and settled trend, not because of any *a priori* truth, for ideas are only accessory to the fact, but because it has proved itself pragmatically.

Such ideas are reminiscent of Lester Ward, but Dewey's emphasis upon individual initiative and "action from below," and his lack of sympathy with governmental planning, gives his liberalism a distinctive quality, and reflects perhaps the gathering difficulties which have enveloped American programs of reform. To achieve broad politico-economic ends it is necessary to adhere to organizations which have a certain momentum of their own, to subscribe to policies which one may not approve in every particular, and which certainly cannot be tested at every stage. The bottleneck of reform is the organization and administration of resources. Raw material, technology, and human resources are not lacking. The problem is to function effectively in organizations which will make proper use of them. Political experience teaches that criticism and the experimental testing of ideas are always important. But so also is loyalty enlisted on the basis of broad objectives. Mistakes of the New Deal needed criticism; its achievements while in progress required unwavering support. In the real political process loyalty to large perspectives, in the spirit of Josiah Royce, is also found necessary.

Dewey's rejection of the dichotomy between extrinsic and intrinsic values, and his doctrine of the continuity of means and ends, were very influential, especially in educational theory and practice. A typical American view had been that education is a preparation for life, and that the normal activity of the adult is to work, and to accumulate wealth, for some remote enjoyment in the future. Since enjoyment was under suspicion, it tended to be deferred. Dewey, in opposition to all this, taught that work bcomes creative when enjoyed, and enjoyment real when consequential. "This redemption of the present from some phantom future," remarks T. V. Smith, "has been John Dewey's greatest contribution to American thought. Ordered by this transforming insight, education becomes not a preparation for life but apprenticeship in the process of living. Assuming the continuity of all values, such a philosophy of education teaches that the best way to prepare for any future stage is to live richly

---

32. *Ibid.*, pp. 145-6.

and sanely in any present moment."[33] The doctrine of the continuity of means and ends, however, had other implications. If the end must resemble the means employed to realize it, undemocratic means, including even wars of self-defense, must have an undemocratic outcome. The means-ends doctrine could thus be used to condemn any forceful action, even though it was retaliatory or defensive in character. This doctrine thus strengthened the purely critical, nonpartisan tendencies of Dewey's philosophy.

There is another side to Dewey's social thought which must be mentioned. The translation of abstract problems of social philosophy into concrete programs of scientific research, which had been forecast by Engels, was also advocated as we have seen by Ward and Veblen and Mead, each in his own way. Professor Dewey has also been a strong proponent of this modern approach. In his *Reconstruction in Philosophy* he states that the common defect of theories from Plato to Bentham is that "they are all committed to the logic of general notions under which specific situations are to be brought." What is needed is light upon particular groups of individuals, particular institutions, and specific social arrangements. Unfortunately "the discussion goes on in terms of *the* state, *the* individual; the nature of institutions as such, society in general."[34]

The task is not to prove deductively that the evils of the world are illusory or necessary, but to locate the social disorders and to find a cure. The problem is not to uphold *the* individual, as against society or institutions, but to see that every individual realizes his full potentialities by participating in social enterprises. The individual becomes an individual only as he is socialized. It is not surprising that one trend of Dewey's thought is toward "socialization" or socialism. In his *Individualism, Old and New* (1930) he bids farewell to *laissez-faire* individualism, and accepts with some apprehension the new collective freedom. We are in for some kind of socialism, he writes, call it what we may. In a later book, *Freedom and Culture* (1939), however, the old individualism seems to be reinstated. The collectivism of Lester Ward gives way again to the individualism of Proudhon. Thus it was possible for Sidney Hook to point out how much Dewey's philosophy resembled that of Marx, and for others to indicate how much it differed. The resolution toward which liberal thought is moving is (1) that freedom and individualism must be brought into harmony with planning and social controls, which have now

---

33. *The Democratic Way of Life,* Revised Ed. (Chicago, the University of Chicago Press, 1939), p. 199.
34. *Reconstruction in Philosophy* (New York, 1930), p. 188.

become necessary, and (2) that other human needs besides free communication must be emphasized. In expansive times, such as the New Deal era, when great gains are made in living standards and social legislation, and material and cultural needs are put first, free communication is at its highest. Communication becomes effective as and when other needs are serviced.

THE SOCIALIZED INDIVIDUAL AND HIS NEEDS

The doctrine that man is formed by his environment, especially by the nature of economic relations, which was pivotal in the thought of Ward, Veblen, and Dewey, received strong support from numerous concrete studies by Franz Boas and his disciples. In a country which has become, in spite of discrimination and immigration restrictions, a real "melting pot" of races, Boas's conclusion that fundamental traits of races are not stable as was supposed, but modifiable by the environment, had decided pertinence. So also his conclusions that the mentality of peoples is evidently not determined by physical traits, and that race mixture is not harmful. Physical and cultural anthropology thus set the stage for the work of the psychologist. His task was to explain the learning process wherein social traits of individuals are acquired. Hereditary differences were still important but for many purposes—both theoretic and practical —could be completely ignored.

A great pioneer in this field was George Herbert Mead, one time colleague of John Dewey at the University of Chicago. One of Mead's objections to the social theories of his predecessors, and he made special reference to Wundt, was that they attempted to derive society from a preexistent self. "The difficulty is that Wundt presupposes selves as antecedent to the social process, whereas, on the contrary, selves must be accounted for in terms of the social process, and in terms of communication . . . ." [35] Since Wundt presupposes the existence of the mind to account for the social process, "the origin of minds and the interaction among minds becomes a mystery." [36] Mead maintained, to the contrary, that if there are selves, there is communication, i.e., socialized behavior. He is careful to distinguish the human level of communication from reaction patterns that sometimes pass for communication among other animals. Ants do not really communicate because they have "no com-

---

35. George Herbert Mead, *Mind, Self, and Society From the Standpoint of Social Behaviorism* (Chicago, the University of Chicago Press, 1946), p. 49.
    36. *Ibid.*, p. 50.

mon symbol that means food." [37]   When a dog by barking at another dog causes it to run away, he may be a little frightened himself (though this reaction is inhibited) but there is no shared meaning.   "Gestures become significant symbols when they implicitly arouse in an individual making them the same responses which they explictly arouse, or are supposed to arouse, in other individuals . . . . In all conversations of gesture within the social process . . . the individual's consciousness of the content and flow of meaning involved depends on his thus taking the attitude of the other toward his own gestures." [38] Mead's account of how the individual internalizes in himself the reactions he produces in other organisms (or tries to produce) in the form of common meanings, is ingenious, but too intricate to describe in this place. There is no reliance on ready-made instincts, such as imitation, to solve the problem, but a straightaway genetic analysis. Mead has shown that behaviorism has subtleties and resources which played no part in Watson's pioneer formulations. Psychologists studying animal learning and the development of social behavior in the child, are now demonstrating how much can be accomplished by a genetic approach. Comparative ethnology has also made a contribution.   It is not unlikely that ultimately socialized behavior will be explained almost entirely in terms of conditioning and selective learning.   The social reactions in any community which survive, as against a great variety of false trials, appear to be those which get associated with habits, or are rewarded.

The reward, however, may be very indirect. Cultures, says Murdock, "contain an immense number of so-called 'instrumental responses' which of themselves reduce no basic drives but merely pave the way for other acts which have rewarding results." [39]   Through association with rewarded acts, or by facilitating and hastening their occurrence,   many response systems become reinforced.   Other writers have contended that such instrumental acts, e.g., making a vessel, or building a house, which at first satisfy no basic drives,   later on prove satisfying in themselves. Acquired or cultural drives thus come to dominate the human organism, directing its major activities, and regulating the basic drives of hunger, thirst, sex, etc. Self-satisfying drives such as Ward and Veblen's "instinct of workmanship" are recognized as valid, though no longer regarded as instincts.   What Perry and Dewey call interests can be conceived as cultural drives or needs acquired in the learning process.   These acquired needs, though always dependent upon biological bases, have an independ-

37. *Ibid.*, p. 56.
38. *Ibid.*, p. 47.
39. George Peter Murdock, "The Common Denominator of Cultures" in *The Science of Man in the World Crisis* (New York, 1945), ed. Ralph Linton, p. 132. See also Clyde Kluckhohn and Wm. H. Kelly, "The Concept of Culture," pp. 89 f., in the same volume.

ent career not to be predicted from mere tissue needs. Hence the wide variety of behavior in different societies, and the feasibility of adjusting populations to social change. The conclusion of American behaviorism (Clark Hull, E. W. Guthrie) is that all acculturation is conditioning or association. It follows *inter alia* that undesirable behavior such as anti-semitic conduct cannot be removed unless social rewards are shifted to other types of behavior.

In this process of acquiring cultural needs, however, the individual is anything but passive. By selecting the stimuli to which it will respond, as William James and Mead emphasized, the organism determines its own environment and organizes its world.[40] By the process of selective learning, perhaps not *essentially* different from what occurs in maze runs, the human individual acquires unique needs and abilities, which in turn reorganize the stimulus field, and determine in advance what behavior will be rewarding.[41] In this way, as Mead suggests, conditioning would be made to account, not only for the conditioned animal, but for the conduct of the experimenter himself. Man, unlike the dog, can control his own conditioning. For example, "it is characteristic of significant speech that just this process of self-conditioning is going on all the time."[42]

A society invests the individual with its approved social patterns, mainly by a process of conditioning. By the same process it also gives him a mind which enables him to respond differently to diverse social issues and attitudes, and thus, in turn, to alter the social structure. Conservatives, Mead says, identify what is a pure convention with the essence of a social situation. Thus "nothing must be changed." But this sanctifying of convention is the work of individuals who have not integrated their isolated demands with the will of the "other," the community, and are therefore scarcely a part of it. The essence of the social situation is the aggregate of social acts expressing community needs. Mead finds some truth in the Marxian economic interpretation of history. If the historian "can get hold of the real economic situation, which is, of course, more accessible than most social expressions, he can work out from that to other expressions and institutions of the community."[43]

Democracy, Mead argues, consists of two factors: "the dominance of the individual or group over other groups," which is a facsimile of the

40. Mead, *op. cit.,* pp. 25 and 94-5.
41. V. J. McGill, "A Psychological Approach to Personality" in *Philosophy for the Future* (New York, 1949), pp. 287-316.
42. Mead, *op cit.,* p. 108.
43. *Ibid.,* p. 264.

economic organization, and "the sense of brotherhood and identity of different individuals in the same group," which was represented by Rousseau's "general will of the community."[44] Together they imply a universal society. Economic competition, though it is self-striving, has brought men together. The sense of being a self arises not only from a felt superiority to others, as Wundt had said. One can also acquire a self by becoming an expert, by performing a necessary task in a complex social organization. In the same way, nations can become experts, each making its valued contribution in a world of experts. Given enough socio-economic interdependence and intercommunication, competition thus becomes cooperation. Mead had some hopes for the League of Nations.

Mead's psychological approach to social philosophy has been called "social behaviorism." It typifies the effort to carry over the results of learning experiments to complex social relations. Although there are countertendencies, the genetic method is gaining ground. In place of catalogues of personality traits, and cross-sectional analysis of institutions, the need is felt for more explanation in terms of the learning process and the historical conditions of development. In theoretic and clinical psychology there is increasing emphasis on adaption through the learning process, and the failure of adaption, namely *frustration*.

Frustration is defined by Dollard and his associates, as "that condition which exists when a goal response suffers interference," whereas aggression is defined as "an act whose goal response is injury to an organism (or organism-surrogate)."[45] Their thesis is that aggression is always the consequence of frustration. It was explicitly stated by Freud, and is also basic, it is claimed, to Marx's doctrine of the class struggle. Frustration is also increasingly recognized as the source of neurosis, the aggression being directed, in this case as in others, toward the frustrating agent, innocent bystanders, or back to the frustrated person himself. There is no question that the phenomenon has importance in most departments of human activity. Dollard and his associates use their frustration-aggression hypothesis to explain the most diverse phenomena: strikes and race prejudice, reformism and criminality, the reading of detective stories and war. In discussing criminality, the authors dismiss such unfounded theories as that the criminal is a special type or mentally disordered. What distinguishes the criminal from the rest of the population, they conclude, is simply that he is more frustrated, or has less fear

---

44. *Ibid.*, pp. 286-8.
45. John Dollard, Leonard Doob, Neal E. Mowrer, O. H. Mower, and Robert W. Sears, *Frustration and Aggression* (New Haven, 1939), p. 11.

of punishment.[46] This behaviorist theory, therefore, is clearly in line with the most enlightened American criminology, which points to re-education and reform of the conditioning environment as the best policy.

The direction that aggression takes in different cultures may determine fundamental reaction patterns. In the United States, with its erstwhile frontier and boundless resources, the idea took root, and was later sedulously propagated, that man is the captain of his ship, the master of his fate. If he was not a wealthy business man, he had only himself to blame. Aggression was thus directed back upon the self. (Erich Fromm, who is intensely aware of this phenomenon, seems to yearn for a restoration of the medieval system of estates which would reimpose status, and thus guarantee security, even at the cost of freedom. He does not appear to realize that security, in the past as in the present, is a function of the percentile freedom achieved.) In this country where there has never been nobility nor orders, and where equal opportunity is the official creed, however, there have been great depressions and severe labor troubles. As a result, the present tendency of American workers is to "direct aggression from themselves on to their employers."[47] The growth of the labor movement since the first Roosevelt administration, has not only maintained living standards, but increased self-respect among the workers.

The importance of self-respect is a theme of Lasswell's recent book. The problem for individuals in a democracy (as for nations in a democratic world) is to develop enough esteem for themselves to be able to esteem others. "The new-born member of society must receive enough positive indulgence from the human environment to enable him to esteem himself and others."[48] This is also stressed by Kardiner and other psychiatrists and anthropologists, who trace almost all hostilities and deformities of character, to infant and childhood frustrations. But Lasswell like Horney, and Alexander and French, wisely recognizes that aggression may also result from adult frustrations. "The hidden destructiveness of our cultural institutions" is a constant menace to the individual. Society, he declares, "needs self-observatories capable of exposing the truth" about this danger and of "reporting experimental efforts at reformation."[49] The great evil of our times, according to Lasswell, is low self-esteem, which leads either to self-destructiveness, or compensatory

---

46. *Ibid.,* pp. 138-9.
47. *Ibid.,* p. 157.
48. Harold Dwight Lasswell, *Power and Personality* (New York, 1948), p. 162.
49. *Ibid.,* p. 173.

power seeking. Power seeking of course cannot be done away with. "The urgent task is to chasten and subordinate power to the service of respect." Lasswell's conception of democracy "is that of a network of congenial and creative interpersonal relations. Whatever deviates from this pattern is both antidemocratic and destructive." [50]

The clinical approach to social problems is now gaining a great deal of attention: Laurence K. Frank has just published his *Society as the Patient,* and Elton Mayo and his associates have brought out a series of books reporting clinical and experimental studies of personnel management problems. Mayo, for example, investigated the causes of absenteeism, high labor turnover, and lessened production in factories. [51] His discovery that higher production can be secured by organizing workers in congenial teams and permitting employees some democratic initiative and control, points the way to improved industrial relations. There is no substitute, however, for adequate wages. Lasswell rightly warns that some of the enthusiasm for "the new human relations" comes from monopolistic business which has an interest in curbing unionization. We must avoid, he says, "the contented cow approach to industrial relations." [52] It is recognized today that self-esteem, as well as self-defense, require strong labor organizations.

The clinical approach is necessary, but limited. It is concerned more with individuals than with institutions, more with symptoms than with causes. Lasswell's book about power phenomena in individuals is well supplemented by institutional studies of power.

A good idea of the massive power of business organizations which now confront labor, the small business men, and the farmer, is supplied by Robert A. Brady in his *Business as a System of Power.* [53] Although as Lynd remarks in the introduction to this book, there is in America "the naive and dangerous popular faith that democracy and capitalist enterprise are two aspects of the same thing," the spirit and structure of capitalist enterprise is anything but democratic. The leadership of such organizations as The National Association of Manufacturers, Brady argues, "is typically self-appointed, self-perpetuating and autocratic . . . . Authority is . . . from the top down and responsibility from the bottom up." Authority in the lower ranks of the business hierarchy coordinates employees, that

50. *Ibid.,* p. 110.
51. See, for example, Elton Mayo, *Social Problems of an Industrial Civilization* (Boston, 1945).
52. *Op. cit.,* p. 193.
53. New York, Columbia University Press, 1943.

in the high ranks "coordinates big and little business in a policy complex forged as a by-product of the *Realpolitik* practiced by their own appointed general staffs. The same individuals, the same groups and cliques, the same interests dominate each sphere; in each the principle of organization . . . is that of an inherently undemocratic, authoritarian hierarchy." [54]

After many years of study, mainly in Germany and the United States, Brady was able to conclude that, in spite of national and competitive differences, this hierarchic autocratic business structure obtains in all highly advanced capitalist countries. There is, in fact, a general tendency toward totalitarianism even in democratic countries. But "contrary to certain implications of current usage, 'totalitarianism' like 'bureaucracy,' is not necessarily undesirable if it is taken to mean a social psychological outlook possessing at once a coherent unifying philosophy and a general program of action which comprehend the totality of organized social life. In this sense, even democracy, as a theoretically coherent web of postulates, freedoms and qualified restraints, is 'totalitarianism.' " [55] Organizations of diverse systems may be similar, or homologous. Their worth depends upon the aim which is declared and pursued. The remedy for the arbitrary power and arrogance of business organizations is more "direct public participation in the formulation of economic policies."

A study of the structure of power in business organizations, when it ignores motivations, can be more objective, more inductive, than any psychological study of power-seeking in individuals. It has also the advantage that it defines a problem which vitally affects the whole community and all the power relations within it. The work of American anthropologists has shown that the amount of tension and anxiety, frustration and aggression, found in any society varies with the politico-economic structure. The belief that psychoneurosis is somehow derivative from the basic conflicts of our own society, is gaining ground,[56] though the theory has not been adequately developed. Psychologists and psycho-therapists are increasingly confronted with problems, the solution of which requires the data and methods which the social sciences are supplying. What is a healthy social attitude? Should the psychotherapist give moral and political guidance is a daring question often raised today. The integration of psychological and sociological methods is more and

---

54. *Ibid.*, p. 313.
55. *Ibid.*, p. 314.
56. See, for example, Karen Horney, *The Neurotic Personality of our Time* (New York, W. W. Norton & Co., 1937).

more felt to be imperative. The social sciences are describing the concrete framework, the complex stimuli, to which socially conditioned individuals respond, whereas psychology is analyzing the mechanism of response. But since stimulus and response are both individual and social, the psychological and sociological approaches must be regarded as interdependent and mutually supplementary.

SUMMARY AND PROSPECTS

It is customary, and perhaps philosophically more interesting, to deal in fine disagreements, and nice distinctions. The present paper, however, had a different aim, namely: to indicate a broad convergence in the philosophy of great American writers. Ward's meliorism, we hold, was as typically American as James's confidence in "the energies of men." His conviction that progress requires planning and increased governmental enterprise and regulation, is now generally conceded though economists such as Hayek and Mises still have many followers. Even Herbert Hoover and Gerard Swope have agreed in principle. Ward's environmentalism, as we have seen, was reinforced by the findings of Boas and his followers, and by the work of the pioneer social behaviorist, Mead. Any suggestion that there is anything wrong with the diverse racial or national stocks which compose the American population, is held not only unscientific but also invidious and un-American. Evidence is accumulating that intelligence and practical aptitude are largely functions of education and training. There is no question that this country has the raw materials, technology, and human resources to cope with all its problems. The bottleneck of progress is now the human organizations which suppress or fail to utilize, the vast resources with which this country is endowed. Here Veblen's criticism of our pecuniary culture, if it did not go to the heart of the matter, was immensely clarifying. A host of writers, such as Mitchell, Hamilton, and Brady, whom we have mentioned, have supplied documentation. But the revamping of human organizations to realize our physical and human resources, in practice, requires obtrusive propaganda and uncustomary coercion. In the New Deal era, consequently, there were many complaints of bureaucracy and regimentation.

Individualism in American thought, whether derivative from Locke in the seventeenth century, or from Thomas Jefferson in the eighteenth century, or from Proudhon in the nineteenth century, has rightly insisted upon public participation, and the individual consent of the governed;

but it has had to adapt itself to the twentieth century need for planning and controls, and government enterprise, all the same. Even American bankers, the most rugged of individualists, as Charles Beard pointed out,[57] do not object to government intervention in crisis and depression, but only when things are going well. The fact is that the rapid concentration of capital, controls, patents, technology, and know-how in a few hands, is an obvious threat to economic efficiency and democracy, which has shaken the old individualism to its foundations. Thus Morris Cohen could call for the socialization of liberalism.

But the problem of cushioning the effects of economic reorganization still remained. There was also the ancient scruple that the best laid plans of mice and men often go awry. Dewey emphasized the uncertainty of political plans and forecasts, and warned that if action was not kept fluid and experimental, responsive to individual communications and claims at every stage, an end might be attained opposite to what was intended. Perry's philosophy indirectly served the same warning. Obviously a great deal of psychological analysis and clinical studies were necessary to prepare the public for impending developments. In the meantime, the broad needs of the American population had been made clear by statistical studies, and were not really in doubt.

We have spoken of prosperity, but not of peace. The two objectives however are inseparable. The world today is divided between two economic systems, each in its way dynamic and expansive. Conflict of interests is inevitable, but peaceful rivalry and cooperation are also possible. As Lasswell says, "The issue of our time is not socialism *or* capitalism, but socialism and capitalism together *against* the annihilation of mankind, or serfdom in a world of garrison-prison states. The issue is progressive democratization of the world."[58] In the world today, however, there are two concepts of democracy.[59] Our own theory emphasizes individual rights and the conflict of parties, whereas that of the Soviets stresses planning, cooperation, and fulfillment of material and cultural needs. Herbert W. Schneider has suggested that the conflict of parties as such, has been exaggerated in our conception of democracy, and work and accomplishments neglected. On the other hand, it is clear that there often has been too little regard for individual rights in the Soviet Union, as even Stalin admitted in reference to the program of collectivizing agriculture. If

---

57. Charles A. Beard, *The Myth of Rugged American Individualism* (New York, 1932).
58. *Op. cit.,* p. 216.
59. V. J. McGill, "Two Concepts of Freedom," *Philosophy and Phenomenological Research,* Vol. VIII, No. 4 (June, 1948), pp. 515-21.

war came, such distinctions would largely disappear. Both individual rights and prosperity would go up in smoke. If peace is maintained, the world will be richer and more interesting for its competing systems.

The problem of formulating a possible *modus vivendi* has engaged the attention of a number of American philosophers. Writing during the recent war, R. B. Perry said: "the bridge between democratic United States and communist Russia must be built from both ends." The communist ideal " 'From each according to his ability, to each according to his needs' is both Christian and democratic as well as Marxist." Thus Christian communism is possible while Christian Nazism "is a contradiction in terms." [60] It is a grave mistake, Perry adds, to suppose that world peace and cooperation depend upon the universal acceptance of a single philosophy. It is enough that America and Russia agree, as they do in fact agree, in a certain common morality and fundamental humanitarian aims. Richard McKeon has made the same point again and again. [61] The problem is not to reduce all national and cultural dispositions to a common philosophy but to build a philosophy of world peace and cooperation on the basis of the present, enriching diversities.

SELECTED BIBLIOGRAPHY

(1) Ward, Lester Frank. *Pure Sociology, A Treatise on the Origin and Spontaneous Development of Society.* Second edition, New York, The Macmillan Co., 1925.

(2) Veblen, T. *The Place of Science in Modern Civilization, and Other Essays.* New York, The Viking Press, 1919, 1930, 1932.

(3) ————. *The Theory of Business Enterprise.* New York, Charles Scribner's Sons, 1904, 1919.

(4) ————. *Absentee Ownership, and Business Enterprise in Recent Times, The Case of America.* New York, B. W. Huebsch, 1923.

(5) Hamilton, Walton. *Patents and Free Enterprise,* TNEC Monograph 31, Senate Committee Print, 76th Congress, 3rd Session, 1941.

---

60. *Our Side is Right* (Cambridge, Harvard University Press, 1942), p. 122.

61. See, for example, "The Rights of Man," *Ethics,* Vol. LVIII (April, 1948); and "A Philosophy for UNESCO," *Philosophy and Phenomenological Research,* Vol. VIII, No. 4 (June, 1948).

(6) Burns, Arthur R. *The Decline of Competition, A Study of the Evolution of American Industry*. Published under the auspices of the Columbia University Council for research in the social sciences. New York, McGraw Hill, 1936.

(7) Boudin, Louis B. *The Theoretical System of Karl Marx in the Light of Recent Criticism*. Chicago, Charles H. Kerr and Co., 1918.

(8) Sweezey, Paul M. *The Nature of Capitalist Development, Principles of Marxian Political Economy*. New York, Oxford University Press, 1942.

(9) Perry, Ralph Barton, *The Present Conflict of Ideals, A Study of the Philosophical Background of the World War*. New York, Longmans, Green and Co., 1922.

(10) ————. *Puritanism and Democracy*. New York, Vanguard Press, 1944.

(11) ————. *Our Side Is Right*. Cambridge, Harvard University Press, 1942.

(12) Dewey, John. *Individualism Old and New*. New York, Balch and Co., 1930.

(13) ————. *Characters and Events, Popular Essays in Social and Political Philosophy*. New York, Henry Holt and Co., 1929.

(14) Mead, George H. *Mind, Self and Society, From the Standpoint of a Social Behaviorist*. Chicago, University of Chicago Press, 1934, 1946.

(15) Brady, Robert A. *Business as a System of Power*. New York, Columbia University Press, 1943.

(16) Lynd, Robert S. *Knowledge for What*. Princeton, Princeton University Press, 1939.

(17) De Leon, Daniel. *Socialist Reconstruction of Society*. New York, Labor News Co., 1938.

TOWARD AN ANALYTIC
PHILOSOPHY OF
HISTORY

*Morton G. White**

T
he philosophy of history has almost disappeared from the list of subjects in which most American philosophers are interested. Indeed, it has never been very actively pursued in America. William James wrote a little on subjects closely allied to it;[1] Santayana has an interesting chapter on history in one of his early works;[2] Dewey occasionally writes about historical method.[3] By and large, however, American philosophers have avoided the subject. A similar lethargy with regard to it characterizes twentieth century British philosophy.[4] Broad, Moore, Russell,[5] and Wittgenstein show little or no concern with the philosophy of history and even contemporary British idealists offer little that is exciting or original. If the phenomenon were restricted to America, we might try to explain it in terms of America's lack of interest in the past and its lack of a past long enough to stimulate historical speculation.

* Born in 1917. Ph.D., Columbia University, 1942. Assistant Professor of Philosophy, Harvard University. Author of: *The Origin of Dewey's Instrumentalism* (1943), "The Revolt Against Formalism in American Social Thought of the Twentieth Century," *Social Thought in America* (1949), and contributions to philosophical publications.
    1. "Great Men and Their Environment" and "The Importance of Individuals," *The Will To Believe* (New York, 1917), pp. 216-254 and 255-262.
    2. *Reason in Science* (New York, 1906), chap. ii.
    3. *Logic: The Theory of Inquiry* (New York, 1938), pp. 230-244.
    4. A change of attitude may be indicated by the appearance of the late Morris R. Cohen's *The Meaning of Human History* (La Salle, Ill., 1947) in America and K. R. Popper's *The Open Society and Its Enemies* (London, 1945) in England. Both authors are distinguished methodologists of science who have turned to problems of history in a spirit of analysis and clarification, although in Popper's case a political purpose is also explicit. Cohen's work is the published version of the sixth in the series of Paul Carus lectures; it is the first in that series on the philosophy of history. Professor Cohen was one of the few philosophers of his generation in America who systematically studied the subject. Popper's work, I believe, is one of the most vigorous and stimulating books in the philosophy of history to appear in many years — an opinion which I hold in spite of sharp differences with him on certain philosophical matters.
    5. Sidney Hook, "Bertrand Russell's Philosophy of History," *The Philosophy of Bertrand Russell,* ed. P. Schilpp (Chicago, 1944), pp. 643-678; also see Russell's reply in the same volume, pp. 734-741.

But such an explanation is obviously incomplete and we must turn to the doctrines and methods which have dominated British and American philosophy in recent years.

Like contemporary England, America today provides a striking example of the decline in metaphysical speculation. In spite of repeated protests in behalf of speculative metaphysics and in spite of periodic calls for its revival in the grand manner, the twentieth century has watched its decline with feelings that range from horror to relief. The dominant philosophies of Americans—pragmatism, naturalism, instrumentalism— have steered large numbers of first-rate American thinkers into logic, epistemology, and the methodology of the sciences; and even those who turn to ethics and esthetics usually do so in the interest of analysis rather than evaluation. Their attitudes have been reenforced by logical positivism and the analytical school of Cambridge, England, both of which exercise considerable influence on American philosophical thought. In America the philosophy of history has been associated with the sweeping generalizations of Spengler and more recently with those of Toynbee, whose *Study of History* has become a best-seller (in an abridged version, of course) and whose prophecies have come to fascinate large and anxious American audiences. But while Toynbee continues at the writing of this essay to keep his hold on a vast reading public, the attitude of historians toward speculative history is the attitude of most analytical philosophers toward speculative philosophy. They look upon the philosophy of history as conceived by Toynbee and Spengler with a mixture of awe and contempt. Although some of America's most distinguished historians of the twentieth century have advanced bold hypotheses about American life (I have Beard and Turner in mind), neither philosophers nor historians show much interest today in the philosophy of history conceived as a speculative study of social development. It is regarded as a field in which geographical determinists, historical materialists, Hegelians, and Spenglerians argue fruitlessly with each other. Even those philosophers who are familiar enough with history to reflect on its course dwell upon the "elements of truth" in all of these rival hypotheses, moved by cautious eclecticism and intellectual sobriety. Most philosophers of history in America today are content with urging that no one cultural factor operates alone in producing historical change. In effect, they have abandoned the philosophy of history as traditionally understood.

What may be salvaged in this situation? Do any serious problems in the philosophy of history remain for those who refuse to deal in obscurity and who prefer the modest but secure achievements of analytic philosophy? I feel that some do remain and that they are very similar to those which analytic philosophers have dealt with for years; they are peculiar only in being connected with historical investigation. The conviction that the philosophy of history ought to be an analytic investigation has grown in recent years. Most American philosophers of history would probably hesitate to identify themselves with what is broadly called "analytic philosophy" but their emphasis is similar. For example, the late Morris R. Cohen urged a distinction between universal history and the philosophy of history which is consistent with the point of view of the present essay.[6] Maurice Mandelbaum, another of the few American workers in this field, says: "A philosophic approach to the knowledge of history must assume one of three forms: it must either commence with a general methodological analysis of historical understanding; or it must attempt to place historical understanding within the context of all human experience; or, finally, it must accept the methods of empirical research and seek to derive some ultimate meaning from the historical process as a whole. Of these three approaches to history we have chosen to follow the first."[7] A similiar outlook dominates much of the work of Sidney Hook.[8]

In spite of the serious difficulties involved in analyzing analysis itself,[9] it will be assumed that there is an important difference, for example, between an interest in clearing up what is meant by the word 'cause' and a scientific interest in finding causes. *How* this distinction is to be drawn and whether it can be drawn sharply will not be discussed here. In a later section of this paper a definition of the word 'history' will be attempted and the reader will be able to examine the procedure himself in order to see that it is quite different from investigations in the speculative

6. Cohen, *op. cit.,* p. 5.
7. *The Problem of Historical Knowledge* (New York, 1938), p. 321.
8. His *Hero in History* (New York, 1943), is his most extended work in this field. Hook has also contributed a series of definitions of terms connected with historical research to *Theory and Practice in Historical Study: A Report of the Committee on Historiography of the Social Science Research Council* (New York, 1946). This pamphlet contains an informative essay on the ideas of some American historians by J. H. Randall, Jr., and George Haines, IV, "Controlling Assumptions in the Practice of American Historians," and a useful reading list compiled by Ronald Thompson, from which the reader interested in American tendencies in the philosophy of history may select relevant items. Also see Morton G. White, "Historical Explanation," *Mind,* Vol. LII, N. S. (1943), pp. 212-229; "The Attack on the Historical Method," *Journal of Philosophy,* Vol. XLII (1945), pp. 314-331, and "The Revolt Against Formalism in American Social Thought of the Twentieth Century," *Journal of the History of Ideas,* Vol. VIII (1947), pp. 131-152. Carl G. Hempel's "The Function of General Laws in History," *Journal of Philosophy,* Vol. XXXIX (1942), pp. 35-48, is an interesting essay by a distinguished analytic philosopher.
9. See, for example, C. H. Langford, "The Notion of Analysis in Moore's Philosophy," *The Philosophy of G. E. Moore,* ed. P. Schilpp (Chicago, 1942), pp. 319-342 and Moore's reply in the same volume, pp. 660-667.

philosophy of history.   Analytic philosophy has been described as a
search for the *meanings* of terms, but this can only serve as a tentative
description since the notion of meaning is not clear in the writer's opinion.
But if this description is tentatively accepted until the analysts of analysis
get clearer, we may distinguish between an analytical philosophy of history
and a Toynbeean, speculative study of civilization.   The first is more
likely to analyze civilization while the second charts its course.   The
difference between a speculative and an analytical philosophy of history
illustrates in many ways the difference between what Broad calls *speculative* and *critical* philosophy.[10]   It is also like the difference between
Carnap's *metaphysics* and his *logical analysis*.[11]   But we need not condemn
the speculative philosophy of history as a collection of meaningless sentences in order to distinguish it from the analytical philosophy of history.
The most ruthless positivist cannot sweep aside *all* of the speculations of
Spengler and Toynbee as meaningless or metaphysical in the sense of
unconfirmable, for some of them are obviously empirical statements about
the history of civilization.   Nor need we condemn it here, as Popper
does,[12] for indulging in unfounded and "dangerous" prophecy.   We
need not condemn historical speculation in this place at all; we simply
need to see how it differs from the analysis of notions connected with
historical investigation.

II

The analytic philosopher ought to approach history as a mode of
discourse, as a kind of language which needs clarification.   If he does,
there are at least two kinds of questions which he may choose to study,
since there are at least two kinds of linguistic expressions which are connected with history.   First there are expressions which occur, to use a
phrase of the logicians, in the *object-language* of history, in the language
which historians use when they are writing directly about the object of
their investigation.   Then there are those which are used to describe
historical writings themselves, which appear in the *metalanguage* of
history.   Let us call the first kind 'historical expressions' and the second
'metahistorical expressions.'   The first kind is illustrated by names of

10.   C. D. Broad, "Critical and Speculative Philosophy," *Contemporary British Philosophy*, First Series, ed. J. H. Muirhead (New York, 1924), pp. 75-100.
11.   *Logical Syntax of Language*, Eng. trans. (New York, 1937).
12.   "A careful examination of this question has led me to the conclusion that such
sweeping historical prophecies are entirely beyond the scope of scientific method," *op. cit.*,
p. 3.   Bertrand Russell has expressed a similar view without seeing as much "danger" in
historical prophecy as Popper does.   Also see Maurice Mandelbaum, "A Critique of Philosophies of History," *Journal of Philosophy*, Vol. XLV (1948), pp. 365-378.

human beings—'Julius Caesar,' 'Abraham Lincoln'—names of countries, and also by names of historical periods like 'The Renaissance,' 'The Dark Ages.' The second kind is illustrated by the word 'history' in one of its uses, by the word 'chronicle,' and several others. This division of terms is regarded by some logicians and philosophers as one of the most important in the history of philosophy, and there is good reason to believe that its application in the philosophy of history will be useful.

Although analytic philosophers have devoted themselves primarily to metahistorical expressions, I do not think that we can generalize from this with certainty that the only task of the analytic philosopher of history is the clarification of expressions which occur in the metalanguage of history rather than in history itself. Philosophers of physics have been interested in defining the physical word 'mass' as well as the *metaphysical* word 'mechanics,' while philosophers of mathematics have been interested in defining mathematical expressions like 'number' and *metamathematical* expressions like 'proof,' 'mathematics,' 'complete,' and 'true.'

The best that may be said for the view that philosophers of history ought to restrict themselves to defining metahistorical expressions is that up to now they have shown more skill at it. The fact is that a philosopher who is not especially well-trained in history is not able to make much of a direct contribution to the definition of phrases like 'The Renaissance' and 'Ancient Culture.' On the other hand, I think that philosophers have been able to say things of great interest in dealing with the word 'cause' as used by historians even when they have not been historians or very familiar with history. It should be remembered that the first succesful definitions of 'mass' and 'simultaneity' were made by Mach and Einstein —physicists interested in the problems of definition rather than philosophers with a reading knowledge of physics. The trained physicist is more likely to be familiar with the various contexts in which the word 'mass' occurs, more familiar with the conditions of adequately defining it than a philosopher with a tourist's acquaintance with physics. The same is true of the historian of the Renaissance who is anxious to make clear what the phrase 'The Renaissance' means to him. He is likely to contribute more to the answer than a philosopher called in for consultation. This does not mean that the philosopher can give no help. On the contrary, he can give information about definition, about analysis, about methods of clarification. But in this respect he is reporting to the historian on a metalinguistic notion—the notion of definition itself.

In the light of these considerations I am inclined to think that the major, though not the sole task of the analytic philosopher of history, is that of defining or clarifying terms in *metahistory*. I do not say that the philosopher of history never does or never ought to try to clarify terms in the object-language of history. There are different kinds of definitional problems in the philosophy of history and they require different kinds of skill and training. One kind of problem is peculiarly suited to the skill and knowledge of philosophers of history who are not historians. Those who are equipped with the tools of logical analysis and with historical learning may carry on all the tasks of definition which concern history, but it would be well to warn those analytic philosophers who hope to perceive "meanings" of historical expressions without studying the historical facts. They must become familiar with the historical material on the Renaissance if they hope to define 'The Renaissance,' but if they prefer ignorance they must recognize the limited function which they can then perform.

If we accept the view of the philosophy of history outlined above and try to settle upon metahistorical terms which deserve philosophical study, we are faced with a curious problem. Which terms in metahistory ought to be studied? Obviously metahistory contains all the names of all the expressions which appear in history. 'Julius Caesar' appears in history, and therefore a name of Caesar's name—"Julius Caesar"— appears in metahistory. But surely these are of little philosophical interest. Most philosophers of history have been interested in *predicates* that may be construed metalinguistically, like 'law,' 'explanation,' 'true,' and 'cause.' But since all the predicates mentioned above appear in the metalanguages of other disciplines as well as in that of history, the question arises as to whether there are metahistorical terms which are specific to metahistory. If there are not, and if all the terms which the philosopher of history selects for clarification appear in *metachemistry, metasociology, metaeconomics,* etc., can we make out a case for any kind of autonomous or independent philosophy of history in the analytical sense? The question leads us to a number of extremely important problems in semantics which cannot be considered here, but I do think that there are terms which are specific to metahistory. One of these is the word 'history' itself and I propose to devote the rest of this paper to an informal discussion of the problems connected with defining it. Many important subsidiary problems in the philosophy of history will be mentioned in passing, and some indication will be given of how problems in the philosophy of history are connected with other kinds of philosophical problems. In this way I will be illustrating what is admittedly a program rather than an accomplishment—an analytical philosophy of history.

Applying the methods of logical analysis to history may appear strange to those who usually put logic and history at opposite poles, and also to those who think of the notion of history as too obscure to be worth analysis. But even if it be admitted that the word 'history' is less clear than some of those with which other analytic philosophers deal, it must be pointed out that philosophers are supposed to make things clear*er*, and that if all words were initially clear in some absolute sense, the need for analysis would disappear. Philosophers may choose to begin analyzing words of no less than a certain pre-analytic clarity, but where one puts the minimum is somewhat arbitrary. One tries to clarify what one finds interesting and obscure. I am inclined to measure the achievement of a philosophical analysis proportionately, since I believe that to start with a term of degree of clarity 99 and to advance it by definition and analysis to degree 100 is a small accomplishment compared to advancing the degree of clarity of a term from 5 to 20. For this reason I would urge analytically minded philosophers to turn to the philosophy of history, for it needs them. Measuring proportionately the chances for success are great, though, measuring absolutely, we rarely reach the summits of clarity. Both of these contentions will be illustrated presently.

III

The major purpose of this part of the paper is to show what problems arise in the course of an attempt to define the word 'history.' Some of them have been discussed for years but as they are presented here they are seen to be closely related to problems in other parts of philosophy with which they have not been associated . It is hoped that their restatement will contribute to their solution, and also that the use of elementary logical techniques will clarify some of the issues that surround the analysis of *history.*

The word 'history' as it is frequently used is part of a relational expression. We are usually interested in a history of some thing, some entity. The fundamental philosophical problem, then, is: how shall we define or make clear the meaning of the statement-form 'x is a history of y'? As in the discussion of other relations it is important to be clear about the kind of entities which are values of the variables in the above statement-form. What kind of entity is a history and what kind of entity has a history? Let us begin with the second question first.

We must remember that the expression 'history' is ambiguous even when it appears in a relational context, so that we cannot assume that every use of it will allow us to answer our question in the same way. But in order to fix our problem, let us give some examples of things which have histories. This desk has a history; this chair does; the region of the earth called 'The United States of America' does. In fact, it would appear proper to speak of every physical object which endures for a reasonable amount of time as having a history. Physical objects are traditionally supposed to exist "in time" and to change in time and histories are generally supposed to be about things that exist and change in time. We will assume, then, that all physical objects have histories in the sense under discussion. Whether any other kind of entity can be said to have a history in the same sense will be left an open question, bound up with problems surrounding Russell's simple theory of types. If we accept the latter it becomes difficult to speak of a history of a *class* of physical objects, of an *idea* construed Platonically. We are also faced with the interesting question of whether we may speak of *institutions* having histories. When the expression 'The United States of America' appears in the sentence 'Charles Beard has written a history of the United States of America' does it denote a physical object—a region of the earth? And if it does not denote a physical object, but rather a "nation," what kind of entity is a nation? Because I think that there are some uses of the phrase 'is a history of' which suggest that physical objects have histories, I will confine myself to this use and leave open the question of whether this *same relation* can include other kinds of entities in its converse domain.

Having fixed the character of the class of things which have histories we may now ask about histories themselves. What kind of thing is a history?

In having previously maintained that the notion of history is metahistorical I have already indicated that a history is a linguistic expression or an entity which is the result of combining linguistic expressions in a certain way. But obviously this is not the only use of the term. The word 'history' is sometimes construed so that it refers to historical discourse and at other times construed so that it refers to what is called 'history as actuality.' In selecting the linguistic version of 'history' I have done so because I think its extra-linguistic counterpart involves ontological commitments which I find obscure. Later, a history will be defined as a sequence of statements (sentences) of a certain kind. Its non-linguistic analogue can vary with one's logical philosophy. Some logicians, following

Frege,[13] might prefer to regard it as a sequence of *propositions,* construing a proposition, with Frege, as the *sense (Sinn)* of a sentence. Others distinguish between the proposition and the *fact* expressed by the sentence, and perhaps they would construe a history as a sequence of facts. Finally there is what Frege called the truth-value of a sentence, which he regarded as its *denotation (Bedeutung)* as distinct from its sense. Since I share the doubt about the status of propositions, facts, and truth-values which a good many philosophers feel,[14] I am inclined to get along without them as much as possible. And since there is a perfectly good use of the word 'history' according to which histories are linguistic entities, I shall accept it as the one I am trying to clarify. My choice is motivated by considerations similiar to those which lead Tarski to construe 'true' as a predicate of sentences rather than propositions,[15] as well as by the fact that historians speak of histories as things that can be written.[16] Because the debates surrounding these questions are still inconclusive, however, I will merely state my own preference for using 'sentences' in the definition of 'history,' recognizing, of course, that others might make an extremely good case for a propositional approach. It will not do to quarrel on this level if agreement may be reached on some of the questions which follow.

As soon as it is agreed that we have to deal with a relation the usual problem of stating some of its properties arises. One of the first steps toward getting an explicit definition of the phrase 'is a history of' is to see what these properties are so that they may be set up as conditions which a satisfactory definition of 'history' must satisfy. Ideally, it would be desirable to state these conditions and then proceed in businesslike fashion to furnish an explicit definition. However, because the problem has not been discussed very much, it seems more feasible to proceed informally, showing how the proposal to state properties of the relation

---

13. "Ueber Sinn und Bedeutung," *Zeitschrift für Philosophie und Philosophische Kritik,* Volume C (New Series, 1892), pp. 25-50. An English translation appeared in *The Philosophical Review,* Volume LVII, No. 3 (1948).

14. W. V. Quine, "Notes on Existence and Necessity," *Journal of Philosophy,* Vol. XXXVI (1943), pp. 113-127. Related questions are considered at length from a different point of view in R. Carnap, *Meaning and Necessity* (Chicago, 1947) and C. I. Lewis, *An Analysis of Knowledge and Valuation* (La Salle, Ill., 1946). Alonzo Church has also considered this question in a number of reviews in *The Journal of Symbolic Logic* and elsewhere.

15. Tarski has given a very lucid, nontechnical exposition of his views in "The Semantic Conception of Truth and the Foundations of Semantics," *Philosophy and Phenomenological Research,* Vol. IV (1944), pp. 341-376.

16. I recognize that some philosophers might argue that there is a sense in which we write propositions, as when Jones writes *that he is ill.*

leads to a number of interesting questions whose answers are by no means definite.

One question of some interest is whether the relation *is a history of* is functional, that is, one-many. Is it the case that every object has no more than one history? In other words, is the relation *history of* like *father of* in one important respect? Can a given entity have many histories as a man can have many brothers, or does it have at most one history as every one has at most one father? Usage is not decisive on this point. Some people speak as though an entity could have no more than one history, while we know, of course, that there is a perfectly good sense in which there are several available histories of France. In this paper I shall try to clarify the usage according to which the relation *is a history of* is functional and to point the way to a definition which satisfies this condition. In doing so I think I can meet some of the difficulties which stand in the way of this view. I want to begin by considering some that are related to more fundamental problems of logic and semantics.

We usually speak of certain *books* as histories and these books are usually printed or written in many copies, so that even if there were only one historical work on a country we would have no more than one written physical object which could be called a history of that country. Consequently, if we construed a history as a particular written or printed object, the relation we have been discussing is plainly not one-many or functional. But we may decide to select only one of the various copies of Herodotus, say, as a history, or we may make it explicit that we are speaking of a historical *work,* understanding by that a class of all written or printed books satisfying a certain condition. The point is that the kind of diversity which is introduced by the existence of more than one copy of a given book is not as serious as some other varieties of diversity which have been urged. Another question arises when we ask whether a history must be a combination of *true* sentences. Of course, if we do not include this condition, we can be sure that the relation is not functional, for obviously there are many works which share all the usual characteristics of histories except that of truth. Therefore we will require that the elements of histories be true.

Before going on I want to summarize the decisions we have made thus far. In speaking of a history we shall mean a historical *work,* and a historical work will be understood as a linguistic entity composed of a certain kind of true declarative sentences in a certain way. Finally, we shall assume that the relation *history of* is one-many. Our chief problem is to state the *kind* of sentences which are elements of history and a mode of combining them into histories which will assure us that there is no more than one history for any given entity.

The expression in common language which comes closest to conveying what I have in mind when I speak of a history is 'story' ('narrative' will also do). The problem, then, is to say what a narrative is, to say what it is composed of and how it is composed. The notion of a story or narrative is to be distinguished from that of a historical statement. One may be curious about what is meant by the expression 'historical statement' just as one may want to define 'physical statement,' 'logical statement,' or 'biological statement.' Usually the answer to questions of this kind are hard to find, and when they are found depend upon an arbitrary selection of terms which are specific to the science in question. From there on it is easy to describe statements of kind S as those in which only terms of kind S occur essentially.[17] Some philosophers who approach the notion of historical statement in this way arrive at the traditional view that a historical statement is any singular statement of fact. In this sense history is simply that vast matrix of factual statements from which the sciences which seek laws get their stimulus and evidence. The observation reports of the chemist, the astronomer, the biologist, and the sociologist are all historical statements in this sense. But I wish to distinguish this sense of 'history' from the one which is under analysis, even though the former will figure in our definition of the latter. First of all, a history of an object is limited to those historical statements which are about that object. Also, a history of an object as we shall understand it involves order, whereas the term 'historical statement' simply denotes a class of statements which are not necessarily ordered. In short, the components of a history of *y* are true singular statements about *y's* characteristics at different times in its career, ordered in a certain way. The question of whether the predicates in these statements ought to be limited in any way will be discussed later.

On the basis of what has been said we may visualize a history of an

---

17. The question of whether the terms of kind *S* can be sharply specified has been considered mainly in connection with logical terms. Tarski, for example, has maintained that the distinction between logical and nonlogical terms is more or less arbitrary "Ueber den Begriff der logischen Folgerung," *Actes du Congrès international de philosophie scientifique*, fasc. VII, (Paris, 1936), where Carnap holds the opposite view (*Introduction to Semantics*, vii). I agree with Tarski and, moreover, feel that the same situation arises in connection with sharply distinguishing terms of any kind from others, e.g., *physical, historical, biological*, etc. For this reason a degree of arbitrariness enters into the definition of any scientific discipline which has a name in ordinary language. For an exact discussion of the idea of essential occurrence see W. V. Quine, "Truth by Convention," *Philosophical Essays for Alfred North Whitehead* (New York, 1936).

entity in a number of ways. First of all we may regard a history of y as a conjunction of all the true singular factual statements about y which could conceivably be made in the language used; the conjunction would be ordered, so that its beginning conjunct would express what was happening to y at time t_1, the next one what was happening to y at t_2, and so on. Or, we may regard a history as a sequence of such sentences written down in consecutive order. This would make it an ordered n-ad in the language of mathematics. The choice as between conjunction or sequence is not dictated by common usage, so far as I can see; I am inclined to view the second alternative as more feasible and will take that approach. The idea which is here expressed in terms of sentences would probably be expressed by those who are not frightened by propositions as a sequence of all the knowable singular true propositions about y, arranged in order of the time in y's career which is being described or, alternatively, as a conjunction of these propositions ordered in that way.

The first statement would take the form: 'y has characteristic R at time t_1,' the next: 'y has characteristic S at time t_2,' and so on. Each statement would sum up all the things happening to y or characteristic of y at the time in question. In fact, it might be better to regard the n-ad or sequence as a sequence of conjunctions of statements which tell what is happening to y at that time. Each conjunction would describe the state of y at the time.[18]

It should be evident that if we define a history of y as a sequence of the kind described above, there could not be more than one history for any given object. For a history of y has been defined so that it contains all the true historical statements about y that could possibly be written. If there are any sequences of this kind in a defensible sense of 'there are,' then surely no entity has more than one. It is also evident that we never write down all possible sentences of this kind. Even if we hesitate to say that these sequences contain an infinite number of elements, we must admit that the number of elements is enormous, and that our frailty pre-

---

18. The notion of a conjunction which describes the state of an object at a given time is closely related to the notion of state-description as it is developed in the work of Carnap, Helmer, Hempel, and Oppenheim on inductive logic and other semantical problems. It is explained by Carnap *(Introduction to Semantics* and *Meaning and Necessity)* who attributes its starting point to ideas of Wittgenstein in his *Tractatus Logico-Philosophicus.* My own use of it requires considerable elaboration and is not to be identified with the notion of the authors mentioned. For a useful bibliography of contributions on semantics, inductive logic, and explanation, some of which are quite important for the kind of questions about history raised here, see C. G. Hempel and Paul Oppenheim, "Studies in the Logic of Explanation," *Philosophy of Science,* Vol. XV (1948), pp. 135-175.

vents us from writing down everything we could conceivably write. The conclusion we must face is that no history book is a history in our sense.

In recent times a great amount of philosophical speculation has arisen because it has been realized that histories conceived in this way are never compressed within the pages of actually printed historical works. Thus Santayana says: "Historical investigation has for its aim to fix the order and character of events throughout past time in all places. The task is frankly superhuman, because no block of real existence, with its infinitesimal detail, can be recorded, nor if somehow recorded could it be dominated by the mind; and to carry on a survey of this social continuum *ad infinitum* would multiply the difficulty." [19] This may serve as a philosophical expression of an attitude which a great number of American historians have come to share; and because of the admitted practical impossibility of achieving histories in the sense defined earlier, they have come to deny that the task of history is to describe things "as they actually happened" in Ranke's phrase. And because of this practical impossibility they have emphasized the need for selection in terms of what they call "a scheme of reference," "interests," and "values." [20]

For this reason the problem of selection is basic to most discussions of historical investigation in America today. Given our inability to present a history in the sense defined, how shall historians proceed? The need for selection has led many philosophers and historians to maintain a kind of relativism, since selection, which is made in terms of *values, interests, schemes of reference, frames of reference,* and problems, will obviously vary with the historian who is doing the selecting. There can be no doubt that many historians are *caused* or led to select their statements in this way, but more has been urged—it has been urged that historians *ought* to select in this way and that such value-dominated selection is part of the accredited procedure of historical investigation. It is important to remember that this hurried flight to schemes of reference starts with a recognition of the fact that we cannot attain what is admittedly the ideal of the historian. But since you cannot achieve your ideal, since you cannot record all the statements about *y,* pick out those statements which are in accord with your scheme of reference, your interest, your problems. In short, this philosophical advice runs: pay no attention

19. *Op. cit.,* pp. 51-53.
20. See Proposition VI, one of a list of "Basic Premises" which a group of American historians have presented as part of their philosophical creed, *Theory and Practice in Historical Study* (full title in note 8). Also Popper, *op. cit.,* Volume II, chap. xxv, in which this position is argued more clearly than it usually is; see note 22 below. Randall and Haines, *op. cit.,* defend a similar position.

to this unattainable ideal; forget about it. But this is a *non sequitur*. It would amount to arguing: we cannot present the whole truth about *y*, therefore let us select those truths about *y* which interest us, which conform to our schemes of reference, which we value. But I do not see how the historian can approach his ideal if he consciously forswears the task of approximating the whole truth and turns to selection guided by his values which may simply register his own prejudices. I do not deny his right to study what he pleases, but I claim that he abandons *for poor reasons,* a task which is usually associated with the study of history. Although I agree that the historian cannot present the enormous sequence here defined as the history of an object, I maintain that the task of the historian is to present a briefer sequence which is *representative* of the enormous sequence he can never attain. His selection, in other words, must be justified on the basis of some connection with the history in a way analogous to (though not identical with) the way in which a good statistical sample is said to represent an infinite population. From my point of view, therefore, one of the great tasks of the philosophy of history today is the analysis of this relation of representation, a relation which underlies the process of historical selection.

In what follows I shall try to suggest a way of beginning on this problem. We ought to start by observing that a history contains true statements about the whole course of the object's existence. True statements about the future of the object will be as much a part of its history as true statements about its remote past. We must observe that some of these statements have causal implications whereas others do not. This distinction is important, as we shall see presently. The next thing to observe is that there are two kinds of historians, two kinds of students who *want* to approximate the whole truth about a given object. First there are those who conceive it as their task to amass as many true singular statements as can be amassed at a given moment, and in this way approach the ideal of the historian. Clearly this seems like the way to approach an infinite or very large number of statements—gather as many as you can. But then there are historians who are more discriminating, who recognize that some singular statements are historically more important than others, not because they fit in with some moral point of view of the historian, but because they are more useful for achieving the history of the object as here defined. The first group is near-sighted. It tries to amass everything in sight on the theory that this is a sure method of getting close to the whole truth. But it fails to realize that those who select facts which seem to have causal significance are more apt to come to know things about the future and past of the object.

There is no denying that the historian who gathers an immense number of true statements about an object will, *a fortiori*, gather those having causal significance. But where both historians have the same limited amount of energy and space for stating their results, the one who selects his statements with the criterion of *causal fertility* in mind is constructing a more representative sequence—a closer approximation to history in the sense defined earlier. It is important to insist that the criterion of causal fertility is not imposed *ab extra* upon the historian. Although it may not be his duty to state and discover the general laws which ground causal connections between singular statements, it is his duty to help increase the number of available true singular statements about the object he is studying. It follows that the historian has an obligation to be familiar with the laws that do or might govern the relations between the singular statements in which he is interested, for it is only by familiarizing himself with these generalizations that he will be able to tell which among the vast quantities of true singular statements are causally fertile. Only in this way will he be able to tell which statements are causally significant for the past and future of the object.[21]

We must remember that this procedure will increase the chances of gaining more knowledge of the object's *past*, lest the view be construed as too 'futuristic' because of its emphasis upon finding causally fertile statements. The inference from the present to the past that is no longer subject to direct observation or memory is in principle similar to the in-

---

21. The problem of defining the so-called causal relation between singular statements is now receiving considerable attention from philosophers who are not especially concerned with. causality in history. In my opinion the problem connected with history is no different from that connected with other disciplines in which causal assertions are made. Moreover, it appears wherever judgments of the form 'since such-and-such happened, then so-and-so must have happened' or 'since such-and-such is happening, then so-and-so will happen' are made. It is not occasioned merely by the appearance of the word 'cause' in history books, so that the attitude of Beard and Vagts *(Theory and Practice in Historical Study)*, who urge historians not to use the word 'cause,' in no way removes the need for a solution of this problem. They say, "When historians are concerned, as they should be, with consequential and coexisting relations between events and personalities and interests, which are intimate in nature and have the appearance of necessity, they can describe such relations in terms more precise than those of causality" (p. 137). But this statement in more precise terms is just what the analysts of causality are searching for, and it is not clear whether Beard and Vagts, when they say that such relations of necessity *can* be stated more clearly, mean simply that it is conceivable that a clear analysis of causality will be given, or that in fact one is available. I believe that no satisfactory analysis has been presented yet because no one has as yet surmounted the difficulties surrounding the definition of 'law,' as Nelson Goodman has so brilliantly shown in his "The Problem of Counterfactual Conditionals," *Journal of Philosophy*, Vol XLIV (1947), pp. 113-128. Hempel and Oppenheim (*op. cit.*) discuss the problem as it bears on the notion of explanation.

ference from the present to the future. The inference from the present to the past takes the form: 'Since this has characteristic *R* now, it must have had characteristic *S* then,' while the inference from the present to the future takes the form: 'Since this has characteristic *T* now it will have characteristic *U* later.' In both cases the inference is grounded by some causal law. For this reason the historian who seeks out statements which are causally fertile not only contributes to our knowledge of the object's future but also to its past.[22]

We may point out some analogies between this view of history and that which stems from deductive approach to mathematics. The brief sequence of statements which our historian tries to formulate as a means of approaching the history of an object has some resemblance to the axioms of a deductive system. The latter is an attempt to formulate a brief number of statements which are *deductively* fertile rather than causally fertile. Both attempts at brevity, however, are motivated by a desire for intellectual economy. And although the axiom sets which a mathematician may use can vary, they can vary only within the limits set by the truths of the mathematical discipline. In other words, the axioms must be able to imply the theorems; they must be deductively powerful. In

---

22. Popper (*op. cit.*, Vol. II, pp. 342-344) deals with the notions of explanation and cause in history. He argues that we must distinguish between the historical and the generalizing sciences and at the same time recognize that causality in history is bound up with universal laws. In the present essay I have limited myself to defining a use of the word 'history' which limits the historian to the search for singular truths. But in accepting this implication of Popper's distinction between two kinds of sciences, I believe that I am clarifying only one use of the word 'history,' since there are historians who do not so limit themselves. I have tried to analyze certain aspects of another use in my "Historical Explanation," cited earlier. What I should like to insist on is that it is futile to argue that any conclusion of this sort stems from the *nature* or *essence* of history. Indeed, I should expect Popper to agree with me on this point in the light of his own opposition to what he calls "essentialism." I believe, incidentally, that analytic philosophy as I conceive it stands in no need of notions like *the nature of* or *the essence of*.

A few other differences between Popper and myself ought to be made explicit, though they should not obscure the sympathy I have for his way of going at some of these problems and for the high standards of clarity he sets himself in a field usually so muddled. For example, I do not agree that the causal laws implicit in the connections between historical statements are always so trivial that they are not mentioned explicitly; indeed I think that the failure to mention them is just as often a result of their being too complicated and difficult to state. Although I agree that there are *histories* rather than *History*, I do so because I believe that different entities have their own histories as different people frequently have different fathers. But given any entity, I have held that it has no more than one history. I have provided for what Popper calls the many histories by introducing the notion of *approximations* to a history, but my view also implies that these different approximations should differ not because of different interests and values on the part of the historians, as Popper does, but because of differing conceptions as to what is a more representative, a closer approximation to the history of the object.

It should be added that the dependence of the notion of causal fertility on that of law leaves my basic notion in an unsettled state, since I believe as Popper evidently does not, that the notion of law is still in need of clarification. (See note 21 above.)

the same way, the brief sequence which aims at a history can vary from historian to historian but this variation ought not be a function of the different *values* of the historian any more than the axiom set which a mathematician uses is a function of *his* values. There is a region of choice but the choices are limited by the responsibility to state briefly the features of a certain domain.

In urging the historian to select according to the principles of causal fertility, I am aware of a possible objection. It might be argued that for any true singular statement chosen there is always some other true singular statement which is causally linked with it, so that even the historian who gathers indiscriminately will be satisfying the principle of causal fertility. It would follow that there is no difference between the method of selection and the method of indiscriminately listing statements. To this I can only reply that even if we were to grant the dubious principle assumed, we must admit that we often have no inkling of the causal connections of statements. In other words, the principle of causal fertility directs us to select our singular statements in accordance with the body of laws accepted and available at the time. On this score the list of singular statements collected by the near-sighted historian will increase constantly and cumulatively; once in his sequence, a singular statement will stay in it unless proven false. But the sequence of the historian who proceeds according to the principle of causal fertility constantly changes. If G, a generalization which had been accepted in 1900, and which had dictated the inclusion of one of its singular antecedent-instances,[23] F, in a history book of 1900, was later shown to be false, F might have to be erased from the sequence unless some other causal connections could vouch for it. Similarly, a statement which was not there in 1900 might be added later if a suitable new generalization came to be accepted. This suggests that we have to revise our sequences constantly if we adopt the methods of the second kind of historian. It provides us with an interpretation and explanation of the slogan 'history is always being rewritten' which does not draw upon the fact that moral values

---

23. My point can be illustrated by considering the generalization "All revolutions are quickly followed by dictatorships." This might have led to including the singular statement "A revolution took place in country A in 1822" in a history book. Now suppose it was shown that the generalization was false. Unless some other generalization about revolutions could be produced, the singular statement would be removed, according to the criterion accepted. The effect of this point of view is to make it unlikely that a statement having no causal significance will be put down in a history when causally fertile ones are clamoring for admission. If we are dealing with an object about which no causal laws are known then, of course, our theory makes no proposals. Under such conditions, I suppose, facts may be put down for "their own sake" and the historian's "interest" may be the complete master of what he writes down, unless he chooses to write everything down.

and schemes of reference are always changing. It even furnishes us with a justification of the view that history *ought* to be rewritten consistent with the kind of view defended in this paper. It should be noticed, however, that, strictly speaking, *history* is not rewritten on this view, but the various approximations to it are.

I wish to emphasize that the principle of selection offered must be distinguished from a good many in the literature. It is particularly important to distinguish it from those which are advanced as evidence of the essentially moral bases for the historian's selection. After he paints the dismal picture of history which I have quoted, Santayana talks about "philosophical history," a study in which we look over the overwhelming number of truths which are available and then pick out those which appear as friends in a crowd. As I have already said, many American philosophers and historians have come to take a position like this. They urge that their selection arises from their own needs, purposes, prejudices, and problems, and feel no shame about the matter. Indeed, they suppose they wash away whatever guilt they may have in holding theories like this by making explicit and willingly confessing to what they call their values. Now I do not deny that some 'historians" write and rewrite history in this way. Nor do I deny that there is an important point in doing this sometimes. But I do deny that this is the way to approach what has been called a history in this essay; I also deny that it is implicit in the procedure of all whom we call historians.

After having written at such length about 'history' it might be fruitful to reflect on the method employed in sketching the definition. Obviously it is highly abstract and idealized, even more idealized than would appear from the fact that it forces us to conclude that we never write down histories. But this is no more puzzling than the fact that the geometry teacher never really draws a Euclidean line-segment or circle on the blackboard. What may be more puzzling is the fact that even our description of something that can be written down—an approximation to a history—does not fit history books perfectly. For example, we have demanded that every statement in a sequence aiming at a history of the United States of America be *about* the United States of America, but obviously this demand is never satisfied.[24] Here, it seems to me, we must recognize the value in the proposal that we regard phil-

---

24. Furthermore, we are faced with the serious problem of clearly defining 'about.' The most obvious proposal, i.e., a statement S is about y just in case S contains a name of y, is subject to numerous difficulties pointed out to me by Professor Nelson Goodman in conversation.

osophy as logically reconstructive in character, and we must not be bound by all aspects of usage. We are trying to clear up the meaning of a very vague word, and it may be fruitful to start with a simple model which we may later enrich and complicate to a point where it is less ideal and remote. On the other hand, philosophical construction must have some foundation in usage. Since the avowed purpose of a good deal of logical analysis is the clarification of terms actually used in science and in every-day language, it must clarify what it aims to clarify. It must steer a course between free formal construction and enslavement to ordinary language. It must try to make a new language which will help us express all the clear parts of ordinary language, but also one which will be fruit-ful in helping us see truths which we had never seen before and which will make us bold enough to discard parts of our supposedly clear original language. For this reason and others, many problems remain in con-nection with defining 'history.' I have suggested several subsidiary prob-lems and lack of space prevents a detailed consideration of others. It may be worthwhile to state briefly a few consequences of the definition outlined here as well as a few open problems which they suggest.

The problem of what kinds of entities have histories is extremely interesting in my opinion. Earlier, the things which had histories were limited to physical objects, with the suggestion that this might be broaden-ed after some study. However, the fact that histories are restricted to sequences of statements about physical objects does not prevent the pre-dicates applied in those statements from being extraphysical. We may say, for example, that the physical region known as the United States of America was the scene of an economic depression in 1932, and yet the predicate 'was the scene of an economic depression in 1932' might not be physical. Because there are different kinds of predicates which may be applied in histories, there are different relations which are intimately con-nected with the one we have been considering. Political histories, economic histories, geological histories are what we get when we limit ourselves to certain statements in what has been called a history in the unqualified sense. We have the relations *is a political history of, is an economic history of, is a geological history of*. These relations may be de-fined similarly in terms of sequences of statements about a physical object where the component statements are of a specific kind—political, eco-nomic, geological.

The decision to study one of these kinds of histories of a given object involves a kind of selection which must be distinguished from that which is forced upon the investigator who is anxious to approximate the history of an object in an unqualified sense. By a history in an unqualified sense, I mean one that is not limited to political, social, economic, etc., statements. When a historian decides to study the economic aspects of an object he still aims at a sequence which is so enormous that he is forced to settle for briefer sequences which are representatives of the economic history he is seeking. This means that a historian who deals with a certain aspect of an object selects in at least two ways: he selects in choosing this aspect rather than others, and he selects his representative, brief sequence just as the historian (in the unqualified sense) does. Limiting the study to an aspect does not eliminate the need for this second kind of selection. Similar considerations apply to relations which differ from *is a history of* in limiting the time interval covered by the history, e.g., x is a history of y from 1789 to 1939.

The present approach also suggests a way of stating the debate between various kinds of historical determinisms. Philosophers of history who maintain that one factor predominates—e.g., economics—may be claiming that a sequence which is arrived at by an economic historian is more representative of the unqualified history of an object that one sought by a political historian.[25] And, they may argue, not only does the economic historian achieve sequences which are more representative than sequences collected by any other kind of historian, but such sequences are, in general, more representative than a sequence which is chosen without any particular aspect in mind. It should be realized that such an analysis of the various kinds of historical determinisms waits upon a further clarification of the notions of representative sequence and causal fertility. However, it has the virtue of uniting a number of problems which have seemed quite separate up to now.

In conclusion it ought to be repeated that the present essay is based upon the firm conviction that the philosophy of history may be approached analytically. It is not intended as a picture of the state of the philosophy of history in America. The number of philosophers who work in this field is so small that we can hardly speak of widespread tendencies today. For this reason I have tried to give some indication of my own views on the subject and to make some proposals for future research. The close connections between the philosophy of history and other parts of philosophy have been stressed, as well as the differences between speculative and analytical philosophy of history. To do this I have tried to an-

---

25. For an attempt at explaining Marx's views see Lewis S. Feuer, "The Economic Factor in History," *Science and Society*, Vol. IV (1940), pp. 168-192. The approach is different from that suggested here.

alyze the notion of history itself, hoping to illustrate a method and to begin work carrying out a program. The method is neither original nor particularly American; and although my conclusions are closely related to those of a number of American philosophers and historians, they are certainly not accepted by all or even a great number of them. I am firmly convinced, however, of the importance of this method and hope that many American philosophers will apply it to history. But I hesitate to speak of the tasks of the philosophy of history *in America* as if its tasks here were any different from what they are elsewhere, for I believe that the tasks of philosophy are the same everywhere—to seek clarity and truth.

SELECTED BIBLIOGRAPHY

Cohen, M. R. *The Meaning of Human History.* La Salle, Ill., Open Court Publishing Co., 1947.

Goodman, Nelson. "The Problem of Counterfactual Conditionals," *Journal of Philosophy,* Vol. XLIV, 1947, pp. 113-128.

Hempel, C. G. "The Function of General Laws in History," *Journal of Philosophy,* Vol. XXXIX, 1942, pp. 35-48.

Hook, Sidney. *The Hero in History.* New York, John Day, 1943

Mandelbaum, Maurice. *The Problem of Historical Knowledge.* New York, Liveright Publishing Corp., 1938.

Popper, K. R. *The Open Society and its Enemies.* London, Routledge, 1945.

Santayana, George. *Reason in Science,* chap. ii. New York, Charles Scribner's Sons, 1906.

Theory and Practice in Historical Study: A Report of the Committee on Historigraphy of the Social Science Research Council, New York, The Council, 1946.

White, Morton G. "Historical Explanation." *Mind,* Vol. LII, N. S., (1943), pp. 212-229.

—————. "The Attack on the Historical Method." *Journal of Philosophy,* Vol. XLII (1945), pp. 314-331.

THE PHILOSOPHY OF
AMERICAN EDUCATION

*Harold Taylor**

I

A philosophy of education, more directly than any other philosophy, reflects and interprets the history, the culture, and the social condition of the country of its origin. On the other hand, the educational system itself, as it works from day to day, in its school buildings with its teachers and students, expresses a philosophy of national aims, cultural aims, political aims, and, to a degree, the ordinary values and hopes of the people. An examination of the educational system of a country, to detect its physical, spiritual, and social strength, can yield, therefore, an insight into the weakness and strength of a nation, as well as an insight into its philosophy. It is of philosophical importance to note such things as the number of schools in proportion to the population, the number of teachers and students, the cost of going to a university, the number of years the average citizen spends in school as a child, the amount of money spent from the national income, the size of the libraries, the number of books, the salaries of teachers, the size of the athletic plant, the facts and content of the curriculum, the human attitudes the teachers are concerned to develop in children, and the beauty and ugliness of the buildings themselves.

These objective items are the reality in which the national value judgments are fixed, and indicate the scope and quality of education, and thus the quality of culture, in the civilization in which they are found. That reality implies a philosophy and a scale of values, which are distinct from those explicitly stated by educators and philosophers, although in many ways they may coincide. The social system and its proclaimed set

* Born in 1914. Ph.D., University of London, 1938. Formerly a member of the Department of Philosophy, University of Wisconsin. President of Sarah Lawrence College since 1945. Author of numerous contributions to philosophical and educational publications including: "Philosophical Aspects of the Harvard Report," *Philosophy and Phenomenological Research*, December, 1946; "Philosophy and World Order," *The Journal of Philosophy*, December, 1946; "Philosophy and Education," *The Journal of Higher Education*, January, 1948; "Education in the Modern World," *The Educational Record*, January, 1948.

of ideals can thus be studied in the educational system, and a philosophy discovered by indirection. In the present century, educators and intellectuals are much more concerned than their predecessors in the past, with the intimate relation between social fact and philosophic statement, and the work of the modern social scientist in the natural history of ideas and ideals has given us a modern truth which has very complex personal and social origins. What is known about society, about nature, about individuals, about God, about the techniques of science, is contained in the minds and works of intellectuals in our universities. The universities provide the only remaining corner in the contemporary world where the passion for inquiry, the re-examination of the known, and the analysis of values, can be indulged in as a professional occupation without serious harm to the passionate. Whatever intellectual leadership a country can give to its social and political aims must be developed through its educational system. That system at the same time is a mirror of the political, psychological, and social forces at work in a given society.

It is also true that a philosophy of education can be used explicitly by political leaders to state and to support national aims, and that, to a large extent in many countries, the philosophies of education are at the mercy of those with political power. The figure of the Minister of Education, like that of the Minister of the Interior, has in some countries become more menacing than liberating; we also have as examples the German professors, and the educational work of Gentile on behalf of the philosophy of facism. There are many other instances, of which the most striking at the moment is that of Russia, of how directly a political philosophy can inspire an educational one. This is a development in the modern world, during that era of the past fifty years in which we have discovered that not only are values not eternal, but that they can be made to suit particular occasions and societies, and that politicians, by inventing them and imposing them through education, can change the course of personal and world history. Such a possibility has been dimly recognized in earlier systems of education, except that before our age, educators and politicians were not as self-conscious about it, and assumed that the values imbedded in the social and economic structure, and thus in the universities and schools, were in fact eternal, and in any case, were those most appropriate for continuing the present society and its present rulers in power. The philosophy of education, has in many ways, become a more and more important matter for contemporary affairs, both for the power of its leadership in the future of civilization, and for the way in which it tells us the news of the direction in which a given society is moving.

II

I would like first to present a philosophy of American education which emerges when some of the historical, economic, and social facts about America are seen in relation to the present condition of education, and then to present some of the more formal philosophies of education about which philosophers and educators are presently concerned.

America's history has been one of an expanding territory, an expanding economy, an expanding population, and an expanding influence. Two items of size will illustrate. From 1775 to 1948, the size of the United States has increased from 892,000 to 3,022,387 square miles. During the same period the population increased from 2,572,000 to roughly 143,000,000 people. I need not mention evidence of the expanding economy and of world influence.

This has meant that since the early settlements in this country, education has been constantly pressed to keep up with demand, first, of aid for the instruction of all children in reading, writing, and calculating, and then for the variety of technical skills needed to man the expanding industrial economy. From the very first, the primary educational demand has been for training to do useful work which could help with the country's development. Education in the beginning was a private matter, later to become a public responsibility, and the ideal of a common school for all our people, where every person could learn the things necessary to take a useful and satisfying place in the economy, had taken hold by the middle of the nineteenth century. This has meant that the curriculum of schools and colleges in America has been designed, not so much to produce rigorously logical minds or to transmit a cultural heritage, but to give the knowledge and skills necessary for making a living, and improving the country. Those without such skills are handicapped in raising their position in American society. The higher the form of education, up to the Bachelor of Arts degree, the more opportunities for the economic success of the one being educated.

This has also meant that the people themselves have for the most part thought of their schools as practical instruments for raising the economic status of their children. Under a rapidly expanding capitalist economy, in which the individual marked his own success and that of others by his economic status, the student worked for his own self-improvement taking from education those things which could help him best with the constant task of getting ahead in his job. The special kind of American individualism which at its best expresses itself in self-confidence, generosity, optimism, independence, and scorn for authority, and at its worst in arrogance, complacency, and philistinism, is a function of that basic historical, economic, and social pattern. So is the attitude of the educator to cultural values.

Since the major concern of education has been, by necessity, to answer the practical needs of a growing country, those values in education which are not directly attached to this concern are either neglected, or considered in the same light as technical subjects, that is, they are considered to be useful pieces of human equipment, and to be contained in subjects, studied just as thoroughly and by the same methods, as those connected with engineering, medicine, or farming. The pressure on the colleges and universities, particularly during the past fifty years, to educate men and women in the sciences, both natural and social, and in the administrative tasks of business and government, has not only overcrowded our buildings with thousands of students, but has overemphasized still further the technical side of the American education. So practical have some universities now become that there are courses, given for academic credit in fulfillment of the Bachelor of Arts degree, in writing advertising copy, and in making one's hair and face more beautiful. One aspect of the philosophy of American education is thus a materialism, to be found in the structure of American life and reflected in the continuously practical emphasis of school and university education. The aim of the student in America has been, for the most part, to learn those things well which will help him to find the kind of position in business or the professions where there is the most opportunity for advancement toward the top income brackets.

There have been two major effects of the philosophy of vocationalism. The first is an emphasis on the practical application of school and college education to the matter of making a good living, with a consequent lack of emphasis on severe intellectual and esthetic standards. The second is that the entire purpose of the American school and college is different from the European, from which the system was originally copied. If the major purpose is to give to each student the skills for livelihood, then the traditional values and methods of the European school system, by which a highly developed curriculum of historical knowledge and the humanities is specified, are no longer of the same importance.

What is more important is that the school and college teach students the difficult art of living together in America, and the necessity of becoming a self-sufficient individual. The educator in America must invent ways in which children of widely different origins and attitudes may come to understand and to accept each other. Since the battle for free education was won, in the middle of the nineteenth century, the children of immigrants, of the wealthy, of the poor, of the well-educated, the poorly educated, the polite, the vulgar, the religious, and the non-religious have gone to school together. It is true that there were, and still are, a good many private schools, and the Roman Catholic Church supports many schools of its own. But most of America is educated in public schools, where the diversity of the student body is both an educational problem and a social opportunity. During the past twenty-five years, the influence of home life and the family in America has declined, and the school has now taken by default certain additional responsibilities for the development of moral character in the young, and the responsibility for educating them in social attitudes and human relations. This is not mere training in etiquette, or in small details of behavior. It is education of the entire child in moral character, a task which was formerly in the hands of the church and family. American education has excluded religious teaching in the public schools, yet at the same time has accepted responsibility for education formerly provided by religion. It has also accepted the responsibility of training the child to think, act, and live democratically, and to learn the social values of his country. This means that the philosophy of education for contemporary America must include a social doctrine, since it is the only medium by which the ethos of democracy can be transmitted consciously, and the expanding and creative spirit of democratic reform kept alive in the younger generation. There are, of course, other agencies in American life, including the family, and community planning, in which the philosophy of democracy is learned and practiced. The main responsibility, however, for the future of the democratic system lies with the educational system.

Thus, a social force and a humanistic philosophy has developed in opposition to the philosophy and practice of materialism. Its philosophical origins undoubtedly lie in the Christian doctrines of the first settlers, modified and changed into secular values, and most often stated as aspects of the philosophy of democracy. On the one hand, the goal of youth is to get ahead in business, to compete for status in the professions, and in industry, to rise from worker to manager, from small income to large, from obscurity to publicized and advertised fame. On the other, the goal of youth is to be loved and admired for the personal virtues of kindliness, liberalism, generosity, understanding, knowledge, and equalitarianism. It is only within the present century that American educators have begun to work specifically at the problem of developing in American youth, the qualities of human character which the country's moral life demands and which the conventional functions of education do not serve.

At the same time, a basic assumption has been made by Americans, whether educators or not, that education should be made available to everyone, regardless of social or economic position, and that it is the duty of the country to provide it whether or not the individual young person anticipates the need and consciously seeks its fulfillment. Any attempt to restrict, on a national scale, the higher education of youth to those who have already shown themselves to be superior scholars, has in recent years been rejected because of the dangers in conceiving education as the creation of an intellectual and social élite. Accordingly, the large public universities financed by the taxes collected in the states, have accepted all students who wish to come, provided they have demonstratd the ability to absorb the regular curriculum of the country's high schools. This means that many young people who are not scholastically superior university students are given the opportunity of higher education, and that, in some instances, the academic standards of American universities for undergraduates are not as high as those existing in the European. It also accounts, in some measure, for the relatively greater interests in nonacademic affairs, such as college sports, parties, games, and entertainment, on the part of American students than on the part of their European contemporaries.

III

There are, in general, three dominant trends in the present development of the philosophy of education in America. The trends receive their most articulate expression in the philosophies developed in colleges and universities. The first of these is closely associated with the pragmatism or instrumentalism inherent in basic modes of American life and thought. The philosophy is most fully expressed in the work of William James and John Dewey, and, at the moment, in a document on higher education by a commission of American educators who were appointed to their task by the President of the United States. The second is the neohumanist or eclectic philosophy expressed in various statements about curriculum reform published by American university faculties whose group membership usually includes one or two philosophers. Principal amongst these statements is that by a group of professors at Harvard University, published under the name of *General Education in a Free*

Society. The third is the neo-scholastic philosophy of the Roman Catholic Church, which underlies the program of Catholic theological schools and undergraduate colleges, and which has been modified in a more secular direction by educators in other colleges where an effort has been made to revive the classical curriculum.

Of these three movements in philosophy, the one which has been most frequently applied in the past ten years to the actual reform of institutions of higher education is that of the eclectics. They have faced the serious problem of the disunity of contemporary knowledge and its separation of spheres of study into rigid,discrete disciplines, by attempting to find a way in which a coherent pattern may be formed for the higher learning. It should be noted that further disunity had already been introduced into higher education by the system of study—each college student chose his own courses from a very large number offered to him, and worked at them in fifteen week sections, receiving a Bachelor of Arts degree when he had studied a sufficient number of subjects for a sufficient length of time. The new pattern, now widely adopted, eliminates a good deal of this confusion of many little courses, by replacing them with programs of general education in each of the four major areas of knowledge, the humanities, the natural sciences, the social sciences, and the arts.

In view of the fact that no young person can expect to know in any detail the whole content of human learning, the general education movement has suggested that an introduction to each of these major fields, with specific study in one of them during the third and fourth year, can constitute the most satisfactory form of higher education. This program is usually known as the core curriculum, since it attempts the union of a common core of knowledge for each student. In most colleges and universities, a serious effort is now being made to find the materials of study in each of the four fields of knowledge which will give the student a sufficient understanding of the major trends and principal items of information in each field, at the same time giving to each, sufficient depth of knowledge to avoid superficiality. The details of this effort are worked out by members of the departments under which the subjects are grouped, in consultation with curriculum committes elected from the whole faculty of each college. Already the reforms have resulted in a greater degree of cooperation amongst the departments, and the present rigid classification of knowledge by departmental subject matter has been modified a little in the direction of greater flexibility of teaching.

The philosophy upon which these reforms rest has not yet been worked out in any detail, since the reforms themselves are more practical than philosophical in nature, and have all been directed against the former evil of disintegrated, separated, units of education. The units themselves have remained, however. That is, the fifteen-week length of courses, the assignment of credits for completion of the units, the evaluation of student ability by grades of A, B, C, D, and F (for failure), are still the basic elements of structure; the content of each unit is the factor which has changed.

However, there are certain philosophical assumptions on which this system rests, which can be stated as follows:

(a)   There is a unity in knowledge which consists in the grouping of the kinds of information available under the heading of various subject matters. Thus there is a body of knowledge called anthropology, psychology, literature, or philosophy, each with its particular known facts and texts. The union of these separate bodies of knowledge under the major divisions of social science, natural science, the arts, and the humanities, is a matter of choosing the material from each separate discipline and embodying such material in textbooks and courses of study.

(b)   A rationalistic conception of the structure of knowledge and its function is therefore assumed, and the communication and discovery of truth, or the heritage of science and culture, consists of lectures upon these subjects by experts, who furnish lists of appropriate reading matter where the things the lecturer has said may be seen repeated or expanded. Once this accredited intellectual material has been surveyed and remembered, the knowledge has become part of the intellectual furniture of the student mind. The latter phrase is often used by educators to describe the knowledge of the student.

(c)   A dualistic epistemology is assumed, which both follows from and adds to the assumption about knowledge as a system of rationally ordered intellectual materials. The practices developed for teaching verify this assumption; the teaching of the surveys of social sciences, or "the humanities," rely upon outlines of the knowledge to be learned; there are books which give in skeleton form the basic facts to be known; students usually make notes on books assigned for reading by classifying facts under a series of numbered headings; students are examined on the "content" of the course; examinations usually consist in questions by the examiner designed to discover the extent of the student's memory for the lectures and books. The terms used by those who speak of reforming the curriculum of higher education imply a stream of dualisms between thought and action, intellect and emotion, past and present, ancient and modern, fact and value.

(d) The metaphysical assumption, as already noted, is that of a reality logically ordered, and forced to assume propositional form in order to be known. This leads to a further practical assumption that once the student has a grasp of some or all the elements comprising the rational order, he is educated in a higher sense. Accordingly, the value systems involved in various forms of knowledge, for example, the philosophical systems, are all equal—they express different points of view, each of them rational and valid, given the equality in status of the values from which they spring.

(e) This means a general distinction between fact and value, which corresponds to the distinctions already made between reason and emotion, science and art, mind and body, knowledge and ignorance. The values which underlie civilization and cultures are assumed to be rationally derived, and for the most part, independent of relative space-time considerations. They become part of a universe in which value is intrinsic.

The debate about philosophical questions of value is seldom found among those who reform university education. Rather, intrinsic rationality, eternal truths and ethical modes are conceived, without serious question, as objective correlatives of a universe rationally contrived and eternally existent. It is regrettable that few of America's keenest contemporary philosophical critics and professional philosophers are not raising epistemological and metaphysical questions in the context of the American educational system.

The practical implications of the eclectic view are that students seldom face live options among values, but are given a continuous stream of facts and interpretations in science, literature, and the arts, from which they may or may not derive value systems of their own. This also means that when philosophy is taught to students, it is taught as a series of disciplined and systematic propositions about various realities conceived in Western thought, with the questions of the claims the systems make for credibility and moral allegiance kept in abeyance and regarded as a private option amongst many possible options. This has the advantage of inducing a sense of the relativism of various philosophical systems in their claims for truth. But it also has the disadvantage of seldom producing original or creative thinking by the students who study philosophy in this way.

The approach of the neo-classicist, who proposed a total revision of the curriculum in terms of classical philosophy, science, and literature, although it shares some of the above assumptions, notably those of rationalistic persuasion, is clearer as to its theory and epistemology. Its philosophy, as already noted, is closest to the neo-Thomist, although with greater emphasis upon Aristotelianism than is usual in that system. It states that, in view of the fact that man is a rational animal, the cultivation of man's reason is the sole aim of higher education, or, for that matter, of life for civilized men. It states that the human reason is everywhere the same, and entails a complete rationalism in theory of education, social philosophy, and theory of culture. The values and truths of Western culture are said to lie in the minds and books of the great thinkers of the past. An objective wisdom, and a set of eternal values, which reflect factors inherent in the universe and in the relation of man to nature, are thus contained in certain specified texts of the Western tradition. It remains to communicate these values and truths to the students by use of one hundred such specified texts, drawn from the history of literature, philosophy, science, and the arts. This is done by lectures, and by discussions in which the students participate. The proposal is that the reading and discussion of these books should occupy students during the four years of their college life. In this way, the wisdom of our cultural heritage is handed on to the youth of the present, and the values by which we in the West live, are then believed to be absorbed by the individual.

The social philosophy implicit here is that of protection and development of a rational society—the aim of education is to educate the student to make rational criticism and to judge fairly of any political or social issue which may arise. It is assumed that the student may apply these moral principles without reference to the specific context in which they appear, since the principles of truth and morality are universal and each situation is therefore covered by a form of natural law.

The total aim of this system is to develop understanding, not action; contemplation, not participation; a knowledge of the past, not of the present; disciplined rather than creative thinkers; conventionally civilized adults, not rebels. The emphasis, both philosophically and practically, is on disciplined rationality. It is for this reason that empirical social science has little place in this system of education, and that the kind of activity known in American colleges as extracurricular, or community life, that is, sports, singing, playing, meeting people, dancing, and organizing affairs, are considered distractions and interruptions of the chief activity, that of learning the laws of reason and of nature.

The influence of the neo-classicists has been indirect, although important. In only one or two instances in institutions has the proposal for reform of the curriculum been accepted as a total answer. On the other hand, in those sections of the eclectic curriculum, as described earlier, which deal with literature, philosophy, and the arts, this philosophy has been a significant factor in reform. Educators have seen in it a clear, unequivocal way of laying a moral basis of a general kind for more specific work in other fields. Many of the units of study designated as surveys of the humanities, take the neo-classical view as to the purpose and scope of study in these areas.

It is perhaps unnecessary to describe the philosophy and curriculum of the church-supported schools, since the characteristics in this case are prescribed by religious doctrine, and rely heavily upon classical learning. In the case of the Roman Catholic colleges, the prescription of subjects and underlying doctrines to be communicated follow a familiar pattern. In the case of the protestant sects, the general undergraduate colleges have become rather like the nonreligious colleges in their educational plan and philosophy, except that in some cases the study of religion or philosophy is required of all students. This, of course, does not apply to the professional schools of theology of any of the churches, which exist in great diversity and which are free to teach their own doctrines, train their own clergy, and solicit funds to support their efforts from any available source.

The philosophy of education implicit in the Report of the President's Commission on Higher Education is more congenial to the philosophical character and political and social thinking of Americans. Whether or not the professed philosophy of colleges and schools is actually instrumentalist, pragmatic, or individualist, as recommended by the Report, the thread running through the whole educational system is of this kind. Religious, rationalistic, and absolutist values, of neo-Thomism or neo-classicism, are either transformed or replaced by an empirical, practical, social value system, in which the chief end of education is said to be, not contemplation or knowledge of absolute value, but the development of citizens who think independently, intelligently, and democratically. The continuous presence of this moral attitude converts most educational systems, from nursery school to graduate study, into some form of preparation for practical affairs, or in the directing of human energies and intellect into socially useful modes. Some of the best work in this philosophy of education is thus found in the nursery and elementary schools, where the concept of high intellectual standards is defined as the full development of the individual character and aptitudes of each child. For it is a corollary moral factor, both for American democracy and for education, that development of the individual in terms of his intrinsic powers is the greatest single aim of the whole social and political system. Education is conceived as the process by which American society reforms itself and applies its own direction and self-correction. It is the ultimate dynamic of social change.

The central force of this philosophy expends itself in the earlier education of the young, and by the time the latter years of high school are reached, the educational practices diverge in the direction either of vocational training, or its counterpart in a different vocational sense, preparation for college entrance. This creates a dilemma which has not yet been solved whether or not to carry out in secondary school education, the aim of developing individual aptitudes in science, the arts, technical skill, or to provide each student with the standard set of knowledge necessary for him to enter college or university. In a genuine sense, opportunity to continue one's education in college is considered a democratic right for every child, regardless of social or economic position, or, in some cases, even of intellectual ability, and the dilemma involves a social distinction, marking those with college degrees as of superior talent and opportunity from those with only technical skills. Serious experiments have shown that the curriculum of the high school can vary according to individual talent and aptitude, while at the same time preparing the student adequately for higher study in American colleges and universities. But the experimental evidence has never been taken seriously by the colleges, which continue to demand uniform entrance requirements of subject matter, which in turn solidify the curriculum for the high school in a standard form. This would be appropriate perhaps in the different conceptions of European education, where the end of secondary school is a terminal point for education, where a body of knowledge is already required, and where much higher levels of intellectual effort are demanded on the part of secondary school students. But in America, there is a contradiction between the philosophy of individual differences and the actual practices of higher education.

During the past ten years, owing to the pressure of external political and social events, American educators have become more conscious of the need for political and social education. Glaring evidence, from our experience with the young Americans of the armed services abroad, and from the lack of social responsibility in students at home, has indicated that the school and college curriculum must, in stronger ways, deal with preparation of American students for life in a political democracy. This need is now being met by an increase in practical studies in the social sciences and by increased research in the problems of contemporary society. In the larger universities there are often Institutes of Human Relations, where research and study in every area of social science is carried on, and teachers are being prepared to work in schools and colleges at the task of increasing social understanding on the part of each student. Accordingly, the impact of the instrumentalist philosophy, with the impact of modern society, on the needs of students, has resulted in social science, particularly psychology, sociology, anthropology, and political science, becoming the most important new development in the curriculum.

If the aim of education is the development of creatively democratic citizens, then the most significant kind of knowledge each student should have is said to be a knowledge of society, of the individuals who compose it and the forces at work which make both modern society and the modern individual behave as they do. The philosophy by which these ends are sought states clearly that knowledge for contemporary students must be related to the present. The history and study of the past is only considered to be significant in this kind of education when the educator makes a conscious effort to relate the past to present issues and problems. The sense of the past is held less valuable than a sense of the present and a knowledge of the things which are now happening. In Europe young people are more conscious, without formal instruction in college, of contemporary social and political history than are the American students, and a great deal of knowledge which the young European normally has, simply from living in Europe, is not available to Americans and must be provided in more academic form in the schools and colleges. Similarly, the European youth feel more deeply their cultural heritage, from the habits of thinking and acting which they have gained in childhood and adolescence. The high value placed upon the new, the fresh, and the young, by Americans, and the general oversimplification of the traditional, means that American young people on the whole regard history as something which happened to people with whom we need no longer be concerned.

If then, the kind of knowledge taught to students must be related to the present, the values by which students are expected to live, unavoidably become relative. The goals of human life can be seen, in actual fact, to be relative to the time and place in which they are conceived, and it becomes literally impossible for educators to set down a complete value system, and then to present it forcefully as a series of unquestionable truths to the young people who are being educated. The whole moral climate of the schools is unfavorable to absolutism, and the tradition of dissent, or rejection of authority, is the central factor around which this education must build itself.

This raises a serious question for American education, in view of the critical need for a youth which not only understands contemporary society, but which must have a set of firm beliefs, solidly held, by which the thinking and acting of the country can be united. For authoritarian philosophies of education this is not a serious question, since the making of firm belief in youth is the entire concern of the educator. It is only in a philosophy of individualism and democracy, where ends are not fixed, and are inextricably bound up with means, that such practical issues arise.

Characteristically, the instrumentalism of American education, and the concern for democratic spirit and behavior, turns to the central fact of democratic method in order to reach its own kind of firm belief. In the schools and colleges it encourages the solution of problems by committees and by discussion, and relies upon joint decisions reached by students and by faculty to represent the truth about a given situation. Often the return to method in place of doctrine induces the notion that a majority of opinion on any question is always right, and that if only enough good-tempered discussion occurs, whether about communism or about the physical universe, the truth will be reached. On the other hand, the genuine effort to achieve understanding and agreement, with minority views influencing radically the quality of conclusion reached, does result in a truth which, although it is not always complete, at least has a better chance of being true in the test of public scrutiny than an *a priori* truth, either revealed or deduced from rational principles.

The philosophy is empirical, practical, and optimistic. The assumption is made, not only that society can be effectively reformed through education, but that the crucial questions of human life can be understood and answers found, if a serious effort is made to understand them by people who have been educated to do so.

The fact that history has yielded to the will and instruments of Americans during the past four hundred years has provided continuous proof that optimism is justified. Here the protestant philosophies of the religious settlers and the secular philosophies of contemporary pragmatists join together, and each suggests salvation through moral, spiritual, and physical effort. The later doctrine, however, makes the assumptions that human nature has intrinsic good, and that the task of education is to release the good by providing the free conditions under which it can grow. The assumption is that the potential goodness in each person is such that freedom of growth can be allowed without destruction of the social system itself. Even among those materialists, naturalists, or positivists, who deny intrinsic values or potentials of any kind to human nature, the assumption is usually made that socially and personally desirable conduct may be developed by the appropriate environment and guidance. The question of what is ultimately desirable conduct is constantly being answered by those who speculate and assert from a variety of points of view. Journalists, radio commentators, politicians, clergymen, business leaders, labor leaders, educators, and philosophers all state their convictions with varying degrees of authority on various occasions.

There is no final authority recognized, nor a philosophical ultimate, except the concept of the free individual. There is of course variation in the concept of freedom, all the way from radical *laisser faire* to government control, in economic matters, and from spontaneous, irresponsible behavior to a disciplined, contemplative life, in personal affairs. This diversity of freedom as an ultimate accounts for the apparent confusion and profusion of American life. Its unity is composed of individual unities, formed into a cohesive society by the tacit agreement that many things can exist together without danger to the whole. The existence of that agreement is again illustrated by the actual diversity among the 1700 colleges and universities of the country.

Finally, the theory of knowledge upon which the philosophy is based is contextualist, and implicitly pragmatic. It relies upon research in psychology for its validation, and, in general, accepts the methods of science as the most appropriate means of discovering knowledge. An experimental mood, in which a good many parts of elementary and secondary schools were reformed, in the 1920's and 1930's, used psychological data, theories, and tests, to advance the science of education. The testing movement itself now occupies a large part of contemporary education and has grown as a result of the confidence educators have placed in psychology as a science useful for the improvement and advance of education. The movement towards psychological testing has also proven itself most adapted to the huge numbers of students at present in colleges and universities, where mass testing of students is a convenient way of classifying individuals. It is, of course, also a dangerous way of classifying individuals, since it reduces human qualities to symbols and numbers, and, in company with other educational methods, tends to mechanize learning and dehumanize education.

When one looks at the less desirable results of this dominant American philosophy, they are seen to fit accurately the less desirable qualities of the American character. The result of the honest democratic effort to educate everyone in sight is to reduce a good deal of education to an inadequate level. The result of the emphasis upon the practical uses of education is to make every form of knowledge justify itself in terms of social or civic utility. The result of the optimism as to knowledge and action is to reduce all of life to a series of soluble problems and minor challenges to be overcome. The result of the emphasis upon the present, in its political, economic, and social dimensions, is to neglect the esthetic and spiritual insights which can make the present and the past the source of spiritual satisfactions.

On the other hand, when one looks at the happier results of the popular American philosophy, the values become clear. Because so many, rather than so few, are educated, more youthful talent is discovered, and more vitality and human energies are released than would be possible in any other system. Because the educational emphasis is upon social usefulness, the arts and sciences must constantly relate themselves to the center of contemporary life, and supply a changing set of needs with a satisfactory solution. Because the philosophy is empirical and optimistic, the younger generation meets the difficulties of its adult life with exuberance and confidence. Because the philosophy emphasizes present issues, values, and goals, young people are more encouraged to think creatively and hard about present issues, than they would be if inhibited by the tradition of acceptance. The indications are that the American educational system will continue its growth with the guidance of these dominant conceptions. It will continue to honor its European origin, it will continue to develop within itself a diversity of philosophies and of institutions, but its main current in the future will be empirical, practical, socially-minded and liberal.

SELECTED BIBLIOGRAPHY

Barzun, J. M. *The Teacher in America*. New York, Little Brown, 1945.
Bode, B., and others. *Modern Education and Human Values,* Pittsburgh, University of Pittsburgh Press, 1947.

Carr, William G., and others. *Education for All American Youth,* Educational Policies Commission, National Educational Association and American Association of School Administrators, 1944.

Harvard University. *General Education in a Free Society*: Report of the Harvard Committee, Cambridge, Harvard University Press, 1945.

Hook, Sidney. *Education for Modern Man.* New York, The Dial Press, 1946.

Jones, Howard M. *Education and World Tragedy.* Cambridge, Harvard University Press, 1946.

Van Doren, Mark. *Liberal Education.* New York, Henry Holt and Co., 1943.

Veblen, Thorstein. *The Higher Learning in America.* New York, Huebsch, 1918.

Brand Blanshard, Curt J. Ducasse, Charles W. Hendel, Arthur E. Murphy, Max C. Otto. *Philosophy in American Education.* New York, Harper's, 1945.

John Dewey. *Democracy and Education.* New York, The Macmillan Co., 1932.

Report of the President's Commission on Higher Education. New York, Harper's 1947.

41st Yearbook, National Society for the Study of Education, *Philosophies of Education.*

REFLECTIONS OF A FRENCH PHILOSOPHER ON THE PRECEDING AMERICAN ESSAYS

André Lalande

I

"Anyone who undertakes to get an understanding of the philosophy of the Ancients," says Renouvier, "is dazzled at the outset by the sight of an illumination which is quite different from that which illuminates us today." But soon, he adds, if the student does not allow himself to be halted by external forms, "he takes part in the speculations of the free and primitive spirits who looked for the reality in things, or the truth in the mind, instead of taking delight in the futile arrangement of the parts of a politically studied system." The situation is a bit the same for a French philosopher invited to participate in a collective work of American philosophy.

The first characteristic which strikes one in these varied contributions is the extreme liberty of approach which almost all of them present. Their authors do not aim at giving a continuing deduction, such as Descartes desired, nor at proceeding dialectically, by thesis, antithesis, and synthesis, nor at constructing what we used to call irreverently, when we were studying for our examinations, "a three-story house": empirical point of view, critical point of view, metaphysical point of view. Such a concern seems entirely contrary to the American genius. When now and then it seems to enter on that path—undoubtedly under Latin or Germanic influences—its spirit of independence reacts quickly. Professor George Boas, in his article on "The History of Philosophy," full of humor and clever insights, remarks that American history of philosophy at first tried to divide the movements of thought into periods, each with one dominant idea, and organized with relation to each other according to a definite rhythm; it passed over as without interest those authors of the epoch which did not fit into the edifice. But shortly afterwards, this architectonic spirit was opposed by the factual and analytical method, which might be called, after Professor Marvin Farber, the phenomenological method, the method which above all records the facts as the investigator finds or discovers them. This is the tendency advocated in Mr. Boas's article, and he is certainly right in doing so. In his judgment it is the dominant tendency at the present time. The entire collection under discussion seems to be a corroboration of that statement.

When reading a French author, it almost always helps to ask, what is he driving at? *Respice finem,* Leibniz said, and this advice is still repeated frequently by the best professors, in a country where philosophy is *taught* more than anywhere else.[1] Most of the American articles collected in this volume give quite the opposite impression. There are undoubtedly notable exceptions, but in general the author goes ahead like an explorer, who follows the natural routes into the interior, rather than like a mountain climber who sets out to scale a given peak. He sometimes ends on a detail, a reservation, even on a complementary thought which did not find its spot in the preceding pages. The same thing is seen often enough in France, but in papers in physics or biology: for it is a way of thinking and of writing which is tied up with the experimental spirit; we shall find other manifestations of it.

Another common trait will strike a French reader, and sometimes embarrass him: the important role played by the names of philosophical parties or tendencies. Not that terms ending in *-ism* are rare among my countrymen; but they are no longer applied to schools, to groups clashing with one another, as was the case with the "materialism" or the "spiritualism" of the nineteenth century. By now one hardly finds philosophical parties with a fixed doctrine, except for Thomism on one side and dialectical materialism on the other. And at that many philosophers would be inclined to say that precisely on account of that property they are rather on

---

1. First in the *lycées* and *collèges,* to young men of 16 or 17, who will be business men, merchants, government officials, judges, or doctors, just as much as to those who later will devote themselves to the sciences or philosophy; then in the classes called *Première Supérieure,* to those of 18 to 20, who go further in their classical studies; then in the Faculties, in preparation for that very comprehensive examination, the *licence de philosophie;* finally, in preparation for an advanced and arduous competition, the *Agrégation,* the usual gateway to upper secondary and university teaching. The Doctorate, however, is not prepared for in any university course; it is obtained by presenting works which are supposed to be entirely personal.

the fringe of genuine philosophy. Positivism, after having been a formally constituted Society, and even a religion, is nothing more today than a certain mental complexion so widespread that it is consistent with the greatest possible variety of attitudes, and no one would dream of discussing it as a fixed doctrine.

The situation in America appears to be different, to judge by the present volume. I see that analogous subdivisions have been made in many doctrines, and that Mr. Arthur Lovejoy speaks wittily of "the thirteenth pragmatism." But what a place these designations occupy in the ensemble of the reports and discussions! One comes across not only all the words in *-ism* which we are familiar with, but also terms rare or all but unknown in France, such as "contextualism," "reductionism," or "primitivism"; and others which are current here, but with a quite different meaning, for example "humanism," whether in the sense of Irving Babbitt and his school[2] or in the sense in which Dr. Robinson speaks of naturalistic humanism; or again "personalism," which hitherto was used to identify Renouvier's second philosophy, or that of M. Emmanuel Mounier, something quite different from E. S. Brightman's "pluralistic personalism" or W. E. Hocking's "absolute personalism." [3] These labels are enigmas for us in many cases, or even pitfalls: when a Frenchman reads, in Prof. Donald C. Williams's penetrating article, that American "positivism" destroys all confidence in reasonable and foresighted conduct, he will recall the celebrated aphorism of Auguste Comte, the founder of positivism: "Science, whence foresight; foresight, whence action"; and he will wonder by what extraordinary semantic metamorphosis the term has ended up having a meaning diametrically opposed to that which its creator had given it.

II

It should not be thought, however, that this unfurling of banners covers discussions which are remote from reality. In this respect, the philosophy of the United States even seems to lie solidly within the framework of certain accepted orientations, technical, political, social. Professor McGill on one hand, in a very concrete, timely, and broadly-documented article on "The Main Trend of Social Philosophy in America," and Pres-

---

2. This, however, is familiar in France, through a work by L. Mercier, *Le mouvement humaniste aux États-Unis* (Paris, Librairie Hachette, 1928), and the doctoral thesis of Christian Richard, *Le movement humaniste en Amérique, et les courants de pensée similaires en France.*

3. Cf. D. S. Robinson's article, "Philosophy of Religion in the United States in the Twentieth Century."

ident Harold Taylor, on the other hand, in his fine article on "The Philosophy of American Education," both vigorously make the point that American philosophy is the philosophy of a people in the fullness of youth, in rapid expansion, whose territory has more than tripled in less than two hundred years, and whose population over the same period increased fifty times. This extraordinary vitality does not manifest itself in an anarchic sprouting of contradictory doctrines: it remains firmly oriented toward certain directives universally held to be good. A philosophy, whatever its tendency, should accept the reality of men as physical bodies, their multiplicity, their material and intellectual relations, the fact that they need to eat in order to live and to wear clothing in order to stand the cold: all this is the very type of existence, and not a world of appearances or illusions. Many Old World philosophers would, no doubt, refuse to insert these obligations as conditions of the articles of agreement of their metaphysics, and think that metaphysics should be constructed without postulating anything. But it may be doubted that it is possible to begin thus in a vacuum, and the duty of the critical spirit may perhaps be confined to being clearly aware of the facts or principles with which one works.

Moreover, philosophy should be democratic: there is nothing more interesting for us than the remarkable activity brought to bear by the philosophers in defining democracy and making explicit its various possible interpretations, as appears in the very penetrating article of Professor McGill: it should be individualistic (in the good sense of the word), favorable to the spirit of enterprise, confident of human power intelligently to improve the physical and social milieu. This "meliorism" is susceptible of many nuances, which are clearly indicated too in Mr. V. J. McGill's article. He even takes note of reservations, like those of John Dewey, who allows the possibility of a checking and a decadence. Men are no longer in the stage of Herbert Spencer's optimistic fatalism, when he wrote: "It is certain that evil and pain must one day disappear; it is certain that the world must become perfect." But without disposing so summarily of those forces within man himself which resist the human order, it is rare for the philosophies of the New World not to show at least a reflection of these magnificent hopes. They are at any rate deeply attached to the vision of a progressive history of humanity whose formation and development through the geological eras constitute the most solid core of reality, and are the condition of all speculative thought.

We will be helped to realize in how different a light these directives show things from that furnished by European philosophies, if we think of the place formerly and still held in the majority of the latter by the notion of *eternity*. Not eternity in the familiar sense of indefinite duration, *nunc currens in tempore sine fine,* as Boethius said, but in the sense of the *nunc stans et permanens.* To escape from this world's evil not only by combatting it in its particular instances, but by rising above time; to grasp, across our fleeting life, and as it were in another dimension, a form of awareness and existence which no longer has any connection with clocks and calendars—this is an orientation which is at right angles to that of meliorism, not excluding it, but going beyond it. This was the key to the spirituality of the great mystics, even when they were men of action as well; and almost every European metaphysics retains an echo of it. No doubt, as Lequier has said, "the succession of things casts its shadow even on God": it is hard to attribute to God a truly intemporal eternity if it is granted that He created free beings which are born and die, that He knows them and is interested in them. But, inversely, is there not all the essential part of that thought which is exterior and superior to time, in the scientist who thinks of the world in his capacity as mathematician?—and also, in an entirely different field, in the meliorist who willingly sacrifices his actual time and labor for the happiness of future generations?—or in the philosophical biologist who conceives the entire history of evolution as a whole and in a sort of synoptic table?

III

Among the characteristics of American philosophy which seems to me to emerge from this collective work, there is another which distinguishes it from French philosophy, and which could usefully be added to the latter: I am referring to the importance which speculations on language have acquired in American philosophy, and the idea that to solve, and even merely define, philosophical problems, the necessary method is to begin with the criticism of the terms and their syntax. Materially, philosophy is discourse: if we pretend to ignore that materiality, we shall only be more completely the dupes of the illusions which it engenders. This question is directly taken up in the interesting article by Mr. Felix Kaufmann, an independent member of the "Wiener Kreis" who emigrated to the United States: "Basic Issues in Logical Positivism," which sums up his discussion with Mr. Carnap, the great promoter of this idea. We find the same question in the article by Mr. F. B. Fitch, a consulting editor of the *Journal of Symbolic Logic,* entitled "Attribute and Class," a remarkable specimen of the amplitude and subtlety with which studies in logic and the theory of meaning have been pursued in the United States. Mr. Victor F. Lenzen's very instructive study on "Philosophy of Science in America" begins by recalling A. B. Johnson's old work, *A Treatise on Language;* another considerable part of it is devoted to the spread of the doctrines of the Vienna School, whose main idea is, according to him, the critical analysis of meanings.   Professor Abraham Edel, in the study which we have already cited, takes up the attempt of certain thinkers to treat morals as a branch of semantics.   Finally, there is a concrete application of the same method in a subject where Frenchmen would hardly expect it: Mr. Morton G. White's lively and up-to-date discussion "Toward an Analytic Philosophy of History."   "To approach history as a mode of discourse, as a form of language which calls for clarification," to distinguish historical from "metahistorical" concepts (in the sense in which we speak of metamathematical language), is a program which gives new life to the traditional aspects of the question.   To be sure, when one goes on to apply it, to the inevitable choice of which facts to retain or to let fall, great difficulties are encountered: the "criterion of causal fertility" raises the question of knowing what the "cause" in history is, and that notion would require a whole new semantic discussion: a valuable attempt will be found in the reports of the *Société française de philosophie,*[4] even though it did not lead to an agreement among the participants in the discussion.

It must be conceded that American philosophy has felt the impact of this criticism of language more than ours has, and taken more interest in it.   It is closely linked, both in the works of writers and the nature of things, to the great activity in mathematical logic, which too has interested only an extremely limited audience in France.   Yet perhaps has not the *Vocabulaire technique et critique* of the *Société de Philosophie* contributed several stones to the edifice?[5]   I do not refer only to the analyses which discriminate among the various meanings of a great number of philosophical terms, and discuss the relations among these meanings (e.g., for the words *amour, évolution, hasard, idéalisme, liberté, nature, personne, vérité*); I am thinking as well of distinction introduced into the body of logic, like the distinction between the "principles" of any body of doctrine, that is, such axioms as that body of doctrine is deduced from; and the "foundation," that is, those propositions to which assent is granted.   This separation is of primary importance in all questions of a normative order, and in that field radically eliminates certain very widely held sophisms.

Another distinction, bound up with this one, but not always observed,

---

4. See the communications of M. Simiand and M. Seignobos in the *Bulletin* of the Society, Séances du 31 mai 1907 and 30 mai 1907, each followed by extended discussions.
5. A fifth edition, entirely revised, appeared in 1947.

even in France,[6] and not appearing in the articles at present under discussion, is the distinction between the algorithm (*combinatoire*) which Logic makes use of, and Logic properly so called, namely as normative science of what we have and what we have not the right to conclude and assert—and consequently what we have and have not the right to demand of others, or to impose on them in the name of the law, if they refuse to recognize it. This leads to a theory which is critical and constructive of certain values—in an axiological sense, altogether different from the sense in which we speak of the different "values" of an independent variable and its function, and even of the "truth-values" of two propositions, as they enter into a table of possible cases; and this very equivocalness of the word "value" has gone far toward creating the illusion that we were already in logic when we had not yet passed the stage of the algorithm (*combinatoire*).

The recognition of the normative character of Logic properly so called, although it has long been theoretically conceded, has been surprisingly neglected in the most celebrated logical treatises; and yet it alone makes possible the solution of a whole series of difficulties which up to the present have been a constant source of skeptical doubts: for instance, it enables us to avoid having the principles of identity and contradiction translated either into tautologies (not in Wittgenstein's sense, but in the primitive sense of the word: silly truisms), or into untenable assertions refuted by the experience of becoming. The same is true of the problem of the nature of error, which always came back to the same paradoxes, and of many others besides.[7] Mr. Kaufmann's remarkable paper, of which we have already spoken, does full justice to this quality in defining the rules of the logic of science; but does not the distinction have a place even in general logic, if the latter is not reduced to a simple collection of matrices?

Again, can everything which purports to be a rule in scientific reasoning derive that authority from convention, as Mr. Kaufmann seems to hold? There is in the status of norms, if analyzed phenomenologically, not an intermediate position between those of Kant and Poincaré, but a *tertium quid* which is quite different, connected with the discovery of the active and directed nature of knowledge, as C. S. Peirce showed. By taking up a position in the domain of values at the outset, we escape from the arbitrariness which is inseparable from the idea of "convention," without ap-

---

6. It is however very clearly defined and applied by M. Morot-Sir in a remarkable work on *La pensée négative* (1947).
7. Cf. *La raison et les normes,* chap. vii: "Les normes et les faits."

pealing to a metaphysical and immovable rationalism whose reflection pure logic would be.[8]

The same distinction and the same relation between the *descriptive* and the *normative,* clearly recognized as such, seem to me the best instrument for clearing up, so far as they can be cleared up, the difficulties encountered in attempting to construct a rationally satisfactory theory of probability. There too we have on the one hand a simple combinatory question—what Le Dantec very illuminatingly used to call the "probability ratio," something in itself useless for determining conduct, and on the other a question of norms (that is, of logical rights and duties), which on the contrary is of remarkable practical efficacy. Professor Donald C. Williams's brilliant article on "Probability, Induction, and the Provident Man" throws full light on these difficulties. He resets this problem in its social, and even religious, setting, with that keen sense of the concrete which is found in almost all American writers, and which it would be desirable to find in all philosophers: does the prudent and active man who enters upon any kind of industry, business, or production, of either material or social nature, reasonably have the right to count on the probabilities indicated by experience? Is this confidence entirely alien to the realm of the intelligence, and would it be just as logical to replace it by faith in one's star, like Caesar and Napoleon, or by a theoretical fatalism, whether it be a fatalism of action or of inaction? Mr. Williams very aptly shows that this problem, which may be called Hume's problem, has not been solved either by the positivists, the pragmatists, the "contextualists," or the mathematical logicians. The solution which he gives, by considering a sample taken from a carload of apples, seems satisfactory for the case he considers, namely the equivalence of the "probability ratio" for the whole and the part, if the sample is correctly taken. But another difficulty arises the moment we pass from the "probability ratio" to the "probability as rule of conduct."

Take a case which is rare, so far as we are concerned, one for which the law of great numbers does not apply for us, or even which is unlikely to arise more than once: a marriage, a choice of profession or location, an industrial speculation on an exceptional situation. Why does it remain *more reasonable* in this case, as common sense grants, to "take the least chances," in other words to act according to the greatest "probability

---

8. Cf. R. Ruyer, *Le monde des valeurs* (1948), and Eugène Dupréel, *Esquisse d'une philosophie des valeurs* (1939).

ratio," rather than acting at random, or trusting a contrary intuition,[9] if we think we have one?

The question can only be solved by going back to the true definition of reason: as may be proved by an analysis of its essential categories,[10] it is not—not even in the physical domain—the statement of a structure constitutive of the world, after the fashion of the "metaphysical principles of a science of nature," but a rule of intellectual conduct and of behavior. What the European tradition calls the problem of the basis of induction mixes two questions which should be kept apart if we wish to find the answers to them, by distinguishing what we have called the foundations and the principles: (1) How do we come to have confidence in experimental induction? If this confidence becomes weaker in ourselves or in others; if we are tempted to act impulsively, without taking into account observed connections, how shall we reinforce it? (2) As philosophers, or as logicians, what is the simplest abstract and general axiom that we can postulate for the "syllogism of action" to furnish a satisfactory conclusion, in the same way that we are satisfied by the proof that the series of prime numbers is unlimited, or that the Euclidean definition of parallels makes the theorem of the three angles of a triangle necessary?

To the first, one should undoubtedly reply with Mr. Williams that to the extent that one discards such a confidence one discards not only intelligent action but life itself. "One has to do it, or die," said Rabelais of the commandment of Messer Gaster, which is a particular case. But the second question is not resolved therewith; and yet this principle is indispensable as something to go by in doubtful cases, as rational conduct requires; Mr. Williams shows well that no descriptive formula gives the solution. But the situation is not the same for a normative solution. Let us take as an axiom: "In the absence of any indication to the contrary, we *should* judge that things will continue to go on as they have gone on up to now, and we *should* act in conformity with that judgment." Immediately, every valid particular judgment will appear as a logical consequence of this statement, provided that the reservation with which the statement begins is taken into account.[11] And this will lead to an understanding of

---

9. Excepting of course the case in which that intuition might have a legitimate basis in our unconscious: Mlles. Renauld and Maire, in their *Psychologie par les textes,* have cited a striking instance. A young man, having made a written comparison of the advantages of the commercial and military careers, and decided in favor of the first, embarked on it. But after a few months, he suddenly abandoned it, enlisted in the army, went through the most trying campaigns, several times had to go home sick and completely exhausted; but none the less, as soon as he recovered, he resumed the same career, and never repented his choice.

10. Cf. *La raison et les normes,* chaps. ii to iv.

11. And which has often been overlooked by critics of the statement made in *Théories de l'induction et de l'expérimentation.* (Published version of a course given at the Sorbonne in 1922).

that paradoxical characteristic of conduct based on experience: that its success is never *guaranteed;* that even in the event of an extremely high probability, one of the unfavorable cases may turn up; and that none the less, even in that event, *it was right and reasonable* to act thus, since it was in conformity with the imperative of reason. In a word, we preserve at once the rational character and the merely probable character of induction by posing its principle as a "rule of law" and making noninduction an *exception,* justified by certain preceding inductions.

IV

Many of the papers which make up the present collection do not call for any discussion: a Frenchman reading them has only to learn what he did not know or knew incompletely. Such is the case, for example, with the article of Mr. F. B. Fitch which we have already mentioned; with that of Mr. Victor Lenzen on the "Philosophy of Science in America," an excellently organized and classified bibliography of the work in this vast field of study. That of Professor Cornelius Benjamin, "Philosophy in America between Two Wars," very lucid and vigorously thought out, is also very symptomatic in our eyes, because of the procedures used to explore his subject: the choices of questions treated in the Carus Lectures; the contents of collective works, including the curious inquiry into *The Philosophy of American Education,* carried out in a way which is singularly reminiscent of the polls of political opinions; a review of the principal philosophical parties; types of outstanding personalities. It is a survey, or more exactly a group of surveys, taken from different angles, opening very suggestive perspectives on the ways and means by which American philosophers tend to take a reflective view of the whole of their activity, more completely and consciously than has been done in any other epoch.

Professor Daniel S. Robinson's study on "Philosophy of Religion in the United States in the Twentieth Century" enables us to see clearly (although showing that was not his purpose) how different the intellectual climate in such a subject is on opposite sides of the Atlantic; this is what brings it about that the doctrines he speaks of are so much less known in France than are American speculations on the nature of knowledge, morality, or logic. The solidly documented historical study of Professor Vernon J. Bourke on "Material Possessions and Thomistic Ethics" has an interest of the same sort, for it brings out the importance which the disciples of St. Thomas in America attach to contrasting their master's doctrine on property, bold as it may be in its principles, to that of communism, to which certain critics seem to have likened it, with a rather hostile intention.

Equally instructive for the French reader, and equally characteristic of the American genius, but in another direction, is the article of Professor Marvin Farber on "Descriptive Philosophy and the Nature of Human Existence." Professor Farber, who is editor of the journal *Philosophy and Phenomenological Research* and president of the International Phenomenological Society, still maintains the most complete freedom of thought with respect to Husserl's doctrines. After discharging the promise he had made to his old teacher, by giving a penetrating description of his ideas in *The Foundation of Phenomenology* (a description already coupled in that work with important reservations), he here sifts what seems to him solid and essential from what appears to him chimerical in that doctrine, which for that matter had been much modified from the *Logische Untersuchungen* to the *Méditations cartésiennes.* His study shows vividly how the most sober and fruitful ideas of phenomenology could find in America a terrain well prepared by the penetrating analyses of C. S. Peirce, with whom we should not have dreamed of connecting him. Professor Farber shows, too, the way in which the philosophy of William James can harmonize with that of the celebrated Freiburg philosopher. It would be misunderstanding the American spirit—and in my opinion the philosophical spirit— to see in these rapprochements a kind of syncretism, a systematic sacrifice of what is original in the doctrines. Eclecticism should not frighten us, when the word is taken in the sense in which it applies to Leibniz, or even to the *first* philosophy of Victor Cousin, whose force and elevation have been well shown by V. Egger. A choice must be made between the taste of those who appreciate individual differences above all and the position of those who put the agreement of intelligences in the front rank values. In France, the introduction of phenomenology was first of all an amazing burgeoning of divergent and occasionally enigmatic interpretations, until Mr. Gaston Berger, in his splendid Husserl studies, opened an accessible and safe road to the knowledge of that philosophy. In *The Foundation of Phenomenology* it was noted that it would not do to take the description of thought as the sole method, and consider as nonexistent any philosophical assertion which did not stem from it. He goes further and now sets forth its essentials, seeking to free them from all the idealist prejudices and transcendental ambitions that the German tradition had mixed in with it, even in Husserl himself; and Mr. Farber does not hesitate to say that these admixtures led Husserl to "an extravagant speculative philosophy." The vision of essences, and of their relations, the

"placing in parentheses" of whatever has not yet been methodically analyzed, the *epoché* of judgments—are the very directives of scientific
method; but it should be realized that the problems they raise are not suspended in a vacuum: they imply first, as La Bruyère said, "that there are
men and they think"; still more, they should not impair our certitude that
there was an epoch, and no doubt one of infinite duration, during which,
although man did not yet exist, there were things and no knowledge of
those things.

Probably a majority of French philosophers would strongly challenge
this attitude, and object that this certitude itself is nothing but a fact of
actual thought, more real than its object. Many of them, I think, would
even refuse to admit that knowledge can exist without a mental function
superior to that very knowledge: the most widespread philosophical ideal
seems still to be a dialectics of the nature of Hegel's, or of Hamelin's, even
if it is modestly admitted, with the latter, that both are but miserably imperfect attempts. But I have too often had occasion to challenge this position not to sympathize with the conviction that the intermental procedures
of science, the only ones which have shown themselves capable of producing a spontaneous and durable agreement among those competent to judge,
are incumbent upon anyone who seeks only the truth. That does not
mean that I wish to accord the genetic and historical attitude the philosophical primacy over the reflective method and the light which each consciousness bears within it. An American reader may recall the enlightening schema by which J. M. Baldwin, in *Thought and Things,* represented
the reciprocal reflection of collective thought on individual thought and of
individual thought on collective thought, a schema in which the super-
position of the two inverse trajectories corresponded to true thought. I
shall try to show, in the conclusion of the present study, how the critique
of the object and method of science opens a window on the nature of the
existences and values it presupposes.

V

One might wonder whether to place Professor C. A. Baylis's article,
"The Given and Perceptual Knowledge," among the documentary studies
or among those which maintain a thesis. On the one hand, he lets us
know very clearly the different answers proposed to the question: "What
is sensibly given, and what does it contain?" and one sees after reading
his article, how fruitfully philosophical work in the United States has been
applied to this problem, which is at the center of the great battle between

the idealist generation (in the gnosiological sense of the word) and the realist generation of American philosophers. On the other hand, he himself does not let any of these theories go without taking note of its weak points; but the partial conclusions at which he stops seem to be rather touchstones than a building whose plan can already be seen.

Although his conclusion expresses certain very decided preferences, the major part of Mr. Thomas Munro's article on "Present Tendencies of American Esthetics" is also in the objective domain. In an extensive paper, the eminent editor of the *Journal of Aesthetics* gives a very rich picture of happenings in this domain. He remarks very justly that a history of esthetics can only be written properly from the international point of view, and should take into account primitive and exotic forms of art; he vigorously stresses the advantages which art derives from democratic liberty; he calls attention to the danger of little researches into details, which replace the true ends of science by what should be only its means; he shows how science is a product which springs from several distinct sources, the point of convergence of multiple currents of thought, which make themselves barren if they do not renew themselves in uniting: I imagine that on these points all French estheticians would agree with him. But there is another aspect. The picture of the present trends of esthetics in the United States is very interesting, and undoubtedly quite exact from the factual point of view, given the high competence of its author. But if some of these trends are obviously commendable, others perhaps are debatable. It is not enough that an intellectual movement exist, nor even that it manifest a great vitality, for it *ipso facto* to merit the support of the philosopher: in the eighteenth century, the cult of nature and faith in the moral superiority of savages made those who adopted the vogue successful; but those who opposed it were right.

A keen interest in the natural and social character of art is certainly good; but should one be glad, as the author of the article is, to see a consequent weakening of the concepts of good taste and bad, of sublimity and mediocrity, of beauty and ugliness (or more exactly, negative esthetic value: for the ugly can have its beauty)? It is a great danger for esthetics —a danger which logic has not escaped—to take the factual part of science for the science itself, and to overshadow or even forget the axiological character, which however alone determines which facts belong in its domain. The esthetic judgment does not rest only on biological, economic, or political circumstances. It is a fact *sui generis,* and it is possible to show in detail by the most positive observation its surprising and suggestive parallelism with the opposition of the true and the false, the good and the evil.

It is quite possible to agree that esthetics should appeal "neither to super-naturalism, nor to transcendentalism, nor to mysticism, nor to (gnosiolog-ical) idealism, nor to metaphysical dualism" (if by this is meant the Car-tesian opposition of body and soul, or the Kantian separation of the phe-nomenon and the noumenon): but it does not follow that works of art, as Herbert Spencer maintained, and as Mr. Munro too seems to hold, should be considered "as natural phenomena, continuous with those studied by the physical and biological sciences and growing out of them by evolu-tion"—unless one grants that evolution is the power of engendering abso-lute novelties at certain moments, and passing to a plane as different from the biological as a four-dimensional volume differs from a Euclidean cube.

It is precisely with the problem of this unity or this duality that Pro-fessor H. G. Townsend's article, "Idealism in America," is concerned. Reading this title, a European philosopher would have expected to see an exposition and discussion of the thesis according to which every reality is a thought, or a product of thought. But this thesis seems to have been abandoned to such a degree in the United States that the word has taken on quite a different connotation. What is involved, under the name of idealism, is essentially a philosophy in which values are not considered as accidental or provisional opinions, comparable to the fashions of dress-makers, tailors, and little literary cliques, but as truths capable of a per-manence and objectivity analogous to those of the great laws of nature. An idealism thus understood does not exclude the reality of the world nor its independence with respect to the mind: for it is necessary there be somehow a matter to which our value-judgments apply, and our action, whether reforming or conservative. Nor is it opposed to science, the necessary instrument of any fruitful undertaking and the limit of what is possible for our will. It is better suited than any other to democracy, in the sense in which it is the recognition of the rights of the human person: for that person is precisely the main point at which the truth of values enters into the reality of existences. It is therefore not at all opposed to realism, but only to those doctrines which subordinate the right to the fact, and which consider man in nature "as the fatal point at which the law is fulfilled." [12]

This is the point on which opinions diverge most notably. I read with great interest and sympathy Professor Roy Wood Sellars's fine article, "Critical Realism and Modern Materialism." My eminent colleague may permit me here to add a postscript to the conversation we had 25 years ago,

---

12. "Comme le point fatal où s'accomplit la loi," a phrase of the poet Edmond Harau-court, in a remarkable little philosophical poem called *Chanson à boire*.

when he was kind enough to come to explain to the *Société française de philosophie* the principles of "critical realism." At that time we spoke principally of the way to conceive of the reality which unfolds by succes-' sive emergences, causing new properties to appear. It is in connection with what he calls "materialism" that I should like now to present a few thoughts. They can apply as well to several other American doctrines presented or supported in the present volume.

The great power of materialism, in every period, has been the satisfaction it offers the mind in quest of explanation: if psychological phenomena could be reduced to the functioning of the nervous system, and if that functioning itself could be *understood,* by a sufficiently developed science, as a physico-chemical ensemble which is very complex, but which does not presuppose any special principle of a different nature from those which the physicist admits—such an intellectual achievement would be comparable to the assimilation of weight to gravitation, or of light to electrical waves. It is this hope, too, which constitutes the attraction of "unitary science," of universal physicalism. Any heterogeneity is an enigma; and every explanation consists in making it enter into a more general order of things, and hence in making it disappear as a datum *sui generis* imposed by experience.

Materialism, says Auguste Comte in a dictum often cited—at least in France—is the explanation of the superior (which he defines: the more complex and special) by the inferior (which he defines: the more general and simple). And such is actually the constant aspiration of reason; and it has often been able to satisfy it.

Matters stand similarly with evolution, as a philosophical doctrine. Its great attraction—which was also that of Hegel's *Logic,* from which in part it stems—was enabling us to understand the world without postulating more than an extremely circumscribed minimum of notions, perhaps even merely the notion of being, and by a necessary differentiation draw from it the prodigious variety of things which our experience shows us. Yes, but on condition that this genesis of the manifold appear logical to our reason: if it is a question of unpredictable emergences, of mutations by means of which a quantitative complexity suddenly gives rise to an absolute novelty which enriches the world, that is undoubtedly a magnificent spectacle:

"Welch' Schauspiel! aber ach! ein Schauspiel nur!"

There is no longer anything intelligible in this flowering; and if it is presented as a fact, it is a fact which we begin to be unsure of once we have discovered its uselessness for purpose of explanation.

Now, "modern materialism" solemnly gives up this advantage; it refuses to allow the reduction of the biological to the physico-chemical, or of "mentation" to physiological phenomena, well-known as such. It recognizes here something entirely new, which appears at a certain point of the preceding development, but which is not deduced from it, which could neither be constructed nor foreseen by a combination of the concepts and laws which served to represent the preceding level. This renunciation might be compared with Marx's criticism of utopian socialism: any attempt to form an idea of the society of the future, he says, should be considered illusory and reactionary, for it could only arise out of our ideological aspirations, themselves suggested by the state of things which is about to disappear. Materialism, in this sense, becomes an ally of irrationalism.

It would still be such an ally in the form under which the modern doctrines which claim this title advise us to use Life as a model — I should be inclined to say, with M. E. Seillière, the goddess Life. Rather than a "materialism," it is now a "biomorphism." Its morality starts from the fact that at each epoch there are in the world institutions and social groups which are in the full period of youth and growth, while others are in a state of decadence; and takes as its rule of action attaching itself to the first and accelerating the aging and the fall of the others. Is this the dominant belief among the American writers studied by Mr. Abraham Edel in the very firm, clear, and well-documented article which he too modestly entitles "Some Trends in American Naturalistic Ethics"? In almost all the authors he cites (and I should be very much tempted to say in himself), we see the combination, or rather the emulsion of two opposed conceptions. One is the tradition inherited from the New England immigrants, the feeling that there are in man, on the one hand an animal, egoistic, impulsive nature, tending toward vital expansion and domination; on the other hand, a nature which is reasonable, objective, reflective, capable of checking its present desire by the thought of a future advantage, and likewise of giving up its individual interest in the name of a rational view of things, of rising above the diversity of peoples and historical events as a spectator might look at and judge the characters of a play, in which he would see himself as one. The second is the philosophy made popular by those who claim Darwin as their chief; it has so deeply impregnated the European and American mentality that most educated men no longer realize the influence it has over them, and consider *élan vital,* expansion, conquest, the struggle for life, as defining values as certain as the existence of the sun and the moon, as impossible to change as the rotation of the earth and the movement of the tides. Thus for instance Mr. Edel shows Mr. R. B. Perry tying up his morality at once with historical materialism and Christianity; thus he himself reproaches Dewey with having attacked a straw man in the belief he was fighting Marxism, and sets perpetuation of life in the front rank of ends, but quite justly objects to Edward C. Tolman that his biologism "leaves up in the air the problem of the satisfaction of an individual or a group of individuals at the expense of another individual or another group," and concludes by strongly emphasizing the rational need, felt by all thinkers, for a universally valid ethic.

But will the principle thereof be found, as he thinks, in the general desire for peace, for increased production, for liberty for the still-oppressed masses? It is true that today most men sincerely dread wars among nations: but ardent instincts of domination and aggressiveness are unceasingly active in other struggles, collective or individual. Mr. John Dewey, as Mr. Sidney Hook recalls very well in the substantial note he devotes to that great mind, has had to struggle on two fronts: against the materialists (that is, in ethics, against those who subordinate reason to biological life), and against the Platonists, partisans of a world of Ideas which we discover by turning our backs on the world of experience. He has brought out well that values are given as facts are given,[13] in judgments of small extension which the disputants are agreed upon: that it is better to be foresighted than unthinking, friends than enemies, sincere than liars, helpful than egoistic, and a host of other elementary and spontaneous judgments, which do not grow dim except in case of bad faith, when people are interested in confusing these intuitive perceptions of value. It is possible to operate scientifically on uncontested evaluations of this kind, as we operate on the sensations which men recognize in common, and which it would be impossible to prove if they were questioned: the fall of a physical body, the appearance of a line in a spectroscope, the presence of a lesion in a cadaver under dissection. Therefore the science of morality, too, will have as its method the construction, on the basis of these normative judgments, of inductive generalizations which can then serve as guides for action.

Well! it will be said, here is a moral empiricism which is not very philosophical! On the contrary, this is what the high road of true rationalism is like; and in it can be found once more that *transverse dimension*

---

13. It should be added that facts cannot be given without certain values being given.

which I have already spoken of in connection with eternity. For in the inner nature of experience, the essential instrument of science, we find upon analysis a "will to reason," at once descriptive and normative.

For, what is the criterion to which this method appeals, in science as in morality? As C. S. Peirce has powerfully pointed out, it is the agreement, the similarity of thought which arises, in the light of the facts, between two or more minds who began with differing opinions. In the factual order, that is true which, once understood, wins one over, by virtue of its own content, without seduction or constraint. Matters do not stand otherwise in the order of appreciations. One may or may not find it; but it is this similarity which one sets himself as goal. But that is the assertion of a judgment of value, which is inherent in the very idea of science and truth: "The answer lies in the question." Anyone who raises it grants that contradiction is the mark of error and that hence, for thought, similitude is better than difference. The world of Ideas is only a myth, tables of categories, after Kant's fashion, express only a passing state of science, the "constituted reason" of a milieu and an epoch; but what does not depend on the time, the milieu, or the economic conditions, is the value of identity, its superiority of value over contrariety: it is implicit in mathematical reasoning, in experimental control; it is implicit as well in the respect for the human person (something quite different from individual caprices or whims), in the condemnation of war, tyranny, lying, the exploitation of men, classes, or peoples by each other — the condemnation of everything which prevents them from being truly "fellowmen."

This value of assimilation without constraint is the only one which is in accord with the ideas of liberty, democracy, equality; whereas the current prejudice, which takes as its type of progress biological life, with its "differentiations" and "integrations," would send us in the opposite direction, toward the totalitarian ideal: it would preach a deep-going, organic inequality between thoroughly and hereditarily specialized individuals, as muscle, nerve, or epithelial cells are differentiated in a living body. It is precisely the contrary — or rather, it should be the contrary — on the specifically human plane.

Reflecting on the cases in which it is satisfied and the cases in which it fails, reason thus can recognize the direction which constitutes it, and without which no opinion would be worth more than another, no experience would be demonstrative, no conduct would be preferable to its opposite. This superior value of identity in comparison to the differences which furnish the material of its work can be verified by studying the history of science, or the line of great moral doctrines.[14] But it would not be verified by economic or political history, which has been so justly called *history as battle*. For man is not all reason, far from it; and even in good citizens this common light of reason flickers and is in danger of going out as soon as the rough voice of the vital instinct of domination, enjoyment, and conquest breaks in. The individual or the group that desires to make itself the center of the world can no longer be the fellow of anybody. It is not impossible that evil should get the upper hand over good, war over peace, the infinite variety of imaginations and interests over the unity of science. Civilization, as Dr. Mochi says, is "a critically sick man." We have no right to rest in a smiling faith in the inevitability of progress; we have only the right to hope that the sick man will get well — and we will have the more reason to believe it, the more we ourselves work toward that end, by grasping as clearly as possible the nature of the fundamental judgment which in societies as in individuals contrasts the good will and the bad.

---

14. In several works, particularly in *La dissolution,* chap. iv, and *Les illusions évolutionnistes,* chaps. v to vii, I have tried to show that the complete program of science is "mutual assimilation of minds, mutual assimilation of things, assimilation between mind and things." All three are particular cases of the general value of identity and its superiority of value over diversities. Here we had occasion to take up only the first; but the second received powerful confirmation in the works of Émile Meyerson; and as to the third, we need only think of the place of mathematics in contemporary science.

SUPPLEMENTARY BIBLIOGRAPHY
1949-1967
*Gilbert Varet**

The Bibliography quotes the main works published in the philosophical
field during the given period by the most distinguished French scholars.
The list of authors is alphabetical. The list of publications is chronological.
The dagger † indicates a deceased author. The name of place under parentheses — e.g. (Paris-Nanterre) — indicates the University in which the
author teaches. The sign (Th.) at the end of the reference signifies that
the work (or even the two works) quoted before is a "Doctorate Thesis"
(Doctorat ès-lettres d'Etat), — practically all Theses of the University of
Paris at the Sorbonne. The "series" are indicated by quotation marks
" . . . "; this is only indicated if significant. The initials under quotation
marks signify:

"B.Ph.C." = "Bibliothèque de Philosophie contemporaine"
"B.Ph.Sc." = "Bibliothèque de Philosophie scientifique"
"N.B.Sc." = "Nouvelle Bibliothèque scientifique"
"N.R.F." = "Nouvelle Revue Francaise"

English translations are given within the range of possibility.

Some authors whose names figure in this Bibliography are not French
according to their "nationality," but their works could not be separated
from the French contemporary literature.

Adam, Michel. *Le sentiment du péché.* Centurion, 1967, 366p. (Th.).
† Alain (1868-1951). *Philosophie,* Textes choisis. P.U.F., 2 vols., 1954-55.
————. *Définitions. Ibid.,* 1955, 250p.
————. *Lettres sur la philosophie première. Ibid.,* 1955, 124p.

---

* Born in 1914. Etudes supérieures en Sorbonne; agrégé de Philosophie (1943); docteur ès
lettres (1956). Professeur aux lycées de Valence, Chambéry, Lyon (1940-47); attaché de recherches au C.N.R.S. (1947-50). Collaborateur de Lavelle, Nabert, Gaston Berger. Assistant, then professor, chef du Département de Philosophie et Psychologie à la Faculté des Lettres et Sciences
humaines de l'Université Besancon (since 1950). International editor of the "Bibliography of
Philosophy" (Paris) under the auspices of Unesco (since 1954). Visiting Professor, State University of New York at Buffalo (1968-69).

—————————. *Propos*, éd. Maurice Savin. Gallimard, 1956, 1.370p., "La Pléiade."

—————————. *Propos sur la religion*. P.U.F., 1957, 288p.

—————————. *Les Arts et les Dieux* (Histoire de mes pensées, Système des Beaux-Arts, Vingt leçons sur les Beaux-Arts, Entretiens chez le sculpteur, La Visite au musicien, Lettre au Dr. Mondor, Stendhal, En lisant Dickens, Avec Balzac, Définitions, Préliminaires à la mythologie, Les Dieux), éd. Georges Bénézé. Gallimard, 1958, 1.488p., "La Pléiade."

—————————. *Portraits de famille*. Mercure de France, 1961, 205p.

—————————. *Propos sur l'esthétique*. P.U.F., 1962, 120p.

—————————. *Esquisses*. Tome I: *Pédagogie enfantine. Ibid.*, 1963, 128p.

—————————. *La théorie de la connaissance chez les stoïciens. Ibid.*, 1963, 76p. Cf.: *Hommage à Alain*. Gallimard, 1952, 371p., "N.R.F.".

Aletheia, No. 4: *Le structuralisme*, Claude Lévi-Strauss, Roland Barthes, Maurice Godelier, Kostas Axelos. 1966, 93p.

Alquié, Ferdinand (Sorbonne). *La nostalgie de l'être*. P.U.F., 1950, 160p.; — *La découverte métaphysique de l'homme chez Descartes. Ibid.*, 1950, 384p. (Th.).

—————————. *Philosophie du surréalisme*. Flammarion, 1956, 238p., "B.Ph.Sc." Engl.: *The Philosophy of Surrealism,* trl. Bernard Waldrop. Ann Arbor, Univ. of Michigan Press, 1965, 196p.

—————————. *L'expérience*. P.U.F., 1957, 103p. (3e éd., 1966).

—————————. *Solitude de la raison*. Losfeld, 1966, 196p., "Le terrain vague."

Althusser, Louis (Ecole Normale Supérieure), éd. trad.: Feuerbach, *Manifestes philosophiques*, textes choisis (1839-45). P.U.F., 1960, 238p. "Epiméthée."

—————————. *Pour Marx*. Maspero, 1965, 258p., "Théorie, I."

—————————, éd.: *Lire Le Capital. Ibid.*, 1966, 2 vols., "Théorie II-III."

Amado-Lévy-Valensi, Eliane (Sorbonne). *La dialogue psychanalytique*. P.U.F., 1962, 222p.; — *Les niveaux de l'être, la connaissance et le mal. Ibid.*, 1962, 674p. (Th.).

————————— et Jean Halperin, edd. *La conscience juive, I. Données et débats;* II. *Face à l'histoire*. P.U.F., 2 vols., 1963-65.

—————————*Le temps dans la vie psychologique*. Flammarion, 1964, 197p. "Nelle. B.sc."

—————————. *La communication*. P.U.F., 1967, 155p., "B.Ph.C.".

Arbousse-Bastide, Paul (Sorbonne). *La doctrine de l'éducation universelle dans la philosophie d'Auguste Comte*. P.U.F., 1956, 2 vols., 735p. (Th.).

Aron, Raymond (Sorbonne). *La sociologie allemande*, 1935. Engl.: *German Sociology*, trl. Mary and Thomas Bottomore. N.Y., Free Press, 1964, 141p.

—————. *La philosophie de l'histoire*, 1935 (3.éd., Vrin, 1964). Engl.: *Introduction to the Philosophy of History, An Essay on the Limits of Historical Objectivity*. Boston, Beacon Press, 1961, 351p.

—————. *L'opium des intellectuels*. Calman-Lévy, 1955, 334p. Engl.: *The Opium of the Intellectuals*, trl. Terence Kilmartin. N.Y., Doubleday, 1957, 340p.

—————. *Espoir et Peur du siècle*. Calman-Lévy, 1957, 367p. "Liberté de l'Esprit."

————— et Arnold Toynbee. *L'histoire et ses interprétations*. La Haye, Mouton, 1961, 237p.

—————. *Dimensions de la conscience historique*. Plon, 1961, 337p., "Recherches en sciences humaines"; — Le livre de poche, 1965, 384p.

—————. *Dix-huit leçons sur la société industrielle. La lutte des classes, nouvelles leçons sur les sociétés industrielles*. Gallimard, 1962-64, 2 vols., 384p. & 384p., "Idées, 19-47."

—————. *Paix et Guerre entre les nations*. Calman-Lévy, 1962, 794p.

—————. *Démocratie et totalitarisme*. Gallimard, 1965, 384p., "Idées."

—————. *Main Currents in Sociological Thought*, trl. R. Howard & H. Weaver. London, Weidenfeld & Nicholson, 1965, 272p.

—————. *Trois Essais sur l'âge industriel*. Plon, 1966, 239p., "Preuves."

—————. *Les étapes de la pensée sociologique*. Gallimard, 1967, 659p.

Arnaldez, Roger (Lyon, Univ.). *Grammaire et Théologie chez ibn-Hazm de Cordoue*, Essai sur les structures et conditions de la pensée musulmane. Vrin, 1955, 336p. (Th.).

—————. Jean Pouilloux, Claud Mondésert, S.J., edd. *Les oeuvres de Philon d'Alexandrie*. Edition du Cerf, 1961—

Arvon, Henri. *Aux sources de l'existentialisme: Max Stirner*. P.U.F., 1954, 188p., "Epiméthée."

—————. *Le marxisme*. A. Colin, 1955, 216p.

—————. *Ludwig Feuerbach ou la transformation du sacré*. P.U.F., 1957, 191p., "Epiméthée."

—————. *La philosophie du travail*. P.U.F., 1961, 112p.

—————. *Feuerbach. Ibid.,* 1964, 114p., "Philosophes."

—————. *Bakounine.* Seghers, 1966, 192p., "Philosophes de tous les temps."

Aubenque, Pierre (Aix-en-Provence, Univ.). *La prudence chez Aristote.* P.U.F., 1963, 192p.

—————. *Le problème de l'être chez Aristote. Ibid.,* 1962, 556p. (Th.).

Audry, Colette. *Léon Blum, ou La Politique du juste.* Julliard, 1955, 200p., "Temps modernes."

—————. *Sartre.* Seghers, 1966, 190p., "Philosophes de tous les temps."

Auger, Pierre (Sorbonne, Sciences). *L'homme microscopique, Essai de monadologie.* Flammarion, 1952, 236p.

Axelos, Kostas. *Héraclite et la philosophie.* Minuit, 1962, 280p., "Arguments"; *Marx, penseur de la technique. Ibid.,* 1961, 328p. (Th.).

—————. *Vers la pensée planétaire.* Ibid., 1963, 336p., "Arguments."

† Bachelard, Gaston (Sorbonne). *L'intuition de l'instant,* 1932. Nouvelle édition par Jean Lescure. Gonthier, 1966, 152p., "Médiations."

—————. *L'eau et les rèves; L'air et les songes; La terre et les rèveries du repos; La terre et les rèveries du mouvement.* José Corti, 1942-48, 4 vols.

—————. *Le rationalisme appliqué.* P.U.F., 1949; 3.éd. 1966, 220p., "B.Ph.C.".

—————. *L'activité rationaliste de la physique contemporaine. Ibid.,* 1951; 2.éd., 1965, 228p., "B.Ph.C.".

—————. *Le matérialisme rationnel. Ibid.,* 1953, 228p., "B.Ph.C."

—————. *La poétique de l'espace. Ibid.,* 1957, 215p., "B.Ph.C." Engl.: *The Poetics of Space,* trl. Maria Jolas. N.Y., Orion, 1964, 241p.

—————. *La poétique de la rêverie.* P.U.F., 1960, 188p., "B.Ph.C."

—————. *La flamme d'une chandelle. Ibid.,* 1961, 116p., "B.Ph.C." Cf.: *Hommage à Gaston Bachelard. Ibid.,* 1957, 216p.

Bachelard, Suzanne (Sorbonne). *La Logique de Husserl, Etude de Logique formelle et transcendentale.* P.U.F., 1957, 316p., "Epiméthée"; *La conscience de rationalité,* Essai phénoménologique sur la physique mathématique. *Ibid.,* 1958, 217p. "B.Ph.C." (Th.).

Bagot, Jean-Pierre. *Connaissance et Amour, Essai sur la philosophie de Gabriel Marcel.* Beauchesne, 1958, 248p. (Th.).

Barthélémy-Madaule, Madeleine (Sorbonne). *Bergson adversaire de Kant.* P.U.F., 1966, 248p., "B.Ph.C." (Th.).

————. *La personne et le drame humain chez Teilhard de Chardin.* Seuil, 1967, 336p.

Barthes, Roland. *Le dégré zéro de l'écriture* (1953), suivi de: *Eléments de séméiologie.* Gonthier, 1965, 192p., "Médiations, 40."

————. *Essais critiques.* Seuil, 1964, 276p., "Tel quel."

————. *Système de la mode.* Gallimard, 1967, "Bibliothèque des sciences humaines."

Bastide, Georges (Toulouse, Univ.). *La conversion spirituelle.* P.U.F., 1955, 104p.

————. *Méditations pour une éthique de la personne.* P.U.F., 1953, 200p., "B.Ph.C.".

————. *Mirages et certitudes de la civilisation. Ibid.,* 1954, 340p. "Nouvelle recherche."

————. *Traité de l'action morale. Ibid.,* 1962, 2 vols., 444 et 424p., "Logos."

† Bataille, Georges (Bibliothèque Nationale.) *Sur Nietzsche, Volonté de chance.* Gallimard, 1945, 285p.

————. *La part maudite, Essai d'économie générale: I. La consumàtion.* Minuit, 1949, 269p., "Critique."

————. *L'érotisme. Ibid.,* 1952, 312p.

————. *Somme athéologique:* I. *L'expérience intérieure* (1943), éd.

————. *Somme athéologique:* I. *L'experieure intérieure* (1943), éd. revue, Gallimard, 1953, 258p.; — II. *Le coupable* (1944), éd. revue, *ibid.,* 1961, 239p.

————. *La littérature et le mal. Ibid.,* 1957, 231p. (Réédition: 1967, 384p., "idées")

————. *L'impossible, histoire de rates* (1947), suivi de *Dianus* et de *Orestie* (1945). Minuit, 1962, 192p.

————. *Le procès de Gilles Rais.* Club Français du Livre, 1959, Pauvert, 1965, 359p.

† Bayer, Raymond (Sorbonne). *Epistémologie et logique depuis Kant.* P.U.F., 1954, 369p.

————. *Traité d'esthétique.* Armand Colin, 1956, 302p.

————. *L'esthétique mondiale au XIXe siècle.* P.U.F., 1961, 238p.

————. *Histoire de l'esthétique.* Armand Colin, 1961, 403p.

Beauvoir, Simone de. *Pour une morale de l'ambiguité* (1947). Engl.: *The Ethics of Ambiguity,* trl. Bernard Frechtman. N.Y., Philosophical Library, 1948.

————. *Le deuxième sexe* (1949-50). Engl.: *The Second Sex,* trl. H. M. Parsley. N.Y., Knopf, 1953; "A Bantam Book," 1961, 705p.

——————. *Mémoires d'une jeune fille rangée,* Gallimard, 1958. Engl.: *Memoirs of a Dutiful Daughter,* trl. James Kirkup, London, Weidenfeld and Nicolson; N.Y., World Publishing Co., 1959.

——————. *La force de l'âge, ibid.,* 1960. Engl.: *The Prime of Life,* trl. Peter Green, *ibid.,* 1962.

——————. *La force des choses, ibid.,* 1964. Engl.: *The Force of Circumstances,* trl. Richard Howard, N. Y., Putnam, 1965.

Belaval, Yvon (Sorbonne). *La recherche de la poèsie.* Gallimard, 1947, 186p., "Les Essais."

——————. *L'esthétique sans paradoxe de Diderot; La morale de Diderot. Ibid.,* 1950, 2 vols., 307 & 310pp. (Th.).

——————. *La pensée de Leibniz.* Bordas, 1952, 288p., "Pour connaître . . . "

——————. *Les philosophes et leur langage.* Gallimard, 1952, 244p., "Les Essais."

——————. *Les conduites d'échec.* Gallimard, 1953, "Les Essais."

——————. *Leibniz critique de Descartes. Ibid.,* 1960, 560p., "Bibliothèque des Idées."

——————. *Remarques. Ibid.,* 1961, 139p.

——————. *Poèmes d'aujourd'hui, essais critiques. Ibid.,* 1964, 222p.

Benvéniste, Emile (Collège de France). *Problèmes de linguistique générale.* Gallimard, 1966, 356p., "Bibliothèque des Sciences humaines."

† Berger, Gaston (1896-1960), éd.: *Philosophie, Religion.* Larousse, 1957, 424p., 'L'Encyclopédie Francaise, Tome XIX."

——————. *L'homme moderne et son éducation,* Introd. par Edouard-Morot-Sir, Bibliographie de Gaston Berger par Gilbert Varet. P.U.F., 1962, 368p.; 2.éd. 1967, 383p.

——————. *Phénoménologie du temps et Prospective. Ibid.,* 1964, 278p.

† Bergson, Henri. *Oeuvres,* édition du Centenaire, par Henri Gouhier et André Robinet. P.U.F., 1959, 1,602p.

——————. *Ecrits et Paroles,* éd. Rose-Marie Mossé-Bastide. *Ibid.,* 1957-58, 3 vols.

Blanché, Robert (Toulouse, Univ.). *L'axiomatique.* P.U.F., 1956, 194p. Engl.: Axiomatics.

——————. *Structures intellectuelles,* Essai sur l'organisation systématique des concepts. Vrin, 1966, 190p., "A la recherche de la vérité."

† Blondel, Maurice (1861-1949). *Exigences philosophiques du christianisme.*
          P.U.F., 1949-50, 308p., "B.Ph.C.".
——————. *Les premiers écrits de Maurice Blondel: L'Action* (1893).
          Ibid., 1950, 521p.
——————. *Lettre sur l'apologétique* (1896). *Ibid.* The Letters on Apolo-
          getics, and History and Dogma, trl. Alexander Dru and
          Illtyd Trethowan. N.Y., Holt, Rinehart & Winston, 1965,
          301p.
——————. *Lettres philosophiques.* Aubier, 1961, 307p.
—————— et Lucien Laberthonière. *Correspondance philosophique.*
          Seuil, 1962, 387p.
——————. *Correspondance* aves le Père Auguste Valensin, éd. H. de
          Lubac. Aubier, 1965, 3 vols.
——————. *Carnets intimes.* Editions du Cerf, T. II, 1966, 404p.
——————. *Dialogues avec les philosophes,* Préface d'Henry Gouhier.
          Aubier, 1966, 294p.
Bouillard, Henri, S. J. (Faculté de Philosophie S.J., Les Fontaines). *Karl
          Barth.* Aubier, 1957, 3 vols., 284 + 288 + 308p., "Thé-
          ologie," (Th.).
——————. *Blondel et le christianisme.* Seuil, 1961, 287p.
Bouligand, Georges (Sorbonne, Sciences) et Jean Desbats. *La mathéma-
          tique et son unité.* Payot, 1947, 311p.
—————— et Jean Desgranges. *Le déclin des absolus mathématico-
          logiques.* S.D.E.S., 1949-50, 270p., "Esprit et méthodes."
——————. *L'accès au principe de la géométrie euclidienne: l'axioma-
          tique du plan.* Vuibert, 1951, 96p.
Bourricaud, Francois (Bordeaux, Univ.). *Esquisse d'une théorie de l'au-
          torité.* Plon, 1961, 422p., "Recherches en sciences hu-
          maines" (Th.).
† Brehier, Emile. *Histoire de la philosophie,* 1926-1948. Engl.: The Univ. of
          Chicago Press, 1965.
——————. *La Philosophie de Plotin,* 1922. Engl.: *Ibid.,* 1958, 212p.
——————. *Transformations de la pensée française.* Flammarion, 1950,
          254p., "B.Ph.Sc.".
——————. *Etudes de philosophie antique.* P.U.F., 1955, 256p., "Univ.
          de Paris."
——————. *Etudes de philosophie moderne. Ibid.,* 1965, 242p., "Univ. de
          Paris."
Breton, Stanislas (Institut Catholique, Paris). *Conscience et intentionnalité.*
          Vitte, 1956, 292p., "Problèmes et Doctrines."

—————. *Approches phénoménologiques de l'idée d'être, ibid.*, 1959, 254p.; — *L'être spirituel,* Recherches sur la philosophie de Nicolai Hartmann, *ibid.,* 1962, 203p. (Th.).

—————. *Essence et Existence.* P.U.F., 1962, 92p.

————— éd.: *Recherches de Philosophie,* Publication de l'Association des Professeurs de Philosophie des Facultés et Instituts Catholiques de France. Bruges-Paris, Desclée De Bruwer, 7 vols.: I. *Histoire de la philosophie et métaphysique;* II. *Aspects de la dialectique,* 1956, 380p.; III. *De la connaissance de Dieu,* 1958, 410p.; V. *La crise de la raison dans la pensée contemporaine;* VI. *S. Thomas aujourd'hui,* 1963; VII. *Idée du monde et philosophie de la nature,* 1966, 215p.

Brillouin, Léon (Collège de France). *La science et la théorie de l'information.* Masson, 1959, 302p. 1st ed.: *Science and Information Theory.* N.Y., Academic Press, 1956.

Broglie, Louis de (de l'Académie Française). *Certitudes et incertitudes de la science.* Albin Michel, 1966, 302p., "Sciences d'aujourd'hui."

Bruaire, Claude. *Logique et Religion chrétienne dans la philosophie de Hegel.* Seuil, 1964, 185p.; — *L'affirmation de Dieu.* Seuil, 1964, 283p. (Th.).

Brun, Jean (Dijon, Univ.). *Prendre et comprendre,* Essai sur les rapports de la main et de l'esprit, P.U.F., 1963, 176p.; — *Les conquêtes de l'homme et la séparation ontologique. Ibid.,* 1961, 300p. (Th.).

Brunet, Olivier. *Philosophie et Esthétique chez David Hume.* Nizet, 1960, 2 vols., 960p. (Th.).

† Brunschvicg, Léon (1869-1944). *Ecrits philosophiques,* textes réunis et annotés par Mme A.-R. Weil-Brunschvicg et Claude Lehec: I. *L'humanisme de l'Occident;* II. *L'orientation du rationalisme;* III. *Science, Religion.* P.U.F., 1951-1954-1958, 3 vols., 342 + 377 + 296p., "B.Ph.C.".

—————. Cf. Deschoux (1949).

† Buber, Martin. *La vie en dialogue* (Je et Tu; Dialogue; La question qui se pose à l'individu; Eléments de l'inter-humain; De la fonction éducatrice), trad. Jean Loewenson-Lavi. Aubier, 1959, 249p.

Burgelin, Pierre (Strasbourg, Univ.). *L'homme et le temps.* Aubier, 1945, 164p.

——————. *La philosophie de l'existence de J.-J. Rousseau.* P.U.F., 1952, 599p. (Th.).

——————. *Commentaire du Discours de Métaphysique de Leibniz. Ibid.*, 1954, 313p. (Th.).

——————. *J.-J. Rousseau et la religion de Genève.* Libraire protestante, 1962, 61p.

Cahiers de Royaumont, Série "Philosophie". Editions de minuit, 6 vols: 1. *Blaise Pascal,* 1956, 472p.; — 2. *Descartes,* 1957, 493p.; — 3. *Husserl,* 1959, 488p.; — 4. *La philosophie analytique,* 1962, 382p.; — 5. *Le concept d'information,* 1965, 423p.; — 6. *Nietzsche,* 1966, 288p.

Caillois, Roger (Unesco). *L'homme et le sacré.* Gallimard, 1949, 272p., "Les Essais."

——————. *Quatre essais de sociologie contemporaine.* Librairie Perrin, 1951.

——————. *Poétique de Saint John Perse.* Gallimard, 1954, 212p.

——————. *Esthétique généralisée.* Gallimard, 1962, 39p.

——————. *Instincts et sociétés.* Gonthier, 1964, 185p., "Médiations."

—————— ed.: *Le Robot, la Bête et l'Homme.* Neuchatel, La Baconnière, 1966, 360p.

——————. *Pierres.* Gallimard, 1966, 127p.

——————. *Les jeux et les hommes, Le masque et le vestige,* nouvelle édition. Gallimard, 1967, 373p., "Idées, 125."

Calvez, Jean-Yves, S.J. (Institut Catholique, Paris). *Droit international et Souveraineté en URSS.* Armand Colin, 1953, 299p.

——————. *La pensée de Karl Marx.* Seuil, 1956, 644p., "Esprit."

——————. *Eglise et Société économique.* Aubier, 1963, 122p., "Théologie, 55."

Camus, Albert (Prix Nobel). *Le mythe de Sisyphe* (1942). Engl.: *The Myth of Sisyphus,* and other Essays, trl. Justin O'Brien. N.Y., Knopf, 1955.

——————. *L'étranger* (1946). Engl.: *The Outsider.* Boston, Houghton-Mifflin, 1956.

——————. *Actuelles:* I. *Chroniques 1944-48;* II. *Chroniques 1948-53.* Gallimard, 1950-53, 2 vols., 276 & 288p.

——————. *L'homme révolté.* Gallimard, 1951, 383p. Engl.: *The Rebel,* trl. Anthony Bower. London, Hamish Hamilton, 1953.

——————. *L'été.* Gallimard, 1954, 192p., "Les Essais."

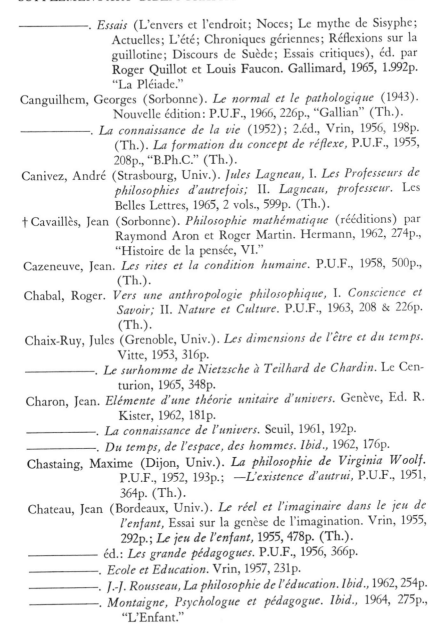

—————. *Essais* (L'envers et l'endroit; Noces; Le mythe de Sisyphe; Actuelles; L'été; Chroniques gériennes; Réflexions sur la guillotine; Discours de Suède; Essais critiques), éd. par Roger Quillot et Louis Faucon. Gallimard, 1965, 1.992p. "La Pléiade."

Canguilhem, Georges (Sorbonne). *Le normal et le pathologique* (1943). Nouvelle édition: P.U.F., 1966, 226p., "Gallian" (Th.).

—————. *La connaissance de la vie* (1952); 2.éd., Vrin, 1956, 198p. (Th.). *La formation du concept de réflexe*, P.U.F., 1955, 208p., "B.Ph.C." (Th.).

Canivez, André (Strasbourg, Univ.). *Jules Lagneau*, I. Les Professeurs de philosophies d'autrefois; II. *Lagneau, professeur.* Les Belles Lettres, 1965, 2 vols., 599p. (Th.).

† Cavaillès, Jean (Sorbonne). *Philosophie mathématique* (rééditions) par Raymond Aron et Roger Martin. Hermann, 1962, 274p., "Histoire de la pensée, VI."

Cazeneuve, Jean. *Les rites et la condition humaine.* P.U.F., 1958, 500p., (Th.).

Chabal, Roger. *Vers une anthropologie philosophique*, I. Conscience et Savoir; II. *Nature et Culture.* P.U.F., 1963, 208 & 226p. (Th.).

Chaix-Ruy, Jules (Grenoble, Univ.). *Les dimensions de l'être et du temps.* Vitte, 1953, 316p.

—————. *Le surhomme de Nietzsche à Teilhard de Chardin.* Le Centurion, 1965, 348p.

Charon, Jean. *Eléménte d'une théorie unitaire d'univers.* Genève, Ed. R. Kister, 1962, 181p.

—————. *La connaissance de l'univers.* Seuil, 1961, 192p.

—————. *Du temps, de l'espace, des hommes. Ibid.,* 1962, 176p.

Chastaing, Maxime (Dijon, Univ.). *La philosophie de Virginia Woolf.* P.U.F., 1952, 193p.; —*L'existence d'autrui*, P.U.F., 1951, 364p. (Th.).

Chateau, Jean (Bordeaux, Univ.). *Le réel et l'imaginaire dans le jeu de l'enfant*, Essai sur la genèse de l'imagination. Vrin, 1955, 292p.; *Le jeu de l'enfant*, 1955, 478p. (Th.).

————— éd.: *Les grande pédagogues.* P.U.F., 1956, 366p.

—————. *Ecole et Education.* Vrin, 1957, 231p.

—————. *J.-J. Rousseau, La philosophie de l'éducation. Ibid.,* 1962, 254p.

—————. *Montaigne, Psychologue et pédagogue. Ibid.,* 1964, 275p., "L'Enfant."

Chatelet, Francois. *Logos et Praxis,* Recherches sur la signification théorique du marxisme. Sedes, 1962, 205p. (Th.).

Chenu, Marie Dominque, O. P. (Le Saulchoir). *Introduction à l'étude de S. Thomas d'Aquin.* Vrin, 1955, 306p.

——————. *Pour une théologie du travail.* Seuil, 1955, 128p., "Esprit."

——————. *La théologie au douzième siècle.* Vrin, 1957, 413p.

——————. *La théologie comme science au XIIIe siècle. Ibid.,* 1957, 111p.

——————. *Saint Thomas et la théologie.* Seuil, 1959, 189p.

—————— éd.: *Bibliothèque thomiste.* Vrin, 36 volumes parus.

† Chevalier, Jacques. *Entretiens avec Bergson.* Plon, 1960, 315p.

——————. *Histoire de la Pensée.* Flammarion, 4 vols.: I. *La pensée antique,* 1955, 761p.; — II. *La pensée chrétienne,* 1956, 844p.; — III. *La pensée moderne,* 1961, 774p.; — IV. *La pensée moderne de Hegel à Bergson,* éd. par Léon Husson, 1966, 756p.

Congar, Y. M. J., O. P. (Le Saulchoir). *Vraie et fausse réforme dans l'Eglise.* Ed. du Cerf, 1950, 650p.

——————. *L'Eglise catholique devant la question raciale.* Unesco, 1953, 64p.

——————. *Esquisse du mystère de l'Eglise.* Ed. du Cerf, 1953, 182p., "Unam Sanctam."

——————. *Le mystère du Temps, ou L'économie de la présence de Dieu à la créature, de la Genèse à l'Apocalypse. Ibid.,* 1958, 342p., "Lectio divina."

——————. *La tradition et les traditions.* Fayard, 1960, 2 vols., 279 & 361p., "Le Signe."

Corbin, Henry (Institut Français, Teheran). *Avicenne et le récit visionnaire.* Adrien-Maisonneuve, 1954, 2 vols.

——————. *L'imagination créatrice dans le soufisme d'ibn-Arabi.* Flammarion, 1958, 285p., "Homo sapiens."

——————. *Histoire de la philosophie islamique.* Gallimard, 1963, 384p., "Idées."

Costa De Beauregard, Oliver. *Le second principe de la science du Temps.* Seuil, 1963, 152p.; — *La notion de temps, Equivalence avec l'espace.* Hermann, 1963, 207p.

Cuénot, Claude. *Pierre Teilhard de Chardin, Les grandes étapes de son évolution.* Club des éditeurs, 1958, 500p. Engl.: *Teilhard de Chardin, A Biographical Study.* Baltimore, Helicon Press, 1965, 492p.

Dagognet, Francois (Lyon, Univ.). *La raison et les remèdes.* P.U.F., 1963, 352p., "Galien"; — *Philosophie et méthodologie de la recherche pastorienne. Ibid.,* 1966, "Galien" (Th.).

Daniélou, Alain (International Institute for Comparative Music Studies, Berlin).

——————. *Traité de musicologie comparé.* Hermann, 1959, 202p.

——————. *Le Polythéisme hindou.* Buchet-Chastel-Corréa, 1960, 597p.

——————. *Les quatre sens de la vie.* Libraire Académique Perrin, 1964, 251p.

——————. *Sémantique musicale,* Essai de psychologie auditive. Herman, 1967, 118p.

Daniélou, Jean (Institut Catholique, Paris). *Sacramentum Futuri, Etudes sur les origines de la typologie.* Beauchesne, 1950, 282p.

——————. *Essai sur le mystère de l'histoire.* Seuil, 1953, 341p.

——————. *Sainteté et Action temporelle.* Desclée & Cie, 1953, "Le monde de la Foi."

——————. *Dieu et nous.* Grasset, 1956, 125p.

——————. *Les saints paiens de l'Ancien Testament.* Seuil, 1956, 175p.

——————. *Histoire des doctrines chrétiennes avant Nicée: la théologie du judéo-christianisme.* Desclée & Cie, 1958, 457p.

——————. *Philon d'Alexandrie.* Fayard, 1958, 230p.

——————. *Scandaleuse vérité. Ibid.,* 1961, 192p., "Les idées et la vie."

——————. *Dialogue avec Israël.* La Palatine, 1963, 162p.

—————— & H. I. Marrou: *Nouvelle Histoire de l'Eglise.* Seuil, 1963.

——————. *Mythes paiens, Mystère chrétien.* Fayard, 1966, 106p.

Davy, Georges, éd. Institut International de Philosophie Politique, *Annales,* P.U.F.: I.-II. *Le pouvoir,* 1957, 2 vols., 192 & 216p.; — III. *Le droit naturel,* 1959; — IV. *La philosophie politique de Kant,* 1962, 188p.; — V. *Rousseau et la philosophie politique,* 1965, 256p.; — VI. *L'idée de philosophie politique,* 1965, 196p.

Davy, Marie-Magdeleine. *Introduction au message de Simone Weil.* Plon, 1954, 288p., "L'Epi."

——————. *Un philosophe itinérant, Gabriel Marcel.* Flammarion, 1959, 352p., "Homo Sapiens."

Deleuze, Gilles (Lyon, Univ.). *Empirisme et subjectivité selon Hume.* P.U.F., 1953, 156p., "Epiméthée."

——————. *Nietzche et la philosophie.* P.U.F., 1962, 232p., "B.Ph.C.".

————. *La philosophie critique de Kant* (Doctrine des Facultés). P.U.F., 1963, 103p.

Delhomme, Jeanne (Poitiers, Univ.). *La pensée interrogative.* P.U.F., 1954, 216p., "Epiméthée"; — *Vie et Conscience de vie,* Essai sur Bergson. *Ibid.,* 1954, 196p., "B.Ph.C.".

————. *Temps et Destin,* Essai sur André Malraux. Gallimard, 1955, 272p., "Les Essais."

————. *La pensée et le réel.* P.U.F., 1966, "Epiméthée."

Derrida, Jacques (Ecole Normale Supérieure). *L'écriture et la différence.* Seuil, 1967, 439p., "Tel quel."

————. *De la Grammatologie.* Minuit, 1967, 447p., "Critique."

————. *Le Voix et le Phénomène,* Introduction au problème du signe dans la phénoménologie de Husserl. P.U.F., 1967, 119p., "Epiméthée."

Deschoux, Marcel (Besançon, Univ.). *La philosophie de Léon Brunschvicg.* P.U.F., 1949, 249p.; — *Essai sur la personnalité.* P.U.F., 1952, 395p. (Th.).

De Waelhens, Alphonse (Louvain, Univ.). *Une philosophie de l'ambiguité: l'existentialisme de Maurice Merleau-Ponty.* Nauwelaerts, 1951, 410p.

————. *Phénoménologie et Vérité. Ibid.,* 1953, 150p.; 2 éd., 1965.

————. *Existence et Signification. Ibid.,* 1958, 289p.

————. *La philosophie et les expériences naturelles.* La Haye, M. Nijhoff, 1961, 212p.

Dufrenne, Mikel (Paris-Nanterre). *Phénoménologie de l'expérience esthétique.* P.U.F., 1953, 2 vols., 416 & 276p., "Epiméthée."

————. *La notion d' a priori. Ibid.,* 1959. Engl.: *The Notion of A Priori,* trl. Edw. Casey, Evanston, Northwestern Univ. Press, 1966, 256p.

————. *Language and Philosophy,* trl. Nehry B. Veatch. Bloomington, Indiana Univ., 1963, 106p.

Duméry, Henry (Paris-Nanterre). *Blondel et la religion,* Essai critique sur la lettre de 1896. P.U.F., 1954, 118p.

————. *Critique et Religion,* Problèmes de méthode en philosophie de la religion. Sedes, 1957, 358p.; — *Philosophie de la Religion, Essai sur la signification du christianisme.* P.U.F., 1957, 2 vols., 317 & 299p., "B.Ph.C." (Th.).

————. *Le problème de Dieu en philosophie de la religion.* Desclée De Brouwer, 1957, 144p., "Textes et Etudes."

—————. *La Foi n'est pas un cri* (1957), suivi de *Foi et Institution,* nouvelle édition. Seuil, 1959, 398p.

—————. *Phénoménologie et Religion,* Structures de l'Institution chrétienne. P.U.F., 1958, 104p.

—————. *Raison et Religion* dans la philosophie de *L'Action*. Seuil, 1963, 640p.

Dupuy, Maurice (Bordeaux, Univ.). *La philosophie de la religion chez Max Scheler*. P.U.F., 1959, "Epiméthée; — *La philosophie de Max Scheler. Ibid.,* 1959, 2 vols., 756p., "Epiméthée" (Th.).

Durand, Gilbert (Grenoble, Univ.). *Les structures anthropologiques de l'imaginaire*. Grenoble, 1961, 514p. (Th.).

—————. *L'imagination symbolique*. P.U.F., 1964, 131p.

Ellul, Jacques (Bordeaux, Univ.). *Le fondement théologique du Droit*. Delachaux & Niestlé, 1946, 112p., "Cahiers théologiques de l'actualité protestante."

—————. *Présence au monde moderne,* Problèmes de civilization post-chrétienne. Genève, Roulet, 1948, 208p.

—————. *L'homme et l'argent*. Delachaux & Niestlé, 1954, 221p.

—————. *La technique ou l'enjeu du siècle*. Armand Colin, 1954, 402p.

—————. *Le vouloir et le faire*. Librairie protestante, 1964, 218p.

Ferrier, Jean-Louis. *L'homme dans le monde* (Th.Litt et J.-P. Sartre). Neuchatel, La Baconnière, 1957, 378p.

Fessard, Gaston, S. J. (Institut Catholique, Toulouse). *De l'actualité historique*. Desclée De Brouwer, 1960, 2 vols., 304 & 524p.

Festugière, André-Jean, O. P. (Institut de France). *La révélation d'Hermès Trismégiste*. Les Belles Lettres, 1944-49-54, 4 vols.

—————. *Epicure et ses Dieux*. P.U.F., 1946. Engl.: Oxford, Blackwell, 1956, 116p.

—————. *Personal Religion among the Greeks*. Berkeley, Univ. of California Press, 1954, 194p., "Sather Classical Lectures."

—————. *Les moines d'Orient*. Ed. du Cerf, 1956-1965, 7 vols.

—————. *Socrate*. Ed. du Fuseau, 1966, 160p.

Février, Paulette (Sorbonne, Sciences). *Déterminisme et indéterminisme*. P.U.F., 1955, 264p.

Finance, Joseph de, S.J. (Univ. Grégorienne, Rome). *Etre et Agir dans la philosophie de S. Thomas d'Aquin*. Beauchesne, 1945. 3.éd., Rome, Univ. Grégorienne, 1966, 381p. (Th.).

—————. *Existence et Liberté*. Beauchesne, 1955, 389p.

——————. *Essai sur l'agir humain*. Rome, Univ. Grégorienne, 1962, 444p.

——————. *Connaissance de l'être,* Traité d'ontologie. Desclée De Brouwer, 1966, 513p.

Foucault, Michel (Paris-Nanterre). *Maladie mentale et Psychologie*. P.U.F., 1954, 114p.; 3.éd., 1966.

——————. *Histoire de la Folie à l'âge classique*. Plon, 1961. Ed. abrégée: *ibid.*, 1964, 308p., "Le monde en 10/18" (Th.).

——————. *Naissance de la clinique*. Une archéologie du regard médical. P.U.F., 1963, 216p., "Galien" (Th.).

——————. *Raymond Roussel*. Gallimard, 1964, 210p., "Le Chemin."

——————. *Les mots et les choses*. Une archéologie des sciences humaines. Gallimard, 1966, 400p., "Bibliothèque des sciences humaines."

Fougeyrollas, Pierre (Dakar, Univ.). *La philosophie en question*. Denoël, 1960, 176p.

——————. *Contradiction et Totalité. Surgissements et déploiements de la dialectique*. Minuit, 1964, 251p., "Arguments, 22."

Fruchon, Pierre. *Création ou Consentement*. Aubier, 1963, 320p.

Garaudy, Roger (Clermont-Ferrand, Univ.). *Les sources françaises du socialisme scientifique*. Hier & Aujourd'hui, 1949, 289p.

——————. *L'Eglise, le communisme et les chrétiens*. Ed. sociales, 1949, 369p.

——————. *La théorie matérialiste de la connaissance*. P.U.F., 1953, 388p., "B.Ph.C." (Th.).

——————. *La liberté*. Moscou, Editions de langues étrangères, 1955, 463p.

—————— et Georges Cogniot. *Mésaventures de l'anti-marxisme: les malheurs de Maurice Merleau-Ponty*. Ed. sociales, 1956, 160p.

——————. *Humanisme marxiste*. Cinq essais polémiques. *Ibid.*, 1957, 315p.

——————. *Questions à Jean-Paul Sartre*. "Clarté," 1962, 115p.

——————. *Perspective de l'homme: existentialisme, pensée catholique, marxisme*. P.U.F., 364p., Nouvelle édition 1962.

——————. *Dieu est mort, Etude sur Hegel*. *Ibid.*, 1962, 440p., "B.Ph.C.". *D'un réalisme sans rivage: Picasso, Saint John Perse, Kafka*. Plon, 1963, 251p.

——————. *Marxisme du XXe siècle*. La Palatine, 1966, 306p.

——————. *La pensée de Hegel*. Bordas, 1967, 207p., "Pour connaître . . ."

Geiger, Louis Bertrand, O.P. (Le Saulchoir). *Philosophie et Spiritualité.* Ed. du Cerf, 1963, 2 vols., 240 & 376p.

Gilson, Etienne (Académie Française). *Le thomisme* (1922). Engl.: *The Christian Philosophy of St. Thomas,* trl. L. K. Shook. N.Y., Random House, 1956, 511p.

—————. *Introduction à l'étude de S. Augustin* (1927). Engl.: *The Christian Philosophy of St. Augustine. Ibid.,* 1961, 398p.

—————. *L'Esprit de la philosophie médiévale* (Gifford Lectures, 1932). *The Spirit of Medieval Philosophy,* trl. A.H.C. Downes. N.Y., Scribner's, 1966, 490p.

—————. *La théologie mystique de S. Bernard* (1947). Engl.: *The Mystical Theology of St. Bernard,* trl. A.H.C. Downes. London, Sheed & Ward, 1955, 266p.

—————. *Christianisme et Philosophie* (1936), 2.éd. revue. Vrin, 1950, 172p.

—————. *L'école des muses.* Vrin, 1951, 270p., "Essais d'art et de philosophie."

—————. *Jean Duns Scot,* Introduction à ses positions fondamentales. *Ibid.,* 1952, 700p.

—————. *Les métamorphoses de la Cité de Dieu. Ibid.* (and Louvain), 1952, 304p.

—————. *God and Philosophy.* New Haven, Yale Univ. Press, 1950, "Powell Lectures on Philosophy at Indiana Univ."; *ibid.,* 1959, "A Yale Paperbound."

—————. *A Gilson Reader,* by Anton Pegis. Garden City, N.Y., Hanover House, 1957, 358p.

—————. *Painting and Reality* (The A. W. Mellon Lectures in the Fine Art, Washington 1955). N.Y., Pantheon Books, 391p., "Bollingen Series." French: *Peinture et Réalité.* Vrin, 1958, 369p., "Problèmes et Controverses."

—————. *Elements of Christian Philosophy.* Garden City, N.Y., Doubleday, 1960, 358p.

—————. *L'être et l'essence* (1947), 2.éd. augmentée. Vrin, 1962, 380p.

—————. *Introduction aux Arts du Beau. Ibid.,* 1963, 277p. *The Arts of the Beautiful.* N.Y., Scribner's, 1965, 189p.

—————. *The Spirit of Thomism.* N.Y., P. J. Kennedy, 1964, 127p.

—————. *Matières et Formes,* Poiétiques particulières des arts majeurs. Vrin, 1964, 272p.

—————. *The Unity of Philosophical Experience.* N.Y., Scribner's, 1965, 331p.

——————— and M. D. Ohenu, O. P. & M.-Th. d'Alverny, edd. *Archives d'Histoire doctrinale et littéraire du Moyen-age*. Vrin, T.I.-XVI, 1926-1948; T.XVII-XXXIV, 1949-67.

——————— and Thomas Langan & Armand Maurer. *History of Philosophy* . . . N.Y., Random House. IV.: *Recent Philosophy, Hegel to Present,* 1966, 876p.

———————. Cf.: *Mélanges offerts à Etienne Gilson*. Toronto-Paris, J. Vrin, 1959, 704p.

Gobry, Ivan (Institut Catholique, Paris). *Le modèle en morale*. P.U.F., 1965, 455p., (Th.).

Goldman, Lucien (Ecole Pratique des Hautes Etudes). *Sciences humaines et Philosophie*. P.U.F., 1952, 148p.

———————. *Le Dieu caché*. Etude sur la vision tragique dans les *Pensées* de Pascal et dans le théâtre de Racine. Gallimard, 1955, 454p., "Bibliothèque des Idées." Engl.: *The Hidden God,* trl. Philipp Thody. N.Y., Humanities Press, 1964, 426p.

———————. *Recherches dialectiques*. Gallimard, 1959, 357p., "Bibliothèques des idées."

Gonseth, Ferdinand (Polytechnicum, Zurich). *La géométrie et le problème de l'espace*. Dunod, 1948-50-53-55, 6 vols., 700p.

———————. *Le problème du temps,* Essai sur la méthodologie de la recherche. Neuchatel, Ed. du Griffon, 1964, 388p., "Bibliothèque scientifique, 36."

Gouhier, Henri (Sorbonne). *La philosophie et son histoire. L'histoire et sa philosophie*. Vrin, 1948-1952, 2 vols., 132 & 152p.

———————. *Le théâtre et l'existence*. Aubier, 1952, 222p.

———————. *Les premières pensées de Descartes, Contribution à l'histoire de l'anti-Renaissance*. Vrin, 1958, 167p.

———————. *Bergson et le Christ des Evangiles*. Fayard, 1961, 224p., "Le Signe."

———————. *La pensée métaphysique de Descartes*. Vrin, 1962, 410p.

———————. *La vie d'Auguste Comte. Ibid.,* 1965, 245p., "3 essais d'Art et de Philosophie."

———————. *Blaise Pascal. Ibid.,* 1966, 404p.

——————— éd.: *Les études Bergsoniennes,* P.U.F. Vol. IV, 1956, 256p.; Vol. V, 1960, 220p.; — Vol. VI, 1961, 212p.; — Vol. VII, 1966, 236p.

Granger, Gilles-Gaston (Aix-en-Provence, Univ.). *La mathématique sociale du marquis de Condorcet; — Méthodologie économique*. P.U.F., 1955-56, 2 vols, 175 & 424p., "B.Ph.C.".

——————. *Pensée formelle et sciences de l'homme.* Aubier, 1960, 228p., "Analyses et Raisons."

Grenier, Jean (Sorbonne). *La Philosophie de Jules Lequier,* P.U.F., 1953, 348p. (Th.).

——————. *A propos de l'humain.* Gallimard, 1955, 203p., "Les Essais."

——————. *Absolu et Choix.* P.U.F., 1961, 119p.

——————. *Entretiens avec 17 peintres non-figuratifs.* Calman-Lévy, 1963, 231p.

† Groethuysen, Bernard. *Anthropologie philosophique.* Gallimard, 1953, 288p.

——————. *Philosophie de la Révolution française,* précédé de *Montesquieu,* éd. Alix Guillain. *Ibid.,* 1956; Nouvelle édition: Gonthier, 1886, "Médiations."

† Grua, Gaston (Grenoble, Univ.). *Jurisprudence universelle et Théodicée selon Leibniz. La justice humaine selon Leibniz.* P.U.F., 1953-57, 2 vols., 548 & 427p.

Gueroult, Martial (Collège de France). *Descartes selon l'ordre des raisons.* Aubier, 1954, 2 vols.

——————. *Nouvelles réflexions sur la preuve ontologique de Descartes.* Vrin, 1955, 150p.

——————. Berkeley, *4 Etudes sur la Perception et sur Dieu.* Aubier, 1956, 192p.

——————. *Malebranche.* Aubier, 1955-59, 3 vols.

——————. Cf.: *Hommage à Martial Gueroult.* Fischbacher, 1965, 227p.

Guitton, Jean (Académie Française). *Pascal et Leibniz.* Aubier, 1951, 183p., "Ph. Esprit."

——————. (Essai sur l'amour humain) Engl.: *Essay on Human Love,* trl. Pearce. London, Rockliff, 1955, 243p.

——————. *Invitation à la pensée et la vie.* A. Blaizot, 1956, 150p.

——————. *Jésus.* Frasset, 1956, 447p.

——————. *La vocation de Bergson.* Gallimard, 1960, 255p., "Vocations, 9."

——————. *Difficultés de croire.* Plon, 1960, 256p., "Présences."

——————. *Dialogue avec les Précurseurs,* Journal oecuménique 1922-1962. Aubier, 1962, 318p.

——————. *Oeuvres complètes,* I. *Portraits.* Desclée De Brouwer, 1967, 943p.

† Gurvitch, Georges. — *La vocation de la sociologie.* P.U.F., 1950, 607p.; 3e éd. refondue: I. *Vers la sociologie différentielle,* 1963, 512p.; II. *Antécédents et perspectives,* 1963, 510p.

——————. *Déterminismes sociaux et liberté humaine.* P.U.F., 1955, 304p.

——————. *Dialectique et Sociologie.* Flammarion, 1962, 242p., "N.B.Sc.".

——————. *Etudes sur les classes sociales.* Gonthier, 1966, 248p., "Médiations."

——————. *Les cadres sociaux de la connaissance.* P.U.F., 1966, 313p., "B.Ph.C.".

Gurwitsch, Aron. *Théorie du champ de la conscience.* Desclée De Brouwer, 1957, 347p. Engl.: *The Field of Consciousness.* Pittsburgh, Duquesne Univ. Press, 1964.

Gusdorf, Georges (Strasbourg, Univ.). *Traité de l'existence morale.* Armand Colin, 1949, 416p.

——————. *Mémoire et Personne.* P.U.F., 1951, 2 vols., 280 & 296p., "B.Ph.C.".

——————. *Mythe et Métaphysique.* Flammarion, 1953, 296p., "B.PH.Sc.".

——————. *La vertu de force.* P.U.F., 1956, 120p.

——————. *Traité de métaphysique.* Armand Colin, 1956, 461p.

——————. *Introduction aux sciences humaines.* Les Belles Lettres, 1961, 523p.

——————. *Dialogue avec le médecin.* Librairie protestante, 1962, 120p.

——————. *Signification humaine de la liberté.* Payot, 1962, 288p.

——————. *De l'histoire des sciences à l'histoire de la pensée, I. Les sciences humaines et la pensée occidentale.* Payot, 1966, 333p.

Heidegger. *De l'essence de la Vérité,* trad. A. De Waelhens. Nauwelaerts, 1949, 108p.

——————. *Lettre sur l'humanisme,* trad. R. Munier. Aubier, 1957, 187p.

——————. *Qu'est-ce que la philosophie?,* trad. Kostas Axelos et Jean Beaufret. Gallimard, 1957, 50p.

——————. *Introduction à la métaphysique,* trad. Gilbert Kahn, P.U.F., 1958, "Epiméthée" Gallimard, 1967, "Classiques de la Philosophie."

——————. *Essais et Conférences,* trad. André Préau. Gallimard, 1958, 350p.

——————. *Qu'appelle-t-on penser?,* trad. Aloys Becker et Gérard Granel. P.U.F., 1959, 272p.

——————. *Approche de Hölderlin.* Gallimard, 1962, 200p.

——————. *Chemins qui ne mènent nulle part. Ibid.,* 1962, 320p.

——————. *Le principe de raison,* Préface de Jean Beaufret. *Ibid.,* 1962, 276p.

—————. *L'être et le temps,* trad. R. Boehm et A. De Waelhens. *Ibid.,* 1958, 350p.

—————. *Questions III: Le chemin de campagne, etc.* . . . Gallimard, 1966, 232p.

Henriot, Jacques. *Existence et Obligation.* P.U.F., 1967, 428p., "B.Ph.C." (Th.).

Henry, Michel (Montpellier, Univ.). *Philosophie et Phénoménologie du corps; L'essence de la manifestation.* P.U.F., 1963-65, 3 vols., 309 & 908p., "Epiméthée" (Th.).

d'Hondt, Jacques. *Hegel, Philosophe de l'histoire vivante. Ibid.,* 1967, 483p. (Th.).

Husserl — *Idées directrices* . . . , trad. P. Ricoeur. Gallimard, 1950, 608p.

—————. *La philosophie comme science rigoureuse,* trad. Q. Lauer. P.U.F., 1955, "Epiméthée."

—————. *Logique formelle et transcendentale,* trad. S. Bachelard. *Ibid.,* 1957, 447p.

—————. *Recherches logiques,* trad. Hubert Elie, Lothar Helkel et René Schérer. *Ibid.,* 4 vols., 1959-1966; "Epiméthée."

—————. *L'origine de la géométrie,* trad. J. Derrida. *Ibid.*

—————. *Leçons pour une phénoménologie de la conscience intime du temps,* trad. H. Dussort et G. Granel. *Ibid.,* 1964, 206p.

Hyppolite, Jean (Collège de France). *Logique et Existence,* Essai sur la *Logique* de Hegel. P.U.F., 1953, 252p., "Epiméthée."

—————. *Etudes sur Marx et Hegel.* Rivière, 1955, 208p.

—————. *Sens et Existence dans la philosophie de Merleau-Ponty.* Oxford, Clarendon, 1963, 29p., "Zaharoff Lecture."

Jalabert, Jacques (Grenoble, Univ.). *Le Dieu de Leibniz.* P.U.F., 1960, 228p., "Univ. de Grenoble."

—————. *L'un et le multiple. Ibid.,* 1960, 169p.

† Jamati, Georges (C.N.R.S.). *La conquête de soi, Méditation sur l'art.* Flammarion, 1961, 474p., "Bibliothèque d'esthétique."

Jankélévitch, Vladimir (Sorbonne). *Traité des Vertus.* Bordas, 1949, 807p.

—————. *Philosophie première.* P.U.F., 1954, 268p., "B.Ph.C.".

—————. *Le "Je ne sais quoi" et le "Presque rien".* P.U.F., 1957, 268p., "Université de Paris."

—————. *La Rhapsodie, Verve et improvisation.* Flammarion, 1955, 251p., "B.Ph.Sc.".

—————. *L'austérité et la vie morale. Ibid.,* 1956, 256p., "B.Ph.Sc.".

—————. *Le pur et l'impur. Ibid.,* 1960, 280p., "B.Ph.Sc.".

—————. *La Musique et l'Ineffable.* Armand Colin, 1961, 198p.

—————. *L'aventure, l'ennui, le sérieux.* Aubier, 1963, 222p., "Présences et Pensées."

—————. *La mauvaise conscience* (1939), nouvelle édition. *Ibid.,* 1966, 218p.

—————. *La mort.* Flammarion, 1966, 426p., "N.B.Sc.".

—————. *Le Pardon.*

Jeanson, Francis. *Le problème moral et la pensée de Sartre.* Lettre préface de J.-P. Sartre (1947), suivi de: Un quidam nommé Sartre. Seuil, 1965, 348p.

—————. *La signification humaine du rire. Ibid.,* 1950, 221p.

—————. *La vraie vérité,* suivie de *La récrimination. Ibid.,* 1954, 192p.

—————. *Sartre par lui-même. Ibid.,* 1955, 192p.

—————. *L'Algérie hors la loi. Ibid.,* 1955.

—————. *Notre guerre.* Editions de Minuit, 1960.

—————. *La révolution algérienne.* Feltrinelli (Milano), 1962.

—————. *Lignes de départ.* Seuil, 1963.

—————. *La Foi d'un incroyant. Ibid.,* 1963, 179p.

—————. *Sartre.* Desclée De Brouwer, 1964, 142p., "Les écrivains devant Dieu."

—————. *Lettre aux femmes.* Seuil, 1965.

—————. *Simone de Beauvoir, ou L'entreprise de vivre,* suivi de *Deux entretiens. Ibid.,* 1966, 302p.

Jerphagnon, Lucien (Besançon, Univ.). *Le caractère de Pascal.* P.U.F., 1962, 320p., "Caractères"; — *De la Banalité.* Vrin, 1965, 418p. (Th.).

† Jolivet, Régis, Mgr. (Institut Catholique, Lyon). *Aux sources de l'existentialisme chrétien: Kierkegaard.* Fayard, "Les idées et la vie." 6e éd., 1958, 288p.

—————. *Essai sur le problème et la condition de la sincérité.* Vitte, 1951, 204p.

—————. *Le Dieu des Philosophes et des Savants.* Fayard, 1956. Engl.: *The God of Reason,* trl. Mark Pontifex. N.Y., Hawthorn Books, 1958, 126p.

—————. *L'homme métaphysique. Ibid.,* 1958, 123p.

—————. *Sartre ou la théologie de l'absurde. Ibid.,* 1965, 168p.

Julia, Didier. *La question de l'homme et le fondement de la philosophie,* Réflexions sur la philosophie pratique de Kant et la philosophie spéculative de Fichte. Aubier, 1964, 421p., "Analyses et Raisons."

† Koyré, Alexandre. *Etudes galiléennes* (1939-40), Nouvelle édition. Hermann, 1966, 344p., "Histoire de la Pensée scientifique, XV."

——————. *Etudes sur l'histoire de la pensée philosophique en Russie.* Vrin, 1951, 326p.

——————. *Mystiques, spirituels, alchimistes au XVIe siècle.* A. Colin, 1955, 117p.

——————. *From the Closed World to the Infinite Universe.* Baltimore, The John's Hopkin's Press, 1957, 313p. (and N.Y., "Harper Torchbooks", 1958, 322p.). French: *Du monde clos à l'univers infini,* trad. Raissa Tarr. P.U.F., 1962, 280p.

——————. *Etudes d'histoire de la pensée philosophique.* A. Colin, 1961, 329p., "Annales."

——————. *La révolution astronomique: Copernic, Kepler, Borelli.* Hermann, 1961, 525p.

——————. *Newtonian Studies.* Cambridge, Mass., Harvard Univ. Press, 1965, 288p.

——————. *Etudes d'histoire de la pensée scientifique.* P.U.F., 1966, 372p., "B.Ph.C.".

Cf.: Braudel (Fernand), Cohen (I. Bernard) & Taton (René), edd. *Mélanges Alexandre Koyré, I. L'aventure de la Science; II. L'aventure de l'Esprit.* Hermann, 1964, 2 vols., 661 & 617p.

Lacan, Jacques. *Ecrits* (Recueil des textes, avec un "Index raisonné" par Jacques-Alain Miller). Seuil, 1966, 912p., "Le champ freudien."

Lacombe, Olivier (Sorbonne). *L'absolu selon le Vedanta* (1937). 2.éd., P. Geuthner, 1966, 416p.

——————. *Existence de l'homme.* Desclée De Brouwer, 1951, 152p., "Courrier des Iles."

——————. *Chemins de l'Inde et Philosophie chrétienne.* Alsatia, 1956, 170p.

Lacroix, Jean (Lyon, Univ.) *Marxisme, existentialisme, personnalisme.* P.U.F., 1950, 124p.; 6.éd., 1966.

——————. *La sociologie d'Auguste Comte.* P.U.F., 1956, 116p.

——————. *Personne et Amour.* Seuil, 1956, 147p., "Esprit."

——————. *Le sens de l'athéisme moderne.* Casterman, 1958, 128p., "Cahiers de l'actualité religieuse, 8."

——————. *Histoire et Mystère. Ibid.,* 1962, 136p., "Cahiers . . . , 18."

——————. *L'échec.* P.U.F., 1964, 177p.

——————. *Panorama de la philosophie française.* P.U.F., 1966, 248p.

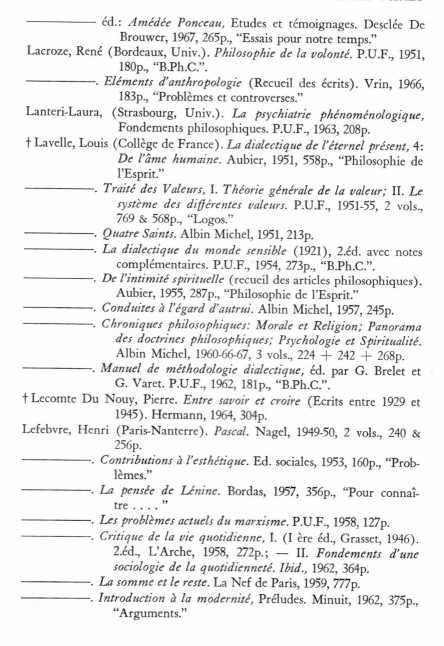

——————— éd.: *Amédée Ponceau,* Etudes et témoignages. Desclée De
      Brouwer, 1967, 265p., "Essais pour notre temps."

Lacroze, René (Bordeaux, Univ.). *Philosophie de la volonté.* P.U.F., 1951,
      180p., "B.Ph.C.".

——————. *Eléments d'anthropologie* (Recueil des écrits). Vrin, 1966,
      183p., "Problèmes et controverses."

Lanteri-Laura, (Strasbourg, Univ.). *La psychiatrie phénoménologique,*
      Fondements philosophiques. P.U.F., 1963, 208p.

† Lavelle, Louis (Collège de France). *La dialectique de l'éternel présent,* 4:
      De l'âme humaine. Aubier, 1951, 558p., "Philosophie de
      l'Esprit."

——————. *Traité des Valeurs,* I. *Théorie générale de la valeur;* II. *Le
      système des différentes valeurs.* P.U.F., 1951-55, 2 vols.,
      769 & 568p., "Logos."

——————. *Quatre Saints.* Albin Michel, 1951, 213p.

——————. *La dialectique du monde sensible* (1921), 2.éd. avec notes
      complémentaires. P.U.F., 1954, 273p., "B.Ph.C.".

——————. *De l'intimité spirituelle* (recueil des articles philosophiques).
      Aubier, 1955, 287p., "Philosophie de l'Esprit."

——————. *Conduites à l'égard d'autrui.* Albin Michel, 1957, 245p.

——————. *Chroniques philosophiques: Morale et Religion; Panorama
      des doctrines philosophiques; Psychologie et Spiritualité.*
      Albin Michel, 1960-66-67, 3 vols., 224 + 242 + 268p.

——————. *Manuel de méthodologie dialectique,* éd. par G. Brelet et
      G. Varet. P.U.F., 1962, 181p., "B.Ph.C.".

† Lecomte Du Nouy, Pierre. *Entre savoir et croire* (Ecrits entre 1929 et
      1945). Hermann, 1964, 304p.

Lefebvre, Henri (Paris-Nanterre). *Pascal.* Nagel, 1949-50, 2 vols., 240 &
      256p.

——————. *Contributions à l'esthétique.* Ed. sociales, 1953, 160p., "Prob-
      lèmes."

——————. *La pensée de Lénine.* Bordas, 1957, 356p., "Pour connaî-
      tre . . . . "

——————. *Les problèmes actuels du marxisme.* P.U.F., 1958, 127p.

——————. *Critique de la vie quotidienne,* I. (I ère éd., Grasset, 1946).
      2.éd., L'Arche, 1958, 272p.; — II. *Fondements d'une
      sociologie de la quotidienneté. Ibid.,* 1962, 364p.

——————. *La somme et le reste.* La Nef de Paris, 1959, 777p.

——————. *Introduction à la modernité,* Préludes. Minuit, 1962, 375p.,
      "Arguments."

——————. *Métaphilosophie.* Prolégomènes. *Ibid.,* 1965, 335p., "Arguments, 26."

—————— éd.: *Le Langage et la Société.* Gallimard, 1966, 384p., "Idées."

——————. *Position: Contre les technocrates, en finir avec l'humanité-fiction.* Gonthier, 1967, 233p., "Médiations."

Lefèvre, Roger (Lille, Univ.). *La vocation de Descartes. L'humanisme de Descartes. La bataille du cogito.* P.U.F., 1956-1960, 3 vols., 228 + 284 + 230p., "B.Ph.C." (Th.).

Leroy, André-Louis. *Hume.* P.U.F., 1953, 342p., "Les Grands Penseurs."

——————. *Georges Berkeley. Ibid.,* 1959, 284p., "Les grands Penseurs."

——————. *Locke. Ibid.,* 1967, "Les Grands Penseurs."

† Le Roy, Edouard (Collège de France). *Essai de philosophie première.* P.U.F., 1958, 2 vols., 881p., "B.Ph.C.".

——————. *La pensée mathématique pure* (1914-1919). *Ibid.,* 1960, 388p., "B.Ph.C.".

† Le Senne, René (Sorbonne). *La destinée personnelle.* Flammarion, 1950, 200p., "B.Ph.Sc.".

——————. *La découverte de Dieu.* Aubier, 1951, "Philosophie de l'Esprit."

Levert, Paule. *L'être et le réel selon Louis Lavelle.* Aubier, 1960, 233p. (Th.).

Lévi-Strauss, Claude (Collège de France). *Les structures élémentaires de la parenté.* P.U.F., 1949, 640p., "B.Ph.C." (Th.).

——————. *Race et Histoire.* Unesco, 1952, 40p.

——————. *Tristes Tropiques.* Plon, 1955, 480p., "Terre humaine."

——————. *Anthropologie structurale. Ibid.,* 1958, 456p.

—————— et Georges Charbonnier. *Entretiens avec Claude Lévi-Strauss.* Plon, 1961.

——————. *Le totémisme aujourd'hui.* P.U.F., 1962, 156p., "Mythes et Religions."

——————. *La pensée sauvage.* Plon, 1962, 395p.

——————. *Mythologiques,* I: *La cuit et le cru;* II: *Le miel et les cendres.* Plon, 1964-1966, 402 & 480p.

Lévinas, Emmanuel (Paris-Nanterre). *La théorie de l'intuition dans la phénoménologie de Husserl.* Ière éd., 1930. 2.éd., Vrin, 1963, 224p.

——————. *En découvrant l'existence, avec Husserl et Heidegger.* Vrin, 1949, 112p.

——————. *Totalité et Infini, Essai sur l'extériorité.* La Haye, M. Nijhoff, 1961, 284p., "Phaenomenologica, 8" (Th.).

——————. *Difficile Liberté,* Essai sur le judaïsme. Albin Michel, 1963, 327p.

Llinarès, Armand (Grenoble, Univ.). *Raymond Lulle.* P.U.F., 1964, 510p. (Th.).

Lubac, Henri de, S.J. (Faculté S.J.). *Histoire et Esprit, Intelligence de l'Ecriture selon Origène.* Aubier, 1949, "Théologie."

——————. *Aspects du bouddhisme.* Seuil, 1951, 201p., "Esprit."

——————. *La rencontre du bouddhisme et de l'Occident.* Aubier, 1952, 288p., "Théologie."

——————. *Nouveaux Paradoxes.* Seuil, 1955, 128p.

——————. *Augustinisme et Théologie moderne.* Aubier, 1965, "Théologie, 63."

——————. *Le mystère du surnaturel.* Aubier, 1965, 300p., "Théologie."

——————. *The Faith of Teilhard,* trl. R. Haugue. London, Burns & Oates, 1965, 206p.

† Madinier, Gabriel (Lyon, Univ.). *Conscience et Signification,* Essai sur la réflection. P.U.F., 1953, 139p.

——————. *La conscience morale. Ibid.,* 1954, 128p. (5e éd., 1966).

——————. *Vers une philosophie réflexive,* Etude liminaire d'Aimé Forest. Neuchatel, La Baconnière, 1960, 171p., "Etre et Penser."

Maire, Gilbert. *Une régression mentale: d'Henri Bergson à J.-P. Sartre.* Grasset, 1958, 210p.

——————. *Les instants privilégiés.* Aubier, 1962, 446p., "Philosophie de l'Esprit."

Marcel, Gabriel. *La métaphysique de Royce* (1917-18). Engl.: *Royce's Metaphysics,* trl. Virginia & Gordon Ringer. Chicago, H. Regnery, 1956, 199p.

——————. *Etre et Avoir* (1935). Engl.: *Being and Having.* N.Y., "Harper Torch Books," 1965, 236p.

——————. *Du refus à l'invocation* (1940; réédition: *Essai de philosophie concrète,* Gallimard, 1967, 376p., "Idées." Engl.: *Creative Fidelity,* trl. Robert Rosthal. N.Y., Farrar & Straus, 1964.

——————. *Homo Viator* (1944). Engl.: *Homo Viator, Introd. to A Metaphysics of Hope,* trl. Emma Craufurd. N.Y., Harper, 1962, "The Cloister Library."

——————. *Le mystère de l'être.* Aubier, 1950, 2 vols., 240p., "Gifford Lecture." Engl.: *The Mystery of Being.* Chicago, H. Regnery, 1960, 2 vols., 284 & 218p., "Getaway Edition."

——————. *Les hommes contre l'humain.* Vieux Colombier, 1951, 208p.

——————. *Le déclin de la sagesse.* Plon, 1954, 128p.

——————. *L'homme problématique.* Aubier, 1955, 118p., "Philosophie de l'Esprit."

——————. *Théâtre et Religion.* Vitte, 1959, 107p.

——————. *Présence et Immortalité.* Flammarion, 1959, 234p., "Homo Sapiens."

——————. *Paix sur la terre.* Aubier, 1965, 175p.

——————. *Foi et Réalité.* Aubier, 1967, 217p., "Foi vivante."

Maritain, Jacques. *Art et scolastique* (1920). Engl.: *The Structure of Poetry,* trl. Marshall Suther. N.Y., Philosophical Library, 1953, 95p.

——————. *Distinguer pour Unir,* ou Les Degrés du Savoir (1932). Engl.: *Distinguish to Unite,* or *The Degrees of Knowledge,* newly trl. under the supervision of Gerald B. Phelan, S.J. N.Y., Ch. Scribner's Sons, 1959, 490p.

——————. *De la philosophie chrétienne* (1933). Engl.: *An Essay on Christian Philosophy,* trl. Edw. H. Flannery. N. Y., Philosophical Library, 1955, 127p.

——————. *Le Docteur angélique* (1930). Engl. trl. J. F. Scalan, 1931, revised by J. W. Evans and Peter O'Reilly: *St. Thomas Aquinas,* N.Y., Meridian Books, 1958, 281p.

——————. *Education at the Crossroads.* New Haven, Yale Univ. Press, 1943, "Terry Lecture" (1960, "A Yale Paperbound," 130p.). French: *Pour une philosophie de l'éducation.* Fayard, 1959, 249p.

——————. *Court traité de l'existence et de l'existant* (1947). Engl.: *Existence and the Existent,* trl. L. Galantière and Gerald B. Phelem. N.Y., Random, 1966, 148p., "Vintage Books."

——————. *La personne et le bien commun* (1939-47). Engl.: *The Person and the Common Good,* trl. J. Fitzgerald. Evanston, Notre Dame, Indiana, Univ. of Notre Dame Press, 1966, 108p.

——————. *L'homme et l'Etat,* trad. de l'anglais par R. et F. Davril. P.U.F., 1953, 222p.

——————. *Approaches de Dieu.* Alsatia, 1953, 140p. Engl.: *Man's Approach to God.* Latrobe, Penns., Archabbey Press, 1961, 153p.

——————. *Creative Intuition in Art and Poetry,* trl. M. H. Carre. London, Harville Press, 1954, 455p. French: *L'intuition créatrice dans l'art.* Desclée De Brouwer, 1966, 432p.

——————. On the Philosophy of History. N.Y., Ch. Scribner's Sons, 1957, 191p. French: Pour une philosophie de l'histoire, trad. Ch. Journet. Seuil, 1959, 192p.

——————. Reflections on America, Ibid., 1958, 205p.

——————. The Sin of the Angel, An Essay on a Re-Interpretation of Some Thomistic Positions, trl. William L. Rossner. Westminster, Md., Newman Press, 1959, 120p.

——————. La philosophie morale, Examen historique des grands systèmes. Gallimard, 1960, 592p., "Bibliothèque des Idées." Engl.: Moral Philosophy. N.Y., Scribner's, 1964, 468p.

——————. The Responsibility of the Artist. N.Y., Scribner's, 1960, 120p. French: La responsabilité de l'artiste, trad. G. et Chr. Brazzola. Fayard, 1961, "Le Signe."

——————. Dieu et la permission du Mal. Desclée De Brouwer, 1963, 111p. Engl.: God and the Permission of Evil, trl. J. W. Evans. London-St. Louis, Herder, 1966, 119p.

——————. Le Mystère d'Israël, et autres essais. Desclée De Brouwer, 1966, 253p.

——————. Challenges and Renewals (Selections), ed. by Leo Ward and Joseph Evans. Notre Dame, Indiana, Univ. of Notre Dame Press, 1966, 389p.

Marrou, Henry Irénée (Sorbonne). Histoire de l'éducation dans l'antiquité. Seuil, 1955. Engl. by George Lamb, N. Y., Sheed & Ward, 1956, 466p.

——————. L'ambivalence du temps de l'histoire chez S. Augustin. Vrin, 1951, 86p.

——————. De la connaissance historique. Seuil, 1954, 300p. The Meaning of History. Baltimore, Helicon Press, 1965, 320p.

——————. S. Augustin et l'augustinisme. Seuil, 1955, 191p. Engl.: St. Augustine and his Influence through the Ages, trl. P. H. Scott. London, Longmans, 1958, 192p.

Martin, Roger (Sorbonne). Logique contemporaine et formalisation. P.U.F., 1964, 222p., "Epiméthée."

Massart, Pierre. La dialectique de la conscience chez J. Paliard. P.U.F., 1959, 358p. (Th.).

Mauchassat, Gaston. La liberté spirituelle. P.U.F., 1961; L'idéalisme de Lachelier. Ibid., 1961, 225p. (Th.).

Mehl, Roger (Strasbourg, Univ.). Images de l'homme. Genève, Labor et Fides, 1953, 64p. Engl.: Images of Man, trl. James H. Farley. Richmond, N.J., John Knox, 1965.

——————. *Du catholicisme romain*. Neuchatel, Delachaux & Niestlé, 1957, 95p.

——————. *De l'autorité des valeurs*. P.U.F., 1957, 271p.

——————. *Société et Amour*, Problèmes éthiques de la vie familiale. Librairie protestante, 1961, 231p.

Merleau-Ponty, Jacques (Paris-Nanterre). *Philosophie et théorie physique chez Eddington*. Les Belles Lettres, 1965; — *Cosmologie du XXe Siècle*. Gallimard, 1965, 533p. "Bibliothèque des idées" (Th.).

† Merleau-Ponty, Maurice (Collège de France). *La structure du comportement* (1942). Engl.: *The Structure of Behavior*, trl. Alden L. Fischer. Boston, Beacon Press, 1963, 256p.

——————. *La phénoménologie de la Perception* (1945). Engl.: *Phenomenology of Perception*, trl. C. Smith. N.Y., Humanities Press, 1962, 466p.

——————. *Les aventures de la dialectique*. Gallimard, 1955, 320p.

——————. *Signes*. *Ibid.*, 1960, 435p. Engl.: *Signs*, trl. Richard C. McCleary. Evanston, The Northwestern Univ. Press, 1964, 355p.

——————. *L'oeil et l'esprit*. Gallimard, 1963.

——————. *Le Visible et l'Invisible*, éd. Claude Lefort. *Ibid.*, 1964, 361p.

——————. *The Primacy of Perception*, and Other Essays (Selections) by James M. Edie. Evanston, Ill., Northwestern Univ. Press, 1964, 228p.

Meyer, Marcel (Aix-en-Provence, Univ.). *L'ontologie d' Unamuno; Problématique de l'évolution*. P.U.F., 1954-55, 148 & 284p., "B.Ph.C." (Th.).

Moles, Abraham (Strasbourg, Univ.). *La création scientifique*. Genève, René Kister, 1957, 243p. (Th.).

——————. *Théorie de l'information et perception esthétique*, Flammarion, 1958, 221p. Engl. trl. Joel E. Cohen. Urbana Univ. Press, 1966, 217p.

Moreau, Joseph (Bordeaux, Univ.). *Réalisme et idéalisme chez Platon*. P.U.F., 1951, 140p.

——————. *L'univers leibnizien*. Vitte, 1956, 256p., "Problèmes et doctrines."

——————. *La connaissance et l'être*. Aubier, 1958, 160p., "Philosophie de l'Esprit."

——————. *L'horizon des esprits*, Essai critique sur la *Phénoménologie de la Perception de Maurice Merleau-Ponty*. P.U.F., 1960, 135p., "B.Ph.C.".

——————. *Aristote et son école.* P.U.F., 1962, 326p., "Les Grands Penseurs."

——————. *L'espace et le temps d'après Aristote.* Antinore (Padova), 1966, 121p.

† Mounier, Emmanuel. *Mounier et sa génération,* Lettres, Carnets et Inédits. Seuil, 1956, 430p.

——————. *Oeuvres.* Seuil, 4 vols., 1963.

Mouloud, Noël (Lille, Univ.). *La peinture et l'espace.* P.U.F., 1964, 341p.; *Formes structurées et modes productifs.* Sedes, 1963, 436p. (Th.).

Moscovici, Serge. *La psychanalyse et son public.* P.U.F., 1960, 650p. (Th.).

Mossé-Bastide, Rose-Marie (Aix-en-Provence, Univ.). *Bergson éducateur; Bergson et Plotin.* P.U.F., 1955-1959, 2 vols., 430 & 468p., "B.Ph.C." (Th.).

† Nabert, Jean. *Eléments pour une éthique* (1943), 2.éd., Préface de Paul Ricoeur. Aubier, 1962, 233p., "Philosophie de l'Esprit."

——————. *Essai sur le Mal.* P.U.F., 1955, 171p., "Epiméthée."

——————. *Le désir de Dieu,* éd. Paul Ricoeur et Paule Levert. Aubier, 1966, 382p.

Naulin, Paul. *Itinéraire de la conscience: Etude sur J. Nabert.* Aubier, 1963, 520p., "Analyses et Raisons" (Th.).

Naville, Pierre. *Le Nouveau Léviathan,* T. I.: *De l'alienation à la jouissance, La genèse de la sociologie du travail chez Marx et Engels.* Rivière, 1957, 514p. (Th.).

Navratil, Michel. (Montpellier). *Introduction critique à une découverte de la pensée; — Les tendances constitutives de la pensée vivante.* P.U.F., 1954, 3 vols., 112 + 348 + 222p., "B.Ph.C." (Th.).

Nédoncelle, Maurice, Chanoine (Strasbourg, Univ.). *Existe-t-il une philosophie chrétienne?* Fayard, 1956, 117p.

——————. *Prière humaine, prière divine,* notes phénoménologiques. Desclée De Brouwer, 1962, 200p.

——————. *Conscience et Logos,* Horizons et méthodes d'une philosophie personnaliste. Ed. de l'Epi, 1962, 240p.

——————. *Personne humaine et nature.* Aubier, 1963, 169p.

Néher, André (Strasbourg, Univ.). *L'essence du prophétisme.* P.U.F., 1955, 360p., "Epiméthée" (Th.).

——————. *L'existence juive,* Souffrance et affrontements. Seuil, 1962, 284p., "Esprit."

——————. *Le puits de l'exil:* la théologie dialectique du Maharal de Prague. Albin Michel, 1965, 244p.

† Paliard, Jacques (Aix-en Provence, Univ.) *Maurice Blondel, ou le dé-passement chrétien.* Juliard, 1949, 304p.

—————. *Pensée implicite et perception visuelle.* P.U.F., 1949, 128p.

—————. *La pensée et la vie,* Recherche sur la logique de la perception. *Ibid.,* 1951, 316p.

—————. *Profondeur de l'âme.* Aubier, 1954, 184p., "Philosophie de l'Esprit."

Pépin, Jean (Ecole Pratique des Hautes Etudes). *Mythe et Allégorie,* Les origines grecques et les contestations judéo-chrétiennes. Aubier, 1958, 522p.

—————. *Les deux approches du christianisme.* Minuit, 1961, 290p., "Arguments."

—————. *Théologie cosmique et théologie chrétienne.* P.U.F., 1964, 598p., "B.Ph.C.".

Piaget, Jean (Genève, Univ., et Paris, Sorbonne). *Introduction à l'épistémologie génétique.* P.U.F., 1950, 3 vols., 361 + 355 + 344p.

—————. *Essai sur les transformations des opérations logiques. Ibid.,* 1952, 240p.

————— éd.: *Etudes d'épistémologie génétique,* publication du "Centre International d'épistémologie génétique de l'Université de Genève." *Ibid.,* 1957-1967, 20 vols., "Bibliothèque scientifique internationale."

—————. *Logic and Psychology* (London, Routledge, 1953), N.Y., Basic Books, 1957.

—————. *The Growth of Logical Thinking from Childhood to Adolescence. Ibid.,* 1958, 382p.

—————. *Le jugement moral chez l'enfant.* P.U.F., 1957, 343p. Engl.: *The Moral Judgment of the Child,* trl. Marjorie Gabain. N.Y., Macmillan, 1965, 410p.

—————. *Six études de psychologie.* Gonthier, 1964, 188p., "Médiations."

—————. *Sagesse et illusions de la philosophie.* P.U.F., 1965, 290p.

—————. *Biologie et connaissance.* Gallimard, 1967, 430p., "L'avenir de la science."

————— éd.: *Logique et connaissance scientifique. Ibid.,* 1967, 1.360p., "Encyclopédie de la Pléiade."

Cf.: *Psychologie et Epistémologie génétique, Thèmes piagétains.* Dunod, 1966, 421p.

Polin, Raymond (Sorbonne). *Politique et Philosophie chez Thomas Hobbes.* P.U.F., 1952, 288p.

—————. *La politique morale de John Locke.* P.U.F., 1960, 320p.

—————. *Du bonheur considéré comme l'un des Beaux-Arts.* P.U.F., 1965, 124p.

Ponceau, Amédée-Jean. *Initiation philosophique.* Rivière, 1947, 298p.

—————. *Timoléon, Réflexions sur la tyrannie.* Ed. du Myrthe, 1949, 239p.

—————. *La musique et l'angoisse.* La Colombe, 1951.

—————. *Le temps dépassé. Ibid.,* 1954, 122p.

Poulet, George (Genève, Univ.). *Etudes sur le temps humain,* Plon. I., 1949, 480p.; II. *La distance intérieure,* 1952, 364p.; III. *Le point de départ,* 1964, 236p. Engl.: *Studies in Human Time,* trl. Eliott Coleman. Baltimore, Johns Hopkins Press, 1956; N.Y., "Harper Torchbooks," 1959, 363p.

—————. *Les métamorphoses du cercle. Ibid.,* 1961, 535p., "Cheminements."

—————. *L'espace proustien.* Gallimard, 1963, 183p.

Pucelle, Jean (Poitiers, Univ.). *L'idéalisme en Angleterre, de Coleridge à Bradley.* Neuchatel, La Baconnière, 1955, 298p. (Th.).

—————. *Le temps.* P.U.F., 1955, 108p.

—————. *Etudes sur la valeur.* Vitte, 1955-64, 3 vols.

Ramnoux, Clémence (Paris-Nanterre). *Héraclite, ou l'homme entre les mots et les choses; — Vocabulaire et structure de pensée archaïque chez Héraclite.* Les Belles Lettres, 1960, 2 vols., 514 & 522p. (Th.).

Ricoeur, Paul (Paris-Nanterre). *Gabriel Marcel et Karl Jaspers.* Seuil, 1949, 456p.

—————. *Le volontaire et l'involontaire.* Aubier, 1950, "Philosophie de l'Esprit" (Th.). Engl.: *The Voluntary and Involuntary,* trl. Erazin V. Kohak. Evanston, Ill., "Northwestern Univ. Studies in Phenomenology and Existential Psychology," 498p.

—————. *Histoire et Vérité.* Seuil, 1955, 269p., "Esprit." Engl.: *History and Truth,* trl. Charles A. Kelbey. *Ibid.,* 1965, 333p.

—————. *Philosophie de la Volonté* II., *Finitude et Culpabilité:* 1. *L'homme faillible;* 2. *La symbolique du Mal.* Aubier, 1960, 2 vols., 164 & 335 p. Engl.: *Fallible Man,* trl. Charles A. Kelbey. Chicago, H. Regnery, 1965.

—————. *De l'interprétation:* Essai sur Freud. Seuil, 1965, 534p., "L'ordre philosophique."

Robinet, André (C.N.R.S.). *Malebranche et Leibniz; — Système et Existence dans l'oeuvre de Malebranche.* Vrin, 1955-1965, 2 vols., 525 & 507p. (Th.).

————— éd.: *Oeuvres complètes de Malebranche.* Vrin-C.N.R.S., 21 vols.

Rolland De Renéville, Jacques (Nantes, Univ.). *L'un-multiple et l'attribution chez Platon et les Sophistes.* Vrin, 1962, 279p. (Th.).

Rostand, Jean (Académie Française). *Ce que je crois.* Grasset, 1953.

—————. *Peut-on modifier l'homme?* Gallimard, 1956, 147p. Engl.: N.Y., Basic Books, 1959.

—————. *Espoir et inquiétudes de l'homme.* Club du meilleur livre, 1959, 286p.

—————. *Science fausse et fausses sciences.* Gallimard, 1958, 304p.

Rougier, Louis (Caen, Univ.). *Traité de la connaissance.* Gauthier-Villars, 1955, 450p.

—————. *La métaphysique et le langage.* Flammarion, 1960, 251p.

Russier, Jeanne (Nantes, Univ.). *La foi selon Pascal.* P.U.F., 1949, 2 vols., 232 & 220p. (Th.).

—————. *Sagesse cartésienne et religion,* Essai sur la connaissance de l'immortalité de l'âme selon Descartes. *Ibid.,* 1958, 163p.

—————. *La souffrance. Ibid.,* 1963, 124p.

Ruyer, Raymond (Nancy, Univ.). *Philosophie de la valeur.* Armand Colin, 1948, 212p.

—————. *L'Utopie et les utopies.* P.U.F., 1950, 295p.

—————. *Néo-finalisme. Ibid.,* 1952, 276p., "B.Ph.C.".

—————. *La cybernétique et l'origine de l'information.* Flammarion, 1955, 237p., "P.Ph.Sc.".

—————. *La genèse des formes vivantes. Ibid.,* 1958, 267p.

—————. *Paradoxes de la conscience et limites de l'automatisme.* Albin Michel, 1966, 286p.

Sargi, Bechara, S.J. *La participation à l'être dans la philosophie de Louis Lavelle,* Préface de Paul Ricoeur. Beauchesne, 1957, 167p. (Th.).

Sartre, Jean-Paul. *La transcendance de l'Ego,* Esquisse d'une description
        phénoménologique, 1936; — Introduction, notes et ap-
        pendices par Sylvie Le Bon. Vrin, 1965, 134p. Engl.: *The
        Transcendence of the Ego, An Existentialist Theory of
        Consciousness,* trl. Forrest Williams & Robert Kirk-
        patrick. N.Y., The Noonday Press, 1957, 119p.

——————. *L'imagination,* 1936. Engl.: Imagination, A Psychological
        Critique, trl. Forrest Williams. Ann Arbor, The Univ.
        of Michigan Press, 1962, 162p.

——————. *La nausée,* 1938. Engl.: Nausea, trl. Lloyd Alexander. Nor-
        folk, Conn., "A New Directions Paperback", 1959, 233p.

——————. *Esquisse d'une théorie des émotions,* 1939. Engl.: *The Emo-
        tions, Outline of A Theory,* trl. Bernard Frechtman. N.Y.,
        Philosophical Library, 1948; *Sketch for a Theory of
        Emotions,* trl. Philip Mairet. London, Methuen, 1962, 92p.

——————. *L'imaginaire,* 1940. Engl.: *The Psychology of Imagination,*
        trl. Bernard Frechtman. N.Y., Philosophical Library,
        1948; Washington Square, 1966.

——————. *L'Etre et le Néant,* 1943. Engl.: *Being and Nothingness, An
        Essay on Phenomenological Ontology,* trl. Hazel Barnes.
        N.Y., Philosophical Library, 1956; Washington Square,
        1966, 738p.

——————. *L'existentialisme est un humanisme,* 1946. Engl.: *Existen-
        tialism,* trl. Bernard Frechtman. N.Y., Philosophical Li-
        brary, 1947; *Existentialism and Humanism,* trl. Philip
        Mairet. London, Methuen, 1948.

——————. *Réflexions sur la question juive,* 1946. Engl.: *Anti-Semite
        and Jew,* trl. George J. Becker. N.Y., Schocken Books,
        1948; *Portrait of the Anti-Semite,* trl. Erik de Mauny,
        London, Secker & Warburg, 1948.

——————. *Matérialisme et Révolution (Les Temps modernes,* I., No.
        9-10, Juin-Juillet 1946). Engl.: *Literary and Philosophical
        Essays,* trl. Annette Michelson. N.Y., Criterion Books, 1955.

——————. *Qu'est-ce que la littérature?, Les temps modernes,* 1947; *Situ-
        ations* II, 1948. Engl.: *What is Literature?,* trl. Bernard
        Frechtman. N.Y., Philosophical Library, 1949; Harper &
        Row, "A Colophon Book," 1965.

——————. *Baudelaire,* 1947. Engl.: *Baudelaire,* trl. Martin Turnell.
        Norfolk, Conn., New Directions, 1950; and "A New
        Directions Paperback, 17."

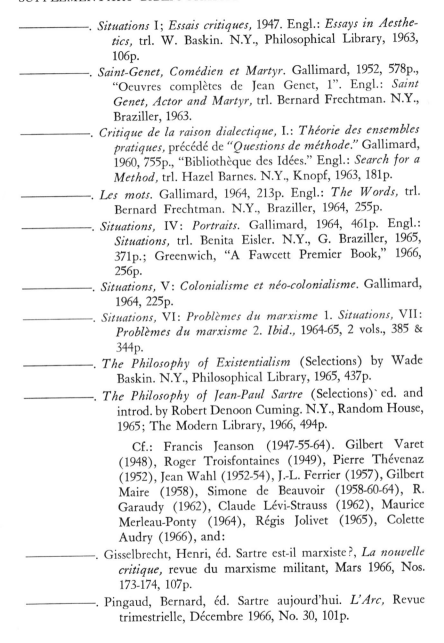

—————————. *Situations* I; *Essais critiques,* 1947. Engl.: *Essays in Aesthetics,* trl. W. Baskin. N.Y., Philosophical Library, 1963, 106p.

—————————. *Saint-Genet, Comédien et Martyr.* Gallimard, 1952, 578p., "Oeuvres complètes de Jean Genet, 1". Engl.: *Saint Genet, Actor and Martyr,* trl. Bernard Frechtman. N.Y., Braziller, 1963.

—————————. *Critique de la raison dialectique,* I.: *Théorie des ensembles pratiques,* précédé de *"Questions de méthode."* Gallimard, 1960, 755p., "Bibliothèque des Idées." Engl.: *Search for a Method,* trl. Hazel Barnes. N.Y., Knopf, 1963, 181p.

—————————. *Les mots.* Gallimard, 1964, 213p. Engl.: *The Words,* trl. Bernard Frechtman. N.Y., Braziller, 1964, 255p.

—————————. *Situations,* IV: *Portraits.* Gallimard, 1964, 461p. Engl.: *Situations,* trl. Benita Eisler. N.Y., G. Braziller, 1965, 371p.; Greenwich, "A Fawcett Premier Book," 1966, 256p.

—————————. *Situations,* V: *Colonialisme et néo-colonialisme.* Gallimard, 1964, 225p.

—————————. *Situations,* VI: *Problèmes du marxisme* 1. *Situations,* VII: *Problèmes du marxisme* 2. *Ibid.,* 1964-65, 2 vols., 385 & 344p.

—————————. *The Philosophy of Existentialism* (Selections) by Wade Baskin. N.Y., Philosophical Library, 1965, 437p.

—————————. *The Philosophy of Jean-Paul Sartre* (Selections)` ed. and introd. by Robert Denoon Cuming. N.Y., Random House, 1965; The Modern Library, 1966, 494p.

Cf.: Francis Jeanson (1947-55-64). Gilbert Varet (1948), Roger Troisfontaines (1949), Pierre Thévenaz (1952), Jean Wahl (1952-54), J.-L. Ferrier (1957), Gilbert Maire (1958), Simone de Beauvoir (1958-60-64), R. Garaudy (1962), Claude Lévi-Strauss (1962), Maurice Merleau-Ponty (1964), Régis Jolivet (1965), Colette Audry (1966), and:

—————————. Gisselbrecht, Henri, éd. Sartre est-il marxiste?, *La nouvelle critique,* revue du marxisme militant, Mars 1966, Nos. 173-174, 107p.

—————————. Pingaud, Bernard, éd. Sartre aujourd'hui. *L'Arc,* Revue trimestrielle, Décembre 1966, No. 30, 101p.

Schérer, René. *La phénoménologie des recherches logiques de Husserl.* P.U.F., 1967, 370p., "Epiméthée"; — *Structure et fondement de la communication humaine,* Essai critique sur les théories contemporaines de la communication. Sedes, 1967, 424p. (Th.).

Schuhl, Pierre-Maxime (Sorbonne). *Le merveilleux, la pensée et l'action.* Flammarion, 1952, 224p., "B.Ph.Sc.".

—————. *L'oeuvre de Platon.* Hachette, 1954, 228p. (2.éd., Vrin).

—————. *Le dominateur et les possibles.* Les Belles Lettres, 1959, 504p.

—————. *Etudes platoniciennes.* P.U.F., 1960, 180p.

—————. *Imaginer et réaliser. Ibid.,* 1963, 148p., "B.Ph.C.".

Simondon, Gilbert (Sorbonne). *Du mode d'existence des objets techniques.* Aubier, 1958, 268p., "Analyses et raisons"; — *L'individu et sa genèse psycho-biologique, L'individuation à la lumière des notions de forme et d'information.* P.U.F., 1963, 312p., "Epiméthée," (Th.).

Solages, Bruno de, Mgr. (Institut Catholique, Toulouse). *L'âme, Dieu, la Destinée.* Spes, 1954, 287p.

—————. *Teilhard de Chardin.* Toulouse, Edouard Privat, 1967, 397p.

Souriau, Etienne (Sorbonne). *Les 100.000 situations dramatiques.* Flammarion, 1949, 288p., "Bibliothèque d'esthétique."

—————. *Mélanges d'esthétique et de science de l'art.* Nizet, 1952, 277p.

—————. *Pensée vivante et perfection formelle.* P.U.F., 1952, 298p.

—————. *L'univers filmique.* Flammarion, 1953, 216p., "Bibliothèque d'esthétique."

—————. *L'ombre de Dieu.* P.U.F., 1955, 376p., "B.Ph.C.".

Starobinsky, Jean (Genève, Univ.). *Jean-Jacques Rousseau, La transparence et l'obstacle.* Plon, 1958, 340p.

Stoetzel, Jean (Sorbonne). *La psychologie sociale.* Flammarion, 1963, 316p.

Taton, René. *L'oeuvre mathématique de Désargues; — L'oeuvre scientifique de Monge.* P.U.F., 1951, 2 vols., 238 & 448p., "B.Ph.C." (Th.).

————— éd.: *Histoire générale des sciences,* P.U.F. T.I, 1957, 724p.; T.II, 1958, 800p.

† Teilhard De Chardin, Pierre, S.J. *Oeuvres,* Ed. du Seuil. 1. *Le phénomène humain,* 347p.; 2. *L'apparition de l'homme,* 375p.; 3. *La vision du passé,* 1957, 391p.; 4. *Le milieu divin,* 203p.; 5. *L'avenir de l'homme;* 1960, 405p.; 6. *La place de l'homme dans la nature;* 7. *L'activation de l'énergie,* 1963, 429p. Engl. trl. published by Harper & Row.

† Thévenaz, Pierre. *De Husserl à Merleau-Ponty: qu'est-ce que la phénoménologie?* (1952), avec une Introduction de Jean Brun. Neuchatel, La Baconnière, 1966, 119p., "Etre et Penser, 52." Engl.: *What is Phenomenology?,* and other Essays, ed. James M. Edie. Chicago, Quadrangle Books, 1962.

——————. *L'homme et sa raison. Ibid.,* 1956, 2 vols. 328 & 192p., "Etre et Penser, 46-47."

——————. *La condition de la raison philosophique. Ibid.,* 120p., "Etre et Penser, 51."

Tilliette, Xavier, S.J. *Karl Jaspers.* Aubier, 1960, 238p., "Théologie."

——————. *Existence et Littérature.* Desclée De Brouwer, 1961, 206p.

——————. *Philosophes contemporains: Gabriel Marcel, Maurice Merleau-Ponty, Karl Jaspers. Ibid.,* 1962, 112p.

——————. *Jules Lequier, ou le tourment de la liberté. Ibid.,* 1963, 210p.

Toinet, Paul, abbé. *Existence chrétienne et Philosophie, Essai sur les fondements de la philosophie chrétienne.* Aubier, 1965, 415p., "Présence et Pensée."

Tresmontant, Claude. *Etudes de métaphysique biblique.* Gabalda, 1955, 261p., "Lectio divina." Engl.: A Study of Hebrew Thought, trl. Michael Gilson. N.Y., Desclée & Co., 1960, 218p.

——————. *Introduction à la pensée de Teilhard de Chardin.* Seuil, 1956, 134p.

——————. *La doctrine morale des prophètes d'Israel. Ibid.,* 1958, 199p.

——————. *Les origines de la philosophie chrétienne.* Fayard, 1962, 113p.

——————. *Les idées maîtresses de la métaphysique chrétienne.* Seuil, 1962, 153p. Engl.: *Christian Metaphysics,* trl. G. Selvin. London, M. H. Gill, 1965.

——————. *Introduction à la métaphysique de Maurice Blondel. Ibid.,* 1963, 336p.

——————. *Comment se pose aujourd'hui le problème de Dieu. Ibid.,* 1966, 409p.

Troisfontaines, Roger, S. J. *Existentialisme et pensée chrétienne.* Nauwelaerts, 1949, 128p.

——————. *De l'existence à l'être, La Philosophie de Gabriel Marcel.* Vrin, 1954, 2 vols., 416 & 432p.

Trouillard, Jean, abbé (Institut Catholique, Paris). *La procession plotinienne; — La purification plotinienne.* P.U.F., 1955, 2 vols., 104 & 247p., "B.Ph.C." (Th.).

——————— éd.: Proclos, *Eléments de théologie.* Aubier, 1965, 193p.

Vajda, Georges (Ecole Pratique des Hautes Etudes). *Juda ben Nissim ibn Malka, philosophe juif marocain.* Larose, 1954, 204p.

——————. *L'amour de Dieu dans la théologie juive du Moyen-age.* Vrin, 1957, 309p.

——————. *Issac Albalag, averroïste juif. Ibid.,* 1960, 292p.

——————. *Recherche sur la philosophie de la Kabbale.* Mouton, 1963, 422p.

† Valéry, Paul. *Les Cahiers de Paul Valéry* (écrits de 1894 à 1945), reproduction photographique du manuscrit. C.N.R.S., 30 vols.

——————. *The Collected Works of Paul Valery,* ed. Jackson Mathews. N.Y., Pantheon Books, 1964, "Bollingen Series."

Vancourt, Raymond (Facultés Catholiques, Lille). *La philosophie et sa structure, Philosophie et Phénoménologie.* Bloud & Gay, 1953, 240p.

——————. *La phénoménologie et la foi.* Desclée & Cie, 1954, 128p.

——————. *Pensée moderne et philosophie chrétienne.* Fayard, 1957, 117p.

Varet, Gilbert (Besancon, Univ.). *L'ontologie de Sartre,* P.U.F., 1949, 196p., "B.Ph.C.".

——————. *L'être et la Valeur à travers l'oeuvre de Louis Lavelle,* J.-B. Baillière, L'information philosophique, 1951.

——————. *Histoire et Savoir.* Les Belles Lettres, 1956, 225p.; *La Réflexion,* Esquisse d'une problématique pure. Besançon, 1956, 432p. (Th.).

——————. *Manuel de bibliographie philosophique.* P.U.F., 1956, 2 vols., 1.058p., "Logos."

——————— éd.: *Bibliographie de la Philosophie.* Vrin, 15 vols., 1951-1967.

Villey, Michel (Paris, Droit) éd.: *Archives de Philosophie du Droit.* Sirey. I. *La distinction du Droit privé et du Droit public,* 1952; II. *La déontologie et la discipline professionnelle,* 1954; III. *Le rôle de la volonté dans le Droit,* 1958; IV. *Droit et Histoire,* 1959; V. *La théologie chrétienne et le Droit,* 1960; VI. *La réforme des études de Droit; Le Droit naturel,* 1961; VII. *Qu'est-ce que la philosophie du droit,*

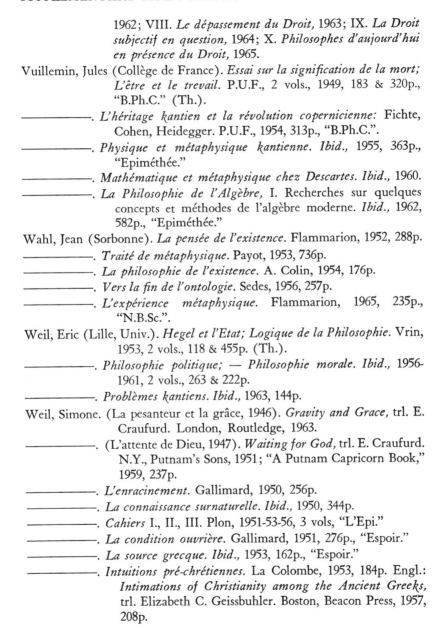

1962; VIII. *Le dépassement du Droit,* 1963; IX. *La Droit subjectif en question,* 1964; X. *Philosophes d'aujourd'hui en présence du Droit,* 1965.

Vuillemin, Jules (Collège de France). *Essai sur la signification de la mort; L'être et le trevail.* P.U.F., 2 vols., 1949, 183 & 320p., "B.Ph.C." (Th.).

——. *L'héritage kantien et la révolution copernicienne:* Fichte, Cohen, Heidegger. P.U.F., 1954, 313p., "B.Ph.C.".

——. *Physique et métaphysique kantienne. Ibid.,* 1955, 363p., "Epiméthée."

——. *Mathématique et métaphysique chez Descartes. Ibid.,* 1960.

——. *La Philosophie de l'Algèbre,* I. Recherches sur quelques concepts et méthodes de l'algèbre moderne. *Ibid.,* 1962, 582p., "Epiméthée."

Wahl, Jean (Sorbonne). *La pensée de l'existence.* Flammarion, 1952, 288p.

——. *Traité de métaphysique.* Payot, 1953, 736p.

——. *La philosophie de l'existence.* A. Colin, 1954, 176p.

——. *Vers la fin de l'ontologie.* Sedes, 1956, 257p.

——. *L'expérience métaphysique.* Flammarion, 1965, 235p., "N.B.Sc.".

Weil, Eric (Lille, Univ.). *Hegel et l'Etat; Logique de la Philosophie.* Vrin, 1953, 2 vols., 118 & 455p. (Th.).

——. *Philosophie politique; — Philosophie morale. Ibid.,* 1956-1961, 2 vols., 263 & 222p.

——. *Problèmes kantiens. Ibid.,* 1963, 144p.

Weil, Simone. (La pesanteur et la grâce, 1946). *Gravity and Grace,* trl. E. Craufurd. London, Routledge, 1963.

——. (L'attente de Dieu, 1947). *Waiting for God,* trl. E. Craufurd. N.Y., Putnam's Sons, 1951; "A Putnam Capricorn Book," 1959, 237p.

——. *L'enracinement.* Gallimard, 1950, 256p.

——. *La connaissance surnaturelle. Ibid.,* 1950, 344p.

——. *Cahiers* I., II., III. Plon, 1951-53-56, 3 vols, "L'Epi."

——. *La condition ouvrière.* Gallimard, 1951, 276p., "Espoir."

——. *La source grecque. Ibid.,* 1953, 162p., "Espoir."

——. *Intuitions pré-chrétiennes.* La Colombe, 1953, 184p. Engl.: *Intimations of Christianity among the Ancient Greeks,* trl. Elizabeth C. Geissbuhler. Boston, Beacon Press, 1957, 208p.

——————. *Oppression et Liberté.* Gallimard, 1955, 273p., "Espoir." *The Need for Roots: Prelude to a Declaration of Duties Toward Mankind,* trl. Arthur Wills. Boston, Beacon Press, 1955, 315p.

——————. *Ecrits de Londres, et dernières lettres.* Gallimard, 1957, 264p., "Espoir."

——————. *Leçons de Philosophie* (1933-34). Plon, 1959, 258p.

——————. *Ecrits historiques et politiques.* Gallimard, 1960, 413p., "Espoir."

——————. *Pensées sans ordre concernant l'amour de Dieu. Ibid.,* 1962, 160p., "Espoir."

——————. *Selected Essays* 1934-1943, trl. R. Rees. Oxford Univ. Press, 1962, 238p.

Zac, Sylvain. *L'idée de vie dans la philosophie de Spinoza; — Signification et valeur de l'interprétation de l'Ecriture chez Spinoza.* P.U.F., 1963-66, 2 vols., 284 & 244p., "B.Ph.C." (Th.).

——————. *La morale de Spinoza,* 2.éd. *Ibid.,* 1966, 124p.